NATIVE AMERICAN LITERATURE

An Anthology

Lawana Trout
Oklahoma City University

NTC *Publishing Group*
a division of NTC/CONTEMPORARY PUBLISHING GROUP
Lincolnwood, Illinois USA

This book is dedicated to the memory of my parents, Pearla M. and Lewis R. Hooper (1909–1998).

Lawana Trout

Sponsoring Editor: Marisa L. L'Heureux
Product Manager: Judy Rudnick
Art Director: Ophelia Chambliss
Production Manager: Margo Goia
Cover art: Inee Yang Slaughter

Acknowledgments begin on page 769, which is to be considered an extension of this copyright page.

ISBN: 0-8442-5985-3 (student text)
ISBN: 0-8442-5986-1 (instructor's edition)

Published by NTC/Contemporary Publishing Group, Inc.,
4255 West Touhy Avenue, Lincolnwood (Chicago), Illinois 60646-1975 U.S.A.

Library of Congress Cataloging-in-Publication Data
Native American literature: an anthology / [compiled by] Lawana
Trout.
p. cm.
Includes index.
ISBN 0-8442-5985-3
1. American literature—Indian authors. 2. Indians of North
America—Literary collections. 3. American literature—Indian
authors—Problems, exercises, etc. 4. Indians of North America—
Problems, exercises, etc. I. Trout, Lawana.
PS508.I5N368   1998
810.8′0897—dc21   98-38987
                                             CIP

8 9 0 VL 0 9 8 7 6 5 4 3 2 1

CONTENTS

CHAPTER TWO

THE SPIRIT WORLD

CHAPTER THREE

CRISIS IN THE HOMELAND

185

CHAPTER FIVE

ALL MY RELATIONS

CHAPTER SIX

GROWING UP   411

CHAPTER SEVEN

AFFAIRS OF THE HEART   493

CHAPTER EIGHT
LANGUAGE AND LEARNING IN TWO WORLDS

CHAPTER NINE

WE SURVIVE

651

CHAPTER TEN
MEMORY ALIVE

715

PREFACE

Will Rogers, Cherokee humorist and author, liked to say, "My ancestors did not come over on the Mayflower, but they were here to meet the ship." Rogers was right. The first Americans arrived thousands of years before other voyagers to this continent. American literature began with the oral traditions of these indigenous peoples, not with the Western Europeans who began to immigrate after 1500. Native American literature is American's first and oldest literature.

Native American Literature will introduce you to a unique literature within its rich cultural and often tragic historical contexts. The recent written literature has its roots in thousands of years of oral stories, ceremonies, and songs. Given the antiquity of oral traditions, the need to introduce this literature may seem strange to you. The truth is, however, that this literary legacy has often been omitted from classrooms and textbooks. This legacy and its descendant, modern Native American literature, are both vital facets of American literature.

This anthology offers you the opportunity to read a wide variety of stories, poems, and essays by authors from many tribes. Their voices include male and female, young and old. They span the past one hundred and seventy years of literary history. To illustrate, the earliest written selection is the text of a speech delivered by Cherokee Elias Boudinot in 1826. This speech is juxtaposed with a scene from *Pushing the Bear,* Diane Glancy's Cherokee-removal novel published in 1996.

What makes *Native American Literature* distinctive is its thematic organization. Each chapter reflects a theme in Indian lives that is special, yet common in terms of connecting with the lives of all people.

Each chapter opens with information about the cultural and historical framework for its theme. Biographical information about the author appears before each selection. This background will help you place the author and text within their contexts.

Following each selection are questions to guide you as you think about the work. They will provide you with some direction as you reflect on the literary and cultural issues raised in the selections. There are discussion questions, which you may discuss with a classmate, in a small group, or with the entire class. The writing topics, on the other hand, are designed to help you respond to the selection on paper. You will probably want to keep a literary response journal in order to review your thoughts.

Varied voices speak to you from this anthology as they tell you about growing up Native American, loving, struggling, losing, and winning. They may surprise, excite, irritate, or delight you. As you listen to the voices and to the responses of your classmates, think of this anthology as a conversation among the authors, you, and your fellow students. This ongoing conversation will spread to other multicultural literature you study. As a citizen of the twenty-first century, you may celebrate multicultural America through its literature. *Native American Literature* allows you to explore a unique part of that America and will no doubt lead you to discover intriguing parts of yourself.

Acknowledgments

I am grateful for the editorial guidance of Marisa L. L'Heureux and Jane Bachman Gordon. My gratitude goes to the National Endowment for the Humanities for funding Summer Institutes in Native American Literature that I directed at the Newberry Library, Chicago, and at Oklahoma City University. Many of the one hundred and fifty teachers who attended seven institutes continue to share insights and ideas with me. They have helped me hone the cross-cultural approach in this anthology. For over twenty years, my students' responses in Native American literature classes have sharpened my thinking.

Many scholars have shared their expertise with me. Thanks to LaVonne Ruoff for her pioneering scholarship; John Aubrey for guiding my research; Raymond Fogelson for background on Cherokee; Raymond DeMallie for background on Sioux; and Kenneth Roemer for information on Native American authors.

I owe a special debt of gratitude to those Native American authors who have given friendship and provided insight about their works: Joy Harjo, Louis Owens, Anna Lee Walters, Albert White Hat, Sr., Luci Tapahonso, Russell Bates, Diane Glancy, Betty Bell, James Welch, and Linda Hogan. Henry F. Dobyns contributed historical and cultural information to this anthology.

Finally, my deep gratitude goes to my husband, Verdine, for his patience and support.

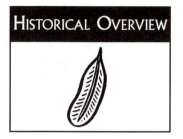

THE FIRST AMERICAN LITERATURE: ORAL TRADITIONS

"American literature begins with the first human perception
of the American landscape expressed and preserved in language."

N. Scott Momaday

Native American literature is the oldest linguistic legacy in North America.
The oral tradition arrived approximately forty thousand years ago, when the
first Americans crossed from Asia to Alaska. They carried old stories from
their homeland and created new tales about their journey. No humans lived
in the Americas until that ancient, arduous journey. Did the early travelers
wonder why they met no new people to share their stories? Ice Age people
began a literary tradition that lived through each new generation for thousands of years. The storytelling never stopped; only the stories changed.

The Paleo-Indians could walk on a land bridge between Siberia and
Alaska because Ice Age glaciers had frozen vast volumes of water, causing
the shallow sea level to fall below what is today the Bering Strait. As giant
glaciers advanced and retreated, water levels rose and fell, causing the Bering
Strait area to fluctuate between water and land. Scientists named the
exposed land *Beringia,* an area approximately one thousand miles wide. We
do not know exact routes or dates for these early explorers, but geologists
have calculated that the land bridge passage opened and closed at least four
times during the late Pleistocene. Melting ice rapidly flooded it for the final
time when climatic changes warmed the earth about fifteen thousand years
ago.

How did the new Americans survive in the harsh, uncharted land?
Unaware that they had entered the crossroads between continents, the pioneer settlers found a familiar landscape and animals in ancient Beringia. They
had already perfected a tool kit for survival in the Arctic environment.

Wearing warm furs and carrying stone weapons, the traveling Homo sapiens were probably following big-game animals. Surviving bitter winters and enjoying brighter summers when the sun slipped along the horizon, families formed small hunting bands who tailored skin clothing, kindled or carried fire, and made tools of wood, bone, and ivory. They created skin shelters to cope with the tundra cold.

What scenes from life near the ice sheets did they dramatize in stories? Brave men must have told exciting stories by firelight. Stone Age hunters no doubt told of the thrill of killing a wooly mammoth. Words captured scenes of wild horses, musk ox, and bison with long, straight horns that attracted dire wolves, saber-toothed tigers, and other predators. In a world where myth and mystery united, rituals linked the spirits of hunters and animals. Sacred stories formed the heart of ceremonies. In a precarious life cycle, fathers and mothers pictured family memories and set cultural lessons in stories for their children.

Over thousands of years, descendants from the first families spread throughout North and South America. Thus, the peopling of two continents gradually occurred as increasing numbers of people colonized frontier territory. Their colonization was the last major dispersal of humans on this planet. D'Arcy McNickle described this long process as "unsealing a continent" in his book *They Came Here First* (1949). "A handful of people standing in a new world! . . . One day the land would be called America, and the people Indians. . . .They were the first to come, the first discoverers, the first settlers."

Some Native Americans reject the scientific theory of Bering Strait migrations. They believe that their Creator placed them on sacred ground where they have always been.

By 2000 B.C., Indians knew every habitable part of North America. Making use of wildlife, water, trees, and plants, these peoples devised a wide range of lifestyles. By 1492, the original, tiny population had grown to over one hundred million people, with about ten million in North America. Throughout the continent, people speaking many different languages taught their children beliefs about a Creator of great power, the spirits that connected with that power, and the future life of souls when life on earth was over. Chapter Two, "The Spirit World," offers examples of such cosmologies.

WRITTEN LITERATURE: 1772–1968

European conquest and colonization put Indian lives and languages at risk. Consequently, American Indian literature may be viewed from a perspective of historical events and their consequences. The establishment of English colonies in Virginia in 1607 and in Massachusetts in 1620 led to English becoming America's national language. Formal English-language instruction for Indians began early in colonial missionary schools. Colonizers taught Indians to read, but historical circumstances delayed the first publication by an Indian until 1772. In that year, Samson Occom, a Mohegan and a Methodist missionary, produced his popular *Sermon Preached at the Execution of Moses Paul,* which became the first Indian bestseller with nineteen printings.

Why did Indians write and publish in English? English was their instrument for protesting injustice and seeking justice. Because English was the conqueror's language, it presented particular problems for native writers. Who was their audience? How could they use English as a weapon in what Gerald Vizenor later called "cultural word wars"? How could they defend Indian traditions and discuss critical issues in "the enemy's language"?

Some natives learned that the written word was powerful in dealing with literate Euro-Americans. William Apess and Elias Boudinot were two eastern Indians who became fluent in spoken and written English. Apess published the first Indian autobiography, *A Son of the Forest,* in 1829. He ultimately published five books and was the most significant Indian author in the early nineteenth century. As an evangelical Christian, Apess was one of the most forceful protest writers of his day and preached against prejudice and injustice. In 1833, he published "An Indian's Looking-Glass for the White Man." In it he held up a literary "looking-glass" for Euro-American Christians in which to view their actions, and he let his readers know in no uncertain terms that their behavior did not measure up to biblical standards, especially their treatment of Native Americans and African Americans. In the late eighteenth and early nineteenth centuries, American Indian authors wrote primarily sermons, protest literature, tribal histories, and autobiographies.

Prominent critic LaVonne Ruoff observed in *Native American Literatures,* "The history of American Indian literature reflects not only tribal cultures and the experience and imagination of its authors but Indian-white relations as well." The theme of Chapter Three, "Crisis in the Homeland," illustrates her observation. The crises arose as the United States government pursued a series of changing policies. As selections in this anthology indicate, the impact of these crises was cumulative. For tribes east of the Mississippi River, the crisis in their homelands began with the Revolutionary War, when they had to choose between fighting with revolutionaries or the British. Because most of the Iroquois and Cherokee aligned with the British, citizens of the new United States felt considerable hostility toward Indians.

The Constitution set the first national policy toward tribes, classing them as nations with which to negotiate treaties. From the beginning, however, treaties typically transferred Indian lands to the United States, reserving reduced areas called "reservations" for natives. Treaties did not transfer Indian lands to land-hungry citizens as rapidly as they desired. In 1830, therefore, Congress passed a Removal Act establishing a policy of forcing all Indian Nations out of their remaining territories east of the Mississippi River into western Indian Territory. President Andrew Jackson told his agent, "Say to them as friends and brothers to listen to their father, and their friend." If Indians moved beyond the Mississippi, Jackson promised, "There their white brothers will not trouble them, and they will have no claim to the land, and they can live upon it, they and all their children, as long as grass grows and waters run." Despite such poetic promises, Cherokee lands would be taken again.

Educated by missionaries and fluent in English, Elias Boudinot was one of the leaders of the Cherokee Nation as it consciously emulated the U.S. constitutional government and futilely protested forced removal. An eloquent spokesman, in 1826 Boudinot gave "An Address to the Whites" to raise funds for a bilingual press in English and Sequoyah's Cherokee syllabary. In 1828, the first copy of *The Cherokee Phoenix* newspaper appeared in both the Cherokee syllabary and the English alphabet. Wide circulation made it a powerful propaganda tool. Ultimately, Boudinot acted on the courage of his convictions and signed the Treaty of New Echota because he believed it was necessary to preserve the Cherokee Nation, knowing that he signed his own death warrant.

Among the Americans who protested Cherokee removal was Ralph Waldo Emerson. On April 23, 1838, Emerson wrote President Martin Van Buren, "Will the American government steal? Will it lie? Will it kill?" Pleading to the president for justice, Emerson admonished, "You sir, will bring down that renowned chair in which you sit into infamy if your seal is set to this instrument of perfidy; and the name of this nation, hitherto the sweet omen of religion and liberty, will stink to the world."

Emerson's letter reminds us that Cherokee removal was taking place during the period when the American nation was beginning to define its own literature. Less than a year earlier, Emerson had delivered "The American Scholar" as the annual Phi Beta Kappa oration at Harvard. The address signaled a turning point in literary history as it began what critics have labeled the "American Renaissance," a flowering of literary art unprecedented in the brief history of the nation. It is an ironic footnote that James Fenimore Cooper created his romantic Leather-Stocking Tales for American readers at the same time Elias Boudinot and others were writing about real Indians.

A decade after Emerson's letter to President Van Buren, the 1848 Treaty of Guadalupe Hidalgo with Mexico brought new territory and numerous tribes under the jurisdiction of the United States. Settling the Oregon dispute with England added more tribes and their territories. The 1848 discovery of gold in California stimulated more encroachments on Indian land as hordes of immigrants traveled to California gold fields or Oregon farm lands. Eventually, the United States reached the Pacific Ocean, so Indians could no longer be removed westward. In forty years, therefore, the U.S. conquered Western Indians and seized most of their lands but reserved segments for them under the reservation system.

As Indians wrote and told about their experiences on reservations and off, they created autobiographies within diverse tribal contexts. Two remarkable women lived in the last half of the nineteenth century—Maria Chona and Sarah Winnemucca. Chona was born about 1845 and grew up in the arid desert of the Papago. The Papago defended their scattered villages against Apaches, who in 1853 destroyed Chona's home village. At ninety, Chona, who did not speak English, told her life history to Ruth Underhill through a thirteen-year-old Papago interpreter, who had learned English at Phoenix Indian School.

Sarah Winnemucca was born about the same time as Chona to a distinguished Northern Paiute family in what later became Nevada. She mastered English, acted as an interpreter, and became a political activist, lecturer, and educator. Even after her mother and brother were massacred by Nevada militia, she sought understanding and peace between her people and outsiders. This fiery crusader for Indian rights presented three hundred lectures from San Francisco to Washington, D.C., and Boston. She spoke at the home of Ralph Waldo Emerson. In *Life Among the Piutes: Their Wrongs and Claims* (1883), Winnemucca wrote a rare eyewitness account of four decades of encounters between Paiutes and Euro-Americans. It is the first autobiography written by an Indian woman.

In the 1870s, policymakers in Washington decided that the best way to "civilize" Indians was through removing children from their homes and placing them in faraway boarding schools. In those schools, "civilizing" Indian children meant suppressing their native languages, teaching them to read English and a vocation, cutting their long hair, dressing them in uniforms, and converting them to Protestantism. Linguistic conquest continued in the classrooms as detailed in Chapter Eight, "Language and Learning in Two Worlds." Established in 1879, Carlisle Indian School in Pennsylvania became the model institution for this policy.

Luther Standing Bear was one of the first students at Carlisle. His transition from traditional plains life, sketched in "At Last I Kill a Buffalo," to an English-language classroom was abrupt. That summer of 1879 he attended a Sioux Sun Dance. Only a few weeks later, he entered Carlisle and the literate world. Coping with boarding school life, Standing Bear "was never the hostage of an education, and he never reduced his various experiences to mere victimage," according to critic Gerald Vizenor in *Native American Literature*. Despite being forbidden to speak Lakota and forced to learn English, Standing Bear used his boarding school education as a springboard for becoming a movie actor and writing four books. *My People the Sioux* (1928) became a landmark in Indian literature as a graphic portrayal of unconquered Northern Plains tribal life. In *Land of the Spotted Eagle* (1933), Standing Bear commented that "all the years of calling the Indian a savage has never made him one." Treasuring tribal values, moreover, he emphatically stated that he would rear his son "to be an Indian!"

Born in 1876, Zitkala-Sa (Gertrude Bonnin) studied at a missionary school in Indiana and at Earlham College. Hired by Carlisle Indian

Industrial School in 1898, she criticized federal Indian assimilation policy. Her writing provides a Sioux teacher's perspective on the early Indian boarding school system. Like Standing Bear, Zitkala-Sa was proud of her accomplishments, but she remained ambivalent about the policy. Leaving federal service, in 1900 Zitkala-Sa published three autobiographical essays in the *Atlantic Monthly*. They were later republished in her 1921 book *American Indian Stories*. She picked up the deceased Winnemucca's torch, claiming in print her heritage as an American Indian woman at a time when few Indian women's works were published. She became an eloquent speaker, campaigning for Indian rights and lobbying Congress for Indian citizenship until the 1924 Citizenship Act was passed.

Caught in the crucible of the Indian Wars, Charles Alexander Eastman forged an impressive literary career. Born in 1858, Eastman was reared as a hunter and warrior until he was fifteen. Attending four schools in ten years, the bright young man became fluent in English. He graduated from Dartmouth in 1887 and from Boston Medical School in 1890. Taking the post of physician at Pine Ridge Agency, Eastman heard Army Hotchkiss guns killing Sioux people eighteen miles away on Wounded Knee Creek. Eastman treated victims, saving as many lives as he could. The massacre ended the Indian Wars. From 1902 to 1918, Eastman published eleven books, including *Indian Boyhood* (1902) and *From the Deep Woods to Civilization* (1916), and became the most popular Indian author of his generation. Through his fiction, nonfiction, and autobiographies, Eastman acted as an effective mediator between Indians and Euro-Americans.

Luther Standing Bear, Zitkala-Sa, and Charles Eastman, like other Indians of their generation, heard oral stories from elders and later published stories based on tribal traditions. They became the first members of their families to write about their experiences and their memories, inasmuch as they belonged to the first generation that was educated at federal and mission boarding schools. These Sioux authors chronicled change and continuity that affected the lives of many Indian people during this period.

Most Indians in the next generation had to adjust to living on reservations. The pioneer novelist of reservation life was D'Arcy McNickle, born on the Flathead Reservation in Montana in 1904. Many critics consider McNickle one of the founders of modern Native American literature. When he published his first novel, *The Surrounded*, in 1936, only a handful of novels by Native Americans existed. Louis Owens wrote in *Other Destinies: Understanding the American Indian Novel* (1992), "More than any other Indian writer, McNickle would prove to be a seminal figure in the new American Indian fiction, publishing three novels over a span of forty years while turning himself into one of the nation's most articulate and knowledgeable spokesmen for Indian concerns."

McNickle left the reservation to attend the University of Montana and later sold his allotted land so he could afford to study at Oxford University. *The Surrounded* appeared in 1936 in the depths of the Depression. That was the year McNickle joined the Bureau of Indian Affairs, where he helped implement the reservation self-governance that Congress authorized in its epochal 1934 Indian Reorganization Act. Federal service prepared and motivated McNickle to write scholarly nonfiction from an Indian perspective: *They Came Here First* (1949) and *Indians and Other Americans: Two Ways of Life Meet* with Harold Fey (1959). McNickle did not, however, hark back to "Old Indian Days," as did Charles Eastman in his book title. In contrast, McNickle analyzed historical events to understand contemporary circumstances. In *Native American Tribalism: Indian Survivals and Renewals* (1973), McNickle analyzed policies from early treaties to removal, reservations, allotment, and the Indian Reorganization Act. As both author and activist, McNickle labored always for a better future for Indians. That future burst upon the literary scene in 1969.

NATIVE AMERICAN LITERARY RENAISSANCE: 1970–PRESENT

In 1969, N. Scott Momaday, a young professor of English at Stanford University, received a Pulitzer Prize for his first novel, *House Made of Dawn*. That same year, he published his autobiography, *The Way to Rainy Mountain*, which interweaves Kiowa myth, history, and family stories. Also in 1969, Vine Deloria, Jr., a young Sioux attorney, published *Custer Died for Your Sins: An Indian Manifesto*. An issue of the *South Dakota Review* that landmark year carried works by Simon Ortiz, James Welch, Janet Campbell, and Phil George. The Native American Literary Renaissance had begun.

Most of the authors in this anthology have contributed to that renaissance. As university professors, some are masters of several genres. Each author crafts a distinctive style and draws from a pool of Native American themes: family and community, sense of place and ties to the land, and tribal cosmologies and histories. Renaissance writers distill scenes from the tragic past and remind modern readers of D'Arcy McNickle's dictum, "The past does not die." For example, James Welch evokes the Baker Massacre of Blackfeet; Diane Glancy revisits the site of the Seventh Cavalry's Washita Massacre of Arapahos; Janet Campbell Hale shares her grandmother's memory of the Nez Perce Battle of Bear Paw.

Contemporary writers are optimistic that they may generate crosscultural understanding by functioning as mediators and cultural translators between natives and nonnatives. They gather inspiration from oral tradition and innovatively integrate it into their texts. In personal narratives, they struggle with their own mixed heritages and, not surprisingly, create fictional characters who struggle to resolve their ethnic identities. They hold a strong belief in the healing power of words expressed in tribal traditions and languages.

N. Scott Momaday has remained at the center of Native American literature since 1969. His poetry collections include *An Angle of Geese* (1974) and *The Gourd Dancer* (1976). As the quintessential "man made of words," Momaday theorizes about the process that transforms oral tradition into written literature. Vine Deloria, Jr.'s teaching, writing, and political activism have informed the American public about the long history and the present state of Indian affairs, correcting misconceptions and exposing stereotypes. A prolific author of more than ten books and eighty articles, Deloria stands as the outstanding nonfiction writer of the renaissance with his personal cascade of titles. *We Talk, You Listen: New Tribes, New Turf* (1970); *God Is Red* (1973); and *Red Earth, White Lies: Native Americans and the Myth of Scientific Fact* (1995) demonstrate that this Sioux author is a formidable phrase maker, eager to heap criticism on federal agencies, religious zealots, and scientists.

Most Indian renaissance authors prefer to fictionalize their pursuit of justice for their peoples. Laguna Pueblo native Leslie Silko, for example, anchors her prose and poetry to a landscape where Puebloan people have lived for about twenty-five hundred years. Silko's first short story, "The Man to Send Rainclouds," launched her literary reputation when editor Kenneth Rosen named his anthology after it, *The Man to Send Rainclouds: Contemporary Stories by American Indians* (1974). In *Ceremony* (1977), she conveyed the same message as Momaday in *House Made of Dawn*—that traditional Pueblo rites function in the contemporary world to restore to mental health Indian veterans of United States wars. In *Storyteller* (1981), she experimented with form, including short stories, poetry, and personal vignettes. Silko's massive novel *Almanac of the Dead* appeared in 1991.

James Welch's surrealist poetry volume *Riding the Earthboy 40* (1971) identified him as one of the initial renaissance writers. The Blackfeet–Gros Ventre poet draws images from a Northern Plains landscape that becomes a metaphor for the interior landscape of humans. From this landscape came the title of Welch's first novel, *Winter in the Blood* (1974), in which a nameless hero seeks the truth about his identity. In his other novels, Welch's lean style and stark images combine tragedy with humor as he creates unforgettable characters. Renaissance authors also write major historical novels about tribal pasts. Welch reconstructed Blackfeet life around 1870 in *Fools Crow* (1986), which portrays a young Blackfeet warrior maturing in traditional culture threatened by Euro-American aggression. Diane Glancy later wrote a gripping reconstruction of Cherokee removal in her historical novel *Pushing the Bear* (1996). Chickasaw Linda Hogan's *Mean Spirit* (1990) follows two Osage families in Oklahoma through the 1920s "Reign of Terror" of oppression, exploitation, and murder to seize tribal oil wealth. Thus, the United States' violent historical treatment of its native peoples continues to generate literary consequences.

Gerald Vizenor is one of America's most distinctive literary voices because he assumes a trickster's mask. Vizenor turns traditional trickster into a postmodern trope. Characters who are "crossbloods" and tricksters dominate his fiction. Vizenor is the first Indian author to celebrate and make a hero of the half-breed. He and his characters are comic liberators and compassionate rebels. This Chippewa author is one of the most prolific and versatile Native American writers, with more than twenty-five books and numerous articles across many genres to his credit. Several of his works combine fiction and nonfiction: *Wordarrows: Indians and Whites in the New Fur Trade* (1978); *Earthdivers: Tribal Narratives on Mixed Descent* (1981); and *The People Named Chippewa: Narrative Histories* (1984). These innovative texts explore traumas Indians suffered as a result of cultural clashes between natives and newcomers. In his novels, Vizenor satirizes both native and newcomer societies through his trickster discourse. He playfully creates cross-blood characters caught in bizarre worlds from *Darkness in Saint Louis Bearheart* (1978) through *The Trickster of Liberty: Tribal Heirs to a Wild Baronage* (1988) to *Hotline Healers: An Almost Browne Novel* (1997).

Acclaimed novelist, poet, essayist, and short story writer Louise Erdrich is one of America's most important contemporary authors. She began her publishing career in 1984 with her first book of poetry, *Jacklight,* followed by *Baptism of Desire* in 1989. This Chippewa author expounds the mixed-ancestry dilemma throughout her fiction. Erdrich weaves an intricate web of family relationships among mixed-heritage characters appearing in a sextet of novels. Her North Dakota saga consists of *Love Medicine* (1984), *The Beet Queen* (1986), *Tracks* (1988), *The Bingo Palace* (1994), *Tales of Burning Love* (1996), and *The Antelope Wife* (1998). Erdrich's sophistication enables her to use multiple narrators, each of whom tells a portion of the story. She skillfully employs irony to create humorous texts. Using many narrative voices makes for episodic narration, but Erdrich staples the episodes together with pervasive themes of place, ethnic identity, and alcohol abuse. The North Dakota landscape to which Erdrich ties her characters is a powerful unifying influence. Going home through her writing is a way for Erdrich to recover and restore parts of her own mixed heritage. The novelist sketches portraits of rampant alcohol abuse. The problem of alcohol abuse is painfully apparent in the work of Erdrich's husband and collaborator, Michael Dorris. In 1989, he completed *The Broken Cord: A Family's On-Going Struggle with Fetal Alcohol Syndrome.* It recounts their family's heartbreaking experiences with an adopted son with FAS. An accomplished novelist, Dorris also published *A Yellow Raft in Blue Water* in 1987 and *Cloud Chamber* in 1997.

Linda Hogan's writing and history have deep roots in Oklahoma. Her Chickasaw ancestors had been removed to Indian territory in the 1830s. Her first book of poetry, *Calling Myself Home* (1978), pays homage to the red earth of Oklahoma, the land she knows and loves. Hogan balances two genetic heritages; a Chickasaw grandmother is an inspiration. *Seeing Through the Sun* (1985) includes a poem agonizing over the poet's mixed heritage. *Eclipse* (1983) conveys Hogan's environmental concerns, fearing war and radioactive waste. Her novel *Solar Storms* (1995) focuses on women and the environment. The teenaged protagonist of that novel journeys from

Oklahoma to Minnesota to find her great-grandmother and great-great-grandmother. Her canoe trip toward the latter's birthplace, which is soon to be destroyed by a dam, enables Hogan to criticize decision makers whose policies and action damage the environment.

Environmental issues also concern Choctaw-Cherokee author Louis Owens. He set his first novel, *Wolfsong* (1991), in the northwest where the characters wrestle with issues of environmental management, specifically the construction of a dam. He set *The Sharpest Sight* (1992) in a small California town where Hispanics and Indians alike believe in very powerful supernatural forces. Ostensibly a murder mystery, *Bone Game* (1994) continues Owens' theme that violence against the land leaves an enduring impact that generates violence against people who live on it. Another mystery, *Nightland* (1996), set in bone-dry New Mexico, traces the troubles of two half-Cherokee ranchers after they see a suitcase containing a million dollars fall from the sky. In all his works, this novelist sprinkles hilarious scenes amid murder and mayhem. Owens also writes brilliant criticism. His *Other Destinies: Understanding the American Indian Novel* (1992) integrates literary and cultural theory in the first book-length analysis of Native American novels.

Momaday believes that "a good many Indian writers rely upon a kind of poetic expression out of necessity, a necessary homage to the native tradition." Three women—Creek Joy Harjo, Cherokee Diane Glancy, and Navajo Luci Tapahonso—stand out as major Indian poets who draw on tradition. Haunted by history, Harjo writes poetry to confront emotional demons, consciously converting hatred into love and turning fear into her ally. In her first book, *The Last Song* (1975), Harjo expressed her strong sense of the Southwestern landscape, its people and history. *She Had Some Horses* (1983) also emphasizes Harjo's lyrical sensitivity to place. A quest for social justice suffuses the robust poems of *In Mad Love and War* (1990) and *The Woman Who Fell from the Sky* (1994). This feminist poet turned editor to recruit more than eighty women to contribute narratives for *Reinventing the Enemy's Language* (1997). Like Harjo, Luci Tapahonso celebrates generations of biological and cultural continuity in women. Tapahonso's *Blue Horses Rush In* (1997) and *Sáanii Dahataal: The Women Are Singing* (1993) reflect the matrilineal kinship matrix of Navajo society. These volumes, much like *Seasonal Woman* (1981) and *A Breeze Swept Through* (1987), reveal the author's sensitivity to the Southwestern landscape and Navajo tradition.

Diane Glancy is a novelist but began her literary efforts with poetry. *Brown Wolf Leaves the Res and Other Poems* (1984) foreshadowed *Firesticks: A Collection of Stories* (1993). *Firesticks* presents nineteen novellas and short stories about urban Indian life today, tied together by a voiceless, powerless female character. Between those publication dates, Glancy combined mythic, historical, and personal viewpoints in six books, including *One Age in a Dream* (1986), *Trigger Dance* (1990), *Iron Woman* (1990), and *Claiming Breath* (1992).

Like many other authors represented in this anthology, Sherman Alexie started his career by publishing poetry. He began with *The Business of Fancydancing: Stories and Poems* (1992), followed by *Old Shirts and New Skins and First Indian on the Moon,* both collections of poems and short prose pieces published in 1993. Alexie's poetry has an attitude—ironical, satirical, and consistently funny. Alexie's humor takes Vine Deloria's humor at least a full stride forward, giving it a different cast.

The youngest major renaissance author, Alexie wrote two humorous contemporary reservation novels. *The Lone Ranger and Tonto Fistfight in Heaven* (1993) and *Reservation Blues* (1995) gently mock reservation residents as earlier Indian authors would scarcely have dared to do. Then Alexie turned to the purely urban setting of Seattle for his putative mystery novel, *Indian Killer.* The book is actually an eloquent and sophisticated protest against non-Indians' adopting of Indian infants, a frequent practice in the mid-twentieth century. As Alexie has said, he definitely does not belong to the "corn pollen school" of Indian literature. He points toward exciting new permutations of the Indian literary renaissance.

Fortunately, the high art of composing new stories in Native American oral tradition thrives. Consider this story told by Wilma Mankiller, former Principal Chief of the Cherokee Nation, about a male student who was driving her from the airport to his college.

> This student clearly didn't approve of me, and after an uncomfortable silence he finally had to say something. "Principal chief is a term for a man. What should I call You? Ms.?"
>
> I looked out of the window for a while. After another pause, he kept at it: "How about chiefess?"
>
> I looked out the window a little longer that time. Finally he announced, "I know—chiefette!"
>
> Well, I looked out of the window a very long time before I said, "You can call me Ms. Chief Mischief."

Tribal Locations

CULTURE AREA BOUNDARY

Tribes are shown in the locations where they initially became important to U.S. history. Consequently, the map has no single date. United States Indian Removal policy forced most Cherokee, Creek, Chickasaw, Choctaw, and many other groups to present-day Oklahoma.

Adapted from Francis Paul Prucha's *Atlas of American Indian Affairs.*
Lincoln: University of Nebraska Press, 1990.

NATIVE AMERICAN LITERATURE

CHAPTER ONE

IMAGES AND IDENTITIES

"Why do you call us Indian?" a puzzled tribesman in 1646 asked John Eliot, a Massachusetts Colony missionary. The initial image of the *Indian*, like the word itself, came from Christopher Columbus. In 1492 there were no *Indians*. Believing he had landed in the Spice Islands, The East Indies, Columbus mistakenly called the peoples he met *Indios* (Indians). He erred because his geography was faulty, but his name for the people endured. Columbus did not know that he had set foot on land where aboriginal people had lived for over forty thousand years. He and subsequent newcomers were unaware that three hundred cultural groups speaking more than two hundred fifty languages lived in North America. Without writing, these first Americans stored their traditions and tribal histories in oral dramas, songs, and stories. Young ones learned from elders who were respected for their wisdom and experience. Contact and trade connected ethnic groups, but the various native peoples dressed, worshipped, spoke, and acted differently. Ignoring this marvelous diversity, Europeans and others have perpetuated misconceptions about "Indians" for five centuries.

To lump these three hundred societies with a rich variety of beliefs and languages into one label—*Indian*—was absurdly unrealistic. All Native Americans never formed a single culture, spoke a single language, or called themselves a single term. Then, as now, each group employed its self-name, such as Lakota or Diné. Recently, *Native American* has appeared as a replacement for *Indian*, but the first Americans remain divided on this issue. Authors in this anthology continue to use both terms, and we will follow their examples.

Native American images and identities have been linked for five hundred years. During that time, two sets of opposing images have prevailed. Others have labeled native peoples as noble/ignoble savages, good/bad natives, real/unreal Indians, and other inaccurate stereotypes. The ambiguity initially appeared in the Columbus letter in 1493. Writing favorably, Columbus described the natives as "so guileless and generous with all they possess, that . . . they refuse nothing . . . and display as much love as if they give their hearts." Columbus did not grasp the concepts of culturally prescribed hospitality and gift exchange. In contrast, Columbus also provided the first bad images when he wrote he had found no human monstrosities except on one island.

Later, during the Renaissance, the noble savage tradition pictured natives dwelling in an idealized landscape and living in harmony with nature, free of European history's burdens and European society's corruptions. In contrast to this image of the inhabitants of a romanticized paradise, Europeans also portrayed them as ignoble savages, mean and treacherous, lacking in scientific knowledge and without religion. During Colonial times, *good* Indians included Pocahontas, who reportedly saved Captain John Smith from execution, and Squanto, who aided the Pilgrims. More than three hundred years later, Michael Dorris pierced the fantasy of Pilgrims and Indians in "For Indians, No Thanksgiving." In nineteenth-century Western history and twentieth-century movies, *bad* Indians appeared as warlike, ignorant, and untrustworthy. Geronimo, Crazy Horse, and other warriors who defended their homelands and families against the invaders fit this stereotype. In "Dear John Wayne," Louise Erdrich deflated Wayne's Hollywood hero image.

The dual system of positive and negative images persists today as Indians are portrayed as real and unreal. If Indians are defined as being frozen in history in a curious timelessness, then real Indians are the ones before European contact or at least those during the early period of that contact. Vine Deloria, Jr., exposes stereotypes of primeval princesses and shiftless half-breeds who are unreal and ahistorical. Choctaw author Louis Owens emphasizes, "The fact that so many people throughout the world have a strangely concrete sense of what a 'real' Indian should be adds still greater stress to the puzzle; woe to him or her who identifies as Indian or mixed blood but does not bear a recognizably 'Indian' name or physiognomy or lifestyle."

In response to the problem of defining Native American identity, tribal and federal agencies have used the individual's quantum of Indian "blood." Before conquest, tribal membership was natural for the people linked by common families, language, and heritage. Native American groups have always had their own definitions of themselves and have always upheld their sovereignty to determine their memberships. The conquest of native peoples created layers of bureaucratic identification problems. When U.S. soldiers forcibly removed the Cherokees and other tribes from their homelands, the government established tribal rolls to count the people; rolls became enduring records. Indians placed on reservations were required to have individual identification in order to receive the recompense guaranteed them in treaties. Federal policy arbitrarily set a racial standard of one-quarter Indian blood as the minimum for receiving federal services. Official Certificates of Degree of Indian Blood (CDIBs) and Bureau of Indian Affairs 4432 forms verifying Indian descent that meet tribal expectations do not eliminate identity problems.

Today, access to health services, scholarships, tribal revenues, and other services requires certification from tribal and federal agencies. To add to the confusion, in the late twentieth century, tribes have determined their memberships according to various requirements. One of them may be a minimum blood quantum. Must one be one-sixteenth Osage, one-eighth Choctaw, one-quarter Blackfeet, or full-blood Sioux to be an Indian? Some tribes, including the Cherokee, have no specific blood quantum and rely on members being descendants of the early tribal rolls. From confusion in genetic makeup, the labels flow: *full-blood, mixed-blood, half-breed*. Central to Indian identity is tribal membership, and Indians themselves typically set qualifications in addition to a certain proportion of Indian genes. Some Kiowas, for example, view speaking the Kiowa language as essential. Others view participating in tribal dances, learning traditional cosmology, and other cultural activities as necessary qualifications. Several groups require participation in reservation society. Since more than fifty percent of contemporary Native Americans live in cities, the issue becomes even more complex for them and their children.

Today, a native person asking, "Who Am I?" inherits centuries of complications. Each one must piece together a giant puzzle to create an identity. At the center of his or her complex answer are six anchors: self, family, community, the land, sovereignty, and culture. As a citizen of the United States, a state, and perhaps an Indian nation (tribe), he or she is subject to three sets of legal and cultural demands.

The identity issue is crucial for Native American authors. Again, no one model holds and no single definition exists. Most have mixed heritages, and it is not surprising that many of the most poignant self-images and powerful characters in Indian literature express the anguish of defining Indian selves. Caught in reservation mathematics in his poem "13/16," Sherman Alexie cuts himself into sixteen equal pieces, keeps thirteen Indian ones and feeds the other three to the dogs. Alexie has described himself as "mixed Blood" and "mixed up." As Linda Hogan, Chickasaw and Euro-American author, testifies, living "two lives" is not easy. Hogan and Alexie refuse to become victims and continue to write their identities through images of pain and pride. Luci Tapahonso celebrates four generations of Navajo family and culture in her testimony, "What I Am."

On a positive note, the identity crisis has inspired some of the great writing in Native American literature, which you will read in this anthology. As you listen to the authors' voices, remember these touchstones, which will help you challenge and understand stereotypical portraits. Native Americans are not and never have been a united, homogeneous population; they are not represented by the stereotypes of Hollywood or most fiction; they are not peoples without history, languages, literatures, sciences, and arts; and they are not vanishing. Native Americans are individuals who share common bonds with other humans, including love for family, a sense of humor, and a wish for the good of their people. They change and adapt, taking that which works for them and leaving the rest from other cultures. As part of multicultural America, they persist in spirit, body, and heart to this moment.

READING POEMS IN PUBLIC

Maurice Kenny

Maurice Kenny, poet, short story writer, and playwright, has traveled across the country many times, usually on a bus, to perform his poetry. Born in 1929, Kenny grew up in northern New York and in the foothills of the Adirondacks. In his writing, this Mohawk author draws inspiration from Iroquois traditions and history. Among his publications are *Between Two Rivers* (1987); *Greyhounding This America* (1988); *Tekonwatonti: Molly Brant, Poems of War, 1735–1795* (1992); and *On Second Thought* (1995). He won the American Book Award for poetry for *The Mama Poems* (1984). Kenny often focuses on a flashpoint between Native Americans and others. In this poem, he creates dramatic tension between the speaker's private hopes and the audience's public responses.

I stand on a stage and read poems,
poems of boys broken on the road;
the audience tosses questions.

I tell of old chiefs swindled of their daughters,
5   young braves robbed of painted shields,
Medicine Man hitting the bottle;
I chant old songs in their language
of the Spirit in wind and water . . .
they ask if Indians shave.

10   I recite old stories,
calendar epics of victory battles,
and cavalry dawn massacres on wintered plains,
villages where war ponies are tethered to snow . . .
and they want to know
15   how many Indians commit suicide.

I read into the microphone,
I read into the camera,
I read into the printed page,
I read into the ear . . .
20 and they say what a pretty ring you wear.
The tape winds, the camera reels,
the newspaper spins
and the headlines read:
Ruffian, the race horse, dies in surgery.

25 At the end of the reading they thank me;
go for hamburgers at McDonalds
and pick up a six-pack to suck
as they watch the death
of Geronimo on the late show.

30 I stand on a stage and read poems,
and read poems, and read . . .

DISCUSSION QUESTIONS

1. Find five Indian images in the poem. Do you consider them positive, negative, or neutral? What is your reaction to the terms *Indian* and *Native American?*
2. What does the reader of poems want his audience to understand? Which lines tell you he is disappointed in their reactions? Give three reasons that you think prevent the audience from "hearing" his message.
3. The poet uses nouns/verbs to structure the poem: "I stand," "I tell," "I recite," "I read." Make a list of the verbs for "they," and for the tape, newspaper, and headlines. Why is this an effective technique for organizing the differences between the speaker and the audience?

WRITING TOPICS

1. Imagine you are a member of the speaker's audience. What questions would you ask him? Write a conversation between you and him in response to his reading this poem to you.

2. Collect information about a Native American leader, artist, or writer from newspapers, journals, books, and Internet sites. Write two paragraphs in which you describe your subject using factual details.
3. Write a poem or story about a time when someone did not listen to your important message. Where were you? Who was your audience? What was your message? Why did they fail to understand? What would you say to them today?

INDIANS TODAY, THE REAL AND UNREAL

Vine Deloria, Jr.

Vine Deloria, Jr., is a forceful, moral voice for Indian rights. As a theologian, attorney, and political scientist, he attacks stereotypes, defends land claims, and proposes Indian policy. A prolific author of more than ten books and eighty articles, Deloria has written on all aspects of contemporary American Indian affairs. In *Custer Died for Your Sins* (1969), from which the following excerpt is taken, he indicts federal policies and proposes actions for twentieth-century Indians. He continues these topics in *We Talk, You Listen* (1970), *God Is Red* (1973), and *American Indian Policy in the Twentieth Century* (1985). In *Red Earth, White Lies* (1995), Deloria challenges scientific theories that ignore wisdom preserved in oral histories and sacred traditions. Born in 1933 in Martin, South Dakota, to a distinguished Sioux family on the Pine Ridge Indian Reservation, Deloria is an enrolled member of the Standing Rock Sioux Tribe.

1   Indians are like the weather. Everyone knows all about the weather, but none can change it. When storms are predicted, the sun shines. When picnic weather is announced, the rain begins. Likewise, if you count on the unpredictability of Indian people, you will never be sorry.

2   One of the finest things about being an Indian is that people are always interested in you and your "plight." Other groups have difficulties, predicaments, quandaries, problems, or troubles. Traditionally we Indians have had a "plight."

3   Our foremost plight is our transparency. People can tell just by looking at us what we want, what should be done to help us, how we feel, and what a "real" Indian is really like. Indian life, as it relates to the real world, is a continuous attempt not to disappoint people who know us. Unfulfilled expectations cause grief and we have already had our share.

4   Because people can see right through us, it becomes impossible to tell truth from fiction or fact from mythology. Experts paint us as they would

like us to be. Often we paint ourselves as we wish we were or as we might have been.

5   The more we try to be ourselves the more we are forced to defend what we have never been. The American public feels most comfortable with the mythical Indians of stereotype-land who were always THERE. These Indians are fierce, they wear feathers and grunt. Most of us don't fit this idealized figure since we grunt only when overeating, which is seldom.

6   To be an Indian in modern American society is in a very real sense to be unreal and ahistorical. In this book we will discuss the other side—the unrealities that face us as Indian people. It is this unreal feeling that has been welling up inside us and threatens to make this decade the most decisive in history for Indian people. In so many ways, Indian people are re-examining themselves in an effort to redefine a new social structure for their people. Tribes are reordering their priorities to account for the obvious discrepancies between their goals and the goals whites have defined for them.

7   Indian reactions are sudden and surprising. One day at a conference we were singing "My Country 'Tis of Thee" and we came across the part that goes:

> Land where our fathers died
> Land of the Pilgrims' pride . . .

Some of us broke out laughing when we realized that our fathers undoubtedly died trying to keep those Pilgrims from stealing our land. In fact, many of our fathers died because the Pilgrims killed them as witches. We didn't feel much kinship with those Pilgrims, regardless of who they did in.

8   We often hear "give it back to the Indians" when a gadget fails to work. It's a terrible thing for a people to realize that society has set aside all non-working gadgets for their exclusive use.

9   During my three years as Executive Director of the National Congress of American Indians it was a rare day when some white didn't visit my office and proudly proclaim that he or she was of Indian descent.

10   Cherokee was the most popular tribe of their choice and many people placed the Cherokees anywhere from Maine to Washington State. Mohawk, Sioux, and Chippewa were next in popularity. Occasionally I would be told about some mythical tribe from lower Pennsylvania, Virginia, or Massachusetts which had spawned the white standing before me.

11   At times I became quite defensive about being a Sioux when these white people had a pedigree that was so much more respectable than mine. But eventually I came to understand their need to identify as partially Indian and did not resent them. I would confirm their wildest stories about their Indian ancestry and would add a few tales of my own hoping that they would be able to accept themselves someday and leave us alone.

12   Whites claiming Indian blood generally tend to reinforce mythical beliefs about Indians. All but one person I met who claimed Indian blood claimed it on their grandmother's side. I once did a projection backward and dis-

covered that evidently most tribes were entirely female for the first three hundred years of white occupation. No one, it seemed, wanted to claim a male Indian as a forebear.

13   It doesn't take much insight into racial attitudes to understand the real meaning of the Indian-grandmother complex that plagues certain whites. A male ancestor has too much of the aura of the savage warrior, the unknown primitive, the instinctive animal, to make him a respectable member of the family tree. But a young Indian princess? Ah, there was royalty for the taking. Somehow the white was linked with a noble house of gentility and culture if his grandmother was an Indian princess who ran away with an intrepid pioneer. And royalty has always been an unconscious but all-consuming goal of the European immigrant.

14   The early colonists, accustomed to life under benevolent despots, projected their understanding of the European political structure onto the Indian tribe in trying to explain its political and social structure. European royal houses were closed to ex-convicts and indentured servants, so the colonists made all Indian maidens princesses, then proceeded to climb a social ladder of their own creation. Within the next generation, if the trend continues, a large portion of the American population will eventually be related to Powhatan.

15   While a real Indian grandmother is probably the nicest thing that could happen to a child, why is a remote Indian princess grandmother so necessary for many whites? Is it because they are afraid of being classed as foreigners? Do they need some blood tie with the frontier and its dangers in order to experience what it means to be an American? Or is it an attempt to avoid facing the guilt they bear for the treatment of the Indian?

16   The phenomenon seems to be universal. Only among the Jewish community, which has a long tribal-religious tradition of its own, does the mysterious Indian grandmother, the primeval princess, fail to dominate the family tree. Otherwise, there's not much to be gained by claiming Indian blood or publicly identifying as an Indian. The white believes that there is a great danger the lazy Indian will eventually corrupt God's hard-working people. He is still suspicious that the Indian way of life is dreadfully wrong. There is, in fact, something *un-American* about Indians for most whites.

17   I ran across a classic statement of this attitude one day in a history book which was published shortly after the turn of the century. Often have I wondered how many Senators, Congressmen, and clergymen of the day accepted the attitudes of that book as a basic fact of life in America. In no uncertain terms did the book praise God that the Indian had not yet been able to corrupt North America as he had South America:

> It was perhaps fortunate for the future of America that the Indians of the North rejected civilization. Had they accepted it the whites and Indians might have intermarried to some extent as they did in Mexico. That would have given us a population made up in a measure of shiftless half-breeds.

I never dared to show this passage to my white friends who had claimed Indian blood, but I often wondered why they were so energetic if they did have some of the bad seed in them.

18 Those whites who dare not claim Indian blood have an asset of their own. They *understand* Indians.

19 Understanding Indians is not an esoteric art. All it takes is a trip through Arizona or New Mexico, watching a documentary on TV, having known *one* in the service, or having read a popular book on *them*.

20 There appears to be some secret osmosis about Indian people by which they can magically and instantaneously communicate complete knowledge about themselves to these interested whites. Rarely is physical contact required. Anyone and everyone who knows an Indian or who is *interested,* immediately and thoroughly understands them.

21 You can verify this great truth at your next party. Mention Indians and you will find a person who saw some in a gas station in Utah, or who attended the Gallup ceremonial celebration, or whose Uncle Jim hired one to cut logs in Oregon, or whose church had a missionary come to speak last Sunday on the plight of Indians and the mission of the church.

22 There is no subject on earth so easily understood as that of the American Indian. Each summer, work camps disgorge teenagers on various reservations. Within one month's time the youngsters acquire a knowledge of Indians that would astound a college professor.

23 Easy knowledge about Indians is a historical tradition. After Columbus "discovered" America he brought back news of a great new world which he assumed to be India and, therefore, filled with Indians. Almost at once European folklore devised a complete explanation of the new land and its inhabitants which featured the Fountain of Youth, the Seven Cities of Gold, and other exotic attractions. The absence of elephants apparently did not tip off the explorers that they weren't in India. By the time they realized their mistake, instant knowledge of Indians was a cherished tradition.

24 Missionaries, after learning some of the religious myths of tribes they encountered, solemnly declared that the inhabitants of the new continent were the Ten Lost Tribes of Israel. Indians thus received a religious-historical identity far greater than they wanted or deserved. But it was an impossible identity. Their failure to measure up to Old Testament standards doomed them to a fall from grace and they were soon relegated to the status of a picturesque species of wildlife.

25 Like the deer and the antelope, Indians seemed to play rather than get down to the serious business of piling up treasures upon the earth where thieves break through and steal. Scalping, introduced prior to the French

and Indian War by the English,* confirmed the suspicion that Indians were wild animals to be hunted and skinned. Bounties were set and an Indian scalp became more valuable than beaver, otter, marten, and other animal pelts.

26 American blacks had become recognized as a species of human being by amendments to the Constitution shortly after the Civil War. Prior to emancipation they had been counted as three-fifths of a person in determining population for representation in the House of Representatives. Early civil rights bills nebulously state that other people shall have the same rights as "white people," indicating there *were* "other people." But civil rights bills passed during and after the Civil War systematically excluded Indian people. For a long time an Indian was not presumed capable of initiating an action in a court of law, of owning property, or of giving testimony against whites in court. Nor could an Indian vote or leave his reservation. Indians were America's captive people without any defined rights whatsoever.

27 Then one day the white man discovered that the Indian tribes still owned some 135 million acres of land. To his horror he learned that much of it was very valuable. Some was good grazing land, some was farm land, some mining land, and some covered with timber.

28 Animals could be herded together on a piece of land, but they could not sell it. Therefore it took no time at all to discover that Indians were really people and should have the right to sell their lands. Land was the means of recognizing the Indian as a human being. It was the method whereby land could be stolen legally and not blatantly.

---

*Notice, for example the following proclamation:

Given at the Council Chamber in Boston this third day of November 1755 in the twenty-ninth year of the Reign of our Sovereign Lord George the Second by the Grace of God of Great Britain, France, and Ireland, King Defender of the Faith.

By His Honour's command
J. Willard, Secry,
God Save the King

Whereas the tribe of Penobscot Indians have repeatedly in a perfidious manner acted contrary to their solemn submission unto his Majesty long since made and frequently renewed.

I have, therefore, at the desire of the House of Representatives . . . thought fit to issue this Proclamation and to declare the Penobscot Tribe of Indians to be enemies, rebels and traitors to his Majesty. . . . And I do hereby require his Majesty's subjects of the Province to embrace all opportunities of pursuing, captivating, killing and destroy-all and every of the aforesaid Indians.

And whereas the General Court of this Province have voted that a bounty . . . be granted and allowed to be paid out of the Province Treasury . . . the premiums of bounty following viz:

For every scalp of a male Indian brought in as evidence of their being killed as aforesaid, forty pounds.

For every scalp of such female Indian or male Indian under the age of twelve years that shall be killed and brought in as evidence of their being killed as aforesaid, twenty pounds.

29   Once the Indian was thus acknowledged, it was fairly simple to determine what his goals were. If, thinking went, the Indian was just like the white, he must have the same outlook as the white. So the future was planned for the Indian people in public and private life. First in order was allotting them reservations so that they could sell their lands. God's foreordained plan to repopulate the continent fit exactly with the goals of the tribes as they were defined by their white friends.

30   It is fortunate that we were never slaves. We gave up land instead of life and labor. Because the Negro labored, he was considered a draft animal. Because the Indian occupied large areas of land, he was considered a wild animal. Had we given up anything else, or had anything else to give up, it is certain that we would have been considered some other thing.

31   Whites have had different attitudes toward the Indians and the blacks since the Republic was founded. Whites have always refused to give nonwhites the respect which they have been found to legally possess. Instead there has always been a contemptuous attitude that although the law says one thing, "we all know better."

32   Thus whites steadfastly refused to allow blacks to enjoy the fruits of full citizenship. They systematically closed schools, churches, stores, restaurants, and public places to blacks or made insulting provisions for them. For one hundred years every program of public and private white America was devoted to the exclusion of the black. It was, perhaps, embarrassing to be rubbing shoulders with one who had not so long before been defined as a field animal.

33   The Indian suffered the reverse treatment. Law after law was passed requiring him to conform to white institutions. Indian children were kidnapped and forced into boarding schools thousands of miles from their homes to learn the white man's ways. Reservations were turned over to different Christian denominations for governing. Reservations were for a long time church operated. Everything possible was done to ensure that Indians were forced into American life. The wild animal was made into a household pet whether or not he wanted to be one.

34   Policies for both black and Indian failed completely. Blacks eventually began the Civil Rights movement. In doing so they assured themselves some rights in white society. Indians continued to withdraw from the overtures of white society and tried to maintain their own communities and activities.

35   Actually both groups had little choice. Blacks, trapped in a world of white symbols, retreated into themselves. And people thought comparable Indian withdrawal unnatural because they expected Indians to behave like whites. . . .

36   One of the foremost differences separating white and Indian was simply one of origin. Whites derived predominantly from western Europe. The earliest settlers on the Atlantic seaboard came from England and the low countries. For the most part they shared the common experiences of their peo-

ples and dwelt within the world view which had dominated western Europe for over a millennium.

37   Conversely Indians had always been in the western hemisphere. Life on this continent and views concerning it were not shaped in a post-Roman atmosphere. The entire outlook of the people was one of simplicity and mystery, not scientific or abstract. The western hemisphere produced wisdom, western Europe produced knowledge.

38   Perhaps this distinction seems too simple to mention. It is not. Many is the time I have sat in Congressional hearings and heard the chairman of the committee crow about "our" great Anglo-Saxon heritage of law and order. Looking about the hearing room I saw row after row of full-blood Indians with blank expressions on their faces. As far as they were concerned, Sir Walter Raleigh was a brand of pipe tobacco that you got at the trading post.

39   When we talk about European background, we are talking about feudalism, kings, queens, their divine right to rule their subjects, the Reformation, Christianity, the Magna Charta and all of the events that went to make up European history.

40   American Indians do not share that heritage. They do not look wistfully back across the seas to the old country. The Apache were not at Runymede to make King John sign the Magna Charta. The Cherokee did not create English common law. The Pima had no experience with the rise of capitalism and industrialism. The Blackfeet had no monasteries. No tribe has an emotional, historical, or political relationship to events of another continent and age.

41   Indians have had their own political history which has shaped the outlook of the tribes. There were great confederacies throughout the country before the time of the white invader. The eastern Iroquois formed a strong league because as single tribes they had been weak and powerless against larger tribes. The Deep South was controlled by three confederacies: the Creeks with their town system, the Natchez, and the Powhattan confederation which extended into tidelands Virginia. The Pequots and their cousins the Mohicans controlled the area of Connecticut, Massachusetts, Rhode Island, and Long Island.

42   True democracy was more prevalent among Indian tribes in pre-Columbian days than it has been since. Despotic power was abhorred by tribes that were loose combinations of hunting parties rather than political entities.

43   Conforming their absolute freedom to fit rigid European political forms has been very difficult for most tribes, but on the whole they have managed extremely well. Under the Indian Reorganization Act Indian people have generally created a modern version of the old tribal political structure and yet have been able to develop comprehensive reservation programs which compare favorably with governmental structures anywhere. . . .

44   Today the Indian people are in a good position to demonstrate to the nation what can be done in community development in the rural areas. With

the overcrowding of the urban areas, rural development should be the coming thing and understanding of tribal programs could indicate methods of resettling the vast spaces of rural America.

45   With so much happening on reservations and the possibility of a brighter future in store, Indians have started to become livid when they realize the contagious trap the mythology of white America has caught them in. The descendant of Pocahantas is a remote and incomprehensible mystery to us. We are no longer a wild species of animal loping freely across the prairie. We have little in common with the last of the Mohicans. We are TASK FORCED to death.

46   Some years ago at a Congressional hearing someone asked Alex Chasing Hawk, a council member of the Cheyenne River Sioux for thirty years, "Just what do you Indians want?" Alex replied, "A leave-us-alone law!!"

47   The primary goal and need of Indians today is not for someone to feel sorry for us and claim descent from Pocahontas to make us feel better. Nor do we need to be classified as semi-white and have programs and policies made to bleach us further. Nor do we need further studies to see if we are feasible. We need a new policy by Congress acknowledging our right to live in peace, free from arbitrary harassment. We need the public at large to drop the myths in which it has clothed us for so long. We need fewer and fewer "experts" on Indians.

48   What we need is a cultural leave-us-alone agreement in spirit and in fact.

DISCUSSION QUESTIONS

1. Deloria refers to "real" and "unreal" Indians. What stereotypical images does he attack? List racist misconceptions that impede understanding between Indians and whites.
2. Deloria uses humor as a weapon. Find humorous lines, such as "we grunt only when overeating, which is seldom." Do you think this technique is effective?
3. The author asks for "a cultural leave-us-alone agreement." Is this request logical? How can understanding be promoted between Indians and other people if they are separated?

WRITING TOPICS

1. Major topics in this essay include Indian stereotypes, conflict over land ownership, and Indians' rights. Select one topic and develop a three-paragraph essay that cites specific evidence from Deloria.
2. Irony is a figure of speech in which the actual intent is expressed in words that carry the opposite meaning. Deloria uses irony throughout the essay. Write a paragraph in which you explain two or more ironic examples that you think help convince the reader of the author's point.
3. Select one argument in the essay that you disagree with and defend your view in a short essay.

FOR INDIANS, NO THANKSGIVING

Michael Dorris

Modoc author Michael Dorris (1945–1997) challenged ignorant and misguided images of Native Americans. A staunch advocate
for respect for Native American cultures, Dorris also supported universal tolerance. When asked about the risk of racist ethnicity, he
replied, "We're all Americans. The common denominator of being
Americans crosses all ethnic lines. A person's ethnic group matters,
but we all have so much in common that it's a bridge." The first step
on that bridge is listening to Native American voices. Acutely aware
of the dangers of subtle or blatant racism for all people, Dorris
shared his convictions in articles for scholarly and popular journals,
novels, short stories, children's books, and nonfiction works. In his
novel *Guests* (1994), a young Wampanoag counteracts the traditional Thanksgiving story by questioning his father's invitation to
hungry, strange-looking immigrants to join their traditional harvest
feast. In the following essay, Dorris asks us to reconsider the facts
and fantasy of the first Thanksgiving.

1   Maybe those Pilgrims and Wampanoags[1] actually got together for a
November picnic, maybe not. It matters only as an ironical footnote.
2   For the former group, it would have been a celebration of a precarious
hurdle successfully crossed on the path to the political domination, first of a
continent and eventually of a planet. For the latter, it would have been, at
best, a naive extravaganza—the last meeting as equals with invaders who,
within a few years, would win King Philip's War[2] and decorate the entrances
to their towns with rows of stakes, each topped with an Indian head.

---

[1] *Wampanoags:* Indians who shared their harvests with the Pilgrims.
[2] *King Philip's War:* To protect Wampanoag homes and land, Metacomet (King Philip) led the resistance
against the colonists.

3   The few aboriginal survivors of the ensuing violence were either sold into Caribbean slavery by their better-armed, erstwhile hosts or ruthlessly driven from their Cape Cod homes. Despite the symbolic idealism of the first potluck, New England—from the emerging European point of view—simply wasn't big enough for two sets of societies.

4   An enduring benefit of success, when one culture clashes with another, is that the victorious group controls the record. It owns not only the immediate spoils but also the power to edit, embellish, and concoct the facts of the original encounter for the generations to come. Events, once past, reside at the small end of the telescope, the vague and hazy antecedents to accepted reality.

5   Our collective modern fantasy of Thanksgiving is a case in point. It has evolved into a ritual pageant that almost everyone of us, as children either acted in or were forced to watch—a seventeenth-century vision that we can conjure whole in the blink of an eye.

6   The cast of stock characters is as recognizable as those in any Macy's parade: dour-faced Pilgrim men, right-to-bear-arms muskets at their sides, sitting around a rude outdoor table while their wives, dressed in long dresses, aprons, and linen caps, bustle about lifting the lids off steaming kettles—pater- and materfamilias of New World hospitality.

7   They dish out the turkey to a scattering of shirtless Indian invitees. But there is no ambiguity as to who is in charge of the occasion, who could be asked to leave, whose protocol prevails.

8   Only "good" Indians are admitted to this tableau, of course, as in those who accept the Manifest Destiny of a European presence and are prepared to adopt English dining customs and, by inference, English everything else.

9   These compliant Hollywood extras are, naturally enough, among the blessings the Pilgrims are thankful for—and why not? Holiday Indians are colorful, bring the food, and vanish after dessert. They are something exotic to write home about, like a visit to Frontierland. In the sound bite of national folklore, they have metamorphosed into totems of America as evocative, and ultimately as vapid, as a flag factory.

10   And members of this particular make-believe tribe did not all repair to the happy hunting grounds during the first Christmas rush. They lived on, smoking peace pipes and popping up at appropriate crowd-pleasing moments.

11   They lost mock battles from coast to coast in Wild West shows. In nineteenth-century art, they sat bareback on their horses and stoically watched a lot of sunsets. Entire professional sports teams of them take the home field every Sunday afternoon in Cleveland, Atlanta, or Washington, D.C.

12   They are the sources of merit badges for Boy Scouts and the emblem of purity for imitation butter. They are, and have been from the beginning, predictable, manageable, domesticated inventions without depth or reality apart from that bestowed by their creators.

13   These appreciative Indians, as opposed to the pesky flesh and blood

native peoples on whom they are loosely modeled, did not question the enforced exchange of their territories for a piece of pie. They did not protest when they died by the millions from European diseases.

14   They did not resist—except for the "bad" ones, the renegades—when solemn pacts made with them were broken or when their religions and customs were declared illegal. They did not make a fuss in courts in defense of their sovereignty. They never expected all the fixings anyway.

15   As for Thanksgiving 1988, the descendants of those first party-goers sit at increasingly distant tables, the pretense of equity all but abandoned. Against great odds, Native Americans have maintained political identity, but, in a country so insecure about heterogeneity that it votes its dominant language as "official," this refusal to melt into the pot has been an expensive choice.

16   A majority of reservation Indians reside in the most impoverished counties in the nation. They constitute the ethnic group at the wrong extreme of every scale: most undernourished, most short-lived, least educated, least healthy. For them, Thanksgiving was perhaps their last square meal.

DISCUSSION QUESTIONS

1. According to Dorris, why do many Native Americans refuse to celebrate Thanksgiving?
2. The author creates images for Thanksgiving: "November picnic," "ironical footnote," "naive extravaganza," "the first potluck," "ritual pageant," "this tableau." How does each of these descriptions relate to his primary argument? Describe some of your cultural images of Thanksgiving. Which of Dorris's images offend you? What would you say to him in defense of your views?
3. In this selection, who are the "good" and "bad" Indians? How does Dorris refer to stereotypical Euro-Americans?
4. What are three examples of ironic humor that the author uses to sharpen his impact?

WRITING TOPICS

1. Select one of these topic sentences to complete a paragraph with details from the selection:

   Holiday Indians are colorful, bring the food, and vanish after dessert.

   It matters only as an ironical footnote.

   An enduring benefit of success, when one culture clashes with another, is that the victorious group controls the record.

2. In the headnote that precedes the essay, Dorris is quoted as saying that "a person's ethnic group matters, but we all have so much in common that it's a bridge." In a brief essay, describe what cultural factors have provided a bridge between ethnic groups, helping to merge all groups into Americans.

13/16

Sherman Alexie

Sherman Alexie, the son of a Spokane father and a part-Coeur d'Alene mother, was born in 1966 and grew up on the Spokane Indian Reservation in Wellpinit, Washington. Alexie has published more than two hundred poems, stories, and translations. A compassionate trickster, Alexie exposes reservation poverty, unemployment, alcoholism, and despair with comic wit. But reservation life means more than pain, as Alexie shows in *First Indian on the Moon* (1993). The reservation is also home for fancydancers, basketball players, book collectors, and dreamers. His poem "13/16" appears in *The Business of Fancydancing* (1992). In the poem, his identity equals reservation mathematics figured in genetic formulas. Alexie quips that Indians learn to love by the measuring cup.

1.

I cut myself into sixteen equal pieces
keep thirteen and feed the other three
to the dogs, who have also grown

tired of U.S. Commodities, white cans
5   black letters translated into Spanish.
"Does this mean I have to learn

the language to eat?" Lester FallsApart asks
but directions for preparation are simple:
a. WASH CAN; b. OPEN CAN; c. EXAMINE CONTENTS

10   OF CAN FOR SPOILAGE; d. EMPTY CONTENTS
OF CAN INTO SAUCE PAN; e. COOK CONTENTS
OVER HIGH HEAT; f. SERVE AND EAT.

2.

It is done by blood, reservation mathematics, fractions:
father (full-blood) + mother (5/8) = son (13/16).

It is done by enrollment number, last name first, first name last:
Spokane Tribal Enrollment Number 1569; Victor, Chief.

It is done by identification card, photograph, lamination:
IF FOUND, PLEASE RETURN TO SPOKANE TRIBE OF INDIANS,
WELLPINIT, WA.

3.

The compromise is always made
in increments. On this reservation
we play football on real grass
dream of deserts, three inches of rain

in a year. What we have lost:
uranium mine, Little Falls Dam
salmon. Our excuses are trapped
within museums, roadside attractions

totem poles in Riverfront Park.
I was there, watching the Spokane River
changing. A ten-year-old white boy asked
if I was a real Indian. He did not wait

for an answer, instead carving his initials
into the totem with a pocketknife: J.N.
We are what we take, carving my name
my enrollment number, thirteen hash marks

into the wood. A story is remembered
as evidence, the Indian man they found dead
shot in the alley behind the Mayfair.
Authorities reported a rumor he had relatives

in Minnesota. A member of some tribe or another
his photograph on the 11 o'clock news. Eyes, hair
all dark, his shovel-shaped incisor, each the same
ordinary identification of the anonymous.

4.

When my father disappeared, we found him
45 years later, in a strange kitchen searching
for footprints in the dust: still

untouched on the shelves all the commodity
cans without labels—my father opened them
one by one, finding a story in each.

DISCUSSION QUESTIONS

1. Alexie structures his poem in four parts, each of which develops related topics of identity and labels. In part 1, the speaker feeds 3/16 of himself to the dogs. What part does he keep? In part 2, how are "blood," "enrollment number," and "identification card" related to identity? In part 3, with all the labels, why is the murdered Indian anonymous? Native Americans treasure their tribal stories because they express survival and tradition. Why is part 4 humorous and positive?

2. Alexie's poem is laced with irony. What is ironic about the name Lester FallsApart and his question? Explain the irony in the poet's juxtaposing simplistic, numbered directions for opening the government-issued commodity cans in part 1 with the government's formulas for identifying Indians in part 2. In part 3, what is ironic about the question of the white boy juxtaposed with the anonymous murdered Indian? In part 4, what is ironic about the unlabeled cans?

WRITING TOPICS

1. Write a short essay exploring Alexie's ironic ideas about reservation identity. Include evidence about "real" Indians, poverty, labels, and stories.

2. In a paragraph or two, describe your genetic "mathematics" that helps establish your identity in school and in your private life. How does your mathematical portrait differ from Alexie's?

THE TRUTH IS

Linda Hogan

Linda Hogan's writing and family history have deep roots in Oklahoma. In her first book of poetry, *Calling Myself Home* (1979) she pays homage to the red earth of Oklahoma, the land she knows and loves. Born in 1947 to a Chickasaw father and Euro-American mother, Hogan is an accomplished fiction writer as well as a fine poet. *Seeing Through the Sun* (1985) won an American Book Award from the Before Columbus Foundation. *The Book of Medicines* (1993) offers healing wisdom emerging from Native American female spirituality. In "The Truth Is," Hogan wrestles with the difficulty of balancing her twin genetic heritages.

In my left pocket a Chickasaw hand
rests on the bone of the pelvis.
In my right pocket
a white hand. Don't worry. It's mine
5 and not some thief's.
It belongs to a woman who sleeps in a twin bed
even though she falls in love too easily,
and walks along with hands
in her own empty pockets
10 even though she has put them in others
for love not money.

About the hands, I'd like to say
I am a tree, grafted branches
bearing two kinds of fruit,
15 apricots maybe and pit cherries.
It's not that way. The truth is
we are crowded together
and knock against each other at night.
We want amnesty.

20 Linda, girl, I keep telling you
this is nonsense
about who loved who
and who killed who.

Here I am, taped together
25 like some old civilian conservation corps
passed by from the great depression
and my pockets are empty.
It's just as well since they are masks
for the soul, and since coins and keys
30 both have the sharp teeth of property.

Girl, I say,
it is dangerous to be a woman of two countries.
You've got your hands in the dark
of two empty pockets. Even though
35 you walk and whistle like you aren't afraid
you know which pocket the enemy lives in
and you remember how to fight
so you better keep right on walking.
And you remember who killed who.
40 For this you want amnesty
and there's that knocking on the door
in the middle of the night.

Relax, there are other things to think about.
Shoes, for instance.
45 Now those are the true masks of the soul.
The left shoe
and the right one with its white foot.

DISCUSSION QUESTIONS

1. Like Sherman Alexie, Linda Hogan is split between two lives. In each of
the six stanzas, find lines that illustrate her division. How do you interpret "it is dangerous to be a woman of two countries" (line 32)?

2. Which lines tell you she is haunted by history? One example is "you
know what pocket the enemy lives in." Why does she talk to herself?
How are poverty and property related to her history?

3. How do you know she is fearful as she tries to resolve the war within herself? Explain "We want amnesty."

WRITING TOPICS

1. Hogan selects specific images to express her divided life. Write a paragraph that develops the following topic sentence: In "The Truth Is," Linda Hogan pairs metaphors to symbolize her inner and outer conflict: two pockets, two shoes, two countries, two kinds of fruit, and two pronouns, "I" (You) and "We."
2. Imagine you and Linda Hogan are friends. As her friend, explain in a letter to her how you see "the truth" about the history you both share. Include information about your family history that compares with hers.
3. Expand the following idea in a few sentences: Pockets and shoes are masks of the soul.

THE TWO LIVES

Linda Hogan

How can one woman live two lives? As she tackles the question of what it is like to be culturally and genetically mixed in the United States, Hogan says, "two lives lived me." Here she also explains there is a bond between her life and other lives of color and without privilege. She considers her writing part of Chickasaw history, but she has also written: "I tell parts of my stories because I have often searched out other lives similar to my own. Telling our lives is important, for those who come after us, for those who will see our experience as part of their own historical struggle." As a teacher of creative writing at the University of Colorado, she encourages her students to consider the impact of oppression, racism, and classism on all people. Always a critic of unequal distribution of wealth, she has noted that the poor who will inherit the earth already work it.

1   November 13, 1984. Today the newspaper contains the usual stories: two countries negotiating money and peace, a space shuttle penetrating the sky, the U.S. government preparing to invade Nicaragua, thousands of Minneapolis teenagers in line to purchase tickets for a Prince concert, an infant girl rejecting the transplanted heart of a baboon. Children are being abused . . . in their families and schools, and by their protectors. There has been a sniper shooting. Two large scorpions guard jewels in Bavaria. Coal miners and other worker struggles are in resistance against governments and police. Microwaves and diamonds are on sale.

2   In the face of this history that goes on minute by minute, the oppression recorded in the papers, human pain and joy, it is a difficult thing to think of autobiography, that telling of our selves or our lives or innerness.

3   I tell parts of my stories here because I have often searched out other lives similar to my own. They would have sustained me. Telling our lives is important, for those who come after us, for those who will see our experience as part of their own historical struggle. I think of my work as part of

the history of our tribe and as part of the history of colonization everywhere. I tell this carefully, and with omissions, so as not to cause any divisions between myself and others. I want it to be understood that the opening paragraph, the news of November 13, 1984, is directly connected to this history, to our stories, to the continuing destruction of Third World and tribal people, and the exploitation of our earth.

4   I come from two different people, from white pioneers who crossed into Nebraska plains and from Chickasaw Indian people from south central Oklahoma.

5   Of the pioneers I know very little except for a journal I have that was written by my maternal great-grandfather during the Depression in 1934. It is a spare book, though it spans the years from 1848 to 1934. His words cover a great movement across the American continent.

6   The journal describes pre-Civil War 1861 when my maternal great-grandfather, W. E. Bower, hoed broom corn, working from dawn to night before he walked home three miles. In 1862 he moved to where a railroad was being constructed, near the Wisconsin River, for hauling wheat. They used wood as fuel for the engines. He cut and hauled wood. At night he worked with his father making shoes until an accident occurred in which the elder Bower was dragged by horses and injured. The younger man then went to work full time for the lumber industry. In three years (1872) he went to Nebraska to homestead. The crops and trees were all eaten by grasshoppers. I have seen this in my own life, so I know it is true. My father tells of seeing plagues of grasshoppers that ate everything made of wood, even shovel handles.

7   Desperate after crop failures, Bower began hunting buffalo in order to sell the meat. The settlers were starving, according to his journal, and the government was sending soldiers out to shoot the buffalo. They also hunted beaver and antelope. He was followed once by hundreds of coyotes and was afraid at night.

8   I see from these words how closely destruction of the land and animal life are linked to the beginning American economy. This continues to be true. I see also how desperate the struggle for survival was for the new white Americans in those days. Their lack of regard for the land and life came out of that desperation. It continues today out of that tradition, but does not work in the service of life.

9   Bower writes about a railroad section boss who refused to give him and his cohunters water from a well and refused them water for their horses, and how the hunters went for their revolvers before they were allowed to drink.

10   I believe he commented upon this cruelty because it surprised him. Historically, the incident took place at a time when major acts of genocide were being committed against tribal people across the country, when Mission Indians were being moved and moved again as settlers began to take over the California lands, when southern tribes were just removed to Indian Territory (Oklahoma), and when numerous other tribes from the North

were being forced into the South, many in resistance. It was a continuing time of great and common acts of cruelty and violence.

11   Bower commented that he saw Indians and they looked friendly. I made this into a poem:

OLD MEN AT WAR, OLD WOMEN

Be silent
old men who live inside me,
dark grandfather that was silent
though I was his blood
5   and wore his black eyes.
He's living in my breath
when it's quiet,
all his people are walking
through my veins without speech.

10   And blonde grandfather
fishing the river for Chubs,
many hunts
to sell buffalo who stood quiet
trusting the settlers
15   starving in Nebraska.
His words:
    We saw Indians but they seemed peaceful.

Red River,
I'm at the red river
20   and it's going dry,
all of us,
we are here,
and I'm drinking your wine for you,
the color of the dawn
25   heading for light
heading for one light.
I'm wearing your love and hate
like silver
and blue stone.

30   This face
this body
this hair
is not mine.
This war inside me
35   is not mine.

I've been waiting,
where are the women?
Are they listening to this
beneath all the soft layers of my skin.
40 Are they listening.
Are they loving each other?

(from *Eclipse*)

12 During the time Bower traveled the continent, my Chickasaw people were trying to make a life in Oklahoma after having been moved forcibly over the Trail of Tears, that trail they began unwillingly and with great sorrow, from our homeland in Mississippi in order that settlers there could have the rich southern lands. That was the trail where soldiers killed children in order to make the journey quick, where women were brutalized, men murdered, where the bodies of living people were left to die as markers along a trail of history, pointing the direction back to our homeland.

13 After Removal, Chickasaws, many of whom had cooperated with whites and been slaveholders in the South before the Removal Act, were told to fight for the South in the Civil War. It is surprising that anyone thought Indian people might want to take up white wars after Removal, which politicized tribes, which Geary Hobson once said was a travesty that turned any white blood running in our veins red.

14 In a November blizzard those Indians who refused to fight were sent into Kansas without rations, horses, shoes, or clothing. Most died, and it was planned that way. As Joy Harjo has said, there are those of us who have survived who were never meant to survive.

15 This was followed by the Dawes Act,[1] by other wars, by one tragedy laid down upon another, by land loss and swindles during the oil boom and the Depression, by continuing struggle, poverty, and loss.

16 My great-grandmother Addie was the granddaughter of Winchester Colbert, head of the Chickasaw Nation. She married Granville Walker Young, a rancher and politician of French-Indian (*métis*) ancestry and as such, in Indian Territory, was considered to be white. As a white intermarried citizen of the Chickasaw Nation, he was given land, and later a place on the Chickasaw legislature, and they built a large home. It is said that as a commissioner of lands, he managed to accumulate money from the tribal holdings. I would like to think this is not true and that I've been misinformed, but historically, it sounds correct. It is not that different today with some Indian leaders.

17 Their daughter, Lucy Young, was my grandmother. When she married a

---

[1] *Dawes Act:* The Dawes Act of 1887 was an attempt to establish private ownership of Indian lands. Indian family heads were to receive 160 acres and others over eighteen years old were to receive eighty acres. This process deprived Native Americans of more than ninety million acres, however.

Chickasaw named Charles Colbert Henderson, her father disowned her, as he did another daughter.

18   My grandmother graduated from the Bloomfield Academy for Chickasaw girls in 1904. In school, she learned to play the violin and the piano. She learned the manners of white upper-class southern women, for this was what the teachers valued in Indian girls, yet when I was a child, she and my grandfather lived in southern poverty, without water or lights, with horse and wagon.

19   That is the history of most of the southern tribes. I believe that when I say the truth, many of my family will feel defensive, as if I am saying that there was something wrong with my grandparents or family that we did not have money. But it is a shared experience. Some Indians built ranches, farms, or nearly comfortable lives only to lose them and return to poverty. We are landless Indians. Most of us continue to live below the poverty level defined by the U.S. government. We often dislike ourselves. We are made to believe that poverty is created by ourselves and not that it is an economic problem existing within the history of the American way of exploiting the colonized.

20   I come from people who have not had privilege. This is because of our histories. Those who are privileged would like for us to believe that we are in some way defective, that we are not smart enough, not good enough. In fact, it may seem that way because we speak separate languages and live a separate way of life. Some of us learn their language, the voice and ways of the educated, and we are then bilingual or trilingual and able to enter their country in order to earn a better living. But seldom do any of them understand our language, and our language goes deeper than words. It goes all the way to meaning and heart.

21   We have not valued the things that are desired by the privileged. We do not assume that we will go to college, or that there are places for us out in the dominant and dominating world, or that if we do certain things we will be taken care of. We generally do not know these "skills," and we often settle for very little because it seems like so much to us. We do not often fight for our rights, nor do we know what they are. We assume we are lucky to be doing so well. Plus, we are accustomed to a "system" that removes small liberties from us when we ask for what we deserve. My ex-husband's father, a non-Indian, worked in Oregon for a grocery firm for less than standard wages. He tried to organize his fellow workers to strike for decent pay and the company threatened to close down. The men, who had no other source of income and lacked also the means to move, had no choice left but to work for substandard wages. And it has been even harder for minority people.

22   For me, when I was a child, two lives lived me. In Gene Autry, Oklahoma, where my grandparents lived, they still went to town in a horse and wagon. They had no water. I wrote a poem about my sister and me in the 1950s in Indian Territory, Oklahoma:

Already you have a woman's hip bones,
long muscles
you slide your dress over
and we brush each other's hair
5   then step out into the blue morning.
Good daughters,
we are quiet
lifting empty milk cans,
silver cans into the wagon.
10   They rattle together
going to town.
(from "Going to Town," *Calling Myself Home*)

23   There was no water, electricity, or plumbing but when we were there we did have Coke, orange soda, and spoonfuls of white sugar. We bathed outside in a galvanized steel tub with Lava soap and water our grandmother heated on the woodstove. Our water came from the pump in town, over the few miles by wagon. My grandmother cooked dozens of eggs in the morning. She raised chickens. She rose from bed before daylight in order to brush her floor-length hair. When I was there, I got up early to help brush out her hair. I have felt this life deeply to be mine; though I lived in many other places and was born in Denver.

24   Outside of Denver, Colorado, in what was then a rapidly changing rural area called Lakewood, my father worked as a carpenter. That place is now city suburbs, but then we lived near a turkey farm. My mother took me a few times on a bus into the city to Woolworth's, and there was a legless man outside on a cart selling red paper poppies. My mother bought me ice cream. Here is an excerpt from around this time. It is from a short story called "Ain't No Indians in Hell (*13th Moon*) and is about our first move into a neighborhood at the time our father was gone to the Korean war:

We were going to talk to my father and we were having a television delivered, all in one day. One of my father's checks had come through and mom's ironing money went for a down payment on the console and the rabbit ear antenna.

The television arrived first and we watched the Fred and Fay show with the clown and just heard Fred say, "You know, boys and girls," when mom shut off the picture.

We all walked together toward the church by the park.

A man with only one leg passed us. I turned to watch him. "Quit staring," Marnie said. "It isn't nice."

In the basement of the church was a large radio with a brown speaker. There were funny sounds coming through it and we waited while a voice took shape in there. The voices were stale and static. A woman standing in front of my mom spoke to the voice and left, crying. Then it was our turn and my mother spoke to a voice she said was my father. "I love you, honey," the voice said. And she told him we had seen grandma, that we had gotten one of the checks, and that the tomatoes were fine but the worms were eating us out of house and home. Marnie told him about the elephant she rode, and said also, "Gracie wouldn't ride him. She was plum afraid." I stared at the box and couldn't speak to it except to say, "Hello" and "Fine."

We walked back home, silent. Mom changed back into her large blue dress and went outside with the rusted rake and began to rake the place where there wasn't even any garden or dry grass.

She raked until it was dark and then she stayed outdoors. Marnie and I had stared at her through the window, raking at nothing, and then we saw her lie down on the grass to watch the stars begin to emerge.

Marnie tucked me in. "Okay," she said. "On the floor is the Kingdom of the Alligators. If you put a foot down there or get out of bed, they will eat you."

When I woke up later, the light in the corner was still lit and there was a small circle of gold on the wall. Marnie was asleep, her arms neatly and perfectly on top of the sheet. Mom was in the living room watching television and ironing. She lifted the iron and placed it back down again and moved rhythmically.

I turned around in my bed so that my head was at the bottom and watched the television. The room was doorless so no one could close me in or out. I heard a sound, a chirping in the bedroom, and followed it. I stood on the bed, careful to not fall into the Kingdom of the Alligators. It was a small green cricket up on the doll shelf. It was rubbing together a wing and leg, over its head. In this way it started a jungle or a fire, and I stood, forgetting the heat and watched it sing with its body, hearing the song of the night.

25   After the Korean War, when my father returned to us and I was eight, my parents moved to Colorado Springs to live in a housing project called Stratton Meadows, a name that signified that the land there was once beautiful. It was near the Fort Carson army base. This was a mixed-race area, and working class. There were a lot of "Spanish" as Mexican-Americans used to call themselves out of their own sense of self-dislike. I wrote a story called "Friends and Fortunes" about Stratton Meadows. One time a woman from National Public Radio read this story and said, I always knew there must be people like this, but I have never read about them. By "them" she meant the Others, those she had never seen. She did not understand that I was one of them, alive and breathing, standing before her.

Where I live, people do things outdoors. Out in the open air, they do what wealthier and more private people hide inside their homes. Young couples neck beside the broken lilac bushes or in old cars parked along the street. Women knead bread on their steps, and sometimes collapse in a fury of weeping on the sidewalk. Boys breaking windows do not hide in the darkness of the night.

We are accustomed to displays, so when Mr. Wrenn across the street has the DTs in front of his house, conversations continue. *What will be will be, and life goes on,* as my mother is fond of saying. The men who are at home go over to convince Mr. Wrenn that the frogs are not really there. If that tack fails, they kill off the frogs or snakes with imaginary machetes or guns. While they are destroying the terrors that crawl out of the mind, the rest of us talk. We visit while the men lift their arms and swing, aiming at the earth, saying there are no more alligators anywhere. "Lovely day, isn't it?" someone says.

26   I am grateful that I have learned how to analyze what happens to us on a daily basis in the form of classism and racism. Otherwise, like many others, I would have destroyed myself out of frustration, pain, and rage. Several times, like so many others, I have bordered on that destruction. We do it with alcohol, suicide, insanity, or other forms of self-hatred: ways of failing in our good, strong living.

27   It is sometimes easier to stay where we are, where we know our place, can breathe, know the language, but for the fact that we are largely powerless there to make any change for ourselves, for others, for our children. It is difficult for us to gather our human forces together because our circumstances force us into divisions and anger and self-destruction.

28   From childhood I believed that oppression (I had no word for it then) was wrong; that the racism I heard daily—all sorts from without and from within my own family—was wrong; that cruelty, all forms of violence and destruction of earth and life, was wrong. I learned every single thing that I know in order to fight these wrongs, and I have not often bothered to learn other things. I began fighting against brutality and oppression when I was still only half-formed in my ideas and language, and sometimes at great risk to my own self. With great courage I began a fight toward growth and integrity, and I am very proud of that young woman I was who believed so strongly in life and had so much hope of change that she found energy and courage and was politicized rather than paralyzed by the struggles.

29   When I began to write, I wrote partly to put this life in order, partly because I was too shy to speak. I was silent and the poems spoke first. I was ignorant and the poems educated me. When I realized that people were going to read the poems, I thought of the best ways to use words, how great

was my responsibility to transmit words, ideas, and acts by which we could live with liberation, love, self-respect, good humor, and joy. In learning that, I also had to offer up our pain and grief and sorrow, because I know that denial and repression are the greatest hindrances to liberation and growth. Simon Ortiz has said that denial is the largest single factor working against us in this country.

30   My life has been a constant effort at self-education, a constant searching and re-searching what was important for me to learn. I went to college as an older student. I had years of work experience behind me. I started work at fifteen as a nurse's aide in Hill Haven Nursing Home, where there were rats and where we aides laundered the sheets and diapers of the patients at 4 A.M. I felt fortunate to have this seventy-five-cents-an-hour job. I did not know how many other girls prepared for college at that age, did not work full time. It was never mentioned to me that I might go to college, although my mother did try to convince me not to quit high school. I was engaged young and I wanted to get married. I didn't know anyone who went to college, or even what it was.

31   I worked many jobs like this. I worked for a dentist at $1.05 an hour. When he praised me for learning to mount X-rays after only one lesson, it made a great difference in my life that he thought I was intelligent and mentioned it to me on several occasions; but in spite of that encouragement, I worked at many other low-paying jobs, in nursing homes, in dental offices, and filing for a collection agency where I occasionally threw away the files of people who called to tell how hard their lives were. I believed them, although the owner said they would manipulate the collectors with their lies about death, poverty, or illness.

32   The poor tell terrible stories, it is true.

33   The last job I had before I went to college was working for an orthodontist who believed Ayn Rand's philosophy,[2] received her *Objectivist Newsletter,* believed I was inferior because I worked for less than his wife's clothing budget or their liquor bill (I paid their bills at the office), and who, when I received money to attend night school and was proud, accused me of being a welfare leech and said, during the first space flight which cost lives in money, that I should be ashamed of myself. He fired me shortly after that for missing a day of work. I yelled at him as I left the office. It was the first time I fought back for myself.

34   That fighting back was an act of strength and self-respect, though I felt badly about it at first. Again, I look back through the years with great love for who I was, for knowing something was wrong, even though it was years before I had words for what it was:

---

[2] *Ayn Rand's philosophy:* Ayn Rand (1905–1982) was a Russian-born American writer and political conservative. She is chiefly known for her novel *The Fountainhead.*

Tell them all
we won't put up with your hard words
and low wages one more day.
Those meek who were blessed
5   are nothing
but meat and potato eaters,
never salsa or any spice.
Those timid are sagging in the soul
and those poor who will inherit the earth
10   already work it
so take shelter
take shelter you
because we are thundering and beating on floors
and this is how walls have fallen in other cities.

(from "Those Who Thunder")

35   When I say that I spent part of my life in self-education, I want people to know that part of this was done even when I went to college. I was a commuter student, attending night classes until my last year or two. There were no classes that made any connection to my own life experience or perception of the world. The closest I came to learning what I needed was in a course on labor literature, and the lesson there was in knowing that there were writers who lived similar lives to ours.

36   This is one of the ways that higher education perpetuates racism and classism. By ignoring our lives and our work, by creating standards for only their own work.

37   Education can be a hard process for minority and women students who have already learned too much of what we don't need to know. As an educator now I use books that are significant for us and are not often found in the university.

38   I find this especially necessary because I am aware of that fact that as a light-skinned Indian person I am seen as a person of betweens, as a person of divided directions. Non-Indians are more comfortable with me than they are with my darker sisters and brothers, for they assume that I am similar to them, or somehow not as real as other Indian people. This preference for light skin is true of other minorities also; the light ones, the mixed ones, are seen as closer, in many ways, to the dominant culture. But I want to point out how exclusion works in a divided society and how color affects us all. To be darker means to experience more pain, more racism, less hope, less self-esteem, less advantage. It means to be vulnerable to attack by police, to be left untreated more often by physicians, and to have less of resources or assistance. . . . These are not isolated or unusual incidents. They happen most often to darker people.

39   My teachers have been those who before me found the first ways to

speak of these things. Writers like the women in *This Bridge Called My Back,* Audre Lorde, Meridel Le Sueur, Tillie Olson, and D'Arcy McNickle, a Flathead Indian writer who documented the truth, as did Gertrude Simmons Bonnin, Zitkala Sa. I have been deeply interested in the work of many writers of the 1930s, and of writers from other countries who are engaged in struggles for survival. I continue to read books from contemporary radical and alternative presses, for those are the books that talk about our lives. I wonder why it is that to be working class or a woman of color in America and to write a book about it is a radical action and one that must be published by the alternative presses. Why is it that telling our lives is a subversive thing to do? Perhaps it is again that burden of denial and of repression. Still, it seems that the covering-up of the truth is the real act of subversion.

40   I read books of feminist theory and often relate that to culture and class. The experience of being a woman has the same elements as being Indian, black, and poor, even though some of the strongest divisions seem to be cultural ones, and some of the most difficult forms of exclusion and misuse that I have felt have come from white women in the women's movement and in the academy where some women have, by necessity and for their own survival, perfected the language of dominance and entered into competition with one another. I believe in the women's movement as another resistance struggle, not as an entering into the ways of the bosses. For many women, their movement is not resistance as much as infiltration. As Audre Lorde has said, "The Master's tools will not dismantle his house." My own efforts have gone into new tools, the dismantling, the rebuilding. Writing is my primary crowbar, saw, and hammer. It is a way of not allowing ourselves to be depowered by disappearance.

41   When I was a child, I knew that my journey through life was going to be a spiritual one.

42   I mention this here because I have met many people on this journey and I know there are those who will find this useful. I am hesitant, however, to go too deeply into it because of the misuse of Indian spiritual beliefs and traditions by those non-Indians who are in spiritual crises, and who hope to gain from the ways of other cultures because they do not find their own ways to be valuable. Searching out "ways" may be a problem in itself, since we are all part of the same motion of life, our work being to serve the planet and its people and creatures, whether we show respect to the life energy through ceremonies or through other kinds of services or through the saying of mass. It seems like people search for ways instead of integrating meaning. North Americans emphasize what they call "method" and "analysis" but do not often get into the center core of living.

43   Also, many spiritual traditions would have us believe so completely in a caste system that we may come to see the paths of others as superior or

inferior to our own. Again, it is because we learn to measure the weight of our accomplishments without learning to love our inner lives. We must learn to see those measurements as meaningless, and to honor that inner-ness as real and as sacred. Here is a poem I wrote about traveling to Chicago:

EVOLUTION IN LIGHT AND WATER

Above gold dragons of rivers
the plane turns.
We are flying in gravity's teeth.
Below us the earth is broken
5   by red tributaries
flowing like melted steel,
splitting the continent apart
and fusing it
in the same touch.

10   It is easier to fall
than to move through the suspended air,
easier to reel toward the pull of earth
and let thoughts drown in the physical rivers of light.
And falling, our bodies reveal their inner fire,
15   red trees in the lungs,
liquids building themselves
light in the dark organs
the way gold-eyed frogs grow legs
in the shallows.

20   Dark amphibians
live in my skin.
I am their country.
They swim in the old quiet seas
of this woman.
25   Salamander and toad
waiting to emerge and fall again
from the radiant vault of myself,
this full and broken continent of living.

(first published in *Denver Quarterly*, Winter 1985)

44   That amphibious woman, the light and dark of myself, the ancient woman I am, comes to be viewed in another way in a later poem that real-izes the essential value and strength of humor as one of the tools the mas-ters have not used in the building of their houses:

And there are days
the old women gossip and sing,
offering gifts of red cloth and cornbread
to one another.
5   On those days I love the ancestors
in and around me,
the mothers of trees and deer
and harvests, and that crazy one
in her nightgown
10 baring herself to the world,
daring the psychiatrists to come
with their couches and theories and rats.
On those days the oldest one is there,
taking stock
in all her shining
and with open hands.

(from "It Must Be")

45   Those on spiritual journeys are often seen to be, or afraid of being, crazy. Contemporary analysis, and I call it that on purpose, has not given people the strength they need, or fed the inner being, the spirit. It has failed to connect people with the world and yet has somehow managed to judge and categorize people who must travel that way, toward connections. I notice how seldom we find it strange that a person decides to specialize in an unusual scholarly career—studying Gawain,[3] for instance—or how little we disdain scientists who perform animal experiments in the name of science, or how we do not find it abnormal that some persons devote their lives to selling insurance or cars or light fixtures. And yet spiritual people are unacceptable in many ways.

46   The poem mentions psychiatrists. It is interesting to note here how many institutionalized people are at poverty level, female, minority, or are men who have verbalized belief systems or religious views that professionals find inappropriate. I think of Nijinsky believing his body was god, and it was, and I think of him dancing "Guernica"[4] in silent protest of war and how that dance made the audience "uncomfortable" and how he died in a mental hospital. He behaved in an insane manner while the sane were enlisting to kill one another. The doubleness of this is intensified in the fact that to be conscious and aware often does make people broken in their Selves.

47   All of the work I do is part of a spiritual journey. "Spirituality is your inner self," a medicine person in New Mexico told me. It is in being. It is in

---

[3] *Gawain:* In Arthurian legend, a knight of the Round Table and a nephew of Arthur.
[4] *Nijinsky . . . "Guernica":* Vaslaw Nijinsky (1890–1950) was a Russian-born dancer and choreographer. Guernica, a town in Spain, was bombed in 1937 by German planes during the Spanish Civil War.

seeing the world, in breathing, talking, cooking. Poetry is a large spiritual undertaking. So are stories, in the telling and the listening. So is being a mother and a caretaker of animals and trees. Doing dishes or painting a wall. More recently, teaching.

48   I have learned that to be spiritually conscious means to undertake a journey that is often a political one, a vision of equality and freedom. It is often to resist, to be a person who has not cooperated in giving up the Self or in joining up with the world that has denied us our full lives and rights. It is to assist others in the first steps of the journey, and to *not* offer assistance where it interferes with growth. It is to pray as well as to fight for the animals, the waters, against all wars, violence, and division. It is to learn clarity and to act out of kindness and compassion. It is to not be involved in conflict except when necessary to grant human and civil rights, animal rights, or to protect the earth from intrusion, poison, or other destruction. It is to pray and offer our breath and songs back to the world.

49   It is a paradox in the contemporary world that in our desire for peace we must willingly give ourselves to struggle. When once the spiritual people could advocate the path of least resistance, now the road to peace is often a path of resistance. This is why we find that in the past years many spiritual people have entered into civil disobedience, have retrained themselves from their previous concepts of religion as a sort of "separate" peace, an *isolated* inner experience, a motion toward acceptance of all things as the will of a creator. We now know that if we want rights we can neither only pray for them nor request them from those who have denied them to us. We know that civil rights and human rights are the same. The struggles of Indian people in Guatemala, El Salvador, Nicaragua, and other countries are the same as our own have been, and we must interfere in the genocide of those living beings that share our continent. We know that the struggles of the hungry are our own. And while we advocate kindness, we also know that for us to continue to practice kindness to oppressors is to act in a way that deprives us of the right to defend ourselves in a situation that remains one of war between nations. It is to cooperate in the violations of our own rights. We are only learning this, and now non-Indians are learning to recognize the sanctity of all life.

50   For my inner growth, it is best when I remember to say "Thank you" to every living thing that graces my eyes or whose sound fills my ears. It is best if I return some of my richness to the spirit world and to the earth, if I feed the birds and carry love into the world. This is all that is required, not elaborate rites and ceremonies, just the need to *be* and to live fully. The healing ceremonies only return us to our being when the busy life and fast world have broken down our inner ways. They return us to our love and connection with the rest of creation. That is their purpose. They remind us of where we are within the framework of all life.

51   Other means that are consciously and actively used for this return to creation are the labor of service, basic and daily work, a strong consciousness of our moment-by-moment living. It is with great meaning that we live,

every minute of our lives, but too seldom do we consider that meaning and the significance of our actions and words.

52   The stories of my life are many. I have omitted the small stories here in favor of the larger story that lays itself down with those of others. The stories of my life:

53   I have loved the songs of the first frogs in springtime, the red light of morning, the red earth, the heartbeat of trees and waters. I have been comforted by human and animal closeness and I have given comfort to the living and to the dying. I have taken care of the bodies and hearts of the sick. I have cooked meals, laid linoleum, cut wood, fixed roofs. I have bathed children, woven wool, made jewelry, painted pictures, and made music. I have lived with old people and with children, with no one too easily. I have worked as a fry cook, a waitress, a nurse's aide, a teacher's aide, a secretary, a dental assistant, and in numerous other jobs. I have protested cruelty and other wars. I have not been afraid to offend the offensive, disturb the disturbed, nor to be kind and loving to the gentle. I have fought and I've given up easily and wondered if I could live one more day, and lived. I have been careless and made separations through my words and actions. I have made healing unions in the same ways. I've listened to the songs of night. I have hated death and taxes and I still do. . . .

DISCUSSION QUESTIONS

1. In "Old Men at War, Old Women," Hogan writes, "This war inside me is not mine." Compare this statement to ideas in "The Truth Is."
2. In "Old Men at War, Old Women," she asks, "Are they loving each other?" Why do you think women may offer Hogan hope for love instead of hate?
3. Note the details Hogan tells you about her relatives on both sides of her family. How are they similar and different?

WRITING TOPICS

1. Select one of the following statements and develop a paragraph with information from the essay:

We are landless Indians.

I come from people who have not had privilege.

Two lives lived me.

Color affects us all.

2. The author tells a story about the first time she fought back for herself. Recall a time you fought for yourself and write the story. Tell how you felt about that experience. Would you act differently now?

3. Hogan supports equality for women. In a brief essay, explain her line, "I believe in the women's movement as another resistance struggle, not as an entering into the ways of the bosses." Cite evidence from the essay.

4. Read again the paragraph that begins, "The stories of my life are many." Which five images do you like best? Make a list of images that give a snapshot of you and develop them into a brief essay.

DEAR JOHN WAYNE

Louise Erdrich

Louise Erdrich grew up in Wahpeton, North Dakota. She was born in 1954 as a member of the Turtle Mountain Band of the Chippewa people. She is also of German-American descent and incorporates mixed-ancestry dilemma into her art. An acclaimed novelist and poet, she published her first book of poetry, *Jacklight,* in 1984. In "Dear John Wayne," Erdrich reverses the traditional adulation of Wayne as western hero. Dramatic contrast exists between the bigger-than-life hero on the gigantic screen and laughing Indians, speechless and small in the audience. Lurking behind the poem is the image of the mystic Plains warrior that has eclipsed the real history of many Native Americans.

August and the drive-in picture is packed.
We lounge on the hood of the Pontiac
surrounded by the slow-burning spirals they sell
at the window, to vanquish the hordes of mosquitoes.
5 Nothing works. They break through the smoke screen for blood.

Always the lookout spots the Indians first,
spread north to south, barring progress.
The Sioux or some other Plains bunch
in spectacular columns, ICBM missiles,
10 feathers bristling in the meaningful sunset.

The drum breaks. There will be no parlance.
Only the arrows whining, a death-cloud of nerves
swarming down on the settlers
who die beautifully, tumbling like dust weeds
15 into the history that brought us all here
together: this wide screen beneath the sign of the bear.

The sky fills, acres of blue squint and eye
that the crowd cheers. His face moves over us,
a thick cloud of vengeance, pitted
20 like the land that was once flesh. Each rut,
each scar makes a promise: *It is*
not over, this fight, not as long as you resist.

Everything we see belongs to us.

A few laughing Indians fall over the hood
25 slipping in the hot spilled butter.
The eye sees a lot, John, but the heart is so blind.
Death makes us owners of nothing.
He smiles, a horizon of teeth
the credits reel over, and then the white fields
30 again blowing in the true-to-life dark.
The dark films over everything.
We get into the car
scratching our mosquito bites, speechless and small
as people are when the movie is done.
35 We are back in our skins.

How can we help but keep hearing his voice,
the flip side of the sound track, still playing:
Come on, boys, we got them
where we want them, drunk, running,
40 *They'll give us what we want, what we need.*
Even his disease was the idea of taking everything.
Those cells, burning, doubling, splitting out of their skins.

▣

DISCUSSION QUESTIONS

1. Imagine this poem is a movie that you are watching. Consider each stanza as a scene and discuss its action. Which images do you consider positive and which negative?

2. The poet creates irony by careful juxtaposition of words and ideas. Hordes of mosquitoes break through the smoke screen for blood. Would her metaphor have been as effective if she had said butterflies flitted through the flowers? Why or why not? How are "whining death-cloud" and "cloud of vengeance" related to "hordes of mosquitoes"? Explain "Plains bunch" (line 8) and "ICBM missiles" (line 9).

3. How can settlers "die beautifully" in a movie? In a small group, discuss the history that brought Indians and settlers together. What is Erdrich's tone about that history? Is it different from your view of Western history?
4. In stanza 4, what is ironic about the crowd cheering?
5. The setting is like a party, but the impact of the movie is deadly serious. In stanza 6, which is the most powerful image? Do you think Erdrich has a successful comparison in "back in our skins" and "splitting out of their skins"?

WRITING TOPICS

1. Erdrich addresses her letter/poem to John Wayne. Write a letter in prose or poetry to "Dear Louise Erdrich" and tell her your response to her poem. Explain why you enjoy or dislike Western movies.
2. Write a review of a film that, in your opinion, portrays Native Americans fairly or unjustly.

I AM NOT A MASCOT

Philip J. Deloria

Philip J. Deloria, a history professor at the University of Colorado, is an advocate for Indian rights. Born in 1959 into a prominent Sioux family, he parallels his father, Vine Deloria, Jr., in challenging insensitive images of Indians. His book *Playing Indian: Making American Identities from the Boston Tea Party to the New Age* (1998) addresses this issue. The topic of Indians as mascots for sports teams is passionately debated by fans and players. "Chiefs," "Redskins," and "Braves" generate anger, pride, and controversy. In this essay, stereotypical warriors are again the major actors.

1   When the Florida State Seminoles football team rushes onto the field, it follows the university's mascot—a stereotyped Indian warrior with colored turkey feathers and a flaming spear, which is planted in the end zone with a whoop. Florida State's fans, many in Indian costumes themselves, then proceed to chant a faux-Indian melody, swinging their arms in a synchronized "tomahawk chop." The Florida State experience is a common one. "Indians"—in a variety of flavors ranging from warriors, red men, braves, and chiefs to "Fighting Sioux" and "Apaches" have been the most consistently popular mascot in American athletic history.

2   The University of Wisconsin at Lacrosse first named its teams Indians in 1909. In 1912. the Boston Braves baseball team followed suit, and three years later, Cleveland's baseball club also became the Indians. During the 1920s, many college and professional teams—including teams at Stanford, Dartmouth, and the University of Illinois, as well as the Chicago Black Hawks hockey club—adopted Indian names. The practice filtered down to thousands of high schools and junior high schools seeking institutional identities. Today, professional sports boast five major clubs that use "the Indian" as a name and mascot. In addition to Chicago and Cleveland, Atlanta has the Braves, Kansas City has the Chiefs, and Washington, D.C., has the Redskins. While some colleges and universities—including Stanford and

Dartmouth—have dropped their Indian logos and mascots, many more continue to insist that their use of Indian stereotypes is harmless fun.

3   Americans' embrace of Indian mascots was only part of a broad, early-twentieth-century primitivist nostalgia that stamped Indian imagery on a nickel, positioned baskets and pottery in the "Indian corners" of arts-and-crafts revival homes, and permeated the rituals of Boy Scouts and Campfire Girls. At the turn of the century, many Americans perceived that the story they had been telling themselves about their origins and character—one of frontier struggle between bold adventurers and savage Indians—had lost much of its cultural power as historians and critics declared the frontier "closed." On the contemporary side of this closed frontier, Americans saw the modern world—a place of cities, immigrants, technology, lost innocence, and limited opportunity. Many Americans used a ritualized set of symbols—cowboys, Indians, scouts, and pioneers—to evoke the bygone "American" qualities of the frontier era: "authenticity," nature, community, and frontier hardiness. Through summer camp and wilderness outings in "nature," touristic contact with the "authenticity" of Indian primitivism in the southwestern deserts, and an increased emphasis on rugged, character-building athletic competition, they sought to reimagine "modern" compensatory experiences that might take the place of the now-lost "frontier struggle."

4   Bringing Indians—potent symbols both of a nostalgic, innocent past and of the frontier struggle itself—into the athletic stadium helped evoke the mythic narrative being metaphorically replayed on the field. It was no accident that many other mascots—mustangs, pioneers, and so on—were also prominent characters in the athletic rendering of the national story. Indian chiefs and braves represented the aggressiveness and fighting spirit that was supposed to characterize good athletic teams. This racial stereotyping justified an American history in which peaceable cowboys and settlers simply defended themselves against innately aggressive Indians in a defensive conquest of the continent. As mascots celebrated "Indian" ferocity and martial (read also athletic) skill, they were at the same time trophies of Euro-American colonial superiority: "Indians were tough opponents, but 'we' prevailed. Now we 'honor' them (and in doing so, celebrate ourselves)."

5   The performative aspects of mascot ritual bring this American narrative to life, and demonstrate to participants that their myths, enacted both on the athletic field and in the stands, remain valid. The virulent response to Indian protests against Indian mascots demonstrates the deep emotional investment many Americans have made both in their imagining of Indian people as ahistorical symbols and in their sports affiliations. In mass society, athletic spectacles have become a deeply ingrained tradition to which many Americans turn for personal and social identities. The Florida State Seminole, then, signifies not only the frontieresque American character sought by early-twentieth-century fans, but also a more contemporary longing for the relative purity, simplicity, and tradition of the early twentieth century itself.

6   Indian people have reacted to the use of Indian mascots differently. While many native people expressed dismay, others saw athletic rituals as truly honoring Indians. American Indian Movement (AIM) leader Dennis Banks, for example, has claimed that, until the late 1950s, Stanford and other schools promoted "positive, respectful images" of Indians. According to Banks, during the 1960s fans became more involved in a disrespectful, racist spectacle, and clubs expanded their mascot activities. In Atlanta, for example, "Chief Noc-a-homa" came out of a tipi and danced wildly each time the Braves hit a home run. So while some Indians have always found the very idea of mascots offensive, others do not find it so even today, and still others join Banks in being most concerned about the positive or negative quality of the stereotyping.

7   In 1972, Banks and other media-conscious Indian activists forcibly brought the mascot issue into public discussion. AIM's Russell Means threatened the Cleveland Indians and the Atlanta Braves baseball clubs with lawsuits, and delegations from AIM, Americans for Indian Opportunity, and the National Congress of American Indians met with Washington Redskins owner William Bennett to ask him to change the team's name. Aside from cosmetic changes to mascot rituals and team songs, however, these efforts proved unsuccessful. Although Indians continued to protest, the effort to eliminate Indian mascots lost momentum for almost twenty years.

8   Then, in October 1991, the Atlanta Braves played the Minnesota Twins in baseball's World Series. Just a few months later, in January 1992, the Washington Redskins competed in football's Super Bowl. Both events took place in Minneapolis, a city with a high concentration of Indian people in a state that had been attempting to eliminate Indian mascots at the college and high school levels. This convergence of place, people, and issue launched a series of protests and an often rancorous national dialogue about the appropriateness of Indian mascots in American sports. . . .

9   The continual use of Indianness as an important American symbol has raised serious questions and dilemmas for native people. Some Indians, for example, have left their communities and performed for white Americans a series of "positive" anti-modern roles—spiritual "teacher," eco-guru, community sage—in order to acquire political and economic power. While such performances indeed generate valuable cultural capital, they also force Indian people to define themselves around non-Indian criteria. For other native people, it has become increasingly apparent that, in an age of mass communication, Indians need to exert some control over—or, at the very least, constantly challenge—any and all ways they are represented in public discourse. As a result, many Indian people—in contrast to many non-Indians—have found struggles against the use of Indian mascots and against the activities of non-Indian countercultural and New Age spokespersons to be critical and significant in terms of social, cultural, and political survival.

DISCUSSION QUESTIONS
---

1. Deloria gives a historical perspective of how and why Indians became symbols for sports teams. How are Indian mascots related to the Western frontier struggle of cowboys, cavalry, settlers, and Indians?
2. Why was the 1991 World Series in Minneapolis particularly explosive for both sides?

WRITING TOPICS
---

1. Survey sports pages in recent newspapers. Imagine you are a fan who supports a particular Indian mascot. In a brief essay, give reasons for your stand.
2. In a brief essay, support one of these thesis statements with examples. (1) Using Indians as mascots is a form of racial stereotyping. (2) Indians as mascots honor the true values of Indian people.
3. Write a satirical essay in which you defend or protest the use of Indian mascots. Set your ironic tone in a beginning sentence such as this one: "Shouting 'Go skins,' wearing war paint, and hopping in a circle are harmless fun."
4. Create a protest or support poster you would carry to a game where one team had an Indian mascot.

Sure You Can Ask Me a Personal Question

Diane Burns

Diane Burns is an artist and author of Chippewa and Chemehuevi heritage. She attended the Institute of American Indian Arts in Santa Fe. In an interview with Joseph Bruchac, she spoke of living in two cultures: "You know, sometimes you feel you're really a freak, a weirdo, you're alienated, alone, and bizarre. Other times, the other side of that is that you're wonderful and unique and brilliant and positive, a marvel and a gem. . . . You can feel like an angel or a worm." In her book of poems, *Riding the One-Eyed Ford* (1981), Burns creates rhythm by combining sounds from contemporary music and images from popular culture. In this poem, she performs a verbal duel with her opponent.

How do you do?
   No, I am not Chinese.
No, not Spanish.
   No, I am American Indi—uh, Native American.
5 No, not from India.
   No, not Apache.
No, not Navajo.
   No, not Sioux.
No, we are not extinct.
10   Yes, Indin.
Oh?
   So that's where you got those high cheekbones.
Your great grandmother, huh?
   An Indian Princess, huh?
15 Hair down to there?
   Let me guess. Cherokee?

Oh, so you've had an Indian friend?
  That close?
Oh, so you've had an Indian lover?
20   That tight?
Oh, so you've had an Indian servant?
  That much?
Yeah, it was awful what you guys did to us.
  It's real decent of you to apologize.
25 No, I don't know where you can get peyote.
  No, I don't know where you can get Navajo rugs real cheap.
No, I didn't make this. I bought it at Bloomingdales.
  Thank you. I like your hair too.
I don't know if anyone knows whether or not Cher is really Indian.
30   No, I didn't make it rain tonight.
Yeah. Uh-huh. Spirituality.
  Uh-huh. Yeah. Spirituality. Uh-huh. Mother
Earth. Yeah. Uh-huh. Uh-huh. Spirituality.
  No, I didn't major in archery.
35 Yeah, a lot of us drink too much.
  Some of us can't drink enough.
This ain't no stoic look.
  This is my face.

DISCUSSION QUESTIONS

1. Burns' poem appears to be a conversation, but it is actually a monologue in which only the Indian woman speaks. Read the poem aloud with a partner and speak the lines for both speakers. What type of speaker did you create for the second person? Irritated? Funny? Naive? How does the Indian woman actually control the poem?

2. What topics does the poet treat humorously? Do you think her sarcasm is overdone?

3. How does Burns achieve rhythm? Find words that beat a predictable rhythm. How does the rhythm convey the tone of the speaker? Read the poem aloud a second time and emphasize the rocking rhythm.

Writing Topics

1. Imagine you are in a tense scene with a friend, family member, teacher, or other person. Adopt an attitude, allow only one person to speak, and imply the other's questions or answers in a written monologue. When you have finished, invite a partner to invent the silent person's lines.

2. Has someone ever made incorrect assumptions about you, your family, your background, or your abilities? If so, write in your journal about the situation and about how you felt.

PLEA TO THOSE WHO MATTER

James Welch

Blackfeet and Gros Ventre poet and novelist James Welch was born in Browning, Montana, in 1940 and attended schools on the Blackfeet and Fort Belknap reservations. His first book of poems *Riding the Earthboy 40* (1971) arose primarily from his experience on the land his father leased from the Earthboy family and the surrounding countryside and small towns. The poems draw images from inside Blackfeet country of unforgiving winds that chill the bone and winters that defy survival. The Northern Plains landscape filled with bones, wind, and snow becomes a metaphor for the interior landscape of the humans. From this place came the title of Welch's first novel, *Winter in the Blood* (1974). He persistently presents the proud Blackfeet, who have claimed that landscape for more than two centuries, in conflict with intolerant invaders, who take the land and seem to own even the winds.

You don't know I pretend my dumb.
My songs often wise, my bells could chase
the snow across these whistle-black plains.
Celebrate. The days are grim. Call your winds
5 to blast these bundled streets and patronize
my past of poverty and 4-day feasts.

Don't ignore me. I'll build my face a different way,
a way to make you know that I am no longer
proud, my name not strong enough to stand alone.
10 If I lie and say you took me for a friend,
patched together in my thin bones,
will you help me be cunning and noisy as the wind?

I have plans to burn my drum, move out
and civilize this hair. See my nose? I smash it
15 straight for you. These teeth? I scrub my teeth
away with stones. I know you help me now I matter.
And I—I come to you, head down, bleeding from my smile,
happy for the snow clean hands of you, my friends.

DISCUSSION QUESTIONS

1. In his "plea," the speaker gives clues about the character of his audience, "those who matter." What are they like? Why would the speaker wish to change himself to meet their expectations?
2. Is this speaker's plea sincere or ironic? Do you think he will civilize his hair, smash his nose straight, and deny his proud identity? Cite details as evidence for your answer.
3. Explain the significance of Welch's beginning the poem "You don't know," and ending it "you, my friends." What kind of friend demands that a person deny his identity and alter his looks?
4. This poem appears in the section of his book called "The Renegade Wants Words." How is this speaker a renegade? Does he have compassion?

WRITING TOPICS

1. Make a list of images from several lines that set the mood for the poem and express the poet's message to "those who matter."
2. Using examples from several lines, write an essay on images and irony in this poem. First, compose a thesis sentence similar to the following: "In 'Plea to Those Who Matter,' James Welch creates irony by having the speaker pretend throughout the poem."
3. In a short paper, compare and contrast "Plea to Those Who Matter" with "Reading Poems in Public."

MY INDIAN NAME AND NAME GIVEAWAY

Phil George

Our names are small capsules of ourselves. They carry our heritage, culture, and identity. As a young Nez Perce Indian, Phil George received his special name during a celebration of dancing, gaming, feasting, and participating in a sacred ceremony. His name binds him to family, tribe, and traditions. His people once occupied a territory that encompassed much of the land drained by the Snake River, in present-day north central Idaho, northeastern Oregon, and southeastern Washington. They called themselves "Numiipu" in their language. In 1805, Meriwether Lewis and William Clark encountered a group of young boys playing near the Clearwater River in present-day Weippe, Idaho. The explorers gave the Numiipu they met a new name: "Nez-Perces" (French for "pierced noses"). Outsiders have referred to the group by that name since that time.

MY INDIAN NAME

1   At birth, my great grandmother gave me the name of my great grandfather, Lah-peh-ya-low-ett. This sacred name refers to two white swans gliding above still waters, symbolic of beauty, grace, purity, and peace. Lahpehyalowett is my heirloom, the war shield to help me withstand evils, particularly during my adolescence.

2   However, it was after I saw my eighth winter that my family officially announced my Indian name. My name ceremony occurred during an annual, intertribal celebration of George Washington's birthday at Lapwai, Idaho.

3   I can remember that event so well! The celebration was a happy time—basketball tournaments, stick games, war dances, and modern dances maintained constant excitement.

4   As is the custom for these name ceremonies, our family sponsored feast after feast for visiting tribes. Attending were members from Colville,

Spokane, Yakima, Warm Springs, Umatilla, Flathead, and Rocky Boy Reservations.

5   On Saturday afternoon, the day before the name ceremony, I started preparing by participating in our ancient sweat bath purification. Then on Medicine Day, or Sunday, Seven Drum Services were held. This particular religious service is an observance of the Seven Drum Services. Even since our old ones can remember, these services have been held in a long lodge, now known as a "longhouse."

6   Longhouses were, originally, constructed from several tepees joined together. Tule mats were tied onto the skeleton-frame poles. Today, our longhouse has the significance of a church and is as modern as any other building. The entrance, as usual, is facing east so dawn's pure light can chase out yesterday's evil spirits.

7   As guests, my relatives from Nespelem on the Colville Reservation conduct the services. These people are direct descendants of war veterans of the Nez Perce War of 1877, and they have not accepted any phase of Christianity.

8   Dress is somewhat uniform. Costumes are all decorated in the finest style of the old way. The men wear bone chokers, bright yellow, blue, and red medallions, beaded belts, vests, and moccasins. The yellow represents the light of the spirit world, the white represents the earthly light, and the red represents dawn's pure light.

9   Only the few old men have their braids wrapped in cloth or yarn. The oldest man wears red paint all over his face and in the part of his silver, braided hair.

10   Black, conical hats hang on the wall behind the old men, and black cowboy hats behind the younger men. An eagle feather set in a beaded band decorates each hat.

11   The women and girls are dressed in cheerful wing-sleeved or "wind" dresses, beaded belts, moccasins, and leggings. They wrap their long, black braids in otter fur and wear pink shell earrings. The old women's dress is subdued. They wear dark scarves on their heads. Middle-aged women wear basket hats. The girls wear beaded headbands.

12   In preparation for activities held outside, wooden benches on either side of the longhouse walls are draped with Pendleton robes and shawls.

13   While the women and girls prepare the foods for the feast, the men sit at the north end of the longhouse. On unpainted hand drums, seven selected drummers drum and chant a song. Then a brass hand bell is rung. They drum and chant the song twice, and the hand bell is rung for each time the song is sung. And so on, until the song is sung and the bell rung seven times.

14   By the time the women set the food on the table, the men are through singing. Long ago, the guests sat on the floor and ate from tule mats. Now, at the signal of a continuous bell, the people line up around tables. The women sit on the east side and the men on the west side of the longhouse.

15   In the preliminary ceremony, the high priest steps forward and gives a prayer of thanks. Then he rings the brass bell, and the people drink fresh mountain water to clean their bodies before eating. A second ringing is the signal for the people to begin eating.

16   After the feast, the people stand and face south to sing the thanksgiving songs. No drum is used, only voices. Again, the priest steps forward to give his message.

17   The people verify his message with an *"Aii."* (Yes, it is so.) They raise their right palms to Sun Father and turn in a small circle as Mother Earth does when she sleeps.

18   Paper sacks and quart jars are given to all the people who want them. They are used to carry away all the surplus food from the table. No food must remain, or the hostesses will be offended.

19   The bell rings and all the people line up for the dance. The men and boys are on the right side of the drummers, facing the women in an opposite line, facing the center. Those in the line are arranged according to stature, the tallest near the drummers.

20   At a stroke on the bell, everyone puts his right hand on his breast. Another tap of the bell and the right hand is brought out in front of the body. The primitive simplicity of the ritual dance involves an abstract flying motion. Standing in one place, the dancers appear to be bouncing on the balls of their feet. In the old days, they held eagle feathers in their right hands. Now, right hands revolve, keeping time with the drums.

21   When everyone sings, the effect is eerie. In the high-pitched portions of the songs, the women seem to be wailing as one would at a funeral. Tears come to the eyes of the older ones. Soon, the singing and banging drums stop.

22   With the help of a wooden cane, the priest steps out into the circle. A stillness falls upon the people. Everyone stands perfectly silent, looking down at the floor.

23   As he speaks, the spring wind caresses our faces, softly so we will always remember. In our native tongue, he speaks on his theory of evolution or on a possible answer to a tribal problem. He describes life in the old days.

24   His interpreter speaks louder than he does, so the oldest woman can hear the message.

25   After the priest concludes his sermon, everyone raises his right palm to Sun Father and, again, turns in a circle. A final *"Aii,"* yes, it is so, ends the sermon.

26   To dismiss the service, the priest rings a continuous bell. The dancers go to the south end of the longhouse, make a turn—a turn to continue their life after death. The service is over.

27   After this service, I went back to my grandmother's house to sleep a couple of hours until the war dances. The evening part of the celebration was the most exciting for me because my name ceremony was to take place then.

28   First, everyone dances for about an hour and a half. The village herald who was then our Master of Ceremonies announced that there would be a name ceremony before the final war dance and beauty contests.

29   The whip woman, a respected elder lady, carrying an old buggy whip tipped with eagle plumes, cleared the dancers from the floor. Wherever she went, all the small children scampered away, running for their lives.

30   After the floor was cleared, my grandfather introduced me to the crowd of spectators and explained the history of his father's name.

31   He explained that Lahpehyalowett lived across from the Palouse grasslands, east from the Kamiah Valley. *Kamiah-pa* means "The green valley with clear waters flowing through." Lewis and Clark named the river The Clearwater. The prairie adjoining pine forests allotted to Lahpehyalowett was perfect for horse raising. Because Lahpehyalowett owned hundreds of Appaloosia horses, the agent at Fort Lapwai named him Phillip, which means in Greek, "Lover of Horses." For reservation records, my great grandfather accepted the name Phillip Williams. William is now my middle name.

32   After my introduction, I stood out on the dance floor. Then all my immediate relatives, dressed in our family's finest trappings, came forward to honor Lahpehyalowett in a circle dance.

33   The Nez Perce have a reputation for proud pageantry. Every dance has a very special meaning. Even the simple circle dance has great significance. Universally danced by Indians, the movement is to the left, following Sun Father's path as he crosses the sky. Our ceremonial circle dance is never complete until the dancers fill in a never-ending circle.

34   The circle dance song, in this case Lahpehyalowett's Honor Song, is sung in a series of threes—for youth, for maturity, and for old age.

35   When the steady drumbeat is interrupted, all the men raise their eagle fans in their right hands toward the center. All then take a few steps forward. After this interrupted rhythm, we step back and continue the dance. This is a ritual salute to Sun Father for his never-ending love.

36   After this circle dance, distinguished old-timers who remembered Lahpehyalowett, came forward to the microphone to wish me some good fortune or success during my life. First one and then another old man related stories about Lahpehyalowett's deeds as an honored chief. They described how people came from miles around to hear him speak in his great *pineewaus,* or longhouse tent.

37   Lahpehyalowett also used to war dance, up until the year that he died. Because he owned many horses and costumes, all the young men would come to his camp to dress up for the ceremonials.

38   Lahpehyalowett was also a kind of general in our Nez Perce war. His father came from the Oregon wilderness, Wallowa country. Like all our people, he loved that beautiful land more than all the rest in the world, and he fought patriotically for it.

39   To all these people who came forward and spoke about Lahpehyalowett's character, my family, as custom requires, gave away gifts. Among these traditional gifts were Pendleton robes and shawls, wampum and dentellium necklaces, beaded bags filled with dried salmon or dried deer meat, and

cornhusk bags filled with dried camas roots or dried bitter-roots. Other gifts were beaded garments and quart jars of canned huckleberries. All of the drummers also received a gift of five dollars each.

40 To conclude the name ceremony, I exhibited our Northwest War Dance. Then I realized the true meaning of the designs and colors in my costume. For me, this was an impressive occasion because Lahpehyalowett was an outstanding warrior, dancer, singer, and messenger-priest to our Seven Drum Services.

41 Time and again, historians have especially praised our tribe's advanced culture and high moral standards. Now, our old ones are gone. Their cultural patterns have all but disappeared, but must their philosophy—a philosophy that took centuries to develop—die with them?

42 I believe that now it is my generation's responsibility to preserve the very best from the old Indian life for use in this, the twentieth century. I study the greatness in our old Nez Perce life, hoping to be a messenger like the swans, like my great grandfather. I write what I love to learn.

43 Yes, I will be faithful to our ancient teachings. Yet, I must live today's life with the conduct and attitude of a genuine Nez Perce. The name-tradition, the same as a dream, is obligating, a strict requirement. Even so, I want to live by Mother Earth's teachings because, since my childhood days, they have been my only way of life.

44 I pray that one day I'll share with Phillip Williams life in our glorious Wallowa. In beauty, grace, purity, and peace. I know these messenger swans will carry my prayer to the Great Spirit.

◉

NAME GIVEAWAY

That teacher gave me a new name . . . again.
She never even had feasts or a giveaway!

Still I do not know what "George" means;
5 and now she calls me: "Phillip."

BAND OF GEESE TWICE ALIGHTING UPON STILL WATERS
must be a name too hard to remember

◉

DISCUSSION QUESTIONS

1. Why does Phil George remain loyal to the ancient teachings of his people?
2. How are the following important to the ceremony and celebration: Sun Father, Mother Earth, honor, stories and songs, gifts, prayers, food, dance and music, and language?
3. What symbols are important to the Nez Perce that are not regarded as sacred or special in other cultures?

WRITING TOPICS

1. Make a chart in which you compare symbols and actions of the Nez Perce celebration/ceremony with a celebration or ceremony you consider important, such as a wedding, a funeral, a church or synagogue service, or a family tradition such as Hanukah, Christmas, or Thanksgiving.
2. Write a brief essay about your full name and how you feel about it. Tell whether you are named for someone in your family or for someone else, the meaning (if you know it) of your full name, whether you feel your name suits you, how you feel when someone mispronounces, misspells, or can't remember your name, and how you feel about women keeping their surnames after marriage.

The Delight Song of Tsoai-Talee

N. Scott Momaday

N. Scott Momaday has been at the center of Native American literature since 1969 when he won a Pulitzer Prize for his novel *House Made of Dawn.* One of the finest works of the twentieth century, the novel has achieved world recognition, being translated into German, Italian, Dutch, Swedish, Norwegian, and Polish. As master storyteller, poet, and novelist, Momaday has influenced an entire generation of Native American writers. Born in 1934 at Lawton, Oklahoma, to Natachee Scott Momaday, mixed French and Cherokee woman, and Alfred Momaday, a full-blooded Kiowa, Momaday received his Kiowa name during the first summer of his life. Pohdlock, an elder of the tribe, held the baby in his arms near the bank of Rainy Mountain Creek and proclaimed him "Tsoai-talee"—"Rock-tree-Boy"—linking the child with that place known as Devil's Tower on the ancient Kiowa migration from the Black Hills country to Rainy Mountain in Oklahoma. The family took Scott on a long journey to Wyoming so he could contact that ancestral landmark, repeatedly honored in Kiowa stories and traditions. Momaday celebrates his heritage in this poem, which defines his identity in relation to family, Kiowa traditions, and the beauty of the earth.

I am a feather on the bright sky
I am the blue horse that runs in the plain
I am the fish that rolls, shining, in the water
I am the shadow that follows a child
5 I am the evening light, the lustre of meadows
I am an eagle playing with the wind
I am a cluster of bright beads
I am the farthest star
I am the cold of the dawn
10 I am the roaring of the rain

I am the glitter on the crust of the snow
I am the long track of the moon in a lake
I am a flame of four colors
I am a deer standing away in the dusk
15 I am a field of sumac and the pomme blanche
I am an angle of geese in the winter sky
I am the hunger of a young wolf
I am the whole dream of these things

You see, I am alive, I am alive
20 I stand in good relation to the earth
I stand in good relation to the gods
I stand in good relation to all that is beautiful
I stand in good relation to the daughter of Tsen-tainte[1]
You see, I am alive, I am alive

DISCUSSION QUESTIONS

1. In his "Delight Song," Momaday describes his identity. Imagine you hear and see the images he calls himself. Which ones do you think express delight with his life?

2. In this poem/song, Momaday creates "music" by repeating words and phrases in particular places and by repeating particular sounds. In stanza one, which words does he repeat to structure the poem?

3. Read the poem aloud and listen for sound repetition. How many examples do you hear repeating long and short *i* sounds in stanzas one and two? (In the title, "delight" and "Tsoai" have long *i* sounds.)

4. Four is a sacred number for many Native American cultures. How does Momaday's chanting in lines 20–23 add to the sacred nature of the poem as a celebration of life?

---

[1] *Tsen-tainte:* famous Kiowa leader and raider.

WRITING TOPICS

1. Both stanzas are like a chant. Select the images you like best and use them as a model for creating a song chant about yourself. Will you use family, community, school, city, or nature images? What sounds, words, and phrases will you repeat for rhythm?
2. Write a four- or six-line poem that tells something about you, following Momaday's style, if you wish.

ADVENTURES OF AN INDIAN PRINCESS

Patricia Riley

Born in 1950, of Cherokee and Irish ancestry, Patricia Riley grew up in Fort Worth, Texas. As a child, she was unaware of her Native American heritage. An avid reader of ten books a week from the bookmobile that serviced her neighborhood, she found books about Indians that bore no resemblance to the lives of her Indian neighbors and friends. She decried this absence in the introduction to her anthology *Growing Up Native American* (1993): "In the books available to me as a child, Native Americans were usually exotic, cultural artifacts from the past, the stereotypical Vanishing Americans, sometimes portrayed as romantic or noble, but always backward savages on their way out." With the anthology, Riley rectified the fallacy for her three children and anyone interested in the "real-life experiences" of Native Americans. Riley continues to share her vision of Native American literature with students at the University of Idaho, where she is a member of the English Department.

1   The dingy blue station wagon lumbered off the road and into the parking lot as soon as its driver spotted the garish wooden sign with the words INDIAN TRADING POST written in three-foot-high, red, white, and blue letters. Beneath the towering letters was the greeting WELCOME TO CHEROKEE COUNTRY, accompanied by a faded and rather tacky reproduction of someone's idea of a Cherokee chief complete with a Sioux war bonnet. A smaller sign stood next to the large one and attested to the authenticity of the "genuine" Indian goods that the store had to offer.

2   The driver, Jackson Rapier, foster parent extraordinaire, assisted by his wife and two teenage daughters, had decided, at first seeing the aforementioned sign from a distance, that coming upon this place must indeed have been an act of providence. Only yesterday they had received their newest addition in a long chain of foster children, a young Cherokee girl, eleven or

twelve years old, called Arletta. The social worker had told them that it was important for the girl to maintain some kind of contact with her native culture. When they saw the sign, they were all agreed that this trading post was just the ticket. It would be good for Arletta and they would all have a good time.

3   Mrs. Rapier twisted around in the front seat and looked at the dark girl wedged between her pale and freckled daughters, the youngest of whom was absorbed in the task of peeling away what remained of a large bubble of chewing gum from around her nostrils. Mrs. Rapier sighed, then tried to smile encouragingly at Arletta as she pushed bobby pins into her wispy red hair. "You're gonna love this place, honey. I just know you will."

4   "Yeah, Arletta," the eldest daughter said, making faces at her sister over Arletta's head. "You ought to feel right at home in a place like this. This looks like just your style."

5   "Just your style," the sister echoed and resumed picking the gum off her face.

6   Arletta looked around her, assessed the situation, and decided she was outnumbered. She knew they wouldn't hear her even if she voiced her objections. They never listened when she talked. When she had arrived at their home, they had seemed to be full of curiosity about what it was like to be Indian. But all the questions they fired at her, they eventually answered themselves, armed as they were with a sophisticated knowledge of Indian people gleaned from old John Wayne movies and TV reruns of "The Lone Ranger."

7   Arletta imagined she could survive this experience. She had survived a great many things these last two years. Her father's death. Her mother's illness. An endless series of foster homes. She was getting tired of being shuffled around like a worn-out deck of cards. All she wanted right now was to be able to stay in one place long enough for her mother to track her down and take her home. She knew her mother must be well by now and probably getting the runaround from the welfare office as to her daughter's whereabouts. For the time being, staying with the Rapiers was the only game in town, and she felt compelled to play along. She arranged what she hoped would pass for a smile on her face and said nothing. Behind the silent mask, she ground her teeth together.

8   The midsummer sun blazed off the shiny chrome hubcaps someone had nailed above the trading post door and reflected sharply into their eyes, making the transition from air-conditioned car to parking lot momentarily unbearable. Mr. Rapier was the first to brave the thick, heated air. He wiped a yellowed handkerchief across his balding head, which had begun to sweat almost immediately upon leaving the car. He adjusted the strap that held his camera around his neck and waited while his wife and daughters quickly climbed out of the car and made their way with swift steps to a battered red Coke machine that stood beside the trading post's open door.

9   Arletta hung back, squinting her eyes against the brightness. She had no interest in the trading post and was determined to stay outside. Off to the

left of the Coke machine, she saw a tall, dark man suddenly walk around the side of the building leading a flea-bitten pinto pony with a blanket draped awkwardly across its back. Arletta had to laugh at the way he looked because a Cherokee, or any other kind of respectable Indian, wouldn't dress like that on his worst day. Before her mother's illness, Arletta had traveled with her throughout the United States, dancing at one powwow or another all summer long. She knew how the people dressed, and she learned to recognize other tribes by the things they wore as well. This man had his tribes all mixed up. He wore a fringed buckskin outfit, with Plains-style geometric beaded designs, a Maidu abalone shell choker, and moccasins with Chippewa floral designs beaded on the toes. On his head was a huge, drooping feather headdress, almost identical to the one pictured in the sign beside the road. Arletta noticed that there was something else not quite right about the way he looked. His skin looked funny, all dark and light, almost striped in places. As he came closer, she could see that the dark color of his skin had been painted on with makeup and that the stripes had been made by the sweat running down his skin and spoiling the paint job. Arletta had never in all her life known an Indian who looked the way this man did.

10   After buying everything they wanted, the Rapier family came spilling out of the trading post just in time to be impressed by the cut-and-paste "Indian."

11   "Oh, Arletta," Mrs. Rapier said. "Look what you found. A real live Indian! Go on over there like a good girl, and I'll have Jackson take a nice picture of the two of you together. It's so seldom you ever see one of your own people."

12   Arletta froze. She couldn't believe Mrs. Rapier was serious, but then she knew she was. Mrs. Rapier and her entire family actually believed that the man they saw before them was a bonafide Cherokee chief. What is wrong with these people? she thought. Can't they see this guy's a fake?

13   Mr. Rapier walked behind Arletta and put his sweaty hands on both her shoulders. For a moment, she thought he was going to give her a reprieve, to tell her that she didn't have to do this, that it was all just a joke. Instead, he pushed her forward, propelling her toward the man with the rapidly melting face. She knew then that they were giving her no choice.

14   Mr. Rapier arranged the girl and the costumed man in what he thought was a suitable pose and stepped back for a look through his camera. Dissatisfied with what he saw, he turned and walked back into the trading post to return minutes later with an enormous rubber tomahawk, a bedraggled turkey feather war bonnet, a smaller version of the one worn by the costumed man, and a shabbily worked beaded medallion necklace with a purple and yellow thunderbird design. He thrust the tomahawk into Arletta's hand, plunked the headdress on her head sideways, and arranged the necklace around her neck with the quickness of a ferret. Surveying his creation, he smiled and returned to his previous position to adjust his camera lens.

15   "Smile real big for me, honey," he said. "And say the magic word. Say Cherokee!"

16   Mr. Rapier grinned, his pale beady eyes twinkled at his clever remark. Arletta felt her mouth go sour and a strange contortion of pain began to move around in the bottom of her belly.

17   The costumed man took her hand and squeezed it. "Come on now, honey. Smile fer the pitcher," he said. His breath was stale rye whiskey and chewing tobacco. Standing next to him, Arletta could smell the pungent sweat that rolled off of him in waves, making his paint job look even worse than it had when she first saw him. Her stomach felt as if she'd swallowed an electric mixer, and she bit her lips to keep the burning in the back of her eyes from sliding down her face. Through her humiliation, Arletta glared defiantly at the man behind the camera and stubbornly refused to utter Mr. Rapier's magic word, no matter how much he coaxed and cajoled. Finally the camera whirred once like a demented bumblebee and it was done.

18   Mrs. Rapier dabbed at the perspiration that puddled in her cleavage with a crumpled tissue and praised her husband's photographic genius. "That was perfect, Jackson," she said. "You got her real good. Why, she looks just like an Indian princess."

19   Appeased by his wife's esteem, Mr. Rapier bought everyone a round of cold drinks and then shepherded Arletta and his rapidly wilting family back into the dilapidated station wagon for the long ride home. The superheated air inside the closed-up car was stifling. Arletta suddenly felt as if she were being walled up alive in some kind of tomb. The syrupy soda that had been so cold when she drank it boiled now as it pitched and rolled inside her stomach. She took off the hideous turkey feather headdress and dropped it, along with the phony rubber tomahawk, onto the floor of the car. Slowly, deliberately, Arletta removed the cheap beaded medallion with its crude rendering of a thunderbird from around her neck. Her fingers trembled as she ran them across the tops of the large, ugly, and uneven beads. Turning the medallion over, she read the tiny words printed faintly on the shiny vinyl backing while the painful turbulence inside her stomach increased.

20   "Mr. Rapier, could you stop the car?" she said. "Mr. Rapier, I don't feel so good."

21   Mr. Rapier adjusted the knob on the air conditioner's control panel to high and drove on without acknowledging that Arletta had ever spoken. He was already envisioning how her picture would look in the photo album where he and his wife kept the captured images of all the foster children they had cared for over the years. He hoped she hadn't spoiled the shot with that stubborn expression of hers. He wanted to put it next to the one of the little black girl they had last year. She sure had looked cute all dressed up in those African clothes standing next to that papier-mâché lion at Jungle World.

22   Mrs. Rapier pulled down the sun visor and began to pull at her perspiration-soaked hair with jerky, irritated movements. She looked at Arletta in the visor's mirror and frowned.

23 "Arletta," she said, "you need to hush. You've just worn yourself out from the heat and playing Indian. You'll be just fine as soon as the car cools off."

24 For an instant, Arletta pleaded with her eyes. Then she threw up all over the genuine Indian goods: "Made in Japan."

25 "Arletta!" Mrs. Rapier screamed. "Look what you've done! You've ruined all those lovely things we bought. Aren't you ashamed of yourself?"

26 Arletta flashed a genuine smile for the first time that day. "No, ma'am," she said. "No, ma'am, I'm not."

DISCUSSION QUESTIONS

1. The author establishes the tone for the entire story with details of the setting. What images contribute to this tone in the first paragraph? Find other adjectives in the description of the Cherokee trading post.
2. The narrator reports the words, actions, and some of the thoughts of the family and Arletta. Is the narrator more favorable to one character than to others? What does the author accomplish by using this point of view? Do you think the narrator is too obvious with the use of prejudiced images?
3. Which character seems the most real? Make a list of details about what you know and don't know about that character. Select lines that reveal qualities of the character, such as Mrs. Rapier's exclaiming, "A real live Indian!"
4. What is significant about the family's having a "chain of foster children"?
5. With three or four of your classmates, improvise a scene in which you are trapped in an event from which you desperately wish to escape. First, decide the plot conflict; then add necessary characters and dialogue.

WRITING TOPICS

1. Imagine you are one of these characters in the trading post scene: Arletta, Mr. Rapier, or the fake Indian chief. In your character's voice, write a first-person view of the scene.
2. Recall vivid details of a time when you encountered prejudice. Use dialogue and dramatic description to set the scene and reveal the personalities of the people with you.

WHAT I AM

Luci Tapahonso

Going home is a recurring theme in Native American literature. Luci Tapahonso's home, the Navajo Reservation, extends over parts of three states: northwestern New Mexico, northeastern Arizona, and southeastern Utah. It covers more than twenty-five thousand square miles, an area slightly larger than the state of West Virginia. There are more than two hundred thousand Navajos today. Tapahonso belongs to a matrilineal society in which women own the property and pass inheritance through their clans. In the Navajo kinship system, each Navajo child is born into four different, unrelated clans: the mother's clan, the father's clan, and the maternal and paternal grandfathers' clans. The kinship system also extends to the natural world and the gods. The Navajos are always among relatives. The tribute to her Navajo family takes place over fifty years and embraces four generations. As a university professor of English and a Navajo writer, Tapahonso celebrates being a daughter, a mother, and a grandmother.

1   1935: Kinlichii'nii Bitsi waited, looking across the snow-covered plain stretching out before her. Snow was falling lightly and the desert was flat and white. From where she stood at the foothills of the Carrizo Mountains, she could see for miles.

2   She would see him when he approached—a small dark speck on the vast whiteness moving slowly but closer. Her son, Prettyboy, tall and lanky on the sure-footed horse. She would see him.

3   All evening, she kept watch. Stepping out every once in a while. He had gone to visit some relatives at Little Shiprock and should have returned by now. It had begun snowing early and continued into the evening. She knew Prettyboy had started home before the storm and would be arriving soon. She kept watch, looking out on the horizon.

4   In those days, hogans had no windows so she stood at the front door, a

shawl around her shoulders. Only her eyes were uncovered as she squinted, looking out into the desert night "Niihiima deesk'aaz," her children called her back in. She would come in for a while and then go back out to watch for him again. All evening she waited, and her children urged her not to worry. He would be home soon. She wasn't cold, she said, and she would wait for him outside.

5   Finally she saw him, a dark speck on the horizon. She rushed in and stirred up the fire, heated up the stew and put on a fresh pot of coffee. She heated the grease for frybread. He came in, damp and cold with snow. They laughed because his eyebrows were frozen white. "Tell us about your trip," they said to him, "tell us everything about your trip." While he ate, he told about their relatives and news he had heard. He said the horse seemed to know the way by itself through the snow and wind. He kept his head down most of the way, he said, it was blowing snow and hard to see.

6   The family finally went to bed, happy and relieved that Prettyboy was safely home. Outside the wind blew and the snow formed drifts around the hogan.

7   In the morning, Kinlichii'nii Bitsi was sick—feverish and dizzy. She didn't get up and they fed her blue corn mush and weak Navajo tea to drink. She slept most of the day and felt very warm. Her family began to worry. The nearest doctor was in Shiprock, forty miles to the east. On horseback, it was a full day's journey. Even then, the doctor was at the agency only two days a week and they couldn't remember which days he was there. The medicine man lived nearby on the mountainside and they decided to wait until morning to go over there and tell him, if they must. She would get better, they said, and they prayed and sang songs for strength and for the children. Very late that night, she became very ill and talked incessantly about her children and grandchildren.

8   She died before morning and Prettyboy went out into the snow and blowing wind to tell other relatives who lived scattered distances from Kinlichii'nii Bitsi's hogan. People gathered quickly despite the snow, they came from all around to help out with the next four days.

9   1968: The granddaughter of Kinlichii'nii Bitsi said:

10   My uncle Prettyboy died today and we went over to his house. His aunt, my grandma, was sweeping out her hogan next door and scolding the young people for not helping out. They were listening to their radios in their pickups and holding hands. You know, they are teenagers. My grandma is 104 years old. My real grandma, Kinlichii'nii Bitsi, would have been 106 if she hadn't died in the 1930s. I know a lot about her and I love her—the stories I know and the way she was. I think I'm like her in some ways.

11   At Prettyboy's house, his wife and children were sitting in the front room and everyone came in and spoke to them quietly. They were crying and crying. Sometimes crying loudly, sometimes sobbing. In the kitchen and outside over open fires, we were all cooking and preparing food for everyone who came for the four days.

12   Prettyboy was a tall man and he died of cancer. It was awful because he didn't even smoke. He worked in the uranium mines near Red Rock.

13   Last week when we were hoeing in the fields, my mother said,

14   "Having a mother is everything. Your mother is your home," she said, "when children come home, the mother is always ready with food, stories and songs for the little ones. She's always happy and glad to see her children and grandchildren." My mother had always told me this as I was growing up. That day when we were hoeing corn, I said, "Tell me that story again about grandmother and how you knew something was wrong that time. Tell me the story, my mother."

15   My mother told me this story. She said:

16   That night, Prettyboy was coming home, I knew something was wrong. The wind blew hard and it roared through the tall pine trees. We lived in the mountains at Oaksprings about ten miles above where my mother lived. We were just married then, our first baby, your oldest sister was a month old. That night the dogs started barking wildly and loudly—they were afraid of something—then they stopped suddenly. Your father and I looked at each other across the room. Then we heard the coyotes barking and yelping outside. He opened the door and they were circling the hogan, running around and around, yelping and howling at the same time. Your father grabbed the rifle and he shot at the two coyotes but he missed each time. He missed. He had been a sharpshooter in the army and he couldn't shoot them. Finally they ran off and we were both afraid that night. We talked about what happened and prayed into the night. We couldn't go anywhere. The snow was deep and even the horses would have a hard time.

17   In the morning, I went out to pray and I saw my brother, Prettyboy, riding up to our hogan. He was still far off and only a small dot on the desert but even then, I knew something had happened. I tried not to cry but I knew in my bones, something had happened. My brother would not ride out just to visit us in that weather. Even though the sun was out, the snow was frozen and the wind blew steadily. I held the baby and prayed, hoping I was wrong.

18   Finally, he came up to our hogan, I went out and saw he was crying. He wasn't looking where he was going. The horse led my brother, who was crying. I watched him and then he saw me. I called out, "Shiinaa, my older brother!" He got off the horse and ran to me crying, "Shideezhi, my baby sister, niihiima adin! Our mother's gone!" My heart fell and we cried. The wind stopped blowing and we went inside.

19   I held my baby girl and told her she would not see her grandmother. None of our children would, either. My mother died and I realized she was my home, she had always welcomed me and since I was the youngest, she called me her baby. "Even if you are a grandmother," she said, "you will be my baby, always."

20   My mother tells me the story and we always cry. Even if I had known Kinlichii'nii Bitsi, I wouldn't love her more than I do now, knowing her only through the stories and my mother's memory.

21 My grandmother had talked to my father about a week before she died. She told him, "Take care of her. She is my youngest, my baby. I trust you and I have faith that you will care for her as I have all these years. She is my baby but she knows what to do. Listen to her and remember a woman's wisdom is not foolish. She knows a lot because I have raised her to be a good and kind person." My father listened and he treats my mother well. He listens to her and abides by her wishes always.

22 1986: The great-granddaughter of Kinlichii'nii Bitsi said:

23 Early in the morning, we went out to pray. The corn pollen drifted into the pool. It became little specks of yellow on the blue water. The water lapped quietly against the edges. We prayed and I asked my ancestors, my grandparents and uncles who died before, to watch over me.

24 I was going so far away—Europe. What a trip it would be. My mother cried when I left and my grandma called me. I was nervous and couldn't sleep. I felt like canceling my plans but my mother had spent all that money already. "Remember who you are," my grandma said, "you're from Oaksprings and all your relatives are thinking about you and praying for you to come back safely. Do well on your trip, my little one."

25 I put the bag of pollen in my purse. At the airport at LaGuardia, I ran to the bathroom and tasted some. My mother, I thought, my grandmother, help me. It was confusing and loud, everyone smoking and talking loudly. I wanted my mother's soft, slow voice then more than anything. I was the only Indian in the group so no one knew how I felt. The other girls were looking at boys and talking and laughing loudly.

26 I had the corn pollen though. I was afraid they would arrest me at customs for carrying an unknown substance, but they didn't. I was meant to go to Paris.

27 I prayed on top of the Eiffel Tower and the pollen floated down to the brick plaza below. I was so far from home—so high above everything—the tower swayed a little in the wind. I never missed Indians until I went abroad; then I was lonely to see an Indian the whole time. People thought I was neat—being a "real" Indian. They wanted to learn Navajo and they asked all kinds of questions. It was weird to be a "real" Indian. All along I was just regular, one of the bunch, laughing with my relatives and friends, mixing Navajo and English. We were always telling jokes about cowboys, computer warriors and stuff.

28 It was while I stood on the top of the Eiffel Tower that I understood that what I am is my mother, her mother, and my great-grandmother, Kinlichii'nii Bitsi, whom I never met but always knew. It was she who made sure I got through customs and wasn't mugged in Paris. My grandmother was at the airport, she hugged me tightly. My mother stood back and then came forward and held me. I was home.

DISCUSSION QUESTIONS

1. Tapahonso ends her story, "I was home." How does this idea echo through the three sections of the story?
2. Give important details about the setting in each section. What do they contribute to the family stories?
3. The author writes, "What I am is my mother, her mother, and my great-grandmother." How do these three women lend a feminine symmetry to the essay?
4. The first two sections are about the death of loved ones. How is the entire selection about life?

WRITING TOPICS

1. Write a brief essay on the role of the sacred, prayer, and song in "What I Am."
2. Interview a family member or friend who belongs to a previous generation. Prepare a list of questions that focus on one or two topics that you would like to know about. Then write about what you learned.

SUMMARY WRITING TOPICS

1. Select one author from "Images and Identities" and write a researched essay on his or her tribal background. In your essay, include some or all of these topics: location of the tribe today; approximate tribal population; significant historical facts involving the tribal-U.S. government relations; information about the tribal ceremonial beliefs; and tribal issues that are relevant to the author's selection in this chapter. Share your paper in a panel discussion with your classmates and invite questions from the audience. (Suggested tribes: Blackfeet, Mohawk, Sioux, Chickasaw, Chippewa, Nez Perce, Navajo, Cherokee, Spokane, Kiowa.)

2. All the Indian authors in this chapter are concerned with their ethnic heritages. They define their identities in relation to heritage in different, yet comparable ways. Reread one autobiographical selection. Then examine autobiographical essays by two authors from different ethnic backgrounds (African American, Asian American, Mexican American, Irish American, and so on). What points do these three authors have in common regarding their heritages? Using these points as an outline, compose an essay in which you compare four major points from the three authors. Topics may include family, special ethnic beliefs and practices, and experiences with people outside their groups. (Suggested authors: Maxine Hong Kingston, Richard Rodriguez, Henry Louis Gates, Jr., Sandra Cisneros, Maya Angelou, James Baldwin.)

3. Write a review of a contemporary movie that involves racial and/or ethnic issues. Evaluate the treatment of the issues and tell what you liked and disliked.

4. Assume that you are a freelance reporter for a national magazine. You are assigned to visit your school and to interview students for a feature article on race relations. Identify the publication you are representing and write an article for it on "Student Voices on Race Relations." Use specific quotations to support your thesis.

5. Assume that you may interview two authors of selections in "Images and Identities." Give reasons for your choices and then compose at least four questions you would like to ask each. Explain why you would want to know the answer to each question.

6. Imagine that you are visiting North America for the first time and have minimal information about American Indians. The voices in "Images and Identities" speak to you through their compositions. Write a letter to a friend in your home country explaining what you have learned about relations between Native Americans and other North Americans and what you think relations will be in the future.

7. Several authors in "Images and Identities" have a keen sense of humor. They employ literary devices of sarcasm, irony, and satire. Select pas-

sages from two authors whom you think used humor effectively and read the passages aloud to your classmates. Then write an analysis of both authors' use of humor, citing examples to support your choices.

8. Recall your perceptions and attitudes toward Native Americans before you studied "Images and Identities." After reading the voices in the selections and discussing the topics, have any of your perceptions and attitudes changed? What new information have you learned about Native Americans? After reviewing the answers to these questions, write a personal essay about your current perceptions and misconceptions of Native Americans.

9. As the ethnic mixture of the American population changes, the information about race collected by the United States Census Bureau has come under scrutiny. Congressional hearings have been held on whether to require the bureau to include a new category in the census questionnaire. This new category would enable persons of mixed racial ancestry to so identify themselves. Write a letter to the Chairperson of the House Census Oversight Committee arguing for or against establishing this new racial category in the census. What name do you suggest for that category? Does implementing it justify the enormous cost? Who would use this information? Why do Americans need to know this information?

CHAPTER TWO

THE SPIRIT WORLD

Once a woman fell from the sky. She had lived in the Sky World with her husband Great Ruler. In the center of that world grew a bright Tree of Light with luminous flowers and rich fruits on its branches. The sacred tree had enormous roots that reached in all directions. Digging among its roots, Great Ruler broke a giant hole in the Sky World floor. He was terrified, but Sky Woman was curious. Bending over, she saw only waters far below; no earth, no day, no night, no humans, only flowing waters. Standing too close to the edge, she slipped and fell. Plunging through space, she cried, "I will die." Iroquois storytellers say that soaring birds caught Sky Woman. Flying wingtip to wingtip, they made a feathery raft and placed her gently on the shell of Great Sea Turtle. Great Turtle floated on the huge ocean with the woman safely on his back.

Falling Sky Woman had frantically grasped roots that stuck between her fingers, and the sea creatures searched for soil so the plants could live. One by one they dove down through dark waters. Then Muskrat dove and disappeared. Suddenly he appeared holding a tiny spot of soil in his paw. The animals pulled him on Great Turtle's back and sang and prayed over him. Finally, he stirred. Thus, Muskrat, Earth Diver, brought soil from the ocean bottom. Then Sky Woman placed the tiny clod of dirt in the middle of Great Sea Turtle's back, and the earth began to grow. Iroquois storytellers say that earth still rests on Great Turtle's shell.

One day twin sons were born to Sky Woman. Good Minded, the Master of Life, created an orderly world for humans. Evil Minded, known as Old Warty, caused chaos and destruction. Good Minded and Evil Minded are locked in cosmic combat for control of the earth and its creatures. During the mythic time, stone giants and flesh eaters preyed on the Iroquois until

Holder of Heavens destroyed them with an earthquake. One giant, Genonsgwa, escaped to instruct a young hunter in curing human illness and carving basswood into the False Face mask a tribal healer wears. Grown old, that hero founded The False Face Society, members of which carry on The Mask-Making Ceremony in their roles as healers. Some monsters lived until an Onondaga warrior had to destroy the Vampire Skeleton.

Thus an extensive set of Iroquois myths and legends explains the core mythistory from the beginning to yesterday's curing ceremony. Told generation after generation, oral histories became increasingly legendary. Excellent examples of such a legendary oral history are "The Council of the Great Peace" edited by the Seneca scholar Arthur C. Parker, and "The Origin of the Long House," concerning the formation of the League of the Iroquois.

The creation myths, hero stories, and legendary histories have sustained and illuminated Iroquois life for centuries. This collection of oral tradition has defined the kind of world in which the Iroquois lived and how it began. It has linked them to the supernatural being who created them. It has given them a sense of who they were and are in their unique ethnic world.

Each Native American group has its own tribal mythology, or cosmology, which describes its origin, explains the genesis of the cosmos, including the earth and its myriad life forms, and provides models for modern behavior. Mythology, or cosmology, is a mirror of and a map for the culture that believes and practices it. Therefore, mythology may be defined as a great body of truth for the people who believe it. Mythology explains the relationship of the people to the cosmos. Some people prefer the word *cosmology* to the term *mythology*.

Each Native American society possesses its distinct cosmology, but groups also share beliefs and practices that illustrate a common spirit world system. The elements of this spiritual framework include the following: (1) a belief that invisible powers operate in the universe; (2) the knowledge that these positive and negative powers of the universe are balanced, and consequently humans must seek balance and harmony in their lives; (3) the need for humans to respect, revere, and be responsible for the earth and its creatures; (4) the belief that healing specialists may acquire knowledge about curing powers; (5) the understanding that one way to communicate with the supernatural beings and powers is to contact them through dreams and visions; (6) a recognition of the spiritual power of words and stories; and (7) the awareness that sacred time, sacred place, and sacred stories unite the spirit world and the natural world for Native Americans today.

Oral literature survived as remembered myths and rituals, songs and poems, narrative tales and legends. Some of the stories and poems you will read in this chapter are very old. Some are sacred myths and others are moral tales. They have been passed down through generations of storytellers to modern authors who wrote them down. Power resides in these stories. They are not simply quaint tales for entertainment, but a great chain of language.

For Native Americans, they are true because they arise from belief. As N. Scott Momaday explains, "In the oral tradition stories are told not merely to entertain or to instruct; they are told to be believed." Words carry power to make things happen. Momaday describes this power in "Carriers of the Dream Wheel."

When a creator descended from the sky, marvelous events happened for the Iroquois. In contrast, the origin story of many Southwestern societies is the myth of emergence, which describes how the ancestors of the present people emerged onto the earth's surface from within the center of the earth. In the origin myths of the Navajos, the people move through four worlds. The sun shone on only the Fifth World, the Glittering World, in which we live. In the Fifth World, White Bead Woman became the mythological mother and protector of the Navajos. Her hero twins, Monster Slayer and Child Born for Water, destroyed terrible monsters who preyed on people. The Navajo and other Native American cosmologies tell of a trying time when monsters devoured humans. Culture heroes, such as the Iroquois and Navajo twins, rescued tribal peoples by slaying these fierce beings. The twins then taught the Navajos healing ceremonies called chants. In "A Prayer from the Night Chant," a patient prays for restored health and happiness. Another prayer, "The War God's Horse Song," celebrates Navajos' love for horses.

The Navajo creation myths also introduce the trickster Coyote. In mythic time Coyote appears as one of the first beings who has both animal and human qualities. Coyote tells stories, plays tricks, and breaks all the rules. Yet there is wisdom in his folly, for his antics generate laughter and learning. In "The Origin of Eternal Death," curious Coyote fails to observe proper taboos and he must lose his wife to Death.

Coyote is only one of numerous Native American tricksters. In "Raven Steals the Light," Raven fills the dark world with light. In "Naanabozho and the Gambler," Gerald Vizenor retells how the Chippewa trickster Naanabozho outwitted the Gambler, another of the monsters luring people to their doom. The life of anyone who lost a game to the Gambler was forfeit. Such narratives are not without a moral. Native American elders over many millennia in North America developed a powerful and extensive repertoire of stories with morals. "The Fawn, the Wolves, and the Terrapin" presents "the fooling fool fooled," as editor Karl Kroeber points out. Kiowa author Russell Bates has Singing-owl, the major character in "Rite of Encounter," turn the tables on Smallpox Death during a mysterious vision quest. Although fictional, Louis Owens' "Soul-Catcher" reads almost like a traditional oral tale, and it drives home a Choctaw belief about relationships between animals and people. In other words, the place of stories in the Spirit World is to teach lessons for proper character and conduct.

Tricksters and heroes, monsters and humans are all part of a universe in which dual forces create balance. Positive and negative powers of creation and destruction are complements. Good health and harmony result not from a final victory of good over evil, but from a balance of good with evil. No sense of punishment or sin operates in this belief system. The kind of world set in motion in the beginning taught Native Americans to practice rituals and conduct ceremonies to preserve the balance of powers.

Sacred time, sacred place, and sacred acts are present in these rituals and ceremonies. One such ceremony is the Plains Sun Dance, which is performed for spiritual strength and physical well being of the community. In "The Sun Dance," Luther Standing Bear describes the Sioux Sun Dance held in 1879, more than a hundred years ago. Standing Bear explains that a dancer made a vow to sacrifice himself in order that the buffalo would give themselves to the hunters and the people would not be hungry, or to request that the spirits would make sick relatives well. The Sun Dance was held each summer on holy ground. According to Standing Bear, "If we ever returned to that sacred spot where the pole was yet standing, with the crosspiece attached, we stood for a long time in reverent attitude, because it was a sacred place to us."

Young John Fire Lame Deer, another Lakota, undertook his vision quest when he was seventeen to become a medicine man, a healer. In "Alone on a Hilltop," Lame Deer tells about his seeking the right ways to perform a ceremony in which each action and every word had its own special meaning. Voices of the winged ones, eagles and owls, spoke to him in his vision. "We are a nation and you shall be our brother. You are going to understand us whenever you come to seek a vision here on this hill. You will learn about herbs and roots, and you will heal people."

Throughout North America, Indians like Luther Standing Bear and Lame Deer purified themselves physically and spiritually in special structures. Pouring water on fire-heated stones filled these sweat lodges with steam, causing participants in the cleansing to perspire profusely. Phil George's "Old Man, the Sweat Lodge" expresses the proper frame of mind for taking part in purification. In "All My Relations," Linda Hogan emphasizes that "story is at the very crux of healing, at the heart of every ceremony and ritual in the older America." For Hogan, all elements of the Spirit World enter the sweat lodge ritual. Wind, animals, willow branches, cedar smoke, thunderclouds, sky, stars, and people gather in intimate kinship. "We sit together in our aloneness and speak, one at a time, our deepest language of need, hope, loss and survival. We remember that all things are connected."

CARRIERS OF THE DREAM WHEEL

N. Scott Momaday

N. Scott Momaday invites us to hear the old stories and sacred songs from the spirit world. He eloquently reminds us that the circle of stories and songs is always old, yet ever new. The carriers of the dream wheel, the keepers of the past, have kept their literature and culture alive for untold generations. This is the oral tradition: voices shaping stories, singing songs, offering prayers, and chanting rituals. The oral tradition is always in motion, moving through time, space, and place. From the time of creation in Kiowa cosmology to this instant, the voices have survived and shaped family and tribal stories. Unlike his ancestral storytellers and singers, Momaday *writes* his words in lyrical form. Yet the oral tradition informs this modern poet who has inherited the legacy of the Dream Wheel carriers. The poem appears in his collection *In the Presence of the Sun* (1992).

This is the Wheel of Dreams
Which is carried on their voices,
By means of which their voices turn
And center upon being.
5 It encircles the First World,
This powerful wheel.
They shape their songs upon the wheel
And spin the names of the earth and sky,
The aboriginal names.
10 They are old men, or men
Who are old in their voices,
And they carry the wheel among the camps,
Saying: Come, come,
Let us tell the old stories,
15 Let us sing the sacred songs.

Discussion Questions
---

1. Who are the carriers and why are they important? What special characteristics do they possess to qualify them for their role in the oral tradition? How is Momaday, the contemporary poet, similar to and different
   from them?
2. The Wheel of Dreams is a symbol. Why is this circular metaphor more
   appropriate for the oral tradition than a straight line moving from point
   A to point B?
3. The Wheel is a powerful, rotating force at the center of the oral tradition.
   What words does the poet choose to convey this motion?

Writing Topic
---

1. Using examples from the poem, develop a brief essay on this topic: In
   "Carriers of the Dream Wheel," N. Scott Momaday uses sound to
   achieve structure in the poem. He creates rhythm by repeating sounds,
   words, and images.

THE CREATION
IROQUOIS MYTHS

Harriet Converse and Arthur Parker

The creation story is the beginning of traditional Iroquois literature. First recorded by Europeans in 1623, the ancient myth has
almost four hundred years of written history. Told by generations of
Iroquois, its oral history is even older. For centuries, learned men
have recited the story of this island, this earth on Turtle's back, after
the first frost when the earth sleeps. The story introduces sacred symbols that underpin modern Iroquois life: the council tree; the Sky
Woman; the earth-bearer turtle; and the rival twins.

Sky Woman became the earth mother of Hah-gweh-di-yu (Good
Minded) and Hah-gweh-da-ĕt-găh (Evil Minded). Good Minded, the
creator, symbolizes growth and fertility. Evil Minded, the destroyer,
is Flint (Ice), patron of winter, the ugly one covered with warts. He
wears a sharp comb of flint on his forehead, a design carved in
Seneca False Faces. In their cosmic combat for the control of the
earth, the twins cause seasons to change. Sky Woman and her sons
demonstrate that life on earth island is a constant struggle between
darkness and light, order and chaos, creation and destruction. Evil
can never be destroyed, but it can be balanced with good.

Sacred trees appear throughout Iroquois literature. The ever-
growing tree symbolizes life, status, and power. In the beginning,
Great Ruler uprooted the celestial tree, cast down the earthbound
woman, and then replanted the tree of heaven. A giant pine grows at
the center of the earth where the False Face Masker acquires healing
power from rubbing his turtle rattle against its bark. Ceremonial
masks, known as False Faces, are carved from living basswood or
other trees for use in healing rituals. In Iroquois society, a pine tree
symbolizes chiefdom, and the tree figuratively falls with the death of
a chief; however, the successor chief ascends with the renewed tree.
Iroquois tribal documents often refer to the "Great Tree of Peace."

THE COUNCIL TREE

1   In the faraway days of this floating island there grew one stately tree that branched beyond the range of vision. Perpetually laden with fruit and blossoms, the air was fragrant with its perfume, and the people gathered to its shade where councils were held.

2   One day the Great Ruler said to his people: "We will make a new place where another people may grow. Under our council tree is a great cloud sea which calls for our help. It is lonesome. It knows no rest and calls for light. We will talk to it. The roots of our council tree point to it and will show the way."

3   Having commanded that the tree be uprooted, the Great Ruler peered into the depths where the roots had guided, and summoning Ata-en-sic, who was with child, bade her look down. Ata-en-sic saw nothing, but the Great Ruler knew that the sea voice was calling, and bidding her carry its life, wrapped around her a great ray of light and sent her down to the cloud sea.

THE TURTLE HAH-NU-NAH

4   Dazzled by the descending light enveloping Ata-en-sic, there was great consternation among the animals and birds inhabiting the cloud sea, and they counseled in alarm.

5   "If it falls it may destroy us," they cried.

6   "Where can it rest?" asked the Duck.

7   "Only the oeh-da (earth) can hold it," said the Beaver, "the oeh-da which lies at the bottom of our waters, and I will bring it." The Beaver went down but never returned. Then the Duck ventured, but soon its dead body floated to the surface.

8   Many of the divers had tried and failed when the Muskrat, knowing the way, volunteered to obtain it and soon returned bearing a small portion in his paw. "But it is heavy," said he, "and will grow fast. Who will bear it?"

9   The Turtle was willing, and the oeh-da was placed on his hard shell.

10   Having received a resting place for the light, the water birds, guided by its glow, flew upward, and receiving the woman on their widespread wings, bore her down to the Turtle's back.

11   And Hah-nu-nah, the Turtle, became the Earth Bearer. When he stirs, the seas rise in great waves, and when restless and violent, earthquakes yawn and devour.

THE SKY WOMAN, ATA-EN-SIC

12   The *oeh-da* grew rapidly and had become an island when Ata-en-sic, hearing voices under her heart, one soft and soothing, the other loud and contentious, knew that her mission to people the island was nearing.

13   To her solitude two lives were coming, one peaceful and patient, the

other restless and vicious. The latter, discovering light under his mother's arm, thrust himself through, to contentions and strife, the right born entered life for freedom and peace.

14   These were the Do-ya-da-no, the twin brothers, Spirits of Good and Evil. Foreknowing their powers, each claimed dominion, and a struggle between them began, Hah-gweh-di-yu claiming the right to beautify the island, while Hah-gweh-da-ĕt-găh determined to destroy. Each went his way, and where peace had reigned discord and strife prevailed.

THE SUN, MOON, AND STARS

15   At the birth of Hah-gweh-di-yu his Sky Mother, Ata-en-sic, had died, and the island was still dim in the dawn of its new life when, grieving at his mother's death, he shaped the sky with the palm of his hand, and creating the Sun from her face, lifted it there, saying, "You shall rule here where your face will shine forever." But Hah-gweh-da-ĕt-găh set Darkness in the west sky, to drive the Sun down behind it.

16   Hah-gweh-di-yu then drew forth from the breast of his Mother, the Moon and the Stars, and led them to the Sun as his sisters who would guard his night sky. He gave to the Earth her body, its Great Mother, from whom was to spring all life.

17   All over the land Hah-gweh-di-yu planted towering mountains, and in the valleys set high hills to protect the straight rivers as they ran to the sea. But Hah-gweh-da-ĕt-găh wrathfully sundered the mountains, hurling them far apart, and drove the high hills into the wavering valleys, bending the rivers has he hunted them down.

18   Hah-gweh-di-yu set forests on the high hills, and on the low plains fruit-bearing trees and vines to wing their seeds to the scattering winds. But Hah-gweh-da-ĕt-găh gnarled the forests besetting the earth, and led monsters to dwell in the sea, and herded hurricanes in the sky which frowned with mad tempests that chased the Sun and the Stars.

THE ANIMALS AND BIRDS

19   Hah-gweh-di-yu went across a great sea where he met a Being who told him he was his father. Said the Being, "How high can you reach?" Hah-gweh-di-yu touched the sky. Again he asked, "How much can you lift?" and Hah-gweh-di-yu grasped a stone mountain and tossed it far into space. Then said the Being, "You are worthy to be my son"; and lashing upon his back two burdens, bade him return to the earth.

20   Hah-gweh-di-yu swam for many days, and the Sun did not leave the sky until he had neared the earth. The burdens had grown heavy but Hah-gweh-di-yu was strong, and when he reached the shore they fell apart and opened.

21   From one of the burdens flew an eagle guiding the birds which followed, filling the skies with their song to the Sun as they winged to the forest. From

the other there came animals led by the deer, and they sped quickly to the mountains. But Hah-gweh-da-ĕt-gǎh followed with wild beasts that devour, and grim flying creatures that steal life without sign, and creeping reptiles to poison the way.

DUEL OF HAH-GWEH-DI-YU AND HAH-GWEH-DA-ĚT-GǍH

22   When the earth was completed and Hah-gweh-di-uy had bestowed a protecting Spirit upon each of his creation, he besought Hah-gweh-da-ĕt-gǎh to reconcile his vicious existence to the peacefulness of his own, but Hah-gweh-da-ĕt-gǎh refused, and challenged Hah-gweh-di-yu to combat, the victor to become the ruler of the earth.

23   Hah-gweh-da-ĕt-gǎh proposed weapons which he could control, poisonous roots strong as flint, monsters' teeth, and fangs of serpents. But these Hah-gweh-di-yu refused, selecting the thorns of the giant crab-apple tree, which were arrow pointed and strong.

24   With the thorns they fought. The battle continued many days, ending in the overthrow of Hah-gweh-da-ĕt-gǎh.

25   Hah-gweh-di-yu, having now become the ruler, banished his brother to a pit under the earth, whence he cannot return. But he still retains Servers, half human and half beasts, whom he sends to continue his destructive work. These Servers can assume any form Hah-gweh-da-ĕt-gǎh may command, and they wander all over the earth.

26   Hah-gweh-di-yu, faithful to the prophesy of the Great Ruler of the floating island, that the earth should be peopled, is continually creating and protecting.

DISCUSSION QUESTIONS

1. The storyteller pictures the creation of the earth and its creatures in imagery that makes the divine events seem real. What is the tone of the selection? Reread the imagery for the sacred council tree; Earth Bearer Turtle; and Sky Woman, and tell how this imagery contributes to the tone.

2. From their birth, the rival twins conduct a cosmic struggle of creation and destruction that affects human lives. Under the headings, " Hah-gweh-di-yu/Good Minded" and "Hah-gweh-da-ĕt-gǎh/Evil Minded" make a chart of actions that describe their struggle.

WRITING TOPICS

1. All societies value the story of their creations or beginnings. Select a creation story from a society that is not American Indian and tell it to a classmate, who should write it down. Revise the written version using lively details. Note the supernatural characters who have natural human traits. How is your story similar to and different from the Iroquois story? Based on your experience of reading a story, telling it to another person, and revising the written version, what observations can you make about "a retold version" of an oral/written story? What literary devices did you use to make your story interesting (figurative language, parallelism, repetition, etc.)?

2. The Iroquois Creation myth presents a process of establishing balance between dual forces: (1) chaos/order, (2) darkness/light, (3) peace/violence, and (4) protection/destruction. Write a brief essay on the role of one of these contrasting pairs in the creation of the world and its creatures. Use at least three examples from the text.

ORIGIN OF THE FALSE FACE COMPANY
SENECA MYTHS

Arthur Parker

Arthur Parker (1881–1955) collected and edited Iroquois literature and culture history. An anthropologist, ethnologist, and archaeologist, Parker was born into a prominent Seneca family as the son of Frederick E. Parker and Geneva Griswold, a Euro-American woman who taught school on the Cattaraugus Indian Reservation. In 1906, Parker became an archaeologist at the New York State Museum. In 1911, he joined with Charles Eastman and others to found the Society of American Indians, and became the editor of its journal, the *American Indian Magazine* in 1915. In 1944, he helped found the National Congress of American Indians. From 1925 to 1944, he served as director of the Rochester Museum of Arts and Sciences. The author of over 250 articles, Parker also wrote and edited several books including *The Code of Handsome Lake, the Seneca Prophet* (1913); *The Constitution of the Five Nations* (1916); and *Seneca Myths & Folk Tales* (1923).

In Parker's "The Origin of the False Face Company," Good Minded continues his struggle to make the world safe for humans. Flesh-eating stone giants mock Good Minded and dare to proclaim, "We have created ourselves!" Finally, all the giants disappear but one, who gradually becomes more like Good Minded. The last of the stone giants reveals his secrets to a young hunter hero. Through dreams and visions, the hero learns the healing ceremonies of the great False Faces, and he gives the laws of the order of the False Faces Society to humans. Today, the Iroquois continue the sacred ceremonies involving the False Faces, or medicine masks, to preserve their well being. These ritual dramas are the heart of *Haudenosaunee* oral literature.

THE STONE GIANTS

1   The stone giants are a kind of men-being that are now gone. What we have heard about them I will tell.

2   There was once a far north country where a race of giants dwelt. They were very tall and bony. It was cold in that north country and the giants lived on fish and raw flesh. When the summer came to that region there was dry sand upon the ground and the giants, it is supposed, taught their children to rub it on their bodies every day until the blood came out where the skin was worn through. After a while the skin became hard and calloused, like a woman's hand when the harvest is over. Each year the young rubbed their bodies with the sand, until when they had grown to be men, it was hard like rawhide and the sand stuck in and made them look like men of stone. This is what some wise men thought, but others said stone giants were born that way.

3   As time went on these giants grew more ferocious and warlike. They became tired of the flesh of beasts and fish and yearned for the flesh of men. Then they sallied forth to the lands south of them and captured Indians and devoured their flesh, tearing it from their living bodies. All the nations and tribes of Indians feared them, for no arrow would pierce their hard stony coats. Thus, secure in their armors of callous and sand, no season was too cold for them, no journey too long and no tribe strong enough to overwhelm them. They became more and more boastful and arrogant until they even laughed at the warnings of the Great Ruler, the Good Minded, and hallooed up to the skies mocking words. "We are as great as the Great Ruler," they said. "We have created ourselves!"

4   When the Confederacy of the five brother nations was young, these terrible stone giants crossed the river of rapids and swept down upon the scattered settlements of the Five Nations. By day they hid in caves and at night they came forth in the darkness and captured men, women and children, rending their bodies apart and chewing up their flesh and bones. When they pointed their fingers at men they fell down dead.

5   The medicine men cried to the Good Minded Spirit until it seemed that prayer was only like hollow talking in one's throat. The giants kept on with their raids and feasted undisturbed. No dark place was secure from their eyes, they penetrated the deepest shadows and found the hiding places of those who fled from them. Villages were destroyed and abandoned, councils were not held, for sachems and chieftains were the victims for the flesh-of-men feasts of the giants. The boldest warriors shot their strongest arrows from their strongest bows upon these invaders, but though the arrow shafts were strong and tipped with the toughest of flint, when they struck the stone-coated giants, the arrows broke and the flints snapped and the giants gathered up the warriors and shredded their meat from their bones with their sharp teeth.

6   At last the Good Ruler saw that men would become exterminated unless

he intervened. Thus, he commanded the Holder of the Heavens to descend from the sky and use his strategy to destroy the entire race of stone giants. Accordingly, the Holder of the Heavens dropped from the place above the clouds, and hiding in a deep forest, took the form of a stone giant and went among the band. Awed by his display of power, his wonderful feats and his marvelous strength they proclaimed the new comer the great chief of all the stone giants. In honor of his installation the Holder of the Heavens swung his huge war club high over his head and roared ferociously, "Now is the time to destroy these puny men, and have a great feast such as never before!" Leading forth the mighty tribe he planned to attack the stronghold of the Onondagas. Arriving at the foot of the great hill on whose summit was the stockade where the Onondagas had assembled, he bade the giants hide in the caves in the hills or make burrows and there hide. They were to await the dawn when they would commence the assault. Having instructed them, the Holder of the Heavens went up the fort hill on a pretense and then gave the whole earth a mighty shake. So mighty was the shaking that the rocks broke from their beds and fell in masses over one another and the earth slid down making new hills and valleys. The caves all collapsed and the crouching stone giants were crushed to bits. You could see bones once in caves among the Onondagas. All but one was killed and he, with a terrible yell, rushed forth and fled with the speed of a being impelled by the Evil Minded to the Allegheny mountains, where, finding a cave, he hid so long in the darkness that he became the Genonsgwa, a new creature to terrify men-being.

THE GENONSGWA

7   The Genonsgwa was a monster terrible for his anger and fierceness. But one spot on his entire being was vulnerable and that was a certain spot on the bottom of his foot. The Holder of the Heavens did not pursue this solitary fugitive, but rested content in the fact that the race of stone giants was destroyed and that this one survivor would not be particularly harmful when his fury subsided and his terror gave way.

8   For many years the Genonsgwa lived in the mountains, or, sallying forth on long journeys, made new abodes where for a time he dwelt. Sometimes in fits of rage he would rush from his cavern in the rocks and hurl stones into the rivers until he had made a waterfall, the booming of whose waters made noises like the voices of the Hi″nos, and then in his madness, he would call up to the father of thunders, and he, looking down, would become enraged at the insolent Genonsgwa and fling his fires down upon his cave retreats in the mountains. Then when the earth shook with the rumbling of thunders, reminding Genonsgwa of the awful day when the Holder of the Heavens shook down the rocks, he would crawl far back into the rocks and the listener miles away might hear his voice as he moaned and pleaded and quarreled with the powers that threatened his life.

9   As the years went by, Genonsgwa became more human and his spirit was quelled, but yet those who sought him found no mercy for he was the last of the stone giants. No one could see him, so terrible was his visage and so strong was his magic.

10   Now at this time a hunter lost his direction in a strange forest and though he traveled far and sought with vision keen the trail that should lead him out, he failed. A terrific hail storm broke from the heavens and snapped the branches and ripped off the leaves of the trees and beat down the underbrush, and the hunter was bruised and dazed by the tumult of the storm. All day he wandered, wading blindly through marshes or stumbling through windfalls, wounded and bleeding. The hail like sharp flints still rained from the skies and the thunders still rumbled their threats and the hunter feared the anger of the heavens. A great rock like a deep shadow loomed up dark against the trees and the hunter hurried to it and found a great cavern for a shelter. When the leaves had been carried into a corner by the wind he made himself a bed and slept.

11   The rock shook and the hunter awoke and thought the great turtle moving from his moorings. A rhythmic roaring filled his mind with fear. A voice cried out, "You are in my lodge without permission! Who was it that bid you enter! Do you know that I kill everybody!"

12   The voice was terrifying and hurt the hunter's ears like thunder when it is very close. Then again it spoke. "Oh warrior, see by my eye-light the bones of people who have sought me to kill me: they are a yellow powder! Listen! I know you came without intent of evil and therefore you shall not suffer. I am the last of the kind of men that were here before men came here, so hearken, for I have seen the earth in its making. When the turtle's back was small I lived here. My brothers are all departed but their spirits still are living. They are in the forest's depths and live within the trees. Only you must dream and you shall see their faces. Some are monsters, some are human, some are like the beasts, but dream and see them. Then go forth and carve their faces on the basswood that speaks when you approach. It is my voice speaking. Be wise and learn my secrets, how disease is healed, how man and beast and plant have the same great kind of life, how man and beast and plant may talk together and learn each other's mission. Go and live with the trees and birds and beasts and fish and learn to honor them as your own brothers. I will be with you always in your learning. Go now and carve the faces that you see in your dreaming and carry back the faces to your people, and you and those that see them shall organize a society to preserve my teaching. Moreover, that posterity may not forget me and these words I speak within the mother turtle's shell. I bid you collect many turtles and make rattles of their shells and when the company of faces shall shake them, let all who know my wisdom and remember you and your adventure and me and who I am."

13   For a long time the hunter meditated upon the wisdom of the giant within the cave and when the wisdom was embedded in his mind he lay

down and slept again and had visions of strange things. When he awoke he found himself lying at the foot of an enormous basswood tree that as he looked at it it transformed itself into a great face like one he had seen in his dreams.

THE FALSE FACE

14   Unfolding from the trunk of the basswood, the great face stared out at the spellbound hunter and opening wide its wide protruding lips began to speak. He told of his wonderful eyesight; its blazing eyes could see behind the moon and stars. His power could summon the storms or push aside the clouds for the sunshine. He knew all the virtues of roots and herbs; he knew all the diseases and knew how to apply the remedies of herbs and roots. He was familiar with all the poisons and could send them through the air and cure the sick. He could breathe health or sickness. His power was mighty and could bring luck in battles. Evil and poison and death fled when he looked, and good health and life came in its stead. He told of the basswood and said that its soft wood was filled with medicine and life. It contained the life of the wind and the life of the sunshine, and thus being good, was the wood for the false faces that the hunter must carve.

15   Long the hunter listened to the words of the giant false face and then he wandered far into the forest until the trees began to speak. Then he knew that there were trees there in which were the spirits of the beings of which he had dreamed and that the Genonsgwa was speaking. He knew that now his task of carving must begin and that the dream-beings, the voices, the birds and the animals that he saw must be represented in the basswood masks that he must make. And so he began, and for a score of years he continued his carving. He lived among the animals and trees and learned all that they could tell, becoming so attached to the things of life that men call beneath them, that he wished forever to stay and be as a brother to the animals and trees. But a day came when the giant's voice spoke from a basswood tree and bade him return to his kinsmen. The hunter who had entered the forest young now was old. He was filled with knowledge and mysteries and was wiser than all men living. Gathering up the many faces that he had carved he made them into one big bundle and lifted it upon his broad shoulders and found the trail that led from the forest to the villages of his people. Of strange appearance and of gigantic proportions, he entered the council hall of his nation and calling a chosen few together told the story of his adventure and related the laws of the order of which he was the delegated founder.

THE FALSE FACE SOCIETY

16   The society, known as the False Face Company, was to be a most secret one and only for a qualified number. Its object was to benefit, protect and help all living things of earth. Its meetings were to be held only when the

moon was away and when there was no light in the night. The hunter taught the chosen band a new dance and a new song and beat time with a large turtle shell as he sang. He explained the meanings of the masks and distributed them among the band, telling each person his special duty to the new society. He explained the relation of mankind to the rest of nature and enjoined all to use every influence to protect all living nature. In return for this kindness he promised that a great power should come upon them, the power of the spirits of the Genonsgwa, and how they should become great medicine men, whose power should be over the spirits of the elements. He unfolded and conducted the band through all the elaborate ceremonies that had been taught him in the forest by the animals and trees and spirits of the Genonsgwa. The Company was to have no outward sign and members were to recognize one another only by having sat together in a ceremony.

17   So deeply was the assembled company impressed by the hunter's words that the new society at once became a strong and well-united organization and other lodges spread rapidly through all the nations of the Iroquois and the False Face Company became one of the greatest factors for good that the people had ever known. They drove all the witches away and cured all the sickness of the people.

THE MASK-MAKING CEREMONY

18   The masks are carved from living basswood trees and are thereby supposed to contain a portion of the life or spirit of the tree. In making these masks the Iroquois select the basswood not alone for its absorbent quality which is supposed to "draw out" disease, but for its remedial values as well. In solution, a tea of its bark will cure a cold and relieve spasmodic affections. Its astringent sap is applied to relieve wounds and bruises, while the mask itself is supposed to be of signal importance in the relief of corruptive diseases.

19   In the ceremonies attending the making of a living mask, the tree is visited for three days. At the dawn of the first day the leaders of the False Face Society gather around the tree and smoke the sacred tobacco into the roots and throughout the branches to their topmost. As the smoke "lifts to the sunrise" songs of incantation are sung and the tree is asked to consent to share its heart with whomsoever the sacred gift is to be sent. At sunrise the ceremony is repeated and the next day continued in the same manner until the three days' propitiation chant is completed and then the axe is lifted to the tree. If at the first stroke of the axe the tree remain firm and unbending it has consented to lend its heart. An outline of the face is then drawn on the bark and cut into the tree to a depth of about six inches. After thanking the tree this block is gouged out to be carved into the desired shape during a final song and dance that concluded the ceremony.

DISCUSSION QUESTIONS

1. The first Stone Giants possess traits of the Evil Minded. Which of their traits are also human traits?
2. Like all mythic heroes, the young hunter must pass trials and tests. What must he perform in order to receive the secrets of healing from Genonsgwa?
3. What is the purpose of the False Face Society? How is this purpose related to the Good Minded twin?

WRITING TOPICS

1. Investigate the topic of the Iroquois False Faces. In an essay, focus on one ceremony of the False Face Society and compare it with a healing ceremony from a different culture, perhaps your own.
2. Imagine you are the young hunter. From your first-person point of view, write about your encounter with the Genonsgwa based on paragraphs 4–7.

THE ORIGIN OF THE LONG HOUSE SENECA LEGEND

Arthur Parker

The longhouse, an extended, bark-covered lodge, is a symbol of the Iroquois Confederacy. Just as Iroquois families lived side by side under the protecting roof of the longhouse, the family nations of the confederacy are geographically linked in union under the great metaphorical longhouse. The confederacy was originally a union of five related nations: the Mohawk, Oneida, Onondaga, Cayuga, and Seneca who lived in what is now upper New York state. In its own separate territory, each nation lived in several forest villages that were tightly stockaded against enemy attacks. No one knows exactly when the Confederacy of the Five Nations was founded, but when the first Europeans met the Iroquois, the confederacy was already quite old. Iroquois scholar Horatio Hale dates the League's founding at approximately 1450. In 1722, the Tuscaroras joined the League, which became known as the Six Indian Nations. The people of the the six nations call themselves *Haudenosaunee,* which translates loosely as "people of the longhouse." Iroquois storytellers and orators have recounted the history of the League's founding in every village year after year, for perhaps five hundred years. Ceremonial speaking and fine oratory have always been honored skills among the Iroquois, and recitation of the Great Law is part of a body of rich oral literature.

In the time before the League, warfare was a way of life for all Iroquois. Their code of honor required revenge for a life taken. Killing led to more killing and to long years of blood feuds. The cycle of perpetual war caused the Iroquois to say that even the sun loved war. The most fearful warriors were the Mohawks, and their enemies gave them the name "Mowak" which translates "Man Eaters."

According to Iroquois tradition, Hiawatha and Deganawida, two peacemakers, persuaded the tribes to end the bloody violence and to form the league of intertribal peace. It was said that during the time of conflict, the demonic Adodarhoh (Tatodaho) took the lives of

Hiawatha's family. Lost in sorrow and rage, the bereaved chief wandered into the depths of the forest where he came upon a lake. From the lake bed, he lifted shining shells and threaded them on rushes. As he held the shell strings in his hand, Hiawatha conceived the first wampum. For him the strings became words. Carrying the wampum from village to village, Deganawida and Hiawatha told the laws of peace and even convinced Adodarhoh to join the Great League of Peace. Modern Iroquois treasure a wampum belt, known as the Hiawatha Belt, which commemorates the founding of the confederacy. At its center, the Ononadaga Nation is represented as a pine tree, and a "chain" connects the tree with four white squares symbolizing the other nations. The account of the legendary heroes Hiawatha and Deganawida is today a vital part of Iroquois oral tradition and written literature.

1   Where the Mohawk river empties into the Hudson in ancient times there was a Mohawk village. The people there were fierce and warlike and were continually sending out war parties against other settlements and returning would bring back long strings of scalps to number the lives they had destroyed. But sometimes they left their own scalps behind and never returned. They loved warfare better than all other things and were happy when their hands were slimy with blood. They boasted that they would eat up all other nations, and so they continued to go against other tribes and fight with them.

2   Now among the Mohawks was a chief named Deganawida, a very wise man, and he was very sad of heart because his people loved war too well. So he spoke in council and implored them to desist lest they perish altogether, but the young warriors would not hear him and laughed at his words; but he did not cease to warn them until at last despairing of moving them by ordinary means, he turned his face to the west and wept as he journeyed onward and away from his people. At length he reached a lake whose shores were fringed with bushes, and being tired he lay down to rest. Presently, as he lay meditating, he heard the soft spattering of water sliding from a skillful paddle and peering out from his hiding place, he saw in the red light of sunset a man leaning over his canoe and dipping into the shallow water with a basket. When he raised it up it was full of shells, the shells of the periwinkles that live in shallow pools. The man pushed his canoe toward the shore and sat down on the beach, where he kindled a fire. Then he began to string his shells and, finishing a string, would touch the shells and talk. Then, as if satisfied, he would lay it down and make another until he had a large number. Deganawida watched the strange proceeding with wonder. The sun had

long since set, but Deganawida still watched the man with the shell strings sitting in the flickering light of the fire that shadowed the bushes and shimmered over the lake.

3   After some deliberation he called out, "Kwē, I am a friend!" and stepping out upon the sand stood before the man with the shells. "I am Deganawida," he said, "and come from the Mohawk."

4   "I am Hiawatha of the Onondaga," came the reply.

5   "The Deganawida inquired about the shell strings for he was very curious to know their import and Hiawatha answered, "They are the rules of life and laws of good government. This all white string is a sign of truth, peace and good will; this black string is a sign of hatred, of war and of a bad heart; the string with the alternate beads, black and white, is a sign that peace should exist between the nations. This string with white on either end and black in the middle is a sign that wars must end and peace declared." And so Hiawatha lifted his strings and read the laws.

6   Then said Deganawida, "You are my friend indeed, and the friend of all nations. Our people are weak from warring and weak from being warred upon. We who speak one tongue should combine against the Hadiondas instead of helping them by killing one another, but my people are weary of my advising and would not hear me."

7   "I, too, am of the same mind," said Hiawatha, "but Tatodaho slew all my brothers and drove me away. So I came to the lakes and have made the laws that should govern men and nations. I believe that we should be as brothers in a family instead of enemies."

8   "Then come with me," said Deganawida, "and together let us go back to my people and explain the rules and laws."

9   So when they had returned, Deganawida called a council of all the chiefs and warriors and the women, and Hiawatha set forth the plan he had devised. The words had a marvelous effect. The people were astonished at the wisdom of the strange chief from the Onondaga, and when he had finished his exposition the chiefs promised obedience to his laws. They delegated Deganawida to go with him to the Oneida and council with them, then to go onward to Onondaga and win over the arrogant erratic Tatodaho, the tyrannical chief of the Onondaga. Thus it was that together they went to the Oneida country and won over their great chief and made the people promise to support the proposed league. Then the Oneida chief went with Hiawatha to the Cayugas and told them how by supporting the league they might preserve themselves against the fury of Tatodaho. So when the Cayuga had promised allegiance, Deganawida turned his face toward Onondaga and with his comrades went before Tatodaho. Now when Tatodaho learned how three nations had combined against him he became very angry and ran into the forest where he gnawed at his fingers and ate grass and leaves. His evil thoughts became serpents and sprouted from his skull and waving in a tangled mass hissed out venom. But Deganawida did not fear him and once more asked him to give his consent to a league of

peace and friendship; but he was still wild until Hiawatha combed the snakes from his head and told him that he should be the head chief of the confederacy and govern it according to the laws that Hiawatha had made. Then he recovered from his madness and asked why the Seneca had not been visited, for the Seneca outnumbered all the other nations and were fearless warriors. "If their jealousy is aroused," he said, "they will eat us."

10   Then the delegations visited the Seneca and the other nations to the west but only the Seneca would consider the proposal. The other nations were exceedingly jealous.

11   Thus a peace pact was made and the Long House built, and Deganawida was the builder, but Hiawatha was its designer.

12   Now moreover, the first council of Hiawatha and Deganawida was in a place now called Albany at the mouth of a small stream that empties into the Hudson.

DISCUSSION QUESTIONS

1. Deganawida is known among the Iroquois for his diplomatic skills. Do you agree that he was a diplomat? If so, describe his skills and their impact.
2. According to Iroquois tradition, Deganawida and Hiawatha joined forces to form a political and social confederation of five Indian tribes. What do you consider the most important contribution of each to this achievement?
3. In paragraph 2, read passages aloud that contain alliteration and comment on their sound and meaning. In paragraph 9, which words and images help you hear and see Tatodaho?

WRITING TOPICS

1. Assume that you are a delegate to a conference on Iroquois literature, history, and culture. You have been asked to speak on a topic of your choice. Investigate one of the following topics, or one you select, and write your speech for the conference. As you read and write, remember the Iroquois admiration for figurative language, especially metaphor, simile, and symbol.

The Confederacy of the Five Nations

Women's Roles in the Iroquois Confederacy

The Use of Wampum and Wampum Belts by the Iroquois

Contributions of Deganawida, Hiawatha, and/or Tatodaho to the Confederacy

2. Locate an important sentence in the preceding selection and use it as the topic sentence for a well developed paragraph.

Examples: I believe that we should be as brothers in a family instead of enemies. (paragraph 7)

He was still wild until Hiawatha combed the snakes from his head. (paragraph 9)

They are the rules of life and laws of good government. (paragraph 5)

THE COUNCIL OF THE GREAT PEACE

Arthur Parker

The formation of the League settled the blood feuds and brought peace to five Iroquois tribes. Deganawida chose as a symbol of the League of the Five Nations the pine tree, the Tree of the Great Long Leaves. Its four symbolic roots, the Great White Roots of Peace, reached to the north, east, south, and west. Deganawida symbolically planted the tree in the land of the Onondagas, the place of the Great Council Fire. There the confederate lords, or peace chiefs, would sit beneath it as caretakers of the Great Peace, acting as mentors and spiritual guides of their people. And these chiefs would figuratively never die, because their chiefly titles would be passed down to their successors forever. In this manner, the League of the Five Nations would always be kept alive.

The meeting was opened with a prayer, offered by the Onondaga delegates, and then each nation sang songs around the fire. A delegate addressing the council held strings of wampum in his hand to show the truth of his words and to help him remember his message. Iroquois chiefs, who were great orators, were rightly renowned for their excellent memories. Although there have been some changes, the confederacy chiefs continue to meet in council and to host a gathering at which the Great Law is recited from memory. The League of the *Haudenosaunee,* now some five or more centuries old, continues to function to this day as a distinct institution.

1. I am Deganawida and with the Five Nations' Confederate Lords I plant the Tree of the Great Peace. I plant it in your territory, Adodarhoh, and the Onondaga Nation, in the territory of you who are Firekeepers.

2. I name the tree the Tree of the Great Long Leaves. Under the shade of this Tree of the Great Peace we spread the soft white feathery down of the globe thistle as seats for you, Adodarhoh, and your cousin Lords.

3   We place you upon those seats, spread soft with the feathery down of the globe thistle, there beneath the shade of the spreading branches of the Tree of Peace. There shall you sit and watch the Council Fire of the Confederacy of the Five Nations, and all the affairs of the Five Nations shall be transacted at this place before you, Adodarhoh, and your cousin Lords, by the Confederate Lords of the Five Nations.

4   **2.**   Roots have spread out from the Tree of the Great Peace, one to the north, one to the east, one to the south and one to the west. The name of these roots is The Great White Roots and their nature is Peace and Strength.

5   If any man or any nation outside the Five Nations shall obey the laws of the Great Peace and make known their disposition to the Lords of the Confederacy, they may trace the Roots to the Tree and if their minds are clean and they are obedient and promise to obey the wishes of the Confederate Council, they shall be welcomed to take shelter beneath the Tree of the Long Leaves.

6   We place at the top of the Tree of the Long Leaves an Eagle who is able to see afar. If he sees in the distance any evil approaching or any danger threatening he will at once warn the people of the Confederacy. . . .

7   **3.**   The Smoke of the Confederate Council Fire shall ever ascend and pierce the sky so that other nations who may be allies may see the Council Fire of the Great Peace. . . .

8   **7.**   Whenever the Confederate Lords shall assemble for the purpose of holding a council, the Onondaga Lords shall open it by expressing their gratitude to their cousin Lords and greeting them, and they shall make an address and offer thanks to the earth where men dwell, to the streams of water, the pools, the springs and the lakes, to the maize and the fruits, to the medicinal herbs and trees, to the forest trees for their usefulness, to the animals that serve as food and give their pelts for clothing, to the great winds and the lesser winds, to the Thunderers, to the Sun, the mighty warrior, to the moon, to the messengers of the Creator who reveals his wishes and to the Great Creator who dwells in the heavens above, who gives all the things useful to men, and who is the source and the ruler of health and life.

9   Then shall the Onondaga Lords declare the council open.

10   The council shall not sit after darkness has set in. . . .

RIGHTS, DUTIES AND QUALIFICATIONS OF LORDS

11   **17.**   A bunch of a certain number of shell (wampum) strings each two spans in length shall be given to each of the female families in which the Lordship titles are vested. The right of bestowing the title shall be hereditary in the family of females legally possessing the bunch of shell strings and the strings shall be the token that the females of the family have the proprietary right to the Lordship title for all time to come, subject to certain restrictions hereinafter mentioned.

12 **18.** If any Confederate Lord neglects or refuses to attend the Confederate Council, the other Lords of the Nation of which he is a member shall require their War Chief to request the female sponsors of the Lord so guilty of defection to demand his attendance of the Council. If he refuses, the women holding the title shall immediately select another candidate for the title.

13 No Lord shall be asked more than once to attend the Confederate Council. . . .

14 **24.** The Lords of the Confederacy of the Five Nations shall be mentors of the people for all time. The thickness of their skin shall be seven spans— which is to say that they shall be proof against anger, offensive actions and criticism. Their hearts shall be full of peace and good will and their minds filled with a yearning for the welfare of the people of the Confederacy. With endless patience they shall carry out their duty and their firmness shall be tempered with a tenderness for their people. Neither anger nor fury shall find lodgement in their minds and all their words and actions shall be marked by calm deliberation.

15 **25.** If a Lord of the Confederacy should seek to establish any authority independent of the jurisdiction of the Confederacy of the Great Peace, which is the Five Nations, he shall be warned three times in open council, first by the women relatives, second by the men relatives and finally by the Lords of the Confederacy of the Nation to which he belongs. If the offending Lord is still obdurate he shall be dismissed by the War Chief of his nation for refusing to conform to the laws of the Great Peace. His nation shall then install the candidate nominated by the female name holders of his family.

16 **26.** It shall be the duty of all of the Five Nations Confederate Lords, from time to time as occasion demands, to act as mentors and spiritual guides of their people and remind them of their Creator's will and words. They shall say:

17 "Hearken, that peace may continue unto future days!

18 "Always listen to the words of the Great Creator, for he has spoken.

19 "United People, let not evil find lodging in your minds.

20 "For the Great Creator has spoken and the cause of Peace shall not become old.

21 "The cause of peace shall not die if you remember the Great Creator."

22 Every Confederate Lord shall speak words such as these to promote peace.

23 **27.** All Lords of the Five Nations Confederacy must be honest in all things. They must not idle or gossip, but be men possessing those honorable qualities that make true royaneh. It shall be a serious wrong for anyone to lead a Lord into trivial affairs, for the people must ever hold their Lords high in estimation out of respect to their honorable positions. . . .

24 **29.** When a Lordship title is to be conferred, the candidate Lord shall furnish the cooked venison, the corn bread and the corn soup, together with other necessary things and the labor for the Conferring of Titles Festival. . . .

OFFICIAL SYMBOLISM

25 **56.**   Five strings of shell tied together as one shell shall represent the Five Nations. Each string shall represent one territory and the whole a completely united territory known as the Five Nations Confederate territory.

26 **57.**   Five arrows shall be bound together very strong and each arrow shall represent one nation. As the five arrows are strongly bound this shall symbolize the complete union of the nations. Thus are the Five Nations united completely and enfolded together, united into one head, one body and one mind. Therefore they shall labor, legislate and council together for the interest of future generations. . . .

27 **65.**   I, Deganawida, and the Union Lords, now uproot the tallest pine tree and into the cavity thereby made we cast all weapons of war. Into the depths of the earth, down into the deep underearth currents of water flowing to unknown regions we cast all the weapons of strife. We bury them from sight and we plant again the tree. Thus shall the Great Peace be established and hostilities shall no longer be known between the Five Nations but peace to the United People. . . .

DISCUSSION QUESTIONS

1. The plan of alliance provided for the establishment of a confederacy that enjoyed a democratic form of government. Civil and legislative power was to be vested in a certain number of wise men, or sachems, and the military and executive power in another set of men. What were the qualifications of the Lords? Explain the image "the thickness of their skin shall be seven spans" in article 24.

2. Specify three characteristics of Tree of the Great Peace.

3. Read articles 26 and 65 aloud in an oratorical voice. What is the impact of the repetition of *peace?* How would the meaning change if *war* were substituted for peace in each instance?

4. The League's constitution specifies how every council assembly shall be opened, with an extended offering of thanks. After studying article 7, draw four inferences regarding how Iroquois viewed their relationship with nature.

WRITING TOPICS

1. Compare the process of selecting league council members with the process established in the U.S. Constitution for selecting members of the United States Congress.

2. In an essay, compare one article from Parker's translation of the Constitution of the League with one article of the United States Constitution. Discuss style, meaning, and audience.

3. Drawing examples from articles I and 65, compose a paragraph on this idea: the Great Tree of Peace is a powerful metaphor in Iroquois tradition.

THE CREATION OR AGE OF BEGINNING
DINÉ (NAVAJO) ORIGIN MYTHS

Hastin Tlo'tsi hee and Aileen O'Bryan

The Navajo singer, Sandoval, Hastin Tlo' tsi hee (Old Man Buffalo Grass) told this version of the Navajo creation myth to Aileen O'Bryan in 1928. "You look at me," he said to her, "and you see only an ugly old man, but within I am filled with great beauty. I sit as on a mountaintop and I look into the future. I see my people and your people living together. So you must write down what I tell you; and you must have it made into a book that coming generations may know this truth."

Sandoval told of the mythic journey of first beings through a series of worlds to the present Glittering World. Since the time of creation, animals, insects, and humans have been equal creatures. In fact, all of them are called *people*. Because of strife in the Second or Blue World, the people moved up into the Third or Yellow World where there was no sun, and again there was suffering and quarreling. Coyote stole the baby of Water Monster, who became angry and threatened the people with a great flood. Escaping from the monster and dangerous waters, First Man and First Woman led the people to the Fourth World, or Glittering World.

Today, traditional Navajos view their emergence myth as sacred history that teaches them lessons for proper living. The myths form the core for ceremonies called Chants, which are performed to renew the sacred patterns set in motion by the creation cycle. The Navajos know that their kinship with the landscape dates back to their arrival in this world. Here are the stories of the First and Second Worlds and the Creation of the Sun and Moon, Earth and Sky.

The First World

1 The First World, Ni′hodilqil, was black as black wool. It had four corners, and over these appeared four clouds. These four clouds contained within themselves the elements of the First World. They were in color, black, white, blue, and yellow.

2 The Black Cloud represented the Female Being or Substance. For as a child sleeps when being nursed, so life slept in the darkness of the Female Being. The White Cloud represented the Male Being or Substance. He was the Dawn, the Light-Which-Awakens, of the First World.

3 In the East, at the place where the Black Cloud and the White Cloud met, First Man, Atse′hastqin, was formed; and with him was formed the white corn, perfect in shape, with kernels covering the whole ear. Dohonot i′ni is the name of this first seed corn, and it is also the name of the place where the Black Cloud and the White Cloud met.

4 The First World was small in size, a floating island in mist or water. On it there grew one tree, a pine tree, which was later brought to the present world for firewood.

5 Man was not, however, in his present form. The conception was of a male and a female being who were to become man and woman. The creatures of the First World are thought of as the Mist People; they had no definite form, but were to change to men, beasts, birds, and reptiles of this world.

6 Now on the western side of the First World, in a place that later was to become the Land of Sunset, there appeared the Blue Cloud, and opposite it there appeared the Yellow Cloud. Where they came together First Woman was formed, and with her the yellow corn. This ear of corn was also perfect. With First Woman there came the white shell and the turquoise and the yucca.

7 First Man stood on the eastern side of the First World. He represented the Dawn and was the Life Giver. First Woman stood opposite in the West. She represented Darkness and Death.

8 First Man burned a crystal for a fire. The crystal belonged to the male and was the symbol of the mind and of clear seeing. When First Man burned it, it was the mind's awakening. First Woman burned her turquoise for a fire. They saw each other's lights in the distance. When the Black Cloud and the White Cloud rose higher in the sky First Man set out to find the turquoise light. He went twice without success, and again a third time; then he broke a forked branch from his tree, and, looking through the fork, he marked the place where the light burned. And the fourth time he walked to it and found smoke coming from a home.

9 "Here is the home I could not find," First Man said.

10 First Woman answered: "Oh, it is you. I saw you walking around and I wondered why you did not come."

11   Again the same thing happened when the Blue Cloud and the Yellow Cloud rose higher in the sky. First Woman saw a light and she went out to find it. Three times she was unsuccessful, but the fourth time she saw the smoke and she found the home of First Man.

12   "I wondered what this thing could be," she said.

13   "I saw you walking and I wondered why you did not come to me," First Man answered.

14   First Woman saw that First Man had a crystal for a fire, and she saw that it was stronger than her turquoise fire. And as she was thinking, First Man spoke to her. "Why do you not come with your fire and we will live together." The woman agreed to this. So instead of the man going to the woman, as is the custom now, the woman went to the man.

15   About this time there came another person, the Great-Coyote-Who-Was-Formed-in-the-Water, and he was in the form of a male being. He told the two that he had been hatched from an egg. He knew all that was under the water and all that was in the skies. First Man placed this person ahead of himself in all things. The three began to plan what was to come to pass; and while they were thus occupied another being came to them. He also had the form of a man, but he wore a hairy coat, lined with white fur, that fell to his knees and was belted in at the waist. His name was Atse'hashke', First Angry or Coyote. He said to the three: "You believe that you were the first persons. You are mistaken. I was living when you were formed."

16   Then four beings came together. They were yellow in color and were called the tsts'na or wasp people. They knew the secret of shooting evil and could harm others. They were very powerful.

17   This made eight people.

18   Four more beings came. They were small in size and wore red shirts and had little black eyes. They were the naazo'zi or spider ants. They knew how to sting, and were a great people.

19   After these came a whole crowd of beings. Dark colored they were, with thick lips and dark, protruding eyes. They were the wolazhi'ni, the black ants. They also knew the secret of shooting evil and were powerful; but they killed each other steadily.

20   By this time there were many people. Then came a multitude of little creatures. They were peaceful and harmless, but the odor from them was unpleasant. They were called the wolazhi'ni nlchu nigi, meaning that which emits an odor.

21   And after the wasps and the different ant people there came the beetles, dragonflies, bat people, the Spider Man and Woman, and the Salt Man and Woman, and others that rightfully had no definite form but were among those people who peopled the First World. And this world, being small in size, became crowded, and the people quarreled and fought among themselves, and in all ways made living very unhappy.

THE SECOND WORLD

22   Because of the strife in the First World, First Man, First Woman, the Great-Coyote-Who-Was-Formed-in-the-Water, and the Coyote called First Angry, followed by all the others, climbed up from the World of Darkness and Dampness to the Second or Blue World.

23   They found a number of people already living there: blue birds, blue hawks, blue jays, blue herons, and all the blue-feathered beings. The powerful swallow people lived there also, and these people made the Second World unpleasant for those who had come from the First World. There was fighting and killing.

24   The first four found an opening in the World of Blue Haze; and they climbed through this and led the people up into the Third or Yellow World. . . .

THE CREATION OF THE SUN AND MOON

25   First Man and First Woman whispered together during many nights. They planned with the help of the All-Wise-Coyote-Who-Was-Formed-in-the-Water. The three devised a scheme that would meet the problems that would later come to pass. They planned that there should be a sun, and day and night. They said that the Coyote, called First Angry, had brought unhappiness and spoiled their life down below, and that he was not the proper person to have with them at this time. He should be kept away.

26   They spread a beautiful buckskin on the ground. This was the skin of a deer not killed by a weapon. On the buckskin they placed a perfect turquoise, round like the sun. It was as large as the height of an average man if he stretched his arm upward. They stood twelve tail feathers from the eagle around it, and also twelve tail feathers from the flicker. On the great turquoise they marked a mouth and nose and eyes. They made a yellow streak below the mouth on top of the chin.

27   Now, although they had stationed four guards to be on the lookout for the Coyote, Atse'hashke', he came and asked them what they were doing. They told him: "Nothing whatsoever". He said: "So I see," and went away. . . .

28   They placed a perfect white shell on the buckskin below the turquoise that was to become the sun. This great, perfect, white shell was to become the moon. First Man planned to heat it with the first crystal that he had used for his fire.

29   By this time they had posted two circles of guards around the place where they were planning; but even with this precaution the Coyote came to them. He appeared in their midst and said: "This must be something that you are planning." But they assured him that he saw nothing; they said that they were just sitting there. And again the Coyote left them. First Man called the guards together and asked them why they had let the one whose name was Atse'hashke' pass. They said that they had not seen the Coyote. First Man then placed three circles of guards around the sacred buckskin.

30   The Holy Ones asked the Turquoise Boy to enter the great, perfect turquoise that was to become the sun; and they asked the White Shell Girl to enter the great, perfect, white shell that was to become the moon. The Turquoise Boy was to carry a whistle made from the Male Reed. This whistle had twelve holes in it, and each time that the Turquoise Boy would blow on his whistle the earth would move one month in time. The White Shell Girl was also to carry a whistle. It was made from the Female Reed, and with it she should move the tides of the sea. . . .

THE SKY AND THE EARTH

31   Then came the Earth Woman, Nahosdzan'esdza'. First Man told her that she was to be the wife of the Sky. She would face the East, and her husband over her, would face the West. And whenever the Fog covered the Earth they would know that the Sky had visited Nahosdzan'esdza'.

32   After that they set the corner posts and stretched the Sky in the four directions.

33   About twenty chants were sung at this time, and after the first ten sections of the first chant, the Sun Chant, the Sun began to move away. The next chant was for the Moon, and after a little time, it also began to move away.

34   Today different medicine men use different chants and prayers for this ceremony; but the chants of the Sun and Moon and Earth are always sung. Some say that black magic and evil entered the plan this time, but others hold that it was not until later.

35   Now, after the Sun rose in the sky, the Dark Cloud that covered the earlier worlds during half periods became the night. The White Cloud was the dawn, and the sun's light became our day. And along the far horizons where the first ones used to see the blue and yellow clouds, there appeared the twilight and the false dawn.

36   The first-day period that the sun was raised in the sky the heat was unbearable. So the Holy Ones stretched out the four corners of the sky and this raised the sun still higher in the heavens. After they had done this four times it was like it is today. There was room on the earth for everyone, and the sun's warmth was right for the growing plants and the animals and the people.

37   Now it was the same with the earth as it was with the sky. They planned just how the earth should be. They made the face of the earth white, with eyes and nose and mouth. They made earrings of turquoise for the ears; and for a border they placed a black ring, a blue ring, a yellow ring, and a white ring, which is the earth's edge. These rings are for the earth's protection; no power shall harm her. . . .

DISCUSSION QUESTIONS

1. For the Navajos, there are four seasons, four directions, and four sacred mountains that mark the boundaries of their homeland. Locate other examples of the sacred number four in the creation story.
2. Corn is one of the sacred cultivated plants that nourish the Navajos. Describe the relationship between first humans and corn.
3. The animals in the origin story have particular characteristics. Coyote, the trickster, is a prominent example. Which of his actions in the first world qualify him as a trickster?
4. Special elements are sacred to the Navajo: turquoise, white shells, eagle feathers, four colors, unblemished deerskin. Cite examples of these elements playing a role in the creation.

WRITING TOPICS

1. Review the order of the things that are created and, in a brief essay, describe the mood or atmosphere. Is it the same throughout the selection?
2. Do some research on legends and myths from other parts of the world about corn (maize) and wheat (often called corn in other countries). Write a brief essay exploring your findings.

WHITE BEAD WOMAN MARRIES THE SUN

THE STORY OF THE TWIN BROTHERS AND THE GIANT YEITSO

As the story is commonly told, First Man and First Woman were near what is now called Huerfano Mountain in New Mexico. Not far away, a baby girl was born from the union of darkness and dawn at Gobernador Knob, a geological formation. Hearing the baby cry one morning, First Man discovered the child and took her home to First Woman. They became the parents of the small holy one, who grew up to become White Bead Woman, mother of hero twins and creator of humans. White Bead Woman arrived in the Navajo world at this time because it was ready for her. With the four sacred mountains and all plants and animals in their proper places, the world achieved beauty and harmony, which, the storytellers say is the opposite of chaos and darkness in the previous worlds.

One day, the sacred Sun visited White Bead Woman and became the father of her twin boys, Monster Slayer and Child Born for Water. The twins' destiny was to slay the monsters killing the Navajo people. First, they had to undergo a difficult and dangerous journey to the house of their father, the Sun, who gave them lightning arrows for weapons and flint armor for protection against the monsters. After meeting their supernatural father, the twins returned to the earth and destroyed the monsters, including the terrible giant Yeitso.

◙

WHITE BEAD WOMAN MARRIES THE SUN

First Man said upon coming home one day: "Over to the east, at the foot of the mesa, there are two different kinds of grass. Their ripening seeds are plentiful." So First Woman and the girl went down to gather the seeds. But when they got there they began to think of the monsters who roamed about the country and became frightened. Looking about them carefully they hurriedly gathered only one kind of seed before they ran back to their home. When they reached their hogan the girl said: "Mother, I want to go back and collect the seeds from the other grass." First Woman said: "No, daughter, you can not go there alone. Some monster might catch you." But the girl insisted. She promised to be careful and to look out for herself. After the request was made four times the old woman let her go, warning her to have great care.

2   The girl went down the mesa as fast as she could and was soon busy gathering seeds from the grass. All of a sudden she heard something behind her. Looking around she saw a great white horse with black eyes. He had a long white mane, and he pranced above the ground not on the earth itself. She saw that the bridle was white too, and that the saddle was white. And there was a young man sitting on the horse. The young man's moccasins and leggings and clothing were all white. All was as for a bride.

3   The holy rider spoke: "You lay towards me each morning until noon. I am he whom you faced. When I am half over the center of the earth you go to the spring. Your wish could not have two meanings." He continued:

> Go home and tell your father to build a brush hogan to the south of your home. Make ready a meal out of the seeds of the grasses that you have gathered. Put this meal into a white bead basket. Have the pollen from a pair of blue birds (pollen which has been sprinkled over them), and use this pollen to draw a line from east to west across the basket on top of the meal. Turn the hand and make a line from north to south, and a line must be drawn around the outer edge of the basket. Set the basket inside the brush hogan. You and your father must sit there late into the night. He will then go home to his wife and you must stay there alone.

4   When the White Bead Girl returned home she told her mother of all that she had seen and all that she had heard. That night when First Man came home his wife told him what the girl had related. First Man said: "I do not believe this thing. We are very poor. Why should we be visited by a Holy Being? I cannot believe what you tell me."

5   Now when the girl told her mother about her experience, First Woman asked if she had acted according to this Holy One's directions each day. The maiden had said: "Yes." So the woman told her husband that indeed it was all true, and that he must go and prepare the brush shelter and not argue. When all was ready First Man took the white bead basket filled with the meal, and he and his foster-daughter went into the brush shelter and sat there.

6   They sat there late into the night, then First Man went home to his wife and left the maiden there alone. The White Bead Girl returned early in the morning, and First Man asked her at once: "Who came last night?" The girl said: "No one came." First Man turned to his wife, "Did I not tell you that it is all a lie?" he said. But the girl said: "Wait, I thought that I

heard someone, and this morning I found just one track, and some of the meal, that towards the east, had been taken." So First Man went with his daughter to the brush hogan and he saw the one track, and also, that the meal towards the east in the basket was gone.

7   That night they prepared another basket of meal, and again First Man took his daughter to the brush shelter, and again they sat there late into the night. He left the maiden there alone. In the morning the girl returned to the home and said: "There are two tracks of a man there now. The meal in the south of the basket is gone."

8   On the third night the same thing happened. In the morning when the girl returned First Man asked: "Who came?" And the girl said: "No one came." Then First Man became angry. "I told you that this thing is all a lie," he said. But the girl answered: "But Father, there are three tracks, and the meal towards the west is gone. And I thought that someone touched me last night."

9   The fourth night they went to the brush shelter as before taking with them fresh meal in the basket. They sat late into the night, then First Man returned to his wife. When the girl entered the home in the early morning her father asked: "Who came?" And the girl answered: "No one." First Man was very angry and insisted that it was all a lie. "But father," said the White Bead Girl, "The meal towards the north is gone, and there are four tracks. I thought that I was moved by someone, and I was all wet when I awakened."

10   Now after the maiden was visited the fourth time by the Holy Being she lived with her foster parents for four days as they had always lived. But at the end of the fourth day the young woman said: "Mother, something moves within me." First Woman answered: "Daughter, that must be your baby moving." . . . After five more days had passed twin boys were born to the White Bead Woman. . . .

11   Later, much later, First Man and First Woman were sent farther east, farther towards the east than where the Sun dwells.

THE STORY OF THE TWIN BROTHERS

12   The Twin Boys were cared for like their mother the White Bead Woman had been; each had a cradle, and when they first laughed, gifts were given to all who came to the home. Not much is told about them until the fifteenth day. By that time they were young men.

13   First Man made bows and arrows for his two grandsons, and they played with them. One day when they were on the south side of the mesa they saw a strange animal with a long nose and a long tail, the coyote. Just as they took aim and were about to shoot, the animal went out of sight over the edge of the cliff. They hurried home and told their mother and First Man and his wife of what they had seen. They were frightened. The old ones said: "That was the spy of the Giant Elk, Anaye'tee'leget." Shortly thereafter when they were on the west side of the mesa they were frightened again, and again they hurried home and said: "We saw a great bird with a red head flying towards us,

but just as we took aim and were about to shoot it flew back to the mesa." The three older people were now frightened. "That was the turkey buzzard," they said. "He is the spy of Tse na'hale, the Giant Birds who devour people." They scolded the boys for having gone so far from home.

14   One day the boys returned from the north side of the mesa and they told of having seen a black bird with shining eyes. Just as they took aim it had flown away, they said. The White Bead Woman and her foster parents warned the boys again and said that the bird was the spy of the monsters. And again they scolded the youths for wandering so far. But they could not keep them at home.

15   Now the boys were afraid to go toward the south, west and north. The only safe place was the east, so they ran eastward chasing chickadees. And someone came to them and said: "Grandchildren, what are you doing?" This was Dotso, the All-Wise Fly who had spoken. He continued: "My grandchildren, your father is the Sun." . . .

16   The three older ones were speechless when the two boys said that they intended to go to the home of their father. The Twins warned their mother and First Man and First Woman not to look at them as they left. With that warning they started out.

17   When the boys stepped outside the hogan they stood side by side. Each had lifted his right foot to take a step. They stepped on the rainbow and were immediately on top of the mountain Chol'i'i where their mother had been found. . . . Then they found themselves way, way to the east in a country that they did not know, a country of nothing but rolling sand. . . .

18   After passing over many difficulties the Twins found themselves way, way, way east standing at the door of a great turquoise house. An old woman asked them where they were going. The boys said that they were going to see their father. She said: "Well, then you are my grandchildren. Come with me." She was the mother of the Sun. She took them to a room, and she wrapped them in the four coverings of the Sky, the dawn, the daylight, the twilight, and the darkness. After a while there was a loud galloping noise. It was the Sun returning home on his big turquoise horse.

19   When the Sun entered his house he said: "Why is there no one here?" His mother said: "Who would be here? There are only ourselves at all times." After asking this question four times the Sun said: "Why mother, at noon I saw two specks coming here. What are they?" . . . Then the grandmother brought the Twins out to their father.

20   The Little Breeze sat behind the boys' ears and told them what to say. They spoke up: "Father, we have come a long way to get help from you." The Sun did not answer them. They repeated their statement four times, but still the Sun did not answer them. . . .

21   The Sun showed the Twins his turquoise house and asked them to choose whatever they wished. One of the Twins said: "Father, we do not wish for anything that you have inside the house." The other brother repeated the same thing. Then they went outside the house. Over toward the East the Sun

showed the Twins all the different kinds of horses that he owned. He asked his sons if they wanted the horses, but they said it was not their wish. Toward the South he showed them all the domestic animals, cattle, sheep, etc. He asked them if they wanted these, but the Twins answered that it was not for these animals that they had come. Over toward the West the Sun showed them all the game animals and the birds, and he asked his sons if they were what they wanted. Again they said that they had not made the journey for these. He showed them the North and all the different kinds of stones, turquoise, white bead, red stone, and he asked them if these stones were what they wanted. But they said: "No, it is not for these that we have come."

22 Now on the outer wall of the Sun's house there hung a weapon. The Twins pointed to this weapon and said that that was what they had come for. The weapon looked like a bow and arrows, but in reality it was the lightning. The Sun asked them what they would do with this weapon. The boys told their father of the suffering on earth, and how men were eaten every day by monsters. They named the monsters, one by one, and they said: "Father, if they eat all the people on the earth, and themselves last, for whom will you travel? What will you receive as a gift for the price of your journey?"

23 The Sun sat with his head down and thought a great thought, for Yeitso, the One-Walking Giant, was also his son. Then he spoke and told the Twins that the Giant was their half brother and that they would be slaying their elder brother. (That is why they say that brothers will sometimes kill one another.)

24 The Sun explained to the Twins that it was not safe for the people on the earth to possess this weapon they asked for. He said that the boys could use the weapon for a little while, but that he would have to reclaim it when they were through with it. "For of a certainty the people on the earth will destroy themselves if they are allowed to keep it," he said. He lifted down the weapon and continued: "Now let us go to the top of the middle of the earth where there is an opening in the sky." The Little Breeze whispered to the Twins: "Now he will ask you questions. He counts on your giving the wrong answers, and he plans on refusing to give you the weapons."

25 The Sun took the weapon and led the Twins to the opening in the sky above Tso dzil, Mt. Taylor. That is where the guessing took place. If the boys did not guess correctly the Sun's plan was to keep them up there and not let them return to earth.

26 First the Sun pointed to the East and said: "What is that object way down on the earth?" Then the elder brother began chanting:

> What is that he asks me?
> That is the mountain called Sis na'jin.
> It is the White Bead Mountain.
> It is the Chief of the Mountain.
> It is like the Most High Power Whose Ways Are Beautiful.
> What is that down below? he asks me.

27   The questions included all the sacred mountains. The questions and the answers were just like, in form, the first verse of the chant, that of the East. The Sun said: "My Sons, your guessing is all correct. I know today that you will kill one of the members of your family." He handed the Elder Brother his weapon, which is the lightning, and to the Younger Brother he also handed his weapon, which is also the lightning. The first weapon is called hat tslin it lish ka', the lightning that strikes crooked. The second weapon is hat tsol ilthe ka', the lightning that flashes straight. They were then lowered with their weapons to the center of the world.

THE TWINS KILL THE GIANT YEITSO

28   Yeitso, the Giant, lived at Tqo'sedo, Hot Springs, and the Twins went there and waited for him to come for water. They saw him coming over the hill from the south. The Elder Brother sang two sections of a chant then and other chants as the Giant came nearer.

29   The Giant went down to the spring and drank four times. He drank all the water, and then he spat it back four times and the spring was as before. He walked back and forth and said: "What are the two beautiful things that I see? And how shall I kill them?" The Twins called back: "What beautiful Big Thing is walking about? And how shall we kill it?" They called to each other four times. Then the Little Breeze, who was with the youths, said: "Ako, look out! Up you go. Jump high in the air." The black knife, the Giant's powerful weapon, passed under the Twins. The Little Breeze said: "Keep low now." And over them passed the blue knife. The youths now got hold of the Giant's two weapons. Now came the time for them to use the sacred feathers that their grandmother, the mother of the Sun, had given them, and when the Little Breeze said: "Jump to this side. Look out!" they were able to do so. This time the Giant had thrown the yellow knife, and it passed them and they recovered it. The fourth time the Little Breeze warned the Twins. "Leap high up now," it said. "Here comes the last weapon." And this time the white knife with the many points passed under them. Then the Breeze said: "He has no more weapons."

30   The Sun had told the Twins that the Giant should be allowed to act first, for he was their elder brother. When their turn came there was a great, blinding flash of lightning and it struck the giant, but he stood there. The Twins aimed the first knife, the black knife, at the Giant. They threw it, but he stood there as before. They aimed and threw the Giant's own blue knife at him. It struck him, but still he stood up. The third knife was yellow, and they hit the Giant with it, but it did not harm him. But when they hit him with the last weapon, the great white knife, he commenced to fall with a terrible noise.

31   Then the blood began to flow from the Giant's mouth and the Little Breeze said: "Stop the blood before it runs into the water." So the Twins placed a stone knife and an arrow point between the blood and the water.

Today you can see a strange formation where the Giant's blood flowed, and also, where the Twins placed the stone knife there is a big, black rock standing. This all happened at Tqo'sedo, beyond Gallup and this (Mesa Verde) side of Tso dzil, Mt. Taylor.

32 The Twins went to the Giant and cut off his scalp. They saw that he was covered with flint armor or clothing made of stone knives. This covered him from his neck to his feet. They gathered some of the stone knives and threw them towards the East, saying: "From now on the people of the earth shall use you. The Giant's spirit has departed from you." They threw the rest of the knives to the South, West and North, and they covered the whole country.

33 The Twins, carrying the Giant's scalp, started for their home. When they reached there they hung the Giant's scalp on a pole to the east of the hogan. And when they entered the home they found the three sitting there. First Man, First Woman and the White Bead Woman were very frightened. They had squeezed themselves against the wall for they thought that some monsters had arrived to kill them. They did not recognize the Twins for they had been reformed in the house of the Sun. They were now tall, handsome young men with long hair and beautiful beads and clothing. The Twins called out: "Mother do not be frightened, we, your sons, are here." They called out to their grandfather and grandmother adding: "We have been to our father's home."

34 The three came forward and looked about them. They were still frightened, for the Twins shone with beauty. The Twins said: "We have killed the Giant, Yeitso." First Man said: "No one can kill the Giant." They said: "But we have the Giant's scalp hanging on the pole outside." . . .

Discussion Questions

1. What is significant about the color of the horse, its trappings, and the young man who appears to White Bead Woman?
2. Consider First Man's reactions to his daughter's story. How are they similar to a human father's responses?
3. Mythological heroes must undertake a dangerous journey and must overcome trials along the way. How are Monster Slayer and Child Born for Water tested?

WRITING TOPICS

1. Locate two other hero or heroine adventures which you enjoy reading. In an essay, compare their stories to that of the Navajo twins. These elements may appear in your comparison: information about their supernatural parents and birth; a dangerous journey to seek their father; trials they must pass and monsters they must defeat; and their gifts to the people.

2. Giants figure in the folklore of many societies. Brainstorm on paper what you know about giants and, in a short poem, speculate on why giants seem to have captured the imagination of human beings the world over.

THE COMING OF HORSES

Hastin Tlo'tsi hee and Aileen O'Bryan

Sandoval told the myth of how White Bead Woman created horses and first gave them to Monster Slayer and Child Born for Water. In a ceremony that the hero twins and other holy beings witnessed, White Bead Woman sang prayers and performed the ritual to bring life to four small stone images of horses. In turn, the hero twins and other holy beings taught humans the sacred prayers for their horses. According to Sandoval, there were eighty-five prayers to be sung for the good of horses. The prayers are part of a longer chant ceremony. This is Sandoval's account of the coming of horses.

1   The White Bead Woman told the boys that they were to learn the Night Chant and all the prayers that went with it. For it was by this ceremony that they should live. So the two boys learned all the chants and the prayers that they were to use in the spring when the plants and the flowers and the young animals come out, and at the time of the harvest.

2   After this the White Bead Woman said: "The Diné shall have horses." And the first chant that she sang is this:

> From the East comes a big black mare.
> Changed into a maiden
> She comes to me.
> From the South comes a blue mare.
> Changed into a maiden
> She comes to me.
> From the West comes a sorrel mare.
> Changed into a maiden
> She comes to me.
> From the North comes a white mare.
> Changed into a maiden
> She comes to me.

The chant is divided into two parts, two sections are sung and then four sections.

3   The White Bead Woman chanted again:

> This is my plan:
> I am the White Bead Woman.
> In the center of my home I planned it.
> On top of the beautiful goods I planned it.
> The white bead basket which contains the horse fetishes,
> They lay before me as I planned it.
> All the beautiful flowers with their pollens
> And the horse fetishes,
> They lay in each other,
> They lay before me as I planned it.
> To increase and to multiply, not to decrease.
> They lay inside (the animals) as I planned it.

There are about twenty sections of this chant. It changes slightly each time.

4   After the White Bead Woman's chanting, the four horses began to move, the white bead horse fetish, the turquoise horse fetish, the white-shell horse fetish and the banded stone horse fetish. These four stone fetishes were made into living horses.

5   Life came into them and they whinnied. Then the White Bead Woman took the horses from her home. She placed them on the white bead plain, on the turquoise plain, on the white bead hill, and on the turquoise hill. Returning, she laid out four baskets—the white bead basket, the turquoise basket, the white shell basket, and the black jet basket. In these she placed the medicine which would make the horses drop their colts. The White Bead Woman then went outside and chanted, and down came the horses from the hills; but instead of four there came a herd.

6   The White Bead Woman told the boys that they were to have the horses in their country; that when she believes it is for their good they will multiply, or again, they will decrease. So they do not always multiply. Some years, when there is poor grass and deep snow, many die. From that time the horses were given to men.

DISCUSSION QUESTIONS

1. For the Navajo, words may be sacred and have power, particularly in prayers or chants. How would you describe the function of powerful words in the creation of horses?

2. In small groups, discuss Sandoval's tale of the coming of horses in comparison with other myths you are familiar with that describe such events. What purpose do you think such tales serve in a culture or society?

WRITING TOPICS

1. After doing some research on the role of horses in Native American history, write a brief essay examining the importance of the horse in Native American culture and how that importance is reflected in the tale of the coming of horses.
2. In small groups, try your hand at writing a brief chant that explains any natural phenomenon of your choosing.

THE WAR GOD'S HORSE SONG

Tall Kia ah ni

The Horse Creation myth is part of an extensive collection of Navajo oral literature. Medicine men have sung songs about sacred horses since the People first acquired these valuable animals in the early seventeenth century. Today, Navajos treasure their horses. Anyone who owns a horse can hold his or her head high. In their stories, prayers, and ceremonies, Navajos continue to pay homage to spirit horses owned by the deities and real horses belonging to humans. During the ceremony, each Navajo singer adheres to the basic mythic patterns, but when his words are written down in English, they still reflect his unique voice. The following version was chanted by Tall Kia ah ni, a medicine man, or singer, who conducted ceremonies in the 1930s. He described the mystical and glorious animal that belonged to one of the Hero Twins, who were also known as the War Gods. The song is an extended metaphor that seems to create the beautiful horse line by line. This prayer continues to bring healthy colts and long life to mortal horses.

I am the Turquoise Woman's son.
On top of Belted Mountain,
Beautiful horse—slim like a weasel.
My horse has a hoof like a striped agate;
5 His fetlock is like a fine eagle plume;
His legs are like quick lightning.
My horse's body is like an eagle-plumed arrow;
My horse has a tail like a trailing black cloud.
I put flexible goods on my horse's back;
10 The Little Holy Wind blows through his hair.
His mane is made of short rainbows.
My horse's ears are made of round corn.
My horses's eyes are made of big stars.

My horses's head is made of mixed waters—
15 From the holy waters—he never knows thirst.
My horse's teeth are made of white shell.
The long rainbow is in his mouth for a bridle, and with it I guide him.
When my horse neighs, different-colored horses follow.
    I am wealthy, because of him.
20   Before me peaceful,
    Behind me peaceful,
    Under me peaceful,
    Over me peaceful,
    All around me peaceful—
25   Peaceful voice when he neighs.
I am Everlasting and Peaceful.
I stand for my horse.

DISCUSSION QUESTIONS

1. The speaker in the poem is one of the Hero Twins, who was the son of Turquoise Woman (also known as White Bead Woman). In one sense, *I* may also refer to the person who has requested the ceremony in which this prayer is chanted. How does the repetition of *I, my,* and *me* accentuate the rhythm and structure of the song?
2. The beautiful horse is pictured for the reader in similes and metaphors. Which comparisons do you think are the most effective?
3. What is the tone of lines 20–24?

WRITING TOPICS

1. In a chanting style, prepare a reading for your classmates that gives your interpretation of the sound and sense of the song.
2. Write a comparison of this song/prayer with one from the Bible or another sacred book. For example, select one of the psalms. What is the theme of the two? From the imagery, draw two inferences about the beliefs of the people who recite the songs. How are they similar and different in form and ideas?

A PRAYER FROM THE NIGHT CHANT

The Navajo Night Chant is one of many healing ceremonies that Monster Slayer and Child Born for Water taught the Navajos. The ceremonies are called chants, such as the Mountain Chant, the Blessing Chant, and the Night Chant. This is one version of a healing prayer from the Night Chant. Like other chants, the Night Chant involves singing prayers, making sand paintings, and invoking the mythic forces of the holy people. The rituals have been handed down for centuries from medicine men who taught the healing powers to a successor in each new generation. A singer, or medicine man, usually is a specialist in one or two chants, for memorizing the complex four- and nine-day rites demands intellectual rigor and dedication. The purpose of these curing ceremonies is to restore beauty and harmony for the patient who has become ill because he or she has slipped out of harmony with the natural universe. A chant ceremony is performed for the sick person who wishes to attain a state of being called *hozho,* which brings peace, happiness, and plenty. Line by line, the patient recites the prayer after the singer, or medicine man. The Navajos believe that the earth and all living things on it as well as the celestial bodies are endowed with spirit and intelligence. Consequently, it is logical that one must respect and revere all creation.

Tségihi.
House made of dawn,
House made of evening light,
House made of dark cloud,
House made of male rain,
House made of dark mist,
House made of female rain,
House made of pollen,

House made of grasshoppers,
10   Dark cloud is at the door.
The trail out of it is dark cloud.
The zigzag lightning stands high upon it.
Male deity!
Your offering I make.
15   I have prepared a smoke for you.
Restore my feet for me,
Restore my legs for me,
Restore my body for me,
Restore my mind for me,
20   Restore my voice for me.
This very day take out your spell for me.
Your spell remove for me.
You have taken it away for me;
Far off it has gone.
25   Happily I recover.
Happily my interior becomes cool.
Happily I go forth.
My interior feeling cool, may I walk.
No longer sore, may I walk.
30   Impervious to pain, may I walk.
With lively feelings, may I walk.
As it used to be long ago, may I walk.
Happily may I walk.
Happily, with abundant dark clouds, may I walk.
35   Happily, with abundant showers, may I walk.
Happily, with abundant plants, may I walk.
Happily, on a trail of pollen, may I walk.
Happily may I walk.
Being as it used to be long ago, may I walk.
40   May it be beautiful before me,
May it be beautiful behind me,
May it be beautiful below me,
May it be beautiful above me,
May it be beautiful all around me.
45   In beauty it is finished.

Discussion Questions

1. In the healing prayer, the patient, who is in ill health, prays to be restored to a state of wholeness and beauty. What happens in the transforming center of the prayer in lines 21–25?

2. Plant pollen is sacred to Navajos, who frequently carry pollen with them in a small pouch or bag. What is the meaning of line 37, and how does it relate to the entire prayer song?
3. Compare the form and content in lines 40–45 with lines 24–28 in "The War God's Horse Song."

Writing Topics

1. The imagery in this prayer is primarily from the natural world. What does this tell you about the Navajo view of life and health? Explore your observations in a few paragraphs.
2. Much Native American oral literature is characterized by parallelism, alliteration, and repetition. Using examples from this selection, write an analysis of the role of these literary devices in the poetic prayer.

THE SUN DANCE

Luther Standing Bear

Born in the 1860s as a Lakota member of the Teton Sioux, Luther Standing Bear led a long and remarkable life. Near the time of his birth, his people were confined in 1868 to the Sioux Reservation. While still a boy, Standing Bear was taught to be a successful hunter and warrior. As an adult living on and away from the reservation at various times, he became an agency clerk, store owner, assistant minister, teacher, rancher, and a member of Buffalo Bill's Wild West Show that toured Europe. Eventually, Standing Bear moved to California, where he appeared in many movies and lectured widely until his death in 1939. During the California years, he wrote four books presenting a unique perspective in American literature: *My People the Sioux* (1928), *My Indian Boyhood* (1931), *Land of the Spotted Eagle* (1933), and *Stories of the Sioux* (1934).

Standing Bear's autobiographical account of the 1879 Sun Dance is a significant contribution to Lakota literature. As one of the last generation of Sioux to be reared in traditional ways, Standing Bear wrote an irreplaceable eyewitness description of the Sun Dance ceremony. The Lakota, like many Native Americans, consider the Sun a divine power. The Sun Dance, a yearly summer ritual lasting three to four days, is performed for the spiritual health and strength of participants and their families. Prior to reservation times, it was the most important religious and social event in the yearly cycle of Sioux life when different bands came together to feast, dance, and practice their religion. From 1881 to 1935, under a policy of legally suppressing Native belief practices, the U.S. Bureau of Indian Affairs (BIA) directed its agents to prohibit Indian "dancing," "giveaways," and other religious behavior. Indian police arrested sundancers and courts of Indian offenses sentenced them to prison terms and to pay fines.

Prohibition against the Sun Dance arose primarily from Euro-Americans who disapproved of the participants making sacrifices with their bodies, and this aspect of the ritual was the principal reason federal officials outlawed the Sun Dance. Despite the ban, however, many tribes, including the Sioux, continued to conduct Sun Dances secretly as underground rites in remote areas of their reservations. In the 1960s, many Plains Indians began conducting their Sun Dances more openly, and in 1978, the Native American Religious Freedom Act guaranteed Indians the right to perform Sun Dances and other religious rites. For contemporary Lakotas as well as other Plains tribes, the ritual continues as a central focus for community devotion and renewal.

1   It was about the middle of the summer of 1879 that I saw the last great Sun Dance of the Sioux. The Brules were holding the dance about six miles southwest of Rosebud Agency, on the place where old Chief Two Strikes's band now have their allotments. As I started for Carlisle Indian School in the fall of 1879, I cannot say whether this was the last dance held or not.

2   I have read many descriptions of this dance, and I have been to different tribes which claimed they did the "real thing," but there is a great difference in their dances from the Sun Dance of the Sioux.

3   The Sun Dance started many years before Christopher Columbus drifted to these shores. We then knew that there was a God above us all. We called God "Wakan Tanka," or the "Big Holy," or sometimes "Grandfather." You call God "Father." I bring this before you because I want you to know that this dance was our religious belief. According to our legend, the red man was to have this dance every summer, to fulfill our religious duty. It was a sacrificial dance.

4   During the winter if any member of the tribe became ill, perhaps a brother or a cousin would be brave enough to go to the medicine man and say, "I will sacrifice my body to the Wakan Tanka, or Big Holy, for the one who is sick." Or if the buffalo were beginning to get scarce, some one would sacrifice himself so that the tribe might have something to eat.

5   The medicine man would then take this brave up to the mountain alone, and announce to the Great Spirit that the young man was ready to be sacrificed. When the parents of this young man heard that he was to go through the Sun Dance, some of his brothers or cousins would sacrifice themselves with him as an honor.

6   If some young man of another band had the desire to go through the Sun Dance, some of his friends or relatives might offer to dance with him. Sometimes as many as thirty or forty braves went into the dance.

7   As soon as the women heard that there was to be a Sun Dance in their band, they began making all the things which were necessary for the ceremony. They placed beautiful porcupine-quill-work on the eagle-bone whistles which the men carried in their mouths during the dance, as well as the beautiful head-dresses for the dancers. These were made from porcupine-

quill-work. The dancer wore a piece of buckskin around the waist, hanging down like a skirt. This also had pretty quill-work decorations. Soon all the things were ready for the dance.

8 When the chiefs learned this dance was coming, they called a meeting and selected a place they thought as best suited to hold it. They then sent word to the other bands to get ready.

9 The main band would move to the place selected, and the other bands would come in one at a time, the boys and warriors mounted on ponies. They would all keep together until they were very near, when they would make an imitation charge on the camp, just as if it were an enemy camp.

10 After this "attack" they would all go up to a hill near by. Four men were then chosen who were to lead the parade. The warriors would now have a chance to show their beautiful war-ponies and good clothes. Then they would all parade into the village. Just about the time the parade was over, the rest of the camp would be moving in. The women would then be very busy erecting the tipis.

11 After the various bands had all arrived, there were some special tipis put up for those who were going to dance. These tipis were not erected in one place, but were sometimes considerably scattered. I have seen a camp of this sort which was a mile and a quarter in diameter. There were from four to six of these special tipis for the dancers. Everybody was allowed to go, and there was always plenty to eat in these tipis.

12 The first day all the people collected at the center of the camp and some scouts were selected to go out and look for the cottonwood pole which was to be used in the dance. After being chosen, these scouts retired to their tipis and dressed in their best clothes, mounted their war-ponies, and rode into the circle. Their parents gave away ponies and other pretty things as a token of respect that their sons had been chosen to act as scouts.

13 Among these scouts were one or two of the old-timers, who were to act as leaders. A fire was now built in the center of the circle, and the scouts rode their ponies around this fire three times, and, after the fourth time, they were off! They rode their ponies at full speed. All those on horseback rode as fast as they could and encircled the scouts as they went on.

14 The scouts would be gone about a half-hour. On their return they would come to the top of a hill and stop. The others in the camp would once more mount their ponies and ride out to meet the scouts. Then they would turn about and race back to the center of the circle, where they would wait for the scouts to ride in.

15 One of the old-timers would then relate how they had found a pole which was considered good enough to be used in the dance. Then everybody got ready to go to the place where the pole had been found.

16 All the various lodges of the tribe now gathered in the timber near the place where the pole was located. There was the White Horse, Bull, Fox, and Short Hair lodges. As each separate tribe had its form of ceremonies, each selected some of its people to go to the tree and "chop it." They did not

really chop the tree, but just simply touched it. As they touched the tree, they gave away ponies or anything they wanted. They stayed here a long time, as they had plenty to eat all the time they were in the timber. If they knew a man who had plenty of ponies, they would select one of his children to come forward and touch the tree, and then he would give away a pony.

17 After all had finished their ceremonies, some one cut the tree down. There were about twenty men to carry this pole, They had long sticks which they put under it, and two men to a stick to carry it. Everybody was carrying something. Some carried forked branches, others limbs of the tree, etc. They had no one to order them around, but every one did his share toward this religious dance.

18 As the twenty men lifted the pole, they walked slowly toward the camp. The rest of the tribe trailed along behind. They stopped three times, and each time a medicine man howled like a wolf. The fourth time they stopped, all the men and boys raced their ponies as fast as they would go, trying to see who would be first to reach the center of the camp. Here they found the effigy of a man made from the limbs of trees. Each tried to be first to touch this. There would be plenty of dust as these men and boys rode in to attack this wooden man. Sometimes two ponies would run together, and then some one was likely to be hurt.

19 At last the men came in with the pole. Then the lodges had some more ceremonies to be gone through with, while some of the men started to dig the hole in which to set the pole. Others would get busy arranging forked poles in a circle. This circle was to serve as our hall.

20 When the hole was ready, all the men from the different lodges got together to help erect the pole, which was sometimes sixty or seventy feet long. They tied two braided rawhide ropes about the middle of the pole, on which some brave was to hang. Other ropes were to be used to hoist the pole into place. These hoisting ropes were tied in such a way as to be easily removed, after the pole was in the right position. We had no stepladders nor any men with climbers on to go up and untie any ropes that might be left up when the pole was in place.

21 When all was ready, some of the men used forked poles, some held on to the ropes, and others got hold of the pole. It required about forty men to do this work properly. The pole must be raised and dropped in the hole at one operation, and with no second lifting. Some pushed, others pulled, while the men with the forked sticks lifted. As the pole dropped in to the hole, everybody cheered.

22 There was a strong superstition regarding this pole. It was believed that if the pole dropped before it was set into the hole, all our wishes and hopes would be shattered. There would be great thunder-storms and high winds; our shade or council hall would be blown away, and there would be no Sun Dance. On top of this, it was believed that the whole tribe would have a run of bad luck.

23 Consequently, when this pole was being erected, every man used all his

strength to ward off any accident or mishap. We were taught to believe that if all minds worked together, it helped a great deal. We were taught this by our parents, and we had strong faith in it.

24 The pole was always a cottonwood tree, as I have previously stated. No other tree would do. It was not always a straight tree, but there was always a branch which extended out from the main trunk. This would be about thirty or forty feet up. This branch would be cut off about four feet from the trunk. On the top of the pole, branches with leaves on would be left.

25 They made a bundle of branches from the tree which were wrapped in bark and tied together. This bundle was placed in the branch which had been cut off about four feet from the trunk. When this bundle was in place, it looked not unlike a huge cross, when viewed from a distance.

26 From this cross-piece hung something which resembled a buffalo and a man. These effigies were cut from rawhide and were tied up with a rawhide rope. They were suspended about ten feet down from the bundle of wood or the cross-piece. Both were painted black, the paint being made from burned cottonwood mixed with buffalo fat.

27 Sometimes there was a small bundle of sticks painted in a variety of colors. At the end of each, a small bag made of buckskin and filled with tobacco was hung. All this was suspended to the cross-piece. Under the pole were many little bags of tobacco, tied on little sticks, as a prayer offering to the spirit.

28 About ten feet to the west of this cross lay the skull of a buffalo on a bed made of sagebrush. The horns were attached to this skull and it was laid facing east. Behind the skull, about two feet, were two forked sticks stuck in the ground, with another stick across them. Against this the pipe of peace rested, with the stem pointing toward the east.

29 The real meaning of having the effigy of the buffalo hanging from the cross was a prayer to the Wakan-Tanka, or Big Holy, for more "pte," or buffalo meat. The effigy of the man meant that in case of war we were to have victory over our enemies.

30 When the main big pole was all completed, the men bent their energies toward the dancing-hall, or shade, as it should rightfully be called. All the forked poles were placed in a double circle, about fifteen feet apart, with an opening left toward the east. Long sticks were laid from one forked pole to another in the inner circle as well as the outside circle. We used no nails in those days, and anything that was to be fastened must be bound with rawhide or tied with bark. In this case, we peeled off the bark of the willow trees and used that to fasten the poles together. Then the longest tipi poles would be brought in, and laid from the inner to the outer circle. The outside wall was made from entwined branches, and on top would be laid the largest tipi coverings, which made a fine shade. This "shade" was about one hundred and fifty feet in diameter, with a depth of about fifteen feet. It was considered a great honor to have one's tipi covering chosen for this purpose.

31 After the shade was completed, if any one wanted to give a piece of buck-

skin, or some red or blue cloth, as an offering to the Great Spirit, he took a long stick and put a cross-piece on it, from which was suspended his offering. These pennants were hung all around the dance-shade. It quite resembled a great convention hall. Several beds of sagebrush were made for the dancers. Sometimes a big dance would precede the Sun Dance. This dance was known as "owanka ona sto wacipi," or "smoothing the floor." It was, in fact, a sort of "house-warming" affair, and was for the braves and young men only. Each carried a weapon and wore his best clothes. The crowd came in from all the different bands in the camp, forming in lines like soldiers as they appeared. Sometimes there were as many as fifteen abreast.

32   Then an old chief came forward with a scalp-lock tied to a pole. He danced before the others, facing them. When he danced backward, the others danced forward, and vice versa. When the old chief led them toward the pole, those carrying guns shot at the buffalo and the effigy of the man, hanging from the pole.

33   While this dance was in progress, different medicine men were in the tipis with the young men who were to do the Sun Dance. From each tipi came six, eight, and sometimes ten from a band to dance. There was a leader, who carried a pipe of peace; the others followed one by one. They wore buffalo robes with the hair outside, and quite resembled a band of buffalo coming to a stream to drink.

34   After these Sun Dance candidates reached the shade from their tipis, they did not go in immediately, but marched around the outside three times. After the fourth time, they went in and took their places. Then the medicine man came forward and took charge of four or eight of the dancers. Four of them must be painted alike. They put on beautiful head-dresses richly ornamented with porcupine quills. Their wrists were wound around with sagebrush, and the eagle-bone whistles they used were likewise decorated.

35   This was a very solemn affair. These men were to dance for three or four days, without food or water. Some of their relatives cried; others sang to praise them and made them feel courageous.

36   The singers were now in their places. They used no tom-tom, but sat around a large buffalo hide which lay flat on the ground, using large sticks to beat upon the dried skin.

37   The braves started dancing as soon as the sun started to rise. They stood facing the sun with both hands raised above their heads, the eagle-bone whistles in their mouths, and they blew on these every time the singers hit the skin with their sticks. All day long they stood in one position, facing the sun, until it set.

38   The sunflower was used by the Sioux in this dance. They cut out a piece of rawhide the shape of a sunflower, which they wore on a piece of braided buckskin suspended around the neck, with the flower resting on the breast. At that time I did not realize the significance of the sunflower, but now I know it is the only flower that follows the sun as it moves on its orbit, always facing it.

39   The dance would be kept up until one of the participants fainted, then he was laid out on one of the sagebrush beds. On the second day of the dance a young man who had started it would come into the shade. First he would walk all around the hall so that all could see him. Then he went straight to the pole. He was giving himself for a living sacrifice. Two medicine men would lift the young man and lay him down under the pole. An old man would then come forward with a very sharp-pointed knife. He would take hold of the breast of the young brave, pull the skin forward, and pierce it through with his knife. Then he would insert a wooden pin (made from the plum tree) through the slit and tie a strong buckskin thong to this pin.

40   From the pole two rawhide ropes were suspended. The candidate would now be lifted up and the buckskin string tied to the rawhide rope. The candidate was now hanging from his breasts, but the rope was long enough for him to remain on the ground. Although the blood would be running down from the knife incision, the candidate would smile, although every one knew he must be suffering intense pain.

41   At this point the friends or relatives of the young brave would sing and praise him for his courage. Then they would give away ponies or make other presents. The singers now began to sing and the young brave to dance. The other dancers were behind him, four in a line, and they accompanied his dancing. These dancers always stood in one spot while they danced, but the candidate danced and at the same time pulled at the rope, trying to tear out the wooden pin fastened through his breasts.

42   If he tried very hard and was unsuccessful, his friends and relatives possibly could not bear to see him suffer any longer; so they would give away a pony to some one who would help him tear loose. This party would stand behind the dancer and seize him around the waist, while the candidate at the same time would throw himself backward, both pulling with all their strength. If they could not yet tear the candidate loose, an old man with a sharp knife would cut the skin off, and the dancer would fall beneath the pole. Then he would be picked up and carried to a sagebrush bed. Occasionally a man with a very strong constitution, after tearing loose, would get off his bed and resume the dancing. I have often seen these braves with their own blood dried to their bodies, yet going on with the dance.

43   This brave candidate fasted three or four days; taking no food or water during that time, instead of the forty days the Saviour did. The candidate had his body pierced beneath the cross. I learned all about this religion in the natural way, but after learning how to read the white man's books I compared your religion with ours; but religion, with us Indians, is stronger.

44   Many things were done during this dance which were similar to what I have read about Christ. We had one living sacrifice, and he fasted three or four days instead of forty. This religious ceremony was not always held in the same place. We did not commercialize our belief. Our medicine men received no salary. Hell was unknown to us. We trusted one another, and

our word was as good as the white man's gold of to-day. We were then true Christians.

45   After the dance was over, everybody moved away, going where he pleased. It was a free country then. But afterward, if we ever returned to that sacred spot where the pole was yet standing, with the cross-piece attached, we stood for a long time in reverent attitude, because it was a sacred place to us.

46   But things have changed, even among the white people. They tear down their churches and let playhouses be built on the spot. What can be your feeling of reverence when you think of the house of God, in which you worshipped, being used to make fun in?

47   As I have many times related in my story, I always wanted to be brave, but I do not think I could ever have finished one of these Sun Dances.

DISCUSSION QUESTIONS

1. Standing Bear organizes his essay according to the chronological events that take place as the Lakotas prepare for and conduct the Sun Dance. Explain one of the major "scenes" or events and tell how it is related to the overall purpose of the ceremony.
2. The author remembers and records distinct details about each part of the Sun Dance. Select one part which you think is well written and give reasons for your choice.
3. According to Standing Bear's account, all members of the various bands played roles in the Sun Dance. Find three examples of this participation. What details does Standing Bear give that helps the reader imagine and understand the roles?

WRITING TOPICS

1. At various times, nonbelievers have viewed the Sun Dance as sacreligious. In a paragraph, explain why some non-Indians thought that the Sun Dance should be prohibited. Also tell why you agree or disagree with the prohibition of the ritual.
2. In a brief essay, compare the Sun Dance with a religious ceremony from another culture. Organize your report by giving three differences in

paragraph one and three similarities in paragraph two. Select specific details to develop each paragraph.

3. Research the Sun Dance. Based on your research and evidence from Standing Bear, write a brief essay on this topic: During the Sun Dance, all participants give their best efforts to renew life for the good of the people. In your essay, explain the purpose of the ceremony within the culture, describe the events that occur, and relate the status of the sun dance within the culture today.

4. Write a paragraph explaining the meaning of Standing Bear's statement, "We were then true Christians." (paragraph 44)

ALONE ON A HILLTOP

John Fire Lame Deer and Richard Erdoes

John Fire Lame Deer was born in 1900 on the Rosebud Sioux Reservation in South Dakota and died in 1976. As a child, Lame Deer listened to his grandfather's first-hand account of the Wounded Knee massacre. During his long life, he became a rodeo clown, a cowhand, a soldier, a spud-picker, a tribal policeman, a prisoner, and a medicine man. Lame Deer wryly observed, "I managed to be both a Christian and a heathen, a fugitive and a pursuer, a lawman and an outlaw." When he was in his seventies, Lame Deer with Richard Erdoes published his autobiography *Lame Deer Seeker of Visions: The Life of a Sioux Medicine Man.* In the book, he recalled being forced to attend boarding school at the age of fourteen. Angered by cruel teachers and insulted by his confinement, Lame Deer ran away, but was caught and returned by authorities. Despite being disciplined with a strap, the young man rebelled: "I felt so lonesome I cried, but I wouldn't cooperate in the remaking of myself." Finally, he was allowed to return home to his family. When he was seventeen, two events made a permanent impact on his life: the death of his mother and the completion of his vision quest. For the rest of his life, he continued to seek knowledge from older Sioux healers and to honor the memory of his relatives, particularly that of his great-grandfather, Tahca Ushte.

In 1877, Tahca Ushte, the elder Lame Deer, and his people had ceased their conflict with the whites and had requested permission to go out on one last hunt during the summer before settling on the reservation. The U.S. government granted permission for the hunt, but at the same time, General Nelson Miles had orders to attack as "hostiles" any Indians hunting off the reservation. Lame Deer recalled his family's account of the scene when Miles' forces found Tahca Uste's camp, "The blue coats came tearing into the camp, shooting and yelling, stampeding the horses and riding down the people. . . . Seeing the peaceful camp from up close, Bear Coat Miles, I believe, changed his mind and regretted what was happening." The General ordered his troops to stop the killing, but bullets struck innocent Indians. One trooper fired his carbine at Tahca Ushte, and Lame Deer continued, "Miles hung onto my great-grandfather's arm with both hands, but the chief tore himself loose and picked up his gun, shooting the man who had fired on him." Many soldiers fired, killing Tahca Ushte and other fleeing victims. In the account of his vision quest, Lame Deer testifies how his family and other Sioux not only survived such tragedies, but also managed to pass sacred objects, such as the pipe, and rituals, such as the seeking of a vision, from generation to generation. Lame Deer promises to pass this special heritage to his descendants.

◉

1   I was all alone on the hilltop. I sat there in the vision pit, a hole dug into the hill, my arms hugging my knees as I watched old man Chest, the medicine man who had brought me there, disappear far down in the valley. He was just a moving black dot among the pines, and soon he was gone altogether.

2   Now I was all by myself, left on the hilltop for four days and nights without food or water until he came back for me. You know, we Indians are not like some white folks—a man and a wife, two children, and one baby sitter who watches the TV set while the parents are out visiting somewhere.

3   Indian children are never alone. They are always surrounded by grandparents, uncles, cousins, relatives of all kinds, who fondle the kids, sing to them, tell them stories. If the parents go someplace, the kids go along.

4   But here I was, crouched in my vision pit, left alone by myself for the first time in my life. I was sixteen then, still had my boy's name and, let me tell you, I was scared. I was shivering and not only from the cold. The nearest human being was many miles away, and four days and nights is a long, long time. Of course, when it was all over, I would no longer be a boy, but a man. I would have had my vision. I would be given a man's name.

5   Sioux men are not afraid to endure hunger, thirst and loneliness, and I was only ninety-six hours away from being a man. The thought was comforting. Comforting, too, was the warmth of the star blanket which old man Chest had wrapped around me to cover my nakedness. My grandmother had made it especially for this, my first *hanblechia*, my first vision-seeking. It was a beautifully designed quilt, white with a large morning star made of many pieces of brightly colored cloth. That star was so big it covered most of the blanket. If Wakan Tanka, the Great Spirit, would give me the vision and the power, I would become a medicine man and perform many ceremonies wrapped in that quilt. I am an old man now and many times a grandfather, but I still have that star blanket my grandmother made for me. I treasure it; some day I shall be buried in it.

6   The medicine man had also left a peace pipe with me, together with a bag of *kinnickinnick*—our kind of tobacco made of red willow bark. This pipe was even more of a friend to me than my star blanket. To us the pipe is like an open Bible. White people need a church house, a preacher and a pipe organ to get into a praying mood. There are so many things to distract you: who else is in the church, whether the other people notice that you have come, the pictures on the wall, the sermon, how much money you should give, and did you bring it with you. We think you can't have a vision that way.

7   For us Indians there is just the pipe, the earth we sit on, and the open sky. The spirit is everywhere. Sometimes it shows itself through an animal, a bird, or some trees and hills. Sometimes it speaks from the Badlands, a stone, or even from the water. That smoke from the peace pipe, it goes straight up to the spirit world. But this is a two-way thing. Power flows down to us through that smoke, through the pipe stem. You feel that power as you hold your pipe; it moves from the pipe right into your body. It makes your hair stand up. That pipe is not just a thing; it is alive. Smoking this pipe would make me feel good and help me to get rid of my fears.

8   As I ran my fingers along its bowl of smooth red pipestone, red like the blood of my people, I no longer felt scared. That pipe had belonged to my father and to his father before him. It would someday pass to my son and, through him, to my grandchildren. As long as we had the pipe there would be a Sioux nation. As I fingered the pipe, touched it, felt its smoothness that came from long use, I sensed that my forefathers who had once smoked this pipe were with me on the hill, right in the vision pit. I was no longer alone.

9   Besides the pipe the medicine man had also given me a gourd. In it were forty small squares of flesh which my grandmother had cut from her arm with a razor blade. I had seen her do it. Blood had been streaming down from her shoulder to her elbow as she carefully put down each piece of skin on a handkerchief, anxious not to lose a single one. It would have made those anthropologists mad. Imagine, performing such an ancient ceremony with a razor blade instead of a flint knife! To me it did not matter. Someone dear to me had undergone pain, given me something of herself, part of her body, to help me pray and make me stronghearted. How could I be afraid with so many people—living and dead—helping me?

10   One thing still worried me. I wanted to become a medicine man, a *yuwipi*, a healer carrying on the ancient ways of the Sioux nation. But you cannot learn to be a medicine man like a white man going to medical school. An old holy man can teach you about herbs and the right ways to perform a ceremony where everything must be in its proper place, where every move, every word has its own, special meaning. These things you can learn—like spelling, like training a horse. But by themselves these things mean nothing. Without the vision and the power this learning will do no good. It would not make me a medicine man.

11   What if I failed, if I had no vision? Or if I dreamed of the Thunder

Beings, or lightning struck the hill? That would make me at once into a *heyoka,* a contrarywise, an upside-down man, a clown. "You'll know it, if you get the power," my Uncle Chest had told me. "If you are not given it, you won't lie about it, you won't pretend. That would kill you, or kill somebody close to you, somebody you love."

12 Night was coming on. I was still lightheaded and dizzy from my first sweat bath in which I had purified myself before going up the hill. I had never been in a sweat lodge before. I had sat in the little beehive-shaped hut made of bent willow branches and covered with blankets to keep the heat in. Old Chest and three other medicine men had been in the lodge with me. I had my back against the wall, edging as far away as I could from the red-hot stones glowing in the center. As Chest poured water over the rocks, hissing white steam enveloped me and filled my lungs. I thought the heat would kill me, burn the eyelids off my face! But right in the middle of all this swirling steam I heard Chest singing. So it couldn't be all that bad. I did not cry out "All my relatives!"—which would have made him open the flap of the sweat lodge to let in some cool air—and I was proud of this. I heard him praying for me: "Oh, holy rocks, we receive your white breath, the steam. It is the breath of life. Let this young boy inhale it. Make him strong."

13 The sweat bath had prepared me for my vision-seeking. Even now, an hour later, my skin still tingled. But it seemed to have made my brains empty. Maybe that was good, plenty of room for new insights.

14 Darkness had fallen upon the hill. I knew that *hanhepi-wi* had risen, the night sun, which is what we call the moon. Huddled in my narrow cave, I did not see it. Blackness was wrapped around me like a velvet cloth. It seemed to cut me off from the outside world, even from my own body. It made me listen to the voices within me. I thought of my forefathers who had crouched on this hill before me, because the medicine men in my family had chosen this spot for a place of meditation and vision-seeking ever since the day they had crossed the Missouri to hunt for buffalo in the White River country some two hundred years ago. I thought that I could sense their presence right through the earth I was leaning against. I could feel them entering my body, feel them stirring in my mind and heart.

15 Sounds came to me through the darkness: the cries of the wind, the whisper of the trees, the voices of nature, animal sounds, the hooting of an owl. Suddenly I felt an overwhelming presence. Down there with me in my cramped hole was a big bird. The pit was only as wide as myself, and I was a skinny boy, but that huge bird was flying around me as if he had the whole sky to himself. I could hear his cries, sometimes near and sometimes far, far away. I felt feathers or a wing touching my back and head. This feeling was so overwhelming that it was just too much for me. I trembled and my bones turned to ice. I grasped the rattle with the forty pieces of my grandmother's flesh. It also had many little stones in it, tiny fossils picked up from an ant heap. Ants collect them. Nobody knows why. These little stones are supposed to have a power in them. I shook the rattle and it made a soothing

sound, like rain falling on rock. It was talking to me, but it did not calm my fears. I took the sacred pipe in my other hand and began to sing and pray: "Tunkashila, grandfather spirit, help me." But this did not help. I don't know what got into me, but I was no longer myself. I started to cry. Crying, even my voice was different. I sounded like an older man, I couldn't even recognize this strange voice. I used long-ago words in my prayer, words no longer used nowadays. I tried to wipe away my tears, but they wouldn't stop. In the end I just pulled that quilt over me, rolled myself up in it. Still I felt the bird wings touching me.

16   Slowly I perceived that a voice was trying to tell me something. It was a bird cry, but I tell you, I began to understand some of it. That happens sometimes. I know a lady who had a butterfly sitting on her shoulder. That butterfly told her things. This made her become a great medicine woman.

17   I heard a human voice too, strange and high-pitched, a voice which could not come from an ordinary, living being. All at once I was way up there with the birds. The hill with the vision pit was way above everything. I could look down even on the stars, and the moon was close to my left side. It seemed as though the earth and the stars were moving below me. A voice said, "You are sacrificing yourself here to be a medicine man. In time you will be one. You will teach other medicine men. We are the fowl people, the winged ones, the eagles and the owls. We are a nation and you shall be our brother. You will never kill or harm any one of us. You are going to understand us whenever you come to seek a vision here on this hill. You will learn about herbs and roots, and you will heal people. You will ask them for nothing in return. A man's life is short. Make yours a worthy one."

18   I felt that these voices were good, and slowly my fear left me. I had lost all sense of time. I did not know whether it was day or night. I was asleep, yet wide awake. Then I saw a shape before me. It rose from the darkness and the swirling fog which penetrated my earth hole. I saw that this was my great-grandfather, Tahca Ushte, Lame Deer, old man chief of the Minneconjou. I could see the blood dripping from my great-grandfather's chest where a white soldier had shot him. I understood that my great-grandfather wished me to take his name. This made me glad beyond words.

19   We Sioux believe that there is something within us that controls us, something like a second person almost. We call it *nagi*, what other people might call soul, spirit, or essence. One can't see it, feel it, or taste it, but that time on the hill—and only that once—I knew it was there inside of me. Then I felt the power surge through me like a flood. I cannot describe it, but it filled all of me. Now I knew for sure that I would become a *wicasa wakan*, a medicine man. Again I wept, this time with happiness.

20   I didn't know how long I had been up there on that hill—one minute or a lifetime. I felt a hand on my shoulder gently shaking me. It was old man Chest, who had come for me. He told me that I had been in the vision pit four days and four nights and that it was time to come down. He would give me something to eat and water to drink and then I was to tell him every-

thing that had happened to me during my *hanblechia*. He would interpret my visions for me. He told me that the vision pit had changed me in a way that I would not be able to understand at that time. He told me also that I was no longer a boy, that I was a man now. I was Lame Deer.

DISCUSSION QUESTIONS

1. Lame Deer tells about several cultural symbols that are part of the tradition of the vision quest and that come from family and tribal history. One example is the star blanket from his grandmother. Find two other examples and explain their significance.
2. How would you describe the function of the vision quest in a young male Lakota's life? What risks are involved?
3. Seeking a vision and acquiring a new name marked the transition from adolescence to adulthood for Lame Deer and others in his society. What are important milestones for you in reaching maturity in your society? Do you and Lame Deer have any similarities? Do you also seek guidance and support from an older generation?

WRITING TOPICS

1. Remember an experience in your life when your family and friends gave you strong support. Write a letter to one of the people involved and explain your feelings about that event.
2. Lame Deer drew on two hundred years of family and tribal traditions. Select the most important parts of that legacy of people and objects, and summarize how each contributed to his vision quest.
3. The appearance of Lame Deer's vision in paragraphs 14–17 is the climax of his story. Assume you are a script writer for the filming of his vision. Write camera directions, dialogue, or interior monologue for the scene.
4. Lame Deer tells about special objects that have been in his family and tribal keeping for generations. Write about a special or sacred object that has been kept in your family for a long time. What makes it special? How long has it been in the family? Do you know its origin? Do you have a special object you wish to pass to your children?

ALL MY RELATIONS

Linda Hogan

This selection appears in *Dwellings: A Spiritual History of the Living World.* In this collection of essays, Hogan centers on two foci that permeate all her works. First, people, animals, and the land are connected. They are all "relations." Second, all living things are sacred. With nature as her teacher, Hogan learns lessons about the earth, our universal home, "We want to live as if there is no other place, as if we will always be here. We want to live with devotion to the world of waters and the universe of life." As an Indian woman, grandmother, and environmentalist, Hogan makes tender arguments on behalf of a fragile, intricate balance between humans and their world. We are responsible for taking care of other species who share our journeys, and women are uniquely qualified to fulfill this promise. As carriers of new life, purveyors of mythological and modern wisdom, and spiritual guardians for the future, women may illuminate a whole vision for life. For Hogan, taking part in a sweat lodge ritual is one way to mend any tear between herself and the universe: "I am within the healing of nature, held in earth's hand."

1   It is a sunny, clear day outside, almost hot, and a slight breeze comes through the room from the front door. We sit at the table and talk. As is usual in an Indian household, food preparation began as soon as we arrived, and now there is the snap of potatoes frying in the black skillet, the sweet smell of white bread overwhelming even the grease, and the welcome black coffee. A wringer washer stands against the wall of the kitchen, and the counter space is taken up with dishes, pans, and boxes of food.

2   I am asked if I still read books and I admit that I do. Reading is not "traditional" and education has long been suspect in communities that were broken, in part, by that system, but we laugh at my confession because a television set plays in the next room.

3   In the living room there are two single beds. People from reservations, travelers needing help, are frequent guests here. The man who will put

together the ceremony I have come to request sits on one, dozing. A girl takes him a plate of food. He eats. He is a man I have respected for many years, for his commitment to the people, for his intelligence, for his spiritual and political involvement in concerns vital to Indian people and nations. Next to him sits a girl eating potato chips, and from this room we hear the sounds of the freeway.

4   After eating and sitting, it is time for me to talk to him, to tell him why we have come here. I have brought him tobacco and he nods and listens as I tell him about the help we need.

5   I know this telling is the first part of the ceremony, my part in it. It is story, really, that finds its way into language, and story is at the very crux of healing, at the heart of every ceremony and ritual in the older America.

6   The ceremony itself includes not just our own prayers and stories of what brought us to it, but also includes the unspoken records of history, the mythic past, and all the other lives connected to ours, our families, nations, and all other creatures.

7   I am sent home to prepare. I tie fifty tobacco ties, green. This I do with Bull Durham tobacco, squares of cotton that are tied with twine and left strung together. These are called prayer ties. I spend the time preparing alone and in silence. Each tie has a prayer in it. I will also need wood for the fire, meat and bread for food.

8   On the day of the ceremony, we meet in the next town and leave my car in public parking. My daughters and I climb into the back seat. The man who will help us is drumming and singing in front of us. His wife drives and chats. He doesn't speak. He is moving between the worlds, beginning already to step over the boundaries of what we think, in daily and ordinary terms, is real and present. He is already feeling, hearing, knowing what else is there, that which is around us daily but too often unacknowledged, a larger life than our own. We pass billboards and little towns and gas stations. An eagle flies overhead. It is "a good sign," we all agree. We stop to watch it.

9   We stop again, later, at a convenience store to fill the gas tank and to buy soda. The leader still drums and is silent. He is going into the drum, going into the center, even as we drive west on the highway, even with our conversations about other people, family, work.

10   It is a hot balmy day, and by the time we reach the site where the ceremony is to take place, we are slow and sleepy with the brightness and warmth of the sun. Others are already there. The children are cooling off in the creek. A woman stirs the fire that lives inside a circle of black rocks, pots beside her, a jar of oil, a kettle, a can of coffee. The leaves of the trees are thick and green.

11   In the background, the sweat lodge structure stands. Birds are on it. It is still skeletal. A woman and man are beginning to place old rugs and blankets over the bent cottonwood frame. A great fire is already burning, and the lava stones that will be the source of heat for the sweat are being fired in it.

12   A few people sit outside on lawn chairs and cast-off couches that have the stuffing coming out. We sip coffee and talk about the food, about recent

events. A man tells us that a friend gave him money for a new car. The creek sounds restful. Another man falls asleep. My young daughter splashes in the water. Heat waves rise up behind us from the fire that is preparing the stones. My tobacco ties are placed inside, on the framework of the lodge.

13   By late afternoon we are ready, one at a time, to enter the enclosure. The hot lava stones are placed inside. They remind us of earth's red and fiery core, and of the spark inside all life. After the flap, which serves as a door, is closed, water is poured over the stones and the hot steam rises around us. In a sweat lodge ceremony, the entire world is brought inside the enclosure. The soft odor of smoking cedar accompanies this arrival. It is all called in. The animals come from the warm and sunny distances. Water from dark lakes is there. Wind. Young, lithe willow branches bent overhead remember their lives rooted in ground, the sun their leaves took in. They remember that minerals and water rose up their trunks, and birds nested in their leaves, and that planets turned above their brief, slender lives. The thunderclouds travel in from far regions of earth. Wind arrives from the four directions. It has moved through caves and breathed through our bodies. It is the same air elk have inhaled, air that passed through the lungs of a grizzly bear. The sky is there, with all the stars whose lights we see long after the stars themselves have gone back to nothing. It is a place grown intense and holy. It is a place of immense community and of humbled solitude; we sit together in our aloneness and speak, one at a time, our deepest language of need, hope, loss, and survival. We remember that all things are connected.

14   Remembering this is the purpose of the ceremony. It is part of a healing and restoration. It is the mending of a broken connection between us and the rest. The participants in a ceremony say the words "All my relations" before and after we pray; those words create a relationship with other people, with animals, with the land. To have health it is necessary to keep all these relations in mind. The intention of a ceremony is to put a person back together by restructuring the human mind. This reorganization is accomplished by a kind of inner map, a geography of the human spirit and the rest of the world. We make whole our broken-off pieces of self and world. Within ourselves, we bring together the fragments of our lives in a sacred act of renewal, and we reestablish our connections with others. The ceremony is a point of return. It takes us toward the place of balance, our place in the community of all things. It is an event that sets us back upright. But it is not a finished thing. The real ceremony begins where the formal one ends, when we take up a new way, our minds and hearts filled with the vision of earth that holds us within it, in compassionate relationship to and with our world.

15   We speak. We sing. We swallow water and breathe smoke. By the end of the ceremony, it is as if skin contains land and birds. The places within us have become filled. As inside the enclosure of the lodge, the animals and ancestors move into the human body, into skin and blood. The land merges with us. The stones come to dwell inside the person. Gold rolling hills take up residence, their tall grasses blowing. The red light of canyons is there.

The black skies of night that wheel above our heads come to live inside the skull. We who easily grow apart from the world are returned to the great store of life all around us, and there is the deepest sense of being at home here in this intimate kinship. There is no real aloneness. There is solitude and the nurturing silence that is relationship with ourselves, but even then we are part of something larger.

16   After a sweat lodge ceremony, the enclosure is abandoned. Quieter now, we prepare to drive home. We pack up the kettles, the coffeepot. The prayer ties are placed in nearby trees. Some of the other people prepare to go to work, go home, or cook a dinner. We drive. Everything returns to ordinary use. A spider weaves a web from one of the cottonwood poles to another. Crows sit inside the framework. It's evening. The crickets are singing. All my relations.

DISCUSSION QUESTIONS

1. Hogan ends her essay with "all my relations." Using information from paragraphs 13, 14, and 15, explain the meaning of what she calls "this intimate kinship."
2. Describe the author's tone. She achieves this tone with carefully selected images. Review the imagery of the setting in paragraphs 1, 10, 11, and 12 and identify the images that contribute to the tone.

WRITING TOPICS

1. Hogan describes the sweat lodge experience as "a sacred act of renewal." In paragraph 4, she writes, "I tell him about the help we need." Using her essay as a model, write an essay about a time when you needed help and received renewal, spiritual or otherwise, from friends and/or relatives. Give detailed description of the setting to establish the tone as background for your feelings and what happened. Weave ordinary observations with your spiritual impressions as Hogan does.
2. Hogan uses the phrase "immense community" to include plants, animals, and the rest of the natural world with the human community. Spend time in a place that gives you this type of connection and jot down images in freewriting. Then, revise your first impressions into a personal narrative or a free verse poem.

OLD MAN, THE SWEAT LODGE

Phil George

As a young man, Phil George honors Nez Perce elders and the ritual sweat bath. He addresses the sweat lodge as an elder that cleanses and renews the poet's spirit, mind, and body. The sweat lodge, a common structure in Indian communities, is typically constructed of young saplings bent to shape a halfdome and covered with skins, canvas, or blankets. Dirt-covered stacked wood may also enclose heat for a sweat bath. Water is poured over hot stones to create steam.

The sweat lodge itself represents the universe and connects the participants to the past, the earth, and the spiritual world. It is a place for teaching, praying, singing, purifying, and communing with others. As participants sing, pray, and meditate, they believe that the ritual sweat bath purges their impurities and brings both spiritual and physical health. Phil George's "Old Man, the Sweat Lodge" expresses the frame-of-mind appropriate for taking part in this ancient purification ceremony.

"This small lodge is now alive,
The womb of our mother, Earth.
The blackness in which we sit,
The ignorance of our impure minds,
5 These burning stones are
The coming of a new life."
Near my heart I place his words.

Naked, like an infant at birth, I crouch,
Cuddled upon fresh straw and boughs.
10 Confessing, I recall all evil deeds.
For each sin I sprinkle water on fire-hot stones;
Their hissing is a special song and I know

The place from which Earth's seeds grow is alive.
Old Man, the Sweat Lodge heals the sick;
15 Brings good fortune to one deserving.
Sacred steam rises—vapor fills my very being—
My pores slime out their dross.
After chanting prayers to the Great Spirit,
I lift a blanket to the East;
20 Through this door dawns wisdom.

Cleansed, I dive into icy waters.
Pure, I rinse away unworthy yesterday.
"My son, walk straight in this new life.
Youth I help to retain in you.
25 Return soon. Visit an old one.
Now, think clean, feel clean, be happy."
I thank you, Old Man, the Sweat Lodge.

Discussion Questions

1. The poem is divided into four stanzas that trace the speaker's physical and spiritual changes that occur during the sweat. How would you describe the difference in the speaker when he enters and when he leaves the lodge? Imagine each stanza as one step in this four-part process. Identify the most significant action or idea in each stanza.
2. Through personification, the young poet presents the sweat lodge as an old man. Contrast four images of youth and age.

Writing Topics

1. In a brief essay, cite lines or images that inform the reader that this is a sacred event.
2. Imagine Phil George is your friend and that he has invited you to be part of a sweat ritual. Write a letter to him explaining why you will or will not accept his invitation.

THE ORIGIN OF ETERNAL DEATH
WISHRAM MYTH

What if humans and animals could escape death and live forever? Once, Eagle and Coyote tested this intriguing idea because their wives and children had died. In their mythic world, death and life were still fluid. Humans and animals exchanged shapes, animals talked, and, most important, animals shared human qualities. According to Wishram tribal storytellers from the Northwest Coast, wily Coyote and wise Eagle tricked death temporarily. But curious Coyote recklessly disobeyed Eagle's warning that he should not look upon their relatives until they had safely completed their journey from death's dark realm back to the light of the living. Filled with human frailty and desire, Coyote made a fatal mistake.

1 Coyote had a wife and two children, and so had Eagle. Both families lived together. Eagle's wife and children died, and a few days later Coyote experienced the same misfortune. As the latter wept, his companion said: "Do not mourn: that will not bring your wife back. Make ready your moccasins, and we will go somewhere." So the two prepared for a long journey, and set out westward.

2 After four days they were close to the ocean; on one side of a body of water they saw houses. Coyote called across, "Come with a boat!" "Never mind; stop calling," bade Eagle. He produced an elderberry stalk, made a flute, put the end into the water, and whistled. Soon they saw two persons come out of a house, walk to the water's edge, and enter a canoe. Said Eagle, "Do not look at those people when they land." The boat drew near, but a few yards from the shore it stopped, and Eagle told his friend to close his eyes. He then took Coyote by the arm and leaped to the boat. The two persons paddled back, and when they stopped a short distance from the other side Eagle again cautioned Coyote to close his eyes, and then leaped ashore with him.

3 They went to the village, where there were many houses, but no people

were in sight. Everything was still as death. There was a very large underground house, into which they went. In it was found an old woman sitting with her face to the wall, and lying on the floor on the other side of the room was the moon. They sat down near the wall.

4   "Coyote," whispered Eagle, "watch that woman and see what she does when the sun goes down!" Just before the sun set they heard a voice outside calling: "Get up! Hurry! The sun is going down, and it will soon be night. Hurry, hurry!" Coyote and Eagle still sat in a corner of the chamber watching the old woman. People began to enter, many hundreds of them, men, women, and children. Coyote, as he watched, saw Eagle's wife and two daughters among them, and soon afterward his own family. When the room was filled, Nikshiámchásht, the old woman, cried, "Are all in?" Then she turned about, and from a squatting posture she jumped forward, then again and again, five times in all, until she alighted in a small pit beside the moon. This she raised and swallowed, and at once it was pitch dark. The people wandered about, hither and thither, crowding and jostling, unable to see. About daylight a voice from outside cried, "Nikshiámchásht, all get through!" The old woman then disgorged the moon, and laid it back in its place on the floor; all the people filed out, and the woman, Eagle, and Coyote were once more alone.

5   "Now, Coyote," said Eagle, "could you do that?" "Yes, I can do that," he said. They went out, and Coyote at Eagle's direction made a box of boards, as large as he could carry, and put into it leaves from every kind of tree and blades from every kind of grass. "Well," said Eagle, "if you are sure you remember just how she did this, let us go in and kill her." So they entered the house and killed her, and buried the body. Her dress they took off and put on Coyote, so that he looked just like her, and he sat down in her place. Eagle then told him to practice what he had seen, by turning around and jumping as the old woman had done. So Coyote turned about and jumped five times, but the last leap was a little short, yet he managed to slide into the hole. He put the moon into his mouth, but, try as he would, a thin edge still showed, and he covered it with his hands. Then he laid it back in its place and resumed his seat by the wall, waiting for sunset and the voice of the chief outside.

6   The day passed, the voice called, and the people entered. Coyote turned about and began to jump. Some thought there was something strange about the manner of jumping, but others said it was really the old woman. When he came to the last jump and slipped into the pit, many cried out that this was not the old woman, but Coyote quickly lifted the moon and put it into his mouth, covering the edge with his hands. When it was completely dark, Eagle placed the box in the doorway. Throughout the long night Coyote retained the moon in his mouth, until he was almost choking, but at last the voice of the chief was heard from the outside, and the dead began to file out. Every one walked into the box, and Eagle quickly threw the cover over and tied it. The sound was like that of a great swarm of flies. "Now, my brother,

we are through," said Eagle. Coyote removed the dress and laid it down beside the moon, and Eagle threw the moon into the sky, where it remained. The two entered the canoe with the box, and paddled toward the east.

7   When they landed, Eagle carried the box. Near the end of the third night Coyote heard somebody talking; there seemed to be many voices. He awakened his companion, and said, "There are many people coming." "Do not worry," said Eagle; "it is all right." The following night Coyote heard the talking again, and, looking about, he discovered that the voices came from the box which Eagle had been carrying. He placed his ear against it, and after a while distinguished the voice of his wife. He smiled, and broke into laughter, but he said nothing to Eagle. At the end of the fifth night and the beginning of their last day of traveling, he said to his friend, "I will carry the box now; you have carried it a long way." "No," replied Eagle, "I will take it; I am strong." "Let me carry it," insisted the other; "suppose we come to where people live, and they should see the chief carrying the load. How would that look?" Still Eagle retained his hold on the box, but as they went along Coyote kept begging, and about noon, wearying of the subject, Eagle gave him the box. So Coyote had the load, and every time he heard the voice of his wife he would laugh. After a while he contrived to fall behind, and when Eagle was out of sight around a hill he began to open the box, in order to release his wife. But no sooner was the cover lifted than it was thrown back violently, and the dead people rushed out into the air with such force that Coyote was thrown to the ground. They quickly disappeared in the west. Eagle saw the cloud of dead people rising in the air, and came hurrying back. He found one man left there, a cripple who had been unable to rise; he threw him into the air, and the dead man floated away swiftly.

8   "You see what you have done, with your curiosity and haste!" said Eagle. "If we had brought these dead all the way back, people would not die forever, but only for a season, like these plants, whose leaves we have brought. Hereafter trees and grasses will die only in the winter, but in the spring they will be green again. So it would have been with the people." "Let us go back and catch them again," proposed Coyote; but Eagle objected: "They will not go to the same place, and we would not know how to find them; they will be where the moon is, up in the sky."

▣

DISCUSSION QUESTIONS

1. In this story, Eagle and Coyote represent two opposing sides of human nature. List five adjectives that describe the opposing characteristics.
2. Despite the serious subject, the story has humorous moments, all arising from Coyote's actions. Retell one incident that has a humorous tone.

3. The idea of a journey often structures a literary work. How does this idea function in this story?

WRITING TOPICS

1. Write a story with animal characters that illustrate a human experience. First, consider the traits associated with one or two animals. Next, create a plot that shows the traits in action. Finally, structure the plot so that insight comes at the end of the story.
2. Research the Greek myth of Demeter and Persephone and, in a brief essay, compare it to "The Origin of Eternal Death."

THE FAWN, THE WOLVES, AND THE TERRAPIN CREEK STORY

Karl Kroeber

This tale comes from the Creek primeval time when metaphorical animals talked and behaved rather like human beings. Reversing the predator-prey relationship, a fawn slays a wolf by using fire, that natural force that humans harnessed early in their evolution. Like arrogant humans, the fawn cannot resist making a necklace of the wolf's bones and wearing it. The fawn's bragging, rhyming song leads to other members of the wolf's pack recognizing its bones and chasing the foolish fawn. The swift fawn eluded the wolf pack, even though two men and the terrapin (turtle) refused to hide it, until it traps itself in a tree. Then archer terrapin kills the fawn with an arrow, and the wolves devour it. The greedy terrapin tries to dupe the grateful wolves into giving him a prime piece of the tender venison, but he carries home only blood-stained leaves.

1   A beautiful Fawn met a Wolf one day who asked how he came to have such pretty spots over his body. "I got under a sieve and they put fire over it, and that made the pretty spots."

2   "Will you show me how I can do that?" asked the Wolf. The Fawn consented. Then the Wolf obtained a large sieve and lay down under it, and the Fawn built a fire and burned him to death. After the flesh had decayed, the Fawn took the bones of the back and made a necklace of them. One day the Fawn met a pack of Wolves, who said to him, "Where did you get that necklace?" But he refused to tell. "What is the song we hear you singing as you gallop over the prairie?" asked the Wolves. "If you will stand here till I get to the top of yonder hill I will sing it for you."

Ya-ha ya-ha	Wolf, wolf
Ef-oo-ne-tul	bones only
Chesarsook, chesarsook	rattle, rattle
Chesarsook	rattle
Kah-ke-tul	The ravens only
Methl-methl	fluttered, fluttered
Soolee-tul	The buzzard only
Methl-methl	fluttered, fluttered
Charnur-tul	The flies only
Sum-sum	buzzed, buzzed
Choon-tah-tul	The worms only
Witter-took	wiggled
Witter-took	wiggled
Witter-took.	wiggled.

3 When the Wolves heard this song they howled in anger and said: "We missed our mate. He is dead and those are his bones. Let us kill his murderer."

4 They started for the Fawn, who, seeing them, sped away for life, the bones rattling as he ran. He came to a basket maker and begged him to place him under a basket, but he refused. Then the Fawn came to a man who was getting bark to cover his house. "Oh, hide me from the Wolves," he begged, but the man would not. He ran on and came to a Terrapin who was making a spoon. "Tell me where to hide from the Wolves," said the Fawn. "No," replied the Terrapin. "I must not take sides." However, the Fawn saw a stream just ahead, and on reaching it he jumped over it and lodged in the fork of a tree and could not extricate himself.

5 The Wolves passed the man who was making baskets and the man who was getting bark to cover his house and came to the Terrapin, who told them the way Fawn had gone.

6 When the Wolves reached the stream, they could trace the Fawn no farther. They looked in the water, and there they saw him. They tried to go into the water to catch the Fawn but failed. In sorrow they began to howl. As they raised their heads in howling, they saw the Fawn in the tree. One Wolf said, "I know a man who can shoot him out"; so he sent for the man. Then he went to the Terrapin and brought him, and the Terrapin said he could kill him. He began to shoot arrows at the Fawn. He shot every arrow away and missed the Fawn. Afterwards, while walking around the tree, Terrapin found one of his old arrows sticking in the ground near an old log. "This was one of my best arrows," said he. So he shot at the Fawn and with this old arrow killed him.

7 Then the Wolves took the body and divided it into pieces. "We must pay the man for shooting him," one said, so they offered the Terrapin a piece of

one leg. But he had some complaint in his leg, and the medicine men had told him not to eat the leg of any animal. He whined out, "I cannot eat leg; it will make my leg hurt, and I shall die."

8   When they offered him a shoulder, he whined out, "I cannot eat shoulder; it will pain my shoulder, and I shall die."

9   "He does not want any," they said, and went away carrying all of the Fawn.

10   After they had gone, the Terrapin looked around and saw that there was blood on the leaves; so he gathered the bloody leaves into a big bundle, saying, "I'll carry them home." He reached his house, threw down the bundle, and said to his wife, "There, cook it for the children." Then she unrolled the bundle but saw nothing. "Where is it?" she asked. "Way inside," replied he; so she separated the leaves, but finding nothing but blood, she threw it in his face. He called to the children to bring him some water; but as they were slow, he crawled around with his eyes closed and found the lye and washed his face in that. Some of this got in his eyes and made them red, and ever since terrapins have had red eyes.

DISCUSSION QUESTIONS

1. The onomatopoeia in the wolves' song creates a humorous effect. Read the Creek version of the poem aloud (pronounce the words phonetically) and emphasize the lighthearted tone. What rhyming sounds do you hear?
2. The tale appears to be only a string of accidental events. Actually, there is a clever structure of three sequential episodes that progressively hit the theme of "the fooling fool fooled." Explain how each animal's weakness makes it behave like a fool.

WRITING TOPICS

1. In addition to the theme of "the fooling fool fooled," this tale also provides an explanation for two things in nature—the spots on a fawn and the terrapin's red eyes. With a partner, devise a tale that explains something else in nature and record the tale on tape or present it orally to the class.
2. In a brief essay, describe the human qualities that the animals in this tale possess.

THE VAMPIRE SKELETON
ONONDAGA STORY

John Bierhorst

This story happened a long time ago. Heading to the Adirondack Mountains to hunt, a couple and an old man take advantage of an empty cabin to sleep in comfort on bedsteads inside it. As their shag-back hickory fire burns out, the couple awaken to the sounds of gnawing and bones rattling. Refueling the fire, the couple discover a skeleton consuming the body of the old man. Building the fire to repel the skeleton, the woman and then the man slip out of the cabin. They run toward the Onondaga village where people are feasting. Warriors respond to the couple's cries of distress, so the skeleton flees.

The narrator of this story took for granted his audience understood Iroquois culture. The Onondaga Reservation is located south of Syracuse, New York, between two of the Finger Lakes. The Adirondack Mountains lie far to the east, and were during historic times frequented by enemies of the Six Nations. Logically, therefore, when the woman character perceived herself in danger, she fled toward her own country.

The storyteller's final two lines underscore a fact of Iroquois culture. Iroquois society recognizes descent matrilineally—through the mother. As in most matrilineal societies, a boy's father does not teach him to hunt or other skills. The mother's brother instructs the young man. Of course, the boy mentioned in passing in this tale parts from his parents to accompany his maternal uncle. The narrator concisely combines ancient and historic elements in relating that the venturesome couple fainted for four hours. Four is a sacred or significant number for nearly all Native American peoples.

◻

1   In old times the Onondagas lived on a much larger reservation than now—a great land—but they made hunting parties to the Adirondacks. A party once went off in which there were an old man, his daughter and her

husband, and their little boy. They went one day and camped, and another day and camped, and then separated. The old man, his daughter, and her husband turned one way, but the little boy accidentally went the other way with his uncle.

2   The three kept on, and late in the day found an empty cabin in a clearing. There was an Indian bedstead on each side within, and as no one seemed to live there, they resolved to stay for the night. They gathered plenty of fuel, stripping long pieces from the shagbark hickory, built a fine fire, spread their deerskins on the bedsteads, and then went to sleep—the old man on one side, and the man and his wife on the other.

3   When the fire became low and it grew dark in the cabin, the young people were awakened by a sound like a dog gnawing a bone. They stirred about, and the noise ceased, but was followed by something like rattling bones overhead. They got up and put on more fuel, and were going back to bed when they saw something like water flowing from the other couch. It was blood, and the old man was dead. His clothes were torn open and his ribs broken and gnawed. They covered him up and lay down again. The same thing happened the second time, and this time they saw it was a terrible skeleton, feeding on the dead man. They were frightened and in whispers devised a plan of escape. They made a great fire, and the wife said, "Husband, I must go to the spring and get some water; I am so thirsty." She went out quietly, but a little way off ran with all her might toward her own country.

4   When her husband thought she had a good start, he made a very big fire, to last a great while, and then he said, "What has become of my wife? I am afraid she is drowned in the spring. I must go and see." So he went out, and a little way off he, too, ran with all his might, and when he overtook his wife he caught her by the arm and they both ran on together. By and by, the fire went down, the skeleton came again, and when he found both were gone he started to give chase. Soon they heard him howling terribly behind them, and they ran faster.

5   It happened that night that the Onondagas were holding a feast, and it now drew near morning. The man and woman heard the drum sounding far off, tum-tum, tum-tum, and they ran harder, and shouted, but the skeleton did the same. Then they heard the drum again, TUM-TUM, tum-tum, and it was nearer, and they shouted again. Their friends heard the distress cry, and came to their rescue with all their arms. The skeleton fled. The fugitives fell down fainting, and did not regain their senses for four hours; then they told their story.

6   A council was held, and the warriors started for the dreadful spot. They found the hut and a few traces of the old man. In the loft were some scattered articles, and a bark coffin. In this was the skeleton of a man left unburied by his friends. They determined to destroy everything, and fuel was gathered on all sides and fire applied. The warriors stood around with bent bows and raised hatchets. The fire grew hot, the cabin fell in, and out

of the flames rushed a fox with red and fiery eyes; it dashed through the ranks and disappeared in the forest. The dreadful skeleton was seen no more.

7 "But what had the little boy to do with all this?"

8 "Oh, that is to show it was well he went the other way."

DISCUSSION QUESTIONS

1. What is your reaction to the last line?
2. If this story were dramatized for television, what kind of rating do you think it would get? Why?
3. What do you think is the purpose of this story?

WRITING TOPIC

1. Recall a scary story from your childhood. Jot down the outline, and then tell it to your classmates in a manner that captures the macabre elements in chilling details.
2. In a brief essay, explore in what ways the setting of this story reflects the life of the Onondagas.

RAVEN STEALS THE LIGHT
HAIDA MYTH

Bill Reid and Robert Bringhurst

Raven, the trickster and culture hero, was and is an extremely powerful being for the Indians living on the Northwest Coast. Listening to mythic storytellers for centuries, audiences imagined Raven shaping the world, creating human beings, and bringing fire. As trickster, Raven also lies, steals, and causes chaos.

Haida artist Bill Reid retells in a jocular, contemporary style, his tribe's myth about Raven stealing light for the world when it was "blacker than a thousand stormy winter midnights." Born in 1920 in Canada, Reid is a sculptor, whose work is included in museums and private collections around the world. Also a writer, he is admired for his poetry and prose. This story appears in *The Raven Steals the Light* (1984), a Reid collaboration with Robert Bringhurst, one of Canada's finest poets.

Raven emerges from the homeland of the Haida, who live off the coast of British Columbia and in modern cities. The dense forest provides a rich natural resource, and the Haida were among the most skilled woodworkers of the region. They built large houses of red cedar with beautifully carved totem poles towering in front, facing the sea. Mild climate and great rainfall support the growth of thick forests of fir, spruce, and cedar trees. Given this, it is not surprising that the old man hides his ball of light within a wooden box.

The story itself is like opening a series of boxes. Raven transforms himself into a single hemlock needle, slowly gains access to the house, and finally opens the box within a box within a box. Ravenchild endears himself to the selfish father who hoards light and has never even seen his own daughter. Raven, like the Haida, longs for sunlight, and he must steal the luminous orb.

1   Before there was anything, before the great flood had covered the earth and receded, before the animals walked the earth or the trees covered the land or the birds flew between the trees, even before the fish and the whales and seals swam in the sea, an old man lived in a house on the bank of a river with his only child, a daughter. Whether she was as beautiful as hemlock fronds against the spring sky at sunrise or as ugly as a sea slug doesn't really matter very much to this story, which takes place mainly in the dark.

2   Because at that time the whole world was dark. Inky, pitchy, all-consuming dark, blacker than a thousand stormy winter midnights, blacker than anything anywhere has been since.

3   The reason for all this blackness has to do with the old man in the house by the river, who had a box which contained a box which contained a box which contained an infinite number of boxes each nestled in a box slightly larger than itself until finally there was a box so small all it could contain was all the light in the universe.

4   The Raven, who of course existed at that time, because he had always existed and always would, was somewhat less than satisfied with this state of affairs, since it led to an awful lot of blundering around and bumping into things. It slowed him down a good deal in his pursuit of food and other fleshly pleasures, and in his constant effort to interfere and to change things.

5   Eventually, his bumbling around in the dark took him close to the home of the old man. He first heard a little singsong voice muttering away. When he followed the voice, he soon came to the wall of the house, and there, placing his ear against the planking, he could just make out the words, "I have a box and inside the box is another box and inside it are many more boxes, and in the smallest box of all is all the light in the world, and it is all mine and I'll never give any of it to anyone, not even to my daughter, because, who knows, she may be as homely as a sea slug, and neither she nor I would like to know that."

6   It took only an instant for the Raven to decide to steal the light for himself, but it took a lot longer for him to invent a way to do so.

7   First he had to find a door into the house. But no matter how many times he circled it or how carefully he felt the planking, it remained a smooth, unbroken barrier. Sometimes he heard either the old man or his daughter leave the house to get water or for some other reason, but they always departed from the side of the house opposite to him, and when he ran around to the other side the wall seemed as unbroken as ever.

8   Finally, the Raven retired a little way upstream and thought and thought about how he could enter the house. As he did so, he began to think more and more of the young girl who lived there, and thinking of her began to stir more than just the Raven's imagination.

9   "It's probable that she's as homely as a sea slug," he said to himself, "but on the other hand, she may be as beautiful as the fronds of the hemlock would be against a bright spring sunrise, if only there were light enough to make one." And in that idle speculation, he found the solution to his problem.

10   He waited until the young woman, whose footsteps he could distinguish by now from those of her father, came to the river to gather water. Then he changed himself into a single hemlock needle, dropped himself into the river and floated down just in time to be caught in the basket which the girl was dipping in the river.

11   Even in his much diminished form, the Raven was able to make at least a very small magic—enough to make the girl so thirsty she took a deep drink from the basket, and in doing so, swallowed the needle.

12   The Raven slithered down deep into her warm insides and found a soft, comfortable spot, where he transformed himself once more, this time into a very small human being, and went to sleep for long while. And as he slept he grew.

13   The young girl didn't have any idea what was happening to her, and of course she didn't tell her father, who noticed nothing unusual because it was so dark—until suddenly he became very aware indeed of a new presence in the house, as the Raven at last emerged triumphantly in the shape of a human boychild.

14   He was—or would have been, if anyone could have seen him—a strange-looking boy, with a long, beaklike nose and a few feathers here and there. In addition, he had the shining eyes of the Raven, which would have given his face a bright, inquisitive appearance—if anyone could have seen these features then.

15   And he was noisy. He had a cry that contained all the noises of a spoiled child and an angry raven—yet he could sometimes speak as softly as the wind in the hemlock boughs, with an echo of that beautiful other sound, like an organic bell, which is also part of every raven's speech.

16   At times like that his grandfather grew to love this strange new member of his household and spent many hours playing with him, making him toys and inventing games for him.

17   As he gained more and more of the affection and confidence of the old man, the Raven felt more intently around the house, trying to find where the light was hidden. After much exploration, he was convinced it was kept in the big box which stood in the corner of the house. One day he cautiously lifted the lid, but of course could see nothing, and all he could feel was another box. His grandfather, however, heard his precious treasure chest being disturbed, and he dealt very harshly with the would-be thief, threatening dire punishment if the Ravenchild ever touched the box again.

18   This triggered a tidal wave of noisy protests, followed by tender importuning, in which the Raven never mentioned the light, but only pleaded for the largest box. That box, said the Ravenchild, was the one thing he needed to make him completely happy.

19   As most if not all grandfathers have done since the beginning, the old man finally yielded and gave his grandchild the outermost box. This contented the boy for a short time—but as most if not all grandchildren have done since the beginning, the Raven soon demanded the next box.

20   It took many days and much cajoling, carefully balanced with well-planned tantrums, but one by one the boxes were removed. When only a few were left, a strange radiance, never before seen, began to infuse the darkness of the house, disclosing vague shapes and their shadows, still too dim to have definite form. The Ravenchild then begged in his most pitiful voice to be allowed to hold the light for just a moment.

21   His request was instantly refused, but of course in time his grandfather yielded. The old man lifted the light, in the form of a beautiful, incandescent ball, from the final box and tossed it to his grandson.

22   He had only a glimpse of the child on whom he had lavished such love and affection, for even as the light was traveling toward him, the child changed from his human form to a huge, shining black shadow, wings spread and beak open, waiting. The Raven snapped up the light in his jaws, thrust his great wings downward and shot through the smokehole of the house into the huge darkness of the world.

23   That world was at once transformed. Mountains and valleys were starkly silhouetted, the river sparkled with broken reflections, and everywhere life began to stir. And from far away, another great winged shape launched itself into the air, as light struck the eyes of the Eagle for the first time and showed him his target.

24   The Raven flew on, rejoicing in his wonderful new possession, admiring the effect it had on the world below, revelling in the experience of being able to see where he was going, instead of flying blind and hoping for the best. He was having such a good time that he never saw the Eagle until the Eagle was almost upon him. In a panic he swerved to escape the savage outstretched claws, and in doing so he dropped a good half of the light he was carrying. It fell to the rocky ground below and there broke into pieces—one large piece and too many small ones to count. They bounced back into the sky and remain there even today as the moon and the stars that glorify the night.

25   The Eagle pursued the Raven beyond the rim of the world, and there, exhausted by the long chase, the Raven finally let go of his last piece of light. Out beyond the rim of the world, it floated gently on the clouds and started up over the mountains lying to the east.

26   Its first rays caught the smokehole of the house by the river, where the old man sat weeping bitterly over the loss of his precious light and the treachery of his grandchild. But as the light reached in, he looked up and for the first time saw his daughter, who had been quietly sitting during all this time, completely bewildered by the rush of events.

27   The old man saw that she was as beautiful as the fronds of a hemlock against a spring sky at sunrise, and he began to feel a little better.

Discussion Questions

1. The setting, characters, and plot of this story depend on the contrast between light and darkness. Locate five references to light and five to dark and relate each reference to a character, the setting, and/or the plot action.
2. How is the plot of this story like "a box within a box within a box"?
3. The authors adopt the voice of a mythic storyteller who uses parallelism and repetition for emphasis. Which example of these literary devices do you consider the best written? Explain the reasons for your choice.

Writing Topics

1. Use this thesis sentence to develop a two-paragraph character analysis: "In 'Raven Steals the Light,' Raven is a trickster and a transformer."
2. Consider how Raven might have told this story. Create a mythic voice for him and retell the action beginning with paragraph 13 and ending with paragraph 22.

NAANABOZHO AND THE GAMBLER

Gerald Vizenor

Gerald Vizenor, the author of more than twenty-five books and numerous articles, is one of the most prolific and versatile Native American writers. Born in 1934, to a Euro-American mother and a father of French and Chippewa ancestry, Vizenor grew up in Minneapolis near his father's relatives living on the White Earth Reservation in Minnesota. There his grandmother told him the adventures of Naanaboozho. Given his genetic heritage and his comic wit, it is not surprising that mixed-bloods and tricksters dominate Vizenor's fiction. Fascinated by the place of the mixed bloods, or "crossbloods" to use his terminology, in modern America, Vizenor denies that they are inevitably victims and claims they can be victors. Vizenor is the first American Indian author to celebrate and make a hero of the half-breed.

Critic Louis Owens notes that the central and unifying figure in all Vizenor's fiction is the trickster: "the mixedblood and the trickster become metaphors that seek to balance contradictions and shatter static certainties." Vizenor's tribal trickster figures are compassionate rebels and comic liberators. They disrupt the ambitions of people, contradict, unsettle, and unglue the creeds. "The characters I admire in my own imagination and the characters I would like to make myself be break out of things," Vizenor writes. "They break out of all restrictions. They even break out of their blood. They break out of the mixture in their blood. They break out of invented cultures and repressions. I think it's a spiritual quest in a way."

Vizenor received the American Book Award and the Fiction Collective Award for his novel *Griever: An American Monkey King in China* (1987). Other major works include *The Trickster of Liberty: Tribal Heirs to a Wild Baronage* (1988); *The Heirs of Columbus* (1992); and *Dead Voices: Natural Agonies in the New World* (1992); and his latest *Hotline Healers: An Almost Browne Novel* (1997). "Naanaboozho and the Gambler" appears in *The People Named the Chippewa: Narrative Histories* (1984).

Odinigun, an elder from the White Earth Reservation, told about the woodland trickster and the creation of the first earth. The people on the first earth were not wise, "they had no clothing . . . they sat around and did nothing. Then the spirit of the creator sent a man to teach them. . . . The first thing he taught them was how to make a fire by means of a bow and stick and a bit of decayed wood. . . . Then he taught them how to cook meat by the fire. They had no axes, but he took a pole and burned it in two over the fire. He taught them to boil meat in fresh birch bark. It was a long time before they had things as he wanted them, but after a while they were made comfortable by his help. They had no minds or ideas of their own. . . ."

This was the time before the appearance of Naanabozho, the woodland trickster, on the first earth. The spirit teacher told the first people on the earth that they "must fast and find out things by dreams and that if they paid attention to these dreams they would learn how to heal the sick. The people listened and fasted and found in dreams how to teach their children and do everything. The young men were taught that they must regulate their lives by dreams, they must live normal lives, be industrious, and be moderate in the use of tobacco when it should be given to them. They were especially taught that their minds would not be clear if they ate and drank too much. . . ." The spirit teacher taught them how to use tobacco and corn.

Naanabozho, the compassionate woodland trickster, wanders in mythic time and transformational space between tribal experiences and dreams. The trickster is related to plants and animals and trees; he is a teacher and healer in various personalities who, as numerous stories reveal, explains the values of healing plants, wild rice, maple sugar, basswood, and birch bark to woodland tribal people. More than a magnanimous teacher and transformer, the trickster is capable of violence, deceptions, and cruelties; the realities of human imperfections. The woodland trickster is an existential shaman in the comic mode, not an isolated and sentimental tragic hero in conflict with nature.

The trickster is comic in the sense that he does not reclaim idealistic ethics, but survives as a part of the natural world; he represents a spiritual balance in a comic drama rather than the romantic elimination of human contradictions and evil.

Naanabozho lived in the woodland with Nookomis, which, in the oral tradition, means *grandmother*. The various mythic genealogies on the trickster reveal that he had a twin brother and that his mother either died or disappeared when the peripatetic comic figure was born. When the trickster learned from his grandmother that his mother was taken from the woodland by a powerful wind spirit, he set out to find her somewhere in a strange and distant place on the earth.

Nookomis warned her trickster grandson that the distant land he intended to visit was infested with hideous humans and "evil spirits and the followers of those who eat human flesh."

"No one who has ever been within their power has ever been known to return," she told her grandson. "First these evil spirits charm their victims by the sweetness of their songs, then they strangle and devour them, but your principle enemy will be the great gambler who has never been beaten in his game and who lives beyond the realm of darkness. . . . Therefore, my grandson, I would beseech you not to undertake so dangerous a journey."

8   Naanabozho listened to his grandmother, but the woodland trickster knew no fear in the world. The warning words of his grandmother were unheeded.

9   Naanabozho first traveled in a birch bark canoe, the first one ever made on the earth, and as he searched for his mother he encountered different animals and birds and spirits. He consulted with the birds and animals and good spirits and it was decided that the owl would lend the trickster his eyes and the firefly would travel with him to light the way through the realms of darkness, where he would encounter the evil gambler. He paddled to the end of the woodland; then he took a path that led him through swamps and over high mountains and by deep chasms in the earth where he saw the hideous stare of a thousand gleaming eyes . . . and he heard the groans and hisses and yells of countless fiends gloating over their many victims of sin and shame . . . and he knew that this was the place where the great gambler had abandoned the spirits of his victims who had lost the game.

10   Naanabozho approached the entrance of the wigwam and raised the mat of scalps that served as the door. Inside he found himself in the presence of the great gambler, who was a curious being, a person who seemed almost round in shape, smooth and white.

11   "So, Naanabozho, you too have come to try your luck, and you think I am not a very expert gambler," the great gambler said, reaching for his war club and chuckling a horrible sound of scorn and ridicule. His round white shape shivered.

12   "All of these hands you see hanging around this wigwam are the hands of your people who came here to gamble. They thought as you are now thinking, they played and lost their lives.

13   "I seek no one to come and gamble with me but those who would gamble their lives. Remember that I demand the lives of those who gamble with me and lose. I keep the scalps and ears and hands, and the rest of the bodies are given to my friends the flesh eaters. . . . The spirit of those who have lost their lives I consign to the land of darkness," the great gambler said, still grinning with confidence. His flesh seemed moist, like a poison mushroom. "Now I have spoken and we will play the game of the four ages of man."

14   The great gambler took in his stout hands the dish game and said this to the woodland trickster: "Here are the four figures, the four ages of man, which I will shake in the dish four times, and if they assume a standing position each time, then I am the winner. . . . Should they fall, then you are the winner."

15   "Very well, we will play," Naanabozho said, his words wedged in nervous laughter. "But it is customary for the party who is challenged to play any

game to have the last play." The trickster looked down at the dish and the figures of the four ages of man. The great gambler shivered in the realm of darkness.

16   The gambler consented to the invitation of the trickster as he took the dish and struck it to the ground for the first time. The four figures remained in the standing position. This was repeated twice more by the great gambler and each time the four figures representing the four ages of man remained in the standing position in the dish. The power of evil was not threatened.

17   The destinies of the trickster and tribal people of the woodland depended upon the one chance remaining, the last throw of the dish. Should the figures of the four ages of man come down in the standing position then the trickster would lose and the spirit of tribal people would be consigned to the *wiindigoo,* the flesh eaters in the land of darkness.

18   When the gambler prepared to make the final shake of the game, the woodland trickster drew near and when the dish came down to the ground he made a teasing whistle on the wind and all four figures of the ages of man fell in the darkness of the dish. The great gambler shivered, his flesh seemed to harden and break into small pieces when he looked up toward the trickster.

19   Naanabozho smiled at the great gambler. The woodland tribes had not lost their spirit to the land of darkness. The trickster had stopped evil for a moment in a game. "Now it is my turn," the woodland trickster said to the great gambler," and should I win, should all the four ages of man stand in the dish, then you will lose your life. . . ."

20   Naanabozho cracked the dish on the earth.

DISCUSSION QUESTIONS

1. Native Americans told trickster stories to teach lessons to the young and to set standards of behavior for adults. Describe three ideals of character and conduct that you notice in the story.
2. This narrative depicts a battle between good and evil. The storyteller accentuates the qualities of good and evil through strong images. What three images do you consider effective for each?
3. The "realm (land) of darkness" image appears six times in the story. Comment on the storyteller's repetition of this image to structure the dramatic action of the plot.

WRITING TOPICS

1. In one or two paragraphs, define the role of the trickster figure in Chippewa culture and illustrate your definition with examples from this story.

2. The struggle between good and evil, the gambler and Naanabozho is on-going. In paragraph 19, Naanabozho has stopped evil "for a moment in a game." Write the next episode in their conflict, using dialogue and imagery. Assume you are the Gambler, Naanabozho, or a *wiindigoo*. Write your story from the point of view of one of these characters. What is the gamble? Who will win? What lesson does your story teach?

3. Coyote is also a trickster figure, particularly in Southwestern Native American cosmologies. Read a coyote story and compare his characterization and actions with those of Naanabozho in this tale. How do both characters fit the trickster model?

4. With your classmates, prepare a dramatic reading of this story. One approach is to add a narrator and actors who pantomime the scenes.

SOUL-CATCHER

Louis Owens

Many Native American peoples viewed large American cats—jaguars, mountain lions, and panthers—as sacred and possessing supernatural powers. Choctaw-Cherokee author Louis Owens focuses on a black panther in the Yazoo River basin in Mississippi. The wounded panther besieges the cabin where a California boy is visiting his Choctaw great-uncle. "Soul-Catcher" revolves around this mixed-heritage youth who learns about his Choctaw identity from ethnography books and folktales. In contrast, his isolated, traditional great-uncle has learned his identity through experience. The cabin sits in Mississippi Delta swampland, ideal panther habitat. Owens says that *nalusachito* is a Choctaw word that translates as soul-catcher, soul-eater, or soul-snatcher. Although Owens terminates this story with suspense, the tale conveys a moral.

According to Owens, his story is based on an event in his childhood. His father had gone hunting along the Yazoo River. On his way home, a black panther, "painter" as he pronounced it, began stalking him. He reached the door of their cabin and shut it behind him before the panther could pounce. The angry animal leapt to the roof, and the family spent the night listening to its footsteps and screams.

Born in 1948, Louis Owens traces his descent from Choctaw, Cherokee, and Irish ancestors. He was reared in Mississippi and California. He has been a wilderness ranger and firefighter for the United States Forest Service, a Fullbright lecturer in American Literature at the University of Pisa, Pisa, Italy, and is now a professor of English at the University of New Mexico. Critic, novelist, educator, and nonfiction writer, Owens is the author of both fiction and critical analysis of fiction. His acclaimed critical study, *Other Destinies: Understanding the American Indian Novel,* was published in 1992. He has also published four novels: *Wolfsong* (1991), *The Sharpest Sight* (1992), *Bonegame* (1994), and *Nightland* (1996).

1   The old man held the rifle in one hand and walked bent over under the weight of the gunnysack on his back, as if studying the tangle of roots that was the trail. Behind him three lanky brown-and-black-and-white hounds crowded close to his thin legs and threw nervous glances at the wet forest all around. The only sound was that of the old man's boots and the occasional whine of one of the dogs. The sliver of moon had set, and the trail was very dark. The light from the carbide lamp on his hat cast a phosphorescent glow around the group, so that the old man, with his long silver hair, might have been one of the Choctaw shadows on the bright path home.

2   Out of the dark to the old man's right came a scream that cut through the swamp like jagged tin and sent the hounds trembling against his legs.

3   "Hah! Get back you!" he scolded, turning to shake his head at the cringing dogs. "That cat ain't going to eat you, not yet."

4   The dogs whined and pushed closer so that the old man stumbled and caught himself and the light from the headlamp splashed upon the trail. He shook his head again and chuckled, making shadows dance around them. He knew what it was that stalked him. The black *koi* hadn't been seen in the swamps during the old man's lifetime, but as a child he'd heard the stories so often that he knew at once what the *koi* meant. It was an old and familiar story. He'd felt the black one out there in the swamps for a long time. The bird, *falachito,* had called from the trees to warn him, and he had listened and gone on because what else was there to do? All of his life he had been prepared to recognize the soul-catcher when it should come.

5   The old man also knew that the screamer was probably the panther that the fool white man, Reeves, had wounded near Satartia a couple of weeks before. He could feel the animal's anger there in the darkness, feel the hatred like grit between his teeth. And he felt great pity for the injured cat.

6   The boar coon in the sack was heavy, and the old man thought that he should have brought the boy along to help, but then the forest opened and he was at the edge of his cabin clearing, seeing the thread of his garden trail between the stubble of the past year's corn and the dried husks of melon and squash vines. Behind him, this time to his left, the panther screamed again. The cat had been circling like that for the past hour, never getting any closer or any farther away.

7   He paused at the edge of the clearing and spoke a few words in a low voice, trying to communicate his understanding and sympathy to the wounded animal and his knowledge of what was there to the soul-catcher. For a moment he leaned the rifle against his leg and reached up to touch a small pouch that hung inside his shirt. All of his life the old man had balanced two realities, two worlds, a feat that had never struck him as particularly noteworthy or difficult. But as the cat called out once more, he felt a shadow fall over him. The animal's cry rose from the dark waters of the swamp to the stars and then fell away like one of the deep, bottomless places in the river.

8   When the old man pulled the leather thong to open the door, the hounds shot past and went to cower beneath the plank beds. He lowered the bag to the puncheon floor and pushed the door closed. After a moment's thought he dropped the bolt into place before reaching with one hand to hang the twenty-two on nails beneath a much larger rifle. Finally, he looked at the teenage boy sitting on the edge of one of the beds with a book in his lap. The lantern beside the boy left half of his upturned face in shadow, as if two faces met in one, but the old man could see one green eye and the fair skin, and he wondered once more how much Choctaw there was in the boy.

9   The boy looked up fully and stared at the old uncle. The distinct epicanthic fold of each eye giving the boy's face an oddly Oriental quality.

10   "*Koi*," the old man said. "A painter. He followed me home."

11   After a moment's silence, the boy said, "You going to keep him?"

12   The old man grinned. The boy was getting better.

13   "Not this one," he replied. "He's no good. A fool shot him, and now he's mad." He studied the air to one side of the boy and seemed to make a decision. "Besides, this black one may be *nalusachito,* the soul-catcher. He's best left alone, I think."

14   The boy's grin died quickly, and the old man saw fear and curiosity mingle in the pale eyes.

15   "Why do you think it's *nalusachito?*" The word was awkward on the boy's tongue.

16   "Sometimes you just know these things. He's been out there a while. The bird warned me, and now that fool white man has hurt him."

17   "*Nalusachito* is just a myth," the boy said.

18   The old man looked at the book in the boy's lap. "You reading that book again?"

19   The boy nodded.

20   "A teacher give that book to your dad one time, so's he could learn all about his people, the teacher said. He used to read that book, too, and tell me about us Choctaws." The old man grinned once more. "After he left, I read some of that book."

21   The old man reached a hand toward the boy. "Here, let me read you the part I like best about us people." He lifted a pair of wire-rimmed glasses from a shelf above the rifles and slipped them on.

22   The boy held the book out and the old man took it. Bending so that the lantern-light fell across the pages, he thumbed expertly through the volume.

23   "This is a good book, all right. Tells us all about ourselves. This writer was a smart man. Listen to this." He began to read, pronouncing each word with care, as though it were a foreign language.

> *The Choctaw warrior, as I knew him in his native Mississippi forest, was as fine a specimen of manly perfection as I have ever beheld.*

24   He looked up with a wink.

> *He seemed to be as perfect as the human form could be. Tall,*
> *beautiful in symmetry of form and face, graceful, active, straight,*
> *fleet, with lofty and independent bearing, he seemed worthy in say-*
> *ing, as he of Juan Fernández fame: "I am monarch of all I survey."*
> *His black piercing eye seemed to penetrate and read the very thoughts*
> *of the heart, while his firm step proclaimed a feeling sense of manly*
> *independence. Nor did their women fall behind in all that pertains*
> *to female beauty.*

25   The old man looked at the boy. "Now there's a man that hit the nail on
the head." He paused for a moment. "You ever heard of this Juan
Fernández? Us Choctaws didn't get along too good with Spanish people in
the old days. Remind me to tell you about Tuscaloosa sometime."

26   The boy shook his head. "Alabama?"

27   The old man nodded. "I read this next part to Old Lady Blue Wood that
lives 'crost the river. She says this is the smartest white man she ever heard
of." He adjusted the glasses and read again.

> *They were of such unnatural beauty that they literally appeared*
> *to light up everything around them. Their shoulders were broad and*
> *their carriage true to Nature, which has never been excelled by the*
> *hand of art, their long, black tresses hung in flowing waves, extend-*
> *ing nearly to the ground; but the beauty of the countenances of many*
> *of those Choctaw and Chickasaw girls was so extraordinary that if*
> *such faces were seen today in one of the parlors of the fashionable*
> *world, they would be considered as a type of beauty hitherto*
> *unknown.*

28   He handed the book back to the boy and removed the glasses, grinning
all the while. "Now parts of that do sound like Old Lady Blue Wood. That
unnatural part, and that part about broad shoulders. But she ain't never had
a carriage that I know of, and she's more likely to light into anybody that's
close than to light 'em up."

29   The boy looked down at the moldy book and then grinned weakly back at
the old uncle. Beneath the floppy hat, surrounded by the acrid smell of the
carbide headlamp, the old man seemed like one of the swamp shadows come
into the cabin. The boy thought about his father, the old man's nephew, who
had been only half Choctaw but looked nearly as dark and indestructible as the
uncle. Then he looked down at his own hand in the light from the kerosene
lantern. The pale skin embarrassed him, gave him away. The old man, his
great-uncle, was Indian, and his father had been Indian, but he wasn't

30   There was a thud on the wood shingles of the cabin's roof. Dust fell from
each of the four corners of the cabin and onto the pages of the damp book.

31   "*Nalusachito* done climbed up on the roof," the old man said, gazing at the ceiling with amusement. "He moves pretty good for a cat that's hurt, don't he?"

32   The boy knew the uncle was watching for his reaction. He steeled himself, and then the panther screamed and he flinched.

33   The old man nodded. "Only a fool or a crazy man ain't scared when soul-catcher's walking around on his house," he said.

34   "You're not afraid," the boy replied, watching as the old man set the headlamp on a shelf and hung the wide hat on a nail beside the rifles.

35   The old man pulled a piece of canvas from beneath the table and spread it on the floor. As he dumped the coon out onto the canvas, he looked up with a chuckle. "That book says Choctaw boys always respected their elders. I'm scared alright, but I know about that cat, you see, and that's the difference. That cat ain't got no surprises for me because I'm old, and I done heard all the stories."

36   The boy glanced at the book.

37   "It don't work that way," the old man said. "You can't read them. A white man comes and he pokes around and pays somebody, or maybe somebody feels sorry for him and tells him stuff and he writes it down. But he don't understand, so he can't put it down right, you see."

38   How do you understand? the boy wanted to ask as he watched the uncle pull a knife from its sheath on his hip and begin to skin the coon, making cuts down each leg and up the belly so delicately that the boy could see no blood at all. The panther shrieked overhead, and the old man seemed not to notice.

39   "Why don't you shoot it?" the boy asked, looking at the big deer rifle on the wall, the thirty-forty Krag from the Spanish-American War.

40   The old man looked up in surprise.

41   "You could sell the skin to Mr. Wheeler for a lot of money, couldn't you?" Mr. Wheeler was the black man who came from across the river to buy the coonskins.

42   The old man squinted and studied the boy's face. "You can't hunt that cat," he said patiently. "*Nalusachito*'s something you got to accept, something that's just there."

43   "You see," he continued, "what folks like that fool Reeves don't understand is that this painter has always been out there. We just ain't noticed him for a long time. He's always there, and that's what people forget. You can't kill him." He tapped his chest with the handle of the knife. "*Nalusachito* comes from in here."

44   The boy watched the old man in silence. He knew about the soul-catcher from the book in his lap. It was an old superstition, and the book didn't say anything about *nalusachito* being a panther. That was something the old man invented. This panther was very real and dangerous. He looked skeptically at the old man and then up at the rifle.

45   "No," the old man said. "We'll just let this painter be."

46   He pulled the skin off over the head of the raccoon like a sweater, leaving the naked body shining like a baby in the yellow light. Under the beds the dogs sniffed and whined, and overhead the whispers moved across the roof.

47   The old man held the skin up and admired it, then laid it fur-side down on the bench beside him. "I sure ain't going out side to nail this up right now," he said, the corners of his mouth suggesting a grin. He lifted the bolt and pushed the door open and swung the body of the coon out into the dark. When he closed the door there was a snarl and an impact on the ground. The dogs began to growl and whimper, and the old man said, "You, Yvonne! Hoyo!" and the dogs shivered in silence.

48   The boy watched the old man wash his hands in the bucket and sit on the edge of the other bed to pull off his boots. Each night and morning since he'd come it had been the same. The old uncle would go out at night and come back before daylight with something in the bag. Usually the boy would waken to find the old man in the other plank bed, sleeping like a small child, so lightly that the boy could not see or hear him breathe. But this night the boy had awakened in the very early morning, torn from sleep by a sound he wasn't conscious of hearing, and he had sat up with the lantern and book to await the old man's return. He read the book because there was nothing else to read. The myths reminded him of fairy tales he'd read as a child, and he tried to imagine his father reading them.

49   The old man was a real Choctaw—*Chahta okla*—a full-blood. Was the ability to believe the myths diluted with the blood, the boy wondered, so that his father could, when he had been alive, believe only half as strongly as the old man and he, his father's son, half as much yet? He thought of the soul-catcher, and he shivered, but he knew that he was just scaring himself the way kids always did. His mother had told him how they said that when his father was born the uncle had shown up at the sharecropper's cabin and announced that the boy would be his responsibility. That was the Choctaw way, he said, the right way. A man must accept responsibility for and teach his sister's children. Nobody had thought of that custom for a long time, and nobody had seen the uncle for years, and nobody knew how he'd even learned of the boy's birth, but there he was come out of the swamps across the river with his straight black hair hanging to his shoulders under the floppy hat and his face dark as night so that the mother, his sister, screamed when she saw him. And from that day onward the uncle had come often from the swamps to take the boy's father with him, to teach him.

50   The old man rolled into the bed, pulled the wool blanket to his chin, turned to the wall, and was asleep. The boy watched him and then turned down the lamp until only a dim glow outlined the objects in the room. He thought of Los Angeles, the bone-dry hills and yellow air, the home where he'd lived with his parents before the accident that killed both. It was difficult to be Choctaw, to be Indian there, and he'd seen his father working hard at it, growing his black hair long, going to urban powwows where the

fancy dancers spun like beautiful birds. His father had taught him to hunt in the desert hills and to say a few phrases, like *Chahta isht ia* and *Chahta yakni,* in the old language. The words had remained only sounds, the pow-wow dancers only another Southern California spectacle for a green-eyed, fair-skinned boy. But the hunting had been real, a testing of desire and reflex he had felt all the way through.

51 Indians were hunters. Indians lived close to the land. His father had said those things often. He thought about the panther. The old man would not hunt the black cat, and had probably made up the story about *nalusachito* as an excuse. The panther was dangerous. For a month the boy had been at the cabin and had not ventured beyond the edges of the garden except to go out in the small rowboat onto the muddy Yazoo River that flanked one side of the clearing. The swampy forest around the cabin was like the river, a place in which nothing was ever clear: shadows, swirls, dark forms rising and disappearing again, nothing ever clearly seen. And each night he'd lain in the bed and listened to the booming and cracking of the swamp like something monstrously evil and thought of the old man killing things in the dark, picturing the old man as a solitary light cutting the darkness.

52 The panther might remain, its soft feet whispering maddeningly on the cabin roof each night while the old man hunted in the swamp. Or it might attack the old man who would not shoot it. For the first time the boy real-ized the advantage in not being really Choctaw. The old uncle could not hunt the panther, but he could, because he knew the cat for what it really was. It would not be any more difficult to kill than the wild pigs he'd hunted with his father in the coastal range of California, and it was no different than the cougars that haunted those same mountains. The black one was only a freak of nature.

53 Moving softly, he lifted the heavy rifle from its nails. In a crate on the floor he found the cartridges and, slipping on his red-plaid mackinaw, he dropped the bullets into his pocket. Then he walked carefully to the door, lifted the bolt, stepped through, and silently pulled the door closed. Outside, it was getting close to dawn and the air had the clean, raw smell of that hour, tainted by the sharp odor of the river and swamp. The trees were unsure outlines protruding from the wall of black that surrounded the cabin on three sides. Over the river the fog hovered in a gray somewhat lighter than the air, and a kingfisher called in a shrill *kree* out across the water.

54 He pushed shells into the rifle's magazine and then stepped along the garden trail toward the trees, listening carefully for the sounds of the woods. Where even he knew there should have been the shouting of crickets, frogs, and a hundred other night creatures, there was only silence beating like the heartbeat drum at one of the powwows. At the edge of the clearing he paused.

55 In the cabin the old man sat up and looked toward the door. The boy had an hour before full daylight, and he would meet *nalusachito* in that tran-sitional time. The old man fingered the medicine pouch on the cord around

his neck and wondered about such a convergence. There was a meaning beyond his understanding, something that could not be avoided.

56 The boy brushed aside a muskedine vine and stepped into the woods, feeling his boots sink into the wet floor. It had all been a singular journey toward this, out of the light of California, across the burning earth of the Southwest, and into the darkness of this place. Beyond the garden, in the uncertain light, the trunks of trees, the brush and vines were like a curtain closing behind him. Then the panther cried in the damp woods somewhere in front of him, the sound insinuating itself into the night like one of the tendrils of fog that clung to the ground. The boy began to walk on the faint trail toward the sound, the air so thick he felt as though he were suspended in fluid, his movements like those of a man walking on the floor of the sea. His breathing became torturous and liquid, and his eyes adjusted to the darkness and strained to isolate the watery forms surrounding him.

57 When he had gone a hundred yards the panther called again, a strange, dreamlike, muted cry different from the earlier screams, and he hesitated a moment and then left the trail to follow the cry. A form slid from the trail beside his boot, and he moved carefully away, deeper into the woods beyond the trail. Now the light was graying, and the leaves and bark of the trees became delicately etched as the day broke.

58 The close scream of the panther jerked him into full consciousness, and he saw the cat. Twenty feet away, it crouched in a clutter of vines and brush, its yellow eyes burning at him. In front of the panther was the half-eaten carcass of the coon.

59 He raised the rifle slowly, bringing it to his shoulder and slipping the safety off in the same movement. With his action, the panther pushed itself upright until it sat on its haunches, facing him. It was then the boy saw that one of the front feet hung limp, a festering wound in the shoulder on that side. He lined the notched sight of the rifle against the cat's head, and he saw the burning go out of the eyes. The panther watched him calmly, waiting as he pulled the trigger. The animal toppled backward, kicked for an instant and was still.

60 He walked to the cat and nudged it with a boot. *Nalusachito* was dead. He leaned the rifle against a tree and lifted the cat by its four feet and swung it onto his back, surprised at how light it was and feeling the sharp edges of the ribs through the fur. He felt sorrow and pity for the hurt animal he could imagine hunting awkwardly in the swamps, and he knew that what he had done was right. He picked up the rifle and turned back toward the cabin.

61 When he opened the cabin door, with the cat on his shoulder, the old man was sitting in the chair facing him. The boy leaned the rifle against the bench and swung the panther carefully to the floor and looked up at the old man, but the old man's eyes were fixed on the open doorway. Beyond the doorway *nalusachito* crouched, ready to spring.

Discussion Questions

1. Owens creates an eerie, ominous setting that hovers close to the old man and the boy. The shadowy spirit world and the foggy swamp scenes emerge from images of darkness and light. Cite five examples by paragraph numbers and explain how they contribute to the mystery.
2. The panther seems poised between the old man and the boy throughout the story. Their reactions to the awesome animal define their characters. Find the lines that reveal their views toward the panther and explain how those views determine their actions.
3. Which adjectives do you think best describe the old man? stubborn, wise, foolish, superstitious, gentle, strong, old-fashioned, mysterious. In contrast, suggest four adjectives to describe the young man.
4. In small groups, discuss the moral of this story and then state it in a sentence.

Writing Topics

1. Select one of the following quotations from the story and explain how it relates to the entire story.

   The old man, his great-uncle, was Indian, and his father had been Indian, but he wasn't. (paragraph 31)

   That cat ain't got no surprises for me because I'm old and I done heard all the stories. (paragraph 37)

   For the first time the boy realized the advantage in not being really Choctaw. (paragraph 52)

   Nalusachito was dead. (paragraph 60)

2. Develop a brief essay with illustrations from the story. Suggested thesis and topic sentences: "Louis Owens uses setting to contrast the differences in the characters of the old man and the boy. First, the boy has been educated in the 'light of California.' The old man has learned to survive in the 'darkness of the swamp.' Second, the two characters respond differently to the panther which punctuates the setting with his screams. The boy is fearful; the old man accepts the panther as a soul-catcher."

RITE OF ENCOUNTER

Russell Bates

Teacher, writer, and performer Russell Bates, Kiowa, was born in 1941 in Lawton, Oklahoma. His grandmother and other relatives schooled him in Kiowa mythology and history. At school, he pursued interests in science, mathematics, and engineering, thanks in some measure to the influence of his father, who was an aerospace inventor. Later, Bates became a missile electronics technician in the U.S. Air Force. In an explosion in a missile facility, he sustained serious injuries and spent nine months in the hospital. To cope with his confinement, he began writing stories on what he calls a "semi-silent typewriter," and he credits writing for having saved his life during his recuperation. For ten hours a day, he wrote primarily science fiction stories, among them a *Star Trek* scenario. One of his scripts for the animated version of *Star Trek* titled "How Sharper Than a Serpent's Tooth," won an Emmy, a Robby Award, a *Melies* Prize, and a Fantasy Film Award and was the American entry for the 15th International TV Film Festival of Monte Carlo. Bates continues to work on film and television projects as well as to write short fiction.

In "Rite of Encounter," he skillfully personifies smallpox. Demographers calculate that the smallpox virus killed more Native Americans than any other single disease. At least forty smallpox epidemics struck Native North Americans between 1520 and the end of the nineteenth century. Some spread to only a few peoples, but others spread to virtually all the native peoples on the continent.

---

1   In the third week of his fasting, Singing-owl found the white men.

2   The young Kiowa awakened that morning to lilting daybreak calls of birds. Rain had fallen in the night; his buffalo robe was soaked and smelly; his buckskin shirt and leggings were clammy wet. He was miserable. A chill wind blew in under the overhanging rocks. Singing-owl shivered, almost forgetting the receding hunger pangs. Almost.

3   At last the sun warmed the rocks around him. Singing-owl sat up wearily, hoping that this new day would finally bring him the vision. He dried his long black hair and braided it loosely on the left side. Then he stared for a long while downward from the rocky cleft. The hillside was unchanging: scattered clumps of scrub oaks, moss-grown boulders thick yellow-green grass and black soil. Hillsides beyond bore the same colors and shapes.

4   Singing-owl had dreamed sometime before dawn. Of deer and clouds and fishes and snow. . . . But the dream had not been the vision he was seeking. When that came, he would speak with spirits and come away with pieces of their wisdom. The wisdom, in songs and chants and riddles, would be his power as a warrior and as a man.

5   At least that was what the medicine man promised to him. But how much longer did he have to wait? The moon had been just past full when Singing-owl started his fast; soon, it would be full once again.

6   Singing-owl thought of the medicine man who slept warm at the camp and had no want of food or clothing.

7   That toothless, half-blind old man! I hope he got bloated on the meat I gave him!

8   The hunger pangs increased at the mention of food. Singing-owl leaned over and pulled a small deerskin parcel from a crack in the rocks. Wrapped inside was a handful of pounded dried meat mixed with suet. He smelled it for a long time, then closed his eyes and tried to swallow. He put the meat away again, feeling very guilty.

9   At length he forced himself to leave the cleft. When he stood, dizziness and nausea made him stagger. He leaned back against the rocks, momentarily unable to see. His arms and legs tingled and a cramp twisted the muscles in his side. Then the white sparkles faded from before his eyes.

10   Water. Must get water.

11   Singing-owl made his way carefully down the hill; the going was harder than the day before. He could no longer jump from boulder to boulder and instead squeezed between them. Sharp rocks hurt his feet through wet moccasins.

12   The slope leveled off, and Singing-owl sat on the ground to catch his breath. He glanced up the hill; it didn't seem any higher than he remembered. But now he regretted having passed by other, more gentle slopes.

13   I chose my suffering spot well. But will I be able to climb it again?

14   He followed a deer trail and walked listlessly among the trees. Twice he stumbled over tree roots. Another time he brushed against a tree and grabbed it desperately to keep from falling. He stopped and looked around.

15   Is this the right trail to the river? It's so long. I'm lost!

16   Singing-owl left the trail and headed away across the clearing. The thick grass slowed him to a stumbling pace. Then he smelled water and knew the river was close.

17   When he reached its muddy bank, he fell to his knees and threw himself forward to drink. The river was cool and slightly muddied. But the water

made him feel better. He washed his face, then stripped off his buckskins to wash the many bruised cuts on his arms, chest and back. His frenzied thrashing against the rocks the evening before had gained him nothing but exhausted sleep; the self-tortures had not made him worthy of the vision. At last, Singing-owl slipped into the water and washed himself vigorously. Some of the fatigue, muscle aches, a lightheadedness flowed away with the sandy mud he used for scrubbing.

18   Then he lay against a log at the water's edge; the river current soothed his body. It was a struggle to stay awake.

19   A dog barked. Singing-owl sat up and listened. Again. Close by. Upstream.

20   He crawled out of the water, grabbed his buckskins, and listened again. The barking broke into howls. Singing-owl scrambled up the bank into bushes and made his way toward the sound, at once curious and afraid.

21   In this isolated land, no other tribes roamed. A dog meant white men.

22   Singing-owl paused to put on his buckskins. Then he crept ahead through the bushes: cautious, patient, silent. A few moments later, he reached the edge of a clearing and could see the camp, the dog, and the white men.

23   The dog was tied to a tree. One white man lay beside a long-dead fire. Another sat against a tree, his arms limp, his head fallen forward to his chest. A third lay sprawled on the riverbank, his head and one arm in the water. All were dressed in dirty gray and brown clothes, with boots scuffed and mud-caked.

24   A breeze fluttered the leaves of cottonwoods around the clearing; it also brought Singing-owl a whiff of decay. The men were dead.

25   The dog sensed Singing-owl and barked louder, leaping to the limit of the rope. Singing-owl stood up slowly, then walked into the camp. The dog retreated a little but kept up its barking. Singing-owl noticed a broken rope between two trees; horses had long since pulled free and wandered off.

26   He stopped at the body laying beside the ashes. The dead man lay face-down, a blanket across his legs. Singing-owl bent down, picked up a fine pistol; it was fully loaded, with light, circular tracings along the barrel. Singing-owl looked around carefully. Perhaps there were other weapons.

27   Singing-owl turned to the dog. It was brown and white spotted; its fur was matted and the mouth was dirty. Starving and dying of thirst, it had been eating mud.

28   Singing-owl put the gun in his shirt and hunted through the men's packs. He found hardtack biscuits and dried meat. He also found metal cans but discarded them because their markings were meaningless. He looked with longing at the food. But another nudge of guilt made him throw it to the dog.

29   It sniffed the morsels suspiciously, then began to eat in great gulps.

30   Singing-owl sighed, then picked up a small pot to get water. He shivered as he passed the man by the tree. At the riverbank he noticed something

strange as he bent to fill the pot. The dead man laying there was covered with sores.

31 He looked closer. The hand that lay out of the water was almost raw; crusted yellow ooze edged what little skin that remained on its back. He looked at the face. The sores there had ragged white strings that waved in the flowing water. Singing-owl filled the pot quickly and stepped away.

32 The dog drank the water and wagged its tail. Then it looked up at him, expectant. Singing-owl reached out carefully, untied the rope. The dog brushed against him, happy.

33 "What killed your people, dog?" Singing-owl said, not truly breaking the ban against speaking to anyone.

34 The dog shook its head and barked. Its tail slapped against Singing-owl's legs.

35 "That was a bad way to meet death. Maybe I'd better not stay here any longer." He skirted wide of the man sitting at the tree. Yes, the sores were there. He did not bother turning over the man under the blanket.

36 Singing-owl remembered the pistol; he took it out with a trembling hand and dropped it. The dog walked with him away from the camp, then stopped.

37 Singing-owl looked back. "Going to stay here, yes? I wouldn't be able to keep you anyway. Hope you find something to eat." He brushed away the obvious and horrible thought, heading back into the hills.

38 When evening came, Singing-owl made a small fire and began his chanting prayers. The wind blew warm over the rocky cleft; stars were glistening in the dying film of twilight. Surely the strange events of the day were signs that the vision was coming. The robes that hid things to come would be lifted and. . . .

39 Singing-owl found himself repeating the words of the medicine man and was disgusted. He waited. Nothing. The air turned cool and the fire slowly fell away.

40 Where is it? The medicine man is a liar! But what of all the other warriors who claim power from a vision?

41 He sat quietly, then decided to fast for only a few more days. If no vision came, he would go back to the Kiowas. He would have to tell them something; exactly what, he did not know.

42 But he would repay the medicine man for many days of discomfort. Singing-owl's brow wrinkled as he half-frowned, half-smiled. His reputation for playing pranks and outwitting his tribesmen was to gain yet another distinction. He would do nothing harmful, to be sure, just a few tricks to upset the old man. Such as: giving him skunk bones if he asked for weasel; hawk meat if he asked for prairie bird; or putting green sticks in his firewood. Singing-owl wanted to laugh, but he could not.

43 He noticed the fire and started to add more wood. But he felt warm enough, in fact, he felt almost too warm. He touched his face: hot.

44   Perhaps I'm tired. All right. I am tired.

45   He lay down to sleep. He remembered the white men and their sores though he really did not want to. Something had killed them. Quickly. Quietly. He tried to think of other things. The vision. The many tricks he had played. Gray Bear's daughters. A running hunt through trees after a deer.

46   But nothing forced the image of the dead men from the edge of sight. Finally, he fell asleep, feeling warmer than before.

47   Singing-owl opened his eyes. The sun was high above the hills. He lay quietly and listened to his body. All was well, apparently. Relieved, he sat up, yawned and stretched. He pushed the buffalo robe away and started to get up.

48   The thing sat a short distance away, watching him. Singing-owl stared, unable to move further. It was shaped like a man. But it was not a man.

49   It was a mass of raw flesh. With a body, and arms and legs, and a head. No skin or hair; just endless running sores. It appeared to be looking at him, but its face was featureless, red, open flesh. Yellow fluids trickled from over its entire body, wet streams ran down the rock on which it sat.

50   Singing-owl crawled backward, pressed himself against the rocks, eyes wide.

51   A ghost? Is it a white man's ghost? Or is . . . is that the vision?

52   He choked on the words: "Are you one of the spirits? Have . . . have you come because I am worthy?"

53   It moved, raised an arm, touched its chest. In a thick, watery voice said, "I am Black Smallpox. And I wish to walk with you."

54   Singing-owl almost fainted. He stared at it, tried to speak.

55   But the creature spoke first. "Do not be afraid. I will not harm you. I only wish to go with you to the Kiowas." It stood, and the yellow streams ran down its legs. "Yes, we will walk together to your people."

56   Singing-owl thought quickly, blinking. It surely was not the vision. Or was it perhaps the vision after all, somehow spoiled by white man's evil? Yes, the white men. Their sores. Death.

57   "No!" he said, feeling for a loose rock. "You came with the white men! You killed them! And now you want to kill . . . !" He found a rock and threw it. Smallpox wavered like a reflection in water, then suddenly was standing a short distance further away. The rock clattered harmlessly to the ground.

58   Smallpox stepped closer. "Come. Let us go."

59   Singing-owl sprang away suddenly and clambered down the hillside. He ran, stumbled, fell, crawled, slid over boulders, ran again. When he reached flatter ground, he broke into a run and did not look back. He staggered and almost tripped several times. He ran past trees, over hills down gullies, into grass and bare ground.

60   At last, he ran, stumbled, ran into a narrow valley. He fell, gasping and crying. He landed on his face and hands at the edge of a rainwater pool. He lay beside a boulder and a small bush. He tried to crawl, but fell back. His

body shook and shivered, though sweat coated him. Then his breathing slowed and he raised himself on one arm.

61   Singing-owl heard wailing and moaning, but very faint. Then he saw people reflected in the pool. They were Kiowas; ragged, wet sores covered their arms and faces. The wailing reflections reached for him, crying louder.

62   Singing-owl jerked himself backward and pushed dirt into the pool with his feet. Something stood at the limit of his side vision, he turned and saw Smallpox standing beside the bush.

63   It stepped toward him. "Why did you stop? We are going to the Kiowas, are we not? The sooner we get there, the better it will please me."

64   Singing-owl scrambled up, backed away in a low crouch. "No! I won't take you! You have no place here! Go away!"

65   It raised a hand. "We must go. The day grows long."

66   Singing-owl turned and ran again.

67   He climbed a cliff. Smallpox walked to the edge above him before he reached the top.

68   He ran over the plateau and dove from more than tree-top height into a lake. Smallpox stood atop the beaver lodge when Singing-owl swam toward the dam.

69   He hid in a box canyon. Smallpox was standing behind him near the sheer rock face. Singing-owl quickly set a grass fire by striking stones together. The flames swept into the canyon, swirling with smoke, trapping Smallpox. But when Singing-owl ran into a forest, Smallpox stepped from behind a tree to meet him.

70   Through the rest of the day, Singing-owl ran, set traps, ran again. But he could neither outrun nor outwit Smallpox, it was always there when he stopped. Night fell and Singing-owl found that he could run no more.

71   He sat on the top of a grassy hill and watched as Smallpox walked slowly toward him. Light from a nearly full moon flashed in sparks from the dripping liquids.

72   I have lost. I have no more tricks. Yet. . .

73   Singing-owl thought hurriedly, formed a plan, then hung his head as Smallpox stopped beside him. "All right," he said, "We will go to the Kiowas."

74   Somewhere, Singing-owl felt a flicker of hope.

75   The lodges were quiet; moonlight revealed a score or more of them built at the base of a tree-lined hill. The main campfire was low. Camp dogs roamed in the spaces between the lodges. Sentries stood unmoving at long intervals around the village.

76   At a distance, Singing-owl circled the camp quietly. Smallpox walked with him.

77   At the far end of the camp, a woman came out of a lodge and threw bones on the ground. The dogs ran toward her and began fighting over the meal.

78 Singing-owl saw his chance and boldly walked in among the lodges where there was no sentry. Then he stopped and abruptly turned to Smallpox. "We are here. Now will you let me go? I am ashamed."

79 It stepped forward and regarded the circle of lodges. "Not just yet. There is still something you must do. Come."

80 He followed it, glancing from side to side, nervous. Smallpox led him to a large deerskin bag that was supported by crossed poles.

81 "This water," it said, standing very close to him and pointing. "Spit into it."

82 Singing-owl stared, not understanding.

83 I said, "Spit into this water."

84 He stepped to the bag, opened a flap near the top, and spat.

85 "Again. That will do it. You are free."

86 Singing-owl moved back. "Free?"

87 Smallpox turned away. "Your usefulness is at an end." It sat down still with its back to him; the open flesh gleamed wetly in the moonlight. "You will not understand, but I will tell you anyway. There are but a few I cannot kill. You are one. But I still lived inside you and thus was my purpose served. Leave me."

88 Singing-owl pretended to walk toward a lodge near a large shade tree. "Yes," he said, looking back. "I must go to my lodge. My family will be glad to see me."

89 But when Smallpox was no longer in sight, Singing-owl ran for the trees. Two dogs ran after him, barking. A sentry shouted and more dogs ran after him. Singing-owl reached the shadows and ran out of camp. He lost his pursuers quickly.

90 I'm free. I'm free! And the Pawnees are no friends to the Kiowas! They deserve Smallpox!

91 Dawn found Singing-owl far away from the Pawnee camp. When he was sure no one followed, he trapped a rabbit and ate his first meal in twenty days. His stomach ached a little when he set out again. But he was still happy at finally outwitting Smallpox

92 He laughed. What a tale he would tell of his vision when he reached the Kiowas!

93 He was almost there when he heard wailing. He stopped and looked around frantically. Nothing else could be seen on the rolling plains except grasses moving in the wind. Then the wailing faded replaced by a laughing taunt. It was the voice of Smallpox.

94 "Where are you?" Singing-owl shouted, turning in circles. "You cannot be here! I outwitted you!"

95 "I told you, but you did not understand. We still walk together. I am part of you. You cannot get rid of me!" And the laughing began again.

96 Then Singing-owl knew the laughing came from inside him. He clutched at himself, tore at his own flesh, and screamed.

97 The laugh rolled on, unstopping.

98   The cleft of rocks offered little protection from the raging thunderstorm. Singing-owl huddled under his buffalo robe and watched the storm. Lightning split trees on far hills and flashed the night away for brief moments. Thunder snapped down from the clouds and shook the ground. Rain splashed on Singing-owl's face and ran in pools under him.

99   He prayed, asking the mercy of the spirits. Small things came back to him: a boy's game with a willow hoop; his mother and stories and songs and gentle scoldings, the self-tortures that had declared him a man, the smiling, teasing daughter of Gray Bear; how fat quail sizzled when roasted. . . .

100   For days, Singing-owl had considered exile or suicide. But he knew the one would be spent in temptation to see loved ones again. And there was no honor in the other.

101   Now Smallpox was to be finally outwitted. Singing-owl was fasting once more. But this time the fasting would go on, until there was nothing left.

102   He smiled faintly and pulled the buffalo robe tighter around him. At least, he thought, the laughing has stopped.

DISCUSSION QUESTIONS

1. The narrator reports details the way a camera might record them. First, he gives a wide-angle view and then he focuses on details within that view. One example is "The dead man . . . was covered with sores" (paragraph 30). Paragraph 31 gives specific images of the dead man. Locate three other examples of this technique of presenting a wide-angle followed by a close-up view. Do you think this is a good technique? What are its advantages and disadvantages?

2. Contrast the two characters Singing-owl and Smallpox according to their actions and attitudes. Which seems the most real to you? What was the most difficult problem Bates had to solve as he developed each character?

3. Bates creates suspense by playing on the theme that appearances are deceptive. At several instances in the story, things are not what they seem. Find examples and tell how you think they are effective or ineffective for lending mystery and suspense.

WRITING TOPICS

1. To achieve unity in the story, the author skillfully integrates *vision, vision quest,* and *lack of vision* (no understanding of reality). Write a critical essay on this topic using illustrations from the story. Begin by studying these scenes. "Singing-owl sat up wearily, hoping that this new day would finally bring him the *vision.*" (paragraph 3); "A ghost? Is it a white man's ghost? Or is . . . that the *vision?*" (paragraph 51); "Then he saw people reflected in the pool" (paragraph 67); "What a tale he would tell of his *vision* when he reached the Kiowas!" (paragraph 92).

2. Review the events in the story and then consider how the title relates to the story. Suggest an alternate title. Which title to you prefer? Explain.

3. In his unique style, Bates does not always follow conventional rules. For example, he does not use quotation marks to indicate interior monologue or dialogue. How do you recognize these conversations? Bates also breaks the narrative with frequent paragraphs that are like snapshots. Does this technique interfere with your understanding or appreciation of the story? In his staccato sentences, the author frequently uses active verbs to carry the sentence. (See paragraphs 19, 59, and others.) What does this technique accomplish? Select one of these techniques and write a brief essay in which you evaluate its success or failure.

SUMMARY WRITING TOPICS

1. Ask five of your classmates these questions: Which selection in "The Spirit World" taught you the most about Native American spirituality? What did you learn? Using three of their answers, write a short article for your school paper on Native American spirituality.

2. Consider the character of the silent daughter in "Raven Steals the Light." Write the story from her point of view.

3. Hero twins are major characters in Navajo and Iroquois mythology. Compare and contrast the purpose and actions of the Navajo mythic twins with the Iroquois rival twins within their respective cultures.

4. Select one story that expresses moral values quite similar to or very different from your own values. Identify the values in the story, and in your journal, compare or contrast those values with your own.

5. Write a story about the adventures of Coyote, Naanabozho, or Raven in modern society. Examples: Coyote Plays Football, Coyote Learns to Dance, Raven Takes a Test.

6. Which character would you most like to meet from "The Spirit World" and why?

7. The storytellers in "The Spirit World" use imagery to help you imagine the supernatural characters. Select three works that use sensory images effectively for this purpose. In an essay, describe the three supernaturals. Examples: White Bead Woman, the Gambler, the False Faces.

8. Write a three-paragraph essay on this thesis. Many Native American societies believe that humans may contact cosmic powers through prayers, dreams, and visions. Use specific examples from the selections and devote one paragraph to each method.

9. Female and male supernaturals play vital roles in preparing the world for humans. Select one male and one female character and write two paragraphs that tell how their roles are similar or different.

CHAPTER THREE

CRISIS IN THE HOMELAND

Miranda: O brave new world, That has such people in't!
Prospero: Tis new to thee.

William Shakespeare wrote these memorable lines in *The Tempest,* which was first performed in 1611. Native American writers have agreed with Shakespeare on both points. First, the Americas were a "new" world only to Europeans; they were an old world to their native peoples. Second, "such people" mattered; they mattered mightily to nineteenth-century Native American authors, and they matter centrally to modern Native American authors.

Some of Shakespeare's English contemporaries in 1607 colonized a bit of swampland on the Virginia coast. *Land* is the key word. The confederacy of Indian villages initially welcomed the colonizers. As the Englishmen expanded their Jamestown beachhead, Pocahontas's people, the Powhatans, recognized that these newcomers treated and managed land in a way fundamentally different from the way Native Americans did.

Native American literature arises from five hundred years of land history, ever since Columbus's 1493 colonizing voyage. Like the English, Columbus started European settlements on Indian land. People from Europe then and since applied their laws written in their languages to lands Native Americans believed they had been placed on by their creators. Authors have always known that literature is never separated from land, law, and language. The lingering impact and trauma of conquest is so great that numerous stories, poems, essays, and novels deal with this trauma. Writing Native American literature is a process of recovering, explaining, and expressing to authors themselves and to others a meaningful past.

What were the causes and consequences of the crisis in the homeland? Tangled answers for five centuries abound but in a simple sense can be boiled down to issues of land, law, and language. Contemporary Native American literature characteristically centers on clashes between natives and newcomers involving these three issues in one way or another.

The history of America can be considered a narrative of intrusions on native lands by many different peoples. In all cases, land was the heart of controversy and conflict. For newcomers, land was property to be bought and sold, fenced and owned. For natives, the people and their land were inseparable. Land was sacred. One could no more sell land than one could sell herself or himself. Just as native literatures were oral, tribal land laws were oral. In contrast, conquering newcomers imposed their written legal system of ownership and played the deed game. This system took the form of treaties, removal, and reservations. The United States Constitution established the federal government's exclusive right to acquire title to Indian lands. The process began with the first treaty negotiated by George Washington in 1789. From then until 1871, the federal government made over 370 treaties. The Constitution declared treaties to be the highest law of the land, equivalent to the Constitution itself. Most importantly, the federal government recognized Indian rights to their tribal territories. When treaty-making ended, there were 187 reservations embracing 181,000 square miles and 243,000 Indians. Citizens raising livestock, prospecting for minerals, and seeking farms and homes frequently ignored Indian rights that were guaranteed by treaties. The U.S. Army was supposed to enforce treaty provisions on both natives and newcomers. It seldom was a double-edged sword, however, usually furthering citizen interests to the cost of Indian lives and property.

For James Welch, the man with rainwater eyes in "The Man from Washington" precisely expresses prevailing Native American attitudes toward the federal government and its futile inoculation against "a world of money, promise, and disease."

In contrast to most tribes, many Cherokees became literate in both English and Cherokee prior to their removal. Elias Boudinot's "Address to the Whites" describes Cherokees rapidly changing their traditional culture, taking U.S. constitutional government as their model. Emulating Americans, however, failed to save Cherokee lands from newcomers like Governor George Gilmer of Georgia, who declared in 1830 that "treaties were expedients by which ignorant, intractable, and savage people were induced without bloodshed to yield up what civilized peoples had a right to possess by virtue of that command of the Creator delivered to man upon his formation—be fruitful, multiply and replenish the earth and subdue it." That same year, Congress passed the Removal Act, directing the president "solemnly to assure the tribe or nation with which the exchange is made, that the United States will forever secure and guarantee to them, and their heirs or successors, the country so exchanged with them." For the

Cherokees, "forever" lasted about seventy years. Boudinot addressed the assembly at the signing of the 1835 Treaty of New Echota: "I know that I take my life in my hand. . . . We will make and sign this treaty. We can die, but the Great Cherokee Nation will be saved. . . . Oh, what is a man worth who will not dare to die for his people?" Cherokee novelist Diane Glancy retells the story of the "Trail of Tears" in her novel, *Pushing the Bear.* Today, Cherokees continue to change in order to cope with current conditions.

Armed confrontations and forced migrations frequently assumed epic proportions in tribal literatures. Navajo authors Luci Tapahonso and Howard Gorman focus on the 1864 forced migration of defeated Navajos from their homeland to the Fort Sumner internment camp. The Navajos returned home in 1868 and became the most populous native group in the United States.

In November of 1868, Lieutenant Colonel George Custer led a detachment of the Seventh Cavalry regiment that massacred peaceful Cheyennes camped on the Washita River. The troops killed Chief Black Kettle and his wife while he waved a United States flag. Most Euro-American historians ignore such events, but poet Diane Glancy remembers and mourns them in "Black Kettle National Grasslands, Western Oklahoma." Other Cheyenne bands escaped; their descendants constitute northern and southern tribes today. Telling how tribal oral literature is transmitted along family lines, Arapaho Debra CallingThunder identifies issues that involve interaction between federal officials and her family that continue to carry their heritage through memories and stories.

Sarah Winnemucca, daughter of a war chief, taught herself fluent English while living among Anglo-American colonists. She wrote about her struggle to achieve justice for her Northern Paiute people. As the first autobiography by a Native American woman, her book is a tribute to her people and testimony of her courage: "Your carbines rise upon the bleak shore, and your so-called civilization sweeps inland from the ocean wave; but, oh, my God! leaving its pathway marked by crimson lines of blood, and strewed by the bones of two races, the inheritor and the invader; and I am crying out to you for justice."

Settler demands for Wallowa Valley land prompted the Nez Perce to flee toward Canada in 1877. Fighting to delay pursuing U.S. Army contingents, the Nez Perce nearly made it. Yellow Wolf, one of the refugees, later told how he preserved his self-respect despite defeat; he did not surrender his rifle. The epic Nez Perce campaign reverberates more than a century later in Coeur d'Alene Janet Hale's moving account of her pilgrimage to the battle site. In 1997, Nez Perce purchased more than ten thousand acres of their treasured Wallowa Valley.

The Northern Paiute anguish of the 1880s that Sarah Winnemucca publicized played its part in the vision that turned Wovoka, another Northern Paiute, into the prophet of the Ghost Dance movement that began in 1889. In December 1890, Sioux physician Charles Eastman saved as many survivors as he could from one Ghost Dancing band massacred by U.S. troops. Eastman heard the Hotchkiss shells bursting among his people eighteen miles from the Agency on Wounded Knee Creek. He rescued from the frozen terrain wounded survivors miraculously alive three days later. He heard their accounts of the massacre while treating them. In 1916, Eastman published his heart-wrenching description of the outcome of the Sioux Ghost Dance.

This chapter closes with Hopi/Miwok Wendy Rose's cry of anguish, "Three Thousand Dollar Death Song." CallingThunder raised the issue of the U.S. Medical Museum and Smithsonian Institution collecting and exhibiting "as curios" skeletons of Native Americans slain by soldiers. The Native American Graves Protection and Repatriation Act reverses how some funded institutions may treat Indian skeletons and grave goods.

Voices rise from the American landscape. Native American authors allow us to hear some of those voices. Their stories are grim. Their words may lie heavy on your heart. The horror they have caught in words may repel you. Yet as part of American literature, they must be heard so old wounds may begin to mend.

THE MAN FROM WASHINGTON

James Welch

Many men came from Washington to the Blackfeet homeland with empty promises. Welch makes a "slouching dwarf" the symbol for glib treaty negotiators, corrupt agents, and ruthless military officers, who brought disease, despair, and death to the Blackfeet people. In only thirteen compact lines, the poet captures the essence of the history of Blackfeet relations with the U.S. government.

Today the Blackfeet live on a reservation in Montana along the eastern slopes of the Rocky Mountains, adjacent to Glacier National Park and the U.S.-Canadian border. Approximately one-third of the land within the reservation is no longer owned by Blackfeet. The reservation is a fifty-mile square of mountains and foothills, lakes and rivers. Tribal land encompassing 1.5 million acres is a small portion of the twenty-six million acres the federal government recognized in an 1855 treaty as Blackfeet territory.

During the first half of the nineteenth century, the Blackfeet traded with Euro-Americans, but because of the isolation of their territory, they encountered outsiders later than most tribes. In 1837, a smallpox pandemic hit Blackfeet camps, and at least one-third of them perished. Then in the 1850s, a flood of prospectors and settlers moved into Blackfeet territory. The newcomers demanded that the U.S. government protect them against the Indians, who resisted encroachment. Consequently, in 1851, the government set the borders of the Blackfeet Nation with the Treaty of Fort Laramie. It was a treaty only in word for the Blackfeet because they were not present, represented, or even consulted during the negotiations.

In 1855, the Blackfeet signed their first mutual treaty with the United States. In return for payment of goods and services, they agreed to give up half their hunting grounds and live in "perpetual peace" with Euro-American neighbors. But the treaty was soon violated as the Blackfeet received spoiled food, damaged wagons, and moldy blankets. With treaties in 1865 and 1868, plus agreements and executive orders until 1895, the Blackfeet were forced gradually to reduce their territory. They resisted and hostilities escalated until on January 6, 1870, Colonel E. M. Baker led his troops in a surprise attack on Heavy Runner's innocent camp and killed approximately two hundred people, primarily elders, women, and children. Most of the men were away hunting. Baker, who attacked the wrong camp, was seeking Mountain Chief's camp to retaliate for raids on settlers. During this dark time, the buffalo, which were the tribe's major source of food, shelter, and clothing, were killed until only a few remained. At last, ravaged by strange diseases and deprived of their primary food supply, the people became dependent upon government rations. When the Blackfeet buffalo hunts failed in 1883–1884, the U.S. government neglected to provide adequate food rations. Over six hundred men, women, and children died in what came to be called the "Starvation Winter."

Welch's great-grandmother survived smallpox and Baker's massacre, and her stories became part of his family history. Clearly, the poet's deadpan tone masks a deeper reality. The "end" could not have been "easy" for his people, who suffered and survived. The nameless man with rainwater eyes offers them a quick-fix promise that life can continue "as usual," despite the loss of buffalo, land, and life. Welch's irony hits hard.

The end came easy for most of us.
Packed away in our crude beginnings
in some far corner of a flat world,
we didn't expect much more
5 than firewood and buffalo robes
to keep us warm. The man came down,
a slouching dwarf with rainwater eyes,
and spoke to us. He promised
that life would go on as usual,
10 that treaties would be signed, and everyone—
man, woman and child—would be inoculated
against a world in which we had no part,
a world of money, promise and disease.

DISCUSSION QUESTIONS

1. Given the losses the Blackfeet people endured, Welch might have justifiably made the representative from Washington a target for rage and hate. Do you think that militant tone would have been more effective for the poet's message? Explain.
2. What does "Washington" in the title stand for?
3. What events marked "the end" for many Native Americans in the nineteenth century?
4. What does the description of "the man" tell you about the kind of representative he was?
5. How can people be "inoculated" against money and promise?

WRITING TOPICS

1. In a paragraph, explain the importance of these words within the context of the poem's message: *promise, treaty, inoculated, money, disease.*
2. Investigate the Blackfeet and their survival from 1850 to the present day. In a short essay, tell what they needed to survive and what happened to them as they met each new challenge. In the final paragraph, give information about contemporary Blackfeet.

AN ADDRESS TO THE WHITES

Elias Boudinot

Elias Boudinot, a pivotal figure in tumultuous times for his people, was caught in the violent conflict between Cherokee and Euro-
American worlds. Buck Watie, who later adopted the name Elias
Boudinot, was born in about 1802 in Georgia. Instead of rearing him
traditionally, his family sent him to a Moravian mission school in
1811. There he received an education in the values and knowledge
of Euro-American society. In 1817, he and other Indian students
attended the American Board of Commissioners for Foreign Missions
school in Cornwall, Connecticut. On their journey to the school,
they stayed at the home of Elias Boudinot, president of the American
Bible Society and a supporter of the Cornwall School. Buck Watie
followed the Cherokee practice of adopting the name of a benefac-
tor and enrolled as Elias Boudinot in the school that he attended until
1826. That year he married Harriet Gold, a Euro-American woman
of Cornwall. The town, however, was unwilling to accept equality
among Indians and Euro-Americans. Outraged citizens declared the
marriage a "criminal act" and burned the couple in effigy on the village green. Later they closed the school in protest against its promo-
tion of racial integration.

In the spring of 1826, the General Council of the Cherokee
Nation sent Boudinot on a tour of the eastern United States to solicit
donations for obtaining a printing press and type in both English and
the Sequoyah syllabary and establishing an academy. As an eloquent
speaker for his people, Boudinot delivered his famous "An Address
to the Whites" in Philadelphia on this tour. He secured the funds and
became the editor of the *Cherokee Phoenix,* the first Indian newspaper. The *Phoenix* became a voice for persuading Americans that the
Cherokees were a "civilized" nation. In the newspaper, Boudinot
protested the encroachments of Georgia citizens on Cherokee lands,
especially after the discovery of gold there.

After Congress passed the 1830 Removal Act, Boudinot at first
resisted removal. He argued that the Cherokee should be allowed to

live in their homeland and preserve their political autonomy. As governmental pressure escalated, Boudinot and a small group holding similar views decided the Nation could not be saved unless it removed to the West. Consequently, about a hundred of them signed the Treaty of New Echota in 1835 providing for the Cherokee to trade lands in the East for land in Indian Territory. Approximately fifteen thousand, almost the entire population, signed a petition protesting the treaty. In fact, Boudinot also signed his death warrant because he violated traditional Cherokee law and the Council law that made selling Cherokee land a crime punishable by death. On June 22, 1839, in Indian Territory, a group of Cherokees executed Boudinot and his relatives Major Ridge and John Ridge in revenge for their having signed the New Echota Treaty. Boudinot believed he had been a patriot. His people believed he had been a traitor.

Boudinot's contribution to Cherokee literature was as editor and translator of English works into Cherokee. In this address, he proves his persuasive skill in English. His logic supported by facts undergirds his question, "Shall red men live?"

1   What is an Indian? Is he not formed of the same materials with yourself? For "of one blood God created all the nations that dwell on the face of the earth. . . ."

2   You here behold an *Indian,* my kindred are *Indians,* and my fathers sleeping in the wilderness grave—they too were *Indians.* But I am not as my fathers were—broader means and nobler influences have fallen upon me. Yet I was not born as thousands are, in a stately dome and amid the congratulations of the great, for on a little hill, in a lonely cabin, overspread by the forest oak, I first drew my breath; and in a language unknown to learned and polished nations, I learnt to lisp my fond mother's name. In after days, I have had greater advantages than most of my race; and I now stand before you delegated by my native country to seek her interest, to labour for her respectability, and by my public efforts to assist in raising her to an equal standing with other nations of the earth. . . .

3   My design is to offer a few disconnected facts relative to the present improved state, and to the ultimate prospects of that particular tribe called Cherokees to which I belong.

4   The Cherokee nation lies within the chartered limits of the states of Georgia, Tennessee, and Alabama. Its extent as defined by treaties is about 200 miles in length from East to West, and about 120 in breadth. This country which is supposed to contain about 10,000,000 of acres exhibits great varieties of surface, the most part being hilly and mountainous, afford-

ing soil of no value. The vallies, however, are well watered and afford excellent land, in many parts particularly on the large streams, that of the first quality. The climate is temperate and healthy. . . . Those advantages, calculated to make the inhabitants healthy, vigorous, and intelligent, cannot fail to cause this country to become interesting. And there can be no doubt that the Cherokee Nation, however obscure and trifling it may now appear, will finally become, if not under its present occupants, one of the Garden spots of America. And here, let me be indulged in the fond wish, that she may thus become under those who now possess her; and ever be fostered, regulated and protected by the generous government of the United States.

5   The population of the Cherokee Nation increased from the year 1810 to that of 1824, 2000 exclusive of those who emigrated in 1818 and 19 to the west of the Mississippi—of those who reside on the Arkansas the number is supposed to be about 5000.

6   The rise of these people in their movement towards civilization may be traced as far back as the relinquishment of their towns; when game became incompetent to their support, by reason of the surrounding white population. They then betook themselves to the woods, commenced the opening of small clearings, and the raising of stock; still however following the chase. Game has since become so scarce that little dependence for subsistence can be placed upon it. They have gradually and I could almost say universally forsaken their ancient employment. In fact, there is not a single family in the nation, that can be said to subsist on the slender support which the wilderness would afford. . . .

7   On the other hand it cannot be doubted that the nation is improving, rapidly improving in all those particulars which must finally constitute the inhabitants an industrious and intelligent people.

8   It is a matter of surprise to me, and must be to all those who are properly acquainted with the condition of the Aborigines of this country, that the Cherokees have advanced so far and so rapidly in civilization. But there are yet powerful obstacles, both within and without, to be surmounted in the march of improvement. The prejudices in regard to them in the general community are strong and lasting. The evil effects of their intercourse with their immediate white neighbours, who differ from them chiefly in name, are easily to be seen, and it is evident that from this intercourse proceed those demoralizing practices which in order to surmount, peculiar and unremitting efforts are necessary. In defiance, however, of these obstacles the Cherokees have improved and are still rapidly improving. To give you a further view of their condition, I will here repeat some of the articles of the two statistical tables taken at different periods.

9   In 1810 there were 19,500 cattle; 6,100 horses; 19,600 swine; 1,037 sheep; 467 looms; 1,600 spinning wheels; 30 waggons; 500 ploughs; 3 sawmills; 13 grist-mills etc. At this time there are 22,000 cattle; 7,600 horses; 46,000 swine; 2,500 sheep; 762 looms; 2488 spinning wheels; 172 waggons; 2,943 ploughs; 10 saw-mills; 31 grist-mills; 62 Blacksmith shops; 8

cotton machines; 18 schools; 18 ferries; and a number of public roads. In one district there were, last winter, upwards of 0000[1] volumes of good books; and 11 different periodical papers both religious and political, which were taken and read. On the public roads there are many decent Inns; and few houses for convenience, etc., would disgrace any country. Most of the schools are under the care and tuition of christian missionaries, of different denominations, who have been of great service to the nation, by inculcating moral and religious principles into the minds of the rising generation. In many places the word of God is regularly preached and explained, both by missionaries and natives; and there are numbers who have publicly professed their belief and interest in the merits of the great Saviour of the world. It is worthy of remark, that in no ignorant country have the missionaries undergone less trouble and difficulty, in spreading a knowledge of the Bible, than in this. . . .

10   There are three things of late occurance, which must certainly place the Cherokee Nation in a fair light, and act as a powerful argument in favor of Indian improvement.

11   First. The invention of letters.

12   Second. The translation of the New Testament into Cherokee.

13   And Third. The organization of a Government.

14   The Cherokee mode of writing lately invented by George Guest,[2] who could not read any language nor speak any other than his own, consists of eighty-six characters, principally syllabic, the combinations of which form all the words of the language.

15   The translation of the New Testament, together with Guest's mode of writing, has swept away that barrier which has long existed, and opened a spacious channel for the instruction of adult Cherokees. Persons of all ages and classes may now read the precepts of the Almighty in their own language. . . .

16   The Government, though defective in many respects, is well suited to the condition of the inhabitants. As they rise in information and refinement, changes in it must follow, until they arrive at that state of advancement, when I trust they will be admitted into all the privileges of the American family.

17   The Cherokee Nation is divided into eight districts, in each of which are established courts of justice, where all disputed cases are decided by a Jury, under the direction of a circuit Judge, who has jurisdiction over two districts. Sheriffs and other public officers are appointed to execute the decisions of the courts, collect debts, and arrest thieves and other criminals. Appeals may be taken to the superior Court, held annually at the seat of

---

[1] *0000:* The number intended is not known.
[2] *George Guest:* The Cherokee known as Sequoyah (c.1760–c.1840), who gave his syllabary to the Cherokees in 1821.

Government. The Legislative authority is vested in a General Court, which consists of the National Committee and Council. The National Committee consists of thirteen members, who are generally men of sound sense and fine talents. The National Council consists of thirty-two members, beside the speaker, who act as the representatives of the people. Every bill passing these two bodies, becomes the law of the land. Clerks are appointed to do the writings, and record the proceedings of the Council. The executive power is vested in two principal chiefs, who hold their office during good behaviour, and sanction all the decisions of the legislative council. Many of the laws display some degree of civilization, and establish the respectability of the nation. . . .

18 From what I have said, you will form but a faint opinion of the true state and prospects of the Cherokees. You will, however, be convinced of three important truths.

19 First, that the means which have been employed for the christianization and civilization of this tribe, have been greatly blessed. Second, that the increase of these means will meet with final success. Third, that it has now become necessary, that efficient and more than ordinary means should be employed.

20 Sensible of this last point, and wishing to do something for themselves, the Cherokees have thought it advisable that there should be established, a Printing Press and a Seminary of respectable character; and for these purposes your aid and patronage are now solicited. They wish the types, as expressed in their resolution, to be composed of English letters and Cherokee characters. These characters have now become extensively used in the nation; their religious songs are written in them; there is an astonishing eagerness in people of all classes and ages to acquire a knowledge of them; and the New Testament has been translated into their language. All this impresses on them the immediate necessity of procuring types. The most informed and judicious of our nation, believe that such a press would go further to remove ignorance, and her offspring superstition and prejudice, than all other means. . . . The simplicity of this method of writing, and the eagerness to obtain a knowledge of it, are evinced by the astonishing rapidity with which it is acquired, and by the numbers who do so. It is about two years since its introduction, and already there are a great many who can read it. In the neighbourhood in which I live, I do not recollect a male Cherokee, between the ages of fifteen and twenty-five, who is ignorant of this mode of writing. But in connexion with those for Cherokee characters, it is necessary to have types for English letters. There are many who already speak and read the English language, and can appreciate the advantages which would result from the publication of their laws and transactions in a well conducted newspaper. . . .

21 The Cherokees wish to establish their Seminary, upon a footing which will insure to it all the advantages, that belong to such institutions in the states. Need I spend one moment in arguments, in favour of such an insti-

tution; need I do more than simply to ask the patronage of benevolent hearts, to obtain that patronage.

22 When before did a nation of Indians step forward and ask for the means of civilization? The Cherokee authorities have adopted the measures already stated, with a sincere desire to make their nation an intelligent and a virtuous people, and with a full hope that those who have already pointed out to them the road of happiness, will now assist them to pursue it. With that assistance, what are the prospects of the Cherokees? Are they not indeed glorious, compared to that deep darkness in which the nobler qualities of their souls have slept? Yes, methinks I can view my native country, rising from the ashes of her degradation, wearing her purified and beautiful garments, and taking her seat with the nations of the earth. I can behold her sons bursting the fetters of ignorance and unshackling her from the vices of heathenism. She is at this instant, risen like the first morning sun, which grows brighter and brighter, until it reaches its fulness of glory.

23 She will become not a great, but a faithful ally of the United States. In times of peace she will plead the common liberties of America. In times of war her intrepid sons will sacrifice their lives in your defence. And because she will be useful to you in coming time, she asks you to assist her in her present struggles. She asks not for greatness; she seeks not wealth, she pleads only for assistance to become respectable as a nation, to enlighten and ennoble her sons, and to ornament her daughters with modesty and virtue. She pleads for this assistance, too, because on her destiny hangs that of many nations. If she completes her civilization—then may we hope that all our nations will—then, indeed, may true patriots be encouraged in their efforts to make this world of the West, one continuous abode of enlightened, free, and happy people.

24 But if the Cherokee Nation fail in her struggle, if she die away, then all hopes are blasted, and falls the fabric of Indian civilization. Their fathers were born in darkness, and have died in darkness; without your assistance so will their sons. You, see, however, where the probability rests. Is there a soul whose narrowness will not permit the exercise of charity on such an occasion? Where is he that can withhold his mite from an object so noble? Who can prefer a little of his silver and gold, to the welfare of nations of his fellow beings? Human wealth perishes with our clay, but that wealth gained in charity still remains on earth, to enrich our names, when we are gone, and will be remembered in Heaven, when the miser and his coffers have mouldered together in their kindred earth. The works of a generous mind sweeten the cup of affliction; they enlighten the dreary way to the cold tomb; they blunt the sting of death, and smooth his passage to the unknown world. When all the kingdoms of this earth shall die away and their beauty and power shall perish, his name shall live and shine as a twinkling star; those for whose benefit be done his deeds of charity shall call him blessed, and they shall add honor to his immortal head.

25 There are, with regard to the Cherokee and other tribes, two alternatives; they must either become civilized and happy, or sharing the fate of many

kindred nations, become extinct. If the General Government continue its protection, and the American people assist them in their humble efforts, they will, they must rise. Yes, under such protection, and with such assistance, the Indian must rise like the Phoenix, after having wallowed for ages in ignorance and barbarity. But should this Government withdraw its care, and the American people their aid, then, to use the words of a writer, "they will go the way that so many tribes have gone before them. . . . They will vanish like a vapour from the face of the earth, their very history will be lost in forgetfulness, and places that now know them will know them no more."

26   There is, in Indian history, something very melancholy, and which seems to establish a mournful precedent for the future events of the few sons of the forest, now scattered over this vast continent. We have seen every where the poor aborigines melt away before the white population. I merely speak of the fact, without at all referring to the cause. We have seen, I say, one family after another, one tribe after another, nation after nation, pass away; until only a few solitary creatures are left to tell the sad story of extinction.

27   Shall this precedent be followed? I ask you, shall red men live, or shall they be swept from the earth? With you and this public at large, the decision chiefly rests. Must they perish? Must they all, like the unfortunate Creeks, (victims of the unchristian policy of certain persons,) go down in sorrow to their grave?

28   They hang upon your mercy as to a garment. Will you push them from you, or will you save them? Let humanity answer.

◉

DISCUSSION QUESTIONS

1. What are some of Boudinot's purposes in this speech?
2. How is his speech organized?
3. Boudinot says that he can see Cherokee sons "bursting the fetters of ignorance." How can ignorance be a fetter?
4. In paragraph 21, what does Boudinot say are the alternatives with "regard to the Cherokee and other tribes"?
5. Non-Indians have often been ignorant about Native Americans. Has this ignorance been a fetter? Why or why not?

Writing Topics

1. Boudinot says that "human wealth perishes . . . but that wealth gained in charity still remains on earth, to enrich our names, . . . and will be remembered in Heaven." These sentiments or similar ones are common to many religions or belief systems. What evidence do you have that proves or disproves that people accept and act on this belief? Present your views in an essay.

2. Ralph Waldo Emerson wrote a letter to President Martin Van Buren protesting Cherokee removal. His letter contains eloquent rhetoric like that of Boudinot's address. Emerson, writing to the president, and Boudinot, speaking to the American public, both presented their arguments in light of "civilization." Find a copy of Emerson's letter. Write an essay in which you support three arguments Emerson makes in support of the notion that Cherokee removal was an uncivilized act on the part of the U.S. government. Use evidence from Emerson and Boudinot to support your essay.

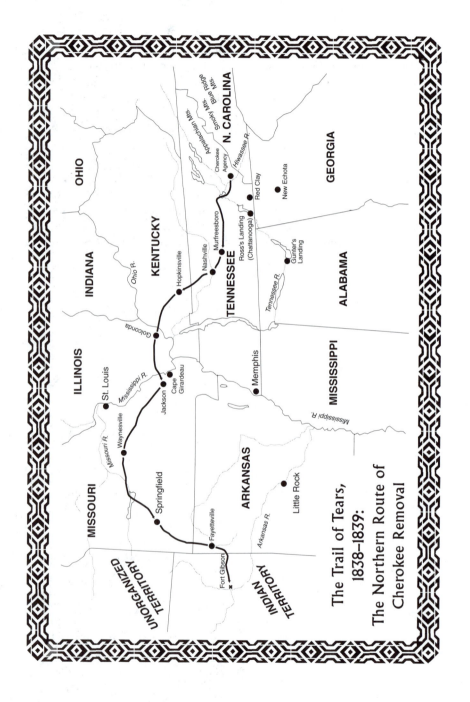

The Trail of Tears, 1838–1839: The Northern Route of Cherokee Removal

FROM *PUSHING THE BEAR*

Diane Glancy

Diane Glancy, poet, fiction writer, essayist, and educator, was born in 1941 to parents of German, English, and Cherokee descent. Her collection of essays *Claiming Breath* (1992) won an American Book Award and the 1992 Native American Prose Award. She received the Five Civilized Tribes Playwriting Prize in 1987 for *Weebjob.* Her other major works include *Firesticks: A Collection of Stories* (1993); *War Cries: A Collection of Plays* (1996); *The Only Piece of Furniture in the House* (1996); and *The West Pole* (1997). Glancy teaches Native American literature and creative writing at Macalester College in St. Paul, Minnesota.

In realistic, sometimes colloquial language, Glancy explores spirituality, family ties, her intimate link to the Great Plains landscape, and her mixed genetic identity. "Out of my eight great-grandparents, only one was Cherokee. How can the influence of one be as strong as seven together? Yet in my writing, as well as in my life . . . it is my Indian heritage that emerges again and again."

In recovering her "Indian voice," the author remembers her grandmother as an inspiration, "My Cherokee grandmother could not write. I have her X on the land deed when the farm was sold in northern Arkansas. . . . Neither did she speak more than a few words when we visited. But not speaking she spoke to me, and it is her quiet influence I feel. . . . I think in some way I am drawn to words because of her."

The parents of Glancy's great-grandfather, Woods Lewis, survived the Trail of Tears. That historical trauma generates struggle within the author. "Part of me came across the sea from Europe to Virginia, then west in a wagon to the Missouri-Kansas border where my mother's family settled. The other part of me walked nine hundred miles on foot during the forced migration of Cherokees from the East to Oklahoma. I do not know why the little storm of words falls upon me. But I hear voices in the grass."

In the novel *Pushing the Bear* (1996), the author imagines courageous voices rising from the Removal. The character Maritole seems to merge with Glancy herself who has observed, "So my structure has always been one of conflict and ambivalence. Aren't all of us made of paradox and diversity, anger, hurt, hope, guilt, endurance . . . especially women? A composite for which we have to provide the connecting threads." She complements passages in English with characters from the Sequoyah syllabary. Glancy dramatizes from the perspective of the 1990s why Cherokees refer to their ancestors' forced march from southeastern homes to Indian Territory as their "Trail of Tears."

On May 23, 1838, about two hundred fifty Cherokees assembled to comply with the federal deadline for their removal to Indian Territory. The rest of the Cherokees, about fifteen thousand souls, remained in their homes. How could they leave their homeland? They believed they were on sacred ground, the center of the world. The spirits of their dead lingered there. The mountains and valleys were holy places. They feared that the native plants used for medicines did not grow in the West. The Cherokees had long struggled against the U.S. government and the southeastern states in disputes over land. Treaties were negotiated with a small fraction of the Indian population. At last the hunger for Indian land led to forceful eviction by the U.S. Army. More than seven thousand federal and state troops were sent to the Cherokee nation to complete removal.

General Winfield Scott and his troops rounded up the dissidents. And so began the Cherokee "Trail of Tears," one of the darkest episodes in the history of United States relations with Native Americans. From October 1838 through March 1839, thirteen Cherokee detachments moved to Indian Territory. Epidemic smallpox, whooping cough, and pneumonia infected and felled many of them. Historians calculate that more than four thousand died from cold, hunger, and disease.

Soldiers arrived at every Cherokee house, often without warning, and forced the people out at bayonet point with only the clothes on their backs. They left behind household goods, farm equipment, seeds, and houses. The captives were marched to stockades and were guarded there under terrible conditions. Food and water were insufficient, and the prisoners suffered from malnutrition and infections. Even the regular Army officers responsible for executing the removal plan were horrified. Soldiers burned many captives' cabins and crops in order to discourage them from escaping and returning home. In other cases, Georgia citizens immediately occupied the Cherokee homes and land. During the swift, brutal sweep of Indian homes, parents and children often became separated.

Removal cast a long shadow, but the Cherokee people gradually rebuilt their lives in Indian Territory. To focus on removal tragedy is to tell only part of the Cherokee story. More than one hundred sixty years later, their descendants number approximately 200,000 tribal members. The Nation's population continues to grow, and it has an annual budget of over $50 million. The Cherokee people continue to renew spirit and culture as they move into the twenty-first century.

MARITOLE

1   "Maritole!" I heard my husband from the field. I sat on the cabin step helping the baby stand. "Maritole," Knobowtee called again. I started to get up, but the baby wobbled at my knees.

2   Dust swarmed over the dried cornstalks in the field by the cabin. Horses were coming. For a moment the woods beyond the cornfield whirled. Knobowtee walked between mounted soldiers into our small clearing. I stood at the cabin step, and the baby sat on the ground.

3   I had seen white men when they came to trade. Sometimes they rode by the farm not seeing our path. Now solders were in the clearing with their rifles and bayonets. I heard their quick words, but I didn't know what they said. They seemed invisible inside their dark clothes.

4   ᎤᎵ, I groaned.

5   We heard that soldiers had rounded up Cherokee in Georgia and Tennessee, but we thought the soldiers would keep riding past the settlements near us: Dústayalun´yi and Egwanulti. Now the soldiers had found us. I stepped on an apple core that fell from my lap. The sun had burned away the morning fog, and the light and the dust blurred the men. I had to wash the baby's clothes. I was going to take the corn to the mill. A basket of apples and peaches from our trees waited by the wagon.

6   The soldiers talked fast. In our language, my husband told me to carry the crying baby. We were going to a stockade in Tennessee.

7   " ᎢᎬᏝᏪᎯᏐᎭᏐᏍ," I told him.

8   "We'll march," Knobowtee answered. "Chief John Ross hoped we could keep our land. But Ridge and Boudinot, the leaders in Georgia, signed the treaty that took our land away."

9   "I won't," I said again to Knobowtee.

10   A soldier with white eyes spoke and gestured to me to take the baby. He dismounted, put his bayonet to my side, and poked. Knobowtee turned and walked ahead of me. I couldn't leave the farm. The cabin in the yellow leaves. My grandmother's spinning wheel and cotton cards. Her copper thimble. I felt my knees fold. The baby screamed and Knobowtee picked her up. The soldier lifted me to my feet, and I knew he said, "March."

11   They couldn't remove us. Didn't the soldiers know we were the land? The cornstalks were our grandmothers. In our story of corn, a woman

named Selu had been murdered by her sons. Where her blood fell, the corn grew. The cornstalks waved their arms trying to hold us. Their voices were the long tassels reaching the air. Our spirits clung to them. Our roots entwined.

12   My feet would not walk, and the soldier held me up by my arm. I walked sideways and fell into the cornstalks at the side of the road. A bird's chirp filled my ears. I wanted to hold the air and the sound of the land. The soldier poked at me with his bayonet. I thought for a moment his face was blue. I tried to get up, but my knees wouldn't hold. I still had the apple core in my hand.

13   "Wagon." The soldier pointed and pulled me out of the cornstalks. I had heard their language from the white minister in church. He read scriptures in English, then one of our holy men would translate: ᎠᏀᎢᏗᏌ, ᏪᏍᎢ. The words spoke of hope but now there was no hope.

KNOBOWTEE

14   Chief John Ross had gone to Washington from Red Clay, Tennessee, to argue against the removal, but the Ridge and Boudinot faction in Georgia knew we had no chance to keep our land and signed the Treaty of New Echota in secret.

15   The white men were still angry that we had joined the British during the Revolutionary War. Then gold was discovered in northern Georgia near Dalonagah, and the white men wanted it. They also wanted our farms.

16   Chief John Ross sent runners to tell us about the men's angry voices in council. They knew Andrew Jackson wouldn't uphold the agreement that kept Cherokee land for Cherokee. Already, Georgia had made Indian meetings illegal other than to sign treaties.

17   I looked at Maritole as she stumbled on the path. I told her again we didn't have a chance.

18   After the Treaty of New Echota passed by one vote in Congress, Ross had gone to Washington to negotiate for us to oversee our own removal. His brother, Lewis Ross, would furnish supplies.

MARITOLE

19   I tried to follow Knobowtee, but the road kept going sideways. I walked like I was my grandmother before she died, when her knees wouldn't hold. I heard the soldiers laugh.

20   "Walk straight," Knobowtee carried the baby and looked at me. "We don't have any choice. There'll be a wagon ahead. You and the baby can ride."

21   I looked back at the cabin, but we had passed the first bend in the wagon ruts. My grandmother's scissors and her bone hairpin and shell beads were on my dresser. The bed my father helped Knobowtee make. The nutting stone and pestles he gave us when we married. Sometimes I still heard my

grandmother's voice in the cabin. I couldn't leave. The sky passed before my eyes, and I felt myself hit the hard ground.

THE SOLDIERS

22 "Corporal, there's another cabin in the trees."

23 "Don't let 'em get out the back."

24 "Harder to stop than horses running loose."

GELEST

25 You soldiers. I knew you were coming. Ha. You didn't startle me. The baby who was born talking said you were coming. It was a Choolaskey. Conjurers. As soon as the baby's head was out, it sang its own birth song. It said its own secret name. ᎠᏬᎠᏎᎢᎫᏍ. It said it was afraid of winter because it didn't want to be one-of-those-who walked.

26 The holy men, ᏗᏴᎣᎠᎤᏴ, made stick-crosses for the four directions, and the crosses fell to the west.

27 Even the birds are quiet. I would run from you, but my legs are stiff as the willow strips I soak in the creek. I hear your horses on the road. I know you stop at my cabin. I hear nothing but my heart beating in my ears. Maybe you are standing still thinking what to do. I could hear your footsteps if you walked to the creek.

28 If I were an animal, the soldiers could not find me. If I hold still I can become a deer. I lean over the creek and lap with my tongue. I feel under my skirt for the hooves. The soft deer tail. ᏝᎩᎣᏝᏃᏢᏎᎣᏝ. My nostrils widen. I smell the wind. I look into the creek and see the downy ears on my head. I lift my head and step through the woods. My deer leavings are all of me you get.

THE SOLDIERS

29 "I think we lost as many as we rounded up."

30 "The corporal don't need to know."

31 "We got more than you think."

32 "Keep your eye on 'em. We're still losing some of 'em."

QUATY LEWIS

33 Of all the trees who spoke it was the pine who said we would go, covering its needles with its hands. The ground seemed to rumble loose our hold. "A whole nation would move," my husband said, sweating though it was no longer hot. Since the 1835 New Echota Treaty, the U.S. government had been trying to push the Cherokee to the new territory. A few had gone, but the rest of us wouldn't leave. Last summer, the soldiers began internment in stockades, but the heat sickened the Cherokee, and we knew they would wait until fall. Each day I looked for soldiers on the road.

MARITOLE

34   The rumble of the wagon startled me from blackness. I sat up. Knobowtee walked beside the wagon. "Some of the Cherokee have already gone west," I heard the men say. "How many trails have there been?"

35   I saw that Anna Sco-so-tah held my baby. "You can't take up the whole wagon." She pushed my feet with hers. The wagon was crowded, and I tried to make room for the others. Kee-un-e-ca and the widow Teehee of the Blue clan. Lacey Woodard of the Long Hair clan. Quaty Lewis, Wolf clan. Mrs. Young Turkey, Blind Savannah clan. The wheels jolted over the ground, and I held to the side.

36   The wagon rattled loose someone's voice. Was it Mrs. Young Turkey? "I seen a bug in the crock. It walk around. Around. It couldn't get out. Har. That's us now. That bug. The trees grow up like sides of a crock. Taller than us. Umgh. Soldiers make us walk in the circle in our heads. We're not getting out."

37   I looked at Knobowtee as he walked beside the wagon. He seemed a stranger to me.

ANNA SCO-SO-TAH

38   The birds called to me across the trees. Even the water spoke. " ᏅᏓᎸᏍᏅᎵᏓᏝᏍ," I told the women bitterly in the wagon. The soldiers came down the road and told me to leave. My legs wouldn't walk. The soldiers grabbed my arms and held me up. The sky was brown as the hen blood on my boots. I tried to call to my neighbor, but my voice cackled. For a moment I thought I was a hen. I flopped on the ground. My brown feathers in the dust.

39   The soldiers let me stop at a stream to drink. "Maybe she'll stop cackling," they said.

MARITOLE

40   I took the baby from Anna Sco-so-tah and held her on my lap. I wanted to ask Knobowtee what stockade we were going to, but I knew he would not want his wife talking.

41   The wagon stopped along the road and was joined by other wagons and columns of men on foot in the thick woods of pine and yellow oak. The soldiers seemed nervous, and some twitched when a woman sobbed or a child cried out. Other soldiers were hard.

42   "Their eyes cut through us like bayonets." The widow Teehee talked under her breath.

43   "My legs trembled and I couldn't stand," Anna Sco-so-tah said to her as we waited in the wagon. "I sat on the ground in front of my cabin. They told me to *get up*. I tried, but my legs wouldn't stand."

44   The wagon started again with a jerk. Lacey Woodard cried out. Mrs. Young Turkey hushed her.

45 "'Up,' the soldiers said." Anna continued twisting the hem of her cotton dress in her hands. "Their voices had vines in them. When they told me to walk, I could feel them pulling me to the wagon. My hands fluttered like they weren't mine. Somewhere the thunder growled."

46 Quaty Lewis had heard that the soldiers separated parents from their children in their hurry. Her voice choked. The men who walked near the wagon looked at the ground. Knobowtee told us all to be quiet. Some of the women cried to themselves. They held their faces in their hands.

> *Listen to that old woman.*
> *She yell over ever bump.*
> *Shud up. Woman.*
> *Umgh.*

47 When we joined another wagon on the main road, a Cherokee called out to a friend. A soldier rode over to him. I knew he'd hit him with his whip. I started to get out of the wagon, but Knobowtee yelled at me. I screamed at the Cherokee who had called. Knobowtee knocked me back into the wagon with his arm. Anna Sco-so-tah held me in her lap. I could hear the soldier hit the man. I could smell the dust from the cornfields on Anna's apron. I could feel her hands clawing my face.

48 There was musket shot, and another soldier ordered the one with the whip to stop. Behind us, a horse reared up and a soldier rushed to hold it. A principal soldier ordered the wagons to start moving, and we leaped forward again with another jerk. The men and women groaned and sobbed. I held the baby so close she fussed.

49 Knobowtee's face was dark with fear.

50 "Where are we going?" I asked him. He didn't answer at first.

51 "I don't know, Maritole. Probably the Hiwassee River."

52 "In Tennessee?" I asked, but he didn't answer. I put my head in Anna's lap and covered my face with her apron. Lights sparked the darkness of Anna's apron when I pushed my fingers into my eyes. The Hiwassee was several days away.

53 *Hey you tree, you going like us?*

54 I had been to Red Clay, Tennessee, when I was a girl. I visited relatives and went to a green corn festival. My great-grandfather came from the old Cherokee capital, Chota, Tennessee. He moved to New Echota, Georgia, and then to North Carolina. Red Clay was now the Cherokee capital. The white men had divided our land among their states and called most of our places by English names.

55 I felt sick in the darkness of Anna's apron and sat up.

56 My mother had wanted to go to Red Clay, but my father was angry with Chief John Ross there. He thought Ross was a dreamer. My father said we would stay in North Carolina and face the loss of our land and whatever came afterward with dignity.

57   Knobowtee kept his dignity. Why didn't he spit on the soldiers? Why didn't everyone stand up to them and say we weren't going? The baby crawled over my lap and struggled to get away, but I held her as the wagon jolted over the road. Knobowtee frowned at me as though there was something I could do to keep her still.

58   I knew the soldiers were rounding up Cherokee all through the woods. Every time we joined another wagon, I looked for my mother and father and Tanner, my older brother, his wife, and two small boys.

59   Behind me, someone was trying to calm a fretting dog, who turned one way, then another, making small, sharp cries.

60   I thought of the birds and geese. The raccoon that came to the cabin step. The curl of wood smoke and the chirp of bugs from the woods. The trees were ancestors. Their roots reached into the creek banks. I wanted to hear the buzz of a fly around me on the cabin step. We were made from the soil we farmed. Now the dust road seemed to flare like cooking fires. I thought once I heard thunder. I looked at the soldiers, their boots dusty from the road, their uniforms like bruises.

61   The wagons passed easier over some pine needles on the road. The baby slept for a moment on my lap but soon woke at a toss of the wagon. I thought of the butter not yet made. Knobowtee was cutting the dried cornstalks for fodder when the soldiers came. Did he leave the horse hitched to the plow? What would happen to it? The Cherokee men walked in their turbans and tunics. The autumn sun shone on our heads, lighting the black hair and eyes that were dark and strained.

QUATY LEWIS

62   The soldiers beat an old man on the road. He bowed under the weight of the bundle on his back. His turban fell. His legs wobbled as he tried to stand but couldn't. The soldiers beat him harder with the whip to make him get up. The women cried, but the Cherokee men looked away. The soldiers didn't stop hitting him. No one could do anything. The old man struggled once more to get up but fell back to the ground. The soldiers told the Cherokee to walk around him and pushed the Cherokee with their bayonets.

63   In the wagon I heard the old man's voice moaning. I put my hand to my neck and felt it stir. I didn't know if it was his voice or my own throat talking.

ANNA SCO-SO-TAH

64   "They got Kinchow, too," I said when I saw my neighbor.

65   Kinchow came to the wagon. "I heard Anna cackle. I knew the soldiers was coming anyway." He looked at the women. I saw the scratches on his face, but he hadn't gotten away through the woods. "I seen Anna, too," he told the women as we waited on the road. "In a dream I was in my cabin and she came to the window. Her arms were short. They was covered with feathers."

66   "He talks all the time," I said.

67   "She a witch," Kinchow said. "That's all I can say."

68   "He's a sorcerer," I told the others. "The chickens cluck when he comes. Sorcerers are night-travelers. Chickens don't like them."

69   "Huh?" Kinchow said. "She only got three chickens. If she eat a chicken one day, I see it walking around again the next. She a witch, I tell you. That's all I can tell."

70   "My chickens would peck him if I didn't chase them with a stick."

71   "Huh?" Kinchow grunted, as the soldiers hurried us on.

72   "That's how I know he's a sorcerer," I said, riding beside him. "The chickens don't like him."

MARITOLE

73   The campfires spoke through the dark woods like stars. I heard Anna's voice. Kinchow's. Quaty Lewis. The widow Teehee. Others. Their voices made a low hum that would rise at times like wind. I think the trees were calling. The baby cried with me. Neither Knobowtee nor the other men could stop us. "What are we going to cook with? Where is our bedding?" We wanted our cabins and belongings.

74   If I slept it was only until the horror stirred me. I woke crying with the others into the dark air.

75   The soldiers ordered us to be quiet with words we didn't always know. They walked among us and poked with bayonets. Some Cherokee men hit their women. It had been agreed in council: We would bear our fate if the removal came.

76   But how could we go without pots to cook with, blankets to sleep in? How could we be quiet when we were being torn away from everything we'd known?

77   Children had been separated from their parents by accident. Wives could not find their husbands. I could not find my own parents in camp. Where was Thomas, my younger brother? Tanner and his family? But I saw no one from my family. Knobowtee looked for his relatives, too. His brother. His mother and sister.

78   In the night a woman cried out. I woke suddenly and listened. I thought I had imagined it, but then I heard another woman scream. A man's angry voice rose above the woman's.

79   "The soldiers killed someone," Knobowtee said, and put his hand over my mouth. He held my head to his chest. The baby was in a sleep of exhaustion. Her small chest jerked in my arms as she dreamed. Soldiers rushed past. After some muffled voices, a hush folded the camp in its darkness.

80   In the morning a soldier was sentenced to ten lashes. He had stabbed the woman with his bayonet.

81   "He lost his head trying to keep order," a soldier told our men. We could hear the whip against his uniform.

82   "But we want our bedding," the women said. The pain of what we lost was worse than the fear of the soldiers. "How can we sleep on the ground? The nights will get cold." The women pleaded with the soldiers, and I cried with them: "We want our cooking pots. How can we eat the army rations? We're sick from salt pork. How can the soldiers feed us along the trails? Our children starve."

83   We kept after the soldiers into the morning. They heard what we said. A ᏗᏝᎣᎤ, a holy man, told them what we said.

84   The holy men and even the white ministers prayed for our loss. They prayed for the return of our land and belongings.

ᎢᏗᎦᏩᎤᏗ
ᎠᏝᎤᎤᏴ

85   They even prayed against the insects that bit us.

Ꭴ	now
ᎲᎤᎠᎪ	insects
ᎣᎥᎮᎾ	ha then
ᎠᎥᎤᏪᎥ°	wood place just
ᎠᎮᎤ	residers
ᎢᎮ4Ꭲ	they certainly being

(Insects are in the woods, but we ask them to stay in their place and not bite us.)

86   One of the principal soldiers talked to the other soldiers. He came to the group of Cherokee, where I stood with Knobowtee. I started to ask Knobowtee what he said, but he put his hand against my mouth.

87   "They'll let the women go back for blankets and cooking pots," he said in a hush.

88   "The men?" I asked.

89   "No, we're under guard. Get ready, Maritole. Go quickly to one of the wagons when the soldiers order. Get the bags of seed-corn. Get my musket and the blankets."

90   The thought of my garden last summer with beans, peas, squash, melon, pumpkin, and potatoes gnawed at my stomach when Knobowtee spoke of corn. I could see my cabin, the bones of dried clay between the logs, the cluttered garden beside the cabin, the cornfields that crowded the garden, the narrow trail through the field, the cabin like a heart, the rows of corn like ribs in the chest of the woods.

91   The soldiers turned the wagons around. The Indians who spoke both languages said a few of the women could go back for whatever belongings they could carry. There was a stampede toward the wagons, then a gunshot

in the air. The soldiers pointed their rifles at us. Not all could go. Too many had escaped already. They rode among us and poked at who could go. They seemed to choose at random. Women who were left behind fell to their knees wailing. The soldier with light eyes rode past me and touched my shoulder with his bayonet. He said something that sounded like Cherokee, but I couldn't understand.

92 "Get whatever will help." Knobowtee held the baby and pushed his hand against my back. I raced for one of the wagons and stood in line panting, thinking of things I would retrieve. A soldier wrote our names. It took him a long time to understand what we said.

93 We rattled back toward our cabins in the dawn. I would have my bowls and the bone-handled forks. My grandmother's bone-carved hairpin I admired since I was a girl. Her scissors. The feather-edge dishes. I thought of Knobowtee's musket and shot pouch and his bullet molds. The bags of seed-corn. Animal traps. Ax. Cooking ladles. My iron pots and kettles. Quilts. Blankets. My garden beside the cabin bordered with blue columbine. The peach and apple trees. The fields and sky. My head scurried like a nest of field mice I had uncovered in the corn.

94 I gripped the side of the wagon so hard my fingers throbbed. I felt my shoulders tighten as if by holding my body stiff the wagon would go faster. I chewed on the sleeves of my blouse. When the wagon stopped, a woman got out and ran to her cabin to grab what she could. The soldiers did not help. The women came tugging their kettles up the wagon ruts. I helped pull things over the sides. The widow Teehee cried when she tumbled back in the wagon empty-handed. Kee-un-e-ca also returned with nothing. Her cabin had burned. Everything was gone. Others said the white men had already auctioned off their farms. Wails filled the sky.

95 I jumped frantically when the wagon came to our path. I raced down the road. Wood smoke was coming from my chimney. I threw back the door and found white people at my table.

96 I screamed at them. ᎤᎾᎥ ᏒᏏ ᎥᏓ. They froze in horror. I pulled the cooking pot out of the hearth with my hands, and it spilled on the floor. "Mine!" I screamed at them in Cherokee. My plates and forks. I turned the table over. The children screamed and danced with terror to their mother. The man got his musket. He aimed it at my head, but the shot went past me. I kicked over a chair in my rage. He loaded his musket again, and the soldier rode his horse nearly into the cabin.

97 "This cabin is mine!" The words spit from my mouth. My body was stiff as a beam. The soldier grabbed me and threw me outside the door. I heard the soldier yell at the people in the cabin. There was a struggle, and he came out with the cooking pot and blankets he ripped from the bed. "The musket," I told him. "My forks and ladles. The quilts my grandmother made. Our corn!"

98 He yelled at me, but I didn't understand his words. He shot into the air,

and another soldier came riding up the wagon ruts. He picked me up and tried to get me on his horse, but I kicked and nearly pulled us both to the ground. It was the same soldier who had tapped my shoulder to let me come. He took his bayonet and held it to my chest. With the point against me, he pushed me away from the cabin. "No!" I held out my arms to the place where I had come as the new wife of Knobowtee. My grandmother's cabin before she died. My baby was born there. It was built near the old ᎠᏏ, the sweat house and storage cellar built after my family came from Georgia. It was my farm! We had not even cleared all the fields yet. Who is the white man to drive us from our land? I spit at the soldier's feet. He stuck me with his bayonet. The sharp point against my breastbone quivered my knees. He turned me away from the cabin and marched me up the road. My legs wobbled and I fell to the ground.

99 I was in the wagon bumping my face against the bed of it. My hands throbbed from the heated handle of the kettle I pulled off the fire. I saw the burn marks. I looked at the sky. It was as though the yellow leaves marched with us, too. The cooking pot next to me was on its side. The blankets thrown in it stained with the white woman's food. I sobbed with the thought of them in my cabin. I retched, but only a thin stream of water came from my stomach. The same soldier rode beside the wagon. I watched him blur into the trees. A streak of blood stained my blouse where his bayonet had stuck me. When he returned he gave me a rag to wrap around my hands.

100 It was as if a bear sat on my chest all the way to camp. I felt air would not come into my lungs. It was a heavy grief I couldn't push away.

DISCUSSION QUESTIONS

1. The author has used multiple narrators in brief passages to tell her story. What are the advantages and disadvantages of this technique for both writer and reader?
2. How do you interpret the title *Pushing the Bear* in relation to the story's action?
3. What is Maritole chiefly concerned about?
4. How does the author convey the distress and fear that people had when they were ordered away from their homes?
5. What do paragraphs 11, 26, and 28 tell you about Cherokee beliefs at this time?
6. Cherokee words and phrases are written in Sequoyah's syllabary. Why do you think the author includes these symbols?

WRITING TOPICS

1. With a small group, prepare a time line of national or world events and people during the years of the Cherokee Removal, 1838–1839.
2. Using print or electronic resources, research one of the following, write a report, and present it to the class:

   Indian Removal Act of 1830

   Cherokee language

   Cherokee myths

   The Treaty of New Echota

   The Eastern Band of Cherokees

   Cherokee Nation in Oklahoma

   Sequoyah syllabary

3. Write a short essay on the character of Maritole. Suggested thesis: Diane Glancy reveals three traits of Maritole in the opening episodes of *Pushing the Bear:* her love for her family, her respect for the land and natural world, and her passionate defense against the soldiers and intruders.

IN 1864

Luci Tapahonso

Luci Tapahonso was born in 1953 in Shiprock, New Mexico, the eleventh child of traditional Navajo parents. Her father Eugene Tapahonso, Sr., is of the Bitter Water clan—one of the four original Navajo clans—and her mother, Lucille Deschenne, of the Salt Water Clan. Navajo is Tapahonso's first language. The roots of her writing reach deep into Navajo heritage and earth. She says in *Saanii Dahataal: The Women Are Singing,* "the place of my birth is the source of the writing."

With the publication of her fifth book, *Blue Horses Rush In* (1997), Tapahonso continues the themes of family and homeland that make her a vital female voice on the Native American literary landscape. Her other works include *One More Shiprock Night: Poems* (1981); *Seasonal Woman* (1981); and *A Breeze Swept Through* (1987). "In 1864" appears in *Saanii Dahataal: The Women Are Singing* (1993), a book of autobiographical prose and narrative poems.

Like Diane Glancy, Luci Tapahonso and Howard Gorman capture the suffering and survival of their people through literary narratives. Twenty-five years after the Cherokees completed their "Trail of Tears" to Indian Territory, the Navajos were beginning their Long Walk to Fort Sumner in New Mexico. Unlike the Cherokees, the Navajos returned to their homeland, where their descendants hear stories that bind generations. Voices of spirits linger and events are imprinted on the landscape. In "Just Past Shiprock," Tapahonso writes, "This land that may seem arid and forlorn to the newcomer is full of stories which hold the spirits of the people, those who live here today and those who lived centuries and other worlds ago." Her words may serve as an introduction to "In 1864."

In 1864, 8,354 Navajos were forced to walk from Dinetah to
Bosque Redondo in southern New Mexico, a distance of three hun-
dred miles. They were held for four years until the U.S. government
declared the assimilation attempt a failure. More than 2,500 died
of smallpox and other illnesses, depression, severe weather conditions,
and starvation. The survivors returned to Dinetah[1] in June of 1868.

While the younger daughter slept, she dreamt of mountains,
the wide blue sky above, and friends laughing.

We talked as the day wore on. The stories and highway beneath
became a steady hum. The center lines were a blurred guide.
5 As we neared the turn to Fort Sumner,[2] I remembered this story:

A few winters ago, he worked as an electrician on a crew
installing power lines on the western plains of New Mexico.
He stayed in his pickup camper, which was connected to a generator.
The crew parked their trucks together and built a fire in the center.
10 The nights were cold and there weren't any trees to break the wind.
It snowed off and on, a quiet, still blanket. The land was like
he had imagined from the old stories—flat and dotted with shrubs.
The arroyos and washes cut through the soft dirt.
They were unsuspectingly deep.
15 During the day, the work was hard and the men were exhausted.
In the evenings, some went into the nearby town to eat and drink
a few beers. He fixed a small meal for himself and tried to relax.
Then at night, he heard cries and moans carried by the wind
and blowing snow. He heard voices wavering and rising
20 in the darkness. He would turn over and pray, humming songs
he remembered from his childhood. The songs returned to him
as easily as if he had heard them that very afternoon.
He sang for himself, his family, and the people whose spirits
lingered on the plains, in the arroyos, and in the old windswept plants.
25 No one else heard the thin wailing.
After the third night, he unhooked his camper, signed his time card,
and started the drive north to home. He told the guys,
"Sure, the money's good. But I miss my kids and it sure gets lonely
out here for a family man." He couldn't stay there any longer.
30 The place contained the pain and cries of his relatives,
the confused and battered spirits of his own existence.

After we stopped for a Coke and chips, the storytelling resumed:

---

[1] *Dinetah:* "Navajo country" or "homeland of The People."
[2] *Fort Sumner:* also called "Bosque Redondo" owing to its location.

My aunt always started the story saying, "You are here
because of what happened to your great-grandmother long ago."

35 They began rounding up the people in the fall.
Some were lured into surrendering by offers of food, clothes,
and livestock. So many of us were starving and suffering
that year because the bilagáana[3] kept attacking us.
Kit Carson and his army had burned all the fields,
40 and they killed our sheep right in front of us.
We couldn't believe it. I covered my face and cried.
All my life, we had sheep. They were like our family.
It was then I knew our lives were in great danger.
We were all so afraid of that man, Redshirt,[4] and his army.
45 Some people hid in the foothills of the Chuska Mountains
and in Canyon de Chelly. Our family talked it over,
and we decided to go to this place. What would our lives
be like without sheep, crops, and land? At least, we thought
we would be safe from gunfire and our family would not starve.

50 The journey began, and the soldiers were all around us.
All of us walked, some carried babies. Little children and the elderly
stayed in the middle of the group. We walked steadily each day,
stopping only when the soldiers wanted to eat or rest.
We talked among ourselves and cried quietly.
55 We didn't know how far it was or even where we were going.
All that was certain was that we were leaving Dinetah, our home.
As the days went by, we grew more tired, and soon,
the journey was difficult for all of us, even the military.
And it was they who thought all this up.

60 We had such a long distance to cover.
Some old people fell behind, and they wouldn't let us go back to help them.
It was the saddest thing to see—my heart hurts so to remember that.
Two women were near the time of the births of their babies,
and they had a hard time keeping up with the rest.
65 Some army men pulled them behind a huge rock, and we screamed out loud
when we heard the gunshots. The women didn't make a sound,
but we cried out loud for them and their babies.
I felt then that I would not live through everything.
When we crossed the Rio Grande, many people drowned.
70 We didn't know how to swim—there was hardly any water deep enough
to swim in at home. Some babies, children, and some of the older men

---

[3] *Bilagáana:* the Navajo word for Anglos.
[4] *Redshirt:* Kit Carson's name was "Redshirt" in Navajo.

and women were swept away by the river current.
We must not ever forget their screams and the last we saw of them—
hands, a leg, or strands of hair floating.

75   There were many who died on the way to Hwééldi.[5] All the way
we told each other, "We will be strong as long as we are together."
I think that was what kept us alive. We believed in ourselves
and the old stories that the holy people had given us.
"This is why," she would say to us. "This is why we are here.
80   Because our grandparents prayed and grieved for us."

The car hums steadily, and my daughter is crying softly.
Tears stream down her face. She cannot speak. Then I tell her that
it was at Bosque Redondo the people learned to use flour and now
fry bread is considered to be the "traditional" Navajo bread.
85   It was there that we acquired a deep appreciation for strong coffee.
The women began to make long, tiered calico skirts
and fine velvet shirts for the men. They decorated their dark velvet
blouses with silver dimes, nickels, and quarters.
They had no use for money then.
90   It is always something to see—silver flashing in the sun
against dark velvet and black, black hair.

Discussion Questions

1. There are three different settings included in the stories of "In 1864."
   Identify the time and the story that accompany each setting.
2. How does the speaker in the poem try to make her daughter feel better?
3. Select three adjectives you think best describe the Navajo people: *religious, courageous, family-centered, resourceful, superstitious,* something else?

---

[5] *Hwééldi:* the Navajo name for Fort Sumner.

WRITING TOPICS

1. Use one of these lines (or select a different one) to tell a story that includes what you have learned about the Long Walk.

   I felt then that I would not live through everything.

   No one else heard the thin wailing.

   The journey began, and the soldiers were all around us.

   We must not ever forget their screams and the last we saw of them.

   We will be strong as long as we are together.

2. Although the general tone of the poem is grim, Tapahonso pictures strong Navajo images. In a brief essay, identify three examples and explain why you think they are positive.
3. Research the life of Kit Carson. Do your sources include his part in the Navajo Long Walk? Present your findings on his life in a report.
4. With a small group, prepare a multimedia presentation of the Navajo Long Walk and its aftermath. Assume that your presentation will air on your local public television or radio station.
5. Recall some stories handed down in your family and record them in your journal, or share them with others in a feature article for a school or local newspaper.

THE NAVAJO LONG WALK

Howard W. Gorman

Howard Gorman, a strong political and cultural leader, was born in 1900 into the Bitter Water clan of the Navajo Nation, Arizona. His constituents reelected him to the Navajo National Council for thirty-six years, and he served as Vice Chairman from 1938 to 1942. He was also a vital member of the first Board of Regents of Navajo Community College. Gorman heard several oral histories of the Long Walk and internment related by his older relatives. At the age of seventy-two, he combined them into his family's account of those traumatic events that affected Navajo history and literature.

Gorman's story and others appear in *Navajo Stories of the Long Walk Period,* a remarkable book published by Navajo Community College Press. This volume encompasses a century of Navajo literature and history. The Press was established in 1968, one hundred years after the Navajos returned to their beloved homeland in 1868 from their incarceration at Fort Sumner. Inasmuch as the Navajos did not have a written language at the time of the Long Walk, the stories were passed down by word of mouth for generations. All the stories were collected by Navajos from Navajo speakers and were then translated into English by Navajos. Consequently, the book is a rare compilation of Navajo voices. Some forty Navajos, most of them elderly, taped their versions of the Long Walk. Navajos fluent in English and Navajo languages translated the tapes. The translations were patiently and painstakingly typed from handwritten manuscripts, with careful editing of the spelling and complex accenting of Navajo words. The English version with Navajo words is reproduced here to preserve the integrity of Gorman's account and to recognize the intent of those who did the tedious and technical work.

Each narrative in the text is personally unique, yet all follow a common road. In the 1850s, as relations between natives and newcomers became increasingly tense, the U.S. Army constructed Fort Defiance in the heart of Navajo country. Determined to eliminate the American presence, a thousand warriors led by Manuelito and Barboncito made a massive attack in 1860 on Fort Defiance. The

Indians almost took the fort, but U.S. troops finally drove them back. As skirmishes continued, federal officials became convinced that only a major military campaign could compel the Navajos to submit to federal authority. Kit Carson, legendary trapper and explorer, spearheaded the campaign to force Navajos to move to Fort Sumner on the Pecos River in eastern New Mexico at a spot called Bosque Redondo, after the round grove of cottonwood trees there.

In 1863, Carson and his men went to Fort Defiance to begin their campaign to subdue the Navajo people. According to his orders, all Indians who refused to surrender and relocate ran the risk of being killed. But the message was never communicated to the Navajos, who fled as the troops entered their country. Soldiers marched through the heart of their country, spoiling wells and burning cornfields and peach orchards. Sometimes they shot Navajos and their livestock without provocation or warning. After their food supply was destroyed, by the end of 1864, some eight thousand Navajos, three-fourths of the total tribe, had surrendered. All were forced to walk to Fort Sumner and confinement.

Once they reached Fort Sumner, the Navajos suffered greatly as they tried to eke out a living by tilling the alkaline soil and protecting their few small flocks of sheep from Comanche raids. Nearly two thousand died, primarily from pneumonia and dysentery. Year after year, crops failed, destroyed by insects or drought. Goods supplied by the government were never adequate, and Navajos were destitute and desperate.

Finally, in 1868, Washington officials recognized that the "civilization" program had failed. General William T. Sherman traveled to Fort Sumner heading a delegation known as the Peace Commission. Sherman proposed that the Navajos move to Indian Territory in what is now Oklahoma, the place where the Cherokees had been moved fifty years earlier. But Navajo Chief Barboncito expressed the wish of all his people, "I hope to God you will not ask me to go to any other country other than my own." After negotiations, the Navajo Treaty of 1868 was signed, and the Navajos returned to live again within the boundaries of their four sacred mountains. Descendants of those who survived the Long Walk, such as Luci Tapahonso and Howard Gorman, continue to tell the stories to their children and grandchildren.

1   The Long Walk to Fort Sumner—what was the cause of it? It began because of the behavior of a few Diné. A handful, here and there, riding horseback, killed white people and others that were traveling overland, and took their belongings. So the soldiers, commanded by Kit Carson, were ordered out. Carson was nicknamed Bi'éé' Łichíí'ii (Red Clothes). . . .

2   Unexpectedly, Bi'éé' Łichíí'i (Red Clothes' Soldiers) arrived, destroying water wells—contaminating them, breaking the rocks edging the water-holes, or filling up the holes with dirt so that they became useless. They also burned cornfields and the orchards of peaches. That is what they did to us unexpectedly and unreasonably, because most of us were not harming anybody. In the open fields we planted squash and corn. And we lived peacefully, not expecting a conflict. We naturally were a peaceful people. We were not warlike; but, still, we had those soldier visitors. . . .

3   Word was sent out warning the Diné that troops were on the move, destroying property, having no pity on anyone. Those living in the area at the time were my closely related clan, such as my uncles; some were of the Ma'ii' Deeshgiizhnii (Coyote Pass) clan and some of the Tódich'íínii (Bitter Water) clan. When the Diné were warned of the invaders, they gathered their bedding and other property and started to move out over the snow-covered ground. I don't know which month it was; it could have been January. The Navajos headed north toward Chííhłgai (Red Clay). Canyon de Chelly[1] was their only hope of survival. You could follow their trail easily because of their plowing through the deep snow. They moved all night, throughout the morning, and into the late afternoon, when they reached a place called Tsé Náá'deezbáál (Blanket Wall Cave) in the canyon, where, below the cliff dwelling, they built a fire to warm themselves. On the steep walls were steps carved into the rock. These steps probably are still there. Down them during the day the ice had melted, and, in the evening, it had frozen again—right after sundown. When the Navajos arrived, the steps were covered with ice, which made it impossible to go up; so they built a fire below the cliff dwelling and settled for the night. Unfortunately, however, the soldiers caught up with them. . . .

4   From Fort Defiance the Navajos started on their journey. That was in 1864. They headed for Shash Bitoo' (Fort Wingate) first, and from there they started on their Long Walk. Women and children traveled on foot. That's why we call it the Long Walk. It was inhuman because the Navajos, if they got tired and couldn't continue to walk farther, were just shot down. Some wagons went along, but they were carrying army supplies, like clothes and food. Jaanééz (mules) pulled the wagons. So the Navajos were not cared for. They had to keep walking all the time, day after day. They kept that up for about eighteen or nineteen days from Fort Wingate to Fort Sumner,[2] or Hwééldi.

---

[1] *Canyon de Chelly:* the site in northeast Arizona of ancient cliff dwellings, built from approximately A.D. 1053 to 1300, and the home of many Navajos. It is about ninety-five miles from Gallup, New Mexico.
[2] *Fort Sumner:* U.S. Army fort in New Mexico.

5   On the journey the Navajos went through all kinds of hardships, like tiredness and having injuries. And, when those things happened, the people would hear gun shots in the rear. But they couldn't do anything about it. They just felt sorry for the ones being shot. Sometimes they would plead with the soldiers to let them go back and do something, but they were refused. This is how the story was told by my ancestors. It was said that those ancestors were on the Long Walk with their daughter, who was pregnant and about to give birth. Somewhere beyond K'aalógii Dził (Butterfly Mountain) on this side of Bilín (Belen), as it is called, south of Albuquerque, the daughter got tired and weak and couldn't keep up with the others or go any farther because of her condition. So my ancestors asked the Army to hold up for a while and to let the woman give birth. But the soldiers wouldn't do it. They forced my people to move on, saying that they were getting behind the others. The soldiers told the parents that they had to leave their daughter behind. "Your daughter is not going to survive, anyway; sooner or later she is going to die," they said in their own language.

6   "Go ahead," the daughter said to her parents, "things might come out all right with me." But the poor thing was mistaken, my grandparents used to say. Not long after they had moved on, they heard a gunshot from where they had been a short time ago.

7   "Maybe we should go back and do something, or at least cover the body with dirt," one of them said.

8   By that time one of the soldiers came riding up from the direction of the sound. He must have shot her to death. That's the way the story goes.

9   These Navajos had done nothing wrong. For no reason they had been taken captive and driven to Hwééldi (Fort Sumner). While that was going on, they were told nothing—not even what it was all about and for what reasons. The Army just rounded them up and herded them to the prison camp. Large numbers of Navajos made the journey. Some of them tried to escape. Those who did, and were caught, were shot and killed.

10   As I said, a large number of our people went on the Long Walk, and, when they started back several years later, more than 7,500 made the return trip. Since many of them had died, this means that there must have been a great number who walked to Fort Sumner. I don't know exactly in what formation they walked. Maybe they marched in two lines or went in single file. That is one thing I never have heard. "We were just being driven," they said afterward. And when they reached Hwééldi, which was located across a river, they saw that, on the other side of the river, some adobe or mud shelters were being started. The Diné helped build those shelters.

11   The Army selected some of the Navajos to be in charge of their people. The captives were divided into groups. The selected men were put in charge—one for each group. If these leaders wanted to go somewhere for a short while, they had to get permission, or a pass, from the Army officers.

They were not allowed to leave confinement without permission, and they had to have good causes and special reasons. The Navajos had hardly anything at that time; and they ate the rations but couldn't get used to them. Most of them got sick and had stomach trouble. The children also had stomach ache, and some of them died of it. Others died of starvation. The prisoners begged the Army for some corn, and the leaders also pleaded for it for their people. Finally, they were given some—one ear of corn for each member of the Diné. Some boys would wander off to where the mules and horses were corraled. There they would poke around in the manure to take undigested corn out of it. Then they would roast the corn in hot ashes to be eaten. They had nothing to grind corn with at that time, like the stone corn grinders that the Navajos have now.

12   Also, the water was bad and salty, which gave them dysentery. They were given medical treatment, but extreme hardships stayed with them for about a year after they arrived at Fort Sumner, and they had a bad time throughout the imprisonment. Large numbers of the Diné lost their lives. A few would ask permission to hunt small game like gah (rabbits), and permission sometimes was granted. The Diné also hunted na'azisi (gophers) along the river bank and used them for food.

13   That's the way it went with our people for at least a year. Then, after about two years, in the autumn, some of them were allowed to leave confinement and were granted permission to go farther to hunt bigger game. There were mountains toward the east, southeast, and south; so the Diné decided to hunt deer in those mountains. Only those who were trusted and "settled" were permitted to hunt, and they were told not to get into trouble. It was said to them, "You Navajos have been in all kinds of trouble back in your homeland—stealing, raiding, and killing the White Men. Many White Men have been killed, and all of these things are charged against you. You are held responsible for them. They charged you people with these things from the east or Wááshindoon (Washington). So now you have to settle down, and some day you might return to your homes and lands. Think about yourselves; think straight!"

14   Although they were told all those things, the Navajos still didn't like what they were being taught. They said among themselves, "What did we do wrong? We people here didn't do any harm. We were gathered up for no reason. The ones that were doing all the killing and raiding of the White Men probably are still doing the same thing back home—raiding and stealing from the White Men, and killing. We harmless people are held here, and we want to go back to our lands right away. . . .

15   In the second and third years the Diné tried to plant corn, but it was no use. It didn't grow. They were told to plant it in the way of the Bilagáana (White Men). But still it didn't grow. So they were given corn from somewhere else which they survived on. . . .

16   Wood became harder and harder to find. There were no trees around, like cedar and piñon. Out at a great distance—many miles—there was some

mesquite, the roots of which were dug out and brought home for firewood. Some little trees were around, but they were not good for firewood, giving a blue flame like butane, and they were tough. Anyway, wood was the hardest thing to get; and the Navajos suffered their worst hardships in winter when it got real cold.

17   Finally, the Diné began to make plans to return to their homeland, and the Army was in contact with Wááshindoon (Washington), explaining that the Diné wanted to make treaties and to go home.

18   One of them, Hastiin Dahghaa'í, said that from the Rio Grande west was their homeland, that what they were staying on was not. A man by the name of Tótsohnii Hastíí (Big Water Clan Man) agreed. He said, "I'm not about to give up my life here—even to think of dying here. I would rather return to my homeland and die there." And that's exactly what happened to him. Years ago, he passed away in Lók'aahnteel (Ganado, Arizona). The Army officials reported these things to Washington, and the result was the old treaty of 1868. It was made at about the end of the fourth year at Fort Sumner, around May or June.

19   Finally, a United States Army general arrived from the east (or Washington), and the treaty began to take shape. On one side sat the general or haskééjínaat'áá' (war chief) and beside him a White Man who spoke Mexican and English. Beside the White Man sat a Navajo by the name of Tsóósí (Tsosie) who spoke Mexican and Diné. At the end of the line sat Hastiin Dahghaa'í (Mr. Mustache), the man also known as Barboncito. When the general spoke it would be to the man who spoke English and Mexican. He would translate in Mexican to Tsóósí, who understood that language; and Tsóósí would translate in the Diné language to Hastiin Dahghaa'í.

20   Then Mr. Mustache would answer in the Navajo language to Tsóósí, and Tsóósí would translate in Mexican to the White Man, who would translate to the general in English. There was no time for the Diné to talk to each other. That was how the treaty was made in 1868—about one hundred and four years ago. . . .

21   On June 2, in the year of 1868, the treaty was made legal for the Navajos; so they started their journey back right away. They went to Shash Bitoo' (Fort Wingate) and then to Tséhootsooí (Fort Defiance), where they were given rations and two sheep to each family. That is how it is said in Navajo history. (Some people don't tell the story right. They just mention that the people were given sheep.) And the Navajos began to take real good care of their sheep. Even if they were hungry and had chapped lips in cold weather, instead of butchering a sheep they would hunt small game, like rabbits, rats and gophers; and they survived on these while they tried hard to increase their livestock. . . .

22   When we were taken to Hwééldi (Fort Sumner), a harmless people, for four years, the White Men got all our land—north to Dibé Nitsaa (the La Plata Mountains), toward the northwest to Dził Ashdlá'ii (La Sal Mountains)

to the Tó Doot*l*izhí (Green River), and beyond to the mountain with no name (Mount Henry). The Navajos used to have, and live on, that whole area. Later, the white people took most of that territory back. . . .

DISCUSSION QUESTIONS

1. What does Gorman say was the cause of the soldiers rounding up the Navajos?
2. How might the military account of the Long Walk have differed from the story handed down orally?
3. Many Navajo words appear in Gorman's narrative. Given the way the book *Navajo Stories of the Long Walk* was compiled, why do you think those words are included? Do you think the editor should have eliminated them? What do they add to the narrative? Explain.
4. Treaty negotiations and other communications between the Navajos and Euro-Americans were complicated by language problems. Refer to paragraphs 19 and 20 and explain the language barriers to effective and fair negotiations.

WRITING TOPICS

1. Research the life of Kit Carson. Do your sources include his part in the Navajo Long Walk? Present your findings on his life in a brief essay.
2. Research one of the following topics for a written report. Organize a panel presentation with your classmates.

   The Navajo Treaty of 1868

   The Navajo Long Walk

   The Navajo leaders Manuelito and Barboncito

   Navajo Life Today

3. With a small group, prepare a multimedia presentation of the Navajo Long Walk and its aftermath. Assume that your presentation will air on your local public television or radio station.
4. Gorman wrote, "I learned it (the story) from my ancestors." Recall some stories handed down in your family and record them in your journal, or share them with others in a feature article for a school or local newspaper.

VOICES OF THE INVISIBLE

Debra CallingThunder

Debra CallingThunder, a member of the Northern Arapaho tribe, has lived most of her life on the Wind River Indian Reservation in Wyoming. She is the former editor of the *WindRiver News* and a regular columnist for the *Salt Lake Tribune*. Enchanted with words, the author informs her readers right at the beginning of "Voices of the Invisible" that words are wondrous even when invisible and unheard. She also alerts her readers that words carrying Arapaho dreams and stories "bind us to eternity."

Then CallingThunder focuses on her family lineage reaching back through time toward eternity. Positioning her story in Arapaho and United States history, CallingThunder layers a ladder of six generations before her. She learned some family history from her ninety-year-old grandmother, Cleone Thunder. Her genealogical ladder climbs back to Cleone's grandfather, Chief Black Coal. Grass Woman, his daughter, was one of the last carriers of the medicine bundles of the Quill Society. Chief Black Coal led his people during their transition from free-ranging bison hunters to ranchers restricted on a reservation. Next, her narrative reaches back two more generations to Black Coal's grandmother Hoh-dah-wan, who told of when the bison still sang to the Arapaho.

CallingThunder's lyrical prose turns somber by the end of her essay. Her turning point in time is November 29, 1864, date of the Sand Creek massacre in Colorado. Eight Arapaho households were camped with the Cheyennes, who were attacked by Colorado militiamen. Hoh-dah-wan witnessed the horror of that assault, which haunted all surviving Arapahos. Her story of the tragedy has been filtered through the oral tradition for more than a century. Six generations later, CallingThunder adds her voice to Hoh-dah-wan's oral story for the written page.

The events leading to the Sand Creek massacre are familiar to all Plains peoples. The surge of settlers, miners, and travelers between the 1840s and 1860s ravaged the heartland of their hunting territory. The Arapahos befriended settlers and fortune hunters attracted by the

Colorado gold rush but eventually lost most of their land to the new-comers. In danger of being fired upon by troops and civilians, the Arapahos frequently avoided hostilities by restricting their movements away from trouble spots. Older leaders usually controlled the young warriors, who were eager to retaliate for the intruders' depredations. By 1861, many Arapahos had died from starvation and from epidemics of smallpox and cholera.

In 1864, a small number of Arapahos joined approximately four hundred fifty Southern Cheyennes led by Black Kettle, who had pledged peace with the Euro-Americans. The Indians thought they were under the protection of the U.S. Army when they were told to camp along Sand Creek where they would be safe. There, on the morning of November 29, 1864, they were attacked without warning by Colonel John M. Chivington with seven hundred troops of the First Colorado Cavalry and one hundred twenty-five regular army troops. At least one hundred thirty Indians were killed. The Sand Creek massacre became infamous not only among Plains Indians but also among citizens of the eastern United States as eyewitness accounts by participants reached the newspapers. On March 3, 1865, Congress created a joint special committee to investigate the behavior of Chivington's command. During the investigation, an agent's testimony confirmed the Arapaho oral tradition account: "Some of the chiefs did not lift an arm, but stood there and were shot down. One of them, Black Kettle, raised the American flag, and raised a white flag. He was supposed to be killed, but was not. They retreated right up the creek. They were followed up and pursued and killed in a brutal manner." Among those who escaped was Hoh-dah-wan. On January 26, 1867, the Congressional committee issued a devastating indictment of the Colorado officials responsible for the militia attack on the peaceful Southern Cheyenne and Arapaho encampment on Sand Creek. Colonel Chivington was never officially censured.

1   There are voices behind the wall—our voices, disembodied, spoken as if by beings unseen.

2   From the silence arise words conjured from invisible mouths, and laughter without smiles, and songs without celebration, and wailing without tears.

3   The air is crowded with words—wondrous and beautiful words that rise invisible and unheard and then are swallowed by time. The air is crowded with words—words that bind us to eternity, that carry the stories and dreams which are gifts from generations unseen, the songs of victory and mourning which compel us to seek tomorrow.

4   We are the invisible ones, the People of the Sky, the people of dreams whose voices cannot be bound by pain. We are the people of prayers, who stand small before the Creator, who entreat him, so that the strand of time that holds us to eternity might not be cut and our words slip into silence.

5   I give this song to Our People, to all the generations, and empty my soul before them.

6   Words are gifts, our grandparents say, and they give us many words so that we will remain a nation, a circle of people.

7   My grandmother, Cleone Thunder, is nearly ninety now, an age she says is not so old. Days disappear, falling furiously into time, but love remains, and words and songs and stories.

8   She tells us the stories of our beginning when the Creator above rejoiced and we and many others came to exist, and the circle of our lodges grew large. Only a short time ago, she says, Our People roamed the Earth, following the great buffalo herds that stormed across the plains, across an expanse of time and dreams.

9   The buffalo sang to us, and their song was their life. The buffalo sang to us so that we would grow strong. And the Old People would gather together many words to make prayers to the Creator. They would gather words as they walked a sacred path across the Earth, leaving nothing behind but prayers and offerings.

10   Now the buffalo days are gone, and we are here, living on a reservation in houses, no longer in a circle of tipis, but still as a tribe. Many of us have fallen into material poverty, but we are rich in relatives and songs and beauty.

11   The transmission of these words is how we keep the oral tradition alive, the gift of the Old People who loved us from long ago even though we did not yet exist upon the Earth. The words of the grandparents have bound us together, those of us who are like a victory song, like an eagle feather, like the thunder when it laughs.

12   When my grandmother was young, she lived in the old way—in a tipi near the Wind River, the river we love—with her great-great-grandmother, Hoh-dah-wan, who gathered wood although she was old.

13   Hoh-dah-wan, the grandmother of Chief Black Coal, lived during a time when the people wandered the Earth, starving because the buffalo were nearly gone. She gave my grandmother the stories of the Sand Creek Massacre of 1864, when the U.S. Cavalry attacked a Cheyenne and Arapaho camp under a white flag of truce and an American flag. . . .

14   She saw the people fleeing in the snow, running to the riverbanks, hoping the Earth would shelter them from the nightmare.

15   After it was done, the soldiers looted the camp, stealing sacred objects and human bodies—including those of my grandmother's two uncles. The elders say that the loss of sacred objects continues to hurt the tribe.

16   The U.S. Army used the beheaded bodies for medical research. It later gave some of the remains to the Smithsonian Institution in Washington, D.C.—our national museum—for display as curios.

17   In October 1992, a Smithsonian anthropologist came to talk to the spiritual elders of our tribe about the repatriation of Arapaho human remains and funerary and sacred objects. My grandmother and I were there.

18   The Smithsonian has made the return of the massacre victims' remains a priority, he told us that day nearly 128 years after the massacre. He said that the government began taking the remains of tribal people to continue medical studies begun on the bodies of Civil War soldiers.

19   No, my grandmother told him, it was because white people considered us savage and uncivilized. But they were wrong.

20   My grandmother is among the first Arapahos to know only the confines of a reservation and not to learn the sacred ways of the women's Quill Society.

21   Her mother, Grass Woman, the daughter of Black Coal, was one of the last of the seven medicine women who carried the Quill Society's medicine bundles. Until her time, the women had passed on knowledge of the society to successive generations.

22   The seven medicine women supervised the making of quill ornaments used to decorate tipis, moccasins, buffalo robes, and cradles with designs representing prayers for health and long life. The women made gifts of the quillwork so that blessings would follow the people as they traveled the four hills of life.

23   The ceremonies of the society have disappeared with other aspects of Arapaho life, and our grandparents say they long for the old ways. There is a loneliness for Arapaho words, they say—the quiet, flowing words of the storytellers that spilled into the thin, winter light and into the hearts of the people, the words that bound generations and were stronger than death.

24   In 1878, the Northern Band of Our People settled on a reservation in Wyoming that they share with an enemy tribe, the Shoshone. The federal government set about turning them into farmers and Christians by allotting families land and outlawing the tribe's ceremonies. Smallpox threatened the tribe, which numbered only several hundred.

25   Black Coal, one of our last traditional chiefs, gave part of his land allotment to the Catholic Church for a school. That way, he said, the children would no longer be sent to faraway boarding schools, banished from the words of Our People.

26   His son, Summer Black Coal, had been one of the first Arapahos to be taken to a boarding school, where the children were punished for speaking their tribal languages. The sons of the Arapaho chiefs and subchiefs were taken so that the people would no longer fight and the future leaders would not learn Our People's way.

27   After the school at St. Stephen's Mission was built, the elders, the chiefs, and the warriors would go into the classrooms and tell the children to get a white man's education. The buffalo days are gone, they told them, and you are the ones who will make a new life for the people.

28   In 1958, the federal government and the state of Wyoming put a radioactive-waste dump near the school. It wasn't cleaned up until thirty years later.

29   The children were not sacred to them.

30   In 1890, Smithsonian ethnologist James Mooney described Our People as "devotees and prophets, continuously seeing signs and wonders."

31   The government had sent him to study our tribe, because it expected us to become extinct and our words to fall into silence. It was during this time that many of the sacred societies, including the Quill Society, began to die out, and soon their ceremonies slipped away and their prayers were heard no more upon the Earth. It was also during this time that Our People began to follow the way of the Ghost Dance,[1] crying out to the Creator, for the return of the buffalo and a way of life.

32   Have pity on us, Father, they prayed. Have pity on us, for we have nothing left.

33   We buried my cousin last month. He was seventeen.

34   Before we buried him, the priest said words, incantations. He told us that all of us were to blame for his death because we failed to speak, we failed to listen. He said that we loved alcohol too much and our young ones too little.

35   His words cut into the silence and into our hearts.

36   Then, we heard the songs given to us by the Old People, the healing words that rose above the circle of the drum. They sang so that we would be strong and the people endure. We have done it many times before—given our young ones back to the Earth who catches our tears and to the Creator above.

37   We have done it many times before, we, the Sky People who are tied together by time and blood, who have shared laughter and tears, life and death.

38   In July 1992, my family visited the Plains Indian Museum in Cody, Wyoming, where traditional cradleboards were on display, including an Arapaho cradleboard made around 1890 from sackcloth and dyed porcupine quills.

---

[1] *Ghost Dance:* the name given to two religious dances, particularly in the 1870s and 1890s. Ghost Dance participants focused on the hope that, by performing a circular dance and other ceremonies, the Indian way of life and Indian lands would be restored.

39   A little girl asked her mother what the quill ornaments were.

40   Toys, her mother said.

41   She did not know that they were the captive prayers the grandmothers had prepared for the young ones.

42   She did not know that like the sacred prayers of the grandmothers and the songs of the buffalo, too many of our children have fallen silent.

DISCUSSION QUESTIONS

1. The author embraces six generations in her story. As a class, make a lineage chart that traces the five ancestors she includes and give one fact about each.
2. Who are the "invisible" of the title?
3. The author says that words are gifts. In what ways are these gifts important?
4. What do you think was the author's purpose in writing this essay?

WRITING TOPICS

1. Investigate the Sand Creek Massacre and the events that surrounded it. Based on your information, write an essay from the viewpoint of a soldier in Chivington's command or from the viewpoint of an Arapaho within the camp.
2. The author says, "I give this song to our people, to all the generations." Read the selection closely and note where the author refers to songs, words, and silence. Write a brief essay on the importance of these three elements in CallingThunder's essay.
3. Write a researched essay on the Northern Arapaho today. Include information about important tribal events since they settled on the Wind River reservation.

BLACK KETTLE NATIONAL GRASSLANDS, WESTERN OKLAHOMA

Diane Glancy

The life of Cheyenne Chief Black Kettle links Diane Glancy's "Black Kettle National Grasslands, Western Oklahoma" to Debra CallingThunder's "Voices of the Invisible." For the Southern Cheyenne "Peace Chief" miraculously survived the 1864 Sand Creek, Colorado, massacre only to die four years later on the Washita River in Indian Territory.

Lieutenant Colonel George A. Custer held his seven hundred troopers through a blizzard all night in order to attack the Cheyennes at dawn. Only three days before the attack, Black Kettle had gone voluntarily to Fort Cobb to pledge peace for his camp of one hundred and eighty lodges. Black Kettle flew a United States flag near his tipi by Washita Creek as a signal that he and his people considered themselves at peace with the United States. Ignoring their own national flag, Seventh Cavalrymen shot Black Kettle and his wife. The morning was bitterly cold with a foot of snow on the ground, and most of the Cheyenne women and children fled to the river bed seeking concealment; the cavalrymen shot them, too. Historians estimate that one hundred Indians died. Many warriors fought desperately to save their families and were determined to exact a heavy toll before they died. They killed nineteen soldiers and wounded thirteen.

More than a century later, poet Glancy creates a verbal landscape of the tragedy. She visits the National Grasslands, an area dedicated to preserving Great Plains grasses and named for Black Kettle. This is the location for the Black Kettle Museum and battle site. According to Glancy, "Indian poetry, especially, should promote stability, precision, hope. It should be salve for the broken race which is enriched by its blood suffering and permanent loss of a way of life." She continues, "Our poetry should rise from despair. . . . If our poetry is a vent for anger, it should also transcend." Glancy does indeed transcend anger and despair in both her prose and poetry.

Her volumes of poetry include *Brown Wolf Leaves the Res and Other Poems* (1984); *Iron Woman* (1990); and *Lone Dog's Winter Count* (1991). She was elected as Five Civilized Tribes poet laureate for 1984–1986.

We feel them for some time now,
a residue as though from a dream,
watching from the crawling hills
and lines of trees in the draw:
5 Chief Black Kettle and his tribe,
frozen white as clouds in the sun.

Gullies gouge the red soil like war-
paint but there was not time for that
when Custer waited the night in a
10 blizzard and rode at dawn from the
ridge into the Cheyenne winter camp.

In the museum: stirrup, bit, rifle-
shells, pouch, arrowheads from the
battle ground; and from the hills,
15 a pack-mule feed-bag and a soldier's
mess kettle, dented as old maps
of attack plans.

Like dreams, it all takes place
in an instant. From the moment
20 I hear the sound until I wake,
you say is only seconds. Between
the cats fighting outside the
window this morning is my long dream.

And here, in glass cases, relics of
25 the Seventh Cavalry and a tribe
of Indians. A chief who wanted peace.
A general who fought for westward
expansion.

Down the road, under a circular
30 break in the clouds, an irrigation-
pipe on crude tractor-wheels
washes their battlefield.

An early morning dream returns:
a werewolf with black hair on its face,
35 tied up, held captive with others
in beds. I walk past them
and someone sprays vinegar-water.
I brush it away with irritation,
and the snarling cats wake me.
40 I cannot sleep again to find what happens.

Black Kettle had his own dream of a
wolf with blood on its face and knew
they would die, like all of us,
but not when.

45 Now I stand on the road where Custer
waited. Some of the artifacts
from two races still buried in the ground.
A strange time warp hidden
like the end of a dream.

50 I look at the Washita Creek where
Black Kettle fell, and his wife with him,
a few yards away. The tribe still
running in all ways.

Before they could bury him, his flesh
55 was torn by wolves
as though he once dreamed he would die,
knowing at last, it would be then.

In the draw, the Indian tribe thaws.
They speak with sign language like trees.
60 The sudden smell of wet buffalo robes,
and a small howl from the soft lining
of the throat.

We listen to winds over the grasslands:
once through this country is enough.

DISCUSSION QUESTIONS

1. There are three settings in this poem: a battlefield, a museum, and a dream. How does the poet tie these three settings together?
2. How have the experiences affected the speaker?

WRITING TOPICS

1. If you could go back to a period in American history that in some way relates to your ancestors or living relatives, what years would you choose and why? Explain in a few paragraphs why this period interests you.
2. Through her dreamlike stanzas, Glancy filters images of soldiers and Indians, Custer and Black Kettle, cats and wolves. She fuses the past and the present. Select three images you think are well written and write a brief essay describing what you like about them. How are the images you chose related to "winds over the grasslands"?
3. If you live near a local history museum, find an exhibit there that intrigues you and write about it in a few paragraphs or a poem. You may want to use Glancy's techniques as a model. She looks at real objects and specific places, and they inspire her to imagine images.

BURIED ALIVE

Sarah Winnemucca

Sarah Winnemucca was born into a distinguished Northern Paiute family in about 1844 near the Humboldt Sink in what became the state of Nevada. In Numic, her first language, her name was Thocmetony, which means "shell flower." Her people call themselves Numa, or "The People." Traditionally, many Numa bands hunted and traveled over a third of present-day Nevada and land in Oregon, southern Idaho, and eastern California. As band chiefs, Winnemucca's father, Old Winnemucca, and her grandfather, Truckee, advocated peaceful coexistence with Euro-Americans. Consequently, Winnemucca mastered English, acted as an interpreter, and spent much of her adult life as a liaison between Paiutes and Euro-Americans. As political activist, lecturer, and educator, this remarkable woman made valuable contributions to her people and to Indian policy in general.

In *Life Among the Piutes, Their Wrongs and Claims* (1883), Winnemucca wrote her personal life story in the context of Paiute history. She is generally recognized as the author of the first autobiography by an Indian woman. Her literary background was scanty, but she developed a strong storytelling voice, turning people in her life into memorable characters within dramatic scenes. The book is a rare eyewitness account of four decades of encounters between Paiutes and Euro-Americans. Through many conflicts and negotiations, Winnemucca sought justice from the federal government. Her feminine voice always rings for peace.

Four years after Winnemucca's birth, gold was discovered in California. Thousands of emigrants crossed Paiute territory, traveling to the California gold fields and Oregon farmlands. Winnemucca began her autobiography when, as a child, she first saw Euro-Americans among the Paiute. She recalls, "They could not get over the mountains, so they had to live with us. It was on Carson River, where the great Carson City stands now. You call my people blood-seeking. My people did not seek to kill them, nor did they steal their horses—no, no, far from it. During the winter my people helped them. They gave them such as they had to eat. They did not hold out their hands and say: 'You can't have anything to eat unless you pay me.'"

Refusing to remain silent, Winnemucca began telling the story of Paiutes' suffering to standing-room only crowds in San Francisco theaters. She delivered nearly three hundred lectures in 1883 and 1884 from Boston to Washington, D.C. She also wrote *Life among the Piutes: Their Wrongs and Claims* as part of her public relations campaign to ameliorate the harsh conditions under which her people lived.

In 1886, the Paiute activist left the lecture circuit to establish a school for Paiute children in Lovelock, Nevada. Local agents of the Office of Indian Affairs were determined to force cultural change among the Paiutes and determined to destroy the power of native leaders like Winnemucca. She struggled with an additional handicap as a female confronting males invested with governmental authority during the late Victorian era. After two years of conflict, her school closed. She moved to live with her sister in Henry's Lake, Idaho, where she died on October 17, 1891.

Winnemucca's legacy as a passionate crusader for Indian rights reaches across more than a century. Her oratorical power continues to arouse the conscience of her audience. One of the best examples of her rhetorical style is this final plea: "For shame! For shame! You dare to cry out Liberty, when you hold us in places against our will, driving us from place to place as if we were beasts . . . if the white people will treat us like human beings, we will behave like a people; but if we are treated by white savages as if we are savages, we are relentless and desperate. . . . I am pleading for God and for humanity."

1   Oh, what a fright we all got one morning to hear some white people were coming. Every one ran as best they could. My poor mother was left with my little sister and me. Oh, I never can forget it. My poor mother was carrying my little sister on her back, and trying to make me run; but I was so frightened I could not move my feet, and while my poor mother was trying to get me along my aunt overtook us, and she said to my mother: "Let us bury our girls, or we shall all be killed and eaten up." So they went to work and buried us, and told us if we heard any noise not to cry out, for if we did they would surely kill us and eat us. So our mothers buried me and my cousin, planted sage bushes over our faces to keep the sun from burning them, and there we were left all day.

2   Oh, can any one imagine my feelings *buried alive*, thinking every minute

that I was to be unburied and eaten up by the people that my grandfather loved so much? With my heart throbbing, and not daring to breathe, we lay there all day. It seemed that the night would never come. Thanks be to God! the night came at last. Oh, how I cried and said: "Oh, father, have you forgotten me? Are you never coming for me?" I cried so I thought my very heartstrings would break.

3   At last we heard some whispering. We did not dare to whisper to each other, so we lay still. I could hear their footsteps coming nearer and nearer. I thought my heart was coming right out of my mouth. Then I heard my mother say, "'Tis right here!" Oh, can any one in this world ever imagine what were my feelings when I was dug up by my poor mother and father? My cousin and I were once more happy in our mothers' and fathers' care, and we were taken to where all the rest were.

4   I was once buried alive; but my second burial shall be for ever, where no father or mother will come and dig me up. It shall not be with throbbing heart that I shall listen for coming footsteps. I shall be in the sweet rest of peace,—I, the chieftain's weary daughter.

5   Well, while we were in the mountains hiding, the people that my grandfather called our white brothers came along to where our winter supplies were. They set everything we had left on fire. It was a fearful sight. It was all we had for the winter, and it was all burnt during that night. My father took some of his men during the night to try and save some of it, but they could not; it had burnt down before they got there.

6   These were the last white men that came along that fall. My people talked fearfully that winter about those they called our white brothers. My people said they had something like awful thunder and lightning, and with that they killed everything that came in their way. . . .

7   Late in that fall, there came news that my grandfather was on his way home. Then my father took a great many of his men and went to meet his father, and there came back a runner, saying, that all our people must come together. It was said that my grandfather was bringing bad news. All our people came to receive their chieftain; all the old and young men and their wives went to meet him. One evening there came a man, saying that all the women who had little children should go to a high mountain. They wanted them to go because they brought white men's guns, and they made such a fearful noise, it might even kill some of the little children. My grandfather had lost one of his men while he was away.

8   So all the women that had little children went. My mother was among the rest; and every time the guns were heard by us, the children would scream. I thought, for one that my heart would surely break. So some of the women went down from the mountain and told them not to shoot any more, or their children would die with fright. When our mothers brought us down to our homes the nearer we came to the camp, the more I cried,

9   "Oh, mother, mother, don't take us there!" I fought my mother—I bit her. Then my father came, and took me in his arms and carried me to the

camp. I put my head in his bosom, and would not look up for a long time. I heard my grandfather say,

10   "So the young lady is ashamed because her sweetheart has come to see her. Come, dearest, that won't do after I have had such a hard time to come to see my sweetheart, that she should be ashamed to look at me."

11   Then he called my two brothers to him, and said to them, "Are you glad to see me?" And my brothers both told him that they were glad to see him. Then my grandfather said to them,

12   "See that young lady; she does not love her sweetheart any more, does she? Well, I shall not live is she does not come and tell me she loves me. I shall take that gun, and I shall kill myself."

13   That made me worse than ever, and I screamed and cried so hard that my mother had to take me away. So they kept weeping for the little one three or four days. I did not make up with my grandfather for a long time. He sat day after day, and night after night, telling his people about his white brothers. He told them that the whites were really their brothers, that they were very kind to everybody, especially to children; that they were always ready to give something to children. He told them what beautiful things their white brothers had—what beautiful clothes they wore, and about the big houses that go on the mighty ocean, and travel faster than any horse in the world. His people asked him how big they were. "Well, as big as that hill you see there, and as high as the mountain over us."

14   "Oh, that is not possible—it would sink, surely."

15   "It is every word truth, and that is nothing to what I am going to tell you. Our white brothers are a mighty nation, and have more wonderful things than that. They have a gun that can shoot a ball bigger than my head, that can go as far off as that mountain you see over there. . . ."

16   He then showed us a more wonderful thing than all the others that he had brought. It was a paper, which he said could talk to him. He took it out and would talk to it, and talk with it. He said, "This can talk to all our white brothers, and our white sisters, and their children. Our white brothers are beautiful, and our white sisters are beautiful, and their children are beautiful! He also said the paper can travel like the wind, and it can go and talk with their fathers and brothers and sisters, and come back to tell what they are doing, and whether they are well or sick."

17   After my grandfather told us this, our doctors and doctresses said,

18   "If they can do this wonderful thing, they are not truly human, but pure spirits. None but heavenly spirits can do such wonderful things. We can communicate with the spirits, yet we cannot do wonderful things like them. Oh, our great chieftain, we are afraid your white brothers will yet make your people's hearts bleed. You see if they don't; for we can see it. Their blood is all around us, and the dead are lying all about us, and we cannot escape it. It will come. Then you will say our doctors and doctresses did know. Dance, sing, play, it will do no good; we cannot drive it away. They have already done the mischief, while you were away."

19 But this did not go far with my grandfather. He kept talking to his people about the good white people, and told them all to get ready to go with him to California the following spring.

20 Very late that fall, my grandfather and my father and a great many more went down to the Humboldt River to fish. They brought back a great many fish, which we were very glad to get; for none of our people had been down to fish the whole summer.

21 When they came back, they brought us more news. They said there were some white people living at the Humboldt sink.[1] They were the first ones my father had seen face to face. He said they were not like "humans." They were more like owls than any thing else. They had hair on their faces, and had white eyes, and looked beautiful.

22 I tell you we children had to be very good, indeed, during the winter; for we were told that if we were not good they would come and eat us up. We remained there all winter; the next spring the emigrants came as usual, and my father and grandfather and uncles, and many more went down on the Humboldt River on fishing excursions. While they were thus fishing, their white brothers came upon them and fired on them, and killed one of my uncles, and wounded another. Nine more were wounded, and five died afterwards. My other uncle got well again, and is living yet. Oh, that was a fearful thing, indeed!

23 After all these things had happened, my grandfather still stood up for his white brothers.

DISCUSSION QUESTIONS

1. Did the narrator have reason to be afraid of white people? Why or why not?
2. What kind of relationship did the narrator and her grandfather have?
3. What are some of the reasons given here for the grandfather's admiration of white people?

---

[1] *sink:* a depression in land.

Writing Topics

1. Recall a time when you were a child and frightened and try to recapture the feelings you had then in a few descriptive paragraphs.
2. Sarah Winnemucca frequently mentions the heart. Find these various passages, and in a brief essay, explore whether they are literal or figurative and explain why they are appropriate and what they contribute to this autobiographical excerpt.

FROM *YELLOW WOLF: HIS OWN STORY*

Yellow Wolf, ed. by L. V. McWhorter

"I did not surrender my rifle," Yellow Wolf recalls his decision on October 5, 1877, at the last stand of Chief Joseph's people at Bear Paw Battlefield. To hear the force of Yellow Wolf's words, we must remember his struggle to stay in the Wallowa Valley of Oregon. Yellow Wolf was born about 1856 in the traditional homeland of Chief Joseph's band of the Nez Perce. His father, known as Horse Blanket, raised Appaloosa horses, and Yellow Wolf excelled as a horse trainer. His mother, Swan Woman, was a cousin of Chief Joseph. Yellow Wolf first told his story to Lucullus V. McWhorter in 1908, and they worked on the warrior's memoirs irregularly for the next twenty-five years. The autobiography appeared in 1940.

At twenty-one, Yellow Wolf fought as a warrior with the Nez Perce during their 1877 flight to Canada. Complex conditions leading to that flight unfolded as the Nez Perce fervently defended their land. Nez Perce territory encompassed land where present-day Idaho, Oregon, and Washington converge. Euro-Americans also coveted this land, and they pressured the government to secure it for them.

In 1855, some Nez Perce chiefs signed their first treaty, which established a reservation one-third the size of their original territory. Outsiders' encroachment accelerated after 1860 when gold was discovered on Nez Perce land, and tribal defiance increased. The government pressured Nez Perce leaders again in 1863 to drastically reduce their reservation to an area around Lapwai, Idaho. Some chiefs signed the landmark treaty. Old Joseph and other chiefs refused to sign, rejecting it as binding on them. Henceforth these bands were known as the "nontreaty Nez Perce." Yellow Wolf and others called this "the thief-treaty." A split developed in the Nez Perce Nation. Old Joseph told Governor Isaac Stevens that no man owned any part of the earth, and a man could not sell what he did not own. He took his people back to their home in Wallowa Valley, a green country of clear waters, wide meadows, and mountain forests. There they raised fine horses and cattle, lived in fine lodges, and sold their livestock for necessities. He would later tell his son Chief Joseph, "This country holds your father's body. Never sell the bones of your father and your mother." In 1871, young Joseph buried his father in the beloved Wallowa and assumed leadership of the band.

The government issued an ultimatum to Chief Joseph and other nontreaty Nez Perce: They must leave their homes and move to the Idaho reservation, where they would settle peacefully within thirty days or face military force. The chiefs protested making the arduous trip across flooding rivers and deep, rugged canyons—all on foot or horseback. Nevertheless, they decided to obey the ultimatum rather than risk worse hardships for their people. Yellow Wolf and others of Joseph's band suffered the greatest loss of personal possessions left behind, of cattle and horses stolen by white settlers, and of belongings and stock lost in the swirling flood waters of the Snake River.

With twelve days remaining, about six hundred Nez Perce gathered at a traditional campground in Oregon to relocate on the reservation. A warlike spirit spread among a few young men, who killed some white men who had treated them unjustly. Joseph, whose wife had a new baby, was away from camp butchering beef. News of the killings created a panic in camp. Other Nez Perce took revenge on white settlers by killing, looting, and burning. Now, the Nez Perce patriots had difficult choices: to fight and die in their homeland, to seek new homes among old friends, the Crows, or to surrender to hostile military forces. They decided to flee to Canada to seek safety with Sitting Bull's exiles.

Led by a council of six band chiefs, the refugees conducted an epic exodus across Idaho and much of Montana. Brigadier General Oliver O. Howard commanded the pursuing army troops. The Nez Perce warriors numbered two hundred fifty at most. Yellow Wolf and other warriors in the rear guard engaged the troops eight times—just often enough to allow four hundred fifty elders, women, and children to stay safely ahead of the soldiers for approximately eleven hundred miles.

The Nez Perce journey ended just forty miles short of the Canadian border after four months of running gun battles. Colonel Nelson A. Miles, with nearly six hundred men, cut the Nez Perce escape route by intercepting them in the Bear Paw Valley of Montana. Miles's Cheyenne scouts picked up the trail of the Nez Perce. On the blustery morning of September 30, Miles ordered an immediate attack. The Indians, wounded, hungry, and cold, suffered intensely. Brought to bay, the refugees dug deep rifle pits for protection and exacted troop casualties about equal to their own. By the time Miles ordered a white flag raised, Chief Joseph was the only surviving member of the council of band chiefs. The sad duty of surrendering to preserve lives fell to him. Surrounded, and worried that his people would starve and freeze in winter weather, Joseph surrendered his rifle to Miles. That is why warrior Yellow Wolf, one of more than three hundred Nez Perce who slipped through the army surveillance to Canada, emphasized "I did not surrender my rifle."

YOUTH OF THE WARRIOR

1   I grew up among warriors, and since old enough to take notice, I made defending myself a study. The whites call me Yellow Wolf, but I take that as a nickname. My true name is different, and is after the Spirit which gave me promise of its power as a warrior.

2   I am Heinmot Hihhih, which means White Thunder. Yellow Wolf is not my chosen name.

3   I was a boy of about thirteen snows when my parents sent me away into the hills. It was to find my *Wyakin*. I saw something—not on the ground, but about four feet up in the air.

4   I took my bow and shot an arrow.

5   It was in moon you call May when my parents again sent me out. This time it was to the wildest part of the mountains. To a place beyond Kemei Koois. Gave me one blanket, but no food. I might go fifteen, maybe twenty, suns with nothing to eat. But could drink water aplenty. Only trees for shelter, and fir brush to sleep on. I might stay in one place three nights, maybe five nights, then go somewhere else. Nobody around, just myself. No weapons, for nothing would hurt me. No children ever get hurt when out on such business.

6   After going so many suns without food I was sleeping. It was just like dreaming, what I saw. A form stood in the air fronting me. It talked to me in plain language, telling me:

7   "My boy, look at me! You do as I am telling you, and you will be as I am. Take a good look at me! I will give you my power; what I have got. You may think I am nothing! You may think I am only bones! But I am alive! You can see me! I am talking to you! I am Hemene Moxmox [Yellow Wolf]."

8   It was a Spirit of a wolf that appeared to me. Yellowlike in color, it sort of floated in the air. Like a human being it talked to me, and gave me its power. . . .

9   That was how I got named Yellow Wolf. Named for that vision-wolf appearing to me. It was yellow-colored, and gave me the power of the wolf. . . .

THE LAST STAND: BEAR PAW'S BATTLEFIELD

10 Evening came, and the battle grew less. Darkness settled and mostly the guns died away. Only occasional shots. I went up toward our camp. I did not hurry. Soldiers guarding, sitting down, two and two. Soldiers all about the camp, so that none could escape from there. A long time I watched. It was snowing. The wind was cold! Stripped for battle, I had no blanket. I lay close to the ground, crawling nearer the guard line

11 It was past middle of night when I went between those guards. I was now back within the camp circle. I went first and drank some water. I did not look for food.

12 On the bluffs Indians with knives were digging rifle pits. Some had those broad-bladed knives [trowel bayonets] taken from soldiers at the Big Hole. Down in the main camp women with camas hooks were digging shelter pits. All this for tomorrow's coming.

13 Shelter pits for the old, the women, the children.

14 Rifle pits for the warriors, the fighters.

15 You have seen hail, sometimes, leveling the grass. Indians were so leveled by the bullet hail. Most of our few warriors left from the Big Hole had been swept as leaves before the storm. Chief Ollokot, Lone Bird, and Lean Elk were gone.

16 Outside the camp I had seen men killed. Soldiers ten, Indians ten. That was not so bad. But now, when I saw our remaining warriors gone, my heart grew choked and heavy. Yet the warriors and no-fighting men killed were not all. I looked around.

17 Some were burying their dead.

18 A young warrior, wounded, lay on a buffalo robe dying without complaint. Children crying with cold. No fire. There could be no light. Everywhere the crying, the death wail.

19 My heart became fire. I joined the warriors digging rifle pits. All the rest of night we worked. Just before dawn, I went down among the shelter pits. I looked around. Children no longer crying. In deep shelter pits they were sleeping. Wrapped in a blanket, a still form lay on the buffalo robe. The young warrior was dead. I went back to my rifle pit, my blood hot for war. I felt not the cold.

20 Morning came, bringing the battle anew. Bullets from everywhere! A big gun throwing bursting shells. From rifle pits, warriors returned shot for shot. Wild and stormy, the cold wind was thick with snow. Air filled with smoke of powder. Flash of guns through it all. As the hidden sun traveled upward, the war did not weaken.

21 I felt the coming end. All for which we had suffered lost!

22 Thoughts came of the Wallowa where I grew up. Of my own country when only Indians were there. Of tepees along the bending river. Of the blue, clear lake, wide meadows with horse and cattle herds. From the mountain forests, voices seemed calling. I felt as dreaming. Not my living self.

23   The war deepened. Grew louder with gun reports. I raised up and looked around. Everything was against us. No hope! Only bondage or death! Something screamed in my ear. A blaze flashed before me. I felt as burning! Then with rifle I stood forth, saying to my heart, "Here I will die, fighting for my people and our homes!"

24   Soldiers could see me. Bullets hummed by me, but I was untouched. The warriors called, "Heinmot! Come back to this pit. You will be killed!"

25   I did not listen. I did not know if I killed any soldiers. To do well in battle you must see what you want to shoot. You glimpse an enemy in hiding and shoot. If no more shots from there, you know you have succeeded.

26   I felt not afraid. Soldier rifles from shelters kept popping fast. Their big gun boomed often but not dangerous. The warriors lying close in dugout pits could not be hit. I know not why the shells never struck our rifle pits on the bluffs. . . .

27   It came morning, third sun of battle. The rifle shooting went on just like play. Nobody being hurt. But soon Chief Looking Glass was killed. Some warriors in same pit with him saw at a distance a horseback Indian. Thinking he must be a Sioux from Sitting Bull, one pointed and called to Looking Glass: "Look! A Sioux!"

28   Looking Glass stepped quickly from the pit. Stood on the bluff unprotected. It must have been a sharpshooter killed him. A bullet struck his left forehead, and he fell back dead.

29   That horseback Indian was a Nez Perce.

30   In the afternoon of this sun we saw the white flag again go up in the soldier camp. Then was heard a voice calling in a strange language, "General [Colonel] Miles would like to see Chief Joseph!"

31   The chiefs held council and Chief Joseph said, "Yes, I would like to see General Miles."

32   Tom Hill, interpreter, went to see what General Miles wanted, to tell General Miles, "Yes, Joseph would like to see you!" After some time, we saw Tom Hill with General Miles and a few men come halfway. They stopped and Tom Hill called to Chief Joseph. Chief Joseph with two or three warriors went to meet them.

33   I did not go where they met. I looked around. There was a hollow place off a distance in the ground. I went there and lay down. I could see General Miles where Chief Joseph met him. I could see all plainly where they stood. I was saying to myself, "Whenever they shoot Chief Joseph, I will shoot from here!"

34   There was talk for a while, and Chief Joseph and General Miles made peace. Some guns were given up. Then there was a trick. *I* saw Chief Joseph taken to the soldier camp a prisoner!

35   The white flag was pulled down!

36   The white flag was a lie!

37   The warriors came back, and right away a soldier officer [Lieutenant

Lovell H. Jerome] rode into our camp. Chief Yellow Bull yelled a warning and grabbed him. I could see them take the officer to the main shelter pit. When I saw all this—Chief Joseph was taken away—I ran to where the captured soldier was being held. Held that Chief Joseph might not be hurt. He had on a yellowcolored outside coat to keep off the wet. A stronglooking young man, he did not say much. Looked around, but seemed not much afraid. I do not think he was bad scared.

38   The chiefs instructed the warriors to guard him. Ordered: "Treat him right! He is one of the commanders."

39   One man, Chuslum Hihhih [White Bull] got mad at this officer and tried to get the best of him. He said, "I want to kill this soldier!"

40   The Indians told him, "No, we do not want you to kill him!"

41   Chuslum Hihhih was mean-minded, had a bad heart. He did no great fighting. Stayed behind where bullets could not reach him. Espowyes, my relation, kept telling him, "Do not hurt the prisoner." Scolding, he said, "Don't you know Chief Joseph is prisoner on other side? We have this officer prisoner here on our side. When they turn Chief Joseph loose, we will turn our prisoner loose at the same time. For this we are holding him, to make the trade. We do not want to kill him. . . .

42   It was about noon of the fourth sun when the officer took paper from his pocket and wrote. I know what he wrote. One Nez Perce understood English very well, and the officer said to him, "You must take my letter to the soldier chief!"

43   The officer read what he wrote on the paper, and when the Indian interpreted it to the chiefs, they said, "All right!"

44   This is what the interpreter said the paper told: "I had good supper, good bed. I had plenty of blankets. This morning I had good breakfast. I am treated like I was at home. I hope you officers are treating Chief Joseph as I am treated. I would like to see him treated as I am treated."

45   But Chief Joseph was not treated right. Chief Joseph was hobbled hands and feet. They took a double blanket. Soldiers rolled him in it like you roll papoose on cradle board. Chief Joseph could not use arms, could not walk about. He was put where there were mules, and not in soldier tent. That was how Chief Joseph was treated all night.

46   When soldier officers received that letter, they took hobbles off Chief Joseph. He could then walk around a little where they let him. Those officers wrote a letter to our prisoner officer. When he read it, he said, "I have not been treated like Chief Joseph!"

47   The officer then read from the letter, "You come across to us. When you get here, then Chief Joseph can go!"

48   The chiefs and warriors replied to the officer, "No! If General Miles is speaking true, he will bring Chief Joseph halfway. To same ground we did that other time. It will be that, if he is speaking true words."

49   This letter was carried to the soldiers by the same interpreter. The soldier officers must have read it, for soon a white flag went up. Then those officers

sent a letter to the Indian chiefs. It said, "Yes, we will bring Chief Joseph halfway. You bring the officer to that same place."

50 The chiefs said, "That is fair enough!"

51 Then we looked across and saw officers and Chief Joseph. They were coming to halfway ground. A buffalo robe was spread there. The chiefs and a few older warriors took our prisoner to meet them. He shook hands with Joseph and those officers. Then each party returned to its own side, Chief Joseph coming back to our camp.

52 The soldiers now pulled down their white flag. When the warriors saw that flag come down, they laughed. They said to each other, "Three times those soldiers lie with the white flag. We can not believe them." We younger warriors had not gone to the meeting place marked by buffalo robe.

53 Chief Joseph now spoke to all headmen: "I was hobbled in the soldier camp. We must fight more. The war is not quit!" . . .

THE LAST DAY: THE SURRENDER

54 Finally the fifth morning of the battle drew on, but no sun could be seen. With first light, the battle began again. It was bad that cannon guns should be turned on the shelter pits where there were no fighters. Only women and children, old and wounded men in those pits. General Miles and his men handling the big gun surely knew no warriors were in that part of camp. The officer we had held prisoner well knew no fighting warriors were where he sheltered. Of course his business was to carry back all news he could spy out in our camp.

55 It was towards noon that a bursting shell struck and broke in a shelter pit, burying four women, a little boy, and a girl of about twelve snows. This girl, Atsipeeten, and her grandmother, Intetah, were both killed. The other three women and the boy were rescued. The two dead were left in the caved-in pit.

56 When a few Indians, mad and wild on white man's whisky, killed mean settlers on Indian lands on the Salmon River, along with one or two women and maybe one child, that was very bad.

57 Soldiers did not need whisky to kill a great many women and children throughout this war.

58 This woman and child, and Chief Looking Glass, were only ones killed in this battle after the first sun's fighting. None even wounded. All those not fighting were in the shelter pits. The warriors in rifle pits could not be seen by the soldiers. Indians are not seen in the fighting. They are hid.

59 The fight went on, but we did not fire continually. We thought the soldiers would get tired, maybe freeze out and charge us. We wanted plenty of ammunition for them if they did.

60 Darkness again settled down, and only occasional shots were heard. These came mostly from soldiers, as if afraid we might slip up on them in their dugout forts.

61 That night, General Howard arrived with two of his scouts, men of our tribe. He did not see much fighting of this battle, and I think maybe he put it wrong in history. Towards noon next day we saw those two Indians coming with a white flag. Heard them calling and I understood. One of them said, "All my brothers, I am glad to see you alive this sun!". . .

62 They carried a white flag, and General Miles had told them to say to us: "I want to speak to Chief Joseph."

63 I heard this message, and I heard Chief Joseph make reply, "We will have council over this. We will decide what to do!"

64 There was a council, and the main messenger talked this way: "Those generals said tell you: 'We will have no more fighting. Your chiefs and some of you warriors are not seeing the truth. We sent our officer to appear before your Indians—sent all our messengers to say to them, "We will have no more war!"'"

65 Then our man, Chief Joseph, spoke, "You see, it is true. I did not say 'Let's quit!'

66 "General Miles said, 'Let's quit.'

67 "And now General Howard says, 'Let's quit!'

68 "You see, it is true enough! I did not say 'Let's quit!'"

69 When the warriors heard those words from Chief Joseph, they answered, "Yes, we believe you now."

70 So when General Miles's messengers reported back to him, the answer was, "Yes."

71 Then Chief Joseph and other chiefs met General Miles on halfway ground. Chief Joseph and General Miles were talking good and friendly when General Howard came speaking loud, commanding words. When General Miles saw this, he held the Indians back from him a little. He said, "I think soon General Howard will forget all this. I will take you to a place for this winter; then you can go to your old home."

72 Chief Joseph said, "Now we all understand these words, and we will go with General Miles. He is a headman, and we will go with him."

73 General Miles spoke to Chief Joseph, "No more battles and blood! From this sun, we will have good time on both sides, your band and mine. We will have plenty time for sleep, for good rest. We will drink good water from this time on where the war is stopped."

74 "Same is here," General Howard said. "I will have time from now on, like you, to rest. The war is all quit." He was in a better humor. General Howard spoke to Chief Joseph, "You have your life. I am living. I have lost my brothers. Many of you have lost brothers, maybe more than on our side. I do not know. Do not worry any more. While you see this many soldiers living from the war, you think of them as your brothers. Many brothers of yours—they are my brothers—living from the war.

75 "Do not worry about starving. It is plenty of food we have left from this war. Any one who needs a sack of flour, anything the people want, come get it. All is yours."

76   The chiefs and officers crossed among themselves and shook hands all around. The Indians lifted their hands towards the sky, where the sun was then standing. This said: "No more battles! No more war!"

77   That was all I saw and heard of chiefs' and generals' ending the war.

78   General Miles was good to the surrendered Indians with food. The little boys and girls loved him for that. They could now have hot food and fires to warm by.

79   What I heard those generals and chiefs say, I have always remembered. But those generals soon forgot their promises. Chief Joseph and his people were not permitted to return to their homes.

80   We were not captured. It was a draw battle. We did not expect being sent to Eeikish Pah [Hot Place]. Had we known this we never would have surrendered. We expected to be returned to our own homes. This was promised us by General Miles. That was how he got our rifles from us. It was the only way he could get them.

81   The fighting was done. All who wanted to surrender took their guns to General Miles and gave them up. Those who did not want to surrender, kept their guns. The surrender was just for those who did not longer want to fight. Joseph spoke only for his own band, what they wanted to do. Of the other bands, they surrendered who wanted to.

82   Chief White Bird did not surrender.

83   When Chief Joseph surrendered, war was quit, everything was quit, for those who surrendered their guns.

84   One side of war story is that told by the white man.

85   The story I have given you is the Indian side. You now have it all, as concerned the war.

86   I did not surrender my rifle. . . .

DISCUSSION QUESTIONS

1. How did Yellow Wolf get his name?
2. How is Chief Joseph taken prisoner, and why is he released?
3. How did Colonel Miles get the rifles away from some of the warriors?
4. What adjectives would you use to describe Yellow Wolf?
5. Suppose that the battle at Bear Paw had been covered by on-the-spot reporters and had been televised, as battles and wars often are today. In a small group, discuss what effect you think this would have had on the Nez Perce and the American public.

WRITING TOPICS

1. Imagine that you were a member of the president's cabinet in 1877 (Rutherford B. Hayes was president). Would you have advised him to intervene in this situation, and if so, how should he have done so? What might have been the consequences of your advice? Examine these questions in an essay.
2. Write an essay in which you examine paragraphs 10–26 and analyze Yellow Wolf's method of telling his story.

RETURN TO BEAR PAW

Janet Campbell Hale

Janet Campbell Hale was born in 1946 in Riverside, California, to Nicholas Pattrick, Coeur d'Alene, and Margaret Campbell of Kootenay, Chippewa, and Euro-American ancestry. Hale attended the Institute of American Indian Arts, Santa Fe, New Mexico, and received a B.A. from the University of California, Berkeley in 1974. She earned an M.A. in English at the University of California, Davis (1984), where she taught literature courses.

Hale began her literary career winning two poetry awards—the Vincent Price Poetry Competition (1963) and the New York Poetry Day Award (1964). She published a poetry collection, *Custer Lives in Humboldt County and Other Poems* in 1978. Hale's first novel, *The Owl's Song,* appeared in 1974, and her second novel, *The Jailing of Cecelia Capture* (1985), was nominated for the Pulitzer Prize.

Hale received the American Book Award for *Bloodlines: Odyssey of a Native Daughter* (1993), a personal chronicle in which she traces the effects of her Coeur d'Alene heritage on her life. In *Bloodlines,* she confronts painful facts not only of her life but also of the difficult lives of several generations of her female relatives, a testimony to the burden and blessing of inheritance.

While on a May 1986 lecture tour in Montana, Hale visited Bear Paw Battlefield. She recalled the experiences of her father's mother, a Coeur d'Alene who had been with Chief Joseph and Yellow Wolf during the entire campaign. The author of "Return to Bear Paw" is two generations removed from the events that carved a costly niche in U.S. history. Hale's grandmother was there, just as Yellow Wolf was there. She told her son and older granddaughters about her experiences as a teenage Coeur d'Alene caught up in the epic Nez Perce journey by happenstance.

Chance circumstances brought Janet Campbell Hale and her grandmother to cold Bear Paw Country over a century apart. In 1877, her grandmother was there by accident because of a clash between soldiers and her people gathering food. In 1986, Hale arrived there when her speech at Fort Belknap Community College was canceled because of freezing weather. Miles, years, and cultural changes separated the two women, yet Hale found part of herself along Snake Creek at the Bear Paw Battleground.

◉

I

1   Montana was startlingly cold for May, especially compared to the mild drizzle I had just left in Seattle. I didn't bring any cold-weather clothing, no coat, no scarf, no gloves, no shoes except for the open-toed pumps I wore on the airplane. Before I went to sleep the first night, I had a sore throat. When I woke, I had a bad cold that would last the length of my stay in Montana.

2   Montana was cold and big and desolate, full of empty, wide-open spaces, no greenery, it seemed (compared to Seattle), very few trees . . . BIG SKY COUNTRY, the license plates proclaimed. Nothing blocked the view of the sky, so it seemed to be bigger than in other places. I kept my speaking engagements, ate in roadside diners, slept in cheap motels, took liberal doses of my cold remedy and endured. Twangy country western music played everywhere in Montana, seemed to permeate the crisp mountain air. The cold weather became even colder. (Hard to believe it was really May.) From the beginning I longed to be home in Seattle.

3   I did not come to Montana to make a pilgrimage to the Bear Paw battleground, to close the circle. I hadn't even realized, at first, that the place where the cavalry finally caught up with the Indians led by Chief Joseph was in Montana. And I hadn't thought of my grandmother, my father's mother, who had been among those Indians, for many years.

4   But now it was impossible not to think of her, not to think of Chief Joseph and the Great Flight of 1877, for often my path and the path of those fugitive Indians would cross. Sometimes a stone or metal "state historical marker" would mark the spot where a skirmish or some other event had occurred. Sometimes my driver would point out a certain place and tell me what had happened there.

5   Near one small town the army had put a barricade of timber to stop the Indians. But when dark fell, the nine hundred and some Indians, including women, children, old people, with their horses and belongings, slipped up along a narrow ledge where it didn't seem a mountain goat could go, up above the heads of the sleeping soldiers, around the white man's barricade and down the other side.

6   "Do you know about Chief Joseph and his war with the government?" asked my driver. I nodded yes. Sure. The government promised Chief Joseph

of the Nez Percé he would be allowed to remain in his homeland, the beautiful, fertile Wallowa Valley in Oregon, but then the government took another look and changed its mind. The Wallowa Valley was good land, too good to be Indian land. They told him he would have to remove himself and his people to a seedy, rocky, arid piece of land in Idaho nobody wanted, but Joseph refused to go there. At first, I think, Joseph intended to fight a war. My father told me how it was said he went to all the tribes of the region—the Coeur d'Alene, Kalispell, Spokane, Kootenay—seeking support, but no one would join forces with him. By 1877 the Indian wars in what would become Washington, Idaho, and Oregon had been fought and lost, treaties had been signed. The great power and ruthlessness of the United States government was well understood by then. Fighting another war would be a futile endeavor. And besides, the other tribes did not get as raw a deal as Chief Joseph.

7 My tribe, the Coeur d'Alene (whose French name, given them in the early 1700s, means "heart of steel"), were never removed from their beautiful ancestral land, only confined to one small corner of it. What the tribes wanted now was peace. No more war. No more bloodshed. No more taking away of land. Chief Joseph and his followers were on their own.

8 He and his chiefs—Looking Glass, Toolhoolzote and the others—decided they would run away from the United States rather than turn themselves in to the soldiers who had hunted them since they left the Wallowa. They would run to Canada and join the Sioux chief, Sitting Bull, who had been granted political asylum there after his defeat of Custer and the 7th Cavalry at the Little Big Horn. The army, led by General Howard, was relentless in its pursuit of Chief Joseph, but not good at keeping up with Indians. For a while the 7th Cavalry, seeking revenge after once having been wiped out by Indians, joined in the chase, but the 7th Cavalry was easily shaken. Four months after the fight began, the Indians stopped and made camp in the Little Bear Paw Mountains just thirty miles from the safety of the Canadian border, unaware that another division, commanded by General Sherman (of Civil War fame), approached from the east. There Sherman's forces found them, and the last battle began.

9 A Nez Percé warrior named Yellow Wolf described his feelings after the Battle at the Bear Paw had begun, but before it was over, when they all knew it could only end in defeat: "I felt the end coming. All for which we had suffered was lost. Thoughts came of the Wallowa where I grew up, of my own country when only Indians were there, of teepees along the bending river, of the blue clear lake, wide meadows with horses and cattle herds. From the mountains and forests, voices seemed to be calling. I felt as though dreaming; not my living self . . . then, with rifle I stood forth, saying to my heart, 'Here I will die fighting for my people and for our home!'"

10 "That place where the last battle was fought," my driver told me, "is right near your last stop, about twenty miles or so from Fort Belknap." But it would be late by then, I thought, and I would still have a trip ahead of me, to Great Falls, where I would spend the night, then board my plane for

Seattle the next morning. And it was cold and getting colder, and I wasn't feeling well.

11 "We could go there if you like. To the Bear Paw." My throat still felt raw.

12 "I don't know," I said. "Maybe. Is there anything there?"

13 "No. An empty field. A stone monument. Nothing."

14 "Maybe. Maybe I'll want to go there. I can't say yet. My grandmother was there, you know. She was with those Chief Joseph people."

15 "Is that so? She was Nez Percé?"

16 "No. How she happened to be with them had to do with a case of mistaken identity."

17 When I was four or five, my father told me how it was: My grandmother, a young girl of fifteen or sixteen in the summer of 1877, had been with a group of Coeur d'Alene root gatherers. As was their custom, they had gone quite a distance from Coeur d'Alene country into what used to be Nez Percé territory to dig camas roots. (Camas was dried and stored, used as winter food.) And, as was also their custom whenever they traveled away from their own home, the camas diggers—women, children, old people— had a small group of armed men watching over them as they worked. This was during the time Chief Joseph and his band hid out and evaded the soldiers who tried to find them.

18 One day while my grandmother and the others dug camas in an open field and warriors watched from hiding places in the hills above, the United States cavalry came riding up.

19 An army translator spoke in Chinook asking the root gatherers to tell them where Chief Joseph was. They were looking for Nez Percé and believed they had found some.

20 One old man spoke Chinook to the translator, explaining the situation, telling him they were Coeur d'Alene root gatherers, not Nez Percé, and they knew nothing about Chief Joseph. The commander yelled in English, "Liar!" and raised his gun, aimed it at the old man, and told the translator to tell him to take him to Chief Joseph or he would kill him.

21 The old man said again he didn't know where Chief Joseph was; the commander shot him dead. The warriors swooped down from their hiding places firing their guns, picking off soldiers. Those few Coeur d'Alene killed a good many soldiers that day and beat the rest into retreat. They were a long way from home. They had no choice after that but to find Chief Joseph and join forces with him. That was how it happened that my grandmother, a Coeur d'Alene, was swept along with the Chief Joseph people pursued by Howard, Miles, the 7th Cavalry, and the Great Warrior himself, Sherman, running for her life for the Canadian border and the camp of Sitting Bull.

II

22 My grandmother, the one who ran with Chief Joseph, died five years before my birth so I have no memories of my own of her. But I heard a lot

about her from both my parents, from my uncle and cousins and sisters who did know her and had memories. My three sisters, who are ten, twelve, and fourteen years older than I, remember a little old woman who liked to joke, who told them Indian stories in our Native language. (She never learned English. They knew Indian as children.) How I envied them. How I wished I, too, had known her, had listened to her stories, had understood the language. I imagined her, though, when I was a child, and she became almost real to me.

23   My family had a photograph of her taken in old age: She is small and thin, her face very wrinkled, her eyes squint in the sun. Her long hair is white. She wears it parted in the middle and in two braids that hang in front to her waist. She is dressed Indian style.

24   She had a fragile appearance, but she was never fragile, they said, never. She was strong and tough, full of energy and industry, she kept busy. She made her own soap and scented it with pine needles. She went berry picking and she made Indian dishes nobody knows how to make anymore. She sewed all her own clothes. One ongoing activity of hers was the making of beautiful, useful articles: deerskin bags decorated with colored glass beads, cornhusk bags, and these, too, with intricate designs, moccasins, and infant cradle boards. She put them away and kept them sort of in the way young girls once kept a hope chest—for a day that would follow her death and funeral—the feast day when her belongings would be given away to friends and family. She wanted them to have something she made herself by which to remember her.

25   She was a rider of horses, too, a great rider of horses. She never gave up riding.

26   Way into old age she would ride, my mother told me, bareback, sometimes long distances. It was twenty miles from their home to the mission village. My grandmother preferred to ride her horse to the village on Sundays rather than go with my parents in their automobile, and she always would if weather permitted. She liked to get an early start, go to an early Mass, eat with friends and relatives, rest, attend a second Mass and visit a bit with her old cronies before heading home. In my mind's eye I can see her riding through the woods and open meadows on Sunday, all decked out in her finery—blue flower-print dress, her long-fringed maroon Spanish trade shawl, a silk scarf tied around her head, riding proud, beautiful, white-haired Indian woman, grandmother I could only know in my mind's eye, in my heart's eye.

27   My grandmother was a very devout Catholic, as were her parents before her. The conversion of the Coeur d'Alene was in response to an ancient prophecy that said three black ravens would come to them one day bringing the sacred word of the Creator. The ravens would only come when the people were ready to receive the new revelations. In time three Jesuit missionaries, or Black Robes, as they were called, did come, and they were welcomed and listened to. The tribe embraced Catholicism. As practiced by the

Coeur d'Alene, it was a rather peculiar brand of Catholicism, and it was not at all "in place of" traditional religious beliefs, but rather an extension of them.

28   My father's generation, though, was of that first generation born *after* the conquest and the advent of the reservation system, the first generation of Indians to have Christianity forced upon it. The Church, for him, was an instrument of assimilation, an authority sponsored and sanctioned by the government whose primary purpose was to "civilize" the Indian and make him as much like a white man as possible. My father could recall, for instance, being beaten by a priest at mission school for speaking his own language. He, unlike his mother, was not a devout Catholic. He was, in fact, about as far from a devout Catholic as one could get.

29   My parents once told me (actually they were retelling each other the story, remembering it, laughing about it, after forty years of marriage) about when they were newlyweds and his mother, who had been living with him prior to his marriage, took extreme measures to get them to marry in the Catholic church.

30   When my father married my mother and brought her, his new part-white, English-speaking wife home, he told his mother they did not intend to marry in the Church. His mother tried to get him to change his mind, but he would not. His mother could not live with the two of them under the circumstances. She moved out—not to live with another son, as she could have, though. She pitched her tepee in the woods behind the house and lived there.

31   She used the same well, the same paths they used. They saw her all the time, coming and going, busy around her home. She would not speak to them, nor look at them, nor acknowledge their presence in any way. To her, they were invisible.

32   They continued to speak to her, to say good morning, how are you, to invite her to go for rides in their automobile, to go into town with them on a hot summer day for some ice cream. But the old lady had a heart of steel. The summer wore on in this way.

33   One month passed. Then two. My grandmother steadfastly continued to live in the woods in her tepee. In the end the old lady won, despite my father's feelings about the Church. Before the first frost my parents married in a Catholic ceremony, and my grandmother moved back into the house and stopped pretending they were invisible.

III

34   The Big Sky Country of Montana, the mountainous terrain, the grey, cold weather, the country western music, the motion of the car took me out of myself and my own petty hardships. (I had a cold, I had to eat in diners and sleep in cheap motels.) I had to speak to nine audiences in eight days (as a single mother I needed the money), though I would rather be

home. I recognized these as petty concerns as we made our way across the big, big state of Montana. I saw her, my grandmother, the young girl she had been in 1877, more and more clearly. I drew closer and closer to her. She was there when they drove their ponies and cattle across a treacherous river and over two mountain ranges (they sometimes reached altitudes of ten thousand feet). Always (until that last day) they managed to keep ahead of the soldiers. In the last month they had no more cattle herds and only a few ponies.

35   Their food supplies ran out. Their clothes and moccasins were worn out. They became ragged, cold and hungry and could not stop to hunt or gather food or make new clothes. They wrapped their bleeding feet in rags and continued. They hurriedly buried their dead in shallow graves along the wayside. Soldiers noted scarred trees where hungry Indians had eaten bark and that they left behind a path marked by blood.

36   I thought of her, the devout Catholic girl she was, swept long with Nez Percé, who were never the friend of the Coeur d'Alene, whose language was not the same or even similar, whose culture was not her own.

37   I remembered something I heard about Chief Joseph when I was a child of eleven: he, always portrayed as "noble" in books, films, poems (in *Bury My Heart at Wounded Knee*), had actually been a mean person, a wicked man who hated women and treated them very badly.

38   My two best friends when I was a girl living on the Yakima Reservation were sisters and they were half Nez Percé. They and their mother were direct descendants of Chief Looking Glass. There was very bad blood between Joseph and Looking Glass (even on that last evening they disagreed). Joseph wanted to let the exhausted people stop and rest at the Bear Paw, then, refreshed, make the thirty miles into Canada in one long march the next day. Looking Glass urged that they push on, despite the belief that no soldiers were near, that they would be safe. They would not be safe, he argued, until they reached Canada. Then they could rest. But Joseph prevailed. Looking Glass, among many others, lost his life at the Bear Paw.

39   The grandfather of my friends was a grandson of Looking Glass. He said (and his mother, who had been there, told him) that Chief Joseph beat women and worse. On one occasion he had one of his wives put to death because he believed she had brought him bad luck at stick games.

40   Whether or not it is true that Chief Joseph was a misogynist, and had had a woman put to death because she brought him bad luck, I'll never know for sure. But I didn't doubt it when I heard it at age eleven, and I've read accounts of Indian chiefs of that region (of an earlier time) having wives put to death for the same reason. It could be true. At any rate the Nez Percé, to my grandmother, were strange people with different beliefs and customs. Maybe their leader held women in low regard, as the grandson of Looking Glass told me. They were not in any way *her people*. Except one: they were Indians and all Indians had in common a powerful enemy who had conquered them and would now hold them in captivity and would not tolerate any defiance.

41   So there she was, a young Catholic Coeur d'Alene, running for her life with Nez Percé (they left a trail marked by blood) from the United States Army (which was commanded by a man who was in fact against the reservation system, who believed Indians should all be killed off lest the government end up supporting "a race of paupers." "The only good Indian is a dead Indian" was a heartfelt sentiment in the America of 1877). And where were they going? To Canada to join the Sioux chief, Sitting Bull. And what kind of a life would she, the little girl who would be my grandmother, have were they to make good their escape? While the Nez Percé were never the friend of the Coeur d'Alene, the Sioux, still polygamous in 1877, were their bitter enemy. The literal translation of the Coeur d'Alene word for "Sioux" is "cutthroat."

42   The last days of the Great Flight were in September, and that year it was, as it often is, very cold in Montana, maybe as cold as the time of my own journey. I know it snowed in the night while they camped and slept in the Little Bear Paw Mountains. I know the snow fell softly throughout the next day.

IV

43   The morning of the last day of my tour I woke in the predawn hours and looked out the motel-room window and saw snow. Three or four inches of snow covered the ground, the rooftops, the cars, weighed heavily upon electrical wires. Somewhere I heard a radio: country western music at five A.M. The snow fell hard. It was time to go.

44   We reached Fort Belknap by noon and found my lecture there had been canceled. Classes had all been canceled, too, due to the heavy snowfall that closed the roads in the northern part of the reservation, where most of the students lived. They were snowed in. I had time now, lots of time. I had noticed a sign that said, TO THE INDIAN BATTLEGROUND. It was twenty-odd miles away. That was all. After eight days' time, all those hours of recalling what I knew about my grandmother and the Great Flight of 1877, and imagining how it must have been, after traveling all those hard Montana miles, I felt compelled to complete the journey now, to close the circle. I asked my driver if, given the snow, it would be possible to visit the Bear Paw. Would the roads be passable? Yes, he said. The roads would be fine. If not, we could turn back. But he thought it would be all right.

45   Those twenty-odd miles were hard ones. The wind blew and the snow drifted across the narrow winding road as we climbed higher and higher. Sometimes the road would be entirely hidden by snowdrifts.

46   The car was small, and I felt our vulnerability, should something go wrong. But my driver was used to bad weather and lonely stretches of country road. This probably wasn't even bad weather to him. Just a light spring snowfall.

47   Cattle lined up against the fence alongside the road, their white faces

watching us. "It's as though they heard we were coming through," I said, "and all turned out to watch us pass."

48 "Maybe," he said, "they heard you were disappointed because you didn't see any buffalo in Montana and came to act as stand-ins. Actually that's what they do when they know a storm is coming."

49 "Why?"

50 "I don't know."

51 I sat back and watched the snow fall as we passed through this desolate area. We passed no house along the way, no filling station. We didn't even pass any other cars on the road. After what seemed like a long time my driver pulled over and stopped the car.

52 "Here we are," he said.

53 We climbed out of the car into the snow, four or five inches deep. I slipped and almost fell. My shoes, my thin high-heeled pumps, filled with snow, and snow fell on my hair and clothes and melted. I clutched my long red cardigan sweater close to me. It didn't keep me warm.

54 How quiet it was now that the car's engine no longer ran. No sound of wind or birds calling or human voices, only the quiet of the softly falling snow.

55 "There"—he indicated the mountains in the distance, barely visible through the veil of falling snow—"is Canada." Their destination.

56 We walked over to the monument, a bronze plate set in stone. On the plate, in relief, were two figures: one a soldier in uniform, presumably General Howard; the other an Indian, naked from the waist up, presumably Chief Joseph. Below the figures, also in relief, the words FROM WHERE THE SUN NOW STANDS I WILL FIGHT NO MORE FOREVER. The last words of Joseph's surrender speech.

57 "Look at this," he said, lightly touching the figure of the Indian. I touched it too. Some kind of blemishes . . . deep scratches on the figure of the Indian.

58 "What is this?"

59 "Bullet nicks," he answered. It took a moment for it to sink in, to imagine good old boys up here drinking beer and getting in a little target practice and expressing themselves. After all these years Indians aren't generally very popular in Montana. FROM WHERE THE SUN NOW STANDS, it said. I WILL FIGHT NO MORE . . ., and there were bullet-nicks, . . .FOREVER, on the bronze monument. FROM WHERE THE SUN, depicting the peace-making SUN NOW STANDS . . . , the final surrender, I WILL FIGHT . . ., after the slaughter, NO MORE. . . . They shot only at FOREVER, the Indian. Not the soldier. Bullet nicks.

60 We stood on a rise above what I realized had to be the battleground. "There it is," he said, "down here." Yes.

61 The Indians had come far, had suffered such great hardships, were so tired and hungry. There would be time enough, or so they thought, to stop for the night, their last night. They knew of Howard, a good long distance away, and they knew they had completely lost the other, the 7th Cavalry. But

they were not aware of a third division, which now came towards them from the east. So they went down there, made their camp in the gulch beside Snake Creek. They hunted, cooked their fresh meat, ate and rested. What did that girl dream of that night as she lay sleeping? Did she dream of the beautiful Coeur d'Alene country that was her home? Did she see the faces of her father and mother? Or did she now dream of her new life in Canada?

62   The cavalry attacked just before dawn while the Indians slept. The battle raged as the snow fell, hour after bloody hour, throughout most of the day. When the Battle at the Bear Paw ended, 419 Indians—88 men, 184 women and 147 children—lay dead on the frozen ground.

63   "Do you want to go down there?" he asked me. I said no. Not in those shoes. Not dressed as I was. I wouldn't be able to take the cold much longer. He went alone. My ears ached in the cold, and my feet felt as though they would turn to ice. I saw him brush the snow from the markers for the communal grave. He stayed there awhile, kneeling in the snow.

64   The cold reached my bones, yet I stood in the snow and felt myself being in that place, that sacred place. I saw how pitifully close lay the mountains of Canada. I felt the biting cold. I was with those people, was part of them. I felt the presence of my grandmother there as though two parts of her met each other that day: the ghost of the girl she was in 1877 (and that part of her will remain forever in that place) and the part of her that lives on in me, in inherited memories of her, in my blood and in my spirit.

65   At length the spell broke. I could take the cold no longer. I went back to the car, to the relative warmth and comfort there.

66   My driver joined me in five or ten minutes. He started the engine, breaking the silence. The tires spun in the mud, but just a bit. Then we pulled forward, made a circle and turned back onto the road, which was easier to travel going down.

67   The snow stopped, turned to rain. We didn't talk much the rest of the way to the highway and then to Great Falls. The day grew dim.

68   Chief Joseph of the Nez Percé was thirty-six years old at the time of the Battle at the Bear Paw. His surrender speech was made through an interpreter and recorded on the spot by an army clerk. It would become one of the most famous of American speeches:

> *Tell General Howard I know his heart. What he told me before I have in my heart. I am tired of fighting. Our chiefs are killed. Looking Glass is dead. Toolhoolzote is dead. The old men are all dead. It is cold and we have no blankets. The little children are freezing to death. My people, some of them, have run away to the hills and have no blankets, no food; no one knows where they are—perhaps freezing to death. I want to have time to look for my children and see how many of them I can find. Maybe I shall find them among the dead. Hear me, my chiefs! From where the sun now stands I will fight no more forever.*

69   After it was all over, my grandmother would return to Coeur d'Alene country in northern Idaho. She would live through a smallpox epidemic that would wipe out most of the tribe, begun when the Coeur d'Alene people, no longer permitted to go to Montana to hunt buffalo, were given small-pox-infected army blankets.

70   She would marry a tall, shrewd Coeur d'Alene man, who would, as a rancher, provide very well for her and the six sons and one daughter they would have together.

71   She would give birth to my father in the mountains one summer day in 1892 while out picking huckleberries. She would tell him about his birth in the mountains and how she came riding down with the basket strapped to her horse on one side filled with huckleberries and the basket on the other side containing her new baby boy.

72   My father would go to mission school at the age of twelve, where he would learn English: to read, to write, to speak. He would become a soldier in the United States Army during World War I (though Indians would not be made citizens until 1924). He would marry and have one son. His first wife would die. He would marry my mother when he was thirty-nine years old, and they would have four daughters together.

73   My paternal grandmother would live to be a very old woman, and she and my three older sisters would know each other very well. She would tell them stories, speaking the old language they would understand as children but forget as adults (and I would never know).

74   The old woman who survived the Great Flight and the Battle at the Bear Paw and the smallpox epidemic would die peacefully in her sleep in her home in Idaho in 1941.

75   I would be born five years later in 1946, shortly after the end of World War II. And though I would live on that same Idaho reservation, and then on the Yakima in Washington State, I would grow up knowing only the English language. I would go to college and law school. Eventually I would become a writer. As a writer I would go back to that hard Montana country, and on a cold day in May 1986, I would, at last, return to the Bear Paw.

DISCUSSION QUESTIONS

1. Hale says that her grandmother was "never fragile." Give examples from the narrative that support this statement.
2. How does the setting affect the author physically, mentally, and spiritually?

3. In a small group, explore the ways that the monument at Bear Paw could stand as a symbol of Indian-white relations.

WRITING TOPICS

1. There were significant changes in Indian life from 1877 to 1992. Reflect on the information about the grandmother, her son, and the author. In a brief essay, identify and discuss three changes within those years. Suggested topics: language, education, cultural experiences.
2. The author refers to the battleground at Bear Paw as a sacred place. In a brief essay, explore the meaning of the word *sacred,* tell in what sense she uses the word, discuss the connotations of the word, and describe one or more places of national importance that you consider sacred.
3. How would you summarize Hale's attitude toward her grandmother? Support your assessment with words, phrases, and sentences from the selection.

DECEMBER 29, 1890

N. Scott Momaday

Momaday's elegy is a memorial to the three hundred women, men, and children who died at Wounded Knee Creek. In stately cadence, his couplets move in lines of seven syllables. Over a hundred years later, his somber words on the Ghost Dance allow us to symbolically bury our collective hearts at Wounded Knee.

Seeking relief from disease, mortality, and land loss, some Sioux had turned to the Ghost Dance movement. The Ghost Dance frightened others in the region. Traveling to the agency to get supplies, Big Foot's Ghost Dancing band learned that Indian police had killed the respected Lakota leader Sitting Bull, who supported the Ghost Dance. Fearing for their safety, Big Foot's band fled southward some two hundred miles over frigid prairie toward the Pine Ridge Agency. Colonel James W. Forsyth's command found their camp on December 28 and surrounded it with four hundred seventy soldiers and thirty Indian scouts. On a hill commanding the camp, soldiers set up four rapid-fire Hotchkiss canons, each able to fire fifty two-pound explosive shells per minute. In the camp were about one hundred warriors and two hundred fifty women and children.

Early on December 29, Forsyth ordered troops to disarm Big Foot's warriors. Tempers flared. Troops ransacked tipis, treated women disrespectfully, and subjected men to body searches. Indian and military reports disagree about what happened next. A shot was fired. Warriors and soldiers promptly began firing at each other. Half the warriors fell. A volley killed Big Foot. Survivors tried to rescue their families. Troops shot down women and children as far as three miles from the camp. Not all the soldiers wanted to annihilate Big Foot's band. One Lakota survivor reported that a soldier, shouting "Remember Custer," shot an elderly woman and a child. Then one of his fellow troopers shot him.

On New Year's Day 1891, hired civilians dug one large pit on the hill where the Hotchkiss guns had been. They threw the frozen bodies of one hundred forty-six men, women, and children into the hole and covered the mass grave.

Wounded Knee Creek

In the shine of photographs
are the slain, frozen and black

on a simple field of snow.
They image ceremony:

5 women and children dancing,
old men prancing, making fun.

In autumn there were songs, long
since muted in the blizzard.

In summer the wild buckwheat
10 shone like fox fur and quillwork,

and dusk guttered on the creek.
Now in serene attitudes

of dance, the dead in glossy
death are drawn in ancient light.

DISCUSSION QUESTIONS

1. How would you describe the tone of this poem? Cite specific images as evidence for your answer.
2. Momaday carefully measures his rhythm in syllables. Read the poem aloud, emphasizing the syllables, and describe the impact of this technique in terms of the purpose of the poem.

WRITING TOPICS

1. In your journal, experiment with a short, image-filled poem modelled on Momaday's.
2. In a brief essay, compare the tone of Momaday's poem with the tone of Luci Tapahonso's "In 1864."

THE GHOST DANCE WAR

Charles Alexander Eastman

Charles A. Eastman, Santee Sioux physician, writer, and lecturer, was the Native American author most widely read in the United States and abroad in the early twentieth century. In his eleven books and numerous articles for national magazines, Eastman explained Sioux mythology, customs, and history to other Americans. His purpose was to tear down the mutual wall of prejudice separating Indians and non-Indians. During his twenty-five year literary career, Eastman informed his readers of the beauty and morality in Indian beliefs and practices. Widely sought after as a public lecturer, Eastman specialized in speaking to Boy and Girl Scouts. Yet he also lectured on Indian culture at Oxford University and the Royal Colonial Institute in Great Britain in 1928.

Indian Boyhood (1902), Eastman's enormously popular first book, is still in print, appearing in more than twenty editions, some in foreign languages. This autobiography describes his growing up in traditional Santee ways. In *From the Deep Woods to Civilization* (1916), he continues the narrative of his experiences as mediator between two conflicting cultures. He also published many works of nonfiction, including *Old Indian Days* (1907); *The Soul of the Indian: An Interpretation* (1911); and *The Indian Today: The Past and Future of the First American* (1915).

Eastman was born in 1858 on the Santee reservation near Redwood Falls, Minnesota. His father was Jacob Eastman (Many Lightnings), a hunter and warrior. His mother, Mary Eastman, daughter of the famous western artist Captain Seth Eastman, died soon after his birth. Driven by destitution, starvation, and government fraud on their reservation, the Santees rebelled in 1862. During the uprising, Many Lightnings's four-year-old child named Ohiyesa (Winner) became separated from his father. Many Lightnings was imprisoned for participating in the rebellion, thus leaving his young son in the care of his paternal grandmother and uncle. In the aftermath of the war, they fled to Canada, where they reared Ohiyesa to become a hunter and warrior.

When Eastman was fifteen, his father, who was believed to have been executed because of his part in the Minnesota Sioux War, unexpectedly appeared. While in confinement, Many Lightnings had converted to Christianity and adopted the name Jacob Eastman. After his release, he established a homestead at Flandreau in Dakota Territory and then traveled to Canada to retrieve his son.

A dramatically different life began when the young man returned with his father. Ohiyesa was baptized and renamed Charles. He graduated from Dartmouth College in 1887; earned an M.D. degree at Boston University in the spring of 1890; and in the fall of that year became agency physician at Pine Ridge Reservation, South Dakota. There he participated in the traumatic events he describes in this selection. Eastman did not witness the massacre on Wounded Knee Creek, but he saw the carnage and did all that he could to save Sioux lives. Thus, he had unique qualifications for writing about the event.

Eastman's clinical tone as the physician tending to the wounded and dying makes his account of the tragedy even more profound. Taking care of their wounded first, cavalrymen loaded them into wagons to be transported to the Pine Ridge Agency. Only afterwards did soldiers load wounded Indians on wagons for the same journey as a blizzard approached. As Eastman relates, the Episcopal missionary opened his church for an emergency Indian hospital. The wounded were laid on hay scattered over the rough floor. As the torn and bleeding bodies were carried into the church, those who were conscious could see in the candlelight a crudely lettered banner reading "Peace on Earth, Good Will to Men."

1   The ghost dancers had gradually concentrated on the Medicine Root creek and the edge of the "Bad Lands," and they were still further isolated by a new order from the agent, calling in all those who had not adhered to the new religion. Several thousand of these "friendlies" were soon encamped on the White Clay creek, close by the agency. It was near the middle of December, with weather unusually mild for that season. The dancers held that there would be no snow so long as their rites continued.

2   An Indian called Little had been guilty of some minor offense on the reservation and had hitherto evaded arrest. Suddenly he appeared at the agency on an issue day, for the express purpose, as it seemed, of defying the authorities. The assembly room of the Indian police, used also as a council room, opened out of my dispensary, and on this particular morning a council was in progress. I heard some loud talking, but was too busy to pay particular attention, though my assistant had gone in to listen to the speeches. Suddenly the place was in an uproar, and George burst into

the inner office, crying excitedly "Look out for yourself, friend! They are going to fight!"

3   I went around to see what was going on. A crowd had gathered just outside the council room, and the police were surrounded by wild Indians with guns and drawn knives in their hands. "Hurry up with them!" one shouted, while another held his stone war-club over a policeman's head. The attempt to arrest Little had met with a stubborn resistance.

4   At this critical moment, a fine-looking Indian in citizen's clothes faced the excited throng, and spoke in a clear, steady, almost sarcastic voice.

5   "Stop! Think! What are you going to do? Kill these men of our own race? Then what? Kill all these helpless white men, women and children? And what then? What will these brave words, brave deeds lead to in the end? How long can you hold out? Your country is surrounded with a network of railroads; thousands of white soldiers will be here within three days. What ammunition have you? What provisions? What will become of your families? Think, think, my brothers! This is a child's madness."

6   It was the "friendly" chief, American Horse, and it seems to me as I recall the incident that this man's voice had almost magic power. It is likely that he saved us all from massacre, for the murder of the police, who represented the authority of the Government, would surely have been followed by a general massacre. It is a fact that those Indians who upheld the agent were in quite as much danger from their wilder brethren as were the whites, indeed it was said that the feeling against them was even stronger. Jack Red Cloud, son of the chief, thrust the muzzle of a cocked revolver almost into the face of American Horse. "It is you and your kind," he shouted, "who have brought us to this pass!" That brave man never flinched. Ignoring his rash accuser, he quietly re-entered the office; the door closed behind him; the mob dispersed, and for the moment the danger seemed over.

7   That evening I was surprised by a late call from American Horse, the hero of the day. His wife entered close behind him. Scarcely were they seated when my door again opened softly, and Captain Sword came in, followed by Lieutenant Thunder Bear and most of the Indian police. My little room was crowded. I handed them some tobacco, which I had always at hand for my guests, although I did not smoke myself. After a silence, the chief got up and shook hands with me ceremoniously. In a short speech, he asked my advice in the difficult situation that confronted them between the ghost dancers, men of their own blood, and the Government to which they had pledged their loyalty.

8   Thanks to Indian etiquette, I could allow myself two or three minutes to weigh my words before replying. I finally said, in substance: "There is only one thing for us to do and be just to both sides. We must use every means for a peaceful settlement of this difficulty. Let us be patient; let us continue to reason with the wilder element, even though some hotheads may threaten our lives. If the worst happens, however, it is our solemn duty to serve the United States Government. Let no man ever say that we were disloyal! Following such a policy, dead or alive, we shall have no apology to make."

9   After the others had withdrawn, Sword informed me confidentially that certain young men had threatened to kill American Horse while asleep in his tent, and that his friends had prevailed upon him and his wife to ask my hospitality for a few days. I showed Mrs. American Horse to a small room that I had vacant, and soon afterward came three strokes of the office bell—the signal for me to report at the agent's office.

10   I found there the agent, his chief clerk, and a visiting inspector, all of whom obviously regarded the situation as serious. "You see, doctor," said the agent, "the occurrence of today was planned with remarkable accuracy, so that even our alert police were taken entirely by surprise and readily overpowered. What will be the sequel we can not tell, but we must be prepared for anything. I shall be glad to have your views," he added.

11   I told him that I still did not believe there was any widespread plot, or deliberate intention to make war upon the whites. In my own mind, I felt sure that the arrival of troops would be construed by the ghost dancers as a threat or a challenge, and would put them at once on the defensive. I was not in favor of that step; neither was Mr. Cook, who was also called into conference; but the officials evidently feared a general uprising, and argued that it was their duty to safeguard the lives of the employees and others by calling for the soldiers without more delay. Sword, Thunder Bear, and American Horse were sent for and their opinions appeared to be fully in accord with those of the agent and inspector, so the matter was given out as settled. As a matter of fact, the agent had telegraphed to Fort Robinson for troops before he made a pretense of consulting us Indians, and they were already on their way to Pine Ridge.

12   I scarcely knew at the time, but gradually learned afterward, that the Sioux had many grievances and causes for profound discontent, which lay back of and were more or less closely related to the ghost dance craze and the prevailing restlessness and excitement. Rations had been cut from time to time; the people were insufficiently fed, and their protests and appeals were disregarded. Never was more ruthless fraud and graft practiced upon a defenseless people than upon these poor natives by the politicians! Never were there more worthless "scraps of paper" anywhere in the world than many of the Indian treaties and Government documents! Sickness was prevalent and the death rate alarming, especially among the children. Trouble from all these causes had for some time been developing, but might have been checked by humane and conciliatory measures. The "Messiah craze" in itself was scarcely a source of danger, and one might almost as well call upon the army to suppress Billy Sunday[1] and his hysterical followers. Other tribes than the Sioux who adopted the new religion were let alone, and the craze died a natural death in the course of a few months.

---

[1] *Billy Sunday:* (1862–1925), an American evangelist known for his dramatic revivalist meetings throughout the United States.

13   Among the leaders of the malcontents at this time were Jack Red Cloud, No Water, He Dog, Four Bears, Yellow Bear, and Kicking Bear. Friendly leaders included American Horse, Young Man Afraid of his Horses, Bad Wound, Three Stars. There was still another set whose attitude was not clearly defined, and among these men was Red Cloud, the greatest of them all. He who had led his people so brilliantly and with such remarkable results, both in battle and diplomacy, was now an old man of over seventy years, living in a frame house which had been built for him within a half mile of the agency. He would come to council, but said little or nothing. No one knew exactly where he stood, but it seemed that he was broken in spirit as in body and convinced of the hopelessness of his people's cause.

14   It was Red Cloud who asked the historic question, at a great council held in the Black Hills region with a Government commission, and after good Bishop Whipple had finished the invocation, "Which God is our brother praying to now? Is it the same God whom they have twice deceived, when they made treaties with us which they afterward broke?"

15   Early in the morning after the attempted arrest of Little, George rushed into my quarters and awakened me. "Come quick!" he shouted, "the soldiers are here!" I looked along the White Clay creek toward the little railroad town of Rushville, Nebraska, twenty-five miles away, and just as the sun rose above the knife-edged ridges black with stunted pine, I perceived a moving cloud of dust that marked the trail of the Ninth Cavalry. There was instant commotion among the camps of friendly Indians. Many women and children were coming in to the agency for refuge, evidently fearing that the dreaded soldiers might attack their villages by mistake. Some who had not heard of their impending arrival hurried to the offices to ask what it meant. I assured those who appealed to me that the troops were here only to preserve order, but their suspicions were not easily allayed.

16   As the cavalry came nearer, we saw that they were colored troopers, wearing buffalo overcoats and muskrat caps; the Indians with their quick wit called them "buffalo soldiers." They halted, and established their temporary camp in the open space before the agency enclosure. The news had already gone out through the length and breadth of the reservation, and the wildest rumors were in circulation. Indian scouts might be seen upon every hill top, closely watching the military encampment.

17   At this juncture came the startling news from Fort Yates, some two hundred and fifty miles to the north of us, that Sitting Bull had been killed by Indian police while resisting arrest, and a number of his men with him, as well as several of the police. We next heard that the remnant of his band had fled in our direction, and soon afterward, that they had been joined by Big Foot's band from the western part of Cheyenne River agency, which lay directly in their road. United States troops continued to gather at strategic points, and of course the press seized upon the opportunity to enlarge upon the strained situation and predict an "Indian uprising." The reporters were among us, and managed to secure much "news" that no one else ever heard

of. Border towns were fortified and cowboys and militia gathered in readiness to protect them against the "red devils." Certain classes of the frontier population industriously fomented the excitement for what there was in it for them, since much money is apt to be spent at such times. As for the poor Indians, they were quite as badly scared as the whites and perhaps with more reason.

18   General Brook undertook negotiations with the ghost dancers, and finally induced them to come within reach. They camped on a flat about a mile north of us and in full view, while the more tractable bands were still gathered on the south and west. The large boarding school had locked its doors and succeeded in holding its hundreds of Indian children, partly for their own sakes, and partly as hostages for the good behavior of their fathers. At the agency were now gathered all the government employees and their families, except such as had taken flight, together with traders, missionaries, and ranchmen, army officers, and newspaper men. It was a conglomerate population.

19   During this time of grave anxiety and nervous tension, the cooler heads among us went about our business, and still refused to believe in the tragic possibility of an Indian war. It may be imagined that I was more than busy, though I had not such long distances to cover, for since many Indians accustomed to comfortable log houses were compelled to pass the winter in tents, there was even more sickness than usual. I had access and welcome to the camps of all the various groups and factions, a privilege shared by my good friend Father Jutz, the Catholic missionary, who was completely trusted by his people.

20   The Christmas season was fast approaching, and this is perhaps the brightest spot in the mission year. The children of the Sunday Schools, and indeed all the people, look eagerly forward to the joyous feast; barrels and boxes are received and opened, candy bags made and filled, carols practiced, and churches decorated with ropes of spicy evergreen.

21   Anxious to relive the tension in every way within his power, Mr. Cook and his helpers went on with their preparations upon even a larger scale than usual. Since all of the branch stations had been closed and the people called in, it was planned to keep the Christmas tree standing in the chapel for a week, and to distribute gifts to a separate congregation each evening. I found myself pressed into the service, and passed some happy hours in the rectory. For me, at that critical time, there was inward struggle as well as the threat of outward conflict, and I could not but recall what my "white mother" had said jokingly one day, referring to my pleasant friendships with many charming Boston girls, "I know one Sioux who has not been conquered, and I shall not rest till I hear of his capture!"

22   I had planned to enter upon my life work unhampered by any other ties, and declared that all my love should be vested in my people and my profession. At last, however, I had met a woman whose sincerity was convincing and whose ideals seemed very like my own. Her childhood had been spent

almost as much out of doors as mine, on a lonely estate high up in the Berkshire hills; her ancestry Puritan on one side, proud Tories on the other. She had been moved by the appeals of that wonderful man, General Armstrong, and had gone to Hampton as a young girl to teach the Indians there. After three years, she undertook pioneer work in the West as teacher of a new camp school among the wilder Sioux, and after much travel and study of their peculiar problems had been offered the appointment she now held.[2] She spoke the Sioux language fluently and went among the people with the utmost freedom and confidence. Her methods of work were very simple and direct. I do not know what unseen hand had guided me to her side, but on Christmas day of 1890, Elaine Goodale and I announced our engagement.

23   Three days later, we learned that Big Foot's band of ghost dancers from the Cheyenne river reservation north of us was approaching the agency, and that Major Whiteside was in command of troops with orders to intercept them.

24   Late that afternoon, the Seventh Cavalry[3] under Colonel Forsythe was called to the saddle and rode off toward Wounded Knee creek, eighteen miles away. Father Craft, a Catholic priest with some Indian blood, who knew Sitting Bull and his people, followed an hour or so later, and I was much inclined to go too, but my fiancée pointed out that my duty lay rather at home with our Indians, and I stayed.

25   The morning of December 29 was sunny and pleasant. We were all straining our ears toward Wounded Knee, and about the middle of the forenoon we distinctly heard the reports of the Hotchkiss guns.[4] Two hours later, a rider was seen approaching at full speed, and in a few minutes he had dismounted from his exhausted horse and handed his message to General Brooke's orderly. The Indians were watching their own messenger, who ran on foot along the northern ridges and carried the news to the so-called "hostile" camp. It was said that he delivered his message at almost the same time as the mounted officer.

26   The resulting confusion and excitement was unmistakable. The white teepees disappeared as if by magic and soon the caravans were in motion, going toward the natural fortress of the "Bad Lands." In the "friendly" camp there was almost as much turmoil, and crowds of frightened women and children poured into the agency. Big Foot's band had been wiped out by the troops, and reprisals were naturally looked for. The enclosure was not

---

[2] *appointment she now held:* Elaine Goodale was superintendent to Indian Education for the reservations in the Dakota Territory.
[3] *Seventh Cavalry:* The Seventh Cavalry under the command of General George A. Custer had been defeated by Sioux and Cheyenne warriors at the Battle of the Little Big Horn in 1876. Three hundred cavalry soldiers were killed, as was Custer. Some commentators think that the Wounded Knee massacre may have been, in part, revenge for Custer's defeat.
[4] *Hotchkiss gun:* a kind of cannon able to fire fifty two-pound shells a minute.

barricaded in any way and we had but a small detachment of troops for our protection. Sentinels were placed, and machine guns trained on the various approaches.

27   A few hot-headed young braves fired on the sentinels and wounded two of them. The Indian police began to answer by shooting at several braves who were apparently about to set fire to some of the outlying buildings. Every married employee was seeking a place of safety for his family, the interpreter among them. Just then General Brooke ran out into the open, shouting at the top of his voice to the police: "Stop, stop! Doctor, tell them they must not fire until ordered!" I did so, as the bullets whistled by us, and the General's coolness perhaps saved all our lives, for we were in no position to repel a large attacking force. Since we did not reply, the scattered shots soon ceased, but the situation remained critical for several days and nights.

28   My office was full of refugees. I called one of my good friends aside and asked him to saddle my two horses and stay by them. "When general fighting begins, take them to Miss Goodale and see her to the railroad if you can," I told him. Then I went over to the rectory. Mrs. Cook refused to go without her husband, and Miss Goodale would not leave while there was a chance of being of service. The house was crowded with terrified people, most of them Christian Indians, whom our friends were doing their best to pacify.

29   At dusk, the Seventh Cavalry returned with their twenty-five dead and I believe thirty-four wounded, most of them by their own comrades, who had encircled the Indians, while few of the latter had guns. A majority of the thirty or more Indian wounded were women and children, including babies in arms. As there were not tents enough for all, Mr. Cook offered us the mission chapel, in which the Christmas tree still stood, for a temporary hospital. We tore out the pews and covered the floor with hay and quilts. There we laid the poor creatures side by side in rows, and the night was devoted to caring for them as best we could. Many were frightfully torn by pieces of shells, and the suffering was terrible. General Brooke placed me in charge and I had to do nearly all the work, for although the army surgeons were more than ready to help as soon as their own men had been cared for, the tortured Indians would scarcely allow a man in uniform to touch them. Mrs. Cook, Miss Goodale, and several of Mr. Cook's Indian helpers acted as volunteer nurses. In spite of all our efforts, we lost the greater part of them, but a few recovered, including several children who had lost all their relatives and who were adopted into kind Christian families.

30   On the day following the Wounded Knee massacre there was a blizzard, in the midst of which I was ordered out with several Indian police, to look for a policeman who was reported to have been wounded and left some two miles from the agency. We did not find him. This was the only time during the whole affair that I carried a weapon; a friend lent me a revolver which I put in my overcoat pocket, and it was lost on the ride. On the third day it cleared, and the ground was covered with an inch or two of fresh snow. We

had feared that some of the Indian wounded might have been left on the field, and a number of us volunteered to go and see. I was placed in charge of the expedition of about a hundred civilians, ten or fifteen of whom were white men. We were supplied with wagons in which to convey any whom we might find still alive. Of course a photographer and several reporters were of the party.

31   Fully three miles from the scene of the massacre we found the body of a woman completely covered with a blanket of snow, and from this point on we found them scattered along as they had been relentlessly hunted down and slaughtered while fleeing for their lives. Some of our people discovered relatives or friends among the dead, and there was much wailing and mourning. When we reached the spot where the Indian camp had stood, among the fragments of burned tents and other belongings we saw the frozen bodies lying close together or piled one upon another. I counted eighty bodies of men who had been in the council and who were almost as helpless as the women and babes when the deadly fire began, for nearly all their guns had been taken from them. A reckless and desperate young Indian fired the first shot when the search for weapons was well under way, and immediately the troops opened fire from all sides, killing not only unarmed men, women, and children, but their own comrades who stood opposite them, for the camp was entirely surrounded.

32   It took all of my nerve to keep my composure in the face of this spectacle, and of the excitement and grief of my Indian companions, nearly every one of whom was crying aloud or singing his death song. The white men became very nervous, but I set them to examining and uncovering every body to see if one were living. Although they had been lying untended in the snow and cold for two days and nights, a number had survived. Among them I found a baby of about a year old warmly wrapped and entirely unhurt. I brought her in, and she was afterward adopted and educated by an army officer. One man who was severely wounded begged me to fill his pipe. When we brought him into the chapel he was welcomed by his wife and daughters with cries of joy, but he died a day or two later.

33   Under a wagon I discovered an old woman, totally blind and entirely helpless. A few had managed to crawl away to some place of shelter, and we found in a log store near by several who were badly hurt and others who had died after reaching there. After we had dispatched several wagon loads to the agency, we observed groups of warriors watching us from adjacent buttes; probably friends of the victims who had come there for the same purpose as ourselves. A majority of our party, fearing an attack, insisted that some one ride back to the agency for an escort of soldiers, and as mine was the best horse, it fell to me to go. I covered the eighteen miles in quick time and was not interfered with in any way, although if the Indians had meant mischief they could easily have picked me off from any of the ravines and gulches.

34   All this was a severe ordeal for one who had so lately put all his faith in the Christian love and lofty ideals of the white man. Yet I passed no hasty

judgment, and was thankful that I might be of some service and relieve even a small part of the suffering. An appeal published in a Boston paper brought us liberal supplies of much needed clothing, and linen for dressings. We worked on. Bishop Hare of South Dakota visited us, and was overcome by faintness when he entered his mission chapel, thus transformed into a rude hospital.

35   After some days of extreme tension, and weeks of anxiety, the "hostiles," so called, were at last induced to come in and submit to a general disarmament. Father Jutz, the Catholic missionary, had gone bravely among them and used all his influence toward a peaceful settlement. The troops were all recalled and took part in a grand review before General Miles, no doubt intended to impress the Indians with their superior force.

DISCUSSION QUESTIONS

1. Eastman divides the Sioux into two categories: "friendly leaders" and "hostile malcontents." What words does he use to describe each group? Do you think his tone or attitude favors one group? Use evidence to support your answer.
2. How can you account for the killing of unarmed people, even to the extent of hunting them down as much as three miles from the scene of the massacre?
3. The wounded and dead of the Seventh Cavalry were hit by so-called friendly fire. What does this imply about the command of the Seventh Cavalry?
4. Eastman describes in detail events leading up to the massacre. What do these events tell about life at the Pine Ridge Agency?

WRITING TOPICS

1. Select one of the following ideas for the topic sentence of a brief essay.

I assured those who appealed to me that the troops were here only to preserve order, but their suspicions were not easily allayed. (paragraph 15)

For me, at that critical time, there was inward struggle as well as the great of outward conflict. (paragraph 21)

I counted eighty bodies of men who had been in the council and who were almost as helpless as the women and babes when the deadly fire began, for nearly all their guns had been taken from them. (paragraph 31)

All this was a severe ordeal for one who had so lately put all his faith in the Christian love and lofty ideals of the white man. (paragraph 34)

2. In a few paragraphs, characterize Eastman based on what you can tell about him from this account.
3. Black Elk, a Lakota Sioux (see page 520), was a witness to the Wounded Knee massacre, coming upon the scene after the shooting had started. He told about his experiences in *Black Elk Speaks.* Find Black Elk's book and, using Eastman's and Black Elk's accounts, write a news story that could have appeared in a newspaper of the day.
4. Research and write a paper on the Wounded Knee takeover by American Indian Movement (AIM) activists in 1973.

THREE THOUSAND DOLLAR DEATH SONG

Wendy Rose

Wendy Rose is a forceful voice for Indian justice, reverence for the earth, and fair treatment of women. Her writing arises from her Hopi/Miwok/Euro-American roots and her life in the San Francisco Bay area. As a poetic activist, Rose forges poems to attack those who sell Indian relics for profit and who desecrate Indian graves. Since 1984, she has been the coordinator of and teacher in American Indian Studies at Fresno City College.

Rose has continued her contribution to American literature through nine volumes of poetry and selections appearing in more than sixty anthologies. Her major works include *Hopi Roadrunner Dancing* (1973); *Long Division: A Tribal History* (1981); *Academic Squaw: Reports to the World from the Ivory Tower* (1977); *Builder Kachina: A HomeGoing Cycle* (1979); *Lost Copper* (1980); *The Halfbreed Chronicles & Other Poems* (1985); *Going to War with All My Relations* (1993); *Now Poof She Is Gone* (1994); and *Bone Dance: New and Selected Poems, 1965–1992* (1994).

Born to a Hopi father and Miwok/Euro-American mother in 1948 in Oakland, California, Rose grew up away from any tribal homeland. Consequently, as a painter and a writer, she has created the identity she claims through her visual and verbal art. Her paintings have been exhibited and have appeared as book illustrations. Her search for identity coincided with her studies in anthropology in the 1970s at the University of California, Berkeley. Receiving an M.A. degree in cultural anthropology in 1978, she later completed the course work for a Ph.D. During that prolific period, she published five volumes of poetry. *Academic Squaw: Reports to the World from the Ivory Tower* (1977) expresses her ironic humor as "a spy" in the academic world. Alienated from most academic anthropologists, she recalls, "The poems were written as a survival kit, really. And in fact one of the most pleasant things I have ever done was the day that the book came out . . . I stuck copies of it in all my professor's mailboxes."

Rose is a renegade scholar, but her insights as an anthropologist have nevertheless inspired and enriched her poetry. As a doctoral student, she recognized the irony of trying to conserve Native American artifacts from within a system that rewarded unethical traders, collectors, and curators. Museums even buy and sell bones, a practice that Native Americans oppose, for Indians are not merely artifacts or specimens, not merely dead bones. For Rose and other Native Americans, bones become metaphors for life, as she explained in an interview with Joseph Bruchac: "Sometimes I feel that I'm a ghost. Similarly, sometimes I feel that I'm alive but there are ghosts all around me . . . as far as the symbols go, of things like the bones . . . I think maybe it's an argument against death. Bones are alive. They're not dead remnants but rather they're alive." Images of life, death, and bones abound in her poems, where Native Americans are not anthropological specimens of the past but are people whose lives and struggles must be respected. She gives them voice, allowing them to speak through her poems.

Rose does more than write words to defend Indian burial grounds. She wrote the poem "Protecting Indian Burial Grounds" in front of a bulldozer, on top of an Indian cemetery, "where we were sitting to prevent the bulldozer from just going through and ripping up Indian graves." Defying the bulldozer as well as the San Jose SWAT team, the protesters saved that burial ground. Rose transformed the literal facts into figurative metaphors.

The theme of "Three Thousand Dollar Death Song" is the desire, indeed obsession, of some people to own "something Indian" from their very bones to their entire history. Defying that obsession, Rose proclaims in one of her poems that there will be no archaeology for her bones: "When I die I ask only to be thrown into the sun."

Nineteen American Indian skeletons from Nevada . . . valued at $3,000.
    —invoice received at a museum as normal business, 1975

Is it in cold hard cash? the kind
that dusts the insides of mens' pockets
laying silver-polished surface along the cloth.
Or in bills? papering the wallets of they
5 who thread the night with dark words. Or
checks? paper promises weighing the same
as words spoken once on the other side
of the mown grass and dammed rivers
of history. However it goes, it goes.
10 Through my body it goes

assessing each nerve, running its edges
along my arteries, planning ahead
for whose hands will rip me
into pieces of dusty red paper,
15 whose hands will smooth or smatter me
into traces of rubble. Invoiced now
it's official how our bones are valued
that stretch out pointing to sunrise
or are flexed into one last fetal bend,
20 that are removed and tossed about,
catalogued, numbered with black ink
on newly-white foreheads.
As we were formed to the white soldier's voice,
so we explode under white students' hands.
25 Death is a long trail of days
in our fleshless prison.
From this distant point
we watch our bones auctioned
with our careful quillwork,
30 beaded medicine bundles, even the bridles
of our shot-down horses. You who have priced us,
you who have removed us—at what cost?
What price the pits
where our bones share
35 a single bit of memory,
how one century has turned
our dead into specimens,
our history into dust,
our survivors into clowns.
40 Our memory might be catching, you know.
Picture the mortars, the arrowheads, the labrets[1]
shaking off their labels like bears suddenly awake
to find the seasons ended while they slept.
Watch them touch each other, measure reality,
45 march out the museum door!
Watch as they lift their faces
and smell about for us. Watch our bones rise
to meet them and mount the horses once again!
The cost then will be paid
50 for our sweetgrass-smelling having-been
in clam-shell beads and steatite, dentalia[2]

---

[1] *labret:* ornament worn in a pierced hole in the lip.
[2] *steatite, dentalia:* Steatite is soapstone, often used for carved ornaments; dentalia are shells of marine mollusks called tooth shells.

and woodpecker scalp, turquoise and copper,
blood and oil, coal and uranium,
children, a universe
55 of stolen things.

DISCUSSION QUESTIONS

1. Why would a monetary value be put on an Indian skeleton?
2. How does the speaker seem to ally herself with the dead bones?
3. Reread line 40. Whose memory is transferable? What does the speaker picture as the result of this millenarian concept?
4. How will line 49 be true if the bones and artifacts disappear out the museum door?

WRITING TOPICS

1. The term *tone* refers to an author's attitude toward his or her subject. In a brief essay, analyze how the author achieves her tone in this poem.
2. In an essay, explain and analyze these metaphors from the poem: "paper promises," "dammed rivers of history," "a universe of stolen things."

SUMMARY WRITING TOPICS

1. If you could interview one of the writers in this chapter, consider in your journal which writer you would choose and why. What is the most important question or statement you would like to ask or make to that person?
2. Was the U.S. government's systematic removal of the Indians westward the same as the so-called ethnic cleansing in Bosnia and the extermination of the Jews in Nazi Germany? Discuss in an essay.
3. Has prejudice and racism toward Indians decreased in the twentieth century? Discuss this question in a persuasive essay.
4. The Sauk chief Black Hawk said, "My reason tells me that land cannot be sold—nothing can be sold but such things as can be carried away." Do you agree? What does his comment tell you about the differences in Native American and Euro-Americans views of land? Consider these questions in a journal entry.
5. Welch, Glancy, and Rose use irony in their poems. In a brief essay, discuss examples and determine which author uses irony most effectively.
6. After Chief Joseph's surrender, Colonel Miles ordered that food, clothing, and tents be given to the starving Nez Perce. In a brief essay, contrast his actions with those of Chivington, Custer, and Forsyth.
7. Research one of the following topics and write a report based on your findings:

   Treaties of Fort Stanwix (1768 and 1784)
   Treaty of Greenville (1795)
   Treaty of Prairie Du Chien (1825)
   Treaty of Dancing Rabbit Creek (1830)
   Treaty of New Echota (1835)
   Treaties of Fort Laramie (1851 and 1868)

8. In 1990 Congress approved the Native American Graves Protection and Repatriation Act. Find out what this act provides for, research the controversy surrounding it, and write a report, including your opinion.
9. Both Sarah Winnemucca and Charles Eastman went to a new school as teenagers. Assume the point of view of Eastman or Winnemucca and write a journal entry about the first and last day in the school.
10. Write an editorial for the Denver paper *Rocky Mountain News* about the Navajo Long Walk. Date your editorial today or in 1864. Compare editorial differences in style and content with your classmates.
11. Assume you and your family are being forcibly removed from your home. You have two hours to collect what you can carry with you. In a brief personal essay, describe three items you select and explain why you chose them.

CHAPTER FOUR

THE REMEMBERED EARTH

N. Scott Momaday reminds us to remember the earth in *The Way to Rainy Mountain:* "Once in his life a man ought to concentrate his mind upon the remembered earth, I believe. He ought to give himself up to a particular landscape in his experience, to look at it from as many angles as he can, to wonder about it, to dwell upon it. He ought to imagine that he touches it with his hands at every season and listens to the sounds that are made upon it. He ought to imagine the creatures that are there and all the faintest motions in the wind. He ought to recollect the glare of noon and all the colors of the dawn and dusk."

Like Momaday, the Native American authors in this chapter write primarily about very specific geographic places, particular plants, single bird species, or one animal. Look at some of the titles: "Wild Strawberry," "Giant Bear," "The Time We Climbed Snake Mountain," "Slim Man Canyon," "Morning Glories and Eastern Phoebes." Native Americans still hold approximately three percent of the American land, which is cherished in each detail and informed with old understandings, still known and used.

A friend's gift of imported strawberries prompts Mohawk Maurice Kenny, ill in New York City, to write his homesick thoughts about a rural tract of wild berries remembered since childhood. Always aware of the fragility of life, Kenny offers a complementary angle to Momaday's thoughts: "We often forget that the earth, Mother Earth, is the flesh of our flesh, the flesh of all creatures great and small, and when her flesh is wounded our flesh is wounded. When Mother Earth dies, we too die."

Leslie Silko also writes about humans' responsibility toward the earth and its natural resources. As a consequence of growing up at Laguna Pueblo, Silko trusts the land but not human beings: "Up in the hills with the birds and animals and my horse, I felt absolutely safe." On the other hand, she saw humans as the most dangerous animals of all. Not firing her .30–.30 at a giant bear marked a milestone in Silko's adolescence. Is deciding when *not* to shoot a Native American lesson or a universal hunting lesson?

Silko's "Slim Man Canyon" lyrically evokes flowing water sustaining riparian trees seven centuries earlier in what is now a severely eroded landscape. She tells of climbing Snake Mountain to warn, "This mountain is his." Silko builds metaphor after metaphor—cold river, mountain lion, spider's web, hummingbirds, lean gray deer, and rainbow—into "Survival." Landscape sits in the center of Pueblo belief and identity for another Laguna author, Paula Gunn Allen. She asserts that Native Americans in the Southwest *are the land* in their own minds.

Mohawk Peter Blue Cloud turns bitter at the sight and smell of a slain hawk. After harvesting its feathers and burying its body with a prayer, he is transformed: "your feathers so close send me no messages of hate." On a lighter note, Geary Hobson celebrates the once indispensable bison on which thirty or more Native American ways of life once depended. Joseph Bruchac tells a modern parable of how Mink the trickster stole the sun and gave humans light. But trickster tricked himself when he stole a metal clock that locked up life.

Master poet Louise Erdrich spins the story of a mythic shape-shifter in "The Strange People." The death of an antelope explodes as a metaphor for the life of Native America. Is this poem really about an animal the poet imbues with mysterious qualities? Erdrich believes that in the tribal view where one place has been inhabited for generations, "the traditional storyteller fixes listeners in an unchanging landscape combined of myth and reality. People and place are inseparable." Erdrich amuses us with pungent skunk images in "Skunk Dreams" and awes us with silken images in "Morning Glories and Eastern Phoebes." James Welch casts a surrealistic tone in his vision of spiders weaving threads to bandage up the day in "Snow Country Weavers." With his concrete poem "Rounds," Lorenzo Baca encircles the bonds of humans and the seasons of planet Earth.

Authors classified as "Native American" writers do not necessarily write about only "Native American" topics. A fourteen-year-old with any ethnic heritage can smile at Louise Erdrich's uninvited visitor in "Skunk Dreams." Women of more than one ethnic heritage can set out to travel waterways, relating legends, sensing strange powers suffusing islands, and "dreaming" medicinal merits of wild plants. Probably only a Native American would, however, talk with the bear from whose hide her coat had been fashioned, like Linda Hogan's character Agnes Iron. Hogan speaks for all writers who remember the earth in words: "the earth writes through me."

FROM "WAITING AT THE EDGE"

Maurice Kenny

Maurice Kenny identifies himself as "a hunter of words." After earning a B.A. in English literature from Butler University in 1956, he attended other colleges. He has taught at several institutions, including the Universities of Oklahoma and British Columbia. Writing poetry and prose for over three decades, this prolific writer has completed more than fifteen volumes. He received Best Anthology Award, *Bloomsbury Review* in 1983 for *Wounds Beneath the Flesh.* In 1976, Kenny founded the Strawberry Press dedicated to publishing works by Native American authors.

Kenny's nature images arise from his youth when he wandered freely in the beauty of Adirondack woodlands. There he lived with his parents Andrew Anthony, Mohawk, and Doris Palmer Kenny, Seneca. His maternal grandmother was related to prominent Senecas Ely and Arthur Parker.

"Wild Strawberry" appears in *Dancing Back Strong the Nation* (1979). In her introduction to this volume, Paula Gunn Allen describes the impact of the poems, "We understand that ache for what is lost, and that strength that comes when it is restored." She continues that alongside Kenny, "we walk each step back home, and we discover how it is that the past in its beauty of wilderness and warmth is part of this present." Kenny's family stories, poetry, and Iroquois traditions are intertwined like wild strawberry vines.

Picking wild strawberries became a ceremony for the Mohawk. A healing ceremony is needed by those in the dark poem "December." This poem appeared in *The Mama Poems,* which won an American Book Award in 1984. Again, grim images of winter and illness contrast with spring green and renewal. In a sense, a ceremonial drum begins the poem. A sick neighbor, dark men in winter kitchens, and uncared for kids all need prayers and the spiritual power of strawberries. With lyrical clarity, Kenny reminds us that we must all remember that our life and the life of the earth are linked.

"WILD STRAWBERRY FOR HELENE"

And I rode the Greyhound down to Brooklyn
where I sit now eating woody strawberries
grown on the backs of Mexican farmers
imported from the fields of their hands,
5   juices without color or sweetness.

     my wild blood berries of spring meadows
     sucked by June bees and protected by hawks
     have stained my face and honeyed
     my tongue . . . healed the sorrow in my flesh

10   vines crawl across the grassy floor
of the north, scatter to the world
seeking the light of the sun and innocent
tap of the rain to feed the roots
and bud small white flowers that in June
15   will burst fruit and announce spring
when wolf will drop winter fur
and wrens will break the egg

     my blood, blood berries brought laughter
     and the ache in the stooped back that vied
20   with dandelions for the plucking,
and the wines nourished our youth and heralded
iris, corn and summer melon

     we fought bluebirds for the seeds
     armed against garter snakes, field mice;
25   won the battle with the burning sun
which blinded our eyes and froze our hands
to the vines and the earth where knees knelt
and we laughed in the morning dew like worms
and grubs; we scented age and wisdom

30   my mother wrapped the wounds of the world
with a sassafras poultice and we ate
wild berries with their juices running
down the roots of our mouths and our joy

I sit here in Brooklyn eating Mexican
35   berries which I did not pick, nor do
I know the hands which did, nor their stories . . .
January snow falls, listen . . .

1   I began this poem in the winter of 1978. January to be exact, living in Brooklyn Heights in New York City; I was ill. A close friend and nearby neighbor had the goodness of heart and thought to bring to my sick bed a basket of cultivated strawberries. Helene knew my fondness for the fruit and just how important the strawberry is to me and my poetry. The wild strawberry is not only the first natural fruit of the eastern spring, but it is the symbol of life to Iroquois people. The strawberry holds strong significance for all the people of the Six Nations and for me as a person, as a Mohawk writer, and as both editor and publisher. In 1976 I established Strawberry Press to be an exclusively Native American press to publish the poetry and art of Native People. . . .

2   As I rallied from the illness, and while biting into those cultivated berries, sucking juices, I began to realize, to remember the many mornings of my childhood at home in northern New York state when I would follow my mother and two older sisters into the flowering fields where the wild strawberry vines crawled under the sun.

> STRAWBERRYING
> morning
> broods
>   in the wide river
> Mama bends
> 5   light
> bleeds
> always
> in her day of
> picking
> 10 (our fields are stained)
> the moon, bats
>   tell us
>   to go
> in the scent of
> 15 berries
> fox
>   awaken
>   in stars

3   With their children, other women, often my mother's friends, would be there picking and filling their baskets. It was a good time. Burning hot as it was in those open meadows, breezes did rush the grasses and flowers from off either Lake Ontario or the St. Lawrence River. It was a time of laughter, jokes and teasing, cries and tears from children bored with the labor and eager for a river swim, and certainly not only a time of filling the belly with the deliciously honeysweet fruit, dripping in ripeness, but a time when the women exchanged what I thought were stories, gossip. I am convinced that was the reason they came to the fields. Even then, in 1934–35, those many

years back, cultivated berries could be bought at roadside stands or in the village markets.

4   Also while eating the berries in my sick bed I recalled a strong sentiment of the Lakota Holy Man, Black Elk:

> When the ceremony was over, everybody felt a great deal bet-
> ter, for it had been a day of fun. They were better able now to see
> the greenness of the world, the wideness of the sacred day, the
> colors of the earth, and to set these in their minds. (*Black Elk
> Speaks*, University of Nebraska Press, 1979)

5   There is no doubt in my mind that picking wild strawberries was a cere-mony, and to this day it has offered me a better look at the grasses of the world, the width of a sacred day, and certainly the "colors of the earth." Picking those berries enriched not only our everyday lives and bellies but our imaginations and spirits as well. We all, even the children, truly felt better later. I wanted to write of this good feeling, this betterment and enrichment.

6   This year, winter 1983, strawberries were shipped air freight to the United States from Chile, in South America—a long way from the home meadows of the north. Obviously, air-freighted fruit must be harvested rather green and needs to complete the cycle en route. And, so, too, the berries in the basket that Helene had brought to me in January of 1978. The straw basket was stamped with purple ink: "Hecho En Mexico"—meaning, made in Mexico. The peaches, watermelons, cantaloupe, and berries are raised in the Mexican state of Sonora. I have spent large chunks of time in Mexico. I also knew that these fruits, and especially the strawberries, were grown with the aid of chemical fertilizers, chemicals that could and surely would cause great pain to the people working those fields with bare hands. So as I am in my bed popping berries into my dry mouth, I recognize the horrendous fact that people were possibly dying, people I did not personally know, nor ever would; people were dying so that I could eat those terrible berries in a winter city, an unnatural time to be eating strawberries. And they were terrible. Large though they were, at least an inch in circumference, they were tasteless. Below the bright red skin the flesh was colorless, pale white. I did thank my friend profusely, but once she had left, I not only threw the wretched fruit out but vowed I'd never eat Mexican strawberries again unless I personally knew the hands that raised and picked them for the table, and especially those harvested in Sonora.

7   Directly, I was not the cause of this pain to the workers in Sonora. I'm sufficiently realistic to comprehend this. But my purchasing these fruits decidedly encouraged the use of not only the chemical fertilizers but the deaths of men and women, probably children as well. I was acutely aware that they, the harvesters, could not enjoy the labors as we had when I was a child of those northern meadows, meadows etched by blackeyed susan, pur-ple clover, dandelion; meadows sung to by wrens, larks, bluejays; meadows

that in the continuum not only supported our desires for fresh fruit but supported our strengths as a people and as a Nation, for the wild strawberry was given to us by the "little people" who live in a quarry, for the pleasure of eating and to be used in a healing ceremony.

DECEMBER
Set up the drum.

Winter's on the creek.

Dark men sit in dark kitchens.
Words move the air
5   A neighbor is sick.
Needs prayer.

Women thaw frozen
strawberries.

In the dark . . . a drum.

10 Kids hang out
eating burgers
at McDonalds.
The Williams boy
is drunk.

15 Set up the drum.

Berries thaw,
are crushed,
    fingers stained, and tongues.

Set up the drum.
20 A neighbor is sick.
Say a prayer.
Dark men sit in dark kitchens.

Wind rattles the moon.

8   While nibbling those horrible cultivated berries I became enraged with the conglomerate fruit companies, as Pablo Neruda[1] had years ago, which control the lives of those Mexican farmers who scratch out a meager livelihood from the sands, and I was discouraged with my own self.

---

[1] *Pablo Neruda:* (1904–1973) Chilean poet.

DISCUSSION QUESTIONS

1. The gift of a basket of strawberries causes several thoughts and reactions on the part of the poet. What are they?
2. The poem "Wild Strawberry" contains images that appeal to several senses. Which images appeal to the senses of taste, touch, and sight?
3. How does the tone of "December" differ from the tone of the other two poems?
4. The author says that the harvesters in Sonora "could not enjoy the labors as we had when I was a child. . . ." What are some differences between the two experiences?

WRITING TOPICS

1. If you have ever picked wild fruit or fruit and vegetables from a garden, recall that time in a poem or a descriptive essay. Include whether you did this alone or with others.
2. In recent years, people have become ill from eating fruit imported into the United States, an ironic footnote to the author's statement that the wild strawberry is "the symbol of life to Iroquois people" and a cure for illness. Research three or four diseases that can be prevented by eating specific fruits and/or vegetables and prepare a report, with graphics if possible.

I STILL TRUST THE LAND

Leslie Silko

Leslie Marmon Silko was born in 1948 in Albuquerque, New Mexico, and grew up at Laguna Pueblo about forty miles to the west. In 1969, she graduated *magna cum laude* from the University of New Mexico, where she continued graduate study in English. After briefly attending law school, she decided to pursue a literary career and has emerged as one of the foremost authors in the Native American Renaissance. Her first book, *Laguna Woman: Poems by Leslie Silko* appeared in 1974. She has published two novels, *Ceremony* (1977) and *Almanac of the Dead* (1991); a multigenre book, *Storyteller* (1981); and *Yellow Woman and a Beauty of the Spirit: Essays on Native American Life Today* (1996). Silko has taught English at the Universities of New Mexico and Arizona. She has received numerous awards and honors including a National Endowment for the Humanities Discovery Grant (1973) and the prestigious MacArthur Foundation Grant (1981).

In "I Still Trust the Land," Silko ties her writing to the Laguna Pueblo landscape, her exploration of that landscape, and her Anglo, Indian, and Hispanic heritage. "All those languages, all those ways of living are combined, and we are like somewhere on the fringes of all three. But I don't apologize for this any more—not to whites, not to full bloods—our origin is unlike any other. My poetry, my storytelling rise out of this source." From early childhood, Silko learned Laguna stories and traditions from her great-grandmother, whom she called "Grandma A'mooh," her grandmother Lily, and "Aunt Susie," who taught school at Laguna in the 1920s. These women profoundly influenced young Silko, passing down to her "an entire culture by word of mouth."

Silko grew up in rural Laguna, a culturally and linguistically diverse community. Her mixed heritage exemplifies the strengths and tensions of Laguna Pueblo for more than a century. In 1869, Walter Marmon arrived at the Pueblo and his brother Robert joined him three years later. The brothers married Laguna women. As prominent members of the community, both served as Pueblo governors. Robert, Silko's great-grandfather, established a trading post, and Walter became a government school teacher at Laguna. Their actions generated political and religious conflicts in the Pueblo. The Anglo Marmons were devout Presbyterians, who spoke English, one of "all those languages." Lagunans speak the Keresan language. Although it is unwritten, it has been spoken for unknown centuries. Spanish has been important in the Laguna area for about three hundred years. When the Marmon brothers arrived, Protestant missionaries were challenging the synthesis of Laguna beliefs and Roman Catholicism that had endured for nearly three centuries. Caught in the conflict between the Christian Bible and Laguna traditions, young Silko chose Pueblo beliefs.

Unlike the Cherokees and other tribes, the Puebloans were never removed from their sacred land. Like Luci Tapahonso and Howard Gorman, Leslie Silko learned that stories connected her family to every place on their Southwestern landscape.

◉

1   When I was four years old I began to climb over the fence and leave the yard where I was supposed to stay. Our house was at the bottom of the hill, by the road everyone took to the post office and store. I watched for people to pass by and I would talk to them; the older kids would tell me all kinds of wild stories because I believed what they told me and I got so excited. I could hear the drumming from the plaza whenever there were ceremonial dances, and I always wanted to go because everyone was gathered around the plaza and the dancers were so powerful to watch.

2   One day the older kids told me that there were special dancers up at the plaza, and these dancers ate wood. I still remember climbing over the fence, because it was a four-foot-high fence but the wire had good spaces to put my feet. I walked quite a distance before Marsalina Thompson saw me. In those days, everyone watched out for everyone else's children, especially the little ones. Marsalina saw me and she knew that I wasn't supposed to be marching along by myself, so she brought me home. I cried and cried and tried to tell her that I must get to the plaza to see the amazing dancers who ate wood, but she was firm.

3   I was never afraid to go anywhere around Laguna when I was growing up. I was never afraid of any person unless the person was an outsider. Outsiders were white people, mostly tourists who drove up and did not stay long. But up in the sandhills and among the sandstone formations around Laguna, I did not see many Laguna people either, only people cutting wood or returning from their sheep-camp. Up in the hills with the birds and animals and my horse, I felt absolutely safe; I knew outsiders and kidnappers

stayed out of the hills. I spent hours and hours alone in the hills southeast of Laguna. After I got my beloved horse, Joey, and before I had to work so much at my grandpa's store, I often spent all day on my horse, riding all around old Laguna. The old folks who did not know my name would refer to me as "the little girl on the horse." I was perfectly happy, lost in my thoughts and imagination as I rode my horse.

4   Sometimes I stopped, tied up my horse, and investigated interesting pet-roglyphs[1] on sandstone cliffs or searched for arrowheads in the ruins of older settlements. I preferred to be without human companions so I could give my complete attention to the hills. Of course, from the time I can remember, I preferred to play alone with my little figures of farm animals, cowboys, and Indians because I liked to make up elaborate dramas in which I whispered what each of the characters was saying; the presence of my sisters and other playmates inhibited these dramas. I was a tomboy who liked to climb cottonwood trees and wade in the river. For real adventure I used to tag along with Gary Fernandez, who was my age, and we would try to keep up with Gary's older brother Ron and his pal Mike Trujillo. The older boys would let us follow for a while before they ditched us.

5   Because our family was such a mixture of Indian, Mexican, and white, I was acutely aware of the inherent conflicts between Indian and white, old-time beliefs and Christianity. But from the start, I had no use for Christianity because the Christians made up such terrible lies about Indian people that it was clear to me they would lie about other matters also. My beloved Grandma A'mooh was a devout Presbyterian, but I can remember, even as a little girl, listening to her read from the Bible and thinking, "I love her with all my heart, but I don't believe in the Bible." I spent time with Aunt Susie and with Grandpa Hank, who was not a Christian. The mesas and hills loved me; the Bible meant punishment. Life at Laguna for me was a daily balancing act of Laguna beliefs and Laguna ways and the ways of the outsiders. No wonder I preferred to wander in the hills by myself, on my horse, Joey, with Bulls-eye, my dog.

6   Grandma Lily took me and my sisters on walks to the river, and as we got older, she took us to hike in the mesas and sandhills as she had done with my father and his brothers when they were young. She wasn't afraid of anything in the hills; she was the horsewoman who would ride any bronco, and she wore a woman's dress and women's shoes only three times a year, to Mass on Christmas Eve and for Palm Sunday and Easter Sunday.

7   I have always felt safer alone in the hills than I feel when I am around people. Humans are the most dangerous of all animals, that's what my mother said. She was fearless with snakes and picked up rattlesnakes with ease. Most of my life I have lived in small settlements or I have lived outside

---

[1] *petroglyph:* an image carved on a rock.

of town, as I do now, in the hills outside of Tucson, where the nearest house is a quarter mile away. I still trust the land—the rocks, the shrubs, the cactus, the rattlesnakes, and mountain lions—far more than I trust human beings. I never feel lonely when I walk alone in the hills: I am surrounded with living beings, with these sandstone ridges and lava rock hills full of life. Luckily I enjoy danger, so I find human beings irresistible; humans are natural forces, just like flash floods or blizzards.

8   I was only five or six years old when my father was elected tribal treasurer. During his term, the Pueblo of Laguna filed a big lawsuit against the state of New Mexico for six million acres of land the state wrongfully took. The land had been granted by the king of Spain to the Pueblo hundreds of years before the United States even existed, let alone the state of New Mexico. The lawyer hired by Pueblo of Laguna and the expert witnesses, archaeologists, used to meet at our house to prepare to testify in court.

9   What made the strongest impression on me, though, were the old folks who also were expert witnesses. For months the old folks and Aunt Susie met twice a week after supper at our house to go over the testimony. Many of them were so aged they could hardly get around; Aunt Susie seemed spry compared to them. She interpreted English for the old folks because she knew them very well; in her own studies of Laguna history she had talked with them many times. Now she helped them prepare their testimony, that from time immemorial the Kawakemeh, the people of the Pueblo of Laguna, had been sustained from hunting and planting on this land stolen by the state of New Mexico. It was explained to me that the old folks testified with stories—stories of childhood outings with adults to gather piñons or to haul wood, stories they had heard as children. The old folks were going up against the state of New Mexico with only the stories.

10   The land claims lawsuit made a great and lasting impression on me. I heard the old folks cry as they talked about the land and how it had been taken from them. To them the land was as dear as a child, and as I listened, I felt the loss and the anger too, as if it all had happened only yesterday.

11   When I was a sophomore in high school I decided law school was the place to seek justice. I majored in English at the University of New Mexico only because I loved to read and write about what I'd read. Sure, I wrote short stories and I'd received a little discovery grant from the National Endowment for the Arts, but my destination was law school, where I planned to learn how to obtain justice. I should have paid more attention to the lesson of the Laguna Pueblo land claims lawsuit from my childhood: The lawsuit was not settled until I was in law school. The U.S. Court of Indian Claims found in favor of the Pueblo of Laguna, but the Indian Claims Court never gives back land wrongfully taken; the court only pays tribes for the land. The amount paid is computed without interest according to the value of the land at the time it was taken. The Laguna people wanted the land they cherished; instead, they got twenty-five cents for each of the six million acres

stolen by the state. The lawsuit had lasted twenty years, so the lawyers' fees amounted to nearly $2 million. . . .

12 One of the advantages that we Pueblos have enjoyed is that we have always been able to stay with the land. Our stories cannot be separated from their geographical locations, from actual physical places on the land. We were not relocated like so many Native American groups who were torn away from their ancestral land. And our stories are so much a part of these places that it is almost impossible for future generations to lose them—there is a story connected with every place, every object in the landscape.

13 Dennis Brutus has talked about the "yet unborn" as well as "those from the past," and how we are still *all* in *this* place, and language—the story-telling—is our way of passing through or being with them, of being together again. When Aunt Susie told her stories, she would tell a younger child to go open the door so that our esteemed predecessors might bring their gifts to us. "They are out there," Aunt Susie would say. "Let them come in. They're here, they're here with us *within* the stories."

14 A few years ago, when Aunt Susie was 106, I paid her a visit, and while I was there she said, "Well, I'll be leaving here soon. I think I'll be leaving here next week, and I will be going over to the Cliff House." She said, "It's going to be real good to get back over there." I was listening, and I was thinking that she must be talking about her house at Paguate village, just north of Laguna. And she went on, "Well, my mother's sister [and she gave her Indian name] will be there. She has been living there. She will be there and we will be over there, and I will get a chance to write down these stories I've been telling you." Now you must understand, of course, that Aunt Susie's mother's sister, a great storyteller herself, has long since passed over into the land of the dead. But then I realized, too, that Aunt Susie wasn't talking about death the way most of us do. She was talking about "going over" as a journey, a journey that perhaps we can only begin to understand through an appreciation for the boundless capacity of language that, through storytelling, brings us together, despite great distances between cultures, despite great distances in time.

DISCUSSION QUESTIONS

1. Find Laguna on a map of New Mexico. What can you tell about the area from the location and from Silko's account of her childhood?
2. How much money was awarded the Laguna people for the six million acres stolen from them, and who got the money?

3. Silko says "there is a story connected with every place, every object in the landscape." Why is storytelling so important in her culture?
4. Do you agree with Silko's mother that "humans are the most dangerous of all animals"?

WRITING TOPICS

1. In an essay, compare and contrast Maurice Kenny's description of the land and the people's connection to it with Leslie Silko's description.
2. Recall carefully the land you occupied as a child, whether your landscape was rural, urban, or suburban, and in a short paper write of your connection to this landscape.

GIANT BEAR

Leslie Silko

When Leslie Silko discovered a sleeping bear while she was deer hunting, she knew she was in a landscape where her father had wandered as a boy and where Puebloan people have lived for about twenty-five hundred years. According to Laguna origin cosmology, Mesa Verde had been the home of their ancestors. Mesa Verde is the well-preserved ruin of a large settlement protected within rock shelters, extending along a canyon in southern Colorado. When it was abandoned late in the thirteenth century, seven clans—Water, Lizard, Snake, Turkey, Eagle, Antelope, and Sun—are said to have migrated from Mesa Verde.

Laguna Pueblo is named from the Spanish mission, San Jose de la Laguna, "Saint Joseph of the Lake." The name was conferred after Laguna people on July 4, 1699, formally requested Spanish colonial recognition. The Pueblo is southeast of its sacred Mount Taylor. Today, the Laguna people of central New Mexico live in six villages on the knoll above the San Jose River. Many of Old Laguna's structures still exist, and the overall view of this Pueblo sitting on a hill crowned with a small church remains beautiful. Approximately one-half of the population of thirty-five hundred lives on the 420,000-acre reservation. Few still depend on agriculture, cattle, or sheep. Most work away from the Pueblo in Albuquerque and elsewhere. Silko's writing ranges from Laguna cosmological time through history to her own lifetime.

1   When I was thirteen I carried an old .30–.30 we borrowed from George Pearl. It was an old Winchester that had a steel ring on its side to secure it in a saddle scabbard. It was heavy and hurt my shoulder when I fired it and it seemed even louder than my father's larger caliber rifle, but I didn't say anything because I was so happy to be hunting for the first time. I didn't get

a deer that year but one afternoon hunting alone on the round volcanic hill we called Chato, I saw a giant brown bear lying in the sun below the hill-top. Dead or just sleeping, I couldn't tell. I was cautious because I already knew what hours of searching for motion, for the outline of a deer, for the color of a deer's hide can do to the imagination. I already knew how easily the weathered branches of a dead juniper could resemble antlers because I had walked with my father on hunts since I was eight. So I stood motion-less for a long time until my breathing was more calm and my heart wasn't beating so hard. I even shifted my eyes away for a moment hoping to see my uncle Polly or my cousin Richard who was hunting the ridges nearby.

2   I knew there were no bears that large on Mt. Taylor; I was pretty sure there were no bears that large anywhere. But when I looked back at the slope above me, the giant brown bear was still lying on the sunny slope of the hill above patches of melting snow and tall yellow grass. I watched it for a long time, for any sign of motion, for its breathing, but I wasn't close enough to tell for sure. If it was dead I wanted to be able to examine it up close. It occurred to me that I could fire my rifle over its head but I knew better than to wake a bear with only a .30–.30. All this time I had only moved my eyes, and my arms were getting numb from holding the rifle in the same position for so long. As quietly and as carefully as I probably will ever move, I turned and walked away from the giant bear, still down wind from it. After I had gone a distance down the slope I stopped to look back to see if it was still a giant brown bear sunning itself on one of the last warm afternoons of the year, and not just damp brown earth and a lightning-struck log above the snow patches. But the big dark bear remained there, on the south slope of Chato, with its head facing southeast, the eyes closed, motionless. I hurried the rest of the way down the ridge, listening closely to the wind at my back for sounds, glancing over my shoulder now and then.

3   I never told anyone what I had seen because I knew they don't let peo-ple who see such things carry .30–30's or hunt deer with them.

Discussion Questions

1. What does "Giant Bear" reveal about the author's relationship with wild things?
2. What keeps the narrator from firing her rifle over the "bear's" head?

WRITING TOPICS

1. In this short essay, Silko appeals to several senses. In a paragraph or two, tell what they are and identify the passages.
2. If you have hunted wild animals or birds, write of one or two experiences in a descriptive essay. Include sensory details.

THE TIME WE CLIMBED SNAKE MOUNTAIN

Leslie Silko

Young Silko intimately identified with rocks, hills, cacti, mountain lions, and other natural elements around Laguna. An important motif in Silko's poetry is her fascination with the animals and landscape of the Southwest. She expresses her love for the region in the titles of her poems: "Deer Song," "Slim Man Canyon," "Where Mountain Lion Lay Down with Deer," and "The Time We Climbed Snake Mountain." Along with bears, deer, and other creatures, reptiles occupy a very important position in Pueblo cosmologies. Southwestern Native Americans generally do not tell certain stories during the warm months when snakes are active. Sacred texts are properly related only during the cold months when snakes go underground seeking warmth to survive the winter.

Specific reptiles serve, in Puebloan conception, as messengers from humans to the powerful spirits who control weather and other natural phenomena. Pueblo water snakes are associated with springs, water sources, and rain. When the poem's speaker reminds the climbers that Snake Mountain belongs to a physical serpent, she is also paying homage to a metaphysical being. Mountain, snake, and human all share a special cosmological niche.

Seeing good places
    for my hands
I grab the warm parts of the cliff
        and I feel the mountain as I climb.

5 Somewhere around here
        yellow spotted snake is sleeping on his rock
        in the sun.

So
    please, I tell them
10   watch out,
don't step on the spotted yellow snake
        he lives here.
The mountain is his.

DISCUSSION QUESTIONS

1. The narrator of "Giant Bear" did not manage to kill a deer, but she was deer hunting. The speaker in the poem argues for respecting the yellow spotted snake, whose mountain it is. How can you account for the difference in actions toward the snake and the deer, considering that both selections were written by the same person?
2. Notice that Silko uses indentation in this poem. Do you think the poem would have been more effective if all the lines had started at the margin, without indentation? Explain.

WRITING TOPICS

1. In stanza one, Silko repeats "l" sounds four times, and in stanzas two and three, she repeats "s" sounds fifteen times. Write a paragraph on this topic: Leslie Silko repeats sounds and uses indentation to achieve rhythm and convey meaning in her poem "The Time We Climbed Snake Mountain."

SLIM MAN CANYON

Leslie Silko

In this lyric poem, landscape reminds Silko and her friend, John, of people who lived in Slim Man Canyon and left their art on its walls centuries ago. The repetition of "700 years ago" frames the poem and lends a chanting quality. Silko blends simple images of gentle water, warm sun, and blue sky with painted stories and songs. Slow lines move across the page in rhythm with the horses' feet through deep white sand. In this ancient landscape, distances in time disappear. The remembered earth endures with the people and their stories.

early summer Navajo Nation, 1972 for John

700 years ago
     people were living here
     water was running gently
     and the sun was warm
⁵   on pumpkin flowers.
It was 700 years ago
     deep in this canyon
     with sandstone rising high above
The rock the silence tall sky and flowing water
¹⁰   sunshine through cottonwood leaves
     the willows smell in the wind
          700 years.
The rhythm
    the horses' feet moving strong through
¹⁵   white deep sand.
Where I come from is like this
   the warmth, the fragrance, the silence.

Blue sky and rainclouds in the distance
　　　　we ride together
20　　　　　　　　　　　　past cliffs with stories and songs
　　　　　　　　　　　painted on rock.
　　　　　　　　　　　　　　　700 years ago.

DISCUSSION QUESTIONS

1. A lyric poem is a short poem that expresses thoughts and emotions, is marked by imagination, and creates a single impression, largely through imagery. Explain how this poem fits the definition of a lyric poem.
2. What is the effect of the repetition in lines 1, 6, 12, and 20?

WRITING TOPICS

1. Imagine that someone seven hundred years ago stood near where you are today. Who might this person have been? What would he or she have seen? Express your imaginings in a few paragraphs or a poem.
2. Read Silko's poem aloud and listen for sounds and images that are repeated. Write a brief essay on this topic: In "Slim Man Canyon," Leslie Silko achieves a synthesis of sound and sense (meaning) through repetition.

INDIAN SONG: SURVIVAL

Leslie Silko

Silko informs us in the title that she will sing a song of survival. In this "song," she weaves strands of mythic, magical, and real landscapes. She shapes the poem as a journey. The journey motif unifies the ten sections that merge metaphorical landscapes with traditional myths. The feminine persona begins her traveling toward the frigid north and ends in sunny warmth. Laguna oral literature records ancestral migration from Mesa Verde south to Laguna. Throughout the journey, she speaks to and is guided and enchanted by mountain lion man, a primordial force.

Knowledge of Yellow Woman as described in Keresan mythology adds another dimension to this poem. For Silko's persona combines elements of several stories about Yellow Woman, who "dares to cross traditional boundaries during times of crisis in order to save the Pueblo." Symbol of fertility, she is also huntress and mother of game. In one traditional myth, Yellow Woman left home with a wilderness spirit, and they traveled mountainous and riverine landscapes. In another, Sun came to Yellow Woman at a river, which also plays a prominent role in "Indian Song." In a third story, Yellow Woman was married to the Ruler of North Mountain, who had a violent temper. They never planted because of the cold. People were forced to live on cacti and other wild plants. One day, she wandered far from home searching for food and water. Yellow Woman met Summer whose moccasins were embroidered with flowers and butterflies. Wearing a yellow shirt woven from corn silk, he carried an ear of green corn. He asked her why she ate only cacti instead of corn and melons. Summer invited her to join him in his home far away in the south, where corn grows and flowers bloom all year. Her husband appeared in a "blinding storm of snow and hail and sleet, in a boisterous mood." Wearing a shirt of icicles, he was covered with frost from head to foot. Winter and Summer fought until Winter, finding himself defeated, called for a truce. Yellow Woman decided that she would spend part of the year with each, so the Pueblo people now experience both seasons.

Knowing these Yellow Woman stories, one hears their echoes through this poem. Knowing that Laguna corn, bean, and squash food production depends not only on summer warmth, but also on irrigation water, one appreciates how central the river is to Laguna survival. No one knows the river's seasons, moods, and spirit as well as those who drink from it and divert its waters to raise their food. Silko's fertile river landscape winds its way through seven stanzas. The poem concludes with a beautiful image of survival.

We went north
　　　　to escape winter
climbing pale cliffs
　　　　　　we paused　to sleep at the river.

5　Cold water　river cold from the north
I sink my body in the shallow
　　　　　　sink into sand and cold river water.

You sleep in the branches of
　　　　　　pale river willows above me.
10　I smell you in the silver leaves, mountain lion man
　　　　　　green willows aren't sweet enough to hide you.

I have slept with the river　and
　　　　　　he is warmer than any man.
At sunrise
15　　　　I heard ice on the cattails.

Mountain lion, with dark yellow eyes
　　　　　　you nibble moonflowers
　　　　　　while we wait.
I don't ask why do you come
20　　　　on this desperation journey north.

I am hunted for my feathers
I hide in spider's web
　　　　hanging　in a thin gray tree
　　　　　　above the river.

25　In the night　I hear music
　　　　song of branches　dry leaves scraping the moon.

Green spotted frogs sing to the river
                    and I know he is waiting.
Mountain lion shows me the way
30   path of mountain wind
                    climbing higher
                    up
                            up to Cloudy Mountain.

It is only a matter of time, Indian
35   you can't sleep with the river forever.
Smell winter and know.

I swallow black mountain dirt
                    while you catch hummingbirds
                    trap them with wildflowers
40   pollen and petals
                            fallen from the Milky Way.

You lie beside me in the sunlight
                    warmth around us and
                    you ask me if I still smell winter.
45 Mountain forest wind travels east and I answer:
                    taste me,
                            I am the wind
                    touch me,
                            I am the lean gray deer
50   running on the edge of the rainbow.

DISCUSSION QUESTIONS

1. Who is making this magical, mythic journey?
2. How is "survival" in the title related to the action in the poem?
3. Two major characters in the poem are the feminine persona and mountain lion. Both behave as spirit beings at times. Find four examples of this transformation between real and magical.
4. With some of your classmates, discuss how this poem might be illustrated, and then paint or draw a mural of the journey. Use each stanza as a reference.

WRITING TOPICS

1. Prepare a reader's theater presentation of the poem, using individual voices and a chorus. You may add music for background.
2. Silko is known for her unusual imagery. In a brief essay, discuss the contribution of the major images in the poem to the magical, mystical mood: winter, the river, mountain lion man, the persona, and others you think are important.

HAWK NAILED TO A BARN DOOR

Peter Blue Cloud

Born in 1933, Peter Blue Cloud was reared on the Mohawk Reservation in Caughnawauga Reserve in Quebec, Canada, as a member of the Turtle Clan. He spoke only the Mohawk language during his childhood until his grandfather introduced him to English, and he subsequently began writing songs and poems in English as a teenager. Responding to an editor's request for biographical information, Blue Cloud once replied, "I'll give you just the basics on myself . . . as I believe in poems speaking & shy away from 'poet as personality.'" Blue Cloud then described himself as "Former ironworker turned logger turned wood carver."

Other poets have been less modest in their praise for his work. Gary Snyder wrote for *Turtle, Bear, and Wolf,* "Blue Cloud's poems are living proof that the power and beauty of the Old Ways cannot be lost." From New York City's high steel construction to quiet mountain tops in Mohawk territory, for almost thirty years, Blue Cloud has been an original voice for natural ways of life. He served as poetry editor for *Akwesasne Notes* from 1975 to 1976. His publications include *Alcatraz Is Not an Island* (1972); *Coyote and Friends* (1976); *Turtle, Bear, and Wolf* (1976); *Back Then Tomorrow* (1978); *Contemporary Coyote Tales* (1982); *Elderberry Flute Song, The Other Side of Nowhere* (1990); and *Clans of Many Nations: Selected Poems of Peter Blue Cloud 1969–94* (1995).

In "Hawk Nailed to a Barn Door," Blue Cloud makes a moral indictment of those who kill hawks, eagles, foxes, coyotes, and other creatures that they consider pests to be eliminated from the environment. Native Americans characteristically consider all creatures valuable for a healthy, balanced environment. The poet contrasts these two systems in a narrative unfolding in two parts. In part one, which presents the killers' system, the speaker discovers the hawk brutally nailed to a barn door. Anger and dismay with anyone who could do such a barbaric act causes him to lose a little more faith in humans. Identifying with the hawk, the poet startles us with strong images of maggots and hollow, eaten eyes. Crucified magnificence has been hammered through wings for flight. Using hyphens as hinges to join two words, Blue Cloud thickens his hawkish images.

In the second part of the poem, the speaker exemplifies the Native American system of respect and reverence for the dead hawk. In a more balanced mood, he staves off the stench, and with pepperwood leaves and a prayer releases the spirit of the hawk.

December 23, 1973

Hawk nailed to a barn door,
and rain makes you small and dark, and my muddy boots
are ankle-deep in ground fog,
far away dog barks sharp as cracking rifles
5   disked earth the hayfield's primal mud
      your brother and sister rough-legged hawks
of quick-beating wings and spread, down-pointed tails
momentarily transfixed in air as if fighting
      an up-slanting gale from earth.
10 Hobbling with practiced dignity, Chauncy, my new dog neighbor
with casts on front legs, limps forward
      to good-morning me the day, hesitant.
Yes, I am trying to fashion a scene to forget the maggots
and the stink, your hollow eaten eyes and tight closed
15 talons in last grasping, nailed through wing muscles,
head down to side, crucified,
      curved beak slightly open to my own questions
who has lost another particle of faith.
      Your wings and claws dry now above the stove,
20 and the rising heat gently revolves them.
It is 4:30 a.m. and cold and dark and your feathers
will be passed on to sky lovers.
      I was choking slightly, deep down, as I removed
your wings, claws, and tail feathers, then one by one
25 I took a handful of breast down,
      so warm looking.
Buried you behind the barn with two pepperwood leaves
and a mumbled se-sa-ton-ti, o-nen,
      go-home, now
30 Sat down in anger for your senseless murder,
all set to write a bitter song,
      it is 5:00 a.m. now
and your feathers so close send me no messages of hate.
I look at your beautiful wings
35   and sense your flight.

DISCUSSION QUESTIONS

1. What clues are there to the fact that the speaker did not kill the hawk?
2. The person who killed the hawk is evidently the one who nailed it to a barn door. Why might someone do this?
3. At 5:00 A.M. the narrator contemplates writing "a bitter song." What changes his mind?
4. How would you describe the tone of this poem? Find five images that support your answer.

WRITING TOPICS

1. Peter Blue Cloud ends his poem with the words "and sense your flight." Reread the poem and write a response about why you think this is or is not an appropriate ending.
2. There are widely divergent viewpoints on hunting wild animals. What are your thoughts on this topic? Plan and write a persuasive paper explaining your point of view.

BUFFALO POEM #1

Geary Hobson

In a burst of humor, Geary Hobson speaks to his buffalo brothers. Albuquerque airport, busy with frantic traffic and scurrying passengers, seems an incongruous spot for a herd of buffalo. But who's to say where buffalo may roam?

Hobson, Cherokee-Chickasaw, is a poet, short story writer, essayist, and editor, who was born in Chicot County, Arkansas, in 1941. He has taught English at the Universities of Arkansas and New Mexico and currently teaches in the English Department at the University of Oklahoma. His landmark *The Remembered Earth: An Anthology of Contemporary Native American Literature* (1979) includes many beginning authors who have since achieved prominence in American literature.

ON HEARING THAT A SMALL HERD OF BUFFALO HAS "BROKEN LOOSE" AND IS "RUNNING WILD" AT THE ALBUQUERQUE AIRPORT—SEPTEMBER 26, 1975

—roam, on brothers . . .

DISCUSSION QUESTIONS

1. How would you characterize the tone of this poem?
2. What, other than the title, makes this brief bit of language a poem?

WRITING TOPICS

1. In the style of Hobson's humorous energy, write a brief "Buffalo #2 Poem." You may try using another animal as the inspiration for an unlikely scene in a short poem.

TIME

Joseph Bruchac

Mythic Mink, trickster for Northwest Coast tribes, was known for his killing of monsters, stealing the Sun, and preparing the world for the arrival of humans. After Mink's gift, early humans lived in days of natural light. Before the arrival of Europeans, Native Americans marked time by the seasons and followed a solar calendar.

Europeans brought with them mechanical devices for measuring life in seconds, minutes, and hours. Once again, Mink stole for his humans, but his gift became a prison. In this brief poem, Bruchac ticks off wind-up-time that owns everyone. "Time" beats through the poem three times.

Mink once stole the Sun
so the People could have light.

Then the Europeans came
and brought with them
5 a new thing called Time.

So Mink stole Time.
He carried it off—
a big metal clock.

But instead of owning it,
10 he soon found out that
it owned him.

To this day he sits
with three big keys
around his neck.

15 Each day he uses them
to wind up Time
which owns us all now
the way we once owned the Sun.

DISCUSSION QUESTIONS

1. In a small group, discuss the appropriateness of this poem in a chapter titled "The Remembered Earth."
2. What can you infer from line 5?
3. How can it be possible to be owned by time?

WRITING TOPICS

1. What are your views on time? Does it own you? Can you take control of time? Can you think of a better way to measure your days? Brainstorm some ideas about time, and write a few paragraphs on this topic.
2. After doing some research, write a brief essay exploring the different views of and relationship to time as experienced by Native Americans and Euro-Americans.

WE ARE THE LAND

Paula Gunn Allen

Acclaimed writer, scholar, and teacher, Paula Gunn Allen has received wide recognition for her contributions to feminist criticism and Native American literature. Allen received a B.A. in English (1966) and an M.F.A. in Creative Writing (1968) from the University of Oregon and a Ph.D. from the University of New Mexico (1975). After teaching at the University of California, Berkeley, in the Native American Studies Department from 1982 to 1990, she moved to the University of California, Los Angeles, to teach in the English Department. In 1990, she was awarded the Native American Literature prize and received the American Book Award for her anthology *Spider Woman's Granddaughters.*

Born in 1939 to a Laguna-Sioux-Scottish mother and a father with Lebanese-American ancestry, Allen describes her birth as a "confluence of cultures." She grew up in Cubero, a small town in northern New Mexico near Laguna Pueblo. Her home environment blended religions, languages, traditional stories, and world views. With good humor, Allen says, "My life was more chaos than order in any ordinary American, Native American, Mexican-American, Lebanese-American, German-American, any heathen, Catholic, Protestant, Jewish, atheistic sense. Fences would have been hard to place without leaving something out." Myriad backgrounds and experiences prepared this author to reflect multiple voices in her writing. On the other hand, Allen describes herself as a "multicultural event" who can "attest to the terrible pain of being a bridge" across cultures.

Allen's cross-cultural works have influenced many writers and scholars. She has published eight volumes of poetry, a novel, a collection of critical essays, and numerous poems and essays in journals and anthologies. *The Sacred Hoop: Recovering the Feminine in American Indian Traditions* (1986) is a landmark study of female power in American Indian traditions and an important text in feminist scholarship. Allen's collections of Native American literature complete her commitment to acquainting a wide audience of readers with other Native American writers. These include *Spider Woman's*

Granddaughters: Traditional Tales and Contemporary Writing by Native American Women (1989); *Voice of the Turtle: American Indian Literature 1900–1970* (1994); and *Song of the Turtle: American Indian Literature 1974–1994* (1996). Her latest book is a collection of poems, *Life Is a Fatal Disease* (1997). In all her works, Allen urges Americans to recognize and respect a Native American world view from which we have much to learn about survival on this planet in the twenty-first century. Laguna's traditions, sacred cosmology, and geography form the philosophical bedrock of Allen's link between land and literature.

1   We are the land. To the best of my understanding, that is the fundamental idea embedded in Native American life and culture in the Southwest. More than remembered, the Earth is the mind of the people as we are the mind of the earth. The land is not really the place (separate from ourselves) where we act out the drama of our isolate destinies. It is not a means of survival, a setting for our affairs, a resource on which we draw in order to keep our own act functioning. It is not the ever-present "Other" which supplies us with a sense of "I." It is rather a part of our being, dynamic, significant, real. It is ourself, in as real a sense as such notions as "ego," "libido" or social network, in a sense more real than any conceptualization or abstraction about the nature of human being can ever be. The land is not an image in our eyes but rather it is as truly an integral aspect of our being as we are of its being. And the integral nature of this fact continues beyond mortal dissolution of bodies—human, beast or plant. The old ones come from Sipap[1] to participate in the eternal living being of the land/people as rain. The gods come from the skies and mountain peaks to participate in the welfare of this immutable gestalt.[2] In this return, the corn and squash, the deer and game, the men and women are renewed. The Shiwana[3] show us what the truth about being, our collective/entire being is. And so, Indian poets of the Southwest return again and again to this relationship, as the singers, the priests, the dancers, the animals and the gods return. It is within this larger being that we are given life, and in the acknowledgment of the singleness of that being that we eat, that we plant, that we harvest, that we build and clean, that we dance, hunt, run, heal, sing, chant and write.

2   Nor is this relationship one of mere "affinity" for the Earth. It is not a matter of being "close to nature." The relationship is more one of identity, in the mathematical sense, than of affinity. The Earth is, in a very real sense, the same as ourself (or selves), and it is this primary point that is made in

---

[1] *Sipap:* mythic place of emergence where humans, animals, and all life emerged from the four worlds below onto this Fifth World.
[2] *immutable gestalt:* a unified whole not susceptible to change.
[3] *Shiwana:* Rain Clouds, defined as the Sun's beloved children and brought by spirits of deceased ancestors.

the fiction and poetry of the Native American writers of the Southwest.

³ On occasion, the point is made by its absence; writers mourn the loss of that unity, or its absence among those who are strangers to the circle, or the person's own distance from that knowledge is chronicled in anger or pain. Yet even despair is a result of known belonging with and to the land: "you can't lose something you never had," as the saying goes, and having known that perfect peace of being together with all that surrounds one, other attempts at gaining satisfaction or joy are too pale to be worth considering. That knowledge, though perfect, does not have associated with it the exalted romance of sentimental "nature lovers," nor does it have, at base, any self-conscious "appreciation" of the land, or even of the primary event of unification. It is a matter of fact, one known equably from infancy, remembered and honored at levels of awareness that go beyond consciousness, and that extend long roots deep into primary levels of mind, language, perception, and all the basic aspects of being that have as one of their expressions our writing.

⁴ Carol Lee Sanchez talks about how deep this awareness goes in a poem for Wendy Rose:

> it seems proper that language should also
> reflect harmony—a giving way;
> a moving in; a coming out.
>
> these things we speak about
> ⁵ (from our respective memories-
> these traditions we keep
> not knowing why we do so
> or even (sometimes-
> how we 'know' the right ways.
> ¹⁰ maybe, that 'racial memory' (he mentioned.
> a genetic imprint
> handed down from many grandmothers
> those grandmothers who watch—over us
> whisper in the wind-
> ¹⁵ remind us of our duties. . . .

⁵ Goweitduweetza (Veronica Riley) writes about this loss, and the knowledge of how it has been/should/will be in "Untitled Journey," saying that after a sojourn in a "peaceful land/Of untouched beauty" a child will return to this place of "lances that pierce/. . . And/Hands that hold/Falsely" who will bring again that beauty and peace to human hearts:

> Child of beauty
> Are you ready?
> Then
> Return my healed heart to earth

5   Bring with you seeds
        Of a new generation

    Begin
    Only when it is safe
    And plant wisely
10 I will guard these seeds
        with my life

6   Her poem speaks to very ancient metaphysical truths of her people, and so
simply, so clearly, that she evokes for us both the reality of the pain of this
strange distance from the Earth and Earth's beauty, and the perfect knowledge
of the kind of unification with the source of our being that is naturally ours.

DISCUSSION QUESTIONS

1. The author says that in Native American life and culture in the Southwest the relationship to the land is one of identity and unity, not appreciation. What is the difference between these two ideas?
2. In the last paragraph, Allen speaks of "ancient metaphysical truths."
   Metaphysics is a division of philosophy that is concerned with the
   nature of reality and being, often beyond what is perceptible to the
   senses. What is the difference between this idea and the ideas of scientists who study the environment and ecosystems?

WRITING TOPICS

1. Allen organizes her essay by contrasting what people's relationship to
   the land is and is not. In your response journal, make two columns with
   the headings "the land is" and "the land is not" and record under each
   heading brief notes about Allen's contrasts. Write a response about people and land based on your notes.
2. Allen describes "that perfect peace of being together" with the earth.
   With this idea in mind, write about a time when you have felt "perfect
   peace" that arose from one earthly place.
3. How would the world today be different if everyone felt a unity with the
   land? Explore this idea in a small group and then outline and compose
   an essay based on your conclusions.

THE STRANGE PEOPLE

Louise Erdrich

Prominent poet Louise Erdrich has published two volumes of poetry *Jacklight* (1984) and *Baptism of Desire* (1989). One of America's most important contemporary authors, Erdrich recalls her early writing efforts: "I was in college and had failed at everything else. I kept journals and diaries when I was a kid, and I started writing when I was nineteen or twenty. After college I decided that that's absolutely what I wanted to do." She earned a B.A. in English (1976) from Dartmouth College and later worked in North Dakota conducting poetry workshops through the Poetry in the Schools program. In 1979, she received an M.F.A. degree from Johns Hopkins University's creative writing program. Her literary career began with publication of *Jacklight.*

The poem "Jacklight" opens the book, and this image shines through the text. *Jacklight* refers to the bright light that hunters use illegally to draw deer and other animals from the forest. In the book, it becomes a metaphor for the destructive lure of American culture and its money, alcohol, cars, and emphasis on greed.

In her 1985 essay "Where I Ought to Be," Erdrich emphasized the impact of place in her prose and poetry: "I grew up in a small North Dakota town, on land that once belonged to the Wahpeton-Sisseton Sioux. . . . Our family of nine lived on the very edge of town in a house that belonged to the Government and was rented to employees of the Bureau of Indian Affairs boarding school, where both my parents worked, and where my grandfather, a Turtle Mountain Chippewa named Pat Gourneau, had been educated." Erdrich dedicates the final poem in *Jacklight,* "Turtle Mountain Reservation," to her aged grandfather, whom she frequently visited on that reservation. His twisted hands are useless, but they are her hands as well: "Hands of earth, of this clay / I'm also made from."

"The Strange People" appears in the section of *Jacklight* that Erdrich named "Myths." She alerts us to expect myth and reality in the quotation she takes from the autobiography of Pretty Shield, a Crow medicine woman. It harks back to a primordial time when people and animals could take one another's shapes and spoke the same language. The poem turns on ambiguous reversals. The hunter does not track the antelope doe; she lures him. In this eerie light, who is the hunter and who is the hunted?

The antelope are strange people . . . they are beautiful to look at, and yet they are tricky. We do no trust them. They appear and disappear; they are like shadows on the plains. Because of their great beauty, young men sometimes follow the antelope and are lost forever. Even if those foolish ones find themselves and return, they are never again right in their heads.
       —*Pretty Shield, Medicine Woman of the Crows,*
       transcribed and edited by Frank Linderman (1932)

All night I am the doe,[1] breathing
his name in a frozen field,
the small mist of the word
drifting always before me.

5 And again he has heard it
and I have gone burning
to meet him, the jacklight[2]
fills my eyes with blue fire;
the heart in my chest
10 explodes like a hot stone.

Then slung like a sack
in the back of his pickup,
I wipe the death scum
from my mouth, sit up laughing,
15 and shriek in my speeding grave.

Safely shut in the garage,
when he sharpens his knife
and thinks to have me, like that,
I come toward him,
20 a lean gray witch,
through the bullets that enter and dissolve.

---

[1] *doe:* here, the female antelope.
[2] *jacklight:* a portable oil-burning lantern or electric light used in hunting or fishing at night.

I sit in his house
drinking coffee till dawn,
and leave as frost reddens on hubcaps.
25 crawling back into my shadowy body.
All day, asleep in clean grasses,
I dream of the one who could really wound me.

DISCUSSION QUESTIONS

1. According to the quotation above the poem, what is it about antelopes that makes them strange?
2. Whose name does the doe breathe in the first stanza, and what does "he" do to the doe?
3. Has the doe been killed or has she merely changed shape?
4. Who might the "one" be in the last line?

WRITING TOPICS

1. This mysterious poem is told from the point of view of a female antelope. Try writing a poem or several paragraphs from the point of view of an animal, wild or domestic, and then analyze what this assignment requires of you.

SKUNK DREAMS

Louise Erdrich

A spraying skunk seems an unlikely subject for an essay, even more unlikely as an inspiration for meditation about afterlife. Yet with delicate humor and pungent images, Erdrich easily connects "my skunk" with mortality and immortality. Mingling her dreams with ponderings about skunk dreams, Erdrich demonstrates why critics have praised her as a fine essayist. "Skunk Dreams" was initially published in the *Georgia Review* in 1993 and subsequently collected in *The Blue Jay's Dance* in 1995, her first book of nonfiction.

Erdrich's awareness of death is never far below the surface of her writing. With sardonic humor, she muses that, if she were an animal, she would prefer to be a skunk: "I wouldn't walk so much as putter, destinationless, in a serene belligerence—past hunters, past death overhead, past death all around." In an interview with Nancy and Allan Chavkin (1992), Erdrich admitted, "I don't want to die. . . . I hope I live long enough to cultivate a civilized attitude about the end of things, because I'm very immature, now, about letting go of what I love."

1 When I was fourteen, I slept alone on a North Dakota football field under cold stars on an early September night. Fall progresses swiftly in the Red River Valley, and I happened to hit a night when frost formed in the grass. A skunk trailed a plume of steam across the forty-yard line near moonrise. I tucked the top of my sleeping bag over my head and was just dozing off when the skunk walked onto me with simple authority.

2 Its ripe odor must have dissipated in the heavy summer grass and ditch weeds, because it didn't smell all that bad, or perhaps it was just that I took shallow breaths in numb surprise. I felt him, her, whatever, pause on the side of my hip and turn around twice before evidently deciding I was a good place to sleep. At the back of my knees, on the quilting of my sleeping bag, it trod out a spot for itself and then, with a serene little groan, curled up and

lay perfectly still. That made two of us. I was wildly awake, trying to forget the sharpness and number of skunk teeth, trying not to think of the high percentage of skunks with rabies, or the reason that on camping trips my father always kept a hatchet underneath his pillow.

Inside the bag, I felt as if I might smother. Carefully, making only the slightest of rustles, I drew the bag away from my face and took a deep breath of the night air, enriched with skunk, but clear and watery and cold. It wasn't so bad, and the skunk didn't stir at all, so I watched the moon—caught that night in an envelope of silk, a mist—pass over my sleeping field of teenage guts and glory. The grass harbored a sere dust both old and fresh. I smelled the heat of spent growth beneath the rank tone of my bag-mate—the stiff fragrance of damp earth and the thick pungency of newly manured fields a mile or two away—along with my sleeping bag's smell, slightly mildewed, forever smoky. The skunk settled even closer and began to breathe rapidly; its feet jerked a little like a dog's. I sank against the earth, and fell asleep too.

Of what easily tipped cans, what molten sludge, what dogs in yards on chains, what leftover macaroni casseroles, what cellar holes, crawl spaces, burrows taken from meek woodchucks, of what miracles of garbage did my skunk dream? Or did it, since we can't be sure, dream the plot of *Moby-Dick*, how to properly age Parmesan, or how to restore the brick-walled tumble-down creamery that was its home? We don't know about the dreams of any other biota, and even much about our own. If dreams are an actual dimension, as some assert, then the usual rules of life by which we abide do not apply. In that place, skunks may certainly dream of themselves into the vests of stockbrokers. Perhaps that night the skunk and I dreamed each other's thoughts or are still dreaming them. To paraphrase the problem of the Taoist philosopher Chuang Tzu, I may be a woman who has dreamed herself a skunk, or a skunk still dreaming that she is a woman.

In a book called *Death and Consciousness,* David H. Lund—who wants very much to believe in life after death—describes human dream life as a possible model for a disembodied existence.

"Many of one's dreams," he says, "are such that they involve the activities of an apparently embodied person whom one takes to be oneself as long as one dreams. . . . Whatever is the source of the imagery . . . apparently has the capacity to bring about images of a human body and to impart the feeling that the body is mine. It is, of course, just an image body, but it serves as a perfectly good body for the dream experience. I regard it as mine, I act on the dream environment by means of it, and it constitutes the center of the perceptual world of my dream."

Over the years I have acquired and reshuffled my beliefs and doubts about whether we live on after death—in any shape or form, that is, besides the molecular level at which I am to be absorbed by the taproots of cemetery elms or pines and the tangled mats of fearfully poisoned, too green lawn grass. I want something of the self on whom I have worked so hard to survive the loss of the body (which, incidentally, the self has done a fairly decent job of looking after, excepting spells of too much cabernet and a few idiotic years of rolling my own cigarettes out of Virginia Blond tobacco). I am put out with the marvelous discoveries of the intricate biochemical configuration of our brains, though I realize that the processes themselves are quite miraculous. I understand that I should be self-proud, content to gee-whiz at the fact that I am the world's only mechanism that can admire itself. I should be grateful that life is here today, though gone tomorrow, but I can't help it. I want more.

8   Skunks don't mind each other's vile perfume. Obviously, they find each other more than tolerable. And even I, who have been in the presence of a direct skunk hit, wouldn't classify their weapon as mere smell. It is more on the order of a reality-enhancing experience. It's not so pleasant as standing in a grove of old-growth cedars, or on a lyrical moonshed plain, or watching trout rise to the shadow of your hand on the placid surface of an Alpine lake. When the skunk lets go, you're surrounded by skunk presence: inhabited, owned, involved with something you can only describe as powerfully *there*.

9   I woke at dawn, stunned into that sprayed state of being. The dog that had approached me was rolling in the grass, half addled, sprayed too. My skunk was gone. I abandoned my sleeping bag and started home. Up Eighth Street, past the tiny blue and pink houses, past my grade school, past all the addresses where I baby-sat, I walked in my own strange wind. The streets were wide and empty; I met no one—not a dog, not a squirrel, not even an early robin. Perhaps they had all scattered before me, blocks away. I had gone out to sleep on the football field because I was afflicted with a sadness I had to dramatize. Mood swings had begun, hormones, feverish and raw. They were nothing to me now. My emotions had seemed vast, dark, and sickeningly private. But they were minor, mere wisps, compared to skunk.

DISCUSSION QUESTIONS

1. Erdrich's images of the skunk are humorous and sometimes almost human ("a serene little groan"). Find four images you think are particularly effective.
2. What prompts the author's speculations about dreams, and how does she lead from dreams to speculation about an afterlife?
3. The author says that she is "put out with the marvelous discoveries of the intricate biochemical configuration of our brains." Why is she annoyed with these discoveries?

WRITING TOPICS

1. If you have had an amusing or annoying encounter with a wild creature or pet, write about it in a letter that could be published in a magazine for travelers.
2. Recall a dream you have had and record it in your journal in as much detail as you can, describing colors, if any, where you were, who, if anyone, was with you, and unexpected or unusual events.

MORNING GLORIES AND EASTERN PHOEBES

Louise Erdrich

What kind of title is "Morning Glories and Eastern Phoebes"? In this small essay, Erdrich starts with simple seeds and grows them into vines that define a natural niche, vibrant with the life of four species. She focuses her sharp word-lens on flourishing morning glories, spiders, and phoebes that are companions for her and her baby. Erdrich's motherhood blends with that of nesting birds, hatching eggs, and maturing spiders.

This essay appears in *The Blue Jay's Dance: A Birth Year* (1995), an eclectic collection about the raptures and ruptures that the birth year of her third daughter brings. Erdrich takes the baby with her to the small gray house where she writes each day. Erdrich describes *The Blue Jay's Dance* as "a set of thoughts from one self to the other—writer to parent, artist to mother." She shares insights about bearing, growing, mothering, and at last letting go of an infant. With a large compass, Erdrich moves beyond herself and the child to explore the world. Her writing illustrates the truth she found in that quest about the ties of humans to their earthly mother: "Once we no longer live beneath our mother's heart, it is the earth with which we form the same dependent relationships, relying completely on its cycles and elements, helpless without its protective embrace."

1   Each spring for the past eight years, I've nicked the tough morning glory seeds with a knife and pushed them deep into the soil beside the doorway. Now I know exactly how it will happen, how they will grow. For two months, the shoots will twist and creep, flowing at last up the trellis in tiny bursts, then wild, incredible twisting ropes, until finally in the last weeks of summer they'll blare open. With the sun's passage, we will watch the blossoms rotate wide in the morning and shut at dusk like silken valves. Their color will be celestial, bluer than their namesake heaven.

2   Within and among the flowers, black and yellow Argiope spiders will set

up their webs. They are swift, streamlined, handsome black and yellow with red-orange bands on their legs. Every year they loom four or five webs in the quiet sunstruck windows facing east, right in the middle of the morning glories. The eggs hatched last winter, the young overwintered in their sacs and even now they are dispersing, already in them the knowledge of how male and female will fix and weave their webs together with an unusual seam—a zigzag up the middle, reinforced, as if stitched by a machine.

3   Walking over to my office, I play a cat and mouse game with a pair of eastern phoebes. The two birds nest every year on a crossbar on the small latticed lean-to outside the door. Each morning, I duck in quickly with baby in my arms, and then all day as I work, they work, building their nest with dabs of mud taken from a low, swampy part of the yard or the pond behind the house. As we all work, as the baby naps restlessly, pouring her cries out from time to time, I learn what they can see, what is in their line of vision. Each time I rise I make myself part of something else—the wall, the door brace—and move with slow care.

4   The nest sprouts moss immediately and becomes an emerald cup. The eggs are laid. I can tell because now the female sits as often as she can, her cool gray back smooth above the moss. When she leaves to hunt with the male they perch together on the electrical wire, a graceful duet. They hover and drop on invisible gnats, snatch food from the air, then exhibit the self-satisfied tail bobbing of their species. Discreet birds, I never know it when the eggs do hatch. I can detect no change in his or her behavior.

5   Two weeks pass and I despair. Though watching carefully, I can see no young. I think perhaps blue jays, the huge feral tomcat that haunts this place, or maybe my own disturbances have doomed the clutch of eggs. And so my curiosity at last overcomes me. One afternoon, when she flies off, I step outside my door and tap my finger lightly on the crosspiece of wood below the nest. At once, four heads shoot out of the nest, beaks open, raving for food.

DISCUSSION QUESTIONS

1. What can you infer about the author from reading this essay?
2. Erdrich uses strong verbs in her descriptions. Give examples of at least six that you think are particularly strong.

WRITING TOPICS

1. Write a short description of a plant, animal, or bird that you have observed over a period of time. Concentrate on using strong and varied verbs.
2. Erdrich seems to have written this essay simply to share an experience that she valued. Recall an out-of-doors experience that you have valued and write about it in from three to five paragraphs.
3. Find a copy of *The Blue Jay's Dance* and read more selections. Choose one to write about or illustrate with line drawings or other art work.

SNOW COUNTRY WEAVERS

James Welch

James Welch can be a playful poet. In this taut, twelve-line poem, he blends real and surreal images of the Montana landscape. In the first stanza, the persona tosses a casual message on the wind—to a friend or to the world? On the wing, a real blue-teal duck flies in with whimsical mother-love news. Reality returns in the second stanza with mention of friends. Winter snow brings a somber scene of wolves dying at the door. From teal to wolves to spiders, the imagery becomes entirely surrealistic. Webs bandage the day. Light-hearted absurdity pervades this poem. The persona begins by sending (or only thinking) words. That same persona ends the poem with ambiguous web-held words blowing in the wind.

"Snow Country Weavers" demonstrates Welch's rich, lyrical art. Listen to the sound and sense the poet hones throughout the poem with precisely selected images: weavers, wing, wild, wolves, winter, webs, words, and wind. Wind blows through many poems in *Riding the Earthboy 40,* in which "Snow Country Weavers" appears. Welch knows Blackfeet country in Montana intimately and survives in it. He recognizes that snow-whitened plains and vast emptiness are indifferent to human beings. No humans are visible in "Snow Country Weavers." He has described winter in Browning, Montana, where he grew up as bleak with "the wind blowing down from the Arctic Circle and the people bundled up. . . . Winter certainly in that country is very treacherous. You're always aware of how vulnerable you are during the winter months."

A time to tell you things are well.
Birds flew south a year ago.
One returned, a blue-wing teal
wild with news of his mother's love.

5 Mention me to friends. Say
Wolves are dying at my door,
the winter drives them from their meat.
Say this: say in my mind

I saw your spiders weaving threads
10 to bandage up the day. And more,
those webs were filled with words
that tumbled meaning into wind.

DISCUSSION QUESTIONS

1. How does the speaker seem to feel about the person to whom the poem is addressed?
2. In your opinion, whose words does the speaker imagine filled the spiders' webs?
3. After discussing surrealistic imagery in this poem, bring to class some song lyrics you like that also have surrealistic imagery. Read them aloud to your classmates and invite them to comment on images they like or dislike.

WRITING TOPICS

1. In a paragraph, speculate about the speaker's circumstances—whether the speaker lives alone, why he mentions the wolves, and why he uses the word *bandage* in line 10.
2. Select a music video that uses surrealistic visual imagery and write a paragraph describing how the imagery supports or detracts from the song lyrics.

FIVE ROUNDS

Lorenzo Baca

Lorenzo Baca is Isleta Pueblo and Mescalero Apache. He was born in Arizona and educated in New Mexico and California. He earned an M.A. degree in Indian Studies from the University of California at Los Angeles. Baca is not only a writer but also an actor and visual artist who does fine art, sculpture, video, and storytelling. His concrete poem appears in *Neon Powwow, New Native American Voices of the Southwest* (1993).

SPRING IS THE TIME OF THE SUN WHEN ALL EARTH MAKES LIFE

SUMMER AFTERNOONS BRING PRAYERS FOR RAIN ON

THE LOVE FOR PEACE IS

DISCUSSION QUESTIONS

1. Has the poet chosen an appropriate form for his statements in your opinion? Explain.
2. What makes these circular bits of language a poem?

WRITING TOPICS

1. Compose your own concrete poems, using any shape you wish, and try to express the interrelatedness of all things in the natural world.

FROM *SOLAR STORMS*

Linda Hogan

Linda Hogan has garnered many distinguished awards, including a National Endowment for the Arts grant in fiction in 1986 and a Guggenheim for fiction in 1990. Her first novel, *Mean Spirit,* was a finalist for a Pulitzer Prize. Critics, teachers, and students have praised her second novel, *Solar Storms,* which focuses on the story of five generations of Native American women in the Boundary Waters between Canada and Minnesota. The novel blends finely honed language, intriguing characters, and remarkable imagery.

A volunteer in wildlife rehabilitation, Hogan envisions the role of women as caretakers of the planet. As bearers of life, women have a special responsibility to take spiritual and political action in their role as custodians. In an introduction to a collection of writings on women's spiritual development, Hogan makes her views explicit: "Earth consciousness is the foundation of women's growing, and it is an honor for us to give back to the earth, to care for animals, plants, people, minerals, to fight with all our will, politics, and the many forms of education we have earned in order to preserve life inside and outside ourselves." In keeping with this philosophy, all the women in *Solar Storms* care for others and the earth and, in doing so, enrich their own lives.

Angel Jensen, the central character and teenage narrator, undertakes a long quest for spiritual purpose in her life. Abused and relinquished by her mother as a child, Angel has shuffled among foster homes. As a rebellious high school drop-out and literally scarred teenager, Angel begins a search for her birth family, her mother, and her inner self. Leaving her foster home in Oklahoma and returning to Adam's Rib, the remote Minnesota village where she was born, Angel meets the brittle cold landscape where her ancestors have endured nature's dangers and hostile invaders. Here she reunites with Dora-Rouge, her great-great-grandmother; Agnes, her great-grandmother; and Bush, the woman who adopted Angel's mother and cared for Angel as a child.

Angel accompanies these woman on a spiritual and physical

journey to their ancestral homeland in the Far North. There, a hydro-electric project is being constructed that will destroy not only the natural beauty but much of the animal and plant life. After reaching this destination, they become entangled in a conflict that threatens two indigenous Indian tribes and their ties to the land. Angel's very essence is endangered as she tries to resolve her inner turmoil over who she is and where she belongs. *Solar Storms,* a story of love and family, is a parable of the Native American quest to preserve a way of life.

In this excerpt from the novel, the women "read" ancient wisdom in the "storied land" of their journey. As they maneuver the canoe through watery pathways, Angel learns lessons taught by the older women and discovers her destiny as one who knows and uses plants for healing. Dora-Rouge encourages Angel to embrace being a dreamer of plants. Bush frees her confined spirit that has been wounded by past wrongs. Agnes remembers a bear she once saved from cruel men and recalls how, after the bear's death, his coat warmed and protected her. With growing insight, Angel says, "We were full and powerful, wearing the face of the world."

1   As we traveled, we entered time and began to trouble it, to pester it apart or into some kind of change. On the short nights we sat by firelight and looked at the moon's long face on water. Dora-Rouge would lie on the beaver blankets and tell us what place we would pass on the next day. She'd look at the stars in the shortening night and say, "the Meeting Place," or "God Island." True to her word, the next day we reached those places.

2   God Island, according to Bush's maps, was now named Smith's Island. It had been an old settlement. We paddled toward it in silence, slowing ourselves as we neared land, drifting toward it. There was s sense of mystery about it. A few tall, moss-covered stone walls remained half-standing at one end of the large island, like a crumbled fortress. A sense of richness dwelled on this island, as if it were inhabited by people to this day unseen but present all the same.

3   A very tall man had gone there in search of copper mines, Dora-Rouge told us. He was part of a tribe from the east, but had become lost, and instead of the copper, he found this island inhabited by small women and only a few short men. Instead of continuing his search for the island of red silver, he remained. Eventually he took several wives, women who bore taller children, all of them beautiful and copper brown. Whenever strangers came, they thought the people were so beautiful and straight they looked like gods.

4   "God Island," said Dora-Rough. "It's an appropriate name. The people there feared no evil and wanted not," she said. "Look, it still has the trees."

5   It was true, there were ancient trees in the center that looked as if they belonged in a southern swamp. They were something like cypress.

6   Even from a distance the island had a feeling of intimacy. It was open and inviting. I thought maybe that was why the tall man had stayed. Or perhaps it was the word "God" that was inviting to me, a word I thought I knew too much about. The one who had tortured Job, who had Abraham lift the ax to his son, who, disguised as a whale, had swallowed Jonah.

7   I know now that the name does not refer to any deity, but means simply to call out and pray, to summon. To use words and sing, to speak. And call out that island did. I heard the sound of this strong land. It was so lovely that, skeptical or not, I wanted to stay there for the night.

8   "No. We should move on," Bush said, even though the island seemed to plead with us to remain. "All the campsites are taken."

9   When I looked back, I agreed with her. Something lived there, something I didn't understand, but would always remember by feel, and when I felt it, I would call it God and that was how I came later to understand that God was everything beneath my feet, everything surrounded by water; it was in the air, and there was no such thing as empty space.

10   Now, looking back, I understand how easily we lost track of things. The time we'd been teasing apart, unraveled. And now it began to unravel us as we entered a kind of timelessness. Wednesday was the last day we called by name, and truly, we no longer needed time. We were lost from it, and lost in this way, I came alive. It was as if I'd slept for years, and was now awake. The others felt it, too. Cell by cell, all of us were taken in by water and by land, swallowed a little at a time. What we'd thought of as our lives and being on earth was gone, and now the world was made up of pathways of its own invention. We were only one of the many dreams of earth. And I knew we were just a small dream.

11   But there was a place inside the human that spoke with land, that entered dreaming, in the way that people in the north found direction in their dreams. They dreamed charts of land and currents of water. They dreamed where food animals lived. These dreams they called hunger maps and when they followed those maps, they found their prey. It was the language animals and humans had in common. People found their cures in the same way.

12   "No one understands this anymore. Once they dreamed lynx and beaver," Agnes said. "It used to be that you could even strike a bargain with the weather."

13   For my own part in this dreaming, as soon as I left time, when Thursday and Friday slipped away, plants began to cross my restless sleep in abundance. A tendril reached through darkness, a first sharp leaf came up from the rich ground of my sleeping, opened upward from the place in my body that knew absolute truth. It wasn't a seed that had been planted there, not a cultivated growing, but a wild one, one that had been there all along, wait-

ing. I saw vines creeping forward. Inside the thin lid of an eye, petals opened, and there was pollen at the center of each flower. Field, forest, swamp. I knew how they breathed at night, and that they were linked to us in that breath. It was the oldest bond of survival. I was devoted to woods the wind walked through, to mosses and lichens. Somewhere in my past, I had lost the knowing of this opening light of life, the taking up of minerals from dark ground, the magnitude of thickets and brush. Now I found it once again. Sleep changed me. I remembered things I'd forgotten, how a hundred years ago, leaves reached toward sunlight, plants bent into currents of water. Something persistent nudged me and it had morning rain on its leaves.

14 Maybe the roots of dreaming are in the soil of dailiness, or in the heart, or in another place without words, but when they come together and grow, they are like the seeds of hydrogen and the seeds of oxygen that together create ocean, lake, and ice. In this way, the plants and I joined each other. They entangled me in their stems and vines and it was a beautiful entanglement.

15 "I knew there'd be another plant dreamer in my family someday," Dora-Rouge said. Her mother, Ek, had been an herb woman. I got it from blood, she said. I came by it legitimately.

16 "Can you draw them?" she asked.

17 We searched the packs for a pencil. But we had forgotten a pencil, along with all the other things we'd left behind: combs, pencils, paper, keys.

18 Bush lit a match, blew it out, and handed it to me. "Here. Try this."

19 I laughed. If the world came to an end, I wanted to be with Bush. She could make do with anything. "What a good idea," I said. I appreciated her. Bush could find water in a desert, food on an iceberg. She knew the way around troubles. These waters were the only things that muddled her.

20 She tore open a brown bag, flattened it out, and laid it before me, almost reverent, a map awaiting creation.

21 I drew carefully, but after a while, the smudges vanished into the paper, so I merely began to remember the plants inside myself and describe them to Dora-Rouge. "This one is the color of sage," I would say, closing my eyes, seeing it. "It opens like a circle. It grows between rocks."

22 "That's an akitsi plant," said Dora-Rouge. "It's good for headaches."

23 Some mornings as we packed our things, set out across water, the world was the color of copper, a flood of sun arrived from the east, and a thick mist rose up from black earth. Other mornings, heating water over the fire, we'd see the world covered with fog, and the birdsongs sounded forlorn and far away. There were days when we traveled as many as thirty miles. Others we traveled no more than ten. There were times when I resented the work, and days I worked so hard even Agnes' liniment and aspirin would not relax my aching shoulders and I would crave ice, even a single chip of it, cold and

shining. On other days I felt a deep contentment as I poled inside shallow currents or glided across a new wide lake.

24   We were in the hands of nature. In these places things turned about and were other than what they seemed. In silence, I pulled through the water and saw how a river appeared through rolling fog and emptied into the lake. One day, a full-tailed fox moved inside the shadows of trees, then stepped into a cloud. New senses came to me. I was equal to the other animals, hearing as they heard, moving as they moved, seeing as they saw.

25   One night we stayed on an island close to the decaying, moss-covered pieces of a boat. Its remains looked like the ribs of a large animal. In the morning, sun was a dim light reaching down through the branches of trees. Pollen floated across the dark water and gathered, yellow and life-giving, along the place where water met land.

26   One day we came to a long swamp that neither Bush nor Dora-Rouge could identify. Agnes looked at us with her arms across her chest. Bush furrowed her brow and looked around as if a clue to our location could be fathomed by the shapes of trees or the sounds of birds. She took out her maps and looked at the lay of the land, trying to decipher any familiar shape. Dora-Rouge rested her scrawny back against a bedroll. "Well, we've passed God Island and the ribs of that boat. We must be at . . ." But just then, before she finished speaking, Bush once more unfolded the map and held it open, and as she did, the creases split, the map came apart, and parts of it fell from her hands.

27   Dora-Rouge laughed. "Throw it away."

28   But even after that, useless as it was, there were many evenings Bush would look at a piece of the map, hold it up in the light and stare.

29   I never understood why she placed so much faith in paper when she trusted nothing else about the world that had created those maps. She wanted to know where she was at any given time, as if not knowing would change everything, should say there was such a thing as being lost. Whenever frogs in the swamp ahead of us began to sing, she fretted. "There's no swamp on any of the maps, not here, anyway," she'd say. Or when we crossed a stream, "I wonder if this is Willow Creek."

30   From the west, soft clouds floated over. We set up camp. I placed stones in a circle and built a fire, then walked across the rocky island and entered the cold water. For a while I floated and dog-paddled and looked at the land on which we were camped. There was smoke from our campfire. It was a place of mosses, lichens, and calm water. From the water I saw Agnes off by herself, singing, walking toward a group of trees.

31   I was swimming stronger than ever. The water was cold and it was sharp against my skin, as if it had blades or edges. But I swam. My arms were lean and newly muscled. I moved through water easily. Then, refreshed, I dried myself, pulled on my jeans and sweater, and went about the job of gather-

ing more wood. We had worked out our routines by now. We had our roles. Wood gathering was one of mine. And fire building. Bush and I set up tents, unrolled sleeping bags. Agnes cooked.

32   Soon we had boiling water and black coffee, and I saw Bush walk toward us with two large fish on a stringer.

33   I teased her. She was a dreamer of walleyes, I told her.

34   Agnes looked at Bush, looked at the two fish, and said, "Where's yours and Angel's?"

35   One evening it seemed cooler. The air had a different feel, rarefied, clean, and thin. Wolves in the distance were singing and their voices made a sound that seemed to lie upon the land, like a cloud covering the world from one edge of the horizon to the other. We sat around the fire and listened, the light on our faces, our eyes soft. Agnes warmed her hands over the flames.

36   There was a shorter time of darkness every night, but how beautiful the brief nights, with the stars and the wolves.

37   The next day, as if we'd become too complacent, a dark cloud of mosquitoes rose up from swamps and marshes. It was late for them, Bush said. Up to now, we'd just been lucky. She reached to the bottom of the clothing pack and took out four white cloth hats and shook them until the brims opened. I laughed but I was grateful she'd brought them. "Where in the world did you get those?" I asked. They looked vaguely like safari hats. Bush was too busy searching among the clothing for veils to answer me.

38   Within a few moments we looked like brides on safari. The insects landed on the netting, attracted by our warm breath. Already the droning of them made me anxious. I was grateful Bush had remembered the nets. We had to cover our hands, as well. The high noise of the mosquitoes, as they came near me, tightened my stomach. I waved them away, but more of them seemed to slip around behind any movement I made.

39   "Don't bother to fight them," Dora-Rouge said. "It only wastes your energy." Then she said, "I don't know what I had in mind. We should have been drinking swamp tea."

40   Yes, I remembered the tea. People in the north had used it for centuries as tonic, as repellent.

41   "We forgot it," Agnes said, but she did not say that Bush, in her zeal to keep our packs light, had probably left it out.

42   Bush set to work making a larger fire, a smudge, and we put green wood on it, grass, and leaves until smoke was all around us.

43   "We need to get the tea leaves," said Dora-Rouge, coughing.

44   My eyes watered.

45   But even if we found swamp tea that day, it had to build up; it would be a few days before enough tea was in our blood to keep the insects away. In the meantime, the insects tortured me the most, flying toward me with an electric sound, finding the places I'd neglected to cover: the hole in my

jeans, the gap between neck and shirt collar. Pant-leg openings. "It's because you eat too much sugar," Agnes said.

46   Later, I heard stories, accounts of caribou and men killed by mosquitoes, almost bloodless or drowned as they submerged themselves to get away from the tiny swarming insects.

47   At darkness, when the mosquitoes abated for a time, Bush went out to gather stalks and leaves of the tea. She was careful in the canoe as she paddled toward the swampy regions where both mosquitoes and swamp tea grew, taking with her a light that would, unfortunately, also wake many of the insects prematurely.

48   I saw her move across the lake, the water silver and heavy as mercury.

49   Mosquitoes are one of the oldest forms of life. They were already there when the first people lit their fires of smoke. That's what Dora-Rouge said. Their ancestors heard the songs of my ancestors, she said, and they were there when the French passed through the broken land singing love songs and ballads of sorrow. They were there when the fur traders paddled swiftly through rivers, up and down, searching for furs and for the dark men who would offer them for trade. The mosquitoes remembered all the letting of blood. They remembered the animals sinking down into earth.

50   Sometimes I thought I could hear these things myself, the lonely, sad songs coming through trees and up from the banks of their destruction. Always, behind those songs, I heard our own deep-pitched songs that were the songs of land speaking through its keepers. Sometimes, too, I heard the old ones in the songs of wolves. It made me think we were undoing the routes of explorers, taking apart the advance of commerce, narrowing down and distilling the truth out of history.

51   We were still and let smoke curl around our bodies. The next day I resorted, finally, to wearing mud in order to protect my too-sweet skin, and to draw the sting from the bites. In what we thought of as evening, the mosquitoes and swarms of black flies were a shadow, a dark cloud, clinging to the tents. I was ashamed to be so afraid of them, more afraid of them than of bears or wolves, or even wolverines. But one evening we looked at each other, our veils covered with alive, dark mosquitoes, mud on our faces, gloves on our hands, and I started laughing. It was contagious, the laughter. Agnes said, "It's not funny," but even she laughed.

52   On our journey, Bush opened like the lilies that flowered on some of our islands, at first tentative and delicate and finally with resolve. It was as if she had needed this place and all the water, to sing in, room to hold out her hands. Water and sky were windows she peered through to something beyond this world. Or perhaps they were mirrors in which she saw herself, her skin, her hands, her thighs, all brand-new. She was as uncontained as she had previously been contained by skin, house, island, and water, Now it seemed there were no borders. In shadows and in deep woods, she vanished, or she danced a slow dance, or she talked to the land. Some nights I sat

beside the fire and saw her against the deepening sky, walking toward us, or sitting on a rock, or moving into the woods, stealthy as an animal. Time dropped away from her. Her eyes softened. She might have been thinking of the things she had been dealt in her life: the betrayals, the unhealable wounds made by Hannah, the loss of me, the solitudes she had needed and thrived on.

53   At times, too, I heard Agnes singing, talking the old language, mumbling inside a tent.

54   Agnes remembered the bear more strongly now and, even without her coat, she talked with it. Dora-Rouge sang low songs that sounded like wind. She read things in the moving of waters; she saw what couldn't be seen by us as the land and soundless mists passed by.

55   As for me, I was awake in time that was measured from before axes, before traps, flint, and carpenter's nails. It was this gap in time we entered, and it was a place between worlds. I was under the spell of wilderness, close to what no one had ever been able to call by name. Everything merged and united. There were no sharp distinctions left between darkness and light. Water and air became the same thing, as did water and land in the marshy broth of creation. Inside the clear water we passed over, rocks looked only a few inches away. Birds swam across lakes. It was all one thing. The canoes were our bodies, our skin. We passed through green leaves, wild rice, and rushes. In small lakes, dense with lily pads, tiny frogs leaped from leaves into the water as we passed.

56   Sometimes I felt there were eyes around us, peering through trees and fog. Maybe it was the eyes of land and creatures regarding us, taking our measure. And listening to the night, I knew there was another horizon, beyond the one we could see. And all of it was storied land, land where deities walked, where people traveled, desiring to be one with infinite space.

DISCUSSION QUESTIONS

1. There is much mention of dreaming in this excerpt. What can you tell about Native American beliefs from these passages?
2. Hogan uses various figures of speech: similes, metaphors, and personification. Find some of these and comment on their effectiveness.
3. In paragraph 55, the narrator says that they entered a "gap in time . . . a place between two worlds." Explain what she means.
4. What about Linda Hogan's writing would make you want to read the novel *Solar Storms,* from which this excerpt is taken?

WRITING TOPICS

1. If you could be in a setting other than the one you are now in, where would you choose to be and why? Would you choose a place you already know or a place you have never been? Consider these questions in an essay.
2. Write a critical essay on Hogan's four women characters. Some topics you may consider are their ages, unique abilities, environmental values, and relationships to one another.
3. Angel narrates the selection from a limited first-person point of view. In a brief essay, discuss what this technique allows you to learn about Angel and what you do not learn.
4. Hogan controls the setting with images of waterways, islands, and plants. Select three places in the setting and discuss them in a three-paragraph essay. Use specific images to support your discussion.

SONG OF THE SKY LOOM

Brian Swann

The oral literatures of numerous Native American groups pair the earth with the sky. Frequently they are addressed as "mother" and "father" to express a family connection among parts of the visible universe. Many of those oral literatures pay homage to these elements. Few can equal, however, this Tewa chanted prayer in its striking imagery, which illuminates the major metaphor.

Pueblo country on the Colorado Plateau is semi-arid; grass is seldom green. Pueblo people invest many resources and much personal effort in rituals, or dance-drama prayers, for precipitation. When enough rain falls to green up the wild grasses growing on the watershed, water flows in the irrigation ditches for the crops central to Pueblo life for centuries. During the hot summer growing season, maize, bean, squash, pumpkin, and other plants require frequent irrigation to grow and mature ears, pods, and fruits for harvesting.

Herbert J. Spinden, archaeologist, first collected this and other Tewa song/poems from 1909 to 1912. The songs were written down in native texts and then translated into English. The songs may reach back to the times when the Puebloans were cliff dwellers. Ceremonial life always included songs and dances that were part of longer dramatic rituals.

Brian Swann created a new version based on Spinden's selection. It appears in *Wearing the Morning Star, Native American Song-Poems* (1996). Swann is professor of English at the Cooper Union in New York City and series editor of *The Smithsonian Series of Studies in Native American Literatures*. He has edited several collections of Native American literatures, including *Coming to Light: Contemporary Translations of the Native Literatures of North America* (1995); *Song of the Sky: Versions of Native American Song-Poems* (1995); *Smoothing the Ground: Essays on Native American Oral Literature* (1982); and *On the Translation of Native American Literature* (1992).

Mother Earth   Father Sky
                    we are your children

            With tired backs we bring you gifts you love

            Then weave for us a garment of brightness,
5   its warp the white light of morning,
                weft the red light of evening,
                fringes the falling rain,
                its border the standing rainbow.

            Thus weave for us a garment of brightness
10   so we may walk fittingly where birds sing,
            so we may walk fittingly where grass is green.

Mother Earth   Father Sky

DISCUSSION QUESTIONS

1. How is the shape of the song appropriate?
2. The Tewa Pueblos are located in New Mexico. What things mentioned in the song might be particularly important to people of the Southwest?

WRITING TOPICS

1. In one or two paragraphs, analyze the structure of this song and explain the images.

SUMMARY WRITING TOPICS

1. Write your impressions of the word *remembered* as it is used in the title of this chapter.
2. In an essay, discuss how the excerpt from *Solar Storms* helps to explain the ideas in "We Are the Land."
3. In a small group, discuss how Anglo-American ideas about the earth and its animals and plants may differ from and be similar to the Native American ideas expressed in this chapter. Write a summary report of your discussion that gives at least two differences and two similarities.
4. What would it take for you to feel at one with the earth? Explain in an essay.
5. Reread the three Welch poems in this anthology: "Plea to Those Who Matter," "The Man from Washington," and "Snow Country Weavers." Write a critical essay in which you discuss Welch's use of surrealistic imagery in these poems.
6. Assume you are the judge of a poetry contest that awards first prize to the poet with the most effective imagery. Hogan, Erdrich, Blue Cloud, and Silko have entered poems included in this chapter. Write a letter to one of the authors explaining why you selected his or her poem for first prize. Cite particular images in your letter.
7. Imagine you are the editor for a revised edition of this chapter. Write a persuasive memo to your publisher explaining why you wish to eliminate one selection from the new edition. Also present your choice for one selection that is your first priority for the new book.

CHAPTER FIVE

ALL MY RELATIONS

Through most of human history, people have lived in families of one kind or another. Native American families historically formed the social bulwark that enabled members to survive the vicissitudes of warfare, defeat and conquest, forced emigration, and other trials and tribulations. Virtually every Native American lived firmly imbedded in his or her network of relatives. Some Native American families met the many challenges of the long interethnic encounter better than others.

In this chapter, Native American authors explore many dimensions of family life. The elder Chona, a Tohono O'odham (Papago), repeats her father's predawn admonitions to his children dating to the time when hostile raiders struck their settlements. She describes a family pattern circa 1850. About a hundred years later, Simon Ortiz, Southwestern Pueblo poet, recalls gentle moments of learning from his father to preserve all forms of life, even voracious field mice that might grow up to pillage the maize crop they were planting. In "Remember," Creek poet Joy Harjo combines typically Native American concerns over the natural environment and one's family, especially involving mother and child. Cherokee author Betty Bell relates in sometimes clinical prose how a mother and daughter who clash may reconcile only when one lies near death. Luci Tapahonso creates a tender scene between mother and daughter in "They Were Alone in Winter." Tapahonso's family portrait in "It Was a Special Treat" depicts her Navajo family with warmth and harmony. Self-confident Tapahonso evokes the pleasure of rural folks going to town. In "Lullaby," Leslie Silko spins the story of persisting love between an elderly Navajo couple caught in winter's brutal, deadly blizzard. In contrast to Tapahonso's real family, this fictional one has been fragmented by outside forces it cannot control.

Coping with mixed family heritages is a prevailing theme in several selections. Who defines a person's identity? Hopi author Wendy Rose describes modern "Neon Scars" inflicted on her by parents from very different ethnic groups. As a Canadian, Maria Campbell writes about her Métis family from the perspective of inner and outer conflicts. The youthful Campbell resolved to walk the streets of the nearest town with her head held high, regardless of the verbal insults townspeople hurled at her as a half-breed. At the heart of Campbell's survival is her great-grandmother Cheechum. For N. Scott Momaday, his grandmother Aho is the most important figure that links him to his Kiowa heritage. Momaday wraps his mourning for her death around a memorial to a Kiowa way of life that ended a few years before Aho's birth.

The deaths of huge numbers of Native Americans stricken by Old World diseases during the Columbian Exchange disrupted many historic families. Those deaths and disruptions made adoption of children by survivors of epidemics frequent and necessary for tribal survival. In the contemporary world, the irresponsibility of some Native American parents keeps adoption a fundamental Native American strategy. Probably no author has written more poignantly about the love between adoptive parents and children than Modoc Michael Dorris. His fundamental message is that parental love, however tender and attentive, cannot alter the harsh physiological realities of fetal alcohol syndrome for its victims. An Abnaki-Slovak poet, Joseph Bruchac, focuses on Ellis Island, the famous U.S. government entry point for millions of late-nineteenth century European immigrants. Then he reveals his divided family loyalties because immigrants invaded his Native American forebears' lands. Bruchac brings home the fact that the continent was not a "vast empty place," as has been claimed since the time of the Pilgrims. For thousands of years, Native American families lived on the land, and these authors are well aware of that ancestral legacy.

MY FATHER'S SONG

Simon Ortiz

Simon Ortiz, Acoma Pueblo poet, wrote his first poem in the fifth grade as a Mother's Day gift. In the seventh grade, he left Acoma to attend St. Catherine's Indian School in Santa Fe. He recalls keeping a secret journal, "Being away from home, family, clan, community, life is very tenuous. . . . You're scared and you're lonely and you're homesick, and so writing is a way to reassure yourself. That was part of it, how I came to be a writer." Continuing his studies at various institutions, Ortiz received an M.A. from the University of Iowa in 1969. From this beginning, Ortiz matured into a talented author of more than a dozen books of poetry, short fiction, and essays. Among them are *A Good Journey* (1977); *Fight Back: For the Sake of the People, for the Sake of the Land* (1980); *Fightin': New and Collected Stories* (1983); and *Woven Stone* (1991). "My Father's Song" appeared in *Going for the Rain* (1976). *From Sand Creek* won the 1981 Pushcart Prize for poetry. In 1993, the Returning the Gift Festival of Native American writers honored Ortiz with a Lifetime Achievement Award.

Born in Albuquerque in 1941, Simon Ortiz grew up in the small Acoma community of McCartys, New Mexico, sixty miles west of Albuquerque. Acoma Pueblo, the oldest continuously inhabited settlement in North America, sits atop a great mesa. There the Acoma people have lived, prayed for rain, and told stories for at least a thousand years, and Ortiz carries on this tradition. In writing, he centers himself in a line of generations with his children and grandchildren at one end and his parents at the other. His mother, Mamie Ortiz, was a member of the Eagle clan. His father, Joe Ortiz, an elder member of the Antelope clan, was keeper of Acoma religious knowledge, history, and stories. He was also a stone mason who enjoyed repairing "stone woven together" in a four-hundred-year-old wall. Jobs in the community were scarce, and the senior Ortiz often left home for railroad work or other employment. Nevertheless, he instilled in his son a love for language, song, and oral stories.

Music made an important impression on the young, developing author. Ortiz remembers his mother singing traditional songs and

Latin chants that fascinated him. In a beautiful voice, his father sang songs in the Acoma, English, Spanish, and Zuni languages; songs he composed are still performed at the Pueblo. Young Ortiz became inspired to write song lyrics and is a renowned singer and teller of stories. Ortiz recognizes that his poetry and prose will always come from Acoma stories because "they aren't just stories; they are the truth which opens our eyes, mind, souls to the world in which we live."

Wanting to say things,
I miss my father tonight.
His voice, the slight catch,
the depth from his thin chest,
5 the tremble of emotion
in something he has just said
to his son, his song:

We planted corn one Spring at Acu—
we planted several times
10 but this one particular time
I remember the soft damp sand
in my hand.

My father had stopped at one point
to show me an overturned furrow;
15 the plowshare had unearthed
the burrow nest of a mouse
in the soft moist sand.

Very gently, he scooped the tiny pink animals
into the palm of his hand
20 and told me to touch them.
We took them to the edge
of the field and put them in the shade
of a sand moist clod.

I remember the very softness
25 of cool and warm sand and tiny alive mice
and my father saying things.

DISCUSSION QUESTIONS

1. What sort of relationship did the speaker seem to have with his father?
2. What has prompted the writing of the poem?
3. The speaker wants "to say things," in the first line, and the poem ends with "my father saying things." What do you think are some words the father might have said to his son?

WRITING TOPICS

1. In lines 6–7, the speaker implies that what his father has said is "his song" and therefore an important part of the father's being or, perhaps, an expression of what he stood for. Recall a time when one of your parents clearly expressed what he or she stood for. What effect did this have on you? Write about this occasion in your journal, in a poem, or in an essay.
2. The speaker has kept his father's memory alive by writing about him. In a poem or in song lyrics, tell how you would like to be remembered.
3. Research Acoma Pueblo and write a report citing information from your notes.

REMEMBER

Joy Harjo

With a vibrant voice, Joy Harjo seems to chant words onto the page. She achieves this lyrical quality through repetition, an approach that echoes tribal songs and ceremonies. Creek scholar C. B. Clark notes that "A cadence marks her work that is reminiscent of the repetitions of the Indian ceremonial drum." Strongly influenced by Creek Stomp Dance songs, jazz, and blues, this unique tribal singer/poet creates new medleys. Harjo emphasizes that her frequent use of repetition is more than a mere literary device: "For me it is a way of speaking that can, if used effectively, make the poem lift off the page and enter into the listener much like a song or a chant." Ceremonial use of repetition in telling stories and in oratory creates "a litany, and gives you a way to enter into what is being said, and a way to emerge whole, but changed." The poet has stated that she wrote "Remember" out of a definite acknowledgment of ceremony.

One of the most important poets in contemporary American litera- ture, Harjo has published six volumes of poetry. All of them reflect her Muskogee Creek heritage, feminist and social issues, and her talents in music, painting, and filmmaking. All her works embrace Native American myths, symbols, and values. Her books include *What Moon Drove Me to This?* (1979); *She Had Some Horses* (1983); *In Mad Love and War* (1990); and *The Woman Who Fell from the Sky* (1992). She edited *Reinventing the Enemy's Language: Contemporary Native Women's Writing of North America* (1997). *In Mad Love and War* won the William Carlos Williams Award from the Poetry Society of America and the Delmore Schwartz Memorial Prize from New York University.

Harjo completed a B.A. in English at the University of New Mexico in 1976 and an M.F.A in creative writing at the University of Iowa in 1978. She has taught at several institutions, including the Universities of Colorado, New Mexico, and Arizona. She received the American Indian Distinguished Achievement Award in 1990 for her writing.

Remember the sky that you were born under,
know each of the star's stories.
Remember the moon, know who she is. I met her
in a bar once in Iowa City.
5   Remember the sun's birth at dawn, that is the
strongest point of time. Remember sundown
and the giving away to night.
Remember your birth, how your mother struggled
to give you form and breath. You are evidence of
10   her life, and her mother's, and hers.
Remember your father. He is your life, also.
Remember the earth whose skin you are:
red earth, black earth, yellow earth, white earth
brown earth, we are earth.
15   Remember the plants, trees, animal life who all have their
tribes, their families, their histories, too. Talk to them,
listen to them. They are alive poems.
Remember the wind. Remember her voice. She knows the
origin of this universe. I heard her singing Kiowa war
20   dance songs at the corner of Fourth and Central once.
Remember that you are all people and that all people
are you.
Remember that you are this universe and that this
universe is you.
25   Remember that all is in motion, is growing, is you.
Remember that language comes from this.
Remember the dance that language is, that life is.
Remember.

DISCUSSION QUESTIONS

1. To whom is the poem addressed, in your opinion?
2. Trace the order of the images in the poem. Is there a pattern, or are the images placed in random order? Support your answer.

WRITING TOPICS

1. Lines 21 and 22 contain a concept that is difficult for many individuals (and nations) to accept. What do these lines mean to you? Is the statement in these lines true, in your opinion, or is it just wishful or poetic thinking? Express your thoughts about these lines in an essay.

2. In line 14, the speaker says "we are earth." Think about this statement and, in a journal entry, reflect on how this could be true.

3. Read the poem aloud, using your voice as an instrument to "color" the repetition. Does the repetition dull or enhance the impact of the poem for you? In a paragraph, state your view and then use examples from the poem to develop it.

THE POWER OF LOVE
AND
A SECOND ADOPTION

Michael Dorris

Award-winning anthropologist, novelist, and nonfiction writer, Michael Dorris focused on family relationships, tribal identities, and Native American history. Born in 1945, Dorris had Irish, French, and Modoc ancestry and was reared in Louisville, Kentucky, and in Washington, Idaho, and Montana. He graduated Phi Beta Kappa with a B.A. from Georgetown University in English and the classics and received an M.Phil. from Yale. From 1972 to 1988, Dorris taught Native American studies and anthropology at Dartmouth College.

Among his impressive works are *Native Americans: Five Hundred Years After* (1975); *A Yellow Raft in Blue Water* (1987); *Rooms in the House of Stone* (1993); *Paper Trail* (1994); and *Cloud Chamber* (1997). Dorris was recognized with numerous honors and awards including a Guggenheim Fellowship in 1978; Woodrow Wilson Faculty Development Fellowships in 1971 and 1980; a Rockefeller Foundation Research Fellowship and an Indian Achievement Award in 1985; and a National Endowment for the Arts grant in 1989.

"The Power of Love" depicts one scene in the unfolding drama that followed Dorris's adoption of a three-year-old Sioux child, whom he named Reynold Abel. In 1971, as a young, unmarried man, Dorris was confident he had the support and ability to begin his own family: "Single-parenthood had, for generations, been the practical norm in my family. My grandfathers and father had all died young, leaving widows to raise children alone. . . . My role models were strong, capable mothers, aunts, and grandmothers, and I saw no compelling reasons not to continue the tradition. . . .Why couldn't a child come for me before a wife?" Dorris later adopted two more Sioux children; "A Second Adoption" tells the tense and tender story of Sava's adoption.

Unknown to his new, optimistic father, Abel suffered from fetal alcohol syndrome (FAS). His brain had been permanently damaged before he was born because his mother consumed alcohol. Mystified and at times terrified by his son's affliction, Dorris fervently sought professional explanations for Abel's severe learning problems, seizures, and dysfunctional actions. Life with Abel was an emotional roller coaster, ranging from his harmless, humorous errors to potentially fatal mistakes. For ten years, Dorris denied the severity of his son's mental and physical disabilities, "I convinced myself that nurture, a stimulating environment, and love could open up life to my little boy. It wasn't true."

After almost two decades of denial, despair, hope, and confusion, Dorris decided to document Abel's life in *The Broken Cord,* a compelling chronicle of the heartbreak and boundless love that engulfed the Dorris family as they coped with daily challenges. Although the story centers on Abel, the book is also the story of thousands of FAS victims. Dorris emphasizes that the consequences of FAS are not limited to its victims: "It's not just a woman's issue, not just a man's. No one is exempted. These are everybody's children." Both of the other adopted children also suffer from fetal alcohol poisoning, but their damage is less severe than Abel's was. *The Broken Cord* was named the Best Nonfiction Book of 1989 by the National Book Critics Circle and was made into an ABC television movie in 1992.

THE POWER OF LOVE

At different stages of our lives, the symptoms of love may vary—dependence, attraction, contentment, worry, loyalty, grief—but at heart, the source is always the same. Human beings occasionally have, among our multiple amazing talents, the capacity to, against every odd and despite any pull otherwise, connect with each other. Like functional crafts that dock in deep space, we blindly reach, touch, and, if we're fortunate, form synapses through which air and light and communication rush. We hurtle, bonded by blood or desire, into the question of "what next?"—our discrete futures temporarily one, our pasts conjoined in unlikely, fragile alliance. Love transforms: it simultaneously makes us larger and limits our possibilities. It changes our history even as it breaks a new path through the present. It may, through accident or inattention, through expediency or necessity, cease, but once in place it can never afterward not have been. Once we love, we are permanently in that love's thrall, caught in its wake, a part of its flow.

2   On the first year's anniversary of our oldest son's death, I collected the dense cube of his ashes at the funeral home where they had resided during our mourning. It was a quiet, overcast September day. Fall was coming, and the grass along the familiar road from Hanover to Cornish had mostly gone to yellow seed.

3   Twelve months before, Abel had as usual risen from his single bed, shaved badly, dressed in a favorite Garfield T-shirt, and eventually made his way to the truck stop where he worked. At twenty-three, he had recently survived a rough transition in his life: two experimental brain surgeries that had at first partially and then ultimately completely separated the left and right hemispheres of his brain so that when he experienced a seizure on one side the other might remain alert. For him, the worst element of each hospital stay—the most dreaded and worried-over procedure—was the implantation of an IV, but for the rest of us who realized the risks, the dangers were far more drastic. Our son could lose memory, the use of limbs, continence, mobility.

4   Since Abel was over eighteen and legally an adult, albeit mentally handicapped as a result of fetal alcohol syndrome, the question of consent had necessitated that my wife and I appear in court to argue that his operations were vital. His seizures had become so frequent and severe, whether due to the natural evolution of his condition or to his chronic failure to remember his various required daily medications, that the chance of his collapse in a hazardous context was increasingly likely. Our petition to act, in this limited capacity, as his legal guardians was granted by the judge, and a week later he underwent the first surgery. It didn't solve the problems.

5   On the morning of the second and more radical operation, a few months later, I picked up Abel at his apartment at dawn and drove him to the hospital. He seemed sluggish from too little sleep, confused and resentful at the idea, I assumed, of having to go through many more weeks of confinement and rehabilitation. At least, I consoled myself, he doesn't completely comprehend what's happening to him. At least his limited imagination doesn't stretch to include the concept of mortality. And then, stopped at a traffic light, I glanced at his face. On his beautifully sculpted cheeks, illuminated by the red glow, there were tears. I had mistaken his silence for fog when, in fact, it was the purest bravery.

6   I was always either over- or underestimating Abel—expecting too much or settling for too little. I had fluctuated for the twenty years since his adoption between the extreme of disappointment and surprise. On the one hand, he possessed traits so rare as to be remarkable: utter loyalty, complete good will, the impulse for wholehearted forgiveness. And yet, on the other, he could often be maddening in his incapacities for sustained motivation, curiosity, and spontaneous intellectual growth. He absorbed without critical thought the dumbest stereotypes and attitudes, the most teeth-grinding vocabulary and obsessions. He stubbornly believed in things that weren't real even as he scoffed in superior doubt at facts that indisputably were. He didn't dream. He didn't complain. He didn't aspire. He didn't despair.

7   Especially during Abel's childhood, before the full magnitude of his learning block was undeniable, I indulged in the persistent fantasy of his brain as a kind of messy room. If I could somehow get inside his head, sweep out the cobwebs, straighten up the clutter, open the windows, organize the files, turn on the lights, suddenly he would become normal. But whether I tapped on it gently, banged at it with a ram, clawed at it with my fingernails, the door stayed firmly, mutely locked. Finally I gave up, let Abel rest. For me, it was defeat. For him, I'm sure it was a great relief.

8   When at last I accepted that I could not affect my by now grown son's life, I elected, instead, to document it. If he could not contribute to society by his actions, then, I reasoned, let him act as example, as a flesh and blood object lesson against the dangers of drinking alcohol during pregnancy. Abel was passively agreeable to this idea, just as he would have been if I had proposed we move to Mars, eat only peanut butter, or go live in a cave.

9   And so together, Abel, Louise,[1] and I wrote *The Broken Cord*. It was published, won a literary prize, and was optioned for a network film. And on the day I arrived in Hollywood to discuss its production with famous actors and directors, I received word that Abel was in critical condition, the victim of a driver who hadn't seen him as he crossed a street at night.

10   After flying the red-eye back to New Hampshire I arrived at his bedside to find him unconscious and bandaged. He had broken bones, a collapsed lung, and unknown internal injuries. Machines assisted his breathing, monitored his pulse, drained his fluids, maintained his temperature. He had suffered no pain, the intensive care doctors promised. Any awareness he might have had after being struck would have been cushioned by shock. He might have heard the trucks on the highway, seen the moon above where he lay, but his mind would have been calm, stunned, almost blank.

11   It was not hard to talk to Abel, even though I didn't know if he could hear me. I had put words in his mouth so often over the years that the process came naturally. I supplied the questions, and I provided the right answers. I knew the skeptical tone his voice would take, the way his mouth would pull down at the ends in a desultory grin. "Here I am," he would half-confess, half-joke. "What a mess, Dad."

12   In the two weeks before Abel's body finally wore out and stopped living, I had many such one-way conversations. I kept apologizing for my constant failures of kindness or understanding, and he, as he surely would have done, kept forgiving me. I kept exhorting him to get better, he kept promising to try his best. He kept slipping away, I kept refusing to let him go. And then he died.

13   Losing a child is an unimaginably painful experience, a moment that calls for privacy and quiet, and yet, through our book, Abel's life had become

---

[1] *Louise:* the author's wife, Louise Erdrich.

something of a public cause. His death was reported in *People* and *Time,* and we received many letters of condolence from strangers as well as from friends. We required time for our grief, time to heal, to accept, and so as a family we followed a tribal tradition and waited for a full year before conducting a memorial service.

14   At last—too soon and not soon enough, as such events inevitably turn out to be—the day arrived. Only seven people were present: Louise and I, three of our daughters, Abel's primary doctor and his wife. We had chosen a spot Abel loved, a little knoll above our pond, and Louise had selected a strong young maple tree to plant as his marker. After the simple ceremony, we stood by the tree in silence for a long time, each reading in the movement of its leaves a different memory. We burned cedar, fanned the smoke upon each other and upon the tree in blessing, and finally each of us in turn, using words Abel would have understood, quietly said good-bye.

15   Because of who our son was, how he was, our sorrow got mixed with humor, for no one could tell a story about Abel that didn't, in one way or another, have a funny twist, a non sequitur, a punch line. He took nothing very seriously, except love—from which he was not for an instant of his existence divided by doubt or meanness of spirit. Spontaneous and direct, love was his true power, the reaction he inspired in others, and love, for those who knew him or read about him or benefited—without ever realizing the source—from the essence of life, is his legacy.

A SECOND ADOPTION

1   There is one feature of single parenthood that any man or woman solely responsible for a young child knows, no matter how the arrangement evolved: dating is next to impossible. By the time a baby-sitter is found, picked up, given instructions, checked upon by telephone, driven home, and paid, your partner for the evening had better have been True Love. If not, you wonder: was it worth it? Furthermore, you become a kind of package deal: like me, like my child. Or forget it.

2   In 1974, with a demanding job, a six-year-old adopted son with special needs, and no fiancée on the horizon, I realized the time had come to recontact my adoption agency. If I was going to spend the next twelve or thirteen years of my life unpartnered—a distinct possibility—I wanted to do so with a larger family.

3   Denis Daigle, Abel's caseworker, was not encouraging. There were so many couples waiting for placements, he said, that it was unlikely that any agency would approve a second child for a single male, especially since this time I requested an infant or toddler. He would submit the paperwork, but I should not count on anything, not get my hopes up.

4   Okay, I promised, and pasted yellow wallpaper with a small green-and-red teddy bear design in the spare bedroom of our house. I watched yard sales for cribs and bassinets, and found a used rocking horse in mint condi-

tion. I put my name on the waiting list for a child-care center and arranged for a lighter teaching load.

5   When Denis called, his voice incredulous, I was ready.

6   "You won't believe it," he said. "There's a little Lakota boy, just over a year old, who's available. They've approved your application."

7   "When does it happen?" I felt the stirrings of the male analog for labor.

8   "He's in South Dakota."

9   I did some geographic calculations. "I'm presenting a paper at a one-day conference in Omaha next Tuesday," I said.

10   "Could you be in Pierre on Wednesday?"

11   *Could* I? I had already chosen his name, Sava, after a Native Alaskan friend who had taken me on as a salmon fishing partner for two summers while I was doing anthropological fieldwork.

12   On Tuesday afternoon the Nebraska weather turned nasty, grounding all planes, so I rented a car, called the caseworker in South Dakota to tell her the name of my motel in Pierre, and drove all night. I checked into my room exhausted, unbathed, and bleary-eyed at 9 A.M., but before I had a chance to unpack my suitcase there was a knock on the door. I opened it to a smiling young blond woman bundled in a green parka.

13   "Hi, I'm Jeanine from SDDSS," she announced. "Are you all set to meet your son?"

14   "Can you wait a few minutes? I want to take a shower, change my clothes, maybe pick up a present for him somewhere."

15   An uneasy expression crossed her face.

16   "Not a good idea?" I asked.

17   "Well . . . *actually* he's waiting in my car right now." Jeanine glanced to her left and, following her look, I saw in the backseat a baby carrier and the top of a purple knitted cap. I didn't want to give the impression of the slightest hesitation, so I said, "Great! Bring him right in."

18   The instant she turned her back I dashed to the bathroom, splashed water on my face, and dabbed some aftershave on my neck. First impressions are imporant and at least I could smell good.

19   When I emerged, Jeanine was standing in the room holding a solid-looking baby whose dark, intelligent eyes regarded me with raw suspicion.

20   "He's very friendly," Jeanine assured me. "He's been so anxious to meet you."

21   I held out my arms, savoring the tender moment of first encounter. He was no lightweight. I cradled him in my arms and lowered my face close to his to get a good look. "Hello Sava," I whispered.

22   His eyes widened, then closed tightly. Simultaneously his jaws opened and opened and opened, revealing a space more like the Grand Canyon than a mouth. I felt him draw a long breath into his lungs, and when he released it in a howl, my mind pictured a cartoon image of pure sound, strong as a hurricane, blowing everything—furniture, hair, trees—in its wake.

23   Jeanine made a step toward us, but I shook my head and spoke more confidently than I felt.

24   "Give us an hour or so." I nodded encouragingly to underscore my words, and she reluctantly departed.

25   Sava's yells did not abate but he didn't struggle as I sat down on the bed, jiggled him on my lap. He was not in the slightest afraid but was simply registering a protest, a critique of my grinning face. I unsnapped his coat, removed it, spoke softly in what I hoped was a comforting tone, and after a few long minutes he opened one eye and gave me a second appraisal.

26   He was a beauty: feathery straight black hair, a sensuous mouth, a strong, broad nose, a clean, sweeping jaw. His torso was wide and his hands were square-shaped with thick, tapering fingers. He opened the other eye and, as abruptly as he had begun to cry, he stopped. We stared at each other, amazed in the sudden silence.

27   "Hello, Sava," I tried again. This time, speculatively, he only blinked.

28   Late the next day we boarded a plane to New Hampshire. By then, I knew Sava's favorite food—mashed green beans mixed with cream of mushroom soup and canned fried onions sprinkled on top—and that he hated to have his hair washed. I knew he was a sound sleeper, that he had a long attention span, and that he was ticklish just below his rib cage on his right side. I knew that he and Abel were profoundly different in their personalities—Abel would leap headfirst into any strange lake, while Sava would always test the water—but I trusted that they would be compatible brothers. And I knew all over again, as if for the first time in human history, the experience of becoming a parent. Within twenty-four hours of meeting my son, I had already forgotten what it felt like not to be his father.

DISCUSSION QUESTIONS

1. What is the connection between paragraph 1 of "The Power of Love" and the rest of the essay?
2. Explain what the author means by the statement "Love . . . simultaneously makes us larger and limits our possibilities." How did this apply to the author's relationship with Abel?
3. Explain the author's metaphor in paragraph 7 of "The Power of Love."
4. How does the author redirect his efforts after he accepts that he cannot affect his son's life?
5. What was Abel's legacy?

6. The author develops his paragraphs with specific details. Select one paragraph from "The Power of Love" or "A Second Adoption" and discuss three specific details that you think make the paragraph interesting.

WRITING TOPICS

1. With a partner, outline and write a research report on fetal alcohol syndrome.
2. Many people have learning disabilities, which are caused by a variety of factors. What qualities and education are necessary for someone who plans a career working with learning disabled people? Express your thoughts in an essay. Begin with a strong topic sentence. You may need to do some research before beginning to write.
3. In a brief essay, analyze the organization of Dorris's essay.

HALFBREED

Maria Campbell

Maria Campbell is a playwright, scriptwriter, editor, and essayist. She is best known for her autobiography *Halfbreed,* which relates her trials and triumphs as a Métis woman in Canadian society. Born in 1940 in northern Saskatchewan, Campbell is of Scots, Indian, and French descent and is the eldest daughter of a family of seven children. She credits her mother with instilling in her a love for books and authors, including Dickens, Longfellow, and Shakespeare. As a child, Campbell played Julius Caesar, wrapped in a long sheet with a willow branch on her head. She recalls that white neighbors shook their heads and laughed when they saw the Campbell children's improvisations: "I guess it was funny—Caesar, Rome and Cleopatra among Halfbreeds in the backwoods of northern Saskatchewan."

Growing up in western Canada, Campbell also survived poverty and prejudice. In the U.S. and Canada, the term *Métis* defines a person of mixed ancestry, usually Indian and French. The Canadian government has refused to recognize the Métis as having special legal status, but the Métis have continued to fight for legal recognition in order to secure land and citizen rights. Their struggle generates both the frustration and motivation for Campbell, who describes her identity crisis in *Halfbreed.* Identifying herself as Indian, or half-breed, exposed her to discrimination. Rejecting the stereotypical label, however, meant turning her back on the love of her family and her cultural traditions. Campbell began writing *Halfbreed* in an attempt to deal with anger, frustration, and loneliness: "I had no money, and I was on the verge of being kicked out of my house, had no food. . . . I started writing a letter to myself because I had to have somebody to talk to, and there was nobody to talk to. And that was how I wrote *Halfbreed.*" A best-seller in Canada, the book is considered a sociological landmark as well as a poignant historical account. Critics have praised its humor, its documentation of Métis rituals, and its loving portrait of the author's great-grandmother Cheechum. This wise Cree woman, who lived to be 104, gave her great-granddaughter strength and hope and taught her to shed prejudice while holding her head high. Cheechum's death in 1966 convinced Campbell that she must become a strong model for future generations.

◎

1 I was born during a spring blizzard in April of 1940. Grannie Campbell, who had come to help my mother, made Dad stay outside the tent, and he chopped wood until his arms ached. At last I arrived, a daughter, much to Dad's disappointment. However this didn't dampen his desire to raise the best trapper and hunter in Saskatchewan. As far back as I can remember Daddy taught me to set traps, shoot a rifle, and fight like a boy. Mom did her best to turn me into a lady, showing me how to cook, sew, and knit, while Cheechum, my best friend and confidante, tried to teach me all she knew about living.

2 I should tell you about our home now before I go any further. We lived in a large two-roomed hewed log house that stood out from the others because it was too big to be called a shack. One room was used for sleeping and all of us children shared it with our parents. There were three big beds made from poles with rawhide interlacing. The mattresses were canvas bags filled with fresh hay twice a year. Over my parents' bed was a hammock where you could always find a baby. An air-tight heater warmed the room in winter. Our clothes hung from pegs or were folded and put on a row of shelves. There were braided rugs on the floor, and in one corner a special sleeping rug where Cheechum slept when she stayed with us, as she refused to sleep on a bed or eat off a table.

3 I loved that corner of the house and would find any excuse possible to sleep with her. There was a special smell that comforted me when I was hurt or afraid. Also, it was a great place to find all sorts of wonderful things that Cheechum had—little pouches, boxes, and cloth tied up containing pieces of bright cloth, beads, leather, jewelry, roots and herbs, candy, and whatever else a little girl's heart could desire.

4 The kitchen and living room were combined into one of the most beautiful rooms I have ever known. Our kitchen had a huge black wood stove for cooking and for heating the house. On the wall hung pots, pans, and various roots and herbs used for cooking and making medicine. There was a large table, two chairs, and two benches made from wide planks, which we scrubbed with homemade lye soap after each meal. On one wall were shelves for our good dishes and a cupboard for storing everyday tin plates, cups, and food.

5 The living-room area had a homemade chesterfield[1] and a chair of carved wood and woven rawhide, a couple of rocking chairs painted red, and an old

---

[1] *chesterfield:* a davenport or sofa.

steamer trunk by the east window. The floor was made of wide planks which were scoured to an even whiteness all over. We made braided rugs during the winter months from old rags, although it often took us a full year to gather enough for even a small rug.

6 There were open beams on the ceiling and under these ran four long poles the length of the house. The poles served as racks where furs were hung to dry in winter. On a cold winter night the smell of moose stew simmering on the stove blended with the wild smell of the drying skins of mink, weasels and squirrels, and the spicy herbs and roots hanging from the walls. Daddy would be busy in the corner, brushing fur until it shone and glistened, while Mom bustled around the stove. Cheechum would be on the floor smoking her clay pipe and the small ones would roll and fight around her like puppies. I can see it all so vividly it seems only yesterday.

7 Our parents spent a great deal of time with us, and not just our parents but the other parents in our settlement. They taught us to dance and to make music on the guitars and fiddles. They played cards with us, they would take us on long walks and teach us how to use the different herbs, roots and barks. We were taught to weave baskets from the red willow, and while we did these things together we were told the stories of our people— who they were, where they came from, and what they had done. Many were legends handed down from father to son. Many of them had a lesson but mostly they were fun stories about funny people.

8 My Cheechum believed with heart and soul in the little people. She said they are so tiny that unless you are really looking for them, you will never find them; not that it matters, because you usually only see them when they want you to.

9 The little people live near the water and they travel mostly by leaf boats. They are a happy lot and also very shy. Cheechum saw them once when she was a young woman. She had gone to the river for water in the late afternoon and decided to sit and watch the sun go down. It was very quiet and even the birds were still. Then she heard a sound like many people laughing and talking at a party. The sounds kept coming closer and finally she saw a large leaf floating to shore with other leaves following behind. Standing on the leaves were tiny people dressed in beautiful colours.

10 They waved to her and smiled as they came ashore. They told her that they were going to rest for the evening, then leave early in the morning to go further downstream. They sat with her until the sun had gone down and then said good-bye and disappeared into the forest. She never saw them again, but all her life she would leave small pieces of food and tobacco near the water's edge for them, which were always gone by morning. Mom said it was only a fairy tale but I would lie by the waters for hours hoping to see the little people.

11 Cheechum had the gift of second sight, although she refused to forecast anything for anyone. Once in a while if someone had lost something she would tell them where to find it and she was always right. But it was something over which she had no control.

12   Once, when we were all planting potatoes and she and I were cutting out the eyes, she stopped in the middle of a sentence and said, "Go get your father. Tell him your uncle is dead." I ran for Dad, and I can remember word for word what she told him. "Malcolm shot himself. He is lying at the bottom of the footpath behind your mother's house. I'll prepare the others. Go!" (Malcolm was Dad's brother-in-law.) Dad took off, with me right behind him. When we reached Grannie Campbell's no one was home. While Dad went to the door I sped down the footpath. Just as Cheechum had said, my uncle's body was lying there just as if he was sleeping.

13   Another time, late at night, Cheechum got up and told Dad that an aunt of ours was very sick and that he should go for Grannie Campbell as there was no time to waste. They arrived a few minutes before the aunt died.

14   She often had this kind of foresight and would tell Mom and Dad days before someone died or something happened. I wanted to be able to see things as she did, but she would reply that it was a sad thing to know that people who are close to you are going to die or have bad fortune—and be unable to do anything to help them because it is their destiny. I am sure that she could see what was in store for me but because she believed life had to take its course she could only try to make me strong enough to get through my difficulties. . . .

15   Summer was always a great time because during those months Dad was home from trapping and could spend most of his time with us. In early June Mom would bake and pack food in the grub box while he would grease the wagon wheels and fit the harness. Then we would leave our house early in the morning and head for the bush to pick seneca root and berries. Our parents sat on the front seat of the wagon, Cheechum and Grannie Campbell and the littlest ones in the middle, Jamie, Robbie and I on top of the grub box, tent, or tailgate. Our four or five dogs and two goats ran behind and away we went.

16   By dinner-time three or four wagons of Halfbreeds had joined us along the way and everyone was talking and yelling and joking, excited at seeing one another and at the prospects of what lay ahead. By the time we pitched our tents for the night there were ten or more families in a long caravan. What a sight we must have been, each family with one or two grannies, grandpas, anywhere from six to fifteen children, four or five dogs, and horses trimmed with bells!

17   The evenings were great. The women cooked while the men pitched the tents and we kids ran about, shouting and fighting, tripping over dogs that barked and circled around us. Parents called to each other and slapped at their young ones, but only halfheartedly, because they too were enjoying themselves. We all sat down to supper outside and ate moose meat, ducks, or whatever the men had killed that day, bannock baked on hot coals, with lard and tea, and all the boiled berries we could eat.

18   Afterwards we helped to clean up and for the rest of the daylight hours the men would wrestle, twist wrists, have target practice or play cards. Someone always had a fiddle and guitar and there was dancing and singing and visiting. We kids played bears and *witecoos* (a white monster who eats children at night)

until it was too dark and we were called in to bed. Inside the tent were our blankets all spread on fragrant spruce boughs, freshly cut. A coal-oil lamp on the grub box gave some light. When we were put to bed the grown-ups would gather outside and an old grandpa or grannie would tell a story while someone built up the fire. Soon everyone was taking turns telling stories, and one by one we would creep out to sit in the background and listen. . . .

19   Some nights there was lots of excitement, like the time a bear crawled into John McAdams' tent and stepped on his wife! She shrieked and her children started screaming and they woke everyone in camp. The bear in his fright stood up and knocked the tent pole and the tent came tumbling down. All the men were trying to get the tent up, McAdams were crawling out from all over, and the poor bear was trapped and growling with rage. Dogs were going crazy and everyone was yelling and talking at once. Needless to say everything was restored to order and we had bear "burgers" for dinner the next day. "Burger" is the right description because the bear was completely chopped up with axes, those being the handiest weapons for the men.

20   We worked like beavers during the daytime. Grown-ups would compete to see whose family picked the most roots or berries and parents would drive the children like slaves, yelling insults to each other all the while. Come supper-time and everyone would gather around while the old people weighed it all to see who had picked the most.

21   We had bad times during those trips too. For as much as we all looked forward to going to town, we knew our fathers would get drunk. The day would come when we had enough seneca roots and berries to sell, so we would all get bathed, load the wagons, and go. The townspeople would stand on the sidewalks and hurl insults at us. Some would say, "Halfbreeds are in town, hide your valuables." If we walked into stores the white women and their children would leave and the storekeepers' wives, sons, and daughters would watch that we didn't steal anything. I noticed a change in my parent's and other adults' attitudes. They were happy and proud until we drove into town, then everyone became quiet and looked different. The men walked in front, looking straight ahead, their wives behind, and, I can never forget this, they had their heads down and never looked up. We kids trailed behind with our grannies in much the same manner.

22   When I first noticed this, I asked Momma why we had to walk as though we had done something bad and she answered, "Never mind, you'll understand when you're older." But I made up my mind then and there that I would never walk like them; I would walk tall and straight and I told my brothers and sisters to do the same. Cheechum heard me, and laying her hand on my head she said, "Never forget that, my girl. You always walk with your head up and if anyone says something then put out your chin and hold it higher."

DISCUSSION QUESTIONS

1. Which of the following does Campbell use in her descriptions: active verbs, strong modifiers, sensory imagery, figurative language? Cite examples.
2. Many people talk and write about family values today. What values can you infer were present in the author's family?
3. What things marred the author's childhood?
4. What is the most important thing you learned from this essay?

WRITING TOPICS

1. In a paragraph or two, describe the author's attitudes toward her childhood. Is she bitter, sentimental, nostalgic, matter-of-fact, puzzled, something else? Support your answers with statements from the author's text.
2. Campbell begins her autobiographical essay with the date and circumstances of her birth. In an autobiographical essay of your own, start with the date and circumstances of your birth and continue with memories of your early childhood, including your physical surroundings.

"INTRODUCTION" FROM
THE WAY TO RAINY MOUNTAIN

N. Scott Momaday

For more than a generation, N. Scott Momaday has been a seminal figure in American literature. His reputation was launched by two remarkable books, a novel, *House Made of Dawn* (1968), and a cultural memoir, *The Way to Rainy Mountain* (1969). Momaday has identified *The Way to Rainy Mountain* as his favorite among his works. His preference seems natural because the slim volume is not only a literary masterpiece but also a testament of his tribal heritage. In lyrical prose, he interweaves three motifs of myth, history, and family stories. He unites this triad by using the structural device of the journey: the historical journey of the Kiowas in the 1700s, his own journey quest in the 1960s, and finally the reader's journey through his words.

The "Introduction" centers on Momaday's grandmother Aho, who dramatically links him to his Kiowa heritage and to the Kiowa golden age. Her unity with the land, her life as journey maker and storyteller, and her role as bearer of tribal images, especially Rainy Mountain, the stars, Tai-me and the Sun Dance, all tie lives and events together. When Aho died, her grandson visited her grave at Rainy Mountain, a sacred place for the Kiowas. There he began a quest for his identity and tells us there are on the way to Rainy Mountain "many journeys in one." One journey began when the Kiowas left their home near the headwaters of the Yellowstone River and migrated east to the Black Hills and down to the Wichita Mountains. Momaday describes their journey as "an evocation of a landscape that is incomparable, a time that is gone forever, and the human spirit, which endures." Along the way, the Kiowas paused in awe at Devil's Tower. They created a story about the seven sisters, their brother, and the origin of this sacred place. Two centuries later, one of their descendants who was named for Tsoai would immortalize their journey and stories in *The Way to Rainy Mountain*. Aho told her grandson how the Kiowas acquired "kinsmen in the night sky" and became related to the stars.

The Kiowas also had a mystical reverence for the Sun, which they expressed in the Sun Dance and Tai-me, the sacred symbol of the Sun. In their calendars, each annual Sun Dance was recorded with radiant images of the summer Sun Dance lodge. During long winter nights, Kiowa calendar-keepers brought out the calendar and told stories of Kiowa history in the circle about the tipi fire. The people living in small, independent bands the rest of the year came together during the Sun Dance time to renew friendships, arrange marriages, trade property, and recite stories. Held when the bison were fat, the ceremony was preceded by a hunt in order to feed the people and to provide the bison skin and head to be honored on the central pole in the Sun Dance lodge. By the summer of 1890, the calendar image "Sun Dance When the Forked Poles Were Left Standing" tells of an Indian agent calling U.S. troops to disband the Kiowas as they were preparing for the ceremony.

Stories lived after the Kiowas reached the Wichita Mountains, and they still tell stories in Rainy Mountain country. In 1923, Big Tree, keeper of a calendar, said of the old ones: "They carried dreams in their voices. . . . They told us the old stories/And they sang the spirit songs."

1   A single knoll rises out of the plain in Oklahoma, north and west of the Wichita Range. For my people, the Kiowas, it is an old landmark, and they gave it the name Rainy Mountain. The hardest weather in the world is there. Winter brings blizzards, hot tornadic winds arise in the spring, and in summer the prairie is an anvil's edge. The grass turns brittle and brown, and it cracks beneath your feet. There are green belts along the rivers and creeks, linear groves of hickory and pecan, willow and witch hazel. At a distance in July or August the steaming foliage seems almost to writhe in fire. Great green and yellow grasshoppers are everywhere in the tall grass, popping up like corn to sting the flesh, and tortoises crawl about on the red earth, going nowhere in the plenty of time. Loneliness is an aspect of the land. All things in the plain are isolate; there is no confusion of objects in the eye, but *one* hill or *one* tree or *one* man. To look upon that landscape in the early morning, with the sun at your back, is to lose the sense of proportion. Your imagination comes to life, and this, you think, is where Creation was begun.

2   I returned to Rainy Mountain in July. My grandmother had died in the spring, and I wanted to be at her grave. She had lived to be very old and at last infirm. Her only living daughter was with her when she died, and I was told that in death her face was that of a child.

3   I like to think of her as a child. When she was born, the Kiowas were living the last great moment of their history. For more than a hundred years

they had controlled the open range from the Smoky Hill River to the Red, from the headwaters of the Canadian to the fork of the Arkansas and Cimarron. In alliance with the Comanches, they had ruled the whole of the southern Plains. War was their sacred business, and they were among the finest horsemen the world has ever known. But warfare for the Kiowas was preeminently a matter of disposition rather than of survival, and they never understood the grim, unrelenting advance of the U.S. Cavalry. When at last, divided and ill-provisioned, they were driven onto the Staked Plains in the cold rains of autumn, they fell into panic. In Palo Duro Canyon they abandoned their crucial stores to pillage and had nothing then but their lives. In order to save themselves, they surrendered to the soldiers at Fort Sill and were imprisoned in the old stone corral that now stands as a military museum. My grandmother was spared the humiliation of those high gray walls by eight or ten years, but she must have known from birth the affliction of defeat, the dark brooding of old warriors.

4   Her name was Aho, and she belonged to the last culture to evolve in North America. Her forebears came down from the high country in western Montana nearly three centuries ago. They were a mountain people, a mysterious tribe of hunters whose language has never been positively classified in any major group. In the late seventeenth century they began a long migration to the south and east. It was a journey toward the dawn, and it led to a golden age. Along the way the Kiowas were befriended by the Crows, who gave them the culture and religion of the Plains. They acquired horses, and their ancient nomadic spirit was suddenly free of the ground. They acquired Tai-me, the sacred Sun Dance doll, from that moment the object and symbol of their worship, and so shared in the divinity of the sun. Not least, they acquired the sense of destiny, therefore courage and pride. When they entered upon the southern Plains they had been transformed. No longer were they slaves to the simple necessity of survival; they were a lordly and dangerous society of fighters and thieves, hunters and priests of the sun. According to their origin myth, they entered the world through a hollow log. From one point of view, their migration was the fruit of an old prophecy, for indeed they emerged from a sunless world.

5   Although my grandmother lived out her long life in the shadow of Rainy Mountain, the immense landscape of the continental interior lay like memory in her blood. She could tell of the Crows, whom she had never seen, and of the Black Hills, where she had never been. I wanted to see in reality what she had seen more perfectly in the mind's eye, and traveled fifteen hundred miles to begin my pilgrimage

6   Yellowstone, it seemed to me, was the top of the world, a region of deep lakes and dark timber, canyons and waterfalls. But, beautiful as it is, one might have the sense of confinement there. The skyline in all directions is close at hand, the high wall of the woods and deep cleavages of shade. There is a perfect freedom in the mountains, but it belongs to the eagle and the

elk, the badger and the bear. The Kiowas reckoned their stature by the distance they could see, and they were bent and blind in the wilderness.

7   Descending eastward, the highland meadows are a stairway to the plain. In July the inland slope of the Rockies is luxuriant with flax and buckwheat, stonecrop and larkspur. The earth unfolds and the limit of the land recedes. Clusters of trees, and animals grazing far in the distance, cause the vision to reach away and wonder to build upon the mind. The sun follows a longer course in the day, and the sky is immense beyond all comparison. The great billowing clouds that sail upon it are shadows that move upon the grain like water, dividing light. Farther down, in the land of the Crows and Blackfeet, the plain is yellow. Sweet clover takes hold of the hills and bends upon itself to cover and seal the soil. There the Kiowas paused on their way; they had come to the place where they must change their lives. The sun is at home on the plains. Precisely there does it have the certain character of a god. When the Kiowas came to the land of the Crows, they could see the dark lees of the hills at dawn across the Bighorn River, the profusion of light on the grain shelves, the oldest deity ranging after the solstices. Not yet would they veer southward to the caldron of the land that lay below; they must wean their blood from the northern winter and hold the mountains a while longer in their view. They bore Tai-me in procession to the east.

8   A dark mist lay over the Black Hills, and the land was like iron. At the top of a ridge I caught sight of Devil's Tower upthrust against the gray sky as if in the birth of time the core of the earth had broken through its crust and the motion of the world was begun. There are things in nature that engender an awful quiet in the heart of man; Devil's Tower is one of them. Two centuries ago, because they could not do otherwise, the Kiowas made a legend at the base of the rock. My grandmother said:

> *Eight children were there at play, seven sisters and their brother. Suddenly the boy was struck dumb; he trembled and began to run upon his hands and feet. His fingers became claws, and his body was covered with fur. Directly there was a bear where the boy had been. The sisters were terrified; they ran, and the bear after them. They came to the stump of a great tree, and the tree spoke to them. It bade them climb upon it, and as they did so it began to rise into the air. The bear came to kill them, but they were just beyond its reach. It reared against the tree and scored the bark all around with its claws. The seen sisters were borne into the sky, and they became the stars of the Big Dipper.*

From that moment, and so long as the legend lives, the Kiowas have kinsmen in the night sky. Whatever they were in the mountains, they could be no more. However tenuous their well-being, however much they had suffered and would suffer again, they had found a way out of the wilderness.

9   My grandmother had a reverence for the sun, a holy regard that now is all but gone out of mankind. There was a wariness in her, and an ancient awe. She was a Christian in her later years, but she had come a long way about, and she never forgot her birthright. As a child she had been to the Sun Dances; she had taken part in those annual rites, and by them she had learned the restoration of her people in the presence of Tai-me. She was about seven when the last Kiowa Sun Dance was held in 1887 on the Washita River above Rainy Mountain Creek. The buffalo were gone. In order to consummate the ancient sacrifice—to impale the head of a buffalo bull upon the medicine tree—a delegation of old men journeyed into Texas, there to beg and barter for an animal from the Goodnight herd. She was ten when the Kiowas came together for the last time as a living Sun Dance culture. They could find no buffalo; they had to hang an old hide from the sacred tree. Before the dance could begin, a company of soldiers rode out from Fort Sill under orders to disperse the tribe. Forbidden without cause the essential act of their faith, having seen the wild herds slaughtered and left to rot upon the ground, the Kiowas backed away forever from the medicine tree. That was July 20, 1890, at the great bend of the Washita. My grandmother was there. Without bitterness, and for as long as she lived, she bore a vision of deicide.[1]

10   Now that I can have her only in memory, I see my grandmother in the several postures that were peculiar to her: standing at the wood stove on a winter morning and turning meat in a great iron skillet; sitting at the south window, bent above her beadwork, and afterwards, when her vision failed, looking down for a long time into the fold of her hands; going out upon a cane, very slowly as she did when the weight of age came upon her; praying. I remember her most often at prayer. She made long, rambling prayers out of suffering and hope, having seen many things. I was never sure that I had the right to hear, so exclusive were they of all mere custom and company. The last time I saw her she prayed standing by the side of her bed at night, naked to the waist, the light of a kerosene lamp moving upon her dark skin. Her long, black hair, always drawn and braided in the day, lay upon her shoulders and against her breasts like a shawl. I do not speak Kiowa, and I never understood her prayers, but there was something inherently sad in the sound, some merest hesitation upon the syllables of sorrow. She began in a high and descending pitch, exhausting her breath to silence; then again and again—and always the same intensity of effort, of something that is, and is not, like urgency in the human voice. Transported so in the dancing light among the shadows of her room, she seemed beyond the reach of time. But that was illusion; I think I knew then that I should not see her again.

11   Houses are like sentinels in the plain, old keepers of the weather watch. There, in a very little while, wood takes on the appearance of great age. All

---

[1] *deicide:* the act of killing a divine being or a symbol of that being.

colors wear soon away in the wind and rain, and then the wood is burned gray and the grain appears and the nails turn red with rust. The window-panes are black and opaque; you imagine there is nothing within, and indeed there are many ghosts, bones given up to the land. They stand here and there against the sky, and you approach them for a longer time than you expect. They belong in the distance; it is their domain.

12   Once there was a lot of sound in my grandmother's house, a lot of coming and going, feasting and talk. The summers there were full of excitement and reunion. The Kiowas are a summer people; they abide the cold and keep to themselves, but when the season turns and the land becomes warm and vital they cannot hold still; an old love of going returns upon them. The aged visitors who came to my grandmother's house when I was a child were made of lean and leather, and they bore themselves upright. They wore great black hats and bright ample shirts that shook in the wind. They rubbed fat upon their hair and wound their braids with strips of colored cloth. Some of them painted their faces and carried the scars of old and cherished enmities. They were an old council of warlords, come to remind and be reminded of who they were. Their wives and daughters served them well. The women might indulge themselves; gossip was at once the mark and compensation of their servitude. They made loud and elaborate talk among themselves, full of jest and gesture, fright and false alarm. They went abroad in fringed and flowered shawls, bright beadwork and German silver. They were at home in the kitchen, and they prepared meals that were banquets.

13   There were frequent prayer meetings, and great nocturnal feasts. When I was a child I played with my cousins outside, where the lamplight fell upon the ground and the singing of the old people rose up around us and carried away into the darkness. There were a lot of good things to eat, a lot of laughter and surprise. And afterwards, when the quiet returned, I lay down with my grandmother and could hear the frogs away by the river and feel the motion of the air.

14   Now there is a funeral silence in the rooms, the endless wake of some final word. The walls have closed in upon my grandmother's house. When I returned to it in mourning, I saw for the first time in my life how small it was. It was late at night, and there was a white moon, nearly full. I sat for a long time on the stone steps by the kitchen door. From there I could see out across the land; I could see the long row of trees by the creek, the low light upon the rolling plains, and the stars of the Big Dipper. Once I looked at the moon and caught sight of a strange thing. A cricket had perched upon the handrail, only a few inches away from me. My line of vision was such that the creature filled the moon like a fossil. It had gone there, I thought, to live and die, for there, of all places, was its small definition made whole and eternal. A warm wind rose up and purled like the longing within me.

15   The next morning I awoke at dawn and went out on the dirt road to Rainy Mountain. It was already hot, and the grasshoppers began to fill the air. Still, it was early in the morning, and the birds sang out of the shadows. The long

yellow grass on the mountain shone in the bright light, and a scissortail[2] hied above the land. There, where it ought to be, at the end of a long and legendary way, was my grandmother's grave. Here and there on the dark stones were ancestral names. Looking back once, I saw the mountain and came away.

DISCUSSION QUESTIONS

1. Momaday's introduction to his book is wide-ranging, encompassing history, geography, myth, reminiscence, and personal feelings. With a small group, discuss how he ties these subjects together.
2. Describe the Kiowa's "golden age" and its end, using specific references to the text.
3. How did the Kiowas explain the scored stone on Devil's Tower in the Black Hills? What other legends have you read that account for the arrangement of certain stars?
4. Does this essay belong in a chapter entitled "All My Relations" or would it be better in a chapter about Native American history? Support your answer with examples from the essay.

WRITING TOPICS

1. In an essay, analyze the effect and appropriateness of the author's similes and metaphors in paragraphs 1, 7, and 8.
2. Two aspects of literary style are sentence construction and word choice (diction). Momaday's prose rhythms and choice of words help to distinguish his style. Reread the first paragraph, noting the figurative language, as well as the colors mentioned. Then, picture a scene that you know well and write about it. If possible, imitate Momaday's sentence rhythms and precise descriptions.
3. Aho is the central figure in this selection. Write a three-paragraph essay about her role. Suggested thesis sentence: In Momaday's "Introduction" Aho is important as (1) the child who attended the 1890 Sun Dance, (2) a symbol of the continuity of Kiowa life at Rainy Mountain, and (3) a family memory for her grandson.
4. Reread paragraph 10. Create a word portrait of a relative or friend whom you have "only in memory."

---

[2] *scissortail:* a bird with a long, scissor-like tail that feeds on insects while in flight.

NEON SCARS

Wendy Rose

Wendy Rose creates poetry and prose out of her experiences as a teenage dropout, a street-life survivor, an anthropologist, a college teacher, and, most of all, a halfbreed woman. In "Neon Scars," she confronts the dilemma of her mixed family heritage and claims she lacks relatives because her parents threw her away. Rose introduced the image "neon scars" in her 1967 poem "Child Held, Child Broken." Twenty years later, it became the title of her personal narrative published in *I Tell You Now,* a volume of autobiographical essays by Native American authors. "Neon Scars" appeared at the same time as "These Bones Are Alive," an interview between Rose and Joseph Bruchac, published in his *Survival This Way, Interviews with American Indian Poets* (1987). She explained to Bruchac: "I was in a situation where I was physically separated from one-half of my family and rejected by the half that brought me up. . . . The first years of writing, perhaps, the motivation from the very beginning was to try to come to terms with being in that impossible situation." Reared by her mother after her parents' divorce, Rose endured rejection by this side of her family. Paradoxically, she displays extensive knowledge of her mother's genealogy, alluding to English, German, Scots, Norman, Irish, and Miwok ancestors. "The colonizer and the colonized meet in my blood," she writes, noting that a mixed heritage is much more complex than white-Indian relations. She was unable to claim the Hopi clan or tradition of her physically absent father because Hopi determine lineage through the mother.

Unwilling to be destroyed by these painful realities, Rose gradually created her own identity through art. Peeling away layers of scar tissue, she began claiming both her urban childhood and Hopi background in her writing: "California moves my pen, but Hotevilla [her father's Hopi village] dashes through my blood." The word *halfbreed* took on a different meaning as the maturing writer composed *The Halfbreed Chronicles*. In this collection, she writes about people from multiethnic backgrounds and concludes that her growing up experiences parallel those of others with mixed ancestry: "History and circumstances have made half-breeds of us all."

⧉

1   I hate it when other people write about my alienation and anger. Even if it's true, I'm not proud of it. It has crippled me, made me sick, made me out of balance. It has also been the source of my poetry.

2   Writing this autobiographical essay has been the most difficult, most elusive task I have faced as a writer. I work hard to be less self-involved, less self-centered, less self-pitying. As readers and listeners have noted the angry or somber tone of my poems, I have struggled to lessen these things, or, at least, keep them in proportion. I work toward balance and attempt to celebrate at least as often as I moan and rage. Everything I have ever written is fundamentally autobiographical, no matter what the topic or style; to state my life now in an orderly way with clear language is actually to restate, simplified, what has already been said. If I could just come right out and state it like that, as a matter of fact, I would not have needed the poetry. If I could look my childhood in the eye and describe it, I would not have needed to veil those memories in metaphor. If I had grown up with a comfortable identity, I would not need to explain myself from one or another persona. Poetry is both ultimate fact and ultimate fiction; nothing is more brutally honest and, at the same time, more thickly coded.

3   When I speak of bruises that rise on my flesh like blue marbles, do you understand that these are real bruises that have appeared on my flesh? Or has the metaphor succeeded in hiding the pain while producing the fact, putting it in a private place just for those readers and listeners who know me well enough to have seen the bruises? I live with ghosts and like anyone who lives with ghosts, I am trapped inside their circle. I long for someone to siphon off the pain, someone to tell it all to, someone to be amazed at how well I have survived. There is both a need for and a revulsion from pity. More than pity, I have needed respect. More than respect, I have needed to be claimed by someone as their own, someone who is wanted. I have survived—and there is pride in that fact—but is my survival of any value? Is my survival different from the millions of survivals in the world? Or is its kinship with them the truth of the matter—that we are growing, reproducing, living together as relations? Is my survival the final proof I have needed that I belong here after all? Will I be missed someday?

4   When I was first approached for this essay, my response (which lasted for several months) was simply to insist that the editor take some body of my poetic work and let it speak for me. I must have decided that there is some

reason to make my pain public, although I am enough of a coward to keep the greatest pain (and the greatest pleasure) to myself. Would releasing the secrets let loose a passion so great and so uncontrolled that it would destroy the poetry? I am told that I take risks. When I am told that, the tellers mean that I take risks artistically, in style or technique, in placing the words on the page just so in a way that other poets would have the sense or the training not to do. It is usually meant as a compliment.

5   Do you know what is the greatest risk of all? Someday I may be forced to see myself as in a sweat vision, wide open to the world. I may find that I am only that one I saw in the vision, no more, no less. I am only what you see. The vision is naked and cannot be tampered with. Is it enough? Will the voices that have always said I am not good enough be quiet? Is this worth the pain and the poetry? Will you be satisfied?

6   Facts: May 7, 1948. Oakland. Catholic hospital. Midwife nun, no doctor. Citation won the Kentucky Derby. Israel was born. The United Nations met for the first time. It was Saturday, the end of the baby boom or the beginning. Boom. Stephen's little sister. Daughter of Betty. Almost named Bodega, named Bronwen instead. Little brown baby with a tuft of black hair. Baptized in the arms of Mary and Joe. Nearly blind for ten years. Glasses. Catholic school. Nuns with black habits to their ankles. Heads encased in white granite. Rosary beads like hard apricots—measuring prayers, whipping wrists. Paced before the blackboard. Swore in Gaelic. Alone. Alone at home. Alone in the play yard. Alone at Mass. Alone on the street. Fed, clothed in World War II dresses, little more. Mom too sick to care; brother raised by grandparents. Alone. Unwatched. Something wrong with me; everyone knows but me. They all leave me alone. No friends. Confirmation. Patron Francis of Assisi.[1] He understands. Public high school. Drugs, dropping out. Finally friends. Getting high, staying high. Very sick, hospital. No more drugs, no more friends. Alone again. Married at eighteen. Tried to shoot me. Lasted three months. Again at nineteen. Lived in basement, then in trailer. Worked in Yosemite. Sold Indian crafts. Went on display. Drinking, fighting, he tried to burn down the house; he gave me the name Rose. Starved in Nevada; nearly died. Home. Eating again; got fat. College. Graduated in ten years. Went to grad school. Alone again. Met Arthur. Fell in love, still happy. Another ten years. Live in a nice house. Fresno. Have a swimming pool. Air conditioning. Have an old cat. Rent a typewriter. Teach. Work on doctorate. Two of us now. Moved to another planet, home.

---

[1] *Patron Francis of Assisi:* A patron saint is regarded as the special guardian of a group, place, country, or, in this case, person. Francis of Assisi (1181?–1226) is a saint and founder of the Franciscan order of monks.

7   Healing.

8   I am probably my mother. She bears my face but is lighter in complexion, taller, long-legged. She was thin enough as a girl to have been teased for it. Her eyebrows each come to a point in the center, little tepees at the top of her face. My brother inherited these, while I got her upward-turned nose and hair that thins at the temple. From my father I have coarse dark hair, a flatness of face and mouth, no waist, a body made of bricks. At different times, I have resembled each of them. I see myself in the old photographs of my mother as a short, stocky, dark version of her, and others have seen my father in me, thinner, younger, lighter, female.

9   As much as I have come from them, the two of them threw me away. I am the part of them that they worked long and hard to cut off. I have never depended on them. I have floated into the distance, alone.

10   I have heard Indians joke about those who act as if they had no relatives. I wince, because I have no relatives. They live, but they threw me away—so, I do not have them. I am without relations. I have always swung back and forth between alienation and relatedness. As a child, I would run away from the beatings, from the obscene words, and always knew that if I could run far enough, then any leaf, any insect, any bird, any breeze could bring me to my true home. I knew I did not belong among people. Whatever they hated about me was a human thing; the nonhuman world has always loved me. I can't remember when it was otherwise. But I have been emotionally crippled by this. There is nothing romantic about being young and angry, or even about turning that anger into art. I go through the motions of living in society, but never feel a part of it. When my family threw me away, every human on earth did likewise.

11   I have been alone too much. I have been bitter too long. This part of me is not in balance. It has made me alien. This is something to pray about.

12   There is only one recent immigrant in my family. Sidney, my mother's father, came from England around the turn of the century. I don't know his father's name, but his mother was Christine. Early pictures of Sidney show a serious English schoolboy intent on his economic future. What he did in America was learn photography and operate a small studio in Berkeley for the rest of his life. He took misty portraits of young girls and babies, Victorian still-lifes, and sweeping panoramas of San Francisco.

13   I don't remember being touched by Sidney at all, but he was my brother's greatest influence. Even today there is a British clip to my brother's speech. When I was in his house, Sidney was always on the other side of some door. I have wondered, too, why his middle name was

"Valdez." And how he came to be so dark and brooding as a young man, so gray when old. Why did he leave England? Where did he meet Clare, the mountain girl from Mariposa, who would give birth to my mother?

14   Clare was born thirty years after the Gold Rush, in Bear Valley. Bear Creek branches from the Merced River near there, just down the mountain from Yosemite, rippling through oak-wooded grassy hills and bullpines. Her mother and father were born there also; he was raised in a house that had belonged to John C. Fremont.[2] Their people had ridden wagons west across the plains or had sailed around the Horn to find prosperity in a land newly claimed from Mexico. Clare's father, Maurice, was the son of German immigrants who had traveled from Missouri in a wagon train; there is a story told by his mother, Margaret, of how one night Indians came to steal the babies. Clare's mother, Elizabeth, had a noble and well-documented lineage. Her people were known by name all the way back to the eighth century on the Scottish side and to the Crusades on the Irish. The dominant thread in her ancestry crossed into Britain with William the Conqueror, part of the family rumored to have been related to him through one of his brothers. The Normans of my mother's background are very well documented and include the modern Lord Dunboyne, although our branch of the Dunboynes split from his during the seventeenth century. This Norman part of the family included Butlers and Massys, Barrets and Percys, Le Petits and de Berminghams—names that fiercely colonized Ireland and settled on stolen land. Among the parts of Ireland that they stole were certain women: O'Brien of Thomond, McCarthy Reagh, Carthach of Muskerry, all representing royal native Irish families. Another thread can be followed to the Scottish Highlands and to royal Celtic and Pictish[3] families via the Clans McInnes and Drummond.

15   By the time Clare was born in the 1880s, the family had included an Indian man, most probably Miwok. Clare's blond hair and transparently blue eyes belied that less well-known (and possibly involuntary) heritage, but the native blood reappeared in my mother. How many almost-comic photographs do I have of the sharp-faced blond and delicate lady who sits before the long-faced mustached Englishman and, between them, holds the chubby little girl with the dark round face, that little Indian baby?

16   Late in the summer of 1984, I received a package from my mother's cousin Joe, who is also my godfather, although I had not seen him for more than thirty years. He was both black sheep and bachelor in the family, a mystery man of whom I have no clear memories. Now I am laughing at myself.

---

[2] *John C. Fremont:* (1813–1890) U.S. general and explorer.
[3] *Pictish:* pertaining to the Picts, ancient people who united with the Scots in the ninth century.

I have always searched for my place and my people, focusing that search on my father. His Hopi people have been sympathetic but silent; they trace their lineage through the mother and I could never be more than the daughter of a Hopi man. How ironic and unexpected Joe's package was! It contained diary excerpts, lists of names and dates, and newspaper clippings about my mother's family. She had always refused to answer my questions about ancestry, citing the melting pot as her excuse. My interest in our heritage was, in her eyes, just an aberration which—like slipping away from the Church—would someday be fixed. Yet the package with its precious communication came to me.

17   Now why didn't Joe send it to my brother? My brother is what they wanted. He is white-looking, with brown hair and green eyes; he has maintained his ties to home and hearth, even while in the Army. He has expressed great interest in his European blood, has dabbled in Druidic and neo-pagan rites, and looks like them. His hair and beard are long, his clothing covered with mystic symbols. The package did not go to him. I gave him and my mother copies of everything; they were as surprised as I that Joe chose me.

18   I learned that the Normans who stole Irish land went bankrupt, lost their land, and booked passage in 1830 for Quebec. The McInnes clan, near that time, was forbidden to wear the tartan and fled Scotland to preserve their heritage. The weekend after Joe's package arrived, Highland Games were held in Fresno. In no other year would it have occurred to me to attend, but Arthur and I walked onto the grounds to search for my roots, he Japanese and I wearing all my turquoise for courage. It may have looked funny to all those Scots to see an Indian looking for a booth with her clan's name on it. The first booth was Irish; I showed my list of ancestral names to the man there, and he pointed to certain ones and said they had stolen his castle. I apologized to all of Ireland on behalf of John Bull[4] and returned his castle to him; I suspect it would not hold up in Parliament and, anyway, they were the ancestors who had gone bankrupt. This is not the heritage I would have picked—to be the daughter of the invaders. It is not where my sympathies lie. Searching the grounds, I found my clan.

19   Great-great-grandmother, Henrietta MacInnes, who came to California for gold from Quebec, you have given me what my own father could not. I learned that I am entitled to wear your tartan, your symbol of a strong arm pointing to the sky with a bow in its hand. I also learned that you were the natives of Scotland, descended from the Pictish king, Onnus, and lent strength to my apology for Ireland. The colonizer and the colonized meet in my blood. It is so much more complex than just white and just Indian. I will pray about this, too.

---

4 *John Bull:* the English people.

20   This year Sidney and Clare, Grandad and Nana, are turning real for me. They have been dead twenty-five years, but my thoughts go to them as I continue to listen to my mother's jokes about their embarrassment. Clare got so angry sometimes! like when people would ask what racial mixture her little girl, my mother, was. Or when that little girl shared a room with a Jew in college. Or when that little girl, who had bobbed her hair and hung out with flappers, married a man with Indian blood and rural background. Clare knew who to blame. My mother told me of her mother's peculiar habit of taking my brother into her home when he was sick to nurse him back to health and, when I was sick, of taking my brother into her home so he wouldn't catch what I had. She was amused by this.

21   Nana! I'm afraid you'll see me cry! I have never been able to cry in front of you, of anyone. Any strong emotion is dangerous, as people are dangerous. Poetry has been the safest way to cry in public. I bristle when people say I'm cold and unfriendly, but they're right. I can't tell you straight out how I feel without putting it into a poem. And I have written some for you, safely cloaked in metaphor or masked by a persona. I hope you understand that the poetry is the only way I can love you. I *do* love. But you are dangerous. Does mom know how much it hurts when she tells me about the way you turned from me? Does she know how much it hurts for me to know that it could have gone unsaid?

22   I am turning numb. I have been educated to put a name to the things that my parents did, but the child within has no such knowledge. I recall that every dirty word I ever knew was first heard from my father's lips, from the man who raised me as he struck over and over. As an adult, I take this apart and study it. . . . There wasno media hype about abuse in those days, no public awareness; I begged the police to put me in a foster home, but I was always sent back. Eventually I learned that I was to blame for all of this, just as I was to blame for my parents' unhappiness.

23   I embarrassed them. They tell me their marriage began to go bad when I was born, although they never divorced. He lives in one room, she in another. How much it must embarrass them now for me to say these things to strangers! I would say something else, be someone else, act some other way—but there is no way I can twist my genes around. There is no sugar sweet enough to smear on the story of our household. These are ghosts that will never leave, the ghosts of knowing how I destroyed their lives. They sent me to social workers and psychiatrists, to priests, to people whose roles or professions I never knew. They told me I was sick and must try to get better so that my family could mend. Everything, they said, depended on me. I just wanted to get out so that the beatings, the obscene language about my body, and the constant knowledge of his hatred would be far away. Didn't they believe what I told them? Couldn't they see the scars? I didn't know that such scars never heal up. It's probably lucky that my nature is a fighting one; otherwise, I would have died.

24   I will just talk about being different, as if I were talking about someone else. My mother said I was born different.

25   Her mother said she was born different. No one ever said what that difference was all about, but everyone knew it when they saw it. They avoided it as if it burned them. And so she was always alone and not just alone, but thrown away. They made sure she knew she was being thrown away. They told her so, over and over, through action and word, until she could see it in no other way. And so she knew she was rejected and she knew she was rejectable. She learned to worship her difference, whatever it was, and this empowered her. She rejected them.

26   Or, I could try this. I'll make up a story about my childhood and see if anyone believes it. I will tell about happy summer days with all my friends. We girls are trying on makeup, combing each other's hair, comparing lies about boyfriends. The boys all want to date me, but I can only choose one at a time. I hate to hurt the others. I have been riding my beautiful stallion on the mountain; alongside is my healthy young collie. I know that when I go home, my parents will be glad to see me; they'll hug me and kiss me and hold me. Uncles and aunts and cousins will be there, too, and they will hug me. They know all about me, what my interests are, what I did that day. I have been placed in the gifted program at school and will be high school valedictorian. I have been skipping grades because everyone thinks I'm so smart. I'm pretty, too. I will enter college at seventeen with an enormous scholarship. I will receive gold jewelry or a diamond for my graduation. My father will kiss me on the cheek and take my picture.

27   I don't want to lie to you, but I don't want to tell the truth. The dirty laundry flaps in the wind, yet the alternative is to go on wearing it. How do you admit in public that you were abused, that the only time your parents ever touched you—that you can remember— was in anger, that your cousins probably don't know you exist, that your own grandparents had no use for you? How do you acknowledge that you were left so alone you never learned to brush your teeth or fix your food? How do you reveal that you were a bag lady at fourteen, having been turned out of the house, or that when you ran away no one looked for you? How do you expect anyone to believe how hungry you were at times, how you nearly died from starvation twice—when they can plainly see how fat you are now? How do you explain that you dropped out of high school, were classified as retarded but educable, and were not allowed to take college-prep classes? How do you reconcile being an "Indian writer" with such a non-Indian upbringing? It is not the Indian way to be left so alone, to be alienated, to be friendless, to be forced to live on the street like a rat, to be unacquainted with your cousins. It would certainly be better for my image as an Indian poet to manufacture something and let you believe in my traditional, loving, spiritual childhood where every winter evening was spent immersed in storytelling and ceremony, where the actions of every day continually told me I was valued.

28   Today I live about fifty miles from Bear Valley. As I write, it is early August and the days are valley-hot, the nights thickly warm and filled with crickets. Although last winter was dry, this summer has found an explosion of toads in my yard. To uncover the memories, I have peeled back layers of scar tissue. I have invoked the ghosts and made them work for me. Is that

the answer? To keep them busy? There is nothing authentic or nice about my past; I am sure that I would be a great disappointment to anthropologists. But then, you know—now—why I write poetry; being Indian was never the reason. I have agonized for months about writing this essay, and now that it is finished I am afraid of it. I am mortified and embarrassed. I am certain I said too much, whined perhaps, made someone squirm. But there is no way I can change the past and the literal fact is that I have tried to forget what is unforgettable; there are few happy moments that I recall— or perhaps, as I have succeeded in forgetting the bad, the good has also been forgotten. Perhaps the editor and the readers will forgive me for using them in an exorcism.

29   My father told me, when I took Arthur down to Hopi to meet him, that Hopi earth does contain my roots and I am, indeed, from that land. Because the roots are there, I will find them. But when I find them, he said, I must rebuild myself as a Hopi. I am not merely a conduit, but a participant. I am not a victim, but a woman.

> I am building myself.
> There are many roots.
> I plant, I pick, I prune.
> I consume.

DISCUSSION QUESTIONS

1. What kind of childhood did the author have?
2. How did her childhood experiences affect her adult life?
3. The author, like many people, has obviously spent some time researching her ancestry. For what reasons might she have done so?
4. What does she say about her Hopi roots?
5. If you had known someone like the author when she was in school, what would you have done and what advice might you have given her?

WRITING TOPICS

1. What do you think it takes to grow up with "a comfortable identity," and why is this important? Express your thoughts in a short essay.
2. How many nationalities or ethnic groups are in your ancestry? In a paragraph or two, describe your background and include a "family tree."
3. Write an essay developing Rose's conclusion, "I am not a victim, but a woman." Support this thesis with at least three examples from the essay.

A SPECIAL TREAT

Luci Tapahonso

As the middle of eleven children, Luci Tapahonso has many family stories. "A Special Treat" appears in *Sáanii Dahataal The Women Are Singing,* a cycle of poetry, prayers, and stories. In her introduction, Tapahonso explains, "To know stories, remember stories, and to retell them well is to have been 'raised right'; the family of such an individual is also held in high esteem. . . . It is with this perspective that I share the following stories, poetry, and prayers."

For a young Navajo girl growing up in rural northwestern New Mexico, going to town was a very special event. Years after that trip, the mature Tapahonso nostalgically describes her family's forays into Farmington, during which each person performed a duty. Her family's first joint task in town was washing clothes at the laundry, which was much easier and effective than washing them at home. In a dry desert land, most Navajo households depended on water that was usually hauled many miles from a deep well and stored in metal barrels for drinking, cooking, and washing. One of her brothers made the trip because he helped carry the laundry; Luci and her siblings helped pull clothes through the wringer. Someone had always to guard the laundry and other things in the open bed of the pickup truck. As was proper in this matrilineal society, Luci's mother carried the money and decided where to spend it and for what. Driving home, they listened to Luci's father sing Navajo songs. Songs are woven into the fabric of everyday Navajo life and are reminders of ancient beliefs as well as entertainment.

⧉

1   Trips to Farmington were a special treat when we were children. Sometimes when we didn't get to go along, we cried so hard that we finally had to draw straws to decide fairly who would get to go. My oldest brother always went because he drove, my other brother went because he helped carry laundry, my father went because he was the father, and my mother

went because she had the money and knew where to go and what to buy. And only one or two kids were allowed to go because we got in the way and begged for things all the time.

2   We got up early on the Saturdays that we were going to town—we would get ready, sort laundry, and gather up pop bottles that we turned in for money. My father always checked the oil and tires on the pickup, and then he and my brothers would load the big laundry tubs, securing the canvas covers with heavy wooden blocks. We would drive out of the front yard, and the unfortunate ones who had to stay home waved good-bye sullenly. The dogs chased the truck down the road a ways before turning home.

3   In Farmington, we would go to the laundry first. It was always dark and clammy inside. We liked pulling the clothes out of the wringer even though my mother was nervous about letting us help. After that, we drove down-town and parked in the free lot north of Main Street. Sometimes my father got off at the library, and we picked him up after we finished shopping. Someone always had to "watch" the pickup, and usually the one who was naughty at the laundry had to sit in the pickup for two or three hours while everyone else got to "see things" around town. If my father didn't go to the library, the kids were off the hook, naughty or not, because he waited in the pickup and read "The Readers Digest."

4   When we stopped at Safeway, our last stop, it was early evening. My mother would buy some bologna or cooked chicken in plastic-wrapped trays and a loaf of bread. We would eat this on our way home. After the groceries were packed securely under the canvas and wooden blocks, we talked about who we saw, what we should have bought instead of what we did buy (maybe we could exchange it next time), then the talking would slow down and by the time we reached the Blue Window gas station, everyone but my father was sleepy.

5   He would start singing in Navajo in a clear, strong voice and once in a while, my mother would ask him about a certain song she heard once. "Do you know it? It was something like this . . ." and she would sing a bit, he would catch it and finish the song. We listened half asleep. I would whisper to my sister, "He sounds like those men on Navajo Hour." "I know. It's so good," she'd answer, and we'd sleep until we reached home.

DISCUSSION QUESTIONS

1. How would you describe this family?
2. Would you like to be a member of this family? Explain your answer.
3. What observations can you make about life on the Navajo reservation from reading this short essay?

WRITING TOPICS

1. Recall a family trip or scene that reveals relationships among members of your family and write a short essay using Tapahonso's model.
2. Do some research on and write an essay about the importance of singing as a Navajo tradition.

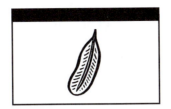

THEY WERE ALONE IN WINTER

Luci Tapahonso

This poem and "A Special Treat" are textual snapshots of Luci Tapahonso's family memories separated and yet bonded by generations. Her work is always autobiographical, shaped and informed by her beliefs and identity as a Navajo daughter, mother, and grandmother. Female relatives appear in her poetry, representing the continuance of the feminine line that is traced back to First Woman. In her poetry collection *One More Shiprock Night* (1981), the author notes, "A lot of my writing has to do with my children, about my daughters who are growing up in a totally different way . . . so my writing has a circular form—it comes back to me through the children and together it becomes a prayer of sorts back to the land, the people, and the families from whence we came originally."

Each night I braid my daughter's hair.
My fingers slip through the thick silkiness,
weaving the strands into a single black stream.

"The air feels like something will happen,"
5   she says. "Maybe it will snow."
The moon outside is a silver arc in the cold sky.
"In the old stories, they say the moon comes as a beautiful horse,"
I tell her. From the bedroom window, we look out
                                    at the glistening night sky.

It is outside the house: the frozen night.
10   It glimmers with her pleas for snow.
It glimmers in her night dreams: a fusing of music, laughter,
                                    talk of boys and clothes.

It glimmers here in the fibers of my bed sheets,
         there above the old roar of the Kaw River.
It glimmers in the western sky where he thinks of me and smiles.

In an old story, a woman and her daughter were alone in the winter
15 and the mother said, "Tomorrow, if the sun rises,
              it will come as many different horses."

DISCUSSION QUESTIONS

1. The persona in the poem is the poet, but she does not identify herself by name. What clues do you find that indicate Navajo traditions?
2. How does the poet create a chantlike poem?

WRITING TOPICS

1. Tapahonso carefully selects words to picture her daughter, the night, and light. What examples do you like? Discuss these images in a paragraph.
2. In a brief essay, compare Tapahonso's stylistic techniques in "A Special Treat" and "They Were Alone in Winter."

Lullaby

Leslie Silko

"Lullaby" is one of several stories that made Leslie Silko a pre-eminent writer of short fiction in what Kenneth Lincoln has called the "Native American Renaissance." Its publication was an important literary event for Silko in 1974, and it was selected for inclusion in *The Best American Short Stories of 1975.* Silko reprinted it in *Storyteller* (1981), a collection of stories, poems, and autobiographical sketches. "Lullaby" carries the familiar Silko theme of traditional Indian lives, especially those of women, in conflict with values and practices of mainstream society.

The Native American and Euro-American actions that color the story parallel the social and cultural contexts in which Silko grew up: "If you want to look at political ideology, I have an awful lot of the old folks' point of view left in me." Considering her work a political act as well as a literary achievement, Silko asserted, "It is more effective to write a story like 'Lullaby' than to rant and rave. . . . Certainly for me the most effective political statement I could make is in my art work."

"Lullaby" reveals the conflicts between an elderly Navajo couple, who live near Laguna, and Euro-American authorities. Instead of directly condemning the latter, Silko shows that the tensions arise from differences in cultural values that neither the Navajos nor the Euro-Americans fully understand. Though the story ends with the old man's death, it also reaffirms life and the power of tradition as Ayah sings a lullaby sung by her mother and grandmother that resembles a chant sung for healing and protection.

In this story, Silko describes the interactions between members of Ayah's Navajo family. Like most Navajo women prior to World War II, the protagonist lacked formal education. Her cowboy husband taught her to sign her name. After the war, Navajo Nation officials demanded that the federal government comply with its 1868 treaty commitment to educate Navajo children.

Like other Native Americans, Navajos served in the U.S. armed forces in disproportionately large numbers during World War II. The

Marine Corps recruited a special "Code Talker" unit deployed in the Pacific theater. Navajo "code talkers" created codes in their own language so that no Japanese hearing their messages radioed in the open could understand them. Consequently, Silko's Navajo family is typical in losing a son overseas.

1   The sun had gone down but the snow in the wind gave off its own light. It came in thick tufts like new wool—washed before the weaver spins it. Ayah reached out for it like her own babies had, and she smiled when she remembered how she had laughed at them. She was an old woman now, and her life had become memories. She sat down with her back against the wide cottonwood tree, feeling the rough bark on her back bones; she faced east and listened to the wind and snow sing a high-pitched Yeibechei[1] song. Out of the wind she felt warmer, and she could watch the wide fluffy snow fill in her tracks, steadily, until the direction she had come from was gone. By the light of the snow she could see the dark outline of the big arroyo a few feet away. She was sitting on the edge of Cebolleta Creek, where in the springtime the thin cows would graze on grass already chewed flat to the ground. In the wide deep creek bed where only a trickle of water flowed in the summer, the skinny cows would wander, looking for new grass along winding paths splashed with manure.

2   Ayah pulled the old Army blanket over her head like a shawl. Jimmie's blanket—the one he had sent to her. That was a long time ago and the green wool was faded, and it was unraveling on the edges. She did not want to think about Jimmie. So she thought about the weaving and the way her mother had done it. On the tall wooden loom set into the sand under a tamarack tree for shade. She could see it clearly. She had been only a little girl when her grandma gave her the wooden combs to pull the twigs and burrs from the raw, freshly washed wool. And while she combed the wool, her grandma sat beside her, spinning a silvery strand of yarn around the smooth cedar spindle. Her mother worked at the loom with yarns dyed bright yellow and red and gold. She watched them dye the yarn in boiling black pots full of beeweed petals, juniper berries, and sage. The blankets her mother made were soft and woven so tight that rain rolled off them like birds' feathers. Ayah remembered sleeping warm on cold windy nights, wrapped in her mother's blankets on the hogan's sandy floor.

3   The snow drifted now, with the northwest wind hurling it in gusts. It drifted up around her black overshoes—old ones with little metal buckles. She smiled at the snow which was trying to cover her little by little. She could remember when they had no black rubber overshoes; only the high buckskin leggings that they wrapped over their elkhide moccasins. If the

---

[1] *Yeibechei song:* Yei or Yeibechei are Holy People who appear in Navajo ceremonials.

snow was dry or frozen, a person could walk all day and not get wet; and in the evenings the beams of the ceiling would hang with lengths of pale buckskin leggings, drying out slowly.

4   She felt peaceful remembering. She didn't feel cold any more. Jimmie's blanket seemed warmer than it had ever been. And she could remember the morning he was born. She could remember whispering to her mother, who was sleeping on the other side of the hogan, to tell her it was time now. She did not want to wake the others. The second time she called to her, her mother stood up and pulled on her shoes; she knew. They walked to the old stone hogan together, Ayah walking a step behind her mother. She waited alone, learning the rhythms of the pains while her mother went to call the old woman to help them. The morning was already warm even before dawn and Ayah smelled the bee flowers blooming and the young willow growing at the springs. She could remember that so clearly, but his birth merged into the births of the other children and to her it became all the same birth. They named him for the summer morning and in English they called him Jimmie.

5   It wasn't like Jimmie died. He just never came back, and one day a dark blue sedan with white writing on its doors pulled up in front of the boxcar shack where the rancher let the Indians live. A man in a khaki uniform trimmed in gold gave them a yellow piece of paper and told them that Jimmie was dead. He said the Army would try to get the body back and then it would be shipped to them; but it wasn't likely because the helicopter had burned after it crashed. All of this was told to Chato because he could understand English. She stood inside the doorway holding the baby while Chato listened. Chato spoke English like a white man and he spoke Spanish too. He was taller than the white man and he stood straighter too. Chato didn't explain why; he just told the military man they could keep the body if they found it. The white man looked bewildered; he nodded his head and he left. Then Chato looked at her and shook his head, and then he told her, "Jimmie isn't coming home anymore," and when he spoke, he used the words to speak of the dead. She didn't cry then, but she hurt inside with anger. And she mourned him as the years passed, when a horse fell with Chato and broke his leg, and the white rancher told them he wouldn't pay Chato until he could work again. She mourned Jimmie because he would have worked for his father then; he would have saddled the big bay horse and ridden the fence lines each day, with wire cutters and heavy gloves, fixing the breaks in the barbed wire and putting the stray cattle back inside again.

6   She mourned him after the white doctors came to take Danny and Ella away. She was at the shack alone that day they came. It was back in the days before they hired Navajo women to go with them as interpreters. She recognized one of the doctors. She had seen him at the children's clinic at Cañoncito about a month ago. They were wearing khaki uniforms and they waved papers at her and a black ballpoint pen, trying to make her understand their English words. She was frightened by the way they looked at the children, like the lizard watches the fly. Danny was swinging on the tire

swing on the elm tree behind the rancher's house, and Ella was toddling around the front door, dragging the broomstick horse Chato made for her. Ayah could see they wanted her to sign the papers, and Chato had taught her to sign her name. It was something she was proud of. She only wanted them to go, and to take their eyes away from her children.

7   She took the pen from the man without looking at his face and she signed the papers in three different places he pointed to. She stared at the ground by their feet and waited for them to leave. But they stood there and began to point and gesture at the children. Danny stopped swinging. Ayah could see his fear. She moved suddenly and grabbed Ella into her arms; the child squirmed, trying to get back to her toys. Ayah ran with the baby toward Danny; she screamed for him to run and then she grabbed him around his chest and carried him too. She ran south into the foothills of juniper trees and black lava rock. Behind her she heard the doctors running, but they had been taken by surprise, and as the hills became steeper and the cholla cactus were thicker, they stopped. When she reached the top of the hill, she stopped to listen in case they were circling around her. But in a few minutes she heard a car engine start and they drove away. The children had been too surprised to cry while she ran with them. Danny was shaking and Ella's little fingers were gripping Ayah's blouse.

8   She stayed up in the hills for the rest of the day, sitting on a black lava boulder in the sunshine where she could see for miles all around her. The sky was light blue and cloudless, and it was warm for late April. The sun warmth relaxed her and took the fear and anger away. She lay back on the rock and watched the sky. It seemed to her that she could walk into the sky, stepping through clouds endlessly. Danny played with little pebbles and stones, pretending they were bird eggs and then little rabbits. Ella sat at her feet and dropped fistfuls of dirt into the breeze, watching the dust and particles of sand intently. Ayah watched a hawk soar high above them, dark wings gliding; hunting or only watching, she did not know. The hawk was patient and he circled all afternoon before he disappeared around the high volcanic peak the Mexicans called Guadalupe.

9   Late in the afternoon, Ayah looked down at the gray boxcar shack with the paint all peeled from the wood; the stove pipe on the roof was rusted and crooked. The fire she had built that morning in the oil drum stove had burned out. Ella was asleep in her lap now and Danny sat close to her, complaining that he was hungry; he asked when they would go to the house. "We will stay up here until your father comes," she told him, "because those white men were chasing us." The boy remembered then and he nodded at her silently.

10   If Jimmie had been there he could have read those papers and explained to her what they said. Ayah would have known then, never to sign them. The doctors came back the next day and they brought a BIA[2] policeman with them. They told Chato they had her signature and that was all they needed.

---

[2] *BIA:* Bureau of Indian Affairs.

Except for the kids. She listened to Chato sullenly; she hated him when he told her it was the old woman who died in the winter, spitting blood; it was her old grandma who had given the children this disease. "They don't spit blood," she said coldly. "The whites lie." She held Ella and Danny close to her, ready to run to the hills again. "I want a medicine man first," she said to Chato, not looking at him. He shook his head. "It's too late now. The policeman is with them. You signed the paper." His voice was gentle.

11 It was worse than if they had died: to lose the children and to know that somewhere, in a place called Colorado, in a place full of sick and dying strangers, her children were without her. There had been babies that died soon after they were born, and one that died before he could walk. She had carried them herself, up to the boulders and great pieces of the cliff that long ago crashed down from Long Mesa; she laid them in the crevices of sandstone and buried them in fine brown sand with round quartz pebbles that washed down the hills in the rain. She had endured it because they had been with her. But she could not bear this pain. She did not sleep for a long time after they took her children. She stayed on the hill where they had fled the first time, and she slept rolled up in the blanket Jimmie had sent her. She carried the pain in her belly and it was fed by everything she saw: the blue sky of their last day together and the dust and pebbles they played with; the swing in the elm tree and broomstick horse choked life from her. The pain filled her stomach and there was no room for food or for her lungs to fill with air. The air and the food would have been theirs.

12 She hated Chato, not because he let the policeman and doctors put the screaming children in the government car, but because he had taught her to sign her name. Because it was like the old ones always told her about learning their language or any of their ways: it endangered you. She slept alone on the hill until the middle of November when the first snows came. Then she made a bed for herself where the children had slept. She did not lie down beside Chato again until many years later, when he was sick and shivering and only her body could keep him warm. The illness came after the white rancher told Chato he was too old to work for him anymore, and Chato and his old woman should be out of the shack by the next afternoon because the rancher had hired new people to work there. That had satisfied her. To see how the white man repaid Chato's years of loyalty and work. All of Chato's fine-sounding English talk didn't change things.

13 It snowed steadily and the luminous light from the snow gradually diminished into the darkness. Somewhere in Ceboletta a dog barked and other village dogs joined with it. Ayah looked in the direction she had come, from the bar where Chato was buying the wine. Sometimes he told her to go on ahead and wait; and then he never came. And when she finally went back looking for him, she would find him passed out at the bottom of the wooden steps to Azzie's Bar. All the wine would be gone and most of the money too, from the pale blue check that came to them once a month in a

government envelope. It was then that she would look at his face and his hands, scarred by ropes and the barbed wire of all those years, and she would think, this man is a stranger; for forty years she had smiled at him and cooked his food, but he remained a stranger. She stood up again, with the snow almost to her knees, and she walked back to find Chato.

14   It was hard to walk in the deep snow and she felt the air burn in her lungs. She stopped a short distance from the bar to rest and readjust the blanket. But this time he wasn't waiting for her on the bottom step with his old Stetson hat pulled down and his shoulders hunched up in his long wool overcoat.

15   She was careful not to slip on the wooden steps. When she pushed the door open, warm air and cigarette smoke hit her face. She looked around slowly and deliberately, in every corner, in every dark place that the old man might find to sleep. The bar owner didn't like Indians in there, especially Navajos, but he let Chato come in because he could talk Spanish like he was one of them. The men at the bar stared at her, and the bartender saw that she left the door open wide. Snowflakes were flying inside like moths and melting into a puddle on the oiled wood floor. He motioned to her to close the door, but she did not see him. She held herself straight and walked across the room slowly, searching the room with every step. The snow in her hair melted and she could feel it on her forehead. At the far corner of the room, she saw red flames at the mica window of the old stove door; she looked behind the stove just to make sure. The bar got quiet except for the Spanish polka music playing on the jukebox. She stood by the stove and shook the snow from her blanket and held it near the stove to dry. The wet wool smell reminded her of new-born goats in early March, brought inside to warm near the fire. She felt calm.

16   In past years they would have told her to get out. But her hair was white now and her face was wrinkled. They looked at her like she was a spider crawling slowly across the room. They were afraid; she could feel the fear. She looked at their faces steadily. They reminded her of the first time the white people brought her children back to her that winter. Danny had been shy and hid behind the thin white woman who brought them. And the baby had not known her until Ayah took her into her arms, and then Ella had nuzzled close to her as she had when she was nursing. The blonde woman was nervous and kept looking at a dainty gold watch on her wrist. She sat on the bench near the small window and watched the dark snow clouds gather around the mountains; she was worrying about the unpaved road. She was frightened by what she saw inside too: the strips of venison drying on a rope across the ceiling and the children jabbering excitedly in a language she did not know. So they stayed for only a few hours. Ayah watched the government car disappear down the road and she knew they were already being weaned from these lava hills and from this sky. The last time they came was in early June, and Ella stared at her the way the men in the bar were now staring. Ayah did not try to pick her up; she smiled at her instead and spoke cheerfully to Danny. When he tried to answer her, he could not seem to remember and he spoke English words with the Navajo.

But he gave her a scrap of paper that he had found somewhere and carried in his pocket; it was folded in half, and he shyly looked up at her and said it was a bird. She asked Chato if they were home for good this time. He spoke to the white woman and she shook her head. "How much longer?" he asked, and she said she didn't know; but Chato saw how she stared at the boxcar shack. Ayah turned away then. She did not say good-bye.

17   She felt satisfied that the men in the bar feared her. Maybe it was her face and the way she held her mouth with teeth clenched tight, like there was nothing anyone could do to her now. She walked north down the road, searching for the old man. She did this because she had the blanket, and there would be no place for him except with her and the blanket in the old adobe barn near the arroyo. They always slept there when they came to Cebolleta. If the money and the wine were gone, she would be relieved because then they could go home again; back to the old hogan with a dirt roof and rock walls where she herself had been born. And the next day the old man could go back to the few sheep they still had, to follow along behind them, guiding them, into dry sandy arroyos where sparse grass grew. She knew he did not like walking behind old ewes when for so many years he rode big quarter horses and worked with cattle. But she wasn't sorry for him; he should have known all along what would happen.

18   There had not been enough rain for their garden in five years; and that was when Chato finally hitched a ride into town and brought back brown boxes of rice and sugar and big tin cans of welfare peaches. After that, at the first of the month they went to Cebolleta to ask the postmaster for the check; and then Chato would go to the bar and cash it. They did this as they planted the garden every May, not because anything would survive the summer dust, but because it was time to do this. The journey passed the days that smelled silent and dry like the caves above the canyon with yellow painted buffaloes on their walls.

19   He was walking along the pavement when she found him. He did not stop or turn around when he heard her behind him. She walked beside him and she noticed how slowly he moved now. He smelled strong of woodsmoke and urine. Lately he had been forgetting. Sometimes he called her by his sister's name and she had been gone for a long time. Once she had found him wandering on the road to the white man's ranch, and she asked him why he was going that way; he laughed at her and said, "You know they can't run that ranch without me," and he walked on determined, limping on the leg that had been crushed many years before. Now he looked at her curiously, as if for the first time, but he kept shuffling along, moving slowly along the side of the highway. His gray hair had grown long and spread out on the shoulders of the long overcoat. He wore the old felt hat pulled down over his ears. His boots were worn out at the toes and he had stuffed pieces of an old red shirt in the holes. The rags made his feet look like little animals up to their ears in snow. She laughed at his feet; the snow

muffled the sound of her laugh. He stopped and looked at her again. The wind had quit blowing and the snow was falling straight down; the southeast sky was beginning to clear and Ayah could see a star.

20   "Let's rest awhile," she said to him. They walked away from the road and up the slope to the giant boulders that had tumbled down from the red sandrock mesa throughout the centuries of rainstorms and earth tremors. In a place where the boulders shut out the wind, they sat down with their backs against the rock. She offered half of the blanket to him and they sat wrapped together.

21   The storm passed swiftly. The clouds moved east. They were massive and full, crowding together across the sky. She watched them with the feeling of horses—steely blue-gray horses startled across the sky. The powerful haunches pushed into the distances and the tail hairs streamed white mist behind them. The sky cleared. Ayah saw that there was nothing between her and the stars. The light was crystalline. There was no shimmer, no distortion through earth haze. She breathed the clarity of the night sky; she smelled the purity of the half moon and the stars. He was lying on his side with his knees pulled up near his belly for warmth. His eyes were closed now, and in the light from the stars and the moon, he looked young again.

22   She could see it descend out of the night sky: an icy stillness from the edge of the thin moon. She recognized the freezing. It came gradually, sinking snowflake by snowflake until the crust was heavy and deep. It had the strength of the stars in Orion, and its journey was endless. Ayah knew that with the wine he would sleep. He would not feel it. She tucked the blanket around him, remembering how it was when Ella had been with her; and she felt the rush so big inside her heart for the babies. And she sang the only song she knew to sing for babies. She could not remember if she had ever sung it to her children, but she knew that her grandmother had sung it and her mother had sung it:

> The earth is your mother,
>   she holds you.
> The sky is your father,
>   he protects you.
> 5 Sleep,
>   sleep.
> Rainbow is your sister,
>   she loves you.
> The winds are your brothers,
> 10   they sing to you.
> Sleep,
>   sleep.
> We are together always
> We are together always
> 15 There never was a time
>   when this
>   was not so.

DISCUSSION QUESTIONS

1. What has happened to all of Ayah's children?
2. Ayah has a great many sorrows. In addition to the loss of her children, what else is cause for worry?
3. This story is told from the third-person limited point of view. That is, the narrator is outside the story and tells only what Ayah thinks and sees. How would the story have changed if Chato's point of view had also been shown?
4. A symbol is an event or object that represents something other than itself. What is the symbolic significance of the season? Of the blanket?
5. In your literary response journal, make notes on the cultural differences between the Navajo couple and the other characters according to medicine, language, religion, and lifestyle. How do these differences create conflict?

WRITING TOPICS

1. Suppose that you were to make a movie based on this story. Would you tell the story in chronological order or use flashbacks? Would you use a voice-over to speak Ayah's thoughts or have her character say the words? Would your film be in color or black and white? When would you use close-up shots and wide-angle shots? Would you want background music? Plan your film on paper, scene by scene, taking these questions (and others you may think of) into consideration.
2. Write an essay, developing the following thesis: In her short story "Lullaby," Leslie Silko uses these important symbols in the setting: the wool blanket, the bar, and the soft, cold snow.
3. With a classmate, compose an essay on this thesis: Ayah's strength and beliefs are revealed in three scenes: her hiding her children to protect them; her entering the bar to find Chato; and her actions as she rested against the boulders with Chato.

WAKE UP! DO NOT BE IDLE!

Maria Chona and Ruth Underhill

Maria Chona was born about 1845 and grew up in the geographic center of the Papaguería, the arid desert homeland of the Tohono O'odham or "Desert People." Two tiny creeks are the only permanent streams in the vast region. In the 1840s and 1850s, the Desert People grew or gathered their vegetable foods, hunted wild game animals, and raised a very few scrawny cattle. They defended their scattered villages against the Apaches, who in 1853 raided and destroyed Chona's home village. As Chona told Ruth Underhill, "Our enemies . . . came every fall, you know when the corn was ripe, to steal corn and women. Right over that mountain they came, and our men would gather to fight them and rescue the women." Chona's father, Con Quien, had excellent reason, therefore, to admonish his children to arise before dawn and to run every day so they could outrun enemies. Chona memorized her father's predawn poetic admonitions.

One summer day in 1930, Chona and Ruth Underhill, an anthropologist, sat with Ella Lopez Antone to begin hearing about events from Chona's life. During that summer, the elderly Chona, who did not speak English, told her life story to Underhill through Ella, a thirteen-year-old interpreter, who had learned English at Phoenix Indian School. Over time, Chona recounted additional details through other interpreters. Chona's life history falls into that class of Native American autobiographies elicited by academic scholars. *The Autobiography of a Papago Woman* was first published in 1936.

Chona lived in harmony with tribal traditions, comfortable and confident of her place within the tribe as a dutiful daughter, responsible wife, loving mother, and successful medicine woman in her later years: "You see, we *have* power. Men have to dream to get power from the spirits and they think of everything they can—song and speeches and marching around, hoping that the spirits will notice them and give them some power. But we *have* power . . . Children. Can any warrior make a child, no matter how brave and wonderful he is?"

1   We lived at Mesquite Root and my father was chief there. That was a good place, high up among the hills, but flat, with a little wash where you could plant corn. Prickly pear grew there so thick that in summer, when you picked the fruit, it was only four steps from one bush to the next. And cholla cactus grew and there were ironwood trees. Good nuts they have! There were birds flying around, doves, and woodpeckers, and a big rabbit sometimes in the early morning, and quails running across the flat land. Right above us was Quijotoa Mountain, the one where the cloud stands up high and white when we sing for rain.

2   We lived in a grass house and our relatives, all around us on the smooth flat land, had houses that were the same. Round our houses were, with no smoke hole and just a little door where you crawled in on hands and knees. That was good. The smoke could go out anywhere through the thatch and the air could come in. All our family slept on cactus fiber mats against the wall, pushed tight against it so centipedes and scorpions could not crawl in. There was a mat for each two children, but no, nothing over us. When we were cold, we put wood on the fire.

3   Early in the morning, in the month of Pleasant Cold, when we had all slept in the house to keep warm, we would wake in the dark to hear my father speaking.

4   "Open your ears, for I am telling you a good thing. Wake up and listen. Open your ears. Let my words enter them." He spoke in a low voice, so quiet in the dark. Always our fathers spoke to us like that, so low that you thought you were dreaming.

5   "Wake up and listen. You boys, you should go out and run. So you will be swift in time of war. You girls, you should grind the corn. So you will feed the men and they will fight the enemy. You should practice running. So, in time of war, you may save your lives."

6   For a long time my father talked to us like that, for he began when it was black, dark. I went to sleep, and then he pinched my ear. "Wake up! Do not be idle!"

7   Then we got up. It was the time we call morning-stands-up, when it is dark but there are white lines in the east. Those are the white hairs of Elder Brother who made us. He put them there so we can know when day is coming and we can go out to look for food.

8   We crawled out the little door. I remember that door so well. I always crawled out of doors till long after I was a married woman and we stopped being afraid of enemies. Then we made houses with white men's doors. But this one was little and when we came out we could see the houses of my relatives nearby among the cactus, and the girls coming out of them, too, to get water. . . .

9   There was no water at Mesquite Root; no water at all except what fell from the clouds, and I am telling about the month of Pleasant Cold when the rains were long over. Then our pond had dried up. If we wanted to stay in our houses, the girls had to run for water far, far up the hills and across

the flat land to a place called Where the Water Whirls Around. That was a low flat place, a good place for corn, and the water ran down to it from all the hills. A big water hole was there full of red mud. Oh yes, our water was always red. It made the corn gruel red. I liked that earth taste in my food. Yes, I liked it.

10   The girls used to crawl laughing out of the houses, with their long black hair hanging to their waists, and they would pick up their carrying nets. Fine nets we used to have in those days, all dyed with red and blue. Shaped like a cone they were, with tall red sticks to keep them in shape. When the net was on a girls' back those red sticks would stand up on either side of her face. We used to think a pretty young girl looked best that way. That was how the men liked to see her. . . .

11   Then the girls put the nets on their backs and if one was married and had a baby, she put that on top in its cradle board. Some men went with them with their war arrows because there were Apaches in the land then. They all went running, running. If they saw dust in the distance that they thought was Apaches, they went dodging behind the giant cactus. You see, women had to run in those days. That was what saved their lives. Many hours they had to run, and when they came back every family had two little jars of water to last for the day. But we did not mind. We knew how to use water. We have a word that means thirst-enduring and that is what we were taught to be. Why, our men, when they went off hunting, never drank at all. They thought it was womanish to carry water with them.

12   My brothers went running off, too. Ah, how we could run, we Desert People; all the morning until the sun was high, without once stopping! My brothers took their bows and arrows and went far off over the flat land.

13   "Run," my father said to them. "Run until you are exhausted. So you will be a strong man. If you fall down tired, far out in the waste land, perhaps a vision will come to you. Perhaps a hawk will visit you and teach you to be swift. Perhaps you will get a piece of the rainbow to carry on your shoulder so that no one can get near to you, any more than to the rainbow itself. Or maybe Coyote himself will sing you a song that has magic in it."

14   So they went off in their breechclouts and bare feet, running in the dark when they could hardly see the cactus joints on the ground and the horned toads—rattlesnakes there were not in that cool weather. One of my brothers did really have visions. The other used to come back without him, bringing jackrabbits for our dinner. The little boy would come in much later and never tell where he had been. But we found out long, long after, when he became a medicine man, that he had been lying dead out on the desert all those hours and that Coyote had come and talked to him.

15   When they were gone my mother would come crawling out. She went to the little enclosure beside our house, made of greasewood bushes piled up in a circle and she got the pot of gruel. We always kept gruel in our house. It was in a big clay pot that my mother had made. She ground up seeds into flour. Not wheat flour—we had no wheat. But all the wild seeds, the good

pigweed and the wild grasses. And corn, too! Some summers we could grow corn. All those things my mother kept in beautiful jars in our storehouse. Every day she ground some more and added fresh flour to the gruel and some boiling water. That pot stood always ready so that whoever came in from running could have some. Oh, good that gruel was! I have never tasted anything like it. Wheat flour makes me sick! I think it has no strength. But when I am weak, when I am tired, my grandchildren make me gruel out of the wild seeds. That is *food.*

DISCUSSION QUESTIONS

1. Judging from this excerpt, do you think Maria Chona had a childhood that prepared her well for adult life?
2. The people in Chona's community obviously lived close together. What would have been some reasons for this?
3. How would your life be different if your family had "two little jars of water to last for the day"?

WRITING TOPICS

1. Research the present-day Papagos and write a feature story that could be published in a newspaper.
2. Write a brief essay exploring how the tone of this excerpt works to create a certain mood. Cite examples from the reading in your essay.

IN THE HOUR OF THE WOLF

Betty Bell

Cherokee author Betty Bell was born in Oklahoma in 1949. She earned a doctorate at Ohio State University and teaches literature at the University of Michigan, Ann Arbor. "In the Hour of the Wolf" is a section from *Faces in the Moon,* her first novel (1994). Bell describes it as fictionalized autobiography because she relied on her own experiences to create characters and actions. In the first chapter she wrote, "I was raised on the voices of women. Indian women. The kitchen table was first a place of remembering, a place where women came and drew their lives from each other. The table was covered with an oilcloth in a floral pattern, large pink and red roses, the edges of the petals rubbed away by elbows." Memories and humorous stories heard at the kitchen table form the core of the novel. Bell weaves together the sounds of women's voices, telling and retelling stories, comforting and seeking comfort. From her own family history, and from the voices of those women as they preserved that history and infused their lives with meaning through the retelling of tales, Bell has shaped an impressive first novel.

⊡

1   Some parents believe children have no memories. They hold their stories and lives until they are ready to return them, with full chronology and interpretation. History is written in this complicity, an infinite regression of children forgetting and remembering. It takes a long time to remember, it takes generations, sometimes nations, to make a story. And sometimes it takes a call in the night before the story is known. . . .

2   The Oklahoma State Indian Hospital was the newest and biggest Indian hospital in the state. It was tucked in the corner of the mammoth health complex, miles and miles of hospitals and clinics and research laboratories quarantined in the northwest corner with the state capitol and government offices. What, I wondered, came first: the government men or the sickness?

I couldn't imagine a better Indian joke, placing the contagions together and hoping they would kill each other off.

3   The Indian hospital covered almost a square mile of prairie at the junction of two interstate highways. At night travelers were pulled toward the white light of a gigantic cross emblazoned across the full six stories of the main building. From the back seat of the cab I saw it appear at the end of the flat and endless highway and knew the sight would have pleased Momma. The cab pulled to a stop under the cross, and I stepped out into the heat of a thousand lights.

4   *Las Vegas. Arriving at night, momma at the wheel of our old Chevrolet and me on the passenger side, face pressed against the window, as we entered the city from the black surrounding desert. Suddenly, there was the glare of a powerful electric sun. "They say you can't tell night from day," momma said, and I knew why we had come. We came to see the miracle of something from nothing.*

5   Comprised of large, blocked interconnecting buildings, the hospital was modern and efficiently planned, with narrow mazelike corridors and directories placed every hundred feet. It was a far cry from the Indian hospitals I had gone to as a child, with their sullen white doctors and their angel-of-mercy sisters giving you the privilege of their time and sympathy, driving each patient further into sickness with gratitude. The hospitals had been army barracks, their walls a pale government green, and the only Indians in the place were in the waiting room, some coughing blood, others dazed by the long wait, even the children hung lifeless from a lap or an arm. In the middle of a waiting room, there had been a large chart: HOW TO DRESS WHEN COMING TO SEE THE DOCTOR. I studied the chart, I wanted to dress right, and any piece of information was appreciated. Over a picture of a man and woman in very fancy dress there was a large X; over a picture of a man and woman in pajamas there was a large X. I looked around, there was not one person in the room in fancy dress or pajamas. But the sign had said nothing about cowboys boots, so I tucked the boots Lizzie had given me under my chair.

6   But the smell was the same. Not just the smell of disease and antiseptic, it was the funky smell of sweat, urine, excrement, and fear, mostly fear. "The smell of white people," Lizzie had said, "the smell of people who drank too much milk." The smell, I held my breath, of rotting spirits.

7   A little woman approached me from the end of the corridor. I watched her come, down the green hall, her steps soundless and her face silent. The width of her face and her sallow skin told me she was Indian. Cherokee, maybe. She paused next to me and whispered.

8   "Are they still killing Indians here?"

9   "Excuse me?"

10   The woman slipped past.

11   "I'm sorry?" I turned and looked for the woman.

12   But she had already vanished down another sick green corridor. I caught the sound of a chant, monotonous and repetitive, fading into the hallways of the building.

13   "Crazy Indians!"

14   At the Intensive Care desk a nurse pointed to a plaque on the opposite wall and said, "Them there are the visiting hours, from one to three and from seven to nine. Visiting hours have been over for almost two hours. You'll have to come back tomorrow."

15   "But I've just arrived. I haven't seen my mother since . . . this thing happened. I came all the way from California. I'd just like to let her know I'm here."

16   "I'm sorry. We have to live by the rules."

17   "Can you tell me how she is? Gracie Khatib?"

18   The nurse picked up a handful of manila folders and thumbed through them. "How're ya spelling that last name?"

19   "K . . . h . . . a . . . t . . . i . . . b."

20   "I don't find anyone here under that name."

21   "Evers. Do you have a Gracie Evers?"

22   "Yep. Room 310, just around the corner. But," she touched my shoulder with the file, "your momma's not going to know if you're here or not. Whyn't you just go on and get some sleep and come back tomorrow?"

23   "I'd like her to know I'm here."

24   "I imagine the good Lord has taken care of that."

25   "Please?"

26   "Alright. But don't make any noise. You can stay for fifteen or twenty minutes, longer if you sit still."

27   With the file she motioned for me to follow her down the corridor. All the doors on either side were open. I heard the beep, beep, beep, and crank of machines, but no sounds of the living. I tried to look inside the rooms but could see only the ends of hospital beds and televisions hanging from the ceiling. In a few rooms the pale light of the television flickered. Now and then, I thought I saw a bundle near the foot of the bed, a few bones wrapped in white sheets. At a door near the end of the corridor, the nurse waited for me.

28   "Now, don't try to disturb her. She can't hear you."

29   Slowly I approached the woman in the bed. Red lights from the machines over her head pulsated across the dark room. I watched her body disappear into darkness, and then resurrect in a luminous red glow. Here, gone, here, gone. Dizziness and nausea threatened, the room spun. Here, gone, here, gone. I closed my eyes and stepped outside. I took a deep breath and reentered. The woman had my mother's dyed yellow hair and heavy body, my mother's pert nose and swollen arthritic hands, but the face was different. I had never seen the face without animation, without laughter, anger, or dream. I had never seen the lips so limp and thin. From moment

to moment, they had shaped words and emotion. Even when she became lost in her own stories, when her face and mind went slack with the past, her eyes burned across the silence.

30   *I wait. She stares into the wall behind me. I wait. Sometimes in the middle of a sentence, in the middle of a story, she drifts into her own dream. I learned to wait, learned to respect the suspension of talk and breath, while she walks through her dream. Then, from somewhere below, she remembers me and continues her story.*

31   I stood over her bed and waited. I watched her flick in and out of the red light and waited for her to remember me and surface. I took her cold hand in mine and ran my fingers over her arthritic joints. All those years of picking cotton and hard living, she said.

32   *"I was pickin cotton, when ya was born. Twelve hours a day in that Oklahoma sun. Without nobody a help but your Auney. And she needed help herself. Going from place to place, living on nothing but beans. And singing "Amazing Grace" from sunup to sundown. A whole field of cotton pickers singing "Amazing Grace." Their hands a-bleeding and calloused. Lookit here, ya think people are born with these kind a hands? All crooked and feeling like the bottom a somebody's shoe. I knowed one thing when ya was born, I knowed I didn't wanna pick no more cotton. Liked to a killed me. Both a y'all.*

33   I tried to slip her wedding ring over the swollen joint. "Arthritis," she said, "they'll have a cut this off a me." Once, she had made love and given birth. Once, she had loved to stomp dance, square dance, any kind of dance with drums and a fiddle. And she loved to talk. In my teens, when we lived alone, she would wake me hours before the sun rose. "Rise and shine!" she called from the kitchen, "Rise and shine!" she called above my pallet. Already, she had had coffee and several cigarettes, already she wanted bright talk and confidences. I sat there, half asleep, while she forced us through the morning's story: her life, Auney's life, her mother's life, Lizzie's life. We never spoke of my life, we knew I had no story. Sometimes, in the middle of recollecting, she would suddenly remember me and say, "Ya mind me a myself." Her claim, my sudden visibility, changed the story for a moment. Only a moment, for we both knew I was biding my time, waiting for my moment of choice.

34   My mother did not choose and so I had to. All her life she had wanted to run away, slip into some magical and quick life, and so I took the first man leaving town. I flew fast and free, only stopping, when I grew tired or unsure, to whisper "Momma." In hard times, I, too, searched the moon for a mother's face.

35   My blood carries the worry and wear that made her middle-aged at thirty and old at forty. Any minute the Oklahoma sun could burn my face into

hide and wrinkles, any minute the bloat and fatigue could fill my body. Already, the mirror catches her. Only some caution, some reticence, keeps me from exhausting all flesh and heart. But any minute, in the flash of a final disappointment. . . .

36   Every year I become more Indian, my hair darkens, my eyes grow fierce and still. Slowly, the blood rises, dragging me into its silence. I try to speak, to force words through thick memory, confounding the blood with pirou-ettes of talk. Every year the blood grows stronger, every year I come a little closer to Lucie who, sitting under the kitchen table, heard her mother tell Auney about Lizzie's death and slipped into months of fearful silence.

37   I began to pray.

38   *Y'all look better'n me, she said, y'all have a easier life. That Christmas I sent her a hundred-dollar jar of anti-wrinkle cream. She covered her face with fistfuls of the magic lanolin. She gave her hair a fresh dye and, anxious to have the full effect, she followed with a tight perm the same afternoon. Her hair burned and fell out. She tied a kerchief around her bald head and returned the jar to me.*

39   *It's too late for me, she said.*

40   Too late.

41   Unconscious, Gracie Evers was not an attractive woman. The wrinkles laid heavier in their folds, the eyes sunk in their bags, and without her teeth, the cheeks collapsed into a moist crevice. Sometimes, if there were no men around, Gracie took out her teeth and smoked cigarette after cigarette, her gums locked hard around the filter and her wide smile stretching from gum to gum.

But there was something else, something besides the teeth missing. And
42   then I knew. She was not snoring, that was it. My mother snored like an infantryman, the rasping wide big-mouthed buzz of the very, very tired. She stood twelve hours behind the cafeteria counter and when she came home, she soaked her feet and passed into sleep. Her boyfriends complained they were unable to sleep, most did not spend a second night. Now, only the machinery, breathing and beeping, filled the room with sound. Hypnotically, the bellows next to the bed expanded and collapsed with per-fect and silent air, the fluids ticked into her nose and wrist, and the moni-tors above the bed pulsed the red glow through the room.

43   I was mesmerized by the machines, her breathing slowed to the bellows, her heart beat to the strobing red light, her body surrendered to the mechanics, the monotony of sustaining and registering life. I watched the bubbles of clear liquid travel through the plastic tubing into Gracie's arm, watched the final suspended drop pause before it fell, carrying sugared water into an inert body. Somehow my loud and vulgar mother had been subdued and sacrificed to this steady drip of fluids.

44   *Beat the drum slowly . . . don't . . . stop . . . too . . . fast.*

45   I watched, her body flashing and disappearing, hearing only the suck and gasp of machines. Here, death would not be the performance she had rehearsed again and again. Here, she was outside the story, simply a heavy prop in death's solo act. Here, there would be no stories of pain endured and fear conquered, only the data of life ending as it has ended billions of times before. For my mother, for whom everything was personal, this was not personal. I watched, unable to turn my eyes from the flickering final drop as it teetered just outside the enlarged bruised vein, then the nausea rose, and I fled the room.

DISCUSSION QUESTIONS

1. What methods does the author use to evoke the life and personality of the mother?
2. What does the sign about how to dress, in the hospital the narrator remembers, imply about the attitude toward Native Americans?
3. Reread paragraph 36 and explain what the narrator means.

WRITING TOPICS

1. The narrator's mother is obviously coming to the end of her life. Is this a good way for her to die? Should her daughter advise alternatives to her mother's care? Write a few paragraphs on your views.
2. In one or two paragraphs, express your reaction to this story.
3. Recall a time when you were really sick. In a brief personal essay, give details about your illness and others' responses to you. If you stayed in a hospital, use Bell's model to create images of sight, smell, and sound for your surroundings and the staff.

ELLIS ISLAND

Joseph Bruchac

Joseph Bruchac was born in 1942 in Saratoga Springs, New York, the son of Joseph E. and Flora Bruchac. Of Slovak, English, and Abenaki heritage, Bruchac was reared by his grandparents near the Adirondack mountains in New York. He was very close to his Abenaki grandfather, whom Bruchac recalls "would never speak of the Indian blood which showed so strongly in him." Bruchac received his B.A. degree from Cornell University in 1965, then attended Syracuse University on a creative writing fellowship. After teaching in Ghana from 1966 to 1969, he earned his doctorate from Union Graduate School in Ohio in 1975. He learned much from his experience in Ghana, including "how human people are every-where—which may be the one grace that can save us all."

Like many other Native American literary renaissance writers, Bruchac began by publishing poetry and subsequently published more than thirty books of poetry, fiction, and Native American folk-tales and legends. *Indian Mountain and Other Poems* appeared in 1971, followed by *The Buffalo in the Syracuse Zoo* (1972). His first book of essays, *The Poetry of Pop,* was published in 1973. Bruchac's first novel, *The Dreams of Jesse Brown,* appeared in 1977. *Breaking Silence: An Anthology of Contemporary Asian American Poets* won an American Book Award in 1984. He is also the founding editor of the Greenfield Review Press, a respected publisher of Native American literature, and he serves on the editorial board of the journal *Studies in American Indian Literatures.*

Beyond the red brick of Ellis Island
where the two Slovak children
who became my grandparents
waited the long days of quarantine,
5   after leaving the sickness,

the old Empires of Europe,
a Circle Line ship slips easily
on its way to the island
of the tall woman, green
10 as dreams of forests and meadows
waiting for those who'd worked
a thousand years
yet never owned their own.

Like millions of others,
15 I too come to this island,
nine decades the answerer
of dreams.

Yet only one part of my blood loves that memory.
Another voice speaks
20 of native lands
within this nation.
Lands invaded
when the earth became owned.
Lands of those who followed
25 the changing Moon,
knowledge of the seasons
in their veins.

DISCUSSION QUESTIONS

1. What thoughts does the sight of Ellis Island stir in the speaker in stanza one?
2. Who is the tall woman in line 9?
3. What is the conflict in the speaker's heritage?

WRITING TOPICS

1. What does land ownership imply in non-Indian societies? Do these implications change according to how much land one owns? In a paragraph or two, explore these questions.
2. Consider Bruchac's choice of the words *Lands invaded* (line 22). In a paragraph, explain why you agree or disagree with the poet's reference.

SUMMARY WRITING TOPICS

1. Are Native American attitudes and ideas about families different from those of the culture in which you grew up? Explain in a brief essay.
2. Should people maintain close ties to the ethnic or cultural group from which they are descended, or is such closeness harmful to maintaining a peaceful society? Consider these issues in a journal entry.
3. Give your definition of family in a poem or a paragraph.
4. In the latter part of the twentieth century, definitions of family have changed. If one has no living relatives, who or what is a family, for example? Explore this question in an essay.
5. There is a passionate debate about how to prevent fetal alcohol syndrome. What are the rights of the unborn child versus the rights of a mother who consumes alcohol during pregnancy? Assume you are a member of a panel advocating solutions. Write a persuasive essay for the panel presentation stating your views regarding if and how the prospective mother should be prevented from having access to alcoholic beverages.
6. Through reading, you have been introduced to several families in this chapter. Assume you can spend three days sharing the lives of any of them. Which would you select to visit? In a personal essay, give reasons for your choice and imagine what would happen.
7. Using photographs, pictures, and your own artwork, create a collage that shows your impressions of one of these titles (or a title of your own): "American Families," "My Family, Then and Now," or "My Fantasy Family."
8. Assume you and some of your classmates have been hired by a theater company to write and perform a one-act play based on a character, an incident, or an idea from one of the selections in "All My Relations." After you have chosen the selection, write dialogue and directions for one or more scenes and perform your creation for an audience of students.

CHAPTER SIX

GROWING UP

The authors who tell us about growing up Native American span more than one hundred and fifty years from William Apess to Tiffany Midge. They range through time, space, and circumstance, through literary styles and genres. It is a long way from the conversion testimony by William Apess in *Son of the Forest* to the irreverent satire of Sherman Alexie in *The Lone Ranger and Tonto Fistfight in Heaven*. The nature of the events they consider also varies, marking milestones in the authors' transition from one stage of life to the next. Witness Luther Standing Bear's killing his first buffalo and Rayona's riding her first bucking bronco. As you will see, growing up Native American has many facets.

Authors in "Growing Up" come from very different types of families. N. Scott Momaday's parents surrounded him with warmth, intellectual stimulation, and economic security. After the murder of Gerald Vizenor's father when he was two, his young mother could provide him none of those parental gifts.

Because of cultural and situational circumstances, many Native Americans grow up in their grandparents' rather than in their parents' homes. Grandparents have provided many Native American children with intellectual and emotional anchoring in their heritages. As several authors in this chapter illustrate, each generation of young Indians needs and seeks family support and love. The selections also reveal that generation after Indian generation wrestles with questions of personal identity.

For these authors, growing up Native American means having a sense of thousands of years of ancestors, yet looking for your place in that chain of generations. It means hearing echoes of a tribal language, but not knowing words in that language for your own voice. It means celebrating ceremonies and stories, yet watching those old cultural legacies conflict with demands from modern society.

Pequot William Apess wrote the earliest autobiography included in this chapter; in contemporary terms, he was a "survivor." His genetically mixed parents and alcoholic grandparents formed a dysfunctional family like any contemporary family plagued by gangs, drug abuse, and child neglect. Kind Euro-Americans and his own logical mind saved young Apess. His 1829 autobiography remains a unique contribution to American literature. Much more fortunate in the grandparents who reared him, Slovak-Abenaki Joseph Bruchac still in mid-twentieth century had to confront deeply disturbing questions concerning his identity. Even at Cornell University, he encountered racial discrimination as he moved toward "mainstream America" via an academic education and career.

Carl Sweezy's essay about the Arapaho illustrates changes across five generations. In his childhood, he heard an old woman tell of her childhood when the Arapaho claimed the Black Hills at the edge of the Northern Plains. The next generation migrated hundreds of miles south, having to learn how to live in different environments. Then the first generation of children born on the Oklahoma reservation that resulted from the 1867 Medicine Lodge Treaty "had everything to learn about the white man's road," but "they had a good time learning it." Sweezy's literary account helps readers comprehend how many cultural changes that "road" required. During Sweezy's boyhood, adults and children alike "were still only beginning to learn" and "fences and farms were only beginning to change the look of the Reservation." In 1891, Arapaho chiefs consented to federal allotment of reserved lands to individuals: "This was the beginning of the end of our tribal life."

Despite having to cope with rapid cultural change, most Native American families in self-governing societies reared children in psychologically healthy environments, instilling in them tribal values. Luther Standing Bear vividly describes the lessons that such northern Plains families taught male children in his account of killing his first buffalo.

Several generations later, Gerald Vizenor and Sherman Alexie belong to generations venturing off reservations to big cities. Early in the twentieth century, Vizenor's French-Chippewa grandmother sold her Minnesota reservation land allotment to finance her move to Detroit Lakes, Minnesota, with eight children. After her son was murdered in Minneapolis, she "cared for" his son Gerald. Are Vizenor's psychological and physical changes limited to Native American rural-urban migrants? Sherman Alexie takes a sardonic view of both reservation and city. The story about the 7-11 comes from Alexie's *The Lone Ranger and Tonto Fistfight in Heaven*. This title itself is funny, twitting a stereotype. Alexie tells two stories in tandem, one current and teasing, one reminiscent and sad. The latter explores a topic to which he returns frequently—his stormy relationship with a non-Indian woman.

Numerous Native American authors have exposed nerves rubbed raw by the emotional stress of growing up in a dual society. Few have illustrated as well as Tiffany Midge how hilarious a simple project of a genetically mixed family with its competing and reinforcing values can be.

Michael Dorris illustrates the persisting importance of relatives to contemporary Native Americans. Doing so, he makes a young woman's failure to ride a bucking bronco during a rodeo a metaphor for personal maturation through persistence. In "Growing Up," Dorris describes achieving emotional fulfillment as a parent.

In his memoir *The Names*, N. Scott Momaday marks the end of his youth with a story of his challenging climb on Jemez mountain. Descending, he becomes trapped in the rock with his life at risk. He survives with new insight: "I should never again see the world as I saw it on the other side of that moment, in the bright reflection of time lost. There are such reflections, and for some of them I have the names." Momaday's words may apply to all the authors in this chapter who have also written of such "moments" in their literary lives.

A SON OF THE FOREST

William Apess

Against strong odds, William Apess overcame poverty, racism, and family abandonment to become an author, activist, and minister. Only a few months after being ordained as a minister in the Methodist church in 1829, he published *A Son of the Forest.* It was the first published Indian life history, and Apess, who ultimately published five books, became the most significant Indian author in the first part of the nineteenth century. In 1831, he was appointed a missionary to his own people, the Pequots. In the 1600s, the Pequots had inhabited southern Connecticut. They lived, therefore, directly in the path of colonial expansion westward. As the victims of the first genocidal war conducted by Englishmen in North America, the Pequot people were decimated by militiamen in 1637. A few Pequot survivors became dependent on New England's dominant group. Dependency does not foster mental health, and William Apess's parents and maternal grandparents were not notably healthy when he was born in 1798, more than a century and a half after the 1637 disaster.

By the time Apess was born, the Pequots had less than five hundred acres left from the thousands they had owned in 1700. The population had dwindled to about one hundred members living on two small reservations. These impoverished people made a bare living from farming, trapping, hunting, and fishing. When his parents left Apess and his siblings with their grandparents, his grandmother supported the family by making brooms and baskets to sell.

The Colrain town selectmen paid for Apess's medical care for a year after his grandmother severely injured him with a beating. At five, the child was bound out to the Furman family, who took care of him for the next six years. Apess became fond of Mrs. Furman, a pious Baptist woman, whom he remembered as "a kind, benevolent, and tender-hearted lady," who taught him about Christianity. Living with the Furmans until he was eleven, Apess attended school for six winters, his only formal schooling, which had an immense impact on his future life and writing.

Mr. Furman sold Apess's indenture to Judge James Hillhouse, who subsequently sold it to General William Williams, who lived in New London. Apess remembered, "I knew nothing of it, and I was greatly mortified to think that I was sold in this way. If my consent had been solicited as a matter of form, I should not have felt so bad. But to be sold to and treated unkindly by those who had got our fathers' lands for nothing was too much to bear." Determined to make "a good boy" of his young charge, Williams whipped him "as if stripes were calculated to effect that which love, kindness, and instruction can only successfully accomplish."

Apess's masters compelled him to attend Baptist and then Presbyterian church services, but he found Methodist congregations more appealing. He was beaten and forbidden to attend the "lowly" Methodist meetings; his masters and others objected to the Methodist practices and their welcoming of different classes and racial groups at their gatherings. Experiencing religious conversion in 1813, Apess was baptized five years later and began feeling the call to preach the Gospel.

A Son of the Forest is a valuable text in American literature that describes New England society from 1800 to 1830 from the viewpoint of a literate Native American. Two parallel themes run through it: one is Apess's journey to salvation and the other is his affirmation of his native heritage and his defense of his people against racism and injustice.

$$\boxed{\square}$$

1 William Apess, the author of the following narrative, was born in the town of Colrain, Massachusetts, on the thirty-first of January, in the year of our Lord seventeen hundred and ninety-eight. My grandfather was a white man and married a female attached to the royal family of Philip, king of the Pequot tribe of Indians, so well known in that part of American history which relates to the wars between the whites and the natives.[1] My grandmother was, if I am not misinformed, the king's granddaughter and a fair and beautiful woman. This statement is given not with a view of appearing great in the estimation of others—what, I would ask, is royal blood?—the blood of a king is no better than that of the subject. We are in fact but one family; we are all the descendants of one great progenitor—Adam. I would not boast of my extraction, as I consider myself nothing more than a worm of the earth. . . .

---

[1] *My grandfather . . . the whites and the natives:* Apess may be deliberately eliding the two great Indian-English wars in seventeenth-century New England—the Pequot War of 1637 and King Philip's War of 1675–76—but I suspect he has just confused them. Philip was not king of the Pequots, a culture located in the south-eastern part of what is now Connecticut, but the sachem of the Pokanokets located in and around Mount Hope in Rhode Island.

2   My father was of mixed blood, his father being a white man and his mother a native or, in other words, a red woman. On attaining a sufficient age to act for himself, he joined the Pequot tribe, to which he was maternally connected. He was well received, and in a short time afterward married a female of the tribe, in whose veins a single drop of the white man's blood never flowed. Not long after his marriage, he removed to what was then called the back settlements, directing his course first to the west and afterward to the northeast, where he pitched his tent in the woods of a town called Colrain, near the Connecticut River, in the state of Massachusetts. In this place, the place of my birth, he continued some time and afterward removed to Colchester, New London County, Connecticut. At the latter place, our little family lived for nearly three years in comparative comfort.

3   Circumstances, however, changed with us, as with many other people, in consequence of which I was taken together with my two brothers and sisters into my grandfather's family. One of my uncles dwelt in the same hut. Now my grandparents were not the best people in the world—like all others who are wedded to the beastly vice of intemperance, they would drink to excess whenever they could procure rum, and as usual in such cases, when under the influence of liquor, they would not only quarrel and fight with each other but would at times turn upon their unoffending grandchildren and beat them in a most cruel manner. It makes me shudder, even at this time, to think how frequent and how great have been our sufferings in consequence of the introduction of this "cursed stuff" into our family—and I could wish, in the sincerity of my soul, that it were banished from our land.

4   Our fare was of the poorest kind, and even of this we had not enough. Our clothing also was of the worst description: Literally speaking, we were clothed with rags, so far only as rags would suffice to cover our nakedness. We were always contented and happy to get a cold potato for our dinners—of this at times we were denied, and many a night have we gone supperless to rest, if stretching our limbs on a bundle of straw, without any covering against the weather, may be called rest. Truly, we were in a most deplorable condition—too young to obtain subsistence for ourselves, by the labor of our hands, and our wants almost totally disregarded by those who should have made every exertion to supply them. Some of our white neighbors, however, took pity on us and measurably administered to our wants, by bringing us frozen milk, with which we were glad to satisfy the calls of hunger. We lived in this way for some time, suffering both from cold and hunger. Once in particular, I remember that when it rained very hard my grandmother put us all down cellar, and when we complained of cold and hunger, she unfeelingly bid us dance and thereby warm ourselves—but we had no food of any kind; and one of my sisters almost died of hunger. Poor dear girl, she was quite overcome. Young as I was, my very heart bled for her. I merely relate this circumstance, without any embellishment or exaggeration, to show the reader how we were treated. The intensity of our sufferings I cannot tell. Happily, we did not continue in this very deplorable

condition for a great length of time. Providence smiled on us, but in a particular manner. . . .

[I]t was deemed expedient to bind me out, until I should attain the age of twenty-one years.[2] Mr. Furman, the person with whom the selectmen had placed me was a poor man, a cooper by trade, and obtained his living by the labor of his hands. As I was only five years old, he at first thought that his circumstances would not justify him in keeping me, as it would be some considerable time before I could render him much service. But such was the attachment of the family toward me that he came to the conclusion to keep me until I was of age, and he further agreed to give me so much instruction as would enable me to read and write. Accordingly, when I attained my sixth year, I was sent to school, and continued for six successive winters. During this time I learned to read and write, though not so well as I could have wished. This was all the instruction of the kind I ever received. Small and imperfect as was the amount of the knowledge I obtained, yet in view of the advantages I have thus derived, I bless God for it. . . .

. . . I well remember the conversation that took place between Mrs. Furman and myself when I was about six years of age; she was attached to the Baptist church and was esteemed as a very pious woman. Of this I have not the shadow of a doubt, as her whole course of conduct was upright and exemplary. On this occasion, she spoke to me respecting a future state of existence and told me that I might die and enter upon it, to which I replied that I was too young—that old people only died. But she assured me that I was not too young, and in order to convince me of the truth of the observation, she referred me to the graveyard, where many younger and smaller persons than myself were laid to molder in the earth. I had of course nothing to say—but, notwithstanding, I could not fully comprehend the nature of death and the meaning of a future state. Yet I felt an indescribable sensation pass through my frame; I trembled and was sore afraid and for some time endeavored to hide myself from the destroying monster, but I could find no place of refuge. The conversation and pious admonitions of this good lady made a lasting impression upon my mind. At times, however, this impression appeared to be wearing away—then again I would become thoughtful, make serious inquiries, and seem anxious to know something more certain respecting myself and that state of existence beyond the grave, in which I was instructed to believe. About this time I was taken to meeting in order to hear the word of God and receive instruction in divine things. This was the first time I had ever entered a house of worship, and instead of

---

[2] *It was deemed . . . twenty-one years:* Being "bound out" was a common practice in New England in the nineteenth century in dealing with people who were indigent, with orphans without relatives willing to take them in, and with those, like Apess, who had been abused. Native Americans, women and children especially, were often bound out—the adults usually for shorter periods, the children often until they reached adulthood. In return for the right to the labor of the indentured, the bondholders undertook to provide food, lodging, and clothing and sometimes other things like education.

attending to what the minister said, I was employed in gazing about the house or playing with the unruly boys with whom I was seated in the gallery. On my return home, Mr. Furman, who had been apprised of my conduct, told me that I had acted very wrong. He did not, however, stop here. He went on to tell me how I ought to behave in church, and to this very day I bless God for such wholesome and timely instruction. In this particular I was not slow to learn, as I do not remember that I have from that day to this misbehaved in the house of God. . . .

7   Shortly after this occurrence I relapsed into my former bad habits—was fond of the company of boys—and in a short time lost in a great measure that spirit of obedience which had made me the favorite of my mistress. I was easily led astray, and, once in particular, I was induced by a boy (my senior by five or six years) to assist him in his depredations on a watermelon patch belonging to one of the neighbors. But we were found out, and my companion in wickedness led me deeper in sin by persuading me to deny the crime laid to our charge. I obeyed him to the very letter and, when accused, flatly denied knowing anything of the matter. The boasted courage of the boy, however, began to fail as soon as he saw danger thicken, and he confessed it as strongly as he had denied it. The man from whom we had pillaged the melons threatened to send us to Newgate,[3] but he relented. The story shortly afterward reached the ears of the good Mrs. Furman, who talked seriously to me about it. She told me that I could be sent to prison for it, that I had done wrong, and gave me a great deal of wholesome advice. This had a much better effect than forty floggings—it sunk so deep into my mind that the impression can never be effaced.

8   I now went on without difficulty for a few months, when I was assailed by fresh and unexpected troubles. One of the girls belonging to the house had taken some offense at me and declared she would be revenged. The better to effect this end, she told Mr. Furman that I had not only threatened to kill her but had actually pursued her with a knife, whereupon he came to the place where I was working and began to whip me severely. I could not tell for what. I told him I had done no harm, to which he replied, "I will learn you, you Indian dog, how to chase people with a knife." I told him I had not, but he would not believe me and continued to whip me for a long while. But the poor man soon found out his error, as *after* he had flogged me he undertook to investigate the matter, when to his amazement he discovered it was nothing but fiction, as all the children assured him that I did no such thing. He regretted being so hasty—but I saw wherein the great difficulty consisted; if I had not denied the melon affair he would have believed me, but as I had uttered an untruth about that it was natural for him to think that the person who will tell one lie will not scruple at two. For a long while after this circumstance transpired, I did not associate with my companions. . . .

---

[3] *Newgate*: the nearest Connecticut state prison, named after the famous English prison.

9   Shortly after this occurrence I was taken ill. I then thought that I should surely die. The distress of body and the anxiety of mind wore me down. Now I think that the disease with which I was afflicted was a very curious one. The physician could not account for it, and how should I be able to do it? Neither had those who were about me ever witnessed any disorder of the kind. I felt continually as if I was about being suffocated and was consequently a great deal of trouble to the family, as someone had to be with me. One day Mr. Furman thought he would frighten the disease out of me. Accordingly, he told me that all that ailed me was this: that the devil had taken complete possession of me, and that he was determined to flog him out. This threat had not the desired effect. One night, however, I got up and went out, although I was afraid to be alone, and continued out by the door until after the family had retired to bed. After a while Mr. F. got up and gave me a dreadful whipping. He really thought, I believe, that the devil was in me and supposed that the birch was the best mode of ejecting him. But the flogging was as fruitless as the preceding threat in the accomplishment of his object, and he, poor man, found out his mistake, like many others who act without discretion. . . .

10   Soon after I recovered from my sickness, I went astray, associating again with my old schoolfellows and on some occasions profaning the Sabbath day. I did not do thus without warning, as conscience would speak to me when I did wrong. Nothing very extraordinary occurred until I had attained my eleventh year. At this time it was fashionable for boys to run away, and the wicked one put it into the head of the oldest boy on the farm to persuade me to follow the fashion. He told me that I could take care of myself and get my own living. I thought it was a very pretty notion to be a man—*to do business for myself and become rich.* Like a fool, I concluded to make the experiment and accordingly began to pack up my clothes as deliberately as could be, and in which my adviser assisted. I had been once or twice at New London, where I saw, as I thought, everything wonderful: Thither I determined to bend my course, as I expected that on reaching the town I should be metamorphosed into a person of consequence; I had the world and everything my little heart could desire on a string, when behold, my companion, who had persuaded me to act thus, informed my master that I was going to run off. At first he would not believe the boy, but my clothing already packed up was ample evidence of my intention. On being questioned I acknowledged the fact. I did not wish to leave them—told Mr. Furman so; he believed me but thought best that for a while I should have another master. He accordingly agreed to transfer my indentures to Judge Hillhouse for the sum of twenty dollars.[4] Of course, after the bargain was made, my consent was to be obtained, but I was as unwilling

---

[4] *He accordingly agreed . . . twenty dollars:* Judge William Hillhouse of New London county, chief judge of the county court. He was one of the most prominent and powerful of the old gentry of Connecticut. He had fought in the Revolution and had sat in the Continental Congress. Twenty dollars would have been in 1804, when the transfer occurred, about two months' salary for a common laborer.

to go now as I had been anxious to run away before. After some persuasion, I agreed to try it for a fortnight, on condition that I should take my dog with me, and my request being granted I was soon under the old man's roof, as he only lived about six miles off. Here everything was done to make me contented, because they thought to promote their own interests by securing my services. They fed me with knickknacks, and soon after I went among them I had a jackknife presented to me, which was the first one I had ever seen. Like other boys, I spent my time either in whittling or playing with my dog and was withal very happy. But I was homesick at heart, and as soon as my fortnight had expired I went home without ceremony. Mr. Furman's family were surprised to see me, but that surprise was mutual satisfaction in which my faithful dog appeared to participate.

11 The joy I felt on returning home, as I hoped, was turned to sorrow on being informed that I had been *sold* to the judge and must instantly return. This I was compelled to do. And, reader, all this sorrow was in consequence of being led away by a bad boy: If I had not listened to him I should not have lost my home. Such treatment I conceive to be the best means to accomplish the ruin of a child, as the reader will see in the sequel. I was sold to the judge at a time when age had rendered him totally unfit to manage an unruly lad. If he undertook to correct me, which he did at times, I did not regard it as I knew that I could run off from him if he was too severe, and besides I could do what I pleased in defiance of his authority. Now the old gentleman was a member of the Presbyterian church and withal a very strict one. He never neglected family prayer, and he always insisted on my being present. I did not believe or, rather, had no faith in his prayer, because it was the same thing from day to day, and I had heard it repeated so often that I knew it as well as he. Although I was so young, I did not think that Christians ought to learn their prayers, and knowing that he repeated the same thing from day to day is, I have no doubt, the very reason why his petitions did me no good. I could fix no value on his prayers.[5]

12 After a little while the conduct of my new guardians was changed toward me. Once secured, I was no longer the favorite. The few clothes I had were not taken care of, by which I mean no pains were taken to keep them clean and whole, and the consequence was that in a little time they were all "tattered and torn" and I was not fit to be seen in decent company. I had not the opportunity of attending meeting as before. Yet, as the divine and reclaiming impression had not been entirely defaced, I would frequently retire behind the barn and attempt to pray in my weak manner. I now became quite anxious to attend evening meetings a few miles off: I asked the judge if I should go and take one of the horses, to which he consented. This

---

[5] *I could fix no value on his prayers:* The issue here is rote, "learned" prayers, as opposed to the spontaneous prayers favored by the evangelical Protestants at whose services Apess felt most moved and at home.

promise greatly delighted me—but when it was time for me to go, all my hopes were dashed at once, as the judge had changed his mind. I was not to be foiled so easily; I watched the first opportunity and slipped off with one of the horses, reached the meeting, and returned in safety. Here I was to blame; if he acted wrong, it did not justify me in doing so; but being successful in one grand act of disobedience, I was encouraged to make another similar attempt, whenever my unsanctified dispositions prompted; for the very next time I wished to go to meeting, I thought I would take the horse again, and in the same manner too, without the knowledge of my master. As he was by some means apprised of my intention, he prevented my doing so and had the horses locked up in the stable. He then commanded me to give him the bridle; I was obstinate for a time, then threw it at the old gentleman and run off. I did not return until the next day, when I received a flogging for my bad conduct, which determined me to run away. Now, the judge was partly to blame for all this. He had in the first place treated me with the utmost kindness until he had made sure of me. Then the whole course of his conduct changed, and I believed he fulfilled only one item of the transferred indentures, and that was work. Of this there was no lack. To be sure I had enough to eat, such as it was, but he did not send me to school as he had promised.

Discussion Questions

1. How would you characterize the Furmans?
2. What effect did Mrs. Furman's talk with young Apess about his "future state of existence" (paragraph 6) have on him?
3. Mr. Furman's solution to any problems with Apess was to flog him. From what you know about this period in history, do you think he did so because Apess was an Indian, because he was a servant, or because this was an acceptable way to discipline any child?
4. How was Apess treated by Judge Hillhouse?
5. What was Apess's general attitude toward his early life?

Writing Topics

1. Were you ever punished unjustly as a child? If so, explain the circumstances in an autobiographical essay.

2. Massachusetts, where Apess was born, has an Indian name, as do more than half the states. Many lakes, rivers, mountains, towns, and counties in the United States also have Indian names. Research some of these names and their meanings in your area and write an article that could be published in a local newspaper.

3. Write a brief essay in which you analyze the diction (choice of words) of this autobiographical excerpt. Make your topic sentence one that states how you would describe the style. For example, would you call it serious, vivid, imitative, original, dignified? A combination of some of these? Support your thesis with examples from the selection.

4. Research the causes and consequences of the Pequot War of 1637. Write a narrative report from the viewpoint of a Pequot or a Puritan.

AT LAST I KILL A BUFFALO

Luther Standing Bear

In this chapter from *My Indian Boyhood* (1931), Luther Standing Bear tells of the test of his hunting skills and his "real character." Born in 1865 or 1868, Young Ota k'te, or Plenty Kill, was one of the last Sioux to be reared to become a warrior and hunter. His Lakota people depended on bison meat and hides, so bison hunting evoked strong emotions. In *Land of the Spotted Eagle* (1933), Standing Bear wrote of the value of buffalo to his people: "Horns were made into spoons, hoofs boiled for glue, ribs turned into sleds, toys, and games, the skull used for ceremonial purposes, the thick hide on the head dried and shaped into bowls and tubs, the large bones broken and boiled to skim for tallow and the hides used for innumerable purposes."

To the Lakota male in the 1870s, killing his first bison marked a turning point, in Standing Bear's case a trial of "the strength of my manhood and my honesty." Describing this experience, Standing Bear tells his readers about his respect for his father and the latter's role as instructor. Standing Bear also pays tribute to the influence of his mother, Wastewin or Pretty Face, "who in her humble way, helped to make the history of her race. For it is the mothers, not the warriors, who create a people and guide their destiny."

The young Plenty Kill learned vital skills by playing games of riding and shooting. In one game, players shot an arrow at a moccasin target placed on top of a pole planted in the earth. The rules called for riding at break-neck speed; if a rider slowed his pony nearing the pole, he was disqualified. Young men also learned other equestrian skills, such as mounting horses running at full speed. Standing Bear explained that the trainee ran a few steps beside the horse "then grasping his mane and springing in the air, he was lifted by the motion of the animal." He also learned to mount behind a rider so another rider could save him in case he were unhorsed during a battle.

These and other experiences from growing up Lakota stayed with Standing Bear all of his life. Long after he left his Lakota home on the Pine Ridge Reservation, he ended his book *Land of the Spotted Eagle* with the conviction that his upbringing had been the best: "So if today I had a young mind to direct, to start on the journey of life, and I was faced with the duty of choosing between the natural way of my forefathers and that of the white man's present way of civilization, I would, for its welfare, unhesitatingly set that child's feet in the path of my forefathers. I would raise him to be an Indian!"

1   At last the day came when my father allowed me to go on a buffalo hunt with him. And what a proud boy I was!

2   Ever since I could remember my father had been teaching me the things that I should know and preparing me to be a good hunter. I had learned to make bows and to string them; and to make arrows and tip them with feathers. I knew how to ride my pony no matter how fast he would go, and I felt that I was brave and did not fear danger. All these things I had learned for just this day when father would allow me to go with him on a buffalo hunt. It was the event for which every Sioux boy eagerly waited. To ride side by side with the best hunters of the tribe, to hear the terrible noise of the great herds as they ran, and then to help bring home the kill was the most thrilling day of any Indian boy's life. The only other event which could equal it would be the day I went for the first time on the warpath to meet the enemy and protect my tribe.

3   On the following early morning we were to start, so the evening was spent in preparation. Although the tipis were full of activity, there was no noise nor confusion outside. Always the evening before a buffalo hunt and when every one was usually in his tipi, an old man went around the circle of tipis calling, "I-ni-la," "I-ni-la," not loudly, but so every one could hear. The old man was saying, "Keep quiet," "Keep quiet." We all knew that the scouts had come in and reported buffalo near and that we must all keep the camp in stillness. It was not necessary for the old man to go into each tipi and explain to the men that tomorrow there would be a big hunt, as the buffalo were coming. He did not order the men to prepare their weapons and neither did he order the mothers to keep children from crying. The one word, "I-ni-la," was sufficient to bring quiet to the whole camp. That night there would be no calling or shouting from tipi to tipi and no child would cry aloud. Even the horses and dogs obeyed the command for quiet, and all night not a horse neighed and not a dog barked. The very presence of quiet was everywhere. Such is the orderliness of a Sioux camp that men, women, children, and animals seem to have a common understanding and sympathy. It is no mystery but natural that the Indian and his animals understand each other very well both with words and without words. There are words, however, that the Indian uses that are understood by both his horses and dogs. When on a hunt, if one of the warriors speaks the word, "A-a-ah" rather quickly and sharply, every man, horse, and dog will stop instantly and listen.

Not a move will be made by an animal until the men move or speak further. As long as the hunters listen, the animals will listen also.

4   The night preceding a buffalo hunt was always an exciting night, even though it was quiet in camp. There would be much talk in the tipis around the fires. There would be sharpening of arrows and of knives. New bow-strings would be made and quivers would be filled with arrows.

5   It was in the fall of the year and the evenings were cool as father and I sat by the fire and talked over the hunt. I was only eight years of age, and I know that father did not expect me to get a buffalo at all, but only to try perhaps for a small calf should I be able to get close enough to one. Nevertheless, I was greatly excited as I sat and watched father working in his easy, firm way.

6   I was wearing my buffalo-skin robe, the hair next to my body. Mother had made me a rawhide belt and this, wrapped around my waist, held my blanket on when I threw it off my shoulders, In the early morning I would wear it, for it would be cold. When it came time to shoot, I should not want my blanket but the belt would hold it in place.

7   You can picture me, I think, as I sat in the glow of the campfire, my lit-tle brown body bare to the waist watching, and listening intently to my father. My hair hung down my back and I wore moccasins and breechcloth of buckskin. To my belt was fastened a rawhide holster for my knife, for when I was eight years of age we had plenty of knives. I was proud to own a knife, and this night I remember I kept it on all night. Neither did I lay aside my bow, but went to sleep with it in my hand, thinking, I suppose, to be all the nearer ready in the morning when the start was made.

8   Father sharpened my steel points for me and also sharpened my knife. The whetstone was a long stone which was kept in a buckskin bag, and sometimes this stone went all over the camp; every tipi did not have one, so we shared this commodity with one another. I had as I remember about ten arrows, so when father was through sharpening them I put them in my rawhide quiver. I had a rawhide quirt,[1] too, which I would wear fastened to my waist. As father worked, he knew I was watching him closely and lis-tening whenever he spoke. By the time all preparations had been made, he had told me just how I was to act when I started out in the morning with the hunters.

9   We went to bed, my father hoping that tomorrow would be successful for him so that he could bring home some nice meat for the family and a hide for my mother to tan. I went to bed, but could not go to sleep at once, so filled was I with the wonderment and excitement of it all. The next day was to be a test for me. I was to prove to my father whether he was or was not justified in his pride in me. What would be the result of my training?

---

[1] *quirt:* a whip with a short handle.

Would I be brave if I faced danger and would father be proud of me? Though I did not know that night I was to be tried for the strength of my manhood and my honesty in this hunt. Something happened that day which I remember above all things. It was a test of my real character and I am proud to say that I did not find myself weak, but made a decision that has been all these years a gratification to me.

10   The next morning the hunters were catching their horses about daybreak. I arose with my father and went out and caught my pony. I wanted to do whatever he did and show him that he did not have to tell me what to do. We brought our animals to the tipi and got our bows and arrows and mounted. From over the village came the hunters. Most of them were leading their running horses. These running horses were anxious for the hunt and came prancing, their ears straight up and their tails waving in the air. We were joined with perhaps a hundred or more riders, some of whom carried bows and arrows and some armed with guns.

11   The buffalo were reported to be about five or six miles away as we should count distance now. At that time we did not measure distance in miles. One camping distance was about ten miles, and these buffalo were said to be about one half camping distance away.

12   Some of the horses were to be left at a stopping place just before the herd was reached. These horses were pack animals which were taken along to carry extra blankets or weapons. They were trained to remain there until the hunters came for them. Though they were neither hobbled nor tied, they stood still during the shooting and noise of the chase.

13   My pony was a black one and a good runner. I felt very important as I rode along with the hunters and my father, the chief. I kept as close to him as I could.

14   Two men had been chosen to scout or to lead the party. These two men were in a sense policemen whose work it was to keep order. They carried large sticks of ash wood, something like a policeman's billy, though longer. They rode ahead of the party while the rest of us kept in a group close together. The leaders went ahead until they sighted the herd of grazing buffalo. Then they stopped and waited for the rest of us to ride up. We all rode slowly toward the herd, which on sight of us had come together, although they had been scattered here and there over the plain. When they saw us, they all ran close together as if at the command of a leader. We continued riding slowly toward the herd until one of the leaders shouted, "Ho-ka-he!" which means, "Ready, Go!" At that command every man started for the herd. I had been listening, too, and the minute the hunters started, I started also.

15   Away I went, my little pony putting all he had into the race. It was not long before I lost sight of father, but I kept going just the same. I threw my blanket back and the chill of the autumn morning struck my body, but I did not mind. On I went. It was wonderful to race over the ground with all these horsemen about me. There was no shouting, no noise of any kind

except the pounding of the horses' feet. The herd was now running and had raised a cloud of dust. I felt no fear until we had entered this cloud of dust and I could see nothing about me—only hear the sound of feet. Where was father? Where was I going? On I rode through the cloud, for I knew I must keep going.

16   Then all at once I realized that I was in the midst of the buffalo, their dark bodies rushing all about me and their great heads moving up and down to the sound of their hoofs beating upon the earth. Then it was that fear overcame me and I leaned close down upon my little pony's body and clutched him tightly. I can never tell you how I felt toward my pony at that moment. All thought of shooting had left my mind. I was seized by blank fear. In a moment or so, however, my senses became clearer, and I could distinguish other sounds beside the clatter of feet. I could hear a shot now and then and I could see the buffalo beginning to break up into small bunches. I could not see father nor any of my companions yet, but my fear was vanishing and I was safe. I let my pony run. The buffalo looked too large for me to tackle, anyway, so I just kept going. Pretty soon I saw a young calf that looked about my size. I remembered now what father had told me the night before as we sat about the fire. Those instructions were important for me now to follow.

17   I was still back of the calf, being unable to get alongside of him. I was anxious to get a shot, yet afraid to try, as I was still very nervous. While my pony was making all speed to come alongside, I chanced a shot and to my surprise my arrow landed. My second arrow glanced along the back of the animal and sped on between the horns, making only a slight wound. My third arrow hit a spot that made the running beast slow up in his gait. I shot a fourth arrow, and though it, too, landed it was not a fatal wound. It seemed to me that it was taking a lot of shots, and I was not proud of my marksmanship. I was glad, however, to see the animal going slower and I knew that one more shot would make me a hunter. My horse seemed to know his own importance. His two ears stood straight forward and it was not necessary for me to urge him to get closer to the buffalo. I was soon by the side of the buffalo and one more shot brought the chase to a close. I jumped from my pony, and as I stood by my fallen game, I looked all around wishing that the world could see. But I was alone. In my determination to stay by until I had won my buffalo, I had not noticed that I was far from every one else. No admiring friends were about, and as far as I could see I was on the plain alone. The herd of buffalo had completely disappeared. And as for father, much as I wished for him, he was out of sight and I had no idea where he was.

18   I stood and looked at the animal on the ground. I was happy. Every one must know that I, Ota K'te, had killed a buffalo. But it looked as if no one knew where I was, so no one was coming my way. I must then take something from this animal to show that I had killed it. I took all the arrows one by one from the body. As I took them out, it occurred to me that I had used

five arrows. If I had been a skillful hunter, one arrow would have been sufficient, but I had used five. Here it was that temptation came to me. Why could I not take out two of the arrows and throw them away? No one would know, and then I should be more greatly admired and praised as a hunter. As it was, I knew that I should be praised by father and mother, but I wanted more. And so I was tempted to lie.

19   I was planning this as I took out my skinning knife that father had sharpened for me the night before. I skinned one side of the animal, but when it came to turning it over, I was too small. I was wondering what to do when I heard my father's voice calling, "To-ki-i-la-la-hu-wo," "Where are you?" I quickly jumped on my pony and rode to the top of a little hill near by. Father saw me and came to me at once. He was so pleased to see me and glad to know that I was safe. I knew that I could never lie to my father. He was too fond of me and I too proud of him. He had always told me to tell the truth. He wanted me to be an honest man, so I resolved then to tell the truth even if it took from me a little glory. He rode up to me with a glad expression on his face, expecting me to go back with him to his kill. As he came up, I said as calmly as I could, "Father, I have killed a buffalo." His smile changed to surprise and he asked me where my buffalo was. I pointed to it and we rode over to where it lay, partly skinned.

20   Father set to work to skin it for me. I had watched him do this many times and knew perfectly well how to do it myself, but I could not turn the animal over. There was a way to turn the head of the animal so that the body would be balanced on the back while being skinned. Father did this for me, while I helped all I could. When the hide was off, father put it on the pony's back with the hair side next to the pony. On this he arranged the meat so it would balance. Then he covered the meat carefully with the rest of the hide, so no dust would reach it while we traveled home. I rode home on top of the load.

21   I showed my father the arrows that I had used and just where the animal had been hit. He was very pleased and praised me over and over again. I felt more glad than ever that I had told the truth and I have never regretted it. I am more proud now that I told the truth than I am of killing the buffalo.

22   We then rode to where my father had killed a buffalo. There we stopped and prepared it for taking home. It was late afternoon when we got back to camp. No king ever rode in state who was more proud than I that day as I came into the village sitting high up on my load of buffalo meat. Mother had now two hunters in the family and I knew how she was going to make over me. It is not customary for Indian men to brag about their exploits and I had been taught that bragging was not nice. So I was very quiet, although I was bursting with pride. Always when arriving home I would run out to play, for I loved to be with the other boys, but this day I lingered about close to the tipi so I could hear the nice things that were said about me. It was soon all over camp that Ota K'te had killed a buffalo.

23   My father was so proud that he gave away a fine horse. He called an old man to our tipi to cry out the news to the rest of the people in camp. The old man stood at the door of our tipi and sang a song of praise to my father. The horse had been led up and I stood holding it by a rope. The old man who was doing the singing called the other old man who was to receive the horse as a present. He accepted the horse by coming up to me, holding out his hands to me, and saying, "Ha-ye," which means "Thank you." The old man went away very grateful for the horse.

24   That ended my first and last buffalo hunt. It lives only in my memory, for the days of the buffalo are over.

DISCUSSION QUESTIONS

1. What adjectives would you use to describe life in the author's village?
2. Killing a buffalo with a bow and arrow while riding a pony bareback seems a remarkable accomplishment, especially when the author was only eight years old at the time. Speculate on how he might have prepared himself to do this.
3. How did the author's father show his pride in his son?
4. What accounts for the difference between the boyhoods of William Apess and Luther Standing Bear?

WRITING TOPICS

1. In your journal, write about a time when you finally achieved something that you had wanted to do for a long time.
2. Using print or electronic sources, research the history of the North American bison, including their near extinction, and report to the class.
3. Luther Standing Bear includes many details that appeal to the senses and add to the vividness of his account. Find the passages that appeal to the senses of hearing, sight, touch, and smell and cite them in a brief essay about the sensory details in this excerpt.

FROM *THE ARAPAHO WAY*

Carl Sweezy and Althea Bass

Artist and author Carl Sweezy was born in 1881 and died in 1953. As a Blue Cloud Arapaho, he grew up in the traditional ways and adjusted to modern life as it replaced the ways of his childhood. He taught himself to paint, and in his illustrations for *The Arapaho Way* he portrays dances, hunts, games, dress, and ceremonies he knew. He saw the Ghost Dance and the Sun Dance. He knew how the Plains Indians made their clothing, their home furnishings, and their war and hunting gear. In his memoir, he recalls sitting with old men who straightened willow rods with their teeth and soaked sinews in their mouth; watching women dress skins and bead moccasins; and learning to shoot with a bow and arrow.

Remembering his childhood on the then-immense Cheyenne-Arapaho Reservation in central Oklahoma, Sweezy made "The Family Tipi" a metaphor for family-centered Arapaho life. A fire constantly burned in the center of the tipi; food simmered in a cooking pot suspended above it. Thus, the central space in the tipi functioned in the same way as the kitchen in most rural Euro-American homes in the late nineteenth century. Family members interacted frequently and intensively in each kind of cooking-eating space.

Arapaho families effectively allocated space within the tipi by gender and age. Plainly aware of Euro-American negative stereotypes of the traditional Plains Indian way of life, Sweezy stressed that every material possession had its assigned place; even air space was used to store dried meat and fruits. He claimed that the family kept everything in its proper place. Describing pitching a tipi and cutting otter grass for winter windbreaks, Sweezy clarified much about the labor the women in a family performed. Women were vital partners in the Arapaho export economy of furs and hides, as well as the emotional mainstays of their families.

1 These Were the Arapaho

My people, the Arapaho, are scattered now. There are fewer than one thousand of us who are full-bloods now living in Oklahoma, and many of us who are left do not know our language or our old ways and our old songs and stories. The Cheyenne-Arapaho Agency at Darlington is gone; Fort Reno, across the river from the old Agency, is no longer a fort; our white lodges no longer stand in circles on the prairie with their poles pointed toward the blue sky. Mornings and evenings no smoke from hundreds of campfires rises into the air; no coyotes howl at night and no prairie dogs build their towns on the uplands. No ponies graze in herds on the open ranges. There are fences dividing the farms, and barns for the cows and horses, and roads marking the land in sections, and highways carrying the people in fast cars from one town to another or from town to their farm homes. A pony carrying an Indian woman on its back, with a travois dragging behind to carry the children and the puppies and the household goods to the hunt or to another village, is never seen.

A boy growing up today has no way of knowing how good life was on the Cheyenne-Arapaho Reservation when I was a boy, or what that life was like, unless he reads about it in books. Even if he should read books about our life, he would miss something. Books could not make him see the sun rising over the land that stretched for miles without fences or roads, or the North Canadian River and the smaller streams winding through that land with trees and brush along their banks and reeds and grass as high as a man's waist in the low places, or feel how friendly the life in our villages was, with children and dogs and ponies outside the tipis, and men and women busy drying meat or beading moccasins or making arrows or dressing skins. But I an old man who can remember all this from my boyhood, before the white man's government and religion and houses and inventions changed everything. The road of the Arapaho was an old and good one, and we believed it had been traveled since the beginning of the world. Now, though we can no longer travel it, it is a good thing to show how that road once ran before we lost it.

In the beginning, we Arapaho called ourselves by a different name that meant "Our Own Kind of People." We had our own kind of lodges and dress, our own societies and beliefs and ways of worship. The Cheyenne called us "Cloud Men," and the Sioux called us "Blue Clouds." We believed that we were the first people created, and that when we were made we were placed in the center of the earth. That was convenient, because we were traders and exchanged goods with all the other Indian tribes around us. The word "Arapaho" means trader. We lived all over the Great Plains, as far west as the Rocky Mountains and east beyond the Mississippi, in the beginning. We hunted and traded there, and got along well with most of the other tribes and held our own against those who were our enemies. After the white men came to the Plains, some of us moved farther south and were separated from the rest of our tribe. Since then we have been called the Southern Arapaho. We never quarreled with the northern division of our tribe, or had any differences with them in our beliefs; we are still one people and we like to visit them in Wyoming and have them visit us in Oklahoma.

4   My people were always known to be friendly and peace-loving. But we had our great war chiefs and our weapons and our dances for war, and when we had to fight we fought hard and well. Long before my day we had been at war with the Ute and the Shoshoni, and when I was a boy we still spoke of the Navajo and the Pawnee as our enemies. But when we made peace, with Indians or with white men, we mean it and we kept it. When our great chief Little Raven signed the treaty at Medicine Lodge, we agreed not to make war again and to sit down on the Reservation with the Cheyenne in what is now Oklahoma. Little Raven saw that the old days were ended, and that we must live at peace with the white men who were coming to the Great Plains with guns and wagons and cattle and machinery. He gave his promise, and we have kept it. Later, when the white men moved their camps to our Reservation and hunted there, or stole our cattle and horses, or held back the rations they had promised to provide for us until we learned to live as they lived, we did not go to war. . . .

5   President Grant was the Great White Father in Washington when we came to the Reservation. . . . He sent Brinton Darlington to be our first Agent. Mr. Darlington belonged to the Society of Friends, the Quakers, and we could tell that he believed many of the things that we believed. He knew, as we did, that there was a good Man-Above and an evil Man-Below, and he worshipped and prayed to the Man-Above. And although he never spoke to my people about his belief in Mother-Earth, he must have believed in her as we did. He and the men he brought with him had strong power in planting and harvesting, while we depended on what Mother-Earth gave us, growing wild. He never spoke to us about the power of the Four Old Men, that comes from the four quarters of the earth, or of the mysteries of Grandfather Sun that lights the day, or of the Moon the Night-Sun, or of the influences of buffalo and eagle and owl and coyote. He had not been trained in our religious societies and did not know our ceremonies. But he did not try to wipe them all out, as some white people believed in doing.

6   Brinton Darlington came to the Agency as our friend and helper, and we liked him. . . . He brought assistants there, many of them Quakers like himself, who built good buildings and started schools and opened trading posts and laid out farms. He planted an orchard and a garden, so that our people might learn how fruits and vegetables grew. He was patient and kind; he managed like a chief; he prayed to the Man-Above when he was thankful and when he needed power. So although he was a white man and did not speak our language, we could understand him. He died in 1872, some years before I was born, and when he was buried in the cemetery on the hill near the road that ran between the Agency and Caddo Spring, there were

Cheyenne and Arapaho chiefs, as well as white men, who wept over his grave. . . .

7   We had everything to learn about the white man's road. We had come to a country that was new to us, where wind and rain and rivers and heat and cold and even some of the plants and animals were different from what we had always know. We had to learn to live by farming instead of by hunting and trading; we had to learn from people who did not speak our language or try to learn it, except for a few words, though they expected us to learn theirs. We had to learn to cut our hair short, and to wear close-fitting clothes made of dull-colored cloth, and to live in houses, though we knew that our long braids of hair and embroidered robes and moccasins and tall, round lodges were more beautiful. . . .

8   We had never made brick or sawed lumber or had a wooden door to open and shut. Although some of us had visited the forts and the trading posts before we came to the Reservation, and a few of us had seen the white man's towns and cities, hardly any of us had ever been in houses where families lived. We thought windows were put in the walls so that we might look in to see how white people did their work and ate their meals and visited with each other. We pulled up some of the first little trees that were planted at Darlington, to see why the white people had put sticks in the ground in rows. There is a story that one of our men, given a little pig to raise so that when it grew up he could have pork and bacon, returned it to the Agency to be kept for him until it grew too big to get through the holes in his fence. He did not realize that he could repair the fence to suit the size of his pig.

9   We knew nothing about how to harness a work horse or turn a furrow in a field or cut and store hay; and today I suppose there are men living in cities who know no more about these things than we did. Our women did not know how to build a fire in a cook-stove or wash clothes in a tub of water. It was a long time before we knew what the figures on the face of a clock meant, or why people looked at them before they ate their meals or started off to church. We had to learn that clocks had something to do with the hours and minutes that the white people mentioned so often. Hours, minutes, and seconds were such small divisions of time that we had never thought of them. When the sun rose, when it was high in the sky, and when it set were all the divisions of the day that we had ever found necessary when we followed the old Arapaho road. When we went on a hunting trip or to a sun dance, we counted time by sleeps.

10   My people had everything to learn about the white man's road, but they had a good time learning it. How they laughed when a war pony, not understanding what it was supposed to do when it was hitched to a plough or a wagon, lunged and jumped away and threw them flat on the ground, with the plough or the wagon riding high in the air. How puzzled they were when they found that old men and women, among the white people, had teeth they could take out of their mouths and put back in again. They gave Brinton Darlington the name "Tosimeea," "He Who Takes Out His Teeth,"

when he showed them he could do this, and they wondered how he had come by that strange power. But when Mr. Miles came, he could do the same thing. It must be, they thought, something all Agents had the power to do; so the movement of taking out and putting back a set of teeth became the word for Agent in our sign language. And stair steps, built to take people up to a house built on top of another house, still amused us. We had never expected to have such things for our own use, on our Reservation.

11   Slowly, the Cheyenne and the Arapaho began to understand some of these things. But when I was a boy at Darlington they were still only beginning to learn. Most of them kept to the old way, in family and village and tribe, and there are a few of us left who can still remember it. We can remember the stretches of prairie where we rode and hunted, mile after mile with no one to stop us; we can remember our villages of tipis, with a crier calling the day's news from one village to the next in the evening quiet; we can remember annuity and issue days, when we dressed in our best robes and moccasins and gathered on the Agency grounds to visit together and receive the goods and the food we needed until we learned to earn money and raise crops and cattle in the white man's way. We can remember our great summer dances, when our whole tribe gathered and put up the medicine lodge and sang and danced and prayed and visited, and made our vows to the Man-Above and received our blessings. Even today, when we pass some spot that is now Geary or Bridgeport or Greenfield, we stop and say, "This is the place where we built the medicine lodge and held the Sun Dance, that summer when we were boys. Remember?"

2   THE FAMILY TIPI

12   I have never known the date of my birth, and I never had a birthday party in my childhood. This was true of all Indian children that I knew when I was growing up, and did not mean that our parents were lacking in love and attention toward us, but only that they knew nothing about dates and had no way of recording them. They usually gave a feast when a new baby was named and one when he first began to walk; and they and our older relatives and friends taught us all we were supposed to know about good manners and the right way to live. We never doubted that they loved us and were concerned for us, even though our birthdays were never celebrated. White people have looked into our school records and tell me I was probably born in 1881, because they find me listed as a child of seven at the Mennonite Mission School in 1888. But I do not know the month or the date of my birth.

13   The first thing I remember about my childhood is the tipi where my family lived. It was one of many that belonged to our band or village, and was always somewhere not far from the Agency. All of our tipis were a good deal alike, and yet none of us children ever made the mistake of getting into the wrong one when we wanted to go home to our mothers, perhaps for the

same reason that prairie dogs never ran into the wrong hole in the ground or cliff swallows never flew into the wrong opening in the river bank. We were within sound of the big bell that hung above the stable at the Agency and was rung at seven in the morning and at noon and at six in the evening, to tell the employees there when to go to work and when to stop. On good days, too, we could hear the bugle calls from Fort Reno, a mile and a half away from the Agency on the high land across the Canadian River. For us in our villages, these bells and bugle calls served as clocks when we needed to take notice of time in the white man's way.

14   Except in midwinter, most of us were stirring in our village long before we heard the Agency bell ring seven o'clock. Our circle of lodges was open to the east, and each one of the lodges within the circle also opened eastward, to the dawn of light and to the sunrise. That was the way the Arapaho had been taught to build their lodges, at the beginning of time, and that was the way we had always built them. I never saw an Arapaho tipi facing any other way, and if I had seen one, even when I was very small, I would have known that something, or everything, about it was wrong.

15   When I was born, most of the Cheyenne and the Arapaho still lived in tipis. Brinton Darlington, when he first came to the Agency, had called our chiefs together and told them he wanted them to live as white people lived, in houses with gardens and orchards and fields around them The Government, he said, would help us build our houses when we were ready to live in them. But this meant a great change, and one we could not make in a hurry. We liked our tipis, with all our things around us in a circle. I have heard white people talk, of late, about the modern circular house, with arrangements for heat and plumbing in the center, new as tomorrow, they say. Well, ours were circular, with a central fire, but I never heard an Arapaho boast that the idea was a new one.

16   The corn road, we found, was different from the buffalo road in more ways than anyone, white or Indian, had realized, and the old people could not learn it in a hurry. But in 1872 a man named John Seger was hired to come to Darlington, to set up a sawmill and a brick plant, and to help build houses and school buildings and offices and a commissary there. He built good buildings, some of them three stories high, and we liked him. He lived among the Cheyenne and the Arapaho for more than fifty years, building and teaching and farming and running a stage and mail line, and he was our friend until he died at Colony in 1928. His children played with us and went to our Arapaho school and learned our language and songs and games and stories. Some people said they even came to look like us.

17   Mr. Seger had a fine memory, and he liked to tell stories about interesting and amusing things that happened on the Reservation. One of the stories he liked to tell was that of how Little Raven objected to the house the Agent proposed to build for him on the Reservation. Little Raven had been taken East, with some other chiefs of the Cheyenne and the Arapaho, to meet the Great White Father and to see the wonders of Washington and

Philadelphia and other cities. The house of the Great White Father was big and fine, he said, and so were the houses of many other people living there. Since he was one of the principal chiefs of the Arapaho, as the President was the principal chief of the white people, would the Agent see that his house was built like the White House in Washington? Such a house, the Agent explained, would cost too much money. Little Raven, enjoying the argument, answered that money was made in Washington; he had been taken to the United States Mint and had seen it made. Would the Agent send word to the Mint to make enough money to build him a house like that of the President? There was a good deal of fun over that argument, and Little Raven enjoyed it as much as the others did. Later, he accepted one of the Government buildings at Cantonment as his house, and he ploughed and planted some of the land around it. But he kept a tipi in his yard, and when he longed for the old ways that were passing, he could stay there.

18   In the winter, our villages stood on low, sheltered ground near the river, where the wind and cold could not reach us; in summer they were moved to higher ground where they could catch the cool winds. We could not only move our houses but could move entire villages, and we often did. In this respect we were better off than the white man is. We moved to suit the seasons, in summer or in winter; we moved to be near a good supply of wood and water, or for fresh pasture for our ponies. All the Reservation, nearly four and a half million acres, was open and free, except for the ground set aside for the Agency and for Fort Reno. To us who were young, its streams and thickets and prairies seemed to stretch to the end of the world, but when we listened to the talk of the old men and women we knew they considered the Reservation small and the white settlements too close to us. When I was little, one of the old women who visited with us in our tipi used to tell us how far the Arapaho traveled in her childhood, hundreds of miles in every direction, hunting deer and buffalo and dressing and trading their skins. She remembered the Black Hills in South Dakota and the country around them, and said it all belonged by right to the Arapaho. She had been born there, and had lived there as a little girl.

19   The buffalo had all gone from our Reservation when I was born, but our band could still go on the hunt for smaller game and stay for weeks, bringing home skins of bear and beaver and wildcat and coon and wolf and deer and badger. These we sold to the traders at the Agency. Fences and farms were only beginning to change the look of the Reservation, in my childhood.

20   I suppose any family's goods could be packed and the tipi taken down for a move in an hour or two. The mother kept the robes and moccasins in heavy skin holders, called parfleches, that were heavier and stiffer than a bag and made like a little trunk; and she kept her few pots and kettles and cooking supplies in two or three boxes that she had got from one of the traders. These, and some skins and low bed frames and willow-rod mattresses that were thin and light enough to roll up easily, were all we had to move except the tipi itself.

21   We never had too much around when I was little; we needed less than people have today. I don't think any Arapaho family had a set of dishes, but we didn't need them for our simple meals. Meat cooked in a big iron pot with vegetables, when we had them, and bread and coffee, made a fine meal. For this food there was some kind of plate for every member of the family, made of polished wood or tin or china, a spoon that might be either horn or metal, and some kind of cup. If a family gave a feast, those that came to it brought their own utensils. Even today, at an Indian gathering, the family or the organization giving it usually announces that the food will be served Indian style. That means "bring your own dishes."

22   The woman of the family had built the lodge, and when we went to a new location she was the one that moved it. We had no architects and no carpenters; we used no nails and needed no saws or hammers to put up our houses. Raising or striking a tipi was not such heavy work as people who have never seen it done suppose it to be, but it was work that needed training and skill. It needed what white people watching it done called know-how. It was women's work, as it always had been, and they took great pride in it. The important thing, besides the know-how, was the lodge poles. These must be long and straight and slender, and for a good family lodge there must be from sixteen to twenty of them. They must be of some wood like cedar that would not rot when they were exposed to rain and snow. Such poles were not easy to find on the Plains, and the women took great care of them.

23   An Arapaho woman, in putting up a tipi, started with three poles that she bound together about three feet from the small end. These she set up on the ground like a big tripod. Then she propped more poles on the ground and rested them above in the fork of the first three. These were spaced evenly in a circle and formed the framework of the tipi. Many buffalo skins sewed together had once made the cover for this frame, but the old lodge skins soon wore out after the buffalo were gone, and then a heavy cloth called lodge cloth or strouding was used. This cloth was cut and sewed in such a way that it formed a kind of cone stretched over the poles. Yet it was not exactly a cone, for two flaps, or ears, were left open at the top, with two more poles thrust through them in such a way that they made the smoke hole above the center of the lodge large or small, depending on how they were braced on the ground. These could be adjusted according to how much wind blew and in what direction.

24   Above the entrance, the cone-shaped canvas was fastened together with wooden pegs about the way an overcoat is fastened with big buttons. The opening that made the entrance was covered with a skin or a length of canvas held down by a strip of wood that weighted the bottom. This was the only kind of door we knew, long ago. In fine weather it was raised on poles to make a kind of awning over the opening. This door could not be locked, of course, like a wooden door on hinges; but the Cheyenne and the Arapaho, like most other Indians, had always respected other people's

houses and never molested them. When they were away from the tipi for any length of time, they placed a stick across the entrance to say that they were not at home. It was not so tight as the locks people have on their doors today, but it made things safer. Our sense of honor protected our property.

25 Our tipis did not need paint as houses made of lumber did. They were white, except for a brown stain at the top made by the smoke from our fires. The tipis of the Cheyenne and the Arapaho were taller than those of other Indians. Anyone traveling the prairies long ago knew one of our villages as soon as he saw it, even before he was near enough to recognize the people or the designs on the chief's tent or the shields and trophies hanging outside. The low, round lodges of the other tribes were never so beautiful as ours; they never stood so white and tall, with the poles crossed so high against the sky, as ours.

26 In a family tipi, everything was neat and orderly. Right by the entrance, as one came in from the east, were the boxes from the trader's store, where sugar and salt and flour and coffee were kept. These things by the door were white man's goods. Beyond that, the furnishings and their arrangement were just as the Arapaho had always had them, made in the old way and placed in the lodge as they had been from the beginning. Our styles in furnishing never changed in the old days. The beds were always around the edge of the circle, and a well-furnished lodge usually had three, one on the south, one on the west, and one on the north. The bed was made of a low wooden frame, with a kind of mattress made of willow twigs laid over it. These twigs were straightened and peeled and polished, and held together by leather thongs run through holes bored near the end of each twig. The mattress was longer than the bed, and narrowed at one or both ends, where it was held up by a kind of tripod to make a back-rest. Painted or rubbed to a high polish, these back-rests looked very fine. Over them, and over the bed itself, robes and skins were laid, and in later years woven blankets, to make a comfortable place to sit during the day and for a covering at night.

27 As you entered the tipi and turned to the left, the first bed belonged to the women of the family. Then the western part of the lodge, opposite the entrance, belonged especially to the father. Here, on a pole or a tripod, were hung his painted shield and his quiver of arrows; here he kept the bundle, wrapped in skin, containing the things that were his particular protection and power, things that the rest of the family never used or handled; and here he kept his saddle. Here was his bed, with its back-rests and robes, where he sat when he worked or entertained his friends; and behind the bed on the wall of the tipi he might have a finely dressed skin painted with designs and figures that represented important happenings and influences in his life. Beyond this, on the north side of the tipi, was the third bed, where the boys in the family slept and where visitors usually sat. A specially honored visitor, or one whose friendship with the father was close, might

sit with him on his bed, at his left. When the family entered the tipi, they turned to the left, while a visitor went to the right.

28   The floor in the center of the lodge was bare earth, scraped smooth and clean; but around the outside of the circle, where the beds were and where the wall of the tipi slanted against them, the grass might be left to cover the ground. Below the smoke hole, a small place was dug out of the ground and lined with stones. Here our fire burned, for heat and for cooking, with the sticks of wood all laid flat and pointing in toward the center, to be pushed farther in as they burned. It is surprising how small a fire was needed even when there was snow on the ground outside. The mother in the family set her cooking pot on the stones or hung it from a stout forked stick above the fire, and some food was always simmering there. Behind this central fire, some stones were laid for a smaller one, which was sacred. Here our offerings to the Man-Above were placed; here, when cedar or sage was burned, such objects as my father's shield or my mother's ceremonial robe or a bundle of arrows were purified and blessed. When we smelled the clean odor burning there, we felt that our home and everything in it had been blessed.

29   There was room for everything in our lodge, and to us it never seemed crowded. Bags of meat and fruit that my mother had dried hung from the lodge poles, out of our way; and around the outer circle of the room, in the space where the beds were and underneath them, folded robes and clothing, our toys, and our mother's tools and materials for handwork were kept. Some of these were laid in parfleches, so that they could be kept clean and handled easily. Except in bad weather, most of our work and play went on outside our tipi. When we came inside, it seemed dim and cool in summer, and rosy and warm in winter. A kettle of food was usually on the fire, ready for us and for any visitors who might come in. It was unheard of among us for visitors to come and leave unfed, as long as there was anything to be had to eat. Sometimes we children brought white playmates, children of Agency employees, to our tipis, knowing our parents would welcome them and make them feel at home, even though the visitors could not speak Arapaho and our parents could speak little or no English. When there is true hospitality, not very many words are needed. Every Arapaho child learned this.

30   The women in our tribe were naturally good housewives. People who laugh at them and say they were dirty and untidy forget how little they had to work with and how much they had to learn when they changed from the buffalo road to the corn road. When I was little, we took for granted our orderly tipis, the kettle of food always ready to eat, and the extra moccasins stored away to replace the ones we wore out. Later I learned, when I went into the world to school and to work, that there are many kinds of housewives, some good and some bad. But the Arapaho women had a gift for making their lodges homelike and caring for their families and showing hospitality. That was why, when schools and teachers came to our Agency,

our girls and women took up the white women's way of doing things and did them well. They had always made beautiful moccasins and belts and robes and leggings, decorated with fine quillwork or with beads. For this work they had used awls made of bone or horn or thorn, and stout string made of deerskin or sinew. Sewing on cloth, with needles and thread and sometimes with a sewing machine to do the stitching, came easy after this. And so did laundering and baking and cleaning, when there were soap and milled flour and iron stoves and straw brooms to make use of.

31 In winter, there were windbreaks to shelter our lodges. The women went to the river in the fall and cut a kind of tall grass that grew in low, wet places along the edge of the water. It grew like reeds or cattails, and we called it otter grass because otters lived among the roots and made their nests there. The women bound this grass into panels and set them up like a stockade fence outside our tipis, to shut out the wind and the snow. Then they pegged down the lodge cloth and laid sod or earth over it to seal it. When that was done, we were snug for the winter, however stormy it might be outside.

32 Winter or summer, our village made a beautiful sight when the sun went down, with the crossed poles pointing up into the dark sky and the fire in the center of each lodge turning it into a big cone of light, with shadows from the furnishings and the people moving about. Sometimes a bell tinkled, where a herd of ponies grazed; sometimes dogs barked, before they settled down for the night; often there was a drum beating, deep and slow or fast and sharp. Sometimes there was the sound of a flute, playing two or three notes over and over, or of men and women singing around a campfire. In the distance there were lights at the Agency and at the Fort, and beyond them the prairie stretched away in the darkness, mile after mile.

DISCUSSION QUESTIONS

1. Why did the Arapahos like Brinton Darlington?
2. What evidence is there that the author and other Arapahos had a sense of humor?
3. The author's earliest memory is of the tipi where his family lived. What would you have liked about living in a tipi in an Indian village? What would you have disliked about it?
4. How did Indians on the reservation eventually change the way they lived? Which changes were necessary and which were not, in your opinion?

WRITING TOPICS

1. Suppose that you have been asked to describe your childhood home in a letter to a correspondent who has never been to North America but has seen American television. Decide how you will organize your letter and then write your description.
2. What changes have taken place in your family from the time your grandparents were growing up, through the time your parents grew up, until the time you have grown up? Choose three topics, such as dress, dating, entertainment, transportation, diet, sports, and so on, and write a brief essay describing those changes.
3. Sweezy speaks of "the corn road" and "the buffalo road" as symbols in his life. Think of your life as a "road." What type of road would you call it? Write about your road and describe three important events on it.

BEETS

Tiffany Midge

The talented young writer Tiffany Midge received the Diane Decorah Memorial Award in 1994 for her *Outlaws, Renegades, and Saints: Diary of a Mixed Up Halfbreed.* Midge is a performance poet and has read for the Red Sky Poetry Theatre, the Live Poet's Society, and Red Eagle Soaring. Her works have appeared in numerous magazines. Midge, who is Hunkpapa Lakota, plans to study Native American studies and creative writing.

In a playful but fully ironic treatment of clichés about Indians arising from history lessons at school, a bumbling father, and American society, Midge centers her story on a saucy young narrator. With broadside humor, the young girl is more savvy than any of the adults as she undercuts the inflated plans of her father, gently prods her reticent mother, and punctures inaccurate Indian images.

The United States Bureau of Indian Affairs strove for decades to convert Northern Plains traditional big-game-hunting Native Americans into self-sufficient farmers. The image of Thomas Jefferson's idealized yeoman farmer fundamentally affected national Indian and land policies. Through the youthful narrator's point of view, Midge skillfully exposes how ridiculously awry that historic ideal worked out in one suburban family. The character of the father symbolizes the whole huge federal policy, illustrating how environmentally ill-advised it was.

As the daughter tells the humorous tale, national "hyperecological awareness" influenced her father to purchase a big pile of manure and draft his Plains Indian wife and daughters to plant maize, radishes, turnips, onions, zucchini squash, and beets, beets, beets! Midge tacks her tale on the prodigious productivity of zucchini and beets and the father's ordering the narrator and her sister to sell the surplus door-to-door. The story becomes a thinly disguised metaphorical game in which the father represents zealous if misinformed "whites" while the narrator, and to some extent her sister and mother, represent more reasonable, realistic Plains Indians.

1   In fourth-grade history class I learned that the Plains Indians weren't cut out to be farmers, that the government tried to get them to plant corn and stuff, but it was one of those no-win situations, meaning that no matter how hard the Indians fought against progress and manifest destiny, they'd never win.

2   This history lesson occurred around the same time the United States began its hyperecological awareness, which soon seeped into the media. Theories and speculations were developed that asserted that the earth was heading for another ice age. Whereas today scientists tell us that the earth is getting hotter. It was during this time that my father's convictions regarding the demise of the twentieth century began tipping toward fanaticism. *The Whole Earth Catalogue* took up residence in our home and he began reciting from it as if it were Scripture. He wanted us all to get back to nature. I think he would have sold the house and moved us all into the mountains to raise goats and chickens, but my mother, who didn't have much of a say in most of the family decisions, must have threatened to leave him for good if he took his plan to fruition. So he settled with gardening. Gardening is too light a word for the blueprints he drew up that would transform our backyard into a small farming community.

3   One day I returned from school and discovered my father shoveling manure from a pile tall as a two-story building. I couldn't help but wonder where he ever purchased such a magnificent pile . . . , and impressive though it was, I doubt the neighbors shared in my father's enthusiasm. I wouldn't have been surprised if they were circulating a petition to have it removed.

4   "Good, you're home!' my father said. "Grab a rake."

5   Knowing I didn't stand a chance in arguing, I did just as he ordered. And I spent the rest of the day raking manure, thinking the Plains Indians opted not to farm because they knew enough not to. I think my father would have kept us out there shoveling and raking till after midnight if my mother hadn't insisted I come in the house and do my homework. The next day I had blisters on my hands and couldn't hold a pencil.

6   "Hard work builds character," my father preached. "Children have it too easy today. All you want to do is sit around and pick lint out of your belly buttons."

7   I was saved from hard labor for the next week because the blisters on my hands burst open and spilled oozy blood all over the music sheets in singing class. The teacher sent me home, back to the plow.

8   "No pain, no gain," Father said, "Next time wear gloves."

9   The following weekend our suburban nuclear unit had transformed into the spitting image of the Sunshine Family dolls. I began calling my sister Dewdrop. Myself, Starshine. I renamed my mother Corn Woman and my father Reverend Buck. Reverend Buck considered it his mission in life to convert us from our heathen Hungry-Man TV dinner, Bisquick and Pop-Tart existence.

10   "Do you realize that with all these preservatives, after you're dead and buried, your body will take an extra few years to completely decompose?" Father preached.

11   "I don't care," my sister said, "I plan on being cremated."

12   As the good reverend's wife and children, we must have represented some deprived tribe of soulless, bereft Indians and he designated himself to take us, the godless parish, under his wing.

13   Mother resigned herself to his plans. And we trudged along behind her. When she was growing up on the reservation, her family had cultivated and planted every season, so gardening wasn't a completely foreign activity. The difference was, her family planted only what could be used. Their gardens were conservative. But my father's plans resembled a large Midwestern crop, minus the tractors. He even drew up sketches of an irrigation system that he borrowed from *The Whole Earth Catalogue*. It was a nice dream. His heart was in the right place. I'm sure the government back in the days of treaties, relocation, and designation of reservation land thought their intentions were noble too. I kind of admired my father for his big ideas, but sided with my mother on this one. Father was always more interested in the idea of something rather than the actuality; to him, bigger meant better. My father liked large things, generous mass, quantity, weight. To him, they represented progress, ambition, trust. Try as he might to be a true renegade, adopt Indian beliefs and philosophies, even go so far as to marry an Indian woman, he still could never avoid the obvious truth. He was a white man. He liked to build large things.

14   "What do you plan to do with all these vegetables?" my mother asked him.

15   "Freeze and can 'em," he replied. Mother was about to say something, but then looked as if she'd better not. I knew what she was thinking. She was thinking that our father expected *her* to freeze and can them. She didn't look thrilled at the prospect. Father may have accused her of being an apple from time to time, even went so far as to refer to her as apple pie, what he thought to be a term of endearment, but Mother must have retained much of that Plains Indian stoic refusal to derive pleasure from farming large acreage.

16   Father assigned each of us a row. Mother was busily stooped over, issuing corn into the soil, as if offering gems of sacrifice to the earth goddess. I was in charge of the radishes and turnips, which up until that day I'd had no previous experience with, other than what I could recall from tales of Peter Rabbit stealing from Mr. McGregor's garden. I bent down over my chore, all the while on keen lookout for small white rabbits accessorized in gabardine trousers.

17   My sister was diligently poking holes in the soil for her onions when our adopted collie began nosing around the corn rows looking for a place to pee. "Get out of the corn, Charlie!" I ordered him.

18   Father chuckled and said, "Hey, look, a scorned corndog!"

19   Mother rolled her eyes and quipped, "What a corny joke!"

20   My sister feigned fainting and said, "You punish me!"

21   Yeah, we were an image right out of a Rockwell classic[1] with the caption reading, *Squawman and family; an American portrait of hope.*

22   In school we learned that the Indians were the impetus behind the Thanksgiving holiday that we practice today. This legend depicts that the Eastern tribes were more reverent and accepting of the white colonists than any fierce and proud Plains Indian ever was. My father challenged this theory by suggesting I take armfuls of our sown vegetables to school. "It'll be like helping out the Pilgrims," he told me. I brought grocery sacks of turnips to class one day and offered them as novelties for our class show-and-tell activity. Everyone was left with the assumption that it was the Sioux Indians who were farmers and who had guided and helped the Pilgrims in their time of need. Mrs. Morton didn't discourage this faux pas but, rather, rattled on about how noble, how Christian, of the Indians to assist the poor colonists in the unsettling and overwhelming wilderness they'd arrived at. My classmates collected my offering of turnips and at recess we rounded up a game of turnip baseball. Lisa Parker got hit in the face with a turnip and went bawling to the school nurse. Mrs. Morton ignored me the rest of the day and sent me home with a note to my parents, which said, *Please do not allow this to happen again.*

23   At Father's suggestion, my sister engineered a baking factory. Every evening after dinner she would bake loaves of zucchini bread. These baked goods went to the neighbors, coworkers, and the public just happening by. My father had suggested she sell them at school, but Mother firmly reminded him that the teachers weren't supportive of free enterprise in the elementary schools. "Well, she could organize a bake sale and the proceeds could go to charity," my father offered. So the following week Helen Keller Elementary School had a bake sale in the school gymnasium. Tables were loaded up with flour-and-sugar concoctions of every creed and color. Cookies, cupcakes, strudel, fudge, brownies, and whole cakes. My sister's table was the most impressive and I felt swelled up with pride at her arrangement. She had a banner struck across the wall behind the table that read *zucchini's R R friends.* And then long with her stacks of loaves she also had our season's bounty of zucchini. I even snuck in a few turnips for color. The teachers milled around her table praising her for her fine ingenuity.

24   Mrs. Morton asked me, "How did your family ever come into so many zucchinis?" As if zucchini was old money we had inherited.

25   "Oh, zucchini is a fast-growing vegetable," I told her "My father says that it breeds in the garden like rabbits . . . , that multiply exponentially."

---

[1] *Rockwell classic:* Norman Rockwell (1894–1978) was an American illustrator whose works depict an idealized view of American life.

26   Mrs. Morton ignored me for the rest of the day and sent a note home to my parents that read, *Please do not allow this to happen again.*

27   In school we learned about the fur trappers and traders who migrated all over the frontier trading with the Indians. We learned about the Hudson's Bay Company and how the Plains Indians bartered with them for the glass beads and shells that modernized and increased the value of their traditional regalia. We learned that before money, folks just traded stuff. Bartered their wares. But then gold was discovered throughout the West and bartering furs and beads took a backseat. The Indians weren't gold diggers.

28   Aside from the Trouble with Tribbles, zucchini problem in our garden, we had another problem to contend with. The beets. Some evenings I would discover my father stooped down over the beet rows, shaking is head and muttering, "Borscht . . . borscht."

29   My sister was encouraged to invent a recipe for beet bread, as she had done with the zucchini, but it kept coming out of the oven soggy and oozing red juice, as if it were hunks of animal flesh trickling trails of blood all over the kitchen counters. Not a very appetizing sight. Father had a bit more success with his beet experimentation. Inventing such delicacies as beetloaf and Sunday morning succotash surprise and beet omelets. He'd counteracted the red by adding blue food coloring, so we ended up with purple tongues after eating. My all-time favorite was beet Jello. And Mother packed our lunches to include bologna-and-beet sandwiches. We took sacks of beets to our grandparents' house and my German grandmother was delighted with our offering. "Oh, I just love beets!" she exclaimed. "I shall make borscht and pickles."

30   The beets were beginning to get on everyone's nerves. But there were other caldrons bubbling in our household; my father's overstimulated dread of waste. He'd been raised by a tough and hearty Montana farm girl, who in turn had been bred from a stock of immigrant Germans from Russia who had escaped the banks of the Volga River after the reign of Catherine the Great. As if injected straight through the bloodline, my grandmother Gertrude instilled a heavy does of "Waste not, want not," medication to my father. My grandfather also ladled out his own brand of practical conservation. But more out of his pennypinching and obsessive attention to dollars and cents, not out of some necessity imprinted from childhood to "Save today, you'll not starve tomorrow." The examination of water and electric bills was one of my grandfather's favorite hobbies. Either wattage fascinated him or he was always expecting to get stiffed. The latter being more true, because he was one of *the* great complainers.

31   It didn't come as much of a surprise when my father promoted his newest scheme: of bartering our surplus beets door to door. The catch was, we were the ones doing the soliciting, he was going to stay home and watch the World Series. He furthered his cause by explaining to us that the Indians traded long ago and this would be our own personal tribute to an old way of life.

32   "Yeah, but they didn't sell beets door to door like encyclopedia sales-men," my sister retorted. "I'll feel so stupid!"

33   "Nonsense!" my father said. "It's a fine idea. Whatever money you make, I'll just deduct from your allowance. And if you make more than your allowance, you can keep the difference. Save up for a bike or mitt or some-thing."

34   I couldn't help thinking that if only my mother had stopped my father when he'd decided to become Reverend Buck and toil and sweat in the gar-den, none of this would be happening. This was a bad episode from *Attack of the Killer Tomatoes,* and my father's ambition and insistence on doing things only on a large scale didn't seem to justify the humiliation and embar-rassment that resulted when we were coaxed to distribute the fruits of our labor. However, his latest plan I was for the most part agreeable to, but only because I was so completely eager to do anything that would levitate me in his eyes as angelic, and perfect and because, secretly, I enjoyed witnessing my sister's discomfort.

35   We filled up grocery sacks with surplus. Father had suggested we fill up the wheelbarrow, but Julie wouldn't hear of it. "For cripe's sake, with that wheelbarrow filled with beets we'd look pathetic!" she argued. "We'd look like Okies from *The Grapes of Wrath!*" My father was a fanatic about Steinbeck. He taught my sister to read "The Red Pony" before she entered the second grade. I, on the other hand, was considered the *slow* one.

36   We set out. Our own personal tribute to Indians of long ago. We weren't very conspicuous. Nothing out of the ordinary, just a couple of brown-skinned kids in braids walking grocery sacks down the suburban street. Indians weren't a common sight in residential neighborhoods, and my sister and I had experienced our share of racial prejudice. When my mother wrote out checks at the grocery store, the store manager was always called by the clerk to verify her driver's license. This occurring immediately after a white woman wrote a check to the same clerk but no verification was asked for. . . . My sister during a Husky game at Hecht Ed Stadium was insulted by a black man when she was buying hot dogs. "Must eat a lot of hot dogs on the reservation, huh?" he told her. Later when we told Father, he responded with "Did you ask him if he ate a lot of watermelon?"

37   We had walked most of a mile to a neighborhood outside the confines of our own, so as not to be further embarrassed by people we actually knew. When we had come to a point where we felt we were at a safe enough dis-tance, my sister told me to go up to the house with the pink flamingos bal-anced in the flower bed. "Only if you come too," I told her. So together we marched up to the door and rang the doorbell.

38   A woman with frizzy red hair answered the door. "Hello?" she asked. "What can I do for you girls?"

39   My sister nudged me with her elbow. "Would you like to buy some beets?" I asked.

40   The woman's brows knitted together. "What's that? What's that you asked?"

41   "BEETS!" I shouted. "WOULD YOU LIKE TO BUY SOME BEETS?"

42   I yelled so loudly that some kids stopped what they were doing and looked toward the house.

43   The woman was having a great deal of difficulty disguising her perplexity. Her brow was so busy knitting together she could have made up an afghan. Finally, some expression resembling resolution passed over her face. "No, not today," and she very curtly closed the door in our faces.

44   I wasn't going to let her go that easily. "BORSCHT, LADY!" I yelled. "YOU KNOW HOW TO MAKE BORSCHT?"

45   My sister threw me a horrified look, shoved me and ran down the street. "HEY JULIE!" I called after her. "YOU SHOULD SEE YOUR FACE, IT'S BEET RED!"

46   We didn't sell any beets that day. Our personal tribute had failed. After I caught up with my sister, I found her sitting on the pavement at the top of a steep hill, with her face in her hands. I didn't say anything because there wasn't anything to say. I knew that she was crying and it was partly my fault. I wanted to make it up to her. Though I wasn't bothered by her pained frustrations, tears were another matter entirely. When she cried, I always felt compelled to cry right along with her. But on this day I didn't. Instead, I took the grocery sacks filled with beets and turned them upside down. The beets escaped from the bags, and as we watched them begin their descent to the bottom of the hill, I noticed the beginning of a smile on my sister's face. When the plump red vegetables had arrived at the bottom of the hill, leaving a bloody pink trail behind, we were both chuckling. And when a Volkswagen bus slammed on its brakes to avoid colliding with our surplus beets, we were laughing. And by the time the beets reached the next block and didn't stop rolling but continued down the asphalt street heading into the day after tomorrow, my sister and I were displaying pure and uncensored hysterics—laughing uncontrollably, holding our bellies as tears ran down our cheeks, pressing our faces against the pavement and rejoicing in the spectacle that we viewed from the top of that concrete hill.

DISCUSSION QUESTIONS

1. How would you describe the narrator's personality?
2. The narrator nicknames her father Reverend Buck. What does she say is his mission?
3. What is the narrator's explanation for why her father liked large things?
4. What would you say is the climax or turning point of the story?

5. Two techniques that Midge uses to create humor are exaggeration and funny actions arranged in a series. Find three examples and read them aloud.

WRITING TOPICS

1. Family schemes, events, or vacations sometimes go awry. Has it happened in your family? If so, write a narrative of what happened and assume your audience to be a reader of a newspaper or general interest magazine.
2. Convert this story into a one-act play suitable for middle-school children. First outline your script. You will have to add some dialogue not present in the story.
3. Write a poem or a paragraph on "My Least Favorite Vegetable."
4. A *caricature* may be defined as description that seizes upon certain individual qualities of a person and through exaggeration or distortion produces a ridiculous effect. Reread the story, concentrating on the character of the father and make notes in your literary journal on this topic: In "Beets," the father is a caricature. Organize your notes in an essay.
5. Write an essay about how the author creates humor in this story. Locate passages you think are humorous and then select some to discuss in your essay. Suggested thesis: Using exaggeration, absurd comparisons, and funny actions, Tiffany Midge creates ironic humor in "Beets."

FROM *INTERIOR LANDSCAPES*

Gerald Vizenor

The gritty kid who stole ski poles from Dayton's Department Store grew up to be a prolific writer, a professor, and a trickster critic— Gerald Vizenor. His father, Clement Vizenor, was born on the White Earth Chippewa Reservation in Minnesota, a descendent of the Crane Clan. After moving to Minneapolis, he married teenager LaVerne Peterson. Clement was murdered when young Gerald was twenty months old; the crime remains unsolved. Later, the fatherless Vizenor recalled, "We were crossbloods, loose families at the end of the depression in the cities." While his mother endured desperate poverty, she shuttled her young son from her care to paternal grandparents and foster families. When she married Elmer Petesch, Gerald had a more stable home for eight years until she abandoned both of them. Petesch died in a fall down an elevator shaft five months later.

At seventeen, Gerald was truly alone. In one dramatic scene from *Interior Landscapes,* when his care was not paid for, his foster family forced him to move out and held his belongings as ransom. The resilient young man worked as a painter, then for an outdoor advertising company to earn money to redeem his belongings. Later Vizenor recalled, "So much depended on a time card then: identity, money, and the need to be distracted by labor." When he writes of his stark poverty, abandonment, and foster homes, he says, "The tricksters raised me in imagination" and " . . . were with me in stories, and we remembered how to turn pain and horror into humor."

Refusing to be destroyed by harsh conditions and lack of a stable family, Vizenor created a vivid fantasy life and turned rebellion into a survival strategy. He dropped out of high school to join the U.S. army and served for three years in Japan. Embracing Japanese culture inspired him to write haiku collected in his first publication, *Two Wings the Butterfly* (1962). Five more Haiku volumes followed: *Raising the Moon Vines and Seventeen Chirps* (1964); *Slight Abrasions (1966); Empty Swings* (1967); and *Matsushima: Pine Island* (1984). Haiku, which resembles Chippewa dream songs for Vizenor, remains one of his important signatures.

About the same time Vizenor was publishing haiku, he began to publish political views as a freelance reporter writer for the *Minneapolis Tribune.* He worked as a reporter (1968–1969) and an editorial writer (1974) for the paper, covering a range of Indian topics including education, treaty rights, child welfare, and the American Indian movement. *Crossbloods, Bone Courts, Bingo, and Other Reports* (1990) includes his best newspaper articles and other essays. From being a poet and journalist, Vizenor has matured into a master of varied styles and genres as a novelist, short story writer, film script author, and postmodern theorist.

Vizenor's autobiography, *Interior Landscapes, Autobiographical Myths and Metaphors,* won the PEN Oakland Book Award (1990). In it, we see not only the young Vizenor, but also the adult Vizenor viewing the young man.

MARCH 1938: CROSSING THE WIRES

1   When my father was murdered, I lived for two more years with my grandmother, aunts, and uncles, in their tenement downtown. Then, with a measure of independence, my mother reclaimed me to begin a new life at the end of the depression.

2   LaVerne rented a cold and coarse two-room apartment above a trunk manufacturing company located on Washington Avenue, near the streetcar barn in north Minneapolis. The small building, close to the street, was covered with dark asphalt paper; the stairs to our apartment were outside, at the back. There were no screens on the windows; the wind rushed at the broken panes, wheezed between the cracks, and pushed under the door. The sound of the wind in that apartment would have been natural in the movies.

3   The tenement with my tribal grandmother, aunts, and uncles, was narrow, crowded, and warm. The apartment with my mother, the source of my earliest memories of loneliness, was dark, cold, and desolate.

4   My mother found a job as a waitress in a restaurant and bar; she worked long hours but her salary was little more than the cost of our rent for the apartment. I was turned over to a neighbor who lived a few doors down the street when my mother was at work, or elsewhere. My first shadow work in the world was being with my mother, and then, without my mother. I remember those long hours in the backyard with no trees or animals; the woman who cared for me did not want me in the house, a miniature frame structure with no more room than our apartment. The earth was hard there. I drove my small metal car for hours between the weeds, down to the mount behind the house. Dandelions bloomed in my hands that spring, my earliest natural pleasure with edible weeds.

5   My mother was always tearful, especially on birthdays and holidays. No one ever visited us over the trunk company. One warm morning late in the spring, I was at the back window at sunrise. Hungry, I climbed on the rough cupboards and searched the shelves for something to eat. I found a box of prunes, which made that morning memorable over the hundreds of others in that apartment. I ate the whole box of prunes, leaned out of the window, and one by one spit the pits like stones at the empty whiskey bottles behind the building. The earth below was soaked with oil, a landscape of ruin and privation. I am haunted by the wind, by the scent of oil; the real world in my memories must be soiled with petroleum. Later, no summer was ever true without a tar truck that sealed the streets. We were the second generation raised on the lure of oil and tar; we chewed a dose of tar in the summer to clean our teeth. I chewed too much once, stained my teeth, and then turned to other habits.

6   Christmas over the trunk company began with music, lights, and humor, turned morose, and then the night passed with bold ornaments. My mother came home with a small tree to celebrate the season. The day after we trimmed the tree with one string of lights, electrical service to the apartment was terminated for nonpayment. We sat in the dark, alone; she cried too much, and she must have promised me more than she had known in her twenty-two years. That higher distance in her voice soon turned to silence.

7   I turned to the windows, to carve the glaciers loose and float them on the lower panes; the ice carried me out on the ocean, back to the woodland, in a burst of light. In "The Snow Queen" by Hans Christian Andersen, the "children warmed coins on the stove and held them against the frosted pane." Gerda might have seen me there, stranded over the trunk company, alive and lonesome in that "lovely round peephole."

8   Sometimes, in that obscure silence with my mother, I would trace the seams and cracks on the rough floor from one room to the next and return. The dirt raised in even rows from the seams was plowed back again with a wedge of cardboard.

9   On the night before Christmas my mother summoned her courage and broke the seal on the electrical meter; she crossed the wires and called me awake to see a lighted tree. She cried with happiness. That little tree with one string of colored lights, more red than green, was her symbolic triumph over poverty, loneliness, and depression. The apartment was cold, but the ornamental lights were warm, and we warmed our hands on the red bulbs. She sat on the rim of the day bed and cried once more, but this time she touched me, hugged me, and kissed me, and she must have told me her material dreams; once upon a time in the summer of our liberation, how our world would be on the ocean, over the rough wood, over the ice, out the round peephole in the frosted window. We were both so young to be poor and alone in the dark. . . .

DECEMBER 1946: SATURNALIA AT DAYTON'S

10   I was invisible when we entered the department store late that afternoon, a mixedblood on the margins with wild hair, dental caries, and the unrestrained manners of a child who lived in a basement. The aisles were packed with festive holiday shoppers; we were pushed aside at the counters, at cosmetics, at confections, misruled in the sundries. No one saw me steal the mittens and baubles, but the ski poles, we were seen with the ski poles, and the rest was made visible. We were arrested on the elevator, held in an executive suite, but no one revealed the punishment. The police would separate and humiliate, my stepfather would beat me, and with no heart my mother would shame me, a burden in the blood.

11   "The principle of moderation in punishment, even when it is a question of punishing the enemy of the social body, is articulated first as a discourse of the heart," wrote Michel Foucault in *Discipline and Punish.* "Or rather, it leaps forth like a cry from the body, which is revolted at the sight or at the imagination of too much cruelty." I was right about the police and my mother, but my stepfather surprised me that night at the saturnalia.[1]

12   "Zero three, come in," said the radio voice.

13   "This is zero three, over."

14   "Two juvenile suspects have removed cartoon films from toys and are leaving the department. They are proceeding to the escalator near aisle seven, zero four out."

15   "This is zero three, have visual contact with suspects, one in brown coat, fake fur collar, and wild hair, and the other suspect in blue parka. Will pursue on escalator."

16   "Check, zero three, zero two will intercept on the next floor. Suspects are heading for winter mittens and the sports department, zero four over."

17   "Check, zero four."

18   "Zero four, juvenile suspects are leaving winter sports department with ski poles and mittens. Advise zero one, we plan immediate interception on the elevator."

19   "Check, zero two, they must think no one can see them."

20   "The invisible shoplifter, zero two over."

21   "Suspects on elevator, notify police, zero three out."

22   "Check, zero two out."

23   "Elevator closed, zero four out."

24   "Main floor, please," said Wilbur Wannum.

25   "We made it," I said with ski poles at my side.

26   "The mittens are mine," he said.

---

[1] *saturnalia:* an unrestrained celebration; originally the festival of Saturn in ancient Rome, involving feasting and gift giving, which began December 17.

27   "But you wanted the ski poles, you got the skis, not me."

28   "No, the mittens."

29   "You already have a pair," I argued.

30   "Let's get another pair then," said Wannum. He smiled, flashed his gold tooth at me on the elevator. Two men at the back moved closer; we were visible between them.

31   "Never mind, dummy."

32   "I see you boys have been shopping for ski poles and mittens," said zero one. Another zero held us by the coat collars when the elevator doors opened on the main floor. "Have you stolen anything else today?"

33   Oh . . ., you . . .," shouted Wannum. He turned his back to me and pleaded with the zeros, the collar tightened around his neck. "This wasn't my idea, I didn't take a thing, nothing," he continued to plead as we were marched from the elevator to the zero one suite.

34   Elmer[2] would beat me, and that bothered me more than the zeros and the police. He would stumble at me in his black boots, with his big hairy arms out, and jerk my body around, and beat me . . . until he was out of breath.

35   "Mister, anything, I'll do anything, but please, do you have to tell my father, do you have to tell him?" Zero one seemed to listen but he did not answer; he never even moved his head. "He's really my stepfather."

36   "Are you ashamed for what you have done?" Zero one leaned back in his executive chair and folded his hands on his chest. "We watched you both for more than an hour." He smiled, at last. . . .

37   "No, I mean yes, but do you have to tell my stepfather?" I pleaded a second time, my heart at the mercy of the zeros. "You don't know what he will do to me when he finds out about this."

38   "Well, I don't think it is my place to tell your father what to do or not to do," said zero one in dictation tones. "At any rate, we are pleased with your confessions and when the police come along any minute now the whole matter will be out of our hands."

39   Minutes later, two stout uniformed police officers came into the zero one suite, out of breath. Zero one gave them the facts while they looked us over. Without a word we were hauled to the police car and driven three blocks to the courthouse. I was invisible; the people on the street could not see me in the backseat.

40   Juvenile officers questioned us in a dark room, they asked us about other crimes, and we were eager to confess to the ski poles, the mittens, and the baubles. Then, the last punishment, the officers called our parents. The scene was not as it should be with parents in the movies. Wannum was an adopted child, and his mother was blue with so much love to lose.

41   Elmer arrived at the courthouse about an hour later. He smelled of boiled cabbage and sulfur from wooden matches. He was my stepfather and

---

[2] *Elmer:* the narrator's stepfather.

had nothing to lose over me. He breathed hard and moved in silence; we marched out the door, around the corner. I waited for the first blow and ducked when he opened the door on the passenger side of the car. He smiled and seemed to be at ease, the worst sign of the storm that would follow once we were at home.

42 He started the engine and drove in silence; right turn, followed the streetcar tracks, but we turned right again, not left, we were not going home. My stepfather was taking me out to eat. We had hamburgers, onions, lemon meringue pie, my favorites then, and a man-to-man talk, the first in our three years together. I measured his gentle manner, however, as a new punishment; I was certain he would beat me when we got home. I asked for a second bottle of Dr Pepper.

43 "Are you going to hit me later?" I asked.

44 "No, not this time, and you know I don't like doing that any more than you like getting it," said my stepfather. Parents and children must bear that platitude as their test of truth.

45 "Does that mean you won't beat me?"

46 "No," he said in a whisper.

47 "Not ever again?"

48 "Well, there might be a time when you'll need it again, but you're old enough now to talk about things man to man." He smiled; the truth had been tested and he survived once more.

49 "When?" I was eager to talk about punishment.

50 "You just eat now, and let's talk about this afternoon before I lose my temper and change my mind." He beat the bottom of the ketchup bottle. "You and that kid you were with have to appear in juvenile court and that will be punishment enough for stealing. The judge will be tough, but you need the lesson."

51 I returned to the basement and listened to my radio. I would travel to those lights and voices in the night, southern, mountain, the great cities on my radio. I ran away at age fifteen to Biloxi, Mississippi, and the Gulf of Mexico, because the south was on my radio and a friend was stationed at a military base near there. I am reminded of that time on the highway now, the glow of the dashboard lights at night, the distant stations on the car radio.

52 Juvenile Court was cold, the wood had no luster, and parents cried over the phrases of punishment. Wannum wore a new necktie his mother bought for the occasion. I wore my best wool shirt. We stood at the bench to hear our punishment, the sentence for our crimes. The judge looked down from his perch, down at the accused, and said that this was not the first time we had stolen. We took the bait and confessed to more than we had stolen, we wanted to please the judge.

53 "Do you want to grow up to be criminals and spend the rest of your natural lives in prison, do you?" He never waited for an answer. The scene was too common. "Let me tell you this, young man," he said and leaned over

the bench. He pointed at me, "And you too, young Wannum. If it were not true that our two juvenile training schools were filled I would send you both there in a minute for your crimes. You deserve no less, but because Glen Lake and Red Wing are filled to the windows, I will give you a chance to do good by placing you both on probation for six months, and if during that time you ever steal, or do anything wrong again, I will let someone out at Red Wing, just to make room to put you in. Do you understand what I have just said?"

54   We nodded at the bench and listened with our heads back. He was serious, that much was clear, but we never understood what he said about institutions and probation. The movie *Boys' Town* came to mind; Father Flanagan, played by Spencer Tracy, rested his warm hand on my shoulder and welcomed me to his school in Nebraska. Mickey Rooney was there too, and we were honored as reformed juvenile delinquents.

55   "You will report to your probation officer every Monday afternoon for six months, and you will tell the principal of your school that you are on probation for stealing and he will permit you to leave early to report. Do you understand what I have just told you?"

56   "Yes, sir," but my tongue wanted to say the opposite.

57   "Have you learned your lesson?"

58   "Yes sir, sir."

59   "No more, sir," said Wannum with a scared smile. His mother had coached him to say the right things, but his gold tooth turned even his best manners into comedies. His mother blamed me as the evil influence, the cause of his brush with the law. She never knew about his revolver, and the things he stole from the grocery and the drug store. The judge and our parents agreed that we were never to see each other again. Close your eyes, they instructed, and turn the other way when you see each other in school or on the street. We listened, nodded, and went on with the legion and our adventures in the cemetery. Monday afternoons, however, we pretended not to be together when we reported to our probation officer at the courthouse.

60   Mondays in the courthouse were given over to juveniles. There were no more than two or three probation officers for the entire city of juvenile criminals. We waited in a line with more than a hundred other criminals that circled one end of the building. Shoplifting was minor compared to the crimes the bandits from northeast claimed. They stood in line and boasted about armed robberies, . . . extortion, burglary, and car theft. Pressed, we told them about the ski poles and mittens. Wannum impressed them with his revolver, but we remained pansies on probation. No matter what time we arrived we were at the end of the line, the last to see the probation officer.

61   His face was ocherous, the color of probation, and his neck was burned and cracked. My probation officer had brown fingernails from cigarette smoke; his teeth were stained and he hacked over his last words.

62   "Did you go to church?" He leaned to the right and waited with his head

down for me to answer; his pencil was aimed at the large yellow card on his desk. His hands were old animals, covered with brown spots.

63 "Yup," I said and watched his hand move over the card.

64 "Attending school every day?"

65 "Yup," I said and wondered what happened to his legs. He sat behind that desk for several hours and never moved. He lighted a cigarette and told me not to smoke.

66 "Staying away from known criminals and juveniles on probation?" He rubbed his forearm on the edge of the desk. There were several other probation officers in the same large room; they sat in the same wooden chairs, behind the same metal desks, and asked the same questions. He marked the card before he heard my answer.

67 "Yup," I said and wondered if he had been wounded in the war.

68 "Staying away from Dayton's?"

69 "Yup," I said and remembered that my mother warned me that no one would ever let me into the store again, that they would never allow me to work there, or open a charge account.

70 "Gerald, you are making very good progress and I think in a month or so, if you behave yourself in school, attend church, and stay out of mischief and follow the rules, we may release you from probation early."

71 "Really?"

72 "Yes, but don't forget to attend church every week," he said. Then he looked up, the only time during the interview, and smiled, a sudden crack on his face. "Keep your nose clean, kid, you know what I mean."

73 "Yup," I said and looked under the desk. He had two legs, and two feet, but no shoes. He wore brown socks and one foot was stacked on top of the other. He moved his toes.

74 "Lose something?"

75 "Nope," I said and turned to leave.

76 "Send in the next boy."

June 1951: One More Good Home

77 Elmer Petesch, the last of my stepfathers, returned home from work on schedule one summer night and found a short departure and disunion note from his wife of eight years. My mother was inspired by a new man who once bought me two bacon, lettuce, and tomato sandwiches. He could have been in movies; his voice was rich and sensuous, and he had a winsome manner.

78 LaVerne wrote to her husband that she would never come back; she had moved to a warmer climate and a better life that very afternoon. The note was concise, written with care, in a poised cursive hand, as she would a sentimental message on a birthday card, and placed in the center of the kitchen table. The gesture was petulant and sarcastic because her husband prepared most of our meals.

79   I came home from school earlier than usual that afternoon. The scent of perfume warmed me at the back door; that special essence was associated with celebrations. Once, in the eighth grade, I borrowed that same perfume to touch a card on Saint Valentine's Day; my mother traced the scent, found the card attached to a shoebox loaded with candy hearts, and read out loud my first love letter to a secret sweetheart.

80   My mother was in the bathroom blotting her lips with a tissue. She wore her best clothes and jewelry, and her suitcase was near the front door. I asked her what happened, "where are you going?" She stared into the bathroom mirror and plucked hairs from her eyebrows. LaVerne was tall, handsome, and nervous.

81   "California," she said. Her breath steamed on the mirror.

82   "Who lives out there?"

83   "Nobody," she said from the side of her mouth.

84   "Why you going then?"

85   "Jerry, I'm leaving for good."

86   "Why?" I pretended to be surprised.

87   "I'm leaving Elmer."

88   "Are you going with someone?"

89   "Do you want to come along?"

90   "Where would we go?" I had no interest in going anywhere, but she was worried so we talked more about me. I was at home, a better home than fosterage, and there were no good reasons for me to leave.

91   "California," she said to the mirror.

92   "No," I said to the doorjamb.

93   "Why not?" My mother would pursue conversations to resolve her worries, but she hesitated the closer we came to maternal responsibilities. Her invitation was insincere; she would have been gone before school ended at the regular time.

94   "Because, my friends are here."

95   "I'll send you postcards," she promised.

96   "Thanks, mother."

97   "I'm going to be late," she said as she put on her shoes. When she turned one last time at the door, there were tears in her eyes. "I wish you could come with me."

98   "You'll be all right," I assured her with a wave and a sudden smile. My mother chose to be lonesome in the movies, in her marriage, even in her own home. The scent of her sweet perfume lingered in the bathroom for several weeks.

99   LaVerne said she was leaving him with a mortgage, a secondhand piano, most of the modest wedding presents, and as a parting gesture of ironic trust and affection, she also left behind her only son. I became a mixedblood fosterling overnight; once more my home was surrendered in the wars of blood and pleasure.

100   Elmer had no legal responsibilities; he had not adopted me, but he was

burdened to remember my mother in me. I renounced his bad memories, denied his power, and escaped, a few weeks later, from his house, his kitchen, his basement, and his garage, lonesome, hurt, and very angry.

101 We had just finished another boiled dinner, ring bologna, potatoes, and onions, when he struck me on the back. I was washing the dishes and talked back to him about the spilled water on the floor under the sink. In his book of manners, children would never talk back to adults, not even expressions of pain over punishment. He cursed me over the sink because of my mother, and he hit me again. I left his house in silence, without a word of pain, determined never to return.

102 Elmer was alone in his house for four days with his memories of my mother. He punished himself with alcohol, and then on the fifth day he started to search for me. He left considerate messages with some of my friends and selected neighbors, that he wanted me to return home; he said our home, but that word had lost value in my survival language. I avoided his rapprochement and peddled my own stories to friends and their parents: stories about his violence to me and my mother, stories that would gain an advantage in the fosterage wars. My mother mismeasured his sentiments because he was older; his emotional distance was cruel, and he blustered at times, but he was not a violent man. He was much wiser in the material world, a pragmatist with machines; but he lost power when he turned, as a last resort, to passion and adoration.

103 Frog invited me to stay at his house. I was pleased because his father told great stories about his adventures in the wilderness, about the time he was shot in the leg in a gunfight at a mining camp in the mountains, and he had a scar, and the gun, to prove the wound, and how he ran bootleg corn whiskey down on rural roads from North Dakota. He told us stories in the basement, in the car, and in the garage, his sacred territories, and winked at us when his wife complained. We were his best listeners and eager conspirators in his great boyhood memories. I pretended he was my father for a time.

104 Elmer found me in the backyard. I was playing basketball when he drove down the alley and stopped by the garage. I told him to leave me alone. "I will never listen to you again," I said and passed the ball. Frog dribbled in a circle and pretended that my stepfather was not there.

105 "Let's just talk it over," said Elmer. I refused to answer him, or even gesture in his direction. Later, he told my friends that he would return the next night to talk with me again. He was defensive, and his appeals to me gave me a sense of personal power.

106 "Here he comes," someone shouted from behind the garage. Elmer met me in the alley on the sixth night. Frog and several other friends were there with me. I told him to listen to my conditions. Elmer said he would stand across the alley, and he agreed that we would listen to each other without interruptions. He was the first to speak that night.

107 "I am very sorry, please believe me," he said from behind his car on the other side of the alley. "I know you want to be with your friends now, but I want you to know how sorry I am for taking your mother out on you. I have

been very lonely since you left and I know it was wrong to hit you. It was not your fault, but sometimes we hurt the people we love the most. You know what I mean?

108   "I want you to come back home. We need each other now. I have never had a good home, and you have never had a good home either, now we need to make one together."

109   Elmer cried. Tears ran down his fat cheeks. He took his glasses off and pleaded to me with his stout hands. I was moved and wanted to reach out to him, but I had been hurt too many times in the past to yield so easily to tears and promises. My thoughts were overburdened with his violence and his weakness. He cried on one side of the alley, and we were silent on the other side; embarrassed to watch a mean, bald man break down with a stained handkerchief.

110   "I wish I could take back all the times I have hurt you," he said and dried his eyes. "Leaving home was the best thing for you to do, and I have no right to expect you to trust me now and come back home, but I do want you to believe me this time." He blew his nose and his voice was a normal tone.

111   "I don't believe you," I said in a cold tone of voice. "You have said all those things before, when I was home. Go take it out on my mother, not me. Go away." I must have sneered too much because my friends were troubled by my mood and manner.

112   "Can we talk tomorrow again?"

113   "Maybe." I would bear the moment but never surrender to tears and sentiments. Frog was there, my best friend, and his father was mine that night; he encouraged me to return home.

114   Elmer faced not only my best friends the next night, but their parents and other neighbors who had learned from gossip about such unusual family negotiations in the alley. He parked near the garage as he had the two previous nights, and stood on the other side of the alley. He wore a starched white shirt, brown suit trousers, and black dress shoes. The women stood behind their children with their arms folded over their breasts. The men stood in the shadows of open garage doors; some chewed toothpicks and looked down at the cement. I was silent; the audience was tense. My mother would have been humiliated by the tableau in the alley; she lacked the courage to face an audience, and she missed the best movie scene of the season.

115   "I will come every night to tell you I want you to come home, but not the way it used to be. I promise you, and you have your friends here listening, that I will never again mistreat you," he said with his hands in his pockets. He was sincere, and eager to taste his promises in public; he was more at ease in the alley, a rural place he must have trusted that night. "We both need a good home, please come back home."

116   "Let me think about it," I said and turned to my friends. Neighbors and friends looked at each other in silence, husbands and wives walked home with their children between them. Screen doors banged closed and lights were turned on in kitchens and bathrooms. I was outside, alone. The trees were

hushed, the leaves were moist. The first fireflies blinked in the dark grass. My hands were clenched, my fingers swollen. No one called my name that night.

117 Elmer was home; his car was parked near the house.

118 The night air was blue, and shadows bounced under the chokecherry tree in the back yard. I circled the house and saw him in his overstuffed chair, asleep with a western novel. I could hear him snore, a primal sound at the windows. I waited in silence near the front door. Mosquitoes landed on my shoulders, out of reach, but I was not ready to open the screen door and return home.

119 I walked toward the river later that night, down the alleys, between houses to avoid the police, and a possible curfew violation. I bought fresh warm sweet rolls from the back door of a local bakery and ate them on the way. I caught the sweet centers in my hand. I was loose, alone, and free that night, a dubious pleasure without a home. I measured my uneven breath with the river, held summer over the thick dark water, and waved moon slivers to tame the shore. I made a bed under the bridge. Overhead demons thundered on the seams, and the animals of the night lettered their escape distances. The tricksters soared in magical flight over the woodland, and the crane must have sounded in my dream that night.

120 I returned home next morning when my stepfather was at work. The air hummed at the back door, the floors creaked and the halls cracked with excitement. I walked through the house and touched handles, cabinets, and furniture, to be sure there was a home there. I imagined my mother in the bathroom, lipstick prints remained in the basket, and my stepfather at the stove, over cabbage steam, over me at the sink. I forgave them both and their problems ended in me.

121 Elmer would be home on schedule for dinner. I cleaned the house, emptied the baskets and trash, washed the dishes, cut the grass, and baked a blueberry pie, his favorite, and then waited on the front steps for him to return. He parked the car and smiled when he noticed the grass, smelled the pie. Without a word he took me by the hand, pulled me from the steps, and embraced me. We both cried and never remembered my mother in our conversations.

122 At last, he was a very compassionate man; his caution was connected to past memories and experiences. He learned to show his love in new ways. I believed the promises he made to me in the alley. I trusted him once more, and learned to share his gentle humor. My trust in him, and his courage to trust me, a mixedblood adolescent son left over from a bum marriage, made me a better person.

123 We decided to share the house, to live together, no hard rules. He paid me an allowance to maintain the house. I would never be his son, and he would never be my father, we agreed; we would be brothers and friends at the same time. . . .

DISCUSSION QUESTIONS

1. What caused the difficult circumstances in the narrator's life when he and his mother lived above the trunk factory?
2. Why is "Saturnalia at Dayton's" an ironic title? What are other examples of irony in the selection?
3. Why did the author invent the dialogue among the four store detectives speaking to one another in paragraphs 12 to 23?
4. Reread the description of the parole officer and the office furniture and make a list of the adjectives. What mood is created by this description? calm? depressing? lively? dull? boring? peaceful? uneasy? something else?
5. What conclusion can you draw from this scene about how the author wants his readers to view "the system"?
6. Who was responsible for the problems between the narrator and his stepfather before the narrator leaves home?
7. What qualities did the narrator have that made him a survivor?

WRITING TOPICS

1. The narrator says that being "loose, alone, and free" is "a dubious pleasure without a home." In one paragraph, tell what he means.
2. Think of someone you see on a regular basis but don't really know. It might be a bus driver, a store clerk, a teacher, or a neighbor, for example. Using Vizenor's descriptions as a model, describe that person's appearance, movements, and any other distinguishing characteristics, conveying, if possible, how this person makes you feel.
3. Read the conversational scenes aloud with a classmate and listen for the tone your voices create. Then write a paper on this idea: Gerald Vizenor creates irony in his dramatic scenes by using exaggeration and sarcasm, and by allowing his reader to know information some of the people in the scenes don't know.

THE LONE RANGER AND TONTO FISTFIGHT IN HEAVEN

Sherman Alexie

According to critic Louis Owens, "Alexie's prose startles and dazzles with unexpected, impossible-to-anticipate moves, like the perfect reservation point guard whose passes sometimes catch you flat-footed and right in the face. It is a prose that takes risks and seldom stumbles." The twenty-two stories in *The Lone Ranger and Tonto Fistfight in Heaven* fit Owens' description well. Alexie's ironic language slips though the hoop easily to score humorous points, but because his laughter comes from irony, it is tinged with darkness. Alexie's writing speaks to the fact that the ability to laugh at life's miseries is necessary for survival.

Alexie, a graduate of "reservation university," writes of his own experiences and heritage. Combining fiction and fact, he presents contemporary Indian life fraught with five hundred years of history. *The Lone Ranger and Tonto Fistfight in Heaven* blends images of hunger and broken treaties, basketball and car wrecks, commodity food and smallpox blankets, love and anger. It demonstrates Alexie's ability to use pop culture icons such as 7-11, Elvis, television, Diet Pepsi, and neon signs in the context of Indian myth, history, and dreams.

In real reservation life, the convenience store is not just convenient. It is often the *only* store for miles with gas, groceries, and magazines. In Alexie's text, the 7-11 becomes a place of necessity and fantasy: "There are so many possibilities in the reservation 7-11, so many methods of survival. Imagine every Skin on the reservation is the new lead guitarist for the Rolling Stones, on the cover of a rock-and-roll magazine. Imagine forgiveness is sold 2 for 1. . . . Imagine a song stronger than penicillin. Imagine a spring with water that mends broken bones. Imagine a drum which wraps itself around your heart."

1   Too hot to sleep so I walked down to the Third Avenue 7-11 for a Creamsicle and the company of a graveyard-shift cashier. I know that game. I worked graveyard for a Seattle 7-11 and got robbed once too often. The last time the bastard locked me in the cooler. He even took my money and basketball shoes.

2   The graveyard-shift worker in the Third Avenue 7-11 looked like they all do. Acne scars and a bad haircut, work pants that showed off his white socks, and those cheap black shoes that have no support. My arches still ache from my year at the Seattle 7-11.

3   "Hello," he asked when I walked into his store. "How you doing?"

4   I gave him a half-wave as I headed back to the freezer. He looked me over so he could describe me to the police later. I knew the look. One of my old girlfriends said I started to look at her that way, too. She left me not long after that. No, I left her and don't blame her for anything. That's how it happened. When one person starts to look at another like a criminal, then the love is over. It's logical.

5   "I don't trust you," she said to me. "You get too angry."

6   She was white and I lived with her in Seattle. Some nights we fought so bad that I would just get in my car and drive all night, only stop to fill up on gas. In fact, I worked the graveyard shift to spend as much time away from her as possible. But I learned all about Seattle that way, driving its back ways and dirty alleys.

7   Sometimes, though, I would forget where I was and get lost. I'd drive for hours, searching for something familiar. Seems like I'd spent my whole life that way, looking for anything I recognized. Once, I ended up in a nice residential neighborhood and somebody must have been worried because the police showed up and pulled me over.

8   "What are you doing out here?" the police officer asked me as he looked over my license and registration.

9   "I'm lost."

10   "Well, where are you supposed to be?" he asked me, and I knew there were plenty of places I wanted to be, but none where I was supposed to be.

11   "I got in a fight with my girlfriend," I said. "I was just driving around, blowing off steam, you know?"

12   "Well, you should be more careful where you drive," the officer said. "You're making people nervous. You don't fit the profile of the neighborhood."

     I wanted to tell him that I didn't really fit the profile of the country but

13   I knew it would just get me into trouble.

14   "Can I help you?" the 7-11 clerk asked me loudly, searching for some response that would reassure him that I wasn't an armed robber. He knew this dark skin and long, black hair of mine was dangerous. I had potential.

15   "Just getting a Creamsicle," I said after a long interval. It was a sick twist to pull on the guy, but it was late and I was bored. I grabbed my Creamsicle

and walked back to the counter slowly, scanned the aisles for effect. I wanted to whistle low and menacingly but I never learned to whistle.

16 "Pretty hot out tonight?" he asked, that old rhetorical weather . . . question designed to put us both at ease.

17 "Hot enough to make you go crazy," I said and smiled. He swallowed hard like a white man does in those situations. I looked him over. Same old green, red, and white 7-11 jacket and thick glasses. But he wasn't ugly, just misplaced and marked by loneliness. If he wasn't working there that night, he'd be at home alone, flipping through channels and wishing he could afford HBO or Showtime.

18 "Will this be all?" he asked me, in that company effort to make me do some impulse shopping. Like adding a clause onto a treaty. *We'll take Washington and Oregon and you get six pine trees and a brand-new Chrysler Cordoba.* I knew how to make and break promises.

19 "No," I said and paused. "Give me a Cherry Slushie, too."

20 "What size?" he asked, relieved.

21 "Large," I said, and he turned his back to me to make the drink. He realized his mistake but it was too late. He stiffened, ready for the gunshot or the blow behind the ear. When it didn't come, he turned back to me.

22 "I'm sorry," he said. "What size did you say?"

23 "Small," I said and changed the story.

24 "But I thought you said large."

25 "If you knew I wanted a large, then why did you ask me again?" I asked him and laughed. He looked at me, couldn't decide if I was . . . just goofing. There was something about him I liked, even if it was three in the morning and he was white.

26 "Hey," I said. "Forget the Slushie. What I want to know is if you know all the words to the theme from 'The Brady Bunch'?"

27 He looked at me, confused at first, then laughed.

28 . . . "I was hoping you weren't crazy. You were scaring me."

29 "Well, I'm going to get crazy if you don't know the words."

30 He laughed loudly then, told me to take the Creamsicle for free. He was the graveyard-shift manager and those little demonstrations of power tickled him. All seventy-five cents of it. I knew how much everything cost.

31 "Thanks," I said to him and walked out the door. I took my time walking home, let the heat of the night melt the Creamsicle all over my hand. At three in the morning I could act just as young as I wanted to act. There was no one around to ask me to grow up.

DISCUSSION QUESTIONS

1. The narrator knows the cashier is wary, but he can't resist making him a little more anxious. Why do you think he does this?
2. Why does the narrator think that he doesn't "fit the profile of the country"?
3. Explain the narrator's sarcastic remark in paragraph 17.
4. Under what circumstances are people usually told to "grow up"?
5. Alexie often uses humor and irony to sharpen the impact of his words. Discuss three examples you think are effective.

WRITING TOPICS

1. Recall a funny or dramatic incident that happened while you were working at a summer or part-time job and write about it. Follow Alexie's example: describe the setting and tell what you were thinking as events progressed.
2. Write about the incident at the 7-11 from the clerk's point of view. Include the events in the order in which they happened and how you, as the clerk, felt.

RAYONA'S RIDE

Michael Dorris

Michael Dorris closes *A Yellow Raft in Blue Water* with Aunt Ida, one of the novel's storytellers, braiding her hair while a priest watches: "As a man with cut hair, he did not identify the rhythm of three strands, the whispers of coming and going, of twisting and tying and blending, of catching and of letting go, of braiding." Braiding is a good metaphor for the interwoven experiences that bind Aunt Ida, Christine, and Rayona in Dorris's book.

Rayona, a spunky fifteen-year-old, has to understand her past in order to make sense of her present life and to be able to walk into her future. As interviewer Bill Moyers commented to Michael Dorris, "Rayona is on a search for her identity. She has to pick here and pluck there and put it together in her own right." Caught between cultures, Rayona is older and wiser than her years.

As the book opens, Dorris introduces Rayona and her mother, Christine, in a Seattle hospital room: "I sit on the bed at a crooked angle, one foot on the floor, my hip against the bent of Mom's legs. . . . Mom has earlier spent twenty minutes pulling my long frizzy hair into a herringbone braid." Christine, an Indian from a reservation in eastern Montana, married Rayona's father, an African-American mail carrier, in Seattle. Their teenage daughter describes her often absent father as "a temp." He jokes about their family, "We may be different shades but look at the blend." Conscious of her color with all its tears and laughter, Rayona found her family's "exact shades" on a mix-tone paint chart: "Mom was Almond Joy, Dad was Burnt Clay, and I was Maple Walnut." Because of her erratic life, Rayona frequently changes schools, never getting past being the new girl, "Too big, too smart, not Black, not Indian, not friendly." Other kids keep their distance, and most teachers are surprised, then annoyed, because she knows the answers on their tests: "I'm not what they expect."

Very ill with cancer, Christine decides to take her daughter back to the reservation and leave her with her grandmother, Aunt Ida. Rayona again faces discrimination, because on the reservation she is the wrong color, has the wrong background, and doesn't speak the language well. Leaving the reservation for a summer does not solve her problems. Without money or a place to live, she arrives at Glacier National Park where a generous Euro-American couple who own a small grocery and gas station take her in, and she finds a job. Coping as usual, Rayona explains this new turn to herself, "It's as though I'm dreaming a lot of lives and I can mix and match the parts into something new each time." The couple, Evelyn and Sky, drive her to an Indian rodeo in Havre, Montana, to search for her mother.

At the rodeo grounds, Rayona meets her cousin Foxy, whom she had already classified as "a snake turned into a human being." When she convinces him that the rodeo officials will not allow him to ride, Foxy pressures her into taking his place. The mare she draws bucks her off three times, but with her typical determination, she climbs on again. Rayona's ride separates her past from her future in this "growing up moment."

1   After we pay admission, Sky and Evelyn stick to me like pennies on a Bingo card. They stand close together, shifting their weight, looking in every direction, and making a point to talk loud to me. They act as though I'm their safe conduct, the reason they're allowed in. For just a flash I see them through Aunt Ida's eyes: a skinny middle-aged hippie and a heavyset woman in Bermuda shorts and a yellow nylon shirt with STAFF written in brown thread across her breast, her gray hair short as a man's, and her mouth blazing with bright lipstick for the occasion. Their skin is colorless and loose over their bones. They're nervous, not used to being strangers surrounded by Indians.

2   But they can relax. They aren't the ones who are about to be challenged.

3   I'm not five feet inside the gate when I come face to face with the last person I want to see. Foxy Cree is standing in the shade under the bleachers, and is in the process of violating the Absolutely No Alcoholic Beverages rule that is posted at every entrance. His half-closed eyes scan the crowd, pass me once, then zero in. He smiles to himself and moves in my direction.

4   "Find some good seats," I tell Sky and Evelyn. "You don't want to have to sit in the sun."

5   At my suggestion, Sky wanders off toward the stands, but not Evelyn. She waves him on when he looks back. "I'll be there, darling," she says, but she's looking at Foxy and knows trouble when she sees it.

6   "Do you know that one coming?" she asks, punching me in the side.

7   I have to admit that if you're not acquainted with Foxy he's handsome. He has a thin straight nose, deep-set black eyes, and long hair, divided today into two leather-wrapped braids. Beneath his weathered blue jeans jacket he

wears an unbuttoned cowboy shirt. On his head is a black Navajo hat with a beadwork band. He's taller than me by a good three inches and so slim he can slip out of the window of a car without opening the door. But once you know him none of that counts.

8   "Rayona," he says, all sly. His voice has a lilt to it that usually shows on people about the same time their vision goes blurry and their drinks spill. It's the voice of a person who thinks he's a lot wilier than the one he's talking to. . . .

9   Evelyn is on red alert. This scene has no part in her vision of family reunions.

10   "We thought you was dead," Foxy goes on. "Or gone back to Africa." He says that last word real slow. . . .

11   "Rayona, Rayona, *Rayona*," Foxy sings. It isn't three o'clock and he's loaded already. His dirty cowboy boots stay in one spot but his body revolves as if moved by a breeze. He sways toward Evelyn.

12   "You here for the show, white lady?" he asks her. . . . He looks her over . . . laughs real low.

13   "Is this the piece of trash you were telling me about?" Evelyn has forgotten about being a stranger. I see her muscles bunching beneath the thin yellow material.

14   "No," I tell her. "Don't. Go with Sky."

15   She doesn't want to leave. She's ready to wipe the floor with Foxy but my look stands in her way. "This is my cousin," I say. "He might know what we came to find out. Let me talk to him."

16   All this time she's staring Foxy down, telling him with her eyes everything she thinks, and I can see she has penetrated his muscatel. His mouth hangs open as though it has been slapped and his face is full of complaint. He's wounded by the injustice of Evelyn's power, but that will turn to spite once he has me alone.

17   Without blinking, Evelyn asks if I'm sure, and when I say yes she suddenly takes a step toward Foxy, which makes him jump back.

18   "Norman and me'll be waiting for you. . . ." With a last, narrow-eyed warning look at Foxy she turns her back and disappears into the crowd.

19   I don't wait for him to recover. "Who's here?" I ask.

20   Foxy's still watching the place where Evelyn was standing and it takes a second for him to swing in my direction. . . . "Where'd you find her?"

21   "What are you doing here?" I ask it a different way. This time it gets through.

22   "I'm here to *ride*, Rayona," he says. My name is ugly in his mouth, just as he means it to be. "I got me entered in the bareback bronc on a hand-picked mount." He reaches into his pocket and draws out a piece of paper with 37 written on it in black Magic Marker.

23   "You'll never make it," I say and laugh at him before I consider what I'm doing.

24   His face clouds over. "You think?"

25   I don't know what to say. He's about to get madder no matter what.

26   He looks blank and rubs his registration paper between his fingers. I think he might pass out on the spot, but instead he's gathering an idea.

27   "Are you here with anybody?" I ask him. "You can't compete."

28   "If I forfeit I'm disqualified for all the . . . rodeos this summer."

29   "Come on, Foxy. They'll bump you anyway. You'd break your neck. You're drinking."

30   The bubble of Foxy's plan has popped in his brain and he's ready to deal. He reaches into his pocket for a piece of paper.

31   "But you're not. Oh no, not Rayona. . . . He balances himself with a hand that weights my shoulder. His fingers dig into me.

32   I go cold. "Shut up." I push him away and he falls heavily onto the ground. He shakes his head as if to clear it, then climbs to his feet. . . .

33   "You're going to ride for me."

34   "Don't be dumb. I've never even been to a rodeo before."

35   "Well, you're here now. All you have to do to keep my qualification is be sober enough to make it through the chute."

36   "No way."

37   "Do it for your mom. My horse belongs to the guy she's shacked up with."

38   Dayton, I think.

39   I want to hit Foxy, to kick the drunken leer off his face. I close my hands into fists and then I see a knife open in his palm. He holds it loose, ready. His legs seem steadier. His eyes are flat and red and I know he'd cut me without thinking twice.

40   I take the easiest way out: I surrender. I don't know whether it's that I'm scared or that I'm defeated by the mention of Mom. I don't really believe they'll let me ride in Foxy's place anyway. When they see I'm a girl they'll disqualify me. And, too, the idea is impossible. The only experience I've had with horses was one summer in Seattle when Mom had a boyfriend who took us to a park where they rented saddle rides and I took a few lessons. I liked it all right, but those ponies were tame, trotted along in a line on paths through the trees. I can't imagine myself on a wild bronc, so I agree.

41   "What time?"

42   "Now you're talking, cousin," Foxy laughs. He clicks the knife closed in one hand, and focuses his eyes on the form he still holds in the other.

43   "Three forty-five," he says. "Number thirty-seven. Horse named Babe."

44   He hands me the registration and then feels into the side of his boot for the long paper bag around the wine held tight against his thin leg. He tips it to his mouth, drinks, then wipes his dripping chin. "I'll be watching, just in case you forget."

45   He starts to walk bowlegged to the stands, when the drink in his brain splashes the other way and he turns back.

46   "If they think you're a girl," he says, figuring it out as he goes along,

"they won't let you ride." He wrestles with this thought, then slips off his jean jacket and hands it to me. "Put this on and button the front."

47   It's large for me, but Foxy is pleased with the effect. He walks behind me and tugs on the thick black braid of my hair.

48   "Now this," he says, and sets the black Navajo on my head. I can't believe Foxy and I have the same size brains, but we must because the hat fits.

49   "They'll just think I sat out in the sun too long." Foxy breaks down at his own joke. He laughs so hard he loses his breath in wheezes and coughs and finally spits on the ground. "You're a real Indian cowboy," he says.

50   It's less than a half hour until the event. I don't look for Sky and Evelyn since I have to figure this out for myself. The news that Mom is still on the reservation is sinking in. There's a part of me that's relieved. Ever since this morning, when Evelyn said Mom was sick, I've been worried in some nameless place, and now that relaxes. I wonder if in the weeks I've been gone, Mom has tried to find me, if she and Aunt Ida have made peace and worried together that I disappeared. No. She's still at this Dayton's and I still don't know how to find him. My one path to his door is through his horse. He's got to be around when she's ridden. Maybe Mom's here with him. Wouldn't she be surprised to see me contest? How would she feel if I got thrown on my head?

51   How will *I* feel? Fear rises in my neck at the thought of actually going through with Foxy's plan. I've seen bronc riding on "Wide World of Sports," and all I can remember is the sound of big men falling hard on the ground, the sight of crazed horses tossing their heads and kicking their hooves.

52   I've been walking toward the stock pens while I think, looking into the crowd for Mom's face, but instead I see Annabelle,[1] and she's spied me first. She's dressed for the rodeo in tight jeans, a purple Bruce Springsteen T-shirt, long silver earrings, a bunch of turquoise bracelets on each arm, and blue Western boots. Her straight black hair hangs below her shoulders and her skin is tan and smooth. She has circled her eyes with dark liner and her fingernails are long and perfectly red. There's something about her that reminds me of Ellen,[2] but then I realize that it's Ellen who's reminded me of Annabelle. Ellen is dim in comparison.

53   Annabelle comes up to me and demands, "Why are you wearing Foxy's hat." If she's surprised to see me, she doesn't let on.

54   "He gave it to me."

55   "Is he drinking?"

56   "He's drunk. . . ."

57   She says, "He's up in a few minutes. He'll get bumped."

---

[1] *Annabelle:* Foxy's girlfriend.
[2] *Ellen:* Rayona's coworker.

58   "He wants me to ride for him." I'm unbelieving all over again at the idea.

59   Annabelle cannot trust her ears. She doesn't know whether to laugh or get mad. She decides to get mad. . . . "I told him to stay straight, at least until after his event. I've had it with him."

60   No matter how many jeans jackets and hats you put on Annabelle, nobody would ever mistake her for a boy. She opens her purse, shakes out a Virginia Slim, and taps it against her lighter. She seems to notice me for the first time.

61   "Where have you been?" She's impatient and pissed off, but all the same this is the friendliest she's ever acted. It's the first time she's talked to me directly and not just to make an impression on whoever else is listening.

62   "Working at Bearpaw Lake State Park." I speak quickly, steeling myself for a mean reply.

63   "Really?" she says. Her imagination is caught. "God, I should get a job and get out of this place."

64   Now I know who Annabelle reminds me of. She's like the pictures I found in Aunt Ida's trailer. This is how Mom must have been, young and pretty, when she left, when she met Dad and they got married.

65   "Well, are you going to?" Annabelle asks.

66   "To what"

67   "To ride for Foxy?"

68   Annabelle will be impressed if I say yes. I'll be different in her eyes, dumb maybe, but worth knowing. I take her question seriously. I consider what Evelyn would do if this was happening to her.

69   "Yes," I say.

70   Dayton could be any one of the men clustered around the corral when I come in answer to the announcer's call and hand over my credentials. The starter pins 37 to the back of Foxy's jacket, and like a robot I mount the fence and stand above the trapped brown horse. Lots of cowboys grow their hair long, and a braid is nothing strange. No one looks at me. Maybe they're embarrassed to see the fear in a rider's eyes.

71   From the instant I lower myself into the stall and onto the mare's broad and sheening back, I buzz with nerves. She inclines her head and regards me with one rolled eye, and I feel her quiver through the inside of my thighs as I grip her high around the shoulders. It's the kind of vibration that comes when you touch a low-voltage electric fence, enough to scare back cows and sheep. Tensing with not even a blanket or saddle between us, her skin seems tight-stretched. With one hand I take the rope that runs from the bit in her mouth and with the other I reach forward to pat her back.

72   "Hey Babe, hey girl," I say.

73   It's a game, I want her to know. We're just playing. We don't mean it for real.

74   She paws her feet, snorts. A cowboy hanging on the fence touches my hat and motions for me to hold it with my free hand. I take it off and am sure that now, at last, they'll get a clear view, realize I'm a girl, see that I don't know how to sit, and call it off. But they still don't see me.

75 I nod to the gate. I'll never be ready, but now is as good a time as any. There are dangers to staying in the chute too long. If the horse panics she'll heave herself against the sides, crushing my legs. Or worse, one buck in that packed space would throw me to the ground with nowhere to roll away from a kick. It's happened more than once on "Wide World." The announcers talk about the metal plates in riders' skulls.

76 The sounds of the rodeo around me fade in my concentration. There's a drone in my ears that blocks out everything else, pasts and futures and long-range worries. The horse and I are held in a vise, a wind-up toy that has been turned one twist too many, a spring coiled beyond its limit.

77 "Now!" I cry, aloud or to myself I don't know. Everything has boiled down to this instant. There's nothing in the world except the hand of the gate judge, lowering in slow motion to the catch that contains us. I see each of his fingers clearly, separately, as they fold around the lever, I see the muscles in his forearm harden as he begins to push down.

78 I never expected the music.

79 Wheeling and spinning, tilting and beating, my breath the song, the horse the dance. Time is gone. All the ordinary ways of things, the gettings from here to there, the one and twos, forgot. The crowd is color, the whirl of a spun top. The noises blend into a waving band that flies around us like a ribbon on a string. Beneath me four feet dance, pounding and leaping and turning and stomping. My legs flap like wings. I sail above, first to one side, then the other, remembering more than feeling the slaps of our bodies together. Things happen faster than understanding, faster than ideas. I'm a bird coasting, shot free into the music, spiraling into a place without bones or weight.

80 I'm on the ground. Unmoving. The heels of my hands sunk in the dust of the arena. My knees sore. Dizzy. Back in time. I shake sense into my head, listen as the loudspeaker brays.

81 "Twenty-four seconds for the young cowboy from eastern Montana. Nice try, son. Hoka-hay."

82 A few claps from the crowd. I know I should move. I've seen riders today limp off when they fall, their heads hung, their mounts kicking two hind legs at the end of the ring until the clowns herd them out.

83 But Babe is calm. She stands next to me, blowing air through her nostrils, looking cross-eyed and triumphant. She wins the hand. Her sides ripple. It could be laughter, it could be disgust for having been touched. Dayton's horse.

84 So I don't leave with a wave to the stands. The first toss is warm-up, practice. I grab the rope, throw my arms around her neck and swing aboard. She stiffens, fuses her joints. The broad muscles of her shoulders turn steel under my gripping legs.

85 And bang! We're off again. This time instead of up and down she bolts straight ahead. The wind whips my braid, blows dust into my eyes till I have to squint them shut. She runs one fast circle around the pen, her body in a low crouch. She's thinking.

86 When you don't know what to expect, you hang on in every way you can. I clasp the rope in one hand, her mane in the other. I dig my heels into the hollows behind the place where her forelegs join her ribs. I lean into her neck, and watch the ground rush by on either side of her ears.

87 Without warning she slows, moves close to the rough plank fence where the Brahmas are milling, and shifts her weight. She stops on a dime and, still clutching her with every part of me, I roll to the left. I'm pinned between Babe and the boards, with my back against the wall. My breath is squeezed out and there's no way I can protect my head, lolling above the pen. Then, without once lightening on the weight she presses against me, Babe walks forward as if to clean herself of me, as if I'm mud on the bottom of a boot.

88 It works. The next thing I know I'm on the ground again, Foxy's jean jacket ripped and torn across the shoulder seam, the air rushing back into my lungs, tears smeared on my cheeks. My ribs hurt, and behind me the bulls knock on the fence with their horns.

89 And before me is Babe, her lips drawn over her yellow teeth, her head low and swinging back and forth, her legs planted far apart. She looks astonished, at herself or me I can't tell.

90 As I stand she begins to retreat, one foot at a time. For an instant, I hear the crowd again, but I can't bother with them. I have Babe in my bead, our eyes in a blinding fix. Our brains lock, and she stops while I grab her mane and hook a leg over her back. Before I'm balanced, she rears. Her front legs climb the air, and I dangle along her back suspended. When at last she drops, I'm low on her flank, our hips one on top of the other, my body fitted into her length. She rears again, and again there is air between us, yet I hang on. I smell her sweat, feel the warmth of her skin beneath my face and hands. There is nothing in the world but her and I think I can stay up forever.

91 When she kicks out her hind legs, though, I slide over her neck, down her long head, and slam into the ground. I concede for the second time today. I'm so winded I can't move, stupid as I must look, my face in the dirt, my ass in the air, and my legs folded beneath me. When my ears stop ringing I hear the loudspeaker again.

92 ". . . give this kid a hand, folks. He may not be much of a rider but he ain't no quitter! Looks like he damn well wore out that wild mare too, even if he didn't bust her."

93 There's real clapping this time, a few whistles, but I get strength more from my curiosity about the last thing he said. I open one eye and the world is upside down, but that isn't the strangest thing. Not ten feet from me, sitting like a big dog and nodding her head, slumps Babe. She looks as bad as I feel, and as it turns out, we both need a hand from the clowns in getting out of the ring.

94 Some of Mom's navy boyfriends in Seattle used to talk about their sea legs and I never knew what they meant. They tried to explain how once you became used to the roll of waves, walking on dry land was never the same again. It felt lifeless.

95   Now I catch on. I'm back from throwing up behind the pens. I've rinsed the dirt from my face and dusted off my pants and jacket and the black hat someone handed to me as I limped out of the corral. Wild horse riding is the next-to-last event in the rodeo. As I lean back against the announcer's stand, I keep shifting my legs and waiting for something to happen under my feet. My muscles haven't yet set into the hard, stiff ache that lies ahead, but all through me I feel a ticking that hasn't run down.

96   There's a part of me that wants to submerge and disappear. Everybody that passes has to say something they think is funny about my ride, and I have to laugh at myself with them or be a bad sport. But there's another part of me that would climb back on Babe in a flash, no waiting, if that horse would appear in front of me. People tell me how lucky I am that I didn't break my neck or my back, or at least bust a shoulder, I fell so hard, but when I was riding I was mindless and beyond hurt. I was connected to a power I never knew existed, and without it I'm unplugged. On Babe, I would have burned out my circuits rather than choose safety. Up there, my only worry was gravity.

97   But on earth, my troubles haven't gone away. I stand, puzzling out what to do next, while the MC reads out the list of winners: Best bull ride. Longest saddle bronc. Fastest hogtie. I can't return to Bearpaw Lake with Sky and Evelyn. At the end of the season, when I would have no choice but to move along, I wouldn't be any closer to knowing what to do than I am now. Already Ellen and Andy and John, even Dave, are as removed and strange, as ancient history, as kids at my schools in Seattle. The ride on Babe is a boundary I can't recross, and I'm stuck on this side for better or worse.

98   Evelyn and Sky are different because they're here, because they brought me, because even though she doesn't know it, Evelyn got me on that horse and kept putting me back, because Sky closed the Conoco and gave up his Christmas money without asking any questions. But I can't live in the trailer with them any longer. . . .

99   Brahma riding. Bareback bronc. The fear comes back.

100   Annabelle pushes through the crowd and walks to face me. She carries two red paper Coke cups and hands one over. Her dark-rimmed eyes are excited.

101   "I wouldn't have believed it. I don't believe it," she says. "You're out of your mind. You're a maniac."

102   This is a compliment from Annabelle. I take a long pull on my Coke and discover it's beer.

103   "Do they know you're a girl?" Annabelle whispers. "You're insane."

104   The MC is about to announce the All-Around, the award for the cowboy who has done the best at the most events. It's what everybody waits to hear, and the crowd noise simmers down.

105   "Before the last prize," he says, "the judges have voted an unscheduled citation, one that's only given on rare occasions."

106   He holds up something shiny and silver that gathers light from the late afternoon sun and reflects it back in a bright beam.

107   "It's engraved special," he goes on. "I wish you folks could see it. This buckle shows a bronc and a rider throwed in the air, with genuine coral and jet inlay. One hundred percent nickel silver plate."

108   I see Evelyn and Sky in the bleachers, straining to hear. Their hands shade their eyes against the afternoon glare, but I'm standing under the judges' box and have my borrowed hat pulled low in front of my face.

109   "So come on, folks, and give a real Havre hand for the roughest, toughest, *clumsiest* cowboy we've seen around here in many a moon. It gives me genuine pleasure to award the hard-luck buckle, for the amazing feat of being bucked off the same horse three times in less than a minute, to a home-grown Indian boy, number thirty-seven, Kennedy 'Foxy' Cree!"

110   Some people let out yells and war whoops, and everybody starts pounding me on the back and shoving me forward. Kennedy Cree is Foxy's real name, and this minute it's mine too. Annabelle gives a sharp piercing whistle through her fingers and stomps her blue boot in the sawdust. I fill my lungs with stockyard air. There's no escape.

111   So I run up the steps and reach to shake the MC's hand. He looks close at me this time, then closer. He realizes I'm no cowboy. I pry the buckle from him anyway and hold it to my right and left for the stands to see. Behind me there are surprised voices talking to each other and when I look down at the other winners assembled nearest to the grandstand I see their eyes are wide too. It's no use pretending. I knock off my hat, undo the rubber band, comb with my fingers, and shake out my braid. With my free hand I unsnap the ruined jacket and shrug it from my shoulders. I thrust out my chest.

112   At first there's silence. Everyone gapes at me and then at each other and then at me again. The quiet hangs like a Seattle fog as we stand there, facing off in the long afternoon light. And finally from far away, clear and proud, Evelyn shouts: "Rayona!" Annabelle whistles again, loud as a siren. And when I raise the silver buckle high above my head, the rest of the crowd joins in.

DISCUSSION QUESTIONS

1. Why does Rayona agree to take Foxy's place in the rodeo?
2. What is the moment of greatest suspense in this narrative?

WRITING TOPICS

1. In a brief essay, analyze the paragraphs that describe Rayona's ride. Consider the diction, sentence length, figurative language, and sensory imagery and what they contribute to the total effect of the scene.
2. An author can use several methods to characterize someone: dialogue, description of appearance and gestures, or what other people say and think about that character. In a brief essay, analyze the methods Dorris uses to characterize Foxy and end your paper with a one-sentence summary of the kind of person he is.

GROWING UP

Michael Dorris

During summers on a Montana reservation, Michael Dorris experienced many of the frustrations that Sherman Alexie and other Indian writers describe. In this autobiographical essay, however, he tells readers about other kinds of frustrations. He describes how he coped with never knowing his father, who died in combat in Europe during World War II, and how he frequently missed him when engaged in "father-son" activities.

Dorris writes about his "growing up" in a different way as the adult parent of adopted children. He almost dismisses the mundane parental responsibilities of toilet training, purchasing expensive shoes, and listening to childhood tales of woe. He finally feels like a parent upon hearing his son Sava boast to a peer about "Dad" performing an ear-piercing that Dad had never anticipated on the basis of his own boyhood daydreams. The author reveals his maturation by recognizing that the fulfilling father-son activities that he had promised himself to engage in were irrelevant to his son's needs.

1   The picture I developed of my late father was a collage of stories I heard from family members who had known him and of my musings upon a series of his photographs—him, at attention in an army uniform, him marrying my mother, him standing arm in arm with two buddies on a Hawaiian beach—as well as from impressions gleaned from observing the fathers of friends and from watching the dads on television.

2   I knew as fact that my father had a wide-ranging military career, always seeming to be at the wrong place at the wrong time. He survived being awakened from sleep in his Pearl Harbor barracks by the Japanese attack in 1941, then came through the Battle of the Bulge without an injury. His only major physical wound was sustained at a baseball game in Texas when another soldier, in excitement over a home run, accidentally shot him in the leg. He was an eldest son, popular in high school. He prized a ruby ring, which failed

to come back with the rest of his things from the town in Germany where, at age twenty-seven, his life ended on an icy mountain road.

3   The father of my imagination, however, took me to the places I hated to go without him—to "males only" grade school sports banquets and to public swimming pool locker rooms. He taught me how to bat one-handed. He advised me how to handle bullies, how to do a box-step, how to impress a date. He was Ward Cleaver, Jim Anderson, Dr. Stone, the Rifleman, and Ricky Ricardo,[1] and when I became a man, I promised myself I would be just like him.

4   As it turned out, it was not impossible to master the arts of changing diapers, kissing scratches, exclaiming at each appropriately timed defecation, and buying increasingly sized—and priced—sneakers. I took pride in my ability to schedule regular physical exams for my two sons and daughter Madeline (whom I had adopted at ten months when Sava was four), to listen to their tales of day-care woes.

5   When my older children were, respectively, thirteen, nine, and five, Louise Erdrich and I got married, and she did her best to be patient with me as I gradually relaxed those solitary prerogatives of decision making and rule setting that are among the advantages of single parenthood. When the time was right, she too, legally adopted our children, and in a few years we had two more babies. With a total of five offspring, I was technically more of a father than I had ever imagined I'd be.

6   But something was missing, some vestigial fantasy from Hollywood or literature, some sense of bridging an archetypal gap. None of our children had ever seemed to require me in quite the vital, aspecific way I had imagined needing my own father.

7   Then one day Sava, just twelve, waited until I was alone and approached me with a body language and verbal hesitation that broadcast that a significant event was about to transpire.

8   "Dad," he said, his voice low, slightly embarrassed. "Would you help me with something?"

9   Instinctively I knew this was it, and prepared myself to don the mantle of true paternity. Every boyhood daydream flooded back: maybe he wanted me to take him for a nature walk in the woods, maybe he desired to know something arcane about human biology, maybe he had been cut from the football team and yearned for a pep talk, maybe he was in love for the first time and feared rejection. I prepared myself to dispense a mixture of wisdom and compassion no matter what the question.

10   "It's like this," he continued, talking to the floor. "A lot of the guys in my class got their ears pierced, but . . . I don't really want to go to a jeweler and I'm kind of nervous to do it myself, so . . . would *you* do it for me?"

---

[1] *Ward Cleaver . . . Ricky Ricardo:* widely varied types of television characters of the 1950s and 1960s.

11   My mouth remained open as I searched for a reply. What would Ward say to the Beaver?[2]

12   "I don't know how," I answered, pedaling as my brain spun calendar pages through the sixties and seventies, scanning for precedents. Of one thing I was certain: if I tried to be reasonable, to talk him out of his plan, he wouldn't soon trust me enough again to ask for something when it wasn't guaranteed that I'd say yes . . . and I didn't want to preempt the opportunity to counsel him on an issue that really mattered.

13   "I found this," Sava offered, and pulled from his pocket a much folded piece of newspaper. It was a "Hints" column that recommended a procedure entailing ice cubes, a sterilized needle, and a raw potato placed directly behind the numbed anatomical part. The piercer was instructed to think of sticking only the potato, not the piercee's skin before it. The result was promised to be an operation painless for both parties.

14   What could I say? "I'll give it a try."

15   Sava had all the tools assembled. I brushed aside his dark hair and held his left lobe between two slivers of ice. His skin was soft to the touch, a pale tan. His ear was so familiar, so cherished, that I could have picked it out of a lineup.

16   Impatient, Sava lit a match, held the point of the needle into its flame until it turned black, then quickly offered it to me. I dropped the ice and fit the brown potato beside my son's head.

17   "Are you sure?" I asked, and our glances met.

18   He was.

19   I followed the Hint and pushed the needle into the potato. I expected a cry of pain, a drop of blood, something dramatic, but Sava didn't flinch, and when I withdrew the needle, a neat puncture remained in his earlobe, perfectly centered.

20   "Did it work?"

21   I nodded, steered him to the bathroom mirror. Sava had a gold post soaking in alcohol, which he fitted into the hole before turning his head left and right to admire the effect.

22   "Thanks, Dad," he said, and was out the door, headed for the telephone.

23   I sat alone, thinking that life was never as you expected it to be, never the same for anyone else as it was for you, never as strange in the imagination as it often turned out to be in reality. But as I overheard Sava bragging to his friend, "My Dad did it. Yeah, my *Dad*," that elusive piece of fatherhood I thought I had missed fell square into place.

---

[2] *Beaver*: son of Ward Cleaver on the television series "Leave It to Beaver."

DISCUSSION QUESTIONS

1. How many of the author's ideas about fathers were based on fiction? Why did this factor leave him unprepared for his son's request?
2. Do you think the author was a good father? Explain.
3. "Growing Up" was originally published in a magazine called *Parents*. For what reasons might the editors have decided to publish this essay?

WRITING TOPICS

1. Why is there sometimes a difference of opinion between parents and children, since parents were themselves once children? Is it a matter of changing times, forgetfulness on the part of parents about their youth, lack of parental trust, untrustworthy children, or the desire of parents to keep their children from making the same mistakes they themselves made? Write an essay exploring these questions.
2. The author says that the picture he had of his father was a "collage of stories." Write a character sketch of your father or mother, based on your first-hand impressions and on stories you have heard.

NOTES OF A TRANSLATOR'S SON

Joseph Bruchac

Joseph Bruchac offers an individual approach to solving the mystery of his mixed ancestry. In *Bowman's Store, A Journey to Myself,* he maps the various roads he traveled searching for his hidden Indian heritage. Over a long time, Bruchac pursued family secrets about his Indian legacy. By interacting with Iroquois and other Indian people and reading books, he gradually reconstructed and created his Abenaki identity.

His grandparents' unspoken rule never to discuss Grandpa's Indian blood impressed and confused the young Bruchac, who grew up with their love and care. His questions remained unanswered until he was adult and his relatives told him that his beloved Grandfather Jesse Bowman had indeed been part Abenaki. Marion Dunham, his grandmother, the well-educated daughter of a prominent family, had married a semiliterate, dark-complexioned hired laborer working for her family. She was sent away to break the relationship, but Jesse joined her and finally found work at the Warm Springs Hotel: "Too light-skinned and too unsophisticated to join the staff of African American hotel waiters, too dark-skinned and too uneducated to work out front where he might be seen, he was given work down back as a teamster." Nevertheless, the couple married and opened Bowman's store. Bruchac and his family live in it today.

Bruchac began his writing career by publishing *Indian Mountain and Other Poems* in 1971. He also began working with native children on Iroquois reservations, where he found people who were proud to be Indians and learned from them. Each year he conducts storytelling and poetry workshops with the children of the Onondaga Nation School. In 1980, an Onondaga clan mother gave him an Iroquois name meaning "The Good Mind" and admonished him, "This name will remind you that you always have to try to use your gift of words in a good way."

Bruchac had already been sharing his gift since 1970 when he began publishing *The Greenfield Review,* a literary quarterly. The next year he established the Greenfield Review Press, publishing anthologies of the works of others. He recalls, "I looked for work by others like myself, people who were seeking out their Native roots along the word trails, people who were unafraid of being Indian." Many of these young writers became his close friends. This led to one of his most valuable books, *Survival This Way, Interviews with American Indian Poets* (1987). For more than four years, Bruchac traveled across America to interview new and established Native American poets. He learned from these authors and continued his own writing odyssey.

Bruchac's writings have appeared in more than four hundred journals and many have been translated from English into other languages. "Notes of a Translator's Son" appears in *I Tell You Now: Autobiographical Essays by Native American Writers.* "Translator" is an appropriate title for Bruchac because he has spent his writing and teaching career learning to understand "the language of both sides to help them understand each other."

1   The best teachers have showed me that things have to be done bit by bit. Nothing that means anything happens quickly—we only think it does. The motion of drawing back a bow and sending an arrow straight into a target takes only a split second, but it is a skill many years in the making. So it is with a life, anyone's life. I may list things that might be described as my accomplishments in these few pages, but they are only shadows of the larger truth, fragments separated from the whole cycle of becoming. And if I can tell an old-time story now about a man who is walking about, *waudjoset ndatlokugan*, a forest lodge man, *alesakamigwi udlagwedewugan*, it is because I spent many years walking about myself, listening to voices that came not just from the people but from animals and trees and stones.

2   Who am I? My name is Joseph Bruchac. The given name is that of a Christian saint—in the best Catholic tradition. The surname is from my father's people. It was shortened from *Bruchacek*—"big belly" in Slovak. Yet my identity has been affected less by middle European ancestry and Christian teachings (good as they are in their seldom-seen practice) than by that small part of my blood which is American Indian and which comes to me from a grandfather who raised me and a mother who was almost a stranger to me. I have other names, as well. One of those names is Quiet Bear. Another, given me by Dewasentah, Clan Mother at Onondaga,[1] is *Gah-neh-go-he-yo*. It means "the Good Mind." There are stories connected to those names, stories for another time.

---

[1] *Onondaga*: The Onondaga were one of the nations of the Iroquois Confederacy, a political group of North American Indian nations. The government of the Onondaga Nation in central New York State continues to be convened by chiefs and clan mothers.

3   What do I look like? The features of my face are big: a beaked nose, lips that are too sensitive, sand-brown eyes and dark eyebrows that lift one at a time like the wings of a bird, a low forehead that looks higher because of receding brown hair, an Adam's apple like a broken bone, two ears that were normal before wrestling flattened one of them. Unlike my grandfather's, my skin is not brown throughout the seasons but sallow in the winter months, though it tans dark and quickly when the sun's warmth returns. It is, as you might gather, a face I did not used to love. Today I look at it in the mirror and say, *Bruchac, you're ugly and I like you.* The face nods back at me and we laugh together.

4   The rest of me? At forty-two I still stand 6'2" tall and weigh the 195 pounds I weighed when I was a heavyweight wrestler at Cornell University. My arms and hands are strong, as strong as those of anyone I've met, though my two sons—Jim who is sixteen and 6'4", and Jesse who is thirteen and close to 6'—smile when I say that. When they were little their games included "Knock Papa Down." Each year they've found it a little easier to do. My physical strength, in part, is from my grandfather, who was never beaten in a fight. Like his, the fingers of my hands are short and thick. I hold them out and see the bulges in the knuckles, the way both my index fingers are skewed slightly and cannot completely straighten. A legacy of ten years of studying martial arts.

5   Do we make ourselves into what we become or is it built into our genes, into the fate spun for us by whatever shapes events? I was a small child, often alone and often bullied. I was different—raised by old people who babied me, bookish, writing poetry in grade school, talking about animals as if they were people. My grandfather joked when he called me a "mongrel," a mixture of English and Slovak and "French," but others said such things without joking. When I was seven I decided I would grow up to be so big and strong that no one would ever beat me up again. It took me nine years to do it. ("Be careful what you really want," a Tai Chi master told me. "If you really want it, you'll get it.") My junior year in high school I was still the strange kid who dressed in weird clothes, had no social graces, and was picked on by the other boys, scored the highest grades in English and biology and almost failed Latin and algebra. That winter of my junior year my grandmother died. My grandfather and I were left alone in the old house. That summer I grew six inches in height. In my senior year, though clothing and social graces showed little evolution, I became a championship wrestler, won a Regents' scholarship, and was accepted by Cornell University to study wildlife conservation. . . .

6   How many memories of my childhood are my own and not those someone else had of me and told me about when I was older? I know that the image of a fence taller than my hands can reach is my own. I can still feel the chill, slightly rusted surface of its wire mesh against my face, my tongue almost freezing to its surface as I taste it on a day when the frost has glazed its red weave to the shimmer of a mirror. Is that my first memory or does

the litter of puppies in Truman Middlebrooks' barn come before it? A warm milk smell of small animals, the sharpness of their teeth, the gentle insistence of their mother's muzzle nudged between me and them, pushing me away to roll on my back in the straw while someone's adult voice laughs. I know I am not being laughed at, so it is my grandfather's laughter that I hear. I never heard my father or my mother laugh when I was a child, and somehow life seemed too serious to my grandmother for her to indulge in much humor, even though she won her battle to keep me from my parents—that battle which I cannot remember but which has been replayed for me from the reluctant memories of those older than I. My grandfather, though, was often joking, often teasing. When he was serious it was a seriousness that no one laughed at.

7 The memory of me climbing the ladder, unafraid and right behind the old man, all the way to the roof forty feet up when I was only two, was my grandfather's. But it was recited about me so often that it became inseparably associated with my thoughts of my childhood. I know that I always dreamed of flight. I still do fly in my dreams. Its secret is simple—just lift your legs when you're falling and you'll never touch the ground until you're ready. To this day I don't understand why I can't continue to do it in the seconds after I wake from such dreams. But I have faith that eventually I will solve that problem one way or another and float away, with my body or without it. And though I've had some spectacular falls—at least one of which I should never have survived—I still love high places, cliffs and trees and resounding waterfalls. I inherited that fearlessness about high places and dying from my grandfather, just as I inherited certain stories. Here is one of them which is as much a part of my own fabric as if I had been there and when that day was being woven:

> *I only went to school until I was in 3rd grade.*
> *What happened then, Grampa?*
> *I jumped out the window of the school and never came back.*
> *Why?*
> *I got in a fight with a boy who called me an Indian.*

8 My grandparents raised me. I grew up only a quarter of a mile away from my mother and father's home on what we always called "The Farm," a plot of ninety acres with several outbuildings, which had been the home of my grandparents when they were first married. My grandfather gave The Farm to them after they'd been married a few years and were still living with my grandparents. The room where I type this was my parents' room when I was a baby. They moved to The Farm with my younger sister, and I stayed "for a while" with my grandparents. I sat with my grandfather in the wooden chairs he had made and painted blue and placed in front of his general store: Bowman's Store. I was wearing shorts and my toes couldn't touch the concrete as I dangled them down, using a stick to keep my balance as I stayed

in the chair. There was a shadow in front of me. My parents. My grandmother took my hand and led me back into the house. "Get to your room, Sonny."

9   There my memory is replaced by that of my other grandmother, the Slovak one who lived three miles away up the South Greenfield road.

> *Your fader, he vas ready to leave your mother. Dere vere so many tears, such crying about you. Ah. Den your fader and mother they come and say they vill take you back, now. Dat is ven your grandfather Bowman, he goes out of the room. Ven he come back it is vith the shotgun. And he hold it to his head and say take him you vill never see me alive again.*

10   Though I did not hear that story until after I was married, I knew that I was important to my grandfather. I realize now I must have been, in part, a replacement for my mother's older brother, who died at birth. I was always close to my grandfather. He delighted in telling how I was his shadow, how I carried my stick just like a spear and followed him everywhere. But, close as I was, he would never speak of the Indian blood which showed so strongly in him. I have a tape recording we made soon after we returned to live with him, back from three years in West Africa to the old house on Splinterville Hill with our new son, his great-grandchild, whose life would start the healing of wounds I had caused by simply being wanted.

> *Are you Indian, Grampa?*
> *No.*
> *Then why is your skin so dark?*
> *Cause I'm French. Us French is always dark.*

11   Yet I was conscious of the difference, of the way people looked at me when I was with my grandfather. When I was a freshman at Cornell University he came to visit, bringing two of my friends from high school, David Phillips and Tom Furlong. They spent two nights in the dorm, all of them sleeping in my room. My grandfather told everyone that David was my younger brother. They looked at my grandfather and then, more slowly, at me. David was black. When they asked me if it was true, I said, "What do you think?" When the fraternity rushing week came later that semester, I was on more than one "black list."

12   There are many people who could claim and learn from their Indian ancestry, but because of the fear their parents and grandparents knew, because of past and present prejudice against Indian people, that part of their heritage is clouded or denied. Had I been raised on other soil or by other people, my Indian ancestry might have been less important, less shaping. But I was not raised in Czechoslovakia or England. I was raised in the foothills of the Adirondack Mountains near a town whose spring waters

were regarded as sacred and healing by the Iroquois and Abenaki alike. This is my dreaming place. Only my death will separate it from my flesh.

13   I've avoided calling myself "Indian" most of my life, even when I have felt that identification most strongly, even when people have called me an "Indian." Unlike my grandfather, I have never seen that name as an insult, but there is another term I like to use. I heard it first in Lakota and it refers to a person of mixed blood, a *métis*. In English it becomes "Translator's Son." It is not an insult, like *half-breed*. It means that you are able to understand the language of both sides, to help them understand each other.

DISCUSSION QUESTIONS

1. What are the similarities and differences between the types of memories the author has about his childhood and the types of memories you have?
2. Why was the author "on more than one 'black list'" at Cornell?
3. How do the incidents in the author's life described here illustrate his contention that "nothing that means anything happens quickly?"

WRITING TOPICS

1. Describe yourself in a paragraph, but don't put your name on your paper. Then, with others in your class, shuffle the paragraphs and have each class member choose a paragraph and read it aloud. Can listeners identify who is being described?
2. When the author was young, he decided how he would become so big and strong that no one would ever beat him up. It took him nine years to do it. What in your life has taken a long time to accomplish? Write about something that you have achieved after a significant period of time. Include why you think the achievement was worthwhile and whether you think this is something you will always continue to do or enjoy.

THE END OF CHILDHOOD

N. Scott Momaday

N. Scott Momaday's adventure that takes him within "an eyelash of eternity" divides his growing up days at Jemez Pueblo from his going out into the world. It is a metaphorical moment. Fortunately, this brush with death does not literally end his life. He tells the story at the end of *The Names, A Memoir,* which continues his exploration of Indian identity begun in *The Way to Rainy Mountain.* In both books, Momaday is fascinated by the miracle of language and explores the way landscape shapes people.

The landscape in "The End of Childhood" is the canyon country beneath the Jemez Mountains west of Santa Fe, New Mexico. Jemez culture is very old, deriving from the cliff dwellers who lived above Jemez Pueblo centuries ago. The Pueblo is located alongside a river in a fertile farming valley hemmed in by peaks and plateaus. Steep escarpments rise at the valley's edge. Momaday no doubt heard Jemez stories about their ancestors retreating to a defensive, ridge-top Pueblo to resist the Spanish reconquest in 1696.

When he was twelve, Momaday moved to Jemez with his parents, who taught at the Jemez Day School for the next twenty-five years. In *The Names,* the author describes his first morning in this magical place. Catching his breath in the cold air at six thousand feet, he recalls a thought from Isak Dinesen, "Here I am, where I ought to be." For the sensitive adolescent, Jemez life was idyllic, filled with feasts, ceremonies, and horseback trips through beautiful country. It was a place for him and his family to grow: "There was at Jemez a climate of the mind in which we, my parents and I, realized ourselves, understood who we were. . . . we invested much of our lives in it, and in it was the remembered place of our hopes, and dreams, and our deep love."

Language in *The Names* is inextricable from identity. It is not surprising that a writer who defines himself as "a man made of words" opens and closes his memoir with *names.* The title of Momaday's memoir underscores a fundamental belief in the miraculous quality of language. In the preface, Momaday asserts that when a person is

given a name, existence is also given him: "My name is Tsoai-talee.
I am, therefore, Tsoai-talee; therefore I am."

◉

1 At Jemez I came to the end of my childhood. There were no schools
within easy reach. I had to go nearly thirty miles to school at Bernalillo, and
one year I lived away in Albuquerque. My mother and father wanted me to
have the benefit of a sound preparation for college, and so we read through
many high school catalogues. After long deliberation we decided that I
should spend my last year of high school at a military academy in Virginia.

2 The day before I was to leave I went walking across the river to the red
mesa, where many times before I had gone to be alone with my thoughts.
And I had climbed several times to the top of the mesa and looked among
the old ruins there for pottery. This time I chose to climb the north end,
perhaps because I had not gone that way before and wanted to see what it
was. It was a difficult climb, and when I got to the top I was spent. I lingered among the ruins for more than an hour, I judge, waiting for my
strength to return. From there I could see the whole valley below, the fields,
the river, and the village. It was all very beautiful, and the sight of it filled
me with longing.

3 I looked for an easier way to come down, and at length I found a broad,
smooth runway of rock, a shallow groove winding out like a stream. It
appeared to be safe enough, and I started to follow it. There were steps
along the way, a stairway, in effect. But the steps became deeper and deeper,
and at last I had to drop down the length of my body and more. Still
it seemed convenient to follow in the groove of rock. I was more than
halfway down when I came upon a deep, funnel-shaped formation in my
path. And there I had to make a decision. The slope on either side was
extremely steep and forbidding, and yet I thought that I could work my way
down on either side. The formation at my feet was something else. It was
perhaps ten or twelve feet deep, wide at the top and narrow at the bottom,
where there appeared to be a level ledge. If I could get down through the
funnel to the ledge, I should be all right; surely the rest of the way down was
negotiable. But I realized that there could be no turning back. Once I was
down in that rocky chute I could not get up again, for the round wall which
nearly encircled the space there was too high and sheer. I elected to go down
into it, to try for the ledge directly below. I eased myself down the smooth,
nearly vertical wall on my back, pressing my arms and legs outward against
the sides. After what seemed a long time I was trapped in the rock. The
ledge was no longer there below me; it had been an optical illusion. Now,
in this angle of vision, there was nothing but the ground, far, far below, and
jagged boulders set there like teeth. I remember that my arms were scraped
and bleeding, stretched out against the walls with all the pressure that I

could exert. When once I looked down I saw that my legs, also spread out and pressed hard against the walls, were shaking violently. I was in an impossible situation: I could not move in any direction, save downward in a fall, and I could not stay beyond another minute where I was. I believed then that I would die there, and I saw with a terrible clarity the things of the valley below. They were not the less beautiful to me. It seemed to me that I grew suddenly very calm in view of that beloved world. And I remember nothing else of that moment. I passed out of my mind, and the next thing I knew I was sitting down on the ground, very cold in the shadows, and looking up at the rock where I had been within an eyelash of eternity. That was a strange thing in my life, and I think of it as the end of an age. I should never again see the world as I saw it on the other side of that moment, in the bright reflection of time lost. There are such reflections, and for some of them I have the names.

DISCUSSION QUESTIONS

1. How does the author make clear his feelings about his homeland?
2. If you could ask Momaday one question, what would it be?

WRITING TOPICS

1. Momaday writes of a significant passage in his life. In a brief personal essay, relate a similarly significant event in your life.
2. If you have ever been in a perilous position, or were very frightened, write about it in three paragraphs.

SUMMARY WRITING TOPICS

1. Many of the authors in this chapter write about a feeling of "not belonging." In an essay, discuss some factors that contribute to this feeling, both as depicted in this chapter and in your own experience.
2. In a paragraph, tell what you think William Apess's reaction would have been to the excerpt from *Interior Landscapes* by Gerald Vizenor.
3. In a short paper, tell who you think were the best parents or grandparents described in this chapter and why you think so.
4. If you are of mixed heritage, write about times when you have felt this to be a mixed blessing. You may make this a poem, a journal entry, or an essay.
5. You have read several autobiographical excerpts in this chapter. In a short paper, tell what you think autobiography ought to contain or reveal (or not reveal).
6. Several authors in this chapter write about turning points in their lives. Recall an experience that you did not recognize as a turning point when it happened. Write a narrative in which you describe what happened then and how you view the experience now.
7. Four essays by Michael Dorris appear in this anthology: "For Indians, No Thanksgiving," "The Power of Love," "A Second Adoption," and "Growing Up." Write an essay contrasting the author's ideas and style in "For Indians, No Thanksgiving" with one of the other essays.

CHAPTER SEVEN

AFFAIRS OF THE HEART

Affairs of the heart surprise and sear, delight and dismay. Trickster love teases. Romance yields to necessity. Loneliness seeks companionship. Writers in this chapter unveil faces of friendship and love. They tell us about native societies and their traditional rules concerning courting and marrying and about modern affairs of the heart.

Nineteenth-century Cheyenne and Sioux marriage customs required that an ardent young man gain approval of the bride's family by proving he was a fine warrior, hunter, and horse raider. In the oldest story in this chapter, Nicholas Black Elk and John Neihardt describe traditional Plains Indian courting behavior, which involved a young man's skulking about a great deal in an effort to talk to a shy young woman.

In an excerpt from his novel, *Fool's Crow*, James Welch, Blackfeet-Gros Ventre twentieth-century novelist, depicts an early Blackfeet courtship and marriage. During the courtship, the prospective groom cheerfully helps to provide for the family of his prospective wife, whose father is unable to do so.

In his story, "Groom Service," Michael Dorris recounts the emotional trials of a reluctant young man who must hunt and fish for and kowtow to members of his future bride's family. Two mothers have negotiated the match, and this story may intrigue readers who have never met a genuine matriarch.

In an excerpt from her autobiography, *Stoney Creek Woman*, Mary John tells how she learned to cope with a husband as shy as she was when a Roman Catholic priest married them in 1929 after a community-arranged union. Love came after marriage for Mary and Lazare John, who celebrated their fiftieth wedding anniversary in 1979. In later years, Mary proudly wrote, "with seven children still living, with thirty-two grandchildren and eighteen great-grandchildren, most of them living close by, our log house near the lake is never lonely."

Unfortunately, not all marriages last as long or are as happy as that of Mary and Lazare. According to Jane Green, Chippewa, in traditional days, if a woman quarreled with her husband and was sent away, both gave a dance and sang divorce songs.

Native American author and activist D'Arcy McNickle grew up before buggies drawn by teams of horses gave way to buggies powered by internal combustion engines. In his story, "Going to School," he reveals what a teenager might have felt and learned about life and love on a seven-mile horse-and-buggy trip between home and school.

Although the automobile has fundamentally changed all Native American cultures, automobile ownership may be especially important to Navajo women, because they traditionally control most property in their matrilineal society. Whatever the cultural background of Luci Tapahonso's "A Classic Drop-Off," it is an amusing anecdote involving a car and a friendship.

During the past twenty years, governments of many reservations have legally opened high-stakes bingo parlors. In "The Bingo Van," Louise Erdrich braids the automotive strand and the bingo strand together with a story of love, desire, and envy that ends in violence and a new awareness for the main character.

The delights and risks of love concern many modern Native American poets. The speaker in Luci Tapahonso's poem "Raisin Eyes" is enamored with a Navajo rodeo cowboy, but she knows she can toss him out, along with his fancy boots, when she is ready to move on.

Donna Whitewing's "Love Song" is serene. Leslie Marmon Silko's "Love Poem" speaks not serenely but searchingly about summer rain that inspires a mythic woman to breathe her "damp earth song" to her lover. Sherman Alexie's "Tiny Treaties" relates some of the trials of a reservation Indian man and an urban white woman loving one another. He treats the danger of death lightly. How does he treat the possibility of her rejection?

While the poems of Whitewing, Silko, and Alexie address the loves of youth, N. Scott Momaday's "Earth and I Gave You Turquoise" foretells the reunion of mature lovers in traditional Navajo metaphors and stately stanzas. His poem is a reminder that affairs of the heart involve not only the self, the community, and the natural world but the spiritual world as well.

A CLASSIC DROP-OFF

Luci Tapahonso

World War II marked the beginning of the end of the horse-and-wagon era in Navajo life. Automobiles, and especially pickup trucks, replaced horses pulling wagons, partly because increasing numbers of Navajos migrated to cities where driving a motor vehicle was the norm. Few writers have written as charmingly about the automobile as has Luci Tapahonso. Tucked neatly and unobtrusively into her story are a few words defining her and her friend's relationships with their respective husbands. The narrative appears in Tapahonso's 1997 collection of poems and stories, *Blue Horses Rush In*.

1   When I lived in Albuquerque, I was going to my part-time job at the bookstore across from the university campus one afternoon. My friend Nita offered to drop me off on her way home. I didn't know she meant that literally.

2   She had just bought a new used convertible and was so excited when she was able to purchase it. She had had her eye on it for months and had even lit candles at church, hoping she could get it. Nita and I were good friends. We had both married young and had our older children about the same time, both life-changing events occurring in quick succession. For years, we both struggled to attend classes, pay day-care bills, dress our kids and ourselves decently. So money was the one thing there was never enough of. Anyway, it felt good when Nita finally saved enough money to buy the car she really wanted, the one she had dreamt about—neither an affordable little compact that got great mileage nor a sturdy car her parents gave her when they bought a larger luxury car.

3   True, it was a used car, but Kharmann Ghias weren't made anymore. "A classic," we kept saying to each other. It was beautiful, a shiny orange body and creamy leather top. The price was good, and at the time we didn't consider the condition of the engine and that sort of thing. We went to the car lot during breaks between classes and simply looked at the car. We ran our hands over the leather interior and imagined driving up the winding roads to Sandia

Crest with the top down. "Do you think I should?" she asked me a hundred times when she finally had the total amount. "Of course, you deserve it," I said, "not to mention I deserve to have a friend with a convertible." We decided not to tell our husbands because we wanted to surprise them. We felt sure they would be happy and proud.

4   After she bought it, the car drove like a dream (her words). I followed her back to campus, and nothing out of the ordinary happened. It drove well that evening when her family saw it for the first time. Her husband wasn't exactly ecstatic. Instead, he said things like, "You mean you just paid the sticker price? Did you try offering less?" "How could I?" Nita said. "That's the price it said, so that's what I paid." Over the years, we've become smarter in these matters.

5   Beginning the next week, the car became unpredictable. Nita drove the car half-time, and the rest of the time it was in an auto mechanic's garage. We found out quickly that a classic car's repair bills hovered near heaven somewhere. I lent Nita some money, but my husband said it wasn't our responsibility. "But I was there the whole time," I said. "I told her she deserved a car like that." "She does," he said. So we had yard sales and sold whatever we found in the remote corners of our homes at the flea market. I couldn't believe how expensive the repairs were. But we kept telling each other that after the brakes were done, it would be a long time before they'd go out again. But after the brakes were replaced, the transmission needed work. It seemed like it would never end. The insurance was high, too. Nevertheless, we remained optimistic that come summer we'd be cruising the Duke City and Santa Fe in the cute orange convertible, our kids tucked in the back seat.

6   The afternoon when Nita offered me the ride to the bookstore, I got in and it was so cool. The top was down and it was a bright spring day. I leaned back and looked at the turquoise sky as Nita was talking. Then in the middle of everything, she said, "Oh, I meant to tell you that once this car starts, I can't stop it. If I stop, it won't start again."

7   "What?" I murmured, trying to comprehend what this meant.

8   "Oh, it's really no problem," she said. "I'll drop you off in the alley behind the store rather than on Central." She paused. "I already thought this through. No problem."

9   "Okay," she continued, "I'll slow down real slow so that you can just get out. I've practiced this. I'll drive so slow that it'll seem like I'm stopped, but of course I won't be."

10   "Well, okay," I said. I could see that there was no other way. Besides, I needed to get to work.

11   We drove through the alley, and Nita told me to throw my shoes and purse out first. "They might weigh you down when you jump," she said. She drove as slowly as she could to show me how simple it would be just to jump out the next time through. After I threw my things out, we turned around in an empty parking lot and came back down, and just before the car was almost stopped, near the bookstore, for some reason I started screaming, "Now? now?"

12   "Go ahead!" Nita yelled.

13   "I can't! Eiyah!" I screamed.

14   "You have to! You have to!" she yelled, her voice rising with panic. Then just before I jumped, she accidentally hit the horn several times. We were both yelling and screaming as I landed on my hands and knees in the gravel right beside my purse. It happened so slowly, I even closed the door as I was leaping out. Then suddenly it was quiet, and Nita sped off, raising a bit of dust and waving. "We did it!" she yelled. I got up and brushed myself off. Then I realized that several people had gathered in the alley to investigate the noises. I was so embarrassed, yet I managed to walk away with one or two shreds of dignity. Later, they said that people thought that we were being attacked in the alley.

15   "Oh no," I said. "Her car wouldn't stop, so I had to jump out when it was still moving."

16   I could tell that they just didn't understand.

DISCUSSION QUESTIONS

1. The narrator says that she and Nita were good friends. How does she support this statement?
2. What is it about the car that both friends like?
3. What adjectives would you use to describe Nita?
4. Tapahonso creates a tone of gentle humor in this personal narrative. Find three examples and read them aloud to your classmates.

WRITING TOPICS

1. Think of an important, amusing, or embarrassing event in your life and write about it. Devote about half a page to events leading up to the event. Tell about the event in about a page, and conclude your narrative in one paragraph. Before you choose a subject, brainstorm on paper about events such as learning to drive, the first day on a job, giving a solo performance, coaching or babysitting, accepting a prize, or finding yourself in trouble.
2. Identify your dream car and describe it in detail—color, model, extras, and so on. Then create an imagined scene in which you drive it. You may wish to use Tapahonso's tone as a model.

TINY TREATIES

Sherman Alexie

"Tiny Treaties" and other love poems appear in a section also titled "Tiny Treaties" in Sherman Alexie's book, *First Indian on the Moon*. The poems describe the anguish resulting from a relationship between an Indian boy and a white girl. Sometimes the couple finds "a continuous grace," but always it is a love that spells trouble.

Because so many treaties were made and broken, the very word *treaty* has explosive connotations for most Native Americans. Many dimensions of their daily lives are shaped by treaties. In "Tiny Treaties," Alexie shifts the term from historic and general to immediate and personal. The lovers' relationship has been predetermined by a history that leaves little room to maneuver for romance.

What I remember most about loving you
that first year is the December night
I hitchhiked fifteen miles through a blizzard
after my reservation car finally threw a rod
5   on my way back home from touching

your white skin again. Wearing basketball shoes
and a U.S. Army Surplus jacket
my hair long, unbraided, and magnified
in headlights of passing cars, trucks, two snowplows
10   that forced me off the road, escaping

into the dormant wheat fields. I laughed
because I was afraid but I wasn't afraid
of dying, just afraid of dying
in such a stupid manner. All the Skins
15   would laugh into their fists

at my wake. All the cousins would tell my story
for generations. I would be the perfect reservation metaphor:
a twentieth century Dull Knife
pulling his skinny ass and dreams
20 down the longest highway in tribal history.

What I imagine now
is the endless succession of white faces
hunched over steering wheels, illuminated
by cigarettes and dashboard lights, white faces
25 pressed against windows as cars passed by me

without hesitation. I waited seconds into years
for a brake light, that smallest possible treaty
and I made myself so many promises
that have since come true
30 but I never had the courage to keep

my last promise, whispered
just before I topped a small hill
and saw the 24-hour lights
of the most beautiful 7-11 in the world.
35 With my lungs aching, my hands and feet

frozen and disappearing, I promised
to ask if you would have stopped
and picked me up if you didn't know me
a stranger Indian who would have fallen in love
40 with the warmth of your car, the radio

and the steady rhythm
of windshield wipers over glass, of tires
slicing through ice and snow. I promised
to ask you that question every day
45 for the rest of our lives

but I won't ask you even
once. I'll just remain quiet
when memories of that first year
come roaring through my thin walls
50 and shake newspapers and skin.

I'll just wrap myself
in old blankets, build fires
from bald tires and abandoned houses
and I won't ask you the question
55 because I don't want to know the answer.

DISCUSSION QUESTIONS

1. To whom is the poem addressed?
2. What can you infer are the reasons no one stops to pick up the speaker?
3. What does the speaker say he was afraid of?
4. What is the speaker afraid to ask?
5. What do lines 47–53 tell you about the speaker? Is he feeling sorry for himself or is he just mocking himself?

WRITING TOPICS

1. In a paragraph, explain the title of the poem and its appropriateness.
2. Examine the images of light in the poem and, in a brief essay, explore what they contribute to the theme.
3. Recall a time when you had a funny, sad, or fantastic experience with someone you were in love with, or wanted to impress. Write a poem, short story, or paragraph telling where you were, who else was there, and what happened. Create a tone that will express your attitude.
4. Think about the historical background for the thoughts in this poem. Then write a paragraph giving reasons why you think the speaker decides not to ask his girlfriend the important question.
5. Alexie structures his poem with five-line stanzas. Frequently the fifth line wraps around to the first line of the next stanza. In your literary journal, write some notes about how this structure contributes to the author's purpose of writing a narrative poem that tells a story.

RAISIN EYES

Luci Tapahonso

A classic Karmann Ghia and Tony Lama boots may be unlikely subjects for literature, but Luci Tapahonso makes them work. She has a knack
for nailing an image. Tony Lamas are fancy handmade footwear, embell-
ished with stitching in high Western style. They come in bright colors and
exotic leathers—snake, lizard, shark, alligator, ostrich, buffalo, and bull-
hide. Boots say plenty about the cowboy who wears them. This cowboy
charms Ella with his winning smile, and he is, of course, Navajo.

Rodeos became popular on many reservations following World War
II. Unlike most spectator sports, rodeos charge contestants entry fees to
finance prizes to the winner or to the top three winners in each event.
The recordings of country-Western singer Gary Stewart (line 27) are
played frequently on radio stations broadcasting to Navajo country.

First published in *Seasonal Woman,* "Raisin Eyes" has frequently
been reprinted, and the audience often requests it at Tapahonso's readings. Anyone hearing the author read "Raisin Eyes" aloud can never
thereafter read this poem without mentally hearing Tapahonso's distinctive voice delivering her special inflections.

I saw my friend Ella
with a tall cowboy at the store
the other day in Shiprock.

Later, I asked her,
5 Who's that guy anyway?

Oh, Luci, she said (I knew what was coming),
it's terrible. He lives with me
and my money and my car.
But just for a while.

10 He's in AIRCA[1] and rodeos a lot.
   And I still work.

This rodeo business is getting to me, you know,
and I'm going to leave him.
Because I think all this I'm doing now
15 will pay off better somewhere else,
but I just stay with him and it's hard
because
     he just smiles that way, you know,
     and then I end up paying entry fees
20   and putting shiny Tony Lamas on lay-away again.
     It's not hard.

But he doesn't know when
I'll leave him and I'll drive across the flat desert
from Red Valley in blue morning light
25 straight to Shiprock so easily.

And anyway, my car is already used
to humming a mourning song with Gary Stewart,
complaining again of aching and breaking,
down-and-out love affairs.

30 Damn.
These Navajo cowboys with raisin eyes
and pointed boots are just bad news,
but it's so hard to remember that all the time,
she said with a little laugh.

DISCUSSION QUESTIONS

1. What does Ella like and dislike about the Navajo cowboy?
2. How does Ella's state of mind and situation compare with the situation and state of mind of the speaker in "Tiny Treaties"?

---

[1] *AIRCA:* An acronym for American Indian Rodeo Circuit of America.

WRITING TOPICS

1. Are Ella's feelings familiar to you? Write a poem modeled after "Raisin Eyes" in which you relate some similar thoughts based on your own experiences.
2. Analyze the situation between Ella and the tall cowboy from his point of view. Write in the form of a poem, a letter, or song lyrics.

THE BINGO VAN

Louise Erdrich

A set of brilliant novels, plus poems, essays, and short stories ensure Louise Erdrich's position in American literature. "The Bingo Van" first appeared in *The New Yorker* in 1990. The author later revised it as a chapter in *The Bingo Palace,* the fourth novel in her quartet set in rural North Dakota. These four novels tell the multivoiced story of five generations of Chippewa and white relatives. Erdrich began the quartet with *Love Medicine* in 1984, followed it with *The Beet Queen* in 1986, *Tracks* in 1988, and then *The Bingo Palace* in 1994.

As the action unfolds, readers discover complex relations among characters who yearn for reciprocal love and understanding. A central character in *Love Medicine* and *The Bingo Palace* is a likeable bumbler named Lipsha Morrissey. Erdrich portrays him as an outsider, hurt at being abandoned by his mother and in search of his father. He is sometimes serious and sometimes amused at his own antics. Erdrich punctuates her serious tone with irony and humor. No voice in the two novels, as in this short story, is as sweetly comic as Lipsha's.

By the end of *Love Medicine,* Lipsha has met his father, Gerry Nanapush, who bears the name of the Chippewa traditional trickster, *nanapush* or *nanabozhu.* Lipsha's grandmother Lulu Lamartine, who plays bingo with a vengeance, finally tells him the story of his parentage. Seeing into the heart of Lipsha's anguish, she says, "Well, I never thought you was odd. . . . Just troubled. You never knew who you were."

In *The Bingo Palace,* Lipsha increases his understanding of his powers, particularly the healing "touch" that he inherited from Old Man Pillager, a shaman, and his father's father. Like most Native American contemporary novelists, Erdrich writes of their inevitable search for identity. "There's a quest for one's own background in a lot of this work," she explained in an interview with Joseph Bruchac. "One of the characteristics of being a mixed-blood is searching. You look back and say, 'Who am I from?' You must question. You must make certain choices. You're able to. And it's a blessing and it's a curse." Lipsha Morrissey feels precisely that way.

1   When I walked into bingo that night in early spring, I didn't have a girl-friend, a home or an apartment, a piece of land or a car, and I wasn't tat-tooed yet, either. Now look at me. I'm walking the reservation road in bor-rowed pants, toward a place that isn't mine, downhearted because I'm left by a woman. All I have of my temporary riches is this black pony running across the back of my hand—a tattoo I had Lewey's Tattoo Den put there on account of a waking dream. I'm still not paid up. I still owe for the little horse. But if Lewey wants to repossess it, then he'll have to catch me first.

2   Here's how it is on coming to the bingo hall. It's a long, low quonset barn. Inside, there used to be a pall of smoke, but now the smoke-eater fans in the ceiling take care of that. So upon first entering you can pick out your friends. On that night in early spring, I saw Eber, Clay, and Robert Morrissey sitting about halfway up toward the curtained stage with their grandmother Lulu. By another marriage, she was my grandma, too. She had five tickets spread in front of her. The boys each had only one. When the numbers rolled, she picked up a dabber in each hand. It was the Earlybird game, a one-hundred-dollar prize, and nobody had got too wound up yet or serious.

3   "Lipsha, go get us a Coke," said Lulu when someone else bingoed. "Yourself, too."

4   I went to the concession with Eber, who had finished high school with me. Clay and Robert were younger. We got our soft drinks and came back, set them down, pulled up to the table, and laid out a new set of tickets before us. Like I say, my grandmother, she played five at once, which is how you get the big money. In the long run, much more than breaking even, she was one of those rare Chippewas who actually profited by bingo. But, then again, it was her only way of gambling. No pull-tabs, no blackjack, no slot machines for her. She never went into the back room. She banked all the cash she won. I thought I should learn from Lulu Larmartine, whose other grandsons had stiff new boots while mine were worn down into the soft shape of moccasins. I watched her.

5   Concentration. Before the numbers even started, she set her mouth, snapped her purse shut. She shook her dabbers so that the foam-rubber tips were thoroughly inked. She looked at the time on her watch. The Coke, she took a drink of that, but no more than a sip. She was a narrow-eyed woman with a round jaw, curled hair. Her eyeglasses, blue plastic, hung from her neck by a gleaming chain. She raised the ovals to her eyes as the caller took the stand. She held her dabbers poised while he plucked the ball from the chute. He read it out: B-7. Then she was absorbed, scanning, dabbing, into the game. She didn't mutter. She had no lucky piece to touch in front of her. And afterward, even if she lost a blackout game by one square, she never sighed or complained.

6   All business, that was Lulu. And all business paid.

7   I think I would have been all business too, like her, if it hadn't been for what lay behind the stage curtain to be revealed. I didn't know it, but that

was what would change the order of my life. Because of the van, I'd have to get stupid first, then wise. You see, I had been floundering since high school, trying to catch my bearings in the world. It all lay ahead of me, spread out in the sun like a giveaway at a naming ceremony. Only thing was, I could not choose a prize. Something always stopped my hand before it reached.

8 "Lipsha Morrissey, you got to go for a vocation." That's what I told myself, in a state of nervous worry. I was getting by on almost no money, relying on my job as night watchman in a bar. That earned me a place to sleep, twenty dollars per week, and as much beef jerky, Beer Nuts, and spicy sausage sticks as I could eat.

9 I was now composed of these three false substances. No food in a bar has a shelf life of less than forty months. If you are what you eat, I would live forever, I thought.

10 And then they pulled aside the curtain, and I saw that I wouldn't live as long as I had coming unless I owned that van. It had every option you could believe—blue plush on the steering wheel, diamond side windows, and complete carpeted interior. The seats were easy chairs, with little headphones, and it was wired all through the walls. You could walk up close during intermission and touch the sides. The paint was cream, except for the design picked out in blue, which was a Sioux Drum border. In the back there was a small refrigerator and a carpeted platform for sleeping. It was a home, a portable den with front-wheel drive. I could see myself in it right off. I could see I *was* it.

11 On TV, they say you are what you drive. Let's put it this way: I wanted to be that van.

12 Now, I know that what I felt was a symptom of the national decline. You'll scoff at me, scorn me, say, What right does that waste Lipsha Morrissey, who makes his living guarding beer, have to comment outside of his own tribal boundary? But I was able to investigate the larger picture, thanks to Grandma Lulu, from whom I learned to be one-minded in my pursuit of a material object.

13 I went night after night to the bingo. Every hour I spent there, I grew more certain I was close. There was only one game per night at which the van was offered, a blackout game, where you had to fill every slot. The more tickets you bought, the more your chances increased. I tried to play five tickets, like Grandma Lulu did, but they cost five bucks each. To get my van, I had to shake hands with greed. I got unprincipled.

14 You see, my one talent in this life is a healing power I get passed down through the Pillager branch of my background. It's in my hands. I snap my fingers together so hard they almost spark. Then I blank out of my mind, and I put on the touch. I had a reputation up to then for curing sore joints and veins. I could relieve ailments caused in an old person by a half century of grinding stoop-over work. I had a power in myself that flowed out, resistless. I had a richness in my dreams and waking thoughts. But I never realized I would have to give up my healing source once I started charging for my service.

15 You know how it is about charging. People suddenly think you are worth something. Used to be, I'd go anyplace I was called, take any price or take nothing. Once I let it get around that I charged a twenty for my basic work, however, the phone at the bar rang off the hook.

16 "Where's that medicine boy?" they asked. "Where's Lipsha?"

17 I took their money. And it's not like beneath the pressure of a twenty I didn't try, for I did try, even harder than before. I skipped my palms together, snapped my fingers, positioned them where the touch inhabiting them should flow. But when it came to blanking out my mind I consistently failed. For each time, in the center of the cloud that came down into my brain, the van was now parked, in perfect focus.

18 I suppose I longed for it like a woman, except I wasn't that bad yet, and, anyway, then I did meet a woman, which set me back in my quest.

19 Instead of going for the van with everything, saving up to buy as many cards as I could play when they got to the special game, for a few nights I went short term, for variety, with U-Pickem cards, the kind where you have to choose the numbers for yourself.

20 First off, I wrote in the shoe and pants sizes of those Morrissey boys. No luck. So much for them. Next I took my birth date and a double of it—still no go. I wrote down the numbers of my grandma's address and her anniversary dates. Nothing. Then one night I realized if my U-Pickem was going to win it would be more like *revealed,* rather than a forced kind of thing. So I shut my eyes, right there in the middle of the long bingo table, and I let my mind blank out, white and fizzing like the screen of a television, until something formed. The van, as always. But on its tail this time a license plate was officially fixed and numbered. I used that number, wrote it down in the boxes, and then I bingoed.

21 I got two hundred dollars from that imaginary license. The money was in my pocket when I left. The next morning, I had fifty cents. But it's not like you think with Serena, and I'll explain that. She didn't want something from me; she didn't care if I had money, and she didn't ask for it. She was seventeen and had a two-year-old boy. That tells you about her life. Her last name was American Horse, an old Sioux name she was proud of even though it was strange to Chippewa country. At her older sister's house Serena's little boy blended in with the younger children, and Serena herself was just one of the teen-agers. She was still in high school, a year behind the year she should have been in, and she had ambitions. Her idea was to go into business and sell her clothing designs, of which she had six books.

22 I don't know how I got a girl so decided in her future to go with me, even that night. Except I told myself, "Lipsha, you're a nice-looking guy. You're a winner." And for the moment I was. I went right up to her at the Coin-Op and said, "Care to dance?", which was a joke—there wasn't any-place to dance. Yet she liked me. We had a sandwich and then she wanted to take a drive, so we tagged along with some others in the back of their car.

They went straight south, toward Hoopdance, off the reservation, where action was taking place.

23   "Lipsha," she whispered on the way, "I always liked you from a distance."

24   "Serena," I said, "I liked you from a distance, too."

25   So then we moved close together on the car seat. My hand was on my knee, and I thought a couple of different ways I could gesture, casually pretend to let it fall on hers, how maybe if I talked fast she wouldn't notice, in the heat of the moment, her hand in my hand, us holding hands, our lips drawn to one another. But then I decided to boldly take courage, to take her hand as, at the same time, I looked into her eyes. I did this. In the front, the others talked among themselves. Yet we just sat there. After a while she said, "You want to kiss me?

26   But I answered, not planning how the words would come out, "Our first kiss has to be a magic moment only we can share."

27   Her eyes went wide as a deer's, and her big smile bloomed. Her skin was dark, her long hair a burnt-brown color. She wore no jewelry, no rings, just the clothing she had sewed from her designs—a suit jacket and a pair of pants that were the tan of eggshells, with symbols picked out in blue thread on the borders, the cuffs, and the hem. I took her in, admiring, for some time on that drive before I realized that the reason Serena's cute outfit nagged me so was on account of she was dressed up to match my bingo van. . . .

28   Well, the money part is not related to that. I gave it all to Serena, that's true. Her intention was to buy material and put together the creations that she drew in her notebooks. It was fashion with a Chippewa flair, as she explained it, and sure to win prizes at the state home-ec. contest. She promised to pay me interest when she opened her own shop. The next day, after we had parted, after I had checked out the bar I was supposed to night-watch, I went off to the woods to sit and think. Not about the money, which was Serena's—and good luck to her—but about her and me.

29   She was two years younger than me, yet she had direction and a child, while I was aimless, lost in hyperspace, using up my talent, which was already fading from my hands. I wondered what our future could hold. One thing was sure: I never knew a man to support his family by playing bingo, and the medicine calls for Lipsha were getting fewer by the week, and fewer, as my touch failed to heal people, fled from me, and lay concealed.

30   I sat on ground where, years ago, my greats and my great-greats, the Pillagers, had walked. The trees around me were the dense birch and oak of old woods. The lake drifted in, gray waves, white foam in a bobbing lace. Thin gulls lined themselves up on a sandbar. The sky went dark. I closed my eyes, and that is when the little black pony galloped into my mind. It sped across the choppy waves like a skipping stone, its mane a banner, its tail a flag, and vanished on the other side of the shore.

31   It was luck. Serena's animal. American Horse.

32   "This is the last night I'm going to try for the van," I told myself. I always kept three twenties stuffed inside the edging of my blanket in back of the bar. Once that stash was gone I'd make a real decision. I'd open the yellow pages at random, and where my finger pointed I would take that kind of job.

33   Of course, I never counted on winning the van.

34   I was playing for it on the shaded side of a blackout ticket, which is always hard to get. As usual, I sat with Lulu and her boys. Her vigilance helped me. She let me use her extra dabber and she sat and smoked a filter cigarette, observing the quiet frenzy that was taking place around her. Even though that van had sat on the stage for five months, even though nobody had yet won it and everyone said it was a scam, when it came to playing for it most people bought a couple of tickets. That night, I went all out and purchased eight.

35   A girl read out the numbers from the hopper. Her voice was clear and light on the microphone. I didn't even notice what was happening—Lulu pointed out one place I had missed on the winning ticket. Then I had just two squares left to make a bingo and I suddenly sweated, I broke out into a chill, I went cold and hot at once. After all my pursuit, after all my plans, I was N-6 and G-60. I had narrowed myself, shrunk into the spaces on the ticket. Each time the girl read a number and it wasn't that 6 or 60 I sickened, recovered, forgot to breathe.

36   She must have read twenty numbers out before N-6. Then, right after that, G-60 rolled off her lips.

37   I screamed. I am ashamed to say how loud I yelled. That girl came over, got the manager, and then he checked out my numbers slow and careful while everyone hushed.

38   He didn't say a word. He checked them over twice. Then he pursed his lips together and wished he didn't have to say it.

39   "It's a bingo," he finally told the crowd.

40   Noise buzzed to the ceiling—talk of how close some others had come, green talk—and every eye was turned and cast on me, which was uncomfortable. I never was the center of looks before, not Lipsha, who everybody took for granted around here. Not all those looks were for the good, either. Some were plain envious and ready to believe the first bad thing a sour tongue could pin on me. It made sense in a way. Of all those who'd stalked that bingo van over the long months, I was now the only one who had not lost money on the hope.

41   O.K., so what kind of man does it make Lipsha Morrissey that the keys did not tarnish his hands one slight degree, and that he beat it out that very night in the van, completing only the basic paperwork? I didn't go after Serena, and I can't tell you why. Yet I was hardly ever happier. In that van, I rode high, but that's the thing. Looking down on others, even if it's only

from the seat of a van that a person never really earned, does something to the human mentality. It's hard to say. I changed. After just one evening riding the reservation roads, passing with a swish of my tires, I started smiling at the homemade hot rods, at the clunkers below me, at the old-lady cars nosing carefully up and down the gravel hills.

42   I started saying to myself that I should visit Serena, and a few nights later I finally did go over there. I pulled into her sister's driveway with a flourish I could not help, as the van slipped into a pothole and I roared the engine. For a moment, I sat in the dark, letting my headlamps blaze alongside the door until Serena's brother-in-law leaned out.

43   "Cut the lights!" he yelled. "We got a sick child."

44   I rolled down my window, and asked for Serena.

45   "It's her boy. She's in here with him." He waited. I did, too, in the dark. A dim light was on behind him and I saw some shadows, a small girl in those pajamas with the feet tacked on, someone pacing back and forth.

46   "You want to come in?" he called.

47   But here's the gist of it. I just said to tell Serena hi for me, and then I backed out of there, down the drive, and left her to fend for herself. I could have stayed there. I could have drawn my touch back from wherever it had gone to. I could have offered my van to take Jason to the I.H.S. I could have sat there in silence as a dog guards its mate, its own blood. I could have done something different from what I did, which was to hit the road for Hoopdance and look for a better time.

48   I cruised until I saw where the party house was located that night. I drove the van over the low curb, into the yard, and I parked there. I watched until I recognized a couple of cars and saw the outlines of Indians and mixed, so I knew that walking in would not involve me in what the newspapers term an episode. The door was white, stained and raked by a dog, with a tiny fan-shaped window. I went through and stood inside. There was movement, a kind of low-key swirl of bright hair and dark hair tossing alongside each other. There were about as many Indians as there weren't. This party was what we call around here a Hairy Buffalo, and most people were grouped around a big brown plastic garbage can that served as the punch bowl for the all-purpose stuff, which was anything that anyone brought, dumped in along with pink Hawaiian Punch. I grew up around a lot of the people, and others I knew by sight. Among those last, there was a young familiar-looking guy.

49   It bothered me. I recognized him, but I didn't know him. I hadn't been to school with him, or played him in any sport, because I did not play sports. I couldn't think where I'd seen him until later, when the heat went up and he took off his bomber jacket. Then "Big Sky Country" showed, plain letters on a bright-blue background.

50   I edged around the corner of the room, into the hall, and stood there to argue with myself. Would he recognize me, or was I just another face, a customer? He probably wasn't really from Montana, so he might not even have

been insulted by our little conversation, or remember it anymore. I reasoned that he had probably picked up the shirt vacationing, though who would want to go across that border, over to where the world got meaner? I told myself that I should calm my nerves, go back into the room, have fun. What kept me from doing that was the sudden thought of Serena. . . .

51   Once I remembered, I was lost to the present moment. One part of me caught up with the other. I realized that I had left Serena to face her crisis, alone, while I took off in my brand-new van.

52   I have a hard time getting drunk. It's just the way I am. I start thinking and forget to fill the cup, or recall something I have got to do, and just end up walking from a party. I have put down a full can of beer before and walked out to weed my grandma's rhubarb patch, or work on a cousin's car. Now I was putting myself in Serena's place, feeling her feelings.

53   *What would he want to do that to me for?*

54   I heard her voice say this out loud, just behind me, where there was nothing but wall. I edged along until I came to a door, and then I went through, into a tiny bedroom full of coats, and so far nobody either making out or unconscious upon the floor. I sat on a pile of parkas and jean jackets in this little room, an alcove in the rising buzz of the party outside. I saw a phone, and I dialed Serena's number. Her sister answered.

55   "Thanks a lot," she said when I said it was me. "You woke up Jason."

56   "What's wrong with him?" I asked.

57   There was a silence, then Serena's voice got on the line. "I'm going to hang up."

58   "Don't."

59   "He's crying. His ears hurt so bad he can't stand it."

60   "I'm coming over there."

61   "Forget it. Forget you."

62   She said the money I had loaned her would be in the mail. She reminded me it was a long time since the last time I had called. And then the phone went dead. I held the droning receiver in my hand, and tried to clear my mind. The only thing I saw in it, clear as usual, was the van. I decided this was a sign for me to get in behind the wheel. I should drive straight to Serena's house, put on the touch, help her son out. So I set my drink on the windowsill. Then I slipped out the door and I walked down the porch steps, only to find them waiting.

63   I guess he had recognized me after all, and I guess he was from Montana. He had friends, too. They stood around the van, and their heads were level with the roof, for they were tall.

64   "Let's go for a ride," said the one from the all-night gas pump.

65   He knocked on the window of my van with his knuckles. When I told him no thanks, he started karate-kicking the door. He wore black cowboy boots, pointy-toed, with hard-edged new heels. They left ugly dents every time he landed a blow.

66   "Thanks anyhow," I repeated. "But the party's not over." I tried to get

back into the house, but, like in a bad dream, the door was stuck, or locked. I hollered, pounded, kicked at the very marks that desperate dog had left, but the music rose and nobody heard. So I ended up in the van. They acted very gracious. They urged me to drive. They were so polite that I tried to tell myself they weren't all that bad. And sure enough, after we had drove for a while, these Montana guys said they had chipped in together to buy me a present.

67 "What is it?" I asked. "Don't keep me in suspense."

68 "Keep driving," said the pump jockey.

69 "I don't really go for surprises," I said. "What's your name, anyhow?"

70 "Marty."

71 "I got a cousin named Marty," I said.

72 "Forget it."

73 The guys in the back exchanged a grumbling kind of laughter, a knowing set of groans. Marty grinned, turned toward me from the passenger seat.

74 "If you really want to know what we're going to give you, I'll tell. It's a map. A map of Montana."

75 Their laughter got wild and went on for too long.

76 "I always liked the state," I said in a serious voice.

77 ". . . Then I hope you like sitting on it." He signalled where I should turn, and all of a sudden I realized that Lewey's lay ahead. Lewey ran his Tattoo Den from the basement of his house, kept his equipment set up and ready for the weekend.

78 "Whoa," I said. I stopped the van. "You can't tattoo a person against his will. It's illegal."

79 "Get your lawyer on it tomorrow." Marty leaned in close for me to see his eyes. I put the van back in gear but just chugged along, desperately thinking. Lewey was a strange kind of guy, an old Dutch sailor who got beached here, about as far as you can get from salt water. I decided that I'd ask Marty, in a polite kind of way, to beat me up instead. If that failed, I would tell him that there were many states I would not mind so much— smaller, rounder ones.

80 "Are any of you guys from any other state?" I asked, anxious to trade.

81 "Kansas."

82 "South Dakota."

83 It wasn't that I really had a thing against those places, understand; it's just that the straight-edged shape is not a Chippewa preference. You look around you, and everything you see is round, everything in nature. There are no perfect boundaries, no borders. Only human-made things tend toward cubes and squares—the van, for instance. That was an example. Suddenly I realized that I was driving a wheeled version of the state of North Dakota.

84 "Just beat me up, you guys. Let's get this over with. I'll stop."

85 But they laughed, and then we were at Lewey's.

86 The sign on his basement door said COME IN. I was shoved from behind and strapped together by five pairs of heavy, football-toughened

hands. I was the first to see Lewey, I think, the first to notice that he was not just a piece of all the trash and accumulated junk that washed through the concrete-floored cellar but a person, sitting still as any statue, in a corner, on a chair that creaked and sang when he rose and walked over.

87 He even looked like a statue—not the type you see in history books, I don't mean those, but the kind you see for sale as you drive along the highway. He was a Paul Bunyan, carved with a chain saw. He was rough-looking, finished in big strokes.

88 "Please," I said, "I don't want . . ."

89 Marty squeezed me around the throat and tousled up my hair, like friendly.

90 "He's just got cold feet. Now remember, Lewey, map of Montana. You know where. And put in a lot of detail."

91 I tried to scream.

92 "Like I was thinking," Marty went on, "of those maps we did in grade school showing products from each region. Cows' heads, oil wells, those little sheaves of wheat, and so on."

93 "Tie him up," said Lewey. His voice was thick, with a commanding formal accent. "Then leave."

94 They did. They took my pants and the keys to the van. I heard the engine roar and die away, and I rolled from side to side in my strict bindings. I felt Lewey's hand on my shoulder.

95 "Be still." His voice had changed, now that the others were gone, to a low sound that went with his appearance and did not seem at all unkind. I looked up at him. A broke-down God is who he looked like from my worm's-eye view. His beard was pure white, long and patchy, and his big eyes frozen blue. His head was half bald, shining underneath the brilliant fluorescent tubes in the ceiling. You never know where you're going to find your twin in the world, your double. I don't mean in terms of looks—I'm talking about mind-set. You never know where you're going to find the same thoughts in another brain, but when it happens you know it right off, just like the two of you were connected by a small electrical wire that suddenly glows red-hot and sparks. That's what happened when I met Lewey Koep.

96 "I don't have a pattern for Montana," he told me. He untied my ropes with a few quick jerks, sneering at the clumsiness of the knots. Then he sat in his desk chair again, and watched me get my bearings.

97 "I don't want anything tattooed on me, Mr. Koep," I said. "It's a kind of revenge plot."

98 He sat in silence, in a waiting quiet, hands folded and face composed. By now I knew I was safe, but I had nowhere to go, and so I sat down on a pile of magazines. He asked, "What revenge?" and I told him the story, the whole thing right from the beginning, when I walked into the bingo hall. I left out the personal details about Serena and me, but he got the picture. I told him about the van.

99   "That's an unusual piece of good fortune."

100   "Have you ever had any? Good fortune?"

101   "All the time. Those guys paid plenty, for instance, though I suppose they'll want it back. You pick out a design. You can owe me."

102   He opened a book he had on the table, a notebook with plastic pages that clipped in and out, and handed it over to me. I didn't want a tattoo, but I didn't want to disappoint this man, either. I leafed through the dragons and the hearts, thinking how to refuse, and then suddenly I saw the horse. It was the same picture that had come into my head as I sat in the woods. Now here it was. The pony skimmed, legs outstretched, reaching for the edge of the page. I got a thought in my head, clear and vital, that this little horse would convince Serena I was serious about her.

103   "This one."

104   Lewey nodded, and heated his tools.

105   That's why I got it put on, that little horse, and suffered pain. Now my hand won't let me rest. It throbs and aches as if it was coming alive again after a hard frost had made it numb. I know I'm going somewhere, taking this hand to Serena. Even walking down the road in a pair of big-waisted green pants belonging to Lewey Koep, toward the So Long Bar, where I keep everything I own in life, I'm going forward. My hand is a ball of pins, but when I look down I see the little black horse running hard, fast, and serious.

106   I'm ready for what will come next. That's why I don't fall on the ground, and I don't yell, when I come across the van in a field. At first, I think it is the dream van, the way I always see it in my vision. Then I look, and it's the real vehicle. Totalled.

107   My bingo van is smashed on the sides, kicked and scratched, and the insides are scattered. Stereo wires, glass, and ripped pieces of carpet are spread here and there among the new sprouts of wheat. I force open a door that is bent inward. I wedge myself behind the wheel, which is tipped over at a crazy angle, and I look out. The windshield is shattered in a sunlight burst, through which the world is cut to bits.

108   I've been up all night, and the day stretches long before me, so I decide to sleep where I am. Part of the seat is still wonderfully upholstered, thick and plush, and it reclines now—permanently, but so what? I relax into the small comfort, my body as warm as an animal, my thoughts drifting. I know I'll wake to nothing, but at this moment I feel rich. Sinking away, I feel like everything worth having is within my grasp. All I have to do is put my hand into the emptiness.

DISCUSSION QUESTIONS

1. How does Lipsha get the money to play bingo?
2. How does he get the $200 he gives to Serena?
3. The narrator says he changed after he won the van. How did he change?
4. What is the climax or point of greatest suspense in the story?
5. What motivates Lipsha to get a tattoo?
6. Is the ending of the story foreshadowed and is it satisfying, or should it have ended differently? Explain.

WRITING TOPICS

1. In a short paper, tell what you think this story reveals about human nature.
2. The author does not tell us much about the white boys who totaled the van. In a paragraph or two, tell why you think they did so. Consider the setting as well as their motivation.
3. The author reveals Lipsha's character through what he does and what he says. Select three sentences from Lipsha's narration that reveal traits in his character. Using ideas from the sentences, write an essay of two or three paragraphs on Lipsha's character. Examples:

   "Because of the van, I'd have to get stupid first, then wise."
   "Our first kiss has to be a magic moment only we can share."
   "I'm ready for what will come next."

LOVE SONG

Donna Whitewing

Donna Whitewing wrote her testament to love while she was a student at the Institute of American Indian Arts in New Mexico, specializing in drama, dance, and writing. Her poem was published in 1972 in *The Whispering Wind,* an anthology of poetry written by young American Indians.

Growing up in a migrant farm-worker family and roaming from her native Nebraska to South Dakota, Whitewing attended elementary schools in Nebraska, St. Augustine's Indian Mission at Winnebago, Assumption Academy at Norfolk, and Flandreau Indian School in South Dakota. Although she wrote about them in her poem, the poet did not see mountains until she went to New Mexico. The "deep dark quiet mountains" in the poem may, however, be internal and not geographic ones at all.

Your being has caused
an indelible line
    through the crimson shadows
      of my past;
5 Over the silent
      white and blue days;
Into,
Merging,
And finally blending
10   with the deep dark quiet
      mountains
        of my life.

DISCUSSION QUESTIONS

1. What does the image of a line being drawn through the speaker's past imply?
2. Why do you think the speaker uses the images of mountains rather than, say, the valleys of her life?

WRITING TOPICS

1. Imagine metaphors that express your feelings for someone you love. Compose a paragraph or poem that expresses your love song.

SONG OF DIVORCE

Traditional Chippewa

Apparently the Chippewas had occasions for newly divorced individuals to hurl insults at each other. Might such socially recognized confrontations benefit American society during a time of rising divorce rates?

This Chippewa divorce song was recorded by Jane Green and translated by Frances Densmore, who was for decades the Smithsonian Institution's foremost musicologist collecting Native American music. She recorded both music and words in cultural contexts, not only among Chippewas, but also among Sioux, Mandan, Hidatsa, Papago, and other tribes.

◰

I guess you love me now.
I guess you admire me now.
You threw me away like something that tasted bad.
You treat me as if I were a rotten fish.

5 I thought you were good at first.
I thought you were like silver and I find you are like lead.
You see me high up.
I walk through the sun.
I am like the sunlight myself.

◰

DISCUSSION QUESTIONS

1. How is the simile in line 4 appropriate?
2. What qualities might a person have who is like silver? who is like lead?
3. Why might the speaker say she is "like sunlight"?

WRITING TOPICS

1. Make a list of items that would be appropriate in your society today that could complete the simile "You threw me away like _____."
2. Imagine you are the speaker in this situation and add a third stanza to the poem.

HIGH HORSE'S COURTING

Black Elk and John Neihardt

Lakotas, Cheyennes, and other Americans have laughed at High Horse's amorous adventures for more than one hundred and fifty years. Black Elk said High Horse's courting story is "absolutely true." The story is quite old. High Horse, a Northern Cheyenne, told Black Elk about his escapades some thirty years before Black Elk, in turn, relayed them to John Neihardt. High Horse was an old man when he told young Black Elk about how he finally won his wife. High Horse and his wife lived together "to a ripe old age."

The story with its moral appears in *Black Elk Speaks,* a famous elicited autobiography of an Oglala Lakota man who lived from 1863 to 1950. John G. Neihardt was a professor of English at the University of Nebraska when he persuaded Nicholas Black Elk to tell his life story. As ethnohistorian Raymond DeMallie concluded, "Neihardt's books are literary interpretations of what he learned from Black Elk. They preserve the details of Lakota culture and yet transcend them, securing a place for Lakota religion in the ranks of recorded tribal traditions." Neihardt, poet laureate of Nebraska, transformed Black Elk's life story into literature.

Black Elk was born in December 1863 on the Little Powder River, probably within the present borders of Wyoming. His father and his father's father were holy men whose healing powers brought recognition to the family. The world into which Black Elk was born was a traditional Lakota world as it was before conquest destroyed it, a sacred world in which Lakotas interacted with the seen and unseen spirit forces of their universe.

A series of vital turning points permanently altered the direction of Black Elk's life. The first was his personal empowering vision in 1872. He traveled with Buffalo Bill's Wild West Show to Europe in 1886–1889 and learned about the outside world. Then he participated in the 1890 Ghost Dance, and survived a soldier's shot during the massacre at Wounded Knee. Finally, he accepted Catholicism around 1904. In 1930 one more crucial event occurred that, like the others, had significant impact on the rest of his life and immortalized him. In August, John Neihardt arrived at Black Elk's house in Manderson, South Dakota. Neihardt was visiting the Sioux country preparing to write the final volume of his epic poem *A Cycle of the West* that would relate the story of the Ghost Dance and end with the massacre at Wounded Knee. Later Neihardt wrote: "The sun was near to setting when Black Elk said: 'There is much to teach you. What I know was given to me for men and it is true and it is beautiful. Soon I shall be under the grass and it will be lost. You were sent to save it, and you must come back so that I can teach you.'" Black Elk asked Neihardt to return in the spring.

Neihardt returned on May 1, 1931. This time he brought his daughter Enid, an accomplished stenographer, who served as his secretary, and his daughter Hilda. Black Elk was then sixty-seven and almost blind. We can imagine the mingling of voices that would eventually create a remarkable book, *Black Elk Speaks*. Nicholas Black Elk made statements in Lakota, which his son Ben then translated into English. Neihardt rephrased Ben's translation, and Enid wrote it down in shorthand. What she wrote was not a verbatim record of Black Elk's words, but her father's rephrasing in standard English. After returning home, Neihardt used his daughter's typewritten text as his source. In other words, when we read High Horse's story today we are reading words that reflect the combined efforts of High Horse, Black Elk, Ben, Enid, and John. Raymond DeMallie has underscored the significance of this collaboration. "Through his remarkable body of teachings, Black Elk truly lives. This is his legacy, passed on to us, the 'future generations,' that we might benefit from knowledge of the old Lakota world and of its sacred power."

1   You know, in the old days, it was not so very easy to get a girl when you wanted to be married. Sometimes it was hard work for a young man and he had to stand a great deal. Say I am a young man and I have seen a young girl who looks so beautiful to me that I feel all sick when I think about her. I can not just go and tell her about it and then get married if she is willing. I have to be a very sneaky fellow to talk to her at all, and after I have managed to talk to her, that is only the beginning.

2   Probably for a long time I have been feeling sick about a certain girl because I love her so much, but she will not even look at me, and her parents keep a good watch over her. But I keep feeling worse and worse all the time; so maybe I sneak up to her tepee in the dark and wait until she comes out. Maybe I just wait there all night and don't get any sleep at all and she does not come out. Then I feel sicker than ever about her.

3   Maybe I hide in the brush by a spring where she sometimes goes to get water, and when she comes by, if nobody is looking, then I jump out and hold her and just make her listen to me. If she likes me too, I can tell that from the way she acts, for she is very bashful and maybe will not say a word or even look at me the first time. So I let her go, and then maybe I sneak around until I can see her father alone, and I tell him how many horses I can give him for his beautiful girl, and by now I am feeling so sick that maybe I would give him all the horses in the world if I had them.

4   Well, this young man I am telling about was called High Horse, and there was a girl in the village who looked so beautiful to him that he was just sick all over from thinking about her so much and he was getting sicker all the time. The girl was very shy, and her parents thought a great deal of her because they were not young any more and this was the only child they had. So they watched her all day long, and they fixed it so that she would be safe at night too when they were asleep. They thought so much of her that they had made a rawhide bed for her to sleep in, and after they knew that High Horse was sneaking around after her, they took rawhide thongs and tied the girl in bed at night so that nobody could steal her when they were asleep, but they were not sure but that their girl might really want to be stolen.

5   Well, after High Horse had been sneaking around a good while and hiding and waiting for the girl and getting sicker all the time, he finally caught her alone and made her talk to him. Then he found out that she liked him maybe a little. Of course this did not make him feel well. It made him sicker than ever, but now he felt as brave as a bison bull, and so he went right to her father and said he loved the girl so much that he would give two good horses for her—one of them young and the other one not so very old.

6   But the old man just waved his hand, meaning for High Horse to go away and quit talking foolishness like that.

7   High Horse was feeling sicker than ever about it; but there was another young fellow who said he would loan High Horse two ponies and when he got some more horses, why, he could just give them back for the ones he had borrowed.

8   Then High Horse went back to the old man and said he would give four horses for the girl—two of them young and the other two not hardly old at all. But the old man just waved his hand and would not say anything.

9   So High Horse sneaked around until he could talk to the girl again, and he asked her to run away with him. He told her he thought he would just fall over and die if she did not. But she said she would not do that; she wanted to be bought like a fine woman. You see she thought a great deal of herself too.

10   That made High Horse feel so very sick that he could not eat a bit, and he went around with his head hanging down as though he might just fall down and die any time.

11   Red Deer was another young fellow, and he and High Horse were great comrades, always doing things together. Red Deer saw how High Horse was

acting, and he said: "Cousin, what is the matter? Are you sick in the belly? You look as though you were going to die."

12 Then High Horse told Red Deer how it was, and said he thought he could not stay alive much longer if he could not marry the girl pretty quick.

13 Red Deer thought awhile about it, and then he said: "Cousin, I have a plan, and if you are man enough to do as I tell you, then everything will be all right. She will not run away with you; her old man will not take four horses; and four horses are all you can get. You must steal her and run away with her. Then afterwhile you can come back and the old man cannot do anything because she will be your woman. Probably she wants you to steal her anyway."

14 So they planned what High Horse had to do, and he said he loved the girl so much that he was man enough to do anything Red Deer or anybody else could think up.

15 So this is what they did.

16 That night late they sneaked up to the girl's tepee and waited until it sounded inside as though the old man and the old woman and the girl were sound asleep. Then High Horse crawled under the tepee with a knife. He had to cut the rawhide thongs first, and then Red Deer, who was pulling up the stakes around that side of the tepee, was going to help drag the girl outside and gag her. After that, High Horse could put her across his pony in front of him and hurry out of there and be happy all the rest of his life.

17 When High Horse had crawled inside, he felt so nervous that he could hear his heart drumming, and it seemed so loud he felt sure it would 'waken the old folks. But it did not, and afterwhile he began cutting the thongs. Every time he cut one it made a pop and nearly scared him to death. But he was getting along all right and all the thongs were cut down as far as the girl's thighs, when he became so nervous that his knife slipped and stuck the girl. She gave a big, loud yell. Then the old folks jumped up and yelled too. By this time High Horse was outside, and he and Red Deer were running away like antelope. The old man and some other people chased the young men but they got away in the dark and nobody knew who it was.

18 Well, if you ever wanted a beautiful girl you will know how sick High Horse was now. It was very bad the way he felt, and it looked as though he would starve even if he did not drop over dead sometime.

19 Red Deer kept thinking about this, and after a few days he went to High Horse and said: "Cousin, take courage! I have another plan, and I am sure, if you are man enough, we can steal her this time." And High Horse said: "I am man enough to do anything anybody can think up, if I can only get that girl."

20 So this is what they did.

21 They went away from the village alone, and Red Deer made High Horse strip naked. Then he painted High Horse solid white all over, and after that he painted black stripes all over the white and put black rings around High Horse's eyes. High Horse looked terrible. He looked so terrible that when

Red Deer was through painting and took a good look at what he had done, he said it scared even him a little.

22   "Now," Red Deer said, "if you get caught again, everybody will be so scared they will think you are a bad spirit and will be afraid to chase you."

23   So when the night was getting old and everybody was sound asleep, they sneaked back to the girl's tepee. High Horse crawled in with his knife, as before, and Red Deer waited outside, ready to drag the girl out and gag her when High Horse had all the thongs cut.

24   High Horse crept up by the girl's bed and began cutting at the thongs. But he kept thinking, "If they see me they will shoot me because I look so terrible." The girl was restless and kept squirming around in bed, and when a thong was cut, it popped. So High Horse worked very slowly and carefully.

25   But he must have made some noise, for suddenly the old woman awoke and said to her old man: "Old Man, wake up! There is somebody in this tepee!" But the old man was sleepy and didn't want to be bothered. He said: "Of course there is somebody in this tepee. Go to sleep and don't bother me." Then he snored some more.

26   But High Horse was so scared by now that he lay very still and as flat to the ground as he could. Now, you see, he had not been sleeping very well for a long time because he was so sick about the girl. And while he was lying there waiting for the old woman to snore, he just forgot everything, even how beautiful the girl was. Red Deer who was lying outside ready to do his part, wondered and wondered what had happened in there, but he did not dare call out to High Horse.

27   Afterwhile the day began to break and Red Deer had to leave with the two ponies he had staked there for his comrade and girl, or somebody would see him.

28   So he left.

29   Now when it was getting light in the tepee, the girl awoke and the first thing she saw was a terrible animal, all white with black stripes on it, lying asleep beside her bed. So she screamed, and then the old woman screamed and the old man yelled. High Horse jumped up, scared almost to death, and he nearly knocked the tepee down getting out of there.

30   People were coming running from all over the village with guns and bows and axes, and everybody was yelling.

31   By now High Horse was running so fast that he hardly touched the ground at all, and he looked so terrible that the people fled from him and let him run. Some braves wanted to shoot at him, but the others said he might be some sacred being and it would bring bad trouble to kill him.

32   High Horse made for the river that was near, and in among the brush he found a hollow tree and dived into it. Afterwhile some braves came there and he could hear them saying that it was some bad spirit that had come out of the water and gone back in again.

33   That morning the people were ordered to break camp and move away from there. So they did, while High Horse was hiding in his hollow tree.

34   Now Red Deer had been watching all this from his own tepee and trying to look as though he were as much surprised and scared as all the others. So when the camp moved, he sneaked back to where he had seen his comrade disappear. When he was down there in the brush, he called, and High Horse answered, because he knew his friend's voice. They washed off the paint from High Horse and sat down on the river bank to talk about their troubles.

35   High Horse said he never would go back to the village as long as he lived and he did not care what happened to him now. He said he was going to go on the war-path all by himself. Red Deer said: "No, cousin, you are not going on the war-path alone, because I am going with you."

36   So Red Deer got everything ready, and at night they started out on the war-path all alone. After several days they came to a Crow camp just about sundown, and when it was dark they sneaked up to where the Crow horses were grazing, killed the horse guard, who was not thinking about enemies because he thought all the Lakotas were far away, and drove off about a hundred horses.

37   They got a big start because all the Crow horses stampeded and it was probably morning before the Crow warriors could catch any horses to ride. Red Deer and High Horse fled with their herd three days and three nights before they reached the village of their people. Then they drove the whole herd right into the village and up in front of the girl's tepee. The old man was there, and High Horse called out to him and asked if he thought maybe that would be enough horses for his girl. The old man did not wave him away that time. It was not the horses that he wanted. What he wanted was a son who was a real man and good for something.

38   So High Horse got his girl after all, and I think he deserved her.

◉

DISCUSSION QUESTIONS

1. High Horse's attempt to win his love's hand in marriage seems quite different from similar situations today, but are the situations so different? Compare High Horse's courtship with a courtship today in your society. Do parents act the way the girl's father acts, but in more subtle ways?
2. Red Deer's advice does not seem of much use. Why is he included in the narrative?
3. This narrative has some humorous moments. Does this surprise you? Explain.
4. This is the second account by a man in this chapter. What are the differences in actions, thoughts, and emotions between Black Elk's account of High Horse's courting and Sherman Alexie's account of the speaker's trials and relationship to his girl friend?

Writing Topics

1. This account has many elements of traditional tales told all over the world. Think about some other tales you have heard or read, and in an essay, point out some similarities and differences.

2. Have you ever felt affection or love for someone who did not return these feelings? Can you express your reactions, or does it make you uncomfortable to do so? Tell in a journal entry or an essay either your reactions or why you would prefer not to express them.

3. Recall a hilarious time when you and your friends or you alone were caught in a scene gone awry. Perhaps it involves love or friendship. Write a journal entry or a personal story that accentuates the humor.

GOING TO SCHOOL

D'Arcy McNickle

Many critics consider D'Arcy McNickle one of the founders of modern Native American literature. When he published his first novel, *The Surrounded,* in 1936, only three novels by Native Americans existed. McNickle's other novels are *Runner in the Sun: A Story of Indian Maize* (1954) and the posthumous *Wind from an Enemy Sky* (1978). According to critic Louis Owens, "More than any other Indian writer, McNickle would prove to be a seminal figure in the new American Indian fiction, publishing three novels over a span of forty years while turning himself into one of the nation's most articulate and knowledgeable spokesmen for Indian concerns."

Although McNickle is best known today for his novels, he also worked tirelessly for many years as a federal official, historian, anthropologist, and Indian-rights advocate. Hired by the Bureau of Indian Affairs in 1936, McNickle worked as a top-level trouble shooter and policy maker until 1952. In 1949 he published an influential nonfiction book drawing on his government experience. *They Came Here First: The Epic of the American Indian* was unique for its time because it was history from an Indian perspective. McNickle's goal was to shatter common stereotypes about Indians and their history. In *Indians and Other Americans: Two Ways of Life Meet* (1959), McNickle and Harold Fey criticized the policy of boarding schools that attempted to erase Indian students' tribal heritage and forbade them to speak their languages.

D'Arcy McNickle was born in St. Ignatius, Montana, in 1904 to a French-Cree mother, Philomean Parenteau, and an Irish rancher father, William McNickle. His mother was adopted into the Flathead tribe. D'Arcy and his two sisters spent their early years on the reservation living near other Indians, but their parents intended to rear the children as Euro-Americans, believing that assimilation would bring a better life. Yet young D'Arcy developed a strong attachment to Indian people and attended the local school for four years. Though he never went back to the reservation to live after he left in 1925, his writing, especially his fiction, was firmly rooted there.

When D'Arcy was ten, his parents divorced, and against his mother's desires, he and his sisters were sent to the Chemawa Indian Boarding School in Oregon. He ran away from the school to return home but was forced to return. After three years at the Chemawa school, he attended public schools in Washington and Montana.

At seventeen, McNickle left the reservation to attend the University of Montana where he studied literature and history. McNickle joined the staff of the university's literary journal, *The Frontier,* in which he published poetry and short stories. His short story "Going to School," appeared in the 1929 issue of the journal. In this early work, McNickle vividly pictures the humdrum farm, bickering parents, and trio of young people going to school in rural Montana.

After three-and-a-half years at the university, McNickle sold his allotment of land near St. Ignatius, which he had received as a member of the Flathead tribe, and used the money to go to Oxford University in England in 1925. When his money ran out the next year, he moved to Paris, determined to become a writer.

Returning to the United States, he worked at several editorial and professional jobs while he tried to sell his novel, short stories, and poetry. In 1936 *The Surrounded* was finally published, but it did not sell well in the Depression book market. That same year, McNickle went to work for the Bureau of Indian Affairs under Commissioner John Collier, a move that changed his life and became the impetus for his landmark historical books.

---

1   Dawn had come but it was still dark. The lights from the houses shone almost as brightly as they would have in the middle of night. A stiff wind came up at intervals and the sky over the eastern mountains was unmistakably growing lighter every minute. Roosters were crowing and occasionally a door opened and a man came out to spit and look at the sky.

2   A young boy stood by the dirt road and peered toward the fringe of timber that lay a quarter of a mile eastward from the town. He could see or hear nothing and was munching on an apple. In one hand he carried a lunch bucket.

3   Suddenly he heard horses snorting and blowing in the cold air. And then he could hear buggy wheels rattling over the frozen ground. He finished his apple in several large bites and tossed the core aside. He wiped his mouth with the sleeve of his coat and put his mitten on the hand that had held the apple. A moment later a team of horses and a buggy materialized out of the mist and gloom and a voice called out sharply:

4   "Whoa, there, cayuses!"

5　　A girl's voice followed immediately after: "Good morning, Joey! Are we late?"

6　　"Naw, you're not late. I just came from the house." He put his lunch pail in the back of the rig and climbed onto the seat.

7　　"Put these blankets around you good. It's terribly cold." The girl helped to wrap the blankets around his legs.

8　　"That's good enough," he said before she had finished.

9　　The scraggy team of mares was put at a trot and the buggy was on its way again. It was precarious footing, however, and though they picked their feet up quickly and made a motion of trotting they couldn't manage anything better than a fast walk.

10　　The sky had turned a shade lighter and the town could be made out more distinctly. It was a forlorn place clinging to the edge of the timber. Not a house was painted; they were all shanties.

11　　On the left the mountains were still black and heavy mist hid their wide bases. High up among the peaks a ray of light gleamed now and then on a snow bank. Off to the right was the rolling prairie land and clumps of trees could be seen along some creek banks. There was a mist over the prairie, too, and it seemed dull and dead out that way. A chill breeze cut into the faces of the tree travelers in the buggy and made them keep their heads pulled low on their shoulders.

12　　Gene, the driver, was a thin-faced youth whose eyes watered constantly in the cold wind. His jaws stood out rigidly and his skin was smooth, for he hadn't yet put a razor to his face. He didn't talk as much as the others; he sat and brooded and wore a long face.

13　　Ada sat in the middle and her blue eyes were always twinkling. She had a clear, healthy complexion and the stinging wind made her cheeks glow warmly. She was eighteen at most, yet she looked older.

14　　Joe, who had waited at the roadside, knew of nothing better in the world than to be sitting where he was, beside Ada. The buggy seat was narrow and he was pressed closely against her; he could feel her warmth up and down his right side. Joe was younger than the others, four years younger than Ada, but he never thought of that.

15　　When they came to the bridge at the end of the first mile the team slowed down and looked cautiously from one side to the other as they went up the approach. The bridge planks were white with frost and after the buggy had passed over, two neat tracks were left behind. When the bridge was crossed, the horses picked up their shambling trot again. The breath came out of their nostrils in white clouds and formed a coating of frost on the hair of their necks. They were an unkempt team of little mares with their long winter's hair; bits of straw and their night's bedding still clung to their sides. Gene forgot to curry them most of the time.

16　　A serious conversation was being carried on in the buggy. Joe had said: "My folks had a fight last night and we may be moving away one of these days."

17　　"No! You don't mean right away—before school is out?" Ada asked.

18   "Well, no, not that soon."

19   "What was they fighting about?" Gene asked.

20   "Why, ma thinks that we made a bad move when we bought lots during the boom. She says we might as well have thrown the money in the river. But pa laughs about it. 'Money's no good if you don't use it,' he says. 'You just as well take a gambling chance once in a while; all you have is a gambling chance; and even then you're bound to lose,' he says."

21   "Were they angry?" Ada wanted to know.

22   "Oh yes, I suppose all the neighbors heard them."

23   "Well," Gene said, "your ma's right. Nobody's going to make any money out of that town!"

24   "You don't know anything about it! You've heard dad say that," his sister reminded him.

25   "We could have made a little money last fall. We were offered three hundred dollars more for the shop than it cost us. But ma said it wasn't enough. She got mad last night when we reminded her of it."

26   Gene went off on a tangent.

27   "Your folks don't fight any more than ours," he said. "There's a wrangle at home every day."

28   "We have dad to thank for that. If it was mother alone it would be different."

29   But Gene couldn't agree with that.

30   "It takes two to make a quarrel and she nags as much as he does. She doesn't do it outright, that's the difference. She goes around complaining until somebody has to get mad."

31   "She has something to complain about, I think! Not one of you kids ever help her and she's had ten of us to take care of."

32   "Well," said Gene. "I'll tell you one thing, Joe, don't get married! A poor man's got to work his fingers to the bone as it is, but if he gets married, he's sunk!"

33   But Joe disagreed. No. It wasn't that bad! It depended on yourself—and, of course, on whom you married.

34   "Do you think married people are never happy? Sure, lots of them are! But you've got to be in love. I don't think my folks were ever in love; they don't act like it, and that's why they row."

35   "You talk like a calf! What's love? I ain't seen any yet," Gene said.

36   What, no love! And Joe sat there burning with it! He knew no unhappiness. It was true that his father and mother made things unpleasant with their misunderstandings and uncharitable accusations. His sister was half an idiot and sat at home laughing and crying by turns and trying to draw pictures on the windowpane with her pencil. There was no money in the home most of the time though his father ran a butcher shop.

37   Joe lived in the midst of many things that might have been thought unpleasant, yet he went through them unscathed. When he sat beside Ada he was content. He thought of finer things; it might even be imagined that

he saw them dancing by like the fence posts on either side that went flying past in an endless chain. For seven months, ever since school opened in September, he had been riding with the Silverthorns, and ever since Christmas when Ada kissed him at the School Entertainment he had been engulfed in a great world of mist and warm dew.

38 The sun had burst over the mountains and the gloom that had lurked in the hollows and over against the timber all disappeared. The few scattered banks of snow that lay in the nearby fields sparkled and looked whiter. The frost disappeared from the horses' necks and they got over the road with a freer gait.

39 On and on the road led in a straight line down the valley. The mountains were always parallel and as one traveled along one could see ever new angles to the peaks and canyons.

40 Gene sat on the driver's side in his peculiar hunched over fashion and he held the lines with listless hands. He hissed at the horses and cursed them soundly when they slowed to catch a breath or when one of them slipped on a patch of ice. He seemed to dream, perhaps of the dreary round of chores that awaited him when he returned at night, perhaps of his father with his savage temper, or perhaps he dreamed of freedom from these things.

41 Ada, as she sat there, wore a half smile and an eager expression as if she expected every moment to come upon some marvellous discovery. No one could think of calling her a girl, exactly; she held her head with the studied grace of a woman; in a few years she would be a little too fleshy and then she would be a woman indeed.

42 For Joe there could be no accounting for her charm. He never relaxed in the seat beside her; he was in a continual flux of emotions. Something happened almost every day that brought him more deeply under her spell. It wasn't much, a mere nothing, but he came to regard each new day with wistful expectation. Anything might happen! In these past few months he had suddenly begun to feel like a matured young man. He looked backward from the pinnacle of his fourteen years and he saw his childhood lying somewhere in the indeterminate past.

43 The conversation had gone to other things.

44 "I've made up my mind to study law when I get to college," Joe said.

45 "Do you really plan to go to college, then?" Ada asked him.

46 "Yes. Ma always wanted me to be a lawyer. When she got her divorce they made her say a lot of things that weren't true but she couldn't help herself. So she's always wanted me to study law and make up for it, though I don't see what can be done now."

47 "That will be fine! When I come to get my divorce I'll see you the first thing. I'll say: 'Joey, my husband's mean to me. Please get me a divorce right away!' And then what will you do?"

48 Joe's tongue failed him and he couldn't think of a witty reply. He said: "I'll go and kick the seat of his pants up between his shoulders!"

49   Ada was surprised and didn't know whether to laugh or not, but Gene roared aloud and the horses threw up their heads and trotted faster.

50   Now they were approaching town. The seven mile ride was ending. The sun was an hour above the mountains and the frostiness had almost gone from the air. The sky was completely free from cloud and mist and a golden effulgence poured down upon the land.

51   The school was the first building on the left as they entered town. It stood by itself in the center of a large yard. There were tall poles standing upright with cross bars over the top, these were the swings where the children played.

52   The school building was long and narrow and built in two stories. The lower half was covered with shingles and painted brown; white clapboards covered the upper half. From all directions one could see pupils coming towards the school in vehicles of all descriptions—some were on horseback, some had single horse rigs, while others drove a team; and now a green and white school-wagon came lumbering down the lane.

53   When Gene stopped his team of brown mares before the entrance gate, there were fully a half-hundred youngsters jumping around; they laughed and shouted and banged one another with their dinner pails. Something as fluid as electricity and as startling took possession of the three in the buggy. They looked at each other, at the crowd of pupils, and began to laugh. This was school! There was nothing else like it!

54   Joe got down and helped Ada from the buggy; then he drove with Gene to the stable to unhitch the horses.

55   It was a strange business, this going to school. Out at home things went their humdrum way; the father would be stamping around the fields to see how near the frost was to leaving the ground or he would be in the granary fanning his seed wheat; the mother would be in the kitchen mixing her bread or else out in the yard feeding the chickens. But in school it was different; they read about the capital of one State and the area of another; they learned about Nigeria and Liberia and Abyssinia and Lake Titicaca high in the mountains; they used words like "hypotenuse" and "congruent" in geometry; they found out that there had been a French Revolution and a War of the Spanish Succession and that Shakespeare had written many plays and was no doubt the greatest man in the world. But when they went home they kept their discoveries under their hats. It would never do to let the old folks feel that they didn't know everything; they would have only one way to answer such a charge, and that was with the stick.

56   Joe knew well enough how it was. He sat in his classroom and swallowed everything greedily. His head was full of things that had happened thousands of miles away and hundreds of years ago. But he knew better than to talk about them when he got home. There was no sense in being laughed at.

57   "Wipe your nose!" his father would say if Joe should tell him that Rome had been a great Empire ruled over by Julius Caesar who talked Latin.

58   The morning's ride had been a pleasant event in its way, and the school hours were themselves filled with moments of ecstasy; but the pleasantest time of all was when they drove home at night.

59   The air was warm then, so warm that coats were left unbuttoned and one could crane one's neck around and have a look at the scenery; and there were heavy shadows lying across the land. At the big cattle ranch along the foothills it was feeding time and the steers could be heard blowing and bellowing. The feeding wouldn't last much longer; soon there would be a coating of green over the hills and prairie and the stockman could leave off measuring his haystacks with his eye.

60   But there was no green grass yet. Indeed, the frost had by no means left the ground. The first few inches were free and soft with mud but down below there was something hard. And when morning came around everything would be stiff with frost again.

61   Everyone felt the glory of those first spring afternoons. Even Gene's shabby mares held their heads with a certain pride and they took to the long road with renewed energy as they swung around the corner and left the school house behind. And Gene himself was not the same. Whatever sparkle of humor his system could muster then came to the surface and played about for a moment like faint blue lightning on the horizon. But he wasn't at home when it came to playing with wit; he would stumble around for a while and before long take to cursing something or other as a more effective way of getting over what he wanted to say. No, Gene didn't fit into this world of youthful thoughts and feelings. He had shrivelled already. He had been broken to the plow when he was too young a colt and now he could never enjoy running wild.

62   Ada was touched by the same searing process. If she escaped at all it was something to marvel at. She was the eldest in the family of ten and she had borne the brunt of it all; she had mothered nine of the ten children; but it hadn't proved too heavy a task for her. She was charming and sprightly for an elderly woman of eighteen!

63   The family of ten was gradually becoming valuable as time went on. Over half of them were working now and if the first ones had been put at it a little too early it was easier for the late comers.

64   Ada had kissed Joe at Christmas time and here it was March and he hadn't awakened from the spell yet! He hadn't enjoyed it at the time, it is true. He had been too ashamed and confused to know just what had happened. Besides, the room had been full of people. Since then the event had revealed its proper significance. He would know how to act the next time.

65   His father and mother spent all their time making life unpleasant for each other. Every night when Joe came home they were at it. He lived his life on the road to school; the night was only spent in waiting for another day. Sometimes he couldn't avoid being drawn into a family melee; he went about looking so dreamy and absent-minded that his parents must turn and attack him occasionally. And he became more pointedly aware of the two

worlds he was attempting to straddle. But on the road to school much was left behind and he dreamed astounding dreams. In fact, it would be hard to say which of Joe's thoughts were real and which were but the froth and mist of some dream pot bubbling over. And on this very day one dream, at least, was to put on a cloak of reality and meet Joe face to face.

66   For over seven months the two brown mares had performed their task in the most irreproachable manner possible. They had trotted mile after mile without complaint—though it is true that a fast-legged man could have kept abreast of them at any time; and as they went they looked neither on one side nor the other but with bowed heads kept the middle of the road. Viewing them critically, they were commonplace and shabby and a whip lash falling on their scrawny backs brought no protest. Yet on this day they did a most unexpected and unreasonable thing.

67   They had been trotting along with their eyes glued to the road and the three young people in the buggy behind them had been engaged in a methodical discussion of the day's events. The mares were shedding heavily and it was really difficult to talk as one had to stop at every other word and spit out a horse hair. Gene sat with the lines held loosely in his hands and he seemed to be pondering things in his uninspired way.

68   And then three pigs appeared suddenly.

69   They had escaped their pen and were in the lane, looking for the feast of green grass they had scented on the wind, no doubt. They had been hidden from view behind a pile of last year's tumble weeds and just as the buggy came abreast of them they ran into the road to sniff the air and decide which way to run. They grunted and squealed and one old sow grew confused and tried to run between the legs of Tricksey, the mare on the rear side.

70   Tricksey was patient enough but she couldn't be expected to allow a pig to run between her legs. She sat back on her haunches for just a second and then she shot ahead like a cannon ball and it was a wonder that the tug straps didn't snap like cotton twine. Tricksey's mate caught the panic too and it took only a moment to get their legs and harness untangled and then they were off!

71   The buggy swayed from side to side; it dashed into the gutter and balanced for a moment on two wheels, then it straightened itself and lurched to the other side of the road. All the loose bolts and rods and wheel spokes were rattling as they never had rattled before.

72   It was strange to see what happened inside the buggy. At the first unexpected move Gene straightened himself in the seat. When the horses took the bits into their teeth and began their mad gallop straight for destruction—he lost no time in contemplation. With one movement he thrust the lines into Ada's hands and with a second motion he had vaulted out of the buggy and clear of the wheels. He landed in a lump on the roadside.

73   Joe sat there in a daze. If he had tried to talk he would have stuttered. The buggy swayed perilously, the slightest obstruction sent the wheels bounding into the air. He probably would have continued to sit in a trance

until they had smashed against a fence or telephone post if he hadn't thrown his hand out involuntarily to balance himself. In doing so he grasped the lines. The next moment he had braced his feet against the dashboard and was pulling for all he was worth. He was thoroughly frightened by now and he had the strength of desperation.

74 Joe stopped the mares by running them into a sand bank at the corner of the lane where the road had been cut through a low hill. The moment they stopped he scrambled out and took them by the bridles. He was trembling. He led them around into the road again before they tried to climb the hill. He kept saying over and over:

75 "You damn mutts! You damn mutts! Hold up now!"

76 Gene didn't overtake them for half an hour. He came up the road with a limp in one leg.

77 Ada looked at him with amazement and contempt. "Why on earth did you jump?" she asked.

78 He didn't answer until he had examined the buggy and harness to see that nothing was broken. He climbed wearily onto the seat and he looked quite an old man.

79 "Why did I jump? What do you suppose! Am I going to risk my neck for a team of scrub cayuses? Not much! I'll die soon enough as it is!"

80 Ada scorned such premature wisdom. "Look at little Joe!" she said. "He isn't thinking of himself all the time! He acts like a little man!—Why Joe!" She turned to him ecstatically. "You're so brave!"

81 With a swift movement she grasped his coat and pulled him close and kissed him, once on the cheek and once on the mouth. Then she laughed gently and let him go.

82 Joe had anticipated her action. He had braced himself to meet it—to no avail. His courage gave way and he turned red; after the second kiss he actually put up his hands to protect himself! And immediately afterwards he felt miserable. He pushed his shoulders up and drew in his head to hide his confusion.

83 "You girls make me sick!" Gene said, "always kissing people!"

84 "We don't kiss everybody, do we, Joe?"

85 What could Joe say!

86 They started down the road again. The mares had spent themselves and were content to go at an ordinary pace though they threw their heads from side to side and blew through their nostrils with the pride of their deed.

87 Darkness was coming now and there was coolness in the air. After the buggy had disappeared in the shadows and mist that arose from the cooling earth, the wheels could still be heard rattling over the graveled road. One more day of school was ending.

DISCUSSION QUESTIONS

1. Joe feels that he must straddle two worlds. What are these two worlds, and why can't the two worlds mesh?
2. Joe's feelings for Ada are somewhat complex. Describe these feelings.
3. What is the climax of the story, the moment of greatest suspense?

WRITING TOPICS

1. Write a poem in which you illustrate one of the relationships in the story. You might choose the relationship between Joe and his parents, between Ada and Joe, or between Ada and her brother Gene. Start with an image that helps to define the relationship. For example, "His parents are fighting again," or "Loud voices fill the night air," or "Two figures share the wagon seat."
2. What will Joe, Ada, and Gene be doing ten years from now? In an essay, tell where you think each will be living, how they will be making a living, and whether they will be married with a family.
3. In a paper, discuss how the time and place setting influence the lives of Gene, Ada, and Joe.

GROOM SERVICE

Michael Dorris

The groom in "Groom Service" literally *serves* not only his bride-to-be but her entire family. Bernard works diligently as a hunter to prove he will be an acceptable son-in-law. Michael Dorris locates his story only in terms of fish and game—beaver, porcupine, caribou, grouse, silver salmon, eel, black bear. Inasmuch as caribou do not range near streams where silver salmon swim, the setting seems to be purely fictional. Dorris included this story in *Working Men*, a collection of short stories about men whose sense of self is synonymous with their work.

In describing the characters' behavior, the author delineates a classic but fictional matrilineal society. Women own the property and prefer female children who can carry on the family heritage. Mothers negotiate and arrange marriages between their offspring. Young men move from their mother's house to their wife's house when they marry. At first glance, Bernard seems to be simply a puppet directed by dominant women. As the story progresses, however, he clearly demonstrates admirable qualities: patience, respect, and persistence. He desires a proper place in his society and is willing to abide by its rules.

Michael Dorris did not have to imagine all of the emotions of a young man adjusting to older women with forceful personalities. The author described his growing up in a household of older female relatives lacking older men: "I come from a family of strong women who had opinions and talked about their opinions all the time. I listened to them and understood how they thought." He concluded, "If I have a point of view to draw on other than myself, it's a woman's point of view."

In "Groom Service," Dorris skillfully creates characters by assuming the voices of both genders and various ages. Inasmuch as Dorris and his wife, Louise Erdrich, stated that they collaborated on most of their literary works, the characterizations in this story may also reflect her impressive ability to use multivoiced narration. Dorris credited Erdrich as being the greatest influence on his writing.

"You can take risks with a trusted co-worker that you couldn't otherwise. . . . You gain freedom when you have someone who knows you and your writing well and who is going to be absolutely honest, even to the point of making you want never to write another sentence." With humor and love, Lipsha, Bernard, Marie, and Serena all reach for maturity in the imagination of these two talented authors.

1

1   "She's a piece of pure quartz," Bernard's mother, Martha, said to Marie's mother, Blanche. "A one-in-a-million that you find after walking the beach for half your life with your eyes on the ground. If I had child like that I would keep her in a safe place."

2   Blanche paused her blade midway down the side of the fish she was scaling. Her face betrayed no expression except exertion, and even in this intermission her teeth remained set, flexing her jaw. The trader steel reflected what little light filtered through the planks of the smokehouse, and the confined air still smelled green. Blanche had hewn the boards with a mallet and chisel in May, as soon as the ground firmed from the spring runoff, and it took a while before the scent of the fire crowded that of drying wood. With her broad thumb she flicked a piece of fin off the carved knife handle, then continued her motion.

3   Martha waited. She had all the time it took.

4   "You don't know," said Blanche. She shook her head as if its secrets rolled like line-weights from side to side. She drew a heavy breath. "You can't imagine. You with such a boy."

5   Martha sat straighter, all ears, while her hands continued to explore, repairing the tears on the net that lay across her lap and hid her pants and boots. Her fingers moved automatically, finding holes, locating the ends of broken cord and twisting them into square knots. She kept her nails sharp and jagged, and when they weren't enough, she bowed her head and bit off any useless pieces. This was mindless work, the labor of ten thousand days, and could be done as easily in the dark as in the light. It required no involvement. Her thoughts were elsewhere.

6   "You mean Bernard?" Her voice was wary. She had three sons and needed to be sure she knew the one Blanche had in mind.

7   "Ber-*nard*," Blanche nodded, giving the knife a last run, then inspecting the fish closely before tossing it into the large basket at her feet. The water slopped onto the floor and, from there, leaked to the shale ground inches below. Blanche arched her back and massaged her spine with her fist. With her other hand she reached for the cup of cooled tea that she had nursed for the past half-hour. Martha let the net rest and joined her.

8   "People talk about him, you know," Blanche said. "His looks, that goes without saying, but the other things too. The respect he pays the old folks. His singing. His calmness. His hunting skill. You must be proud."

9   Martha closed her eyes as if in great pain. "He is my punishment," she confessed, "but I don't know what I could have done so terrible as to deserve him. He stays out until morning. His hair is always tangled. I sometimes think that the game he brings home has died before he found it, the meat is so tough. You must have him confused with another boy. Or perhaps, with a girl like Marie, you find it hard to think ill of any child."

10   "Now you make fun of me," Blanche said. "It is well known that Marie has turned out badly. She is lazy and disrespectful, conceited and stubborn. I try my best to teach her, and so do my sisters and even my mother, but she folds her arms and stares at nothing. Hopeless. And she will never find a husband. A boy's mother would have to be desperate to send her son courting at my house."

11   "But not as desperate as the mother who could tolerate the thought of Bernard as a son-in-law," Martha said. "That would be true desperation. I will never be free of him. I will grow old with him at my side, and with no granddaughters or grandsons to comfort me."

12   "If only someone like your Bernard would find an interest in Marie," Blanche said as if she had not heard Martha. "If only some young man exactly like him would consent to live in my house, how I would welcome him. I would treat him as my own blood."

13   The two women met each other's gaze at last. Each held a cup to her lips, and after a few seconds, each drank. Each replaced her cup on the table between them. Each held her mouth firm. Blanche found her knife and reached for a new fish, cool and slippery as a stone over which much water has rushed. Martha shifted the net in her lap, moving a new section to the center. The smell of salt rose like steam as her hands went to work.

14   "I will speak to him," Martha said.

15   "And I to her," Blanche replied. "But I know her answer already. I have seen how she regards him."

16   "She will not be disappointed." Martha allowed one wave of pride to crest. "He's not so bad."

17   Blanche glanced up at Martha, then looked quickly back to her work. Bernard must be good indeed, she thought, if Martha could not better contain herself.

2

18   Bernard was drawing with charcoal on a piece of driftwood when his mother returned home. He was twenty-two, lean, and had large teeth. His eyes were dark beneath unusually thick brows, and his hands were long and broad. At the sound of Martha's step, he jumped to his feet and assumed the air of a person about to do something important. His fingers curved as if to

hold a tool or a weapon and his eyes narrowed as if to see something far away. He was busy at nothing, his energy humming, ready for a focus. But for once she made no comment about his sloth. She did not despair at the time he wasted scratching on any smooth surface. She did not inspect his sketch and then toss it into the cooking fire. In fact, this afternoon she dealt with him rather mildly.

19   "Well, it's arranged," she announced. "I spent an endless morning with your future mother-in-law and before I left she had agreed to let you come to see Marie. Don't think it was easy."

20   Bernard's eyes followed his mother's movements as she crossed the floor and sat in exhaustion on the bed. She pushed off her boots, still caked with beach mud, and rubbed her feet together. She wore no socks.

21   "Marie?" he said at last. "She's too young. You should have asked me first."

22   Martha's glare clapped a hand over his mouth. In a moment, Bernard tried again.

23   "I know they're a good family. I know you want to do right for me. But you could . . . *we* could have discussed this. I mean, I think of her as a little girl, not a *wife*." The word, a stranger on Bernard's tongue, vibrated in the air.

24   "Stop whining," Martha lost patience. "Who do you 'think of' as a wife? *Doris?*"

25   Bernard blushed. He wasn't surprised that his mother knew about him and Doris, but it did not seem fair for her to mention it. Doris was a widow whose name brought nervous laughs to teenage boys and smiles of disapproval to everyone else. She was a woman almost twice Bernard's age with a missing front tooth and eyes that sparked in his memory, a woman who had summoned him for an errand six months ago and whom he now loved better than he would have thought possible. But it was true: he had never thought of Doris as a wife.

26   "You should see yourself," Martha said. "Keep that face and you won't have to worry about marrying anyone. But don't expect me to support you forever." She noticed the driftwood, still on the floor, and nudged it with her toe to get a better view. Bernard had outlined the mountain across the bay from the village, and tucked a large sun behind its peak. When he drew it he thought it was his best work, but now its lines looked smudged and shaky. Martha leaned forward to pick it up and turn it over, as if expecting another illustration on the back. Finding none, she held it out for Bernard to take.

27   "Give this to your Doris," she said. "It looks like her under the blanket where she spends her time."

28   Bernard didn't move, but he watched the wood until his mother let it fall to the floor. He was angry at the shame he felt. He was angry that he knew it was just a matter of time until he would have to call on Marie. He was angry that his mother was right: his mountain *did* look like Doris, turned on her side.

3

29 When Blanche went into the house and told Marie that their problems were over, that Bernard, the catch of the village, would be courting, she expected some reaction, but her daughter simply folded her arms and stared at the fire.

30 "Don't you hear me?" Blanche demanded. "Bernard. Coming to see you. Can't you be happy? Can't you say something?"

31 Marie, however, only rolled her eyes and drummed her fingers against the pine bench upon which she sat. She wore a close-knit woven cap that, in combination with her unfortunately weak chin, made her head resemble an acorn. She was fifteen, just out of her confinement, trained for adulthood to the limits of Blanche and her sister's patience, but still a sulking child. At length she drew up her knees, circled them with her arms, and watched her mother from the corner of her eye.

32 Blanche stood across the long room, talking to her older sister Bonnie. She was not hard to overhear.

33 "Does she say 'thank you'? Does she appreciate what it means to her, to all of us, to get that damn Martha to agree? Does she care that Bernard could have any girl, from any family?"

34 Bonnie shook her head sadly. Her surviving children had all been boys and had long since moved to the houses of their wives' families, so she had no experience with reluctant girls, unless, she thought, she counted her memories of Blanche. But that would not do to say, especially not in earshot of Marie, who sat with her head cocked in their direction. Blanche's daughter was the hope of the next generation, the one who had to bring in a husband and produce more daughters than her mother or aunt, if the family was to regain its position. For a moment Bonnie thought of suggesting to Blanche that they present that information to Marie directly, to drop the shadows and point out both her responsibility and her power, but then she rejected the idea. The girl was impressed enough with herself as it was. Instead, Bonnie sympathized with her sister and cast occasional looks at her niece in hopes of catching on Marie's face a secret, a streak of pleasure.

4

35 "What am I supposed to do?" Bernard asked the next time his uncle visited. Bernard had waited for a private moment, and it came when, just before sleep, Theodore had stepped outside to relieve himself. The trees around the village seemed closer at night, taller, like the sides of a box.

36 From the darkness came rattling sounds of strangulation that Bernard eventually identified as the older man's yawn. When it, and the noise of splashing water, had abated, Theodore spoke. It was clear that he understood Bernard's problem.

37 "You do whatever they tell you and you hope they're not as bad as they

could be," Theodore said. "You don't complain. You don't assume anything. You stay out of the way, because you never know what they're going
to find to dislike. You be what they want."

38   "It's not fair." Bernard leaned against the side of the house and searched
the sky. Thin clouds, silver as wet spiderwebs, passed in the night wind.

39   "That's true, but there are other things in the world besides owning real
estate. Your true home will remain here at your mother's, just as it has been for
me, but you can't *live* here forever. You need independence, distance, the
chance to be a man in a place where you were never a boy. Once you get yourself established, you'll understand what I mean. Your life is not all indoors.
You'll hang around with your brothers-in-law, your uncles, your friends. Spend
time at the men's house. Go to the sweat bath and gripe, or listen to the com-
plaints of others and make jokes. In a year all your wife's family will care about
is whether or not you bring in your share. By then you'll know what's what."

40   "But what if I don't get along with Marie?"

41   "*Do* get along with her. Get along with her mother. Get along with her
auntie. But on your own time do what you want. It's not a big price to pay.
It's a daughter-poor clan and the one they've picked out for you is going to
control everything someday: rich fishing sites, a big house. Behave yourself
now and you'll get your reward. It's not like you're marrying a youngest sister with no prospects."

42   Which was, Bernard knew, what had happened to Theodore. No wonder
he was not more sympathetic.

43   "How do I tell Doris?" Bernard asked. This was something he had struggled with for days.

44   "Doris! She could have told *you*. It's good news to her. She gets a
younger guy, fresh the way she likes them, and no hard feelings between
you." Theodore laughed, and put an arm around Bernard's shoulders.
"Listen to some advice, from your great-uncle through me to you," he said.
"Groom service is the worst part, so make it as short as possible. Convince
her family you won't be a pain in the ass to live with. Rule number one:
appreciate everything they do. Compliment, compliment, compliment."

45   "Did you do that?" Bernard asked. "Did my mother's husband do that?"

46   "Do fish fry in hot grease? But don't take my word for it. Ask Pete. He's
your father."

47   "I'd be embarrassed," Bernard said. "He and I never talk about serious
matters. He's not of the clan."

48   "A man's a man," Theodore said.

5

49   "This is what you do," Martha instructed.

50   It was not yet light and she had awakened Bernard from a sound sleep.
He blew into a cup of hot tea as he listened, let the darkness hide the resent-
ment in his face.

51   "You go hunting and you catch something *good*. I don't care what. Something a little unusual. A beaver, maybe, or a goose. *Not* something small and easy. *Not* a squirrel. *Not* fish. You bring it home and I'll help you clean it. You leave a portion for me as if that's what you always do, to help provide for your family, but you take the best part and you set yourself in front of Blanche's door. You only speak if you're spoken to. You wait for *them* to ask *you*. And if they don't, which they won't right away, you act unconcerned. You do this every day until they invite you in, and then I'll tell you what to do next. This is your chance, so don't ruin it. Now move."

52   Bernard stepped out into the chill morning grayness, thought briefly of visiting Doris before he went hunting, but then abandoned the idea. He had heard through his mother's husband that Doris had made friends with a seventeen-year-old boy named James.

53   The dew from high grass had soaked through to Bernard's feet before he reached the edge of the woods. He realized his mother had forgotten to feed him breakfast, forgotten to make him a lunch. He heard a duck call from the lake and paused, but then continued on. He could hear his mother in his mind, and she said a duck wouldn't do.

6

54   "He's *there*!" Bonnie dropped the firewood she was carrying and rushed to Blanche's side.

55   Her sister was stirring a pot on the fire, as if what it contained were all that concerned her. "I have eyes," Blanche said. "Keep your voice down. He'll hear you."

56   "Did you see what he had?" Bonnie asked. "I got a glimpse of something flat and dark, but I didn't want him to catch me looking."

57   "I think it was a beaver tail. Would you believe, he had the nerve to hold it up to me and smile the first time I passed."

58   "No!"

59   "I thought he was better trained. It simply means he'll have to wait longer."

60   "Did Marie see him yet?"

61   "She won't go outside." Both sisters turned to the gloom in the rear of the room where Marie crouched, her head lowered over a stick game. Her long hair was loose and covered her shoulders like a shawl, her back to the doorway.

7

62   "Well, what happened?" Martha demanded when Bernard returned home late in the evening.

63   "Nothing happened," Bernard said, and threw himself down on his blankets. He raised an arm to cover his eyes, then turned to face the wall.

64   Martha spotted the sack her son had dropped on the floor and looked

inside. The beaver tail and quarters were exactly as she had cleaned them that afternoon, and she took them out to add to the broth she had prepared.

65 "At least we'll eat well for a while," she said.

66 "I'm not hungry," Bernard replied, but his mother ignored him.

67 "Tell me everything."

68 "There's nothing to tell. I walked over there, dressed like I was going to a feast, carrying that beaver. I trapped it clean, surprised it so completely, there wasn't even adrenaline in its flesh. I thought they'd taste it, invite me to supper, but they walked by me like I wasn't there, their noses in the air."

69 "Whose noses?" Martha wanted to know.

70 "The mother and the aunt."

71 "Not the girl?"

72 "I saw no girl. I heard no girl."

73 "Ah," said Martha. "So she's shy. Good."

74 "Why good?"

75 "Because then she won't bully you at first, stupid boy. I've seem what happens to the husbands of the bold ones."

76 The smell of stewing meat filled the room, warm, rich, brown. Martha's husband Pete came into the house at the scent, tipped his head in his son's direction, and asked, "Hard day?"

8

77 For a week, then two weeks, the same pattern was repeated. Only the animals changed: they ranged from a porcupine to a hind quarter of caribou, from a fat grouse on a bad day to a string of matched silver salmon on a good one. Once Bernard thought he saw a black bear dive into the brush at the side of a stream, but he was momentarily afraid to investigate, and later berated himself. With a bear skin, he thought too late, he would have been irresistible and his long afternoons and evenings at Blanche's closed door would have been over.

78 As a month passed, Bernard gave up hope. He lost the alertness he had once felt when Blanche or Bonnie or Marie, the most unsympathetic of them all, approached, and he soon tired of the commiseration that Blanche's and Bonnie's husbands cast in his direction as they went about their business. They could remember, their expressions said, what it was to wait outside this house, but there was nothing they could do. A word from them might slow the process rather than speed it up, might do more damage than good. If boredom was patience, Bernard achieved patience. If learning to exist without expectation of fulfillment was maturity, Bernard matured. At first he used his time to remember Doris, to wonder what she was doing and to regret not doing it with her. Later he thought about hunting, how he could have succeeded the times he had failed, how the animals behaved, how they smelled and sounded. Finally he found himself thinking about Pete, his father, in different ways than he ever had before. In Bernard's mind Pete

became more than just his mother's husband; he became another man, an earlier version of Bernard, a fellow sufferer. It had not previously occurred to Bernard how hard it was to be forever a stranger in the house where you lived, to be always a half-visitor. He wondered how Pete stayed so cheerful, and wondered if his grandmother had kept his father waiting long at the doorway before inviting him inside. On an afternoon late in the second week, Bernard had a thought so profound, so unprecedented, that it straightened his back. What if, he wondered, his grandmother had not let Pete in at all? What if Pete had been judged inadequate? Where would that have left Bernard?

79   The next morning when he went hunting, Bernard returned to the place where he had seen the bear, hid himself behind a log, and waited.

9

80   "Did you hear?" Pete asked Theodore as they walked the trail from the sweat bath to their wives' houses.

81   "About Bernard's bear?"

82   "It must have weighed three hundred pounds. I didn't know Bernard had it in him."

83   "Have you forgotten what sitting in front of a house will drive you to? What did you catch to get inside Blanche's?"

84   "Nothing," Pete said. "It was me she couldn't resist."

85   "You forget," Theodore replied. "I was still a boy in that house. I recall their words of you. . . ."

86   "Poor brother-in-law," Pete said. "You still don't realize the lengths to which they went to avoid hurting your feelings! And how *is* your wife? How is the health of her many elder sisters? Is it true that they become stronger and more robust with every year?"

10

87   On the second day of the fifth week, just as she passed through the door, Blanche reached down her right hand and snagged one of the bear claws that rested in the basket by Bernard's leg. So quick was her movement, so apparently disconnected to the intent of her mind, so complete her distraction, that Bernard had to look twice to make sure it was gone. All the same, he felt a warm flush spread beneath the skin of his neck, and a feeling of inordinate pride suffused him so thoroughly that he had difficulty remaining still. He had been found worthy, and now it was only a matter of time.

88   Every day, with more pause and deliberation, Blanche browsed through his offerings and always selected some choice token. Her expression betrayed no gratitude, yet Bernard was sure that occasionally she was pleasantly surprised. Afraid to unbalance their precarious arrangement, he sat still as a listening hare in her presence. He kept his eyes lowered and held his

breath until she had departed, but remained ever watchful for any cue that his probation had progressed. At last it came.

89   "Bernard!" Blanche said one day. She stood in the doorway, her hands on her hips, her head cocked to the side in amazement. "Is that you crouching there so quietly? Please, come in and share our supper, poor as it is. What a pleasure to see you."

90   Bernard rose slowly, stiff in his joints and half-skeptical that this was some joke, some new test, but when he entered the house, Blanche's hospitality continued and was joined by that of Bonnie, who sat by the fire trimming her husband's hair with a squeaking scissors. "Sit, sit," she motioned to a bench near the door. "What a shy boy you are. Luckily we have some nice moose to feed you."

91   Indeed they did. Bernard recognized the remains of the foreleg he had offered yesterday. Bonnie passed him a plate with a small portion of tough gristle, gray and cooled. He knew what to say.

92   "This is wonderful," he exclaimed. "The best I've ever tasted. What cooks you are. But you are too generous. Let me put some back in the pot."

93   When they refused, politely and with many denials of his compliments, Bernard made a great show of eating. The act of digestion absorbed his total concentration. He rubbed his stomach and cast his eyes to the ceiling in delight. With great subtlety he periodically raised his hand to his mouth, as if to wipe some grease, and used that motion to conceal the small bits of undigestible food he removed from his cheeks and tucked secretly into his pockets.

94   When he finished, Bernard sat nervously, breathless with anxiety. From the corner of the room he detected a space so devoid of movement that it attracted his attention. He looked, then quickly looked away. Yet his eyes still registered the image of Marie, her hair oiled and braided, wearing a new dress and a necklace made of bear claws, sitting as composed and shaded as a perfect charcoal sketch.

11

95   "You know, Pete," Martha said as she lay by her husband's side under a robe, "watching Bernard lately brings back memories."

96   "To me too. Your mother was a terror."

97   "I notice you still whisper such words, even though she's more than four years gone."

98   Pete shifted his position and propped on an elbow. In the moonlight Martha's face was seamless and young. A beam like the hottest part of a coal danced off her dark eye. He ran his fingers along her cheek and she turned her head in comfort. "You look the same as then," he said.

99   Martha caught his hand and brought it to her mouth, let it feel the smile.

100   "I pestered her, you know, to let you in," she said.

101   "You didn't care."

102   "I didn't care the day you found the eagle feathers? I didn't care the day you came an hour later than always?"

103   "It was raining," Pete said. "The ground was soft and I kept sinking to my knees. I couldn't arrive at your door covered in mud."

104   "I thought you weren't coming. I confronted my mother and told her that her slowness had cost me . . ."

105   "Cost you what?" Pete asked, when Martha's silence persisted.

106   "Enough talk."

12

107   Marie watched the back of Bernard's head and admired the sleek sheen of his long hair, the play of muscles in his arms at his every movement. During the last month she had studied every part of him so completely that she could create him in her imagination whenever she chose, and lately she chose often. She had to fight not to laugh when they gave him the worst meat and he had to spit into his hand and act as though it were delicious. She watched the way his fingers held the plate, the way he sat so compact and attentive. She waited for the sound of his soft voice and wondered what he would say when he could speak in private. She made a game of observing his eyes until just the second before they turned to her, and believed she'd been discovered only once.

13

108   Bernard ate almost all of his meals at Blanche's house now, and gradually became more relaxed. For one thing, his distribution increased in both quality and quantity, and he could now expect a reasonable piece of meat or salmon. For another, Blanche's and Bonnie's husbands had begun to join him on his hunts, to show him places to fish that only members of this household knew. He found he liked these men and began to call them "uncle."

109   Blanche herself still frightened him, but not all the time. There were moments when he found approval in her gaze, times when some word of hers sounded almost like a joke. Bonnie was warmer, more solicitous of his needs, more delighted at the food he brought, and Bernard regarded her as an ally.

110   As far as Marie was concerned, he still had no clue to her feelings. Even Pete and Theodore observed that this game was lasting longer than the usual and debated whether something might be wrong. They were full of advice for Bernard, full of ideas of how to please Marie, full of reminders that it was her agreement, more than anyone's, that was necessary. But no matter what Bernard did, Marie would not look at him or give him any sign of encouragement. He grew despondent, lost his appetite, found himself thinking once again of Doris and the ease of their association. Marie

seemed totally beyond his reach, the focus of mystery and impossible desire. And so he was unprepared on the night, just before the first frost of winter, when, with shaking hands, Marie herself passed him a plate of food.

111 "This is for you," she said so softly he could barely hear, and she sat beside him while, slowly and with great emotion, he ate.

14

112 A year later, while waiting for the birth of Marie's first child, Blanche and Martha passed the time by nibbling strips of dried eel. Martha, who had no love for the oily skin, threw hers into the fire, where it sizzled briefly.

113 "The midwife predicts a girl," Blanche said. "When she spun the charm above Marie's stomach, it revolved to the left."

114 "A girl is most rewarding," Martha nodded. "But there is a special satisfaction in raising boys. So often I think of times when Bernard was young, so often I miss him around the house."

115 Blanche reached for another stick of *baleek* and did not answer. Her silence was immediately noticed, as she knew it would be.

116 "How is he doing?" Martha asked at last.

117 "He will learn," Blanche said. "He has potential. It is clear he cares greatly for Marie, and she is patient."

118 "That is one word for it." Martha tossed a handful of scraps into the flame and watched the light flare and dance. "Of course, Bernard was used to . . ." She shifted her weight, cleared her throat. "He had such a *happy* home that I'm sure it has taken some adjusting on his part in new surroundings."

119 "Yes, he *was* somewhat spoiled. But I think he has a good heart."

120 "As well he must, to remain loyal to such a chinless girl."

121 "One only hopes their child will inherit the mother's disposition and not be sulky and resentful of every request."

122 "One can but pray it will have the father's looks and personality."

123 A single rope of eel remained on the plate. Both women extended a hand toward it, hesitated, and withdrew. It rested between them as they cleaned their teeth with fine bone picks, carefully wiped their fingers, and when, at the sound of Marie's first muffled protest, the rose together and rushed to her side, it remained behind.

DISCUSSION QUESTIONS

1. In Part 1 of the story, how are Marie and Bernard characterized by their own mothers?
2. Since both mothers want Marie and Bernard to marry each other, why do you think they don't praise their children?
3. What does the contrast between the apparently modern setting of the story and the kind of courtship Bernard must adhere to tell you about this society and who directs it?
4. What qualities do Blanche, Bonnie, and Marie seem to admire most in a man?
5. How have the mothers' remarks changed at the end of the story?

WRITING TOPICS

1. In an essay, discuss the plot of this story, including the exposition, rising action, climax, falling action, and resolution.
2. With a partner, adapt the story into a radio play. Write the script, recruit actors and actresses to read the parts, prepare sound effects, and audio-tape the play.
3. Marie speaks only once in the entire story. In your literary journal, write a letter from Marie to Bernard.
4. Examine the structure of this story. The author divides it into fourteen sections. Each section highlights one or two characters and their views on their roles regarding love, marriage, and tradition. Select seven sections and describe the characters and compare and contrast their views about love, marriage, and tradition.

FROM STONEY CREEK WOMAN

Mary John and Bridget Moran

Mary John was born in 1913 on the Stoney Creek Reserve in British Columbia, Canada. She is one-half Carrier from her mother's ancestry. When an older woman, she told her life story to Bridget Moran, and it appeared as *Stoney Creek Woman* in 1988.

At age seven in 1920, Mary traveled two days by wagon to Fort St. James and a mission boarding school staffed by four nuns of the Sisters of Child Jesus. There she feared that she would never see her family again. The nuns forbade pupils to speak their native language, so Mary complained, "I'm always hungry" in English. She saw many pupils whipped for speaking their language, for stealing food, and for running away. Boys were whipped for speaking to girls and girls for writing notes to boys. Mary missed her family's meat diet: fish caught and dried during the summer, roast grouse, rabbit stew, venison, and moose-meat of winter hunting camp. "At school it was porridge, porridge, porridge, and if it wasn't that, it was boiled barley or beans, and thick slices of bread spread with lard."

In 1922, the school moved into a new building at Lejac, but food and regime did not change. During seven years at boarding school Mary felt "always the same longing to be at home with my family." In 1927, her mother allowed her to stay at home for two happy years before arranging her marriage.

When she was sixteen in 1929 "The chief and my parents talked together." She did not even know the chief's son chosen as her husband. Nonetheless, when a Roman Catholic priest next visited Stoney Creek Village, he married Mary and Lazare John.

Mary John's reminiscences make clear that their marriage endured because she and Lazare both worked at it, quite literally. Between 1930 and 1949, Mary bore a dozen children, half boys and half girls. Three died young. Lazare built them a succession of houses. "No housing subsidies in those days!" according to Mary. To support his large family, Lazare worked as a harvest hand, sold hay and firewood, made railroad ties, cleared land for cash, and hunted, fished, and trapped.

Proud of her heritage, Mary John worked as an activist in preserving the Carrier language and technology. Half a century after Mary John left the Lejac school with its draconian punishment for speaking the Carrier language, the priest in charge of her local St. Joseph's school in 1972 recruited her as its Carrier language instructor to teach Carrier young people, most of whose parents had lost their native language. "So there I was, Mary John, formerly a student in Lejac, now a teacher of the Carrier language and songs and dances in a Catholic school."

1   The village of Stoney Creek was my world and I loved it. I loved the log houses all set out in rows and the little hillocks and the creek which ran through the village. Without that creek, the elders said, there would have been no village, for that was where the fish spawned. Years before, the Indians had lived further along Nulki Lake, but around 1890, families moved to the rolling land through which the creek flowed. In those years, fish was the staple in our diet, and wherever the fish were, there you would find the Natives.

2   Our day-to-day life, what we did, where we were located, the food we ate, all of these things depended on the season.

3   In the summer we were in Stoney Creek village. Oh, the village in the hot months of summer was an active place! Berries were picked and fish were caught. The men and women, and the children too, were busy with drying and canning and smoking. This work would go on throughout the daylight hours, and sometimes into the night—our central British Columbian winters were harsh and a family's survival depended on a good store of food laid up for months ahead.

4   My role in the family was established when I was still very young. I looked after Mark and the babies who came after him, and wherever we were, I spent much of my time indoors, looking after our home. Johnny, my grandmother, the elders, all used to say, "Mary is a real little mother!" Bella, my stepsister, worked with my mother and learned early to treat hides, to dry and smoke fish, to trap and shoot and do all the things which Native women have done for centuries, and which were so necessary for their families' survival. I had to learn these things when I was much older.

5   But it wasn't all work. Once or twice during the summer, Johnny would harness the horses and we would jump into the wagon and travel to Vanderhoof, nine miles away.

6   How exciting it was when the horses reached the top of the hill and we could look down on Vanderhoof with its sidewalks and buildings! Johnny drove the team of horses to the edge of town and, in amongst the willows, he tied the horses on a long rope so that they could graze.

7   When the horses were settled, Bella and I helped my mother to gather kindling for a campfire. We always had a campfire when we went to town—in those days there were no signs telling us that campfires were prohibited! Besides, we had no money to spend in a restaurant, and even if our pockets had been full of dollar bills, we weren't allowed to enter any of the cafes in Vanderhoof. Natives knew that if they walked into a restaurant, they would be asked to leave, and if they refused, the police would be called. When I was a little girl, this didn't bother me—I wouldn't have traded the campfire and the willows and the sounds of the horses grazing for the most expensive dining room in the world!

8   When the campfire was ablaze, my mother put a kettle on to boil water for tea. She spread a tarp in the shade, and then we all went into the town. Sometimes we did nothing but walk along the wooden sidewalks, looking into the store windows and imagining what we would buy if we had money. Sometimes, if my mother had a little spare cash, we might buy a loaf of store bread—that was a great treat for us—or some goodies from the bakery. Then we would go back to the campfire in amongst the willows and have our tea and treats. Sometimes we'd stay there until dark, driving home to Stoney Creek when the stars were out and the heat of the day was done.

9   I loved those trips to town! Tea never tasted so good as it did there on the edge of town, with our campfire burning and the horses snorting and grunting as they grazed in the long grass, with my mother and Johnny and Bella and Mark on the tarp beside me, our teacups steaming in our hands.

10   When I was a little girl, I believe I thought that the long hot days of summer would last forever. Then suddenly—as I grew older I came to know that it would happen but in those early years it was always a surprise to me—there was the first frost early in September and with it, the village emptied of people. One by one the families loaded their wagons with tents and bedding and supplies, and left for their hereditary hunting grounds.

11   And the village was silent.

12   Just after my sixteenth birthday in 1929, I went to the home of our band chief with my parents. I did not know that this visit had anything to do with my future. I don't think I ever considered the future; the present was enough for me. I believe I thought that I would go on forever living with my parents, looking after the young ones, following the family on its seasonal wanderings. I should have known better. After all, I was now sixteen and I knew that marriages had been arranged for many girls who were my age and younger.

13   In our village we had watchmen. These were villagers who were appointed by the chief to arrange marriages, guard the morals of the young people, and watch over the people of the reserve. The watchmen were sometimes stern and hard. A few were different: they were appointed by the chief because they felt a concern for the welfare of the people. After 1940, we no

longer had watchmen on the reserve, but when I was a girl they were powerful. Their word was law.

14 Walking to the chief's home, entering his house, I did not expect my parents to tell me why we were making this visit. I'm sure that it didn't occur to my parents to tell me that my marriage was about to be arranged. No, just as when I first went to school, an announcement would be made when the plans were final. That is the way it was done in our village.

15 The chief and my parents talked together. I stayed in the background, as was expected of a young girl in the presence of her parents and the chief. I heard my parents tell the chief that they had talked to the watchmen and that they agreed to my marriage with Lazare John.

16 "When next the priest says Mass in the village, they will be married," said the chief.

17 "I agree," said my mother.

18 Johnny nodded.

19 And still no one spoke to me. No one asked me, "Mary, do you agree? Do you wish to marry this young man? Do you, Mary, even know Lazare John?"

20 Now, when I remember the days before my marriage, I think of a moth beating its wings against a lighted lamp. I knew that there was no escape for me. The chief, my parents, and the watchmen had decided that I was to marry Lazare John, and from that decision there was no appeal.

21 I did not dream of questioning the decision or of saying to my mother, "I don't want to get married! I want to go to work in a hotel or a hospital or in somebody's house, a house with nice things that I can take care of! I want a career. I don't know anything about being married! I don't know this Lazare! I have seen him but I have never spoken to him. Please, please, don't make me get married!" Still less did it occur to me to say, "I won't get married! I refuse!" These things, and many more, I said to myself day and night, but I never said them to my mother, to the chief, or to the watchmen.

22 Day by day, with the arrival of the priest approaching, I grew more scared. I knew that when I married Lazare I would have to leave my family and live in the John home. I didn't know anyone in his family. How could I suddenly go into the home of strangers and live as if I was one of them?

23 Worse still, I knew nothing about sex—what would happen to me when suddenly I was this man's wife? I had never been alone with a boy in my life. Apart from my family and relatives, I had hardly exchanged a word with someone of the opposite sex. And if my shyness had not made me avoid boys, my early training at Lejac and the knowledge that I would be the talk of the village if I was seen with a boy kept me silent. I had danced with them, but this was always under the watchful eyes of my mother and the elders.

24 In our culture, sex was never discussed. Most young girls were told what happened to their bodies when they became women. Young people might be warned that if they slept with an unclean person, they would get a disease. But that was all.

25 Lazare John was seven years older than me. I knew that he was the son of a chief, that he was considered a "mother's boy" and that his family lived across the village from us. I had often seen him with a group of boys, but until the day we were married, I had never exchanged a word with him.

26 Lazare's father was Chief Vital John. His mother Margaret came from a reserve far to the south of our village. The John family, along with the Antoine family, were considered to be at the top of the social scale in the village, because both families were headed by hereditary chiefs. This gave them a good deal of status on the reserve.

27 Lazare was one of six children, two boys and four girls. He was the youngest son; for some reason, his mother favoured him over his older brother Felix. I had heard that when Lazare went to the Mission School in Fort St. James, his mother moved to that village to be near him. He was so unhappy away from Stoney Creek that he and his mother returned to our village after one year, and Lazare never went to school again.

28 Poor Lazare . . . in my distress at being ordered to marry and leave my family, it did not occur to me that he might be equally unhappy. He was no more consulted about his wishes than I was. As I was to discover, he was just as shy as his reluctant bride.

29 The day I dreaded arrived. The priest came to the village to say Mass. I felt as if this must be happening to someone else—it couldn't be me, Mary Paul, the girl who wanted nothing more than to live with her parents forever, who, if she left them, yearned for a career in a hospital or in a home with nice things. It couldn't be me putting on my Sunday dress and the coat I had bought so happily from the Army and Navy Store two years before. Could it be me walking to the Catholic Church in our village to be united in matrimony with a man named Lazare John? But it was.

30 I had gained only one small victory. A widow was going steady with my mother's first cousin, and I convinced the two of them that they should be married on the same day as me. At least there would be others in the front of the church; everyone wouldn't be looking at me.

31 After the ceremony, I ran home alone. I crouched in a corner of our cabin and I cried with such violence that my chest hurt. I felt as if my world had come to an end, that I had been condemned to some terrible fate that would go on forever and ever.

32 My parents, my relatives, came in. They tried to comfort me. Nothing helped. To me it was just like going away to school again, but now I knew that from this journey I was taking, across the village and into the house of strangers, there was no return. Finally, in an effort to cheer me, my aunt called out to me, "Why are you crying? Tonight you are going to sleep with your husband!"

33 I cried louder than ever.

34 In a few minutes, Lazare came to our cabin. He didn't look at me. He said, "Come."

35 And I went with him, away from my parents' home.

36   Looking back, I think that I was lucky. If I had to marry—and I know that given the times and our culture, there was no escape from the decision of my parents and the watchmen—I was fortunate to marry a man as kind and decent as Lazare John. Many young Native girls were not as lucky.

37   So there I was, sixteen years old, married to a man who was a stranger to me. I was so ignorant, shy, afraid. All I wanted was to turn the clock back to the good old days before I knew that I would have to stand up in our little Catholic Church and find myself turned into a married woman.

38   It was like going away to school all over again. Now I lived only a walk of five minutes from my parents' home, just across the village, and I was as homesick as if I was one hundred miles away. I missed caring for my half-brothers and sisters, I missed Johnny's loud voice and Bella's companionship, and above all, I missed my mother.

39   As if this wasn't bad enough, my new mother-in-law showed from the beginning that she did not think I was good enough for her son. Her attitude was confusing to me because she and her husband, like my parents, must have talked to the watchmen and agreed to the marriage. "I agree," Chief John must have said when the band chief discussed the marriage with him. Mrs. John, like my stepfather, must have nodded agreement.

40   But once I was in her home, it was clear to me that she did not approve of the marriage. From the first day I walked into the John cabin, I knew she felt that because of my background, I was not good enough for her son.

41   Looking back now, I wonder if any girl would have been good enough for Lazare in her eyes. Perhaps the most highly born princess from the richest Native band would not have suited her. I had always heard that she was possessive and that Lazare was a "mother's boy." I soon found out that village gossip was right. Lazare was the most important person in her life. I think that she had great ambitions for Lazare. If he had to marry, she wanted him to marry someone with Native parents.

42   My parentage was not the only thing about me that Mrs. John did not like. In her eyes a good Native wife learned early how to dry fish and meat, how to prepare hides, how to trap and set nets and find the places where the berries grew. She came to believe that her son was saddled with a wife who would be a burden to him and to the John family.

43   I realize now how useless I must have seemed to her. In Native families it was the women, as much as the men, who made certain that there was plenty of dried meat and fish and berries. Most of the meat and fish were brought home by the men, but after that, almost all of the work—the drying, the smoking, the canning—was done by women.

44   Native women did more than make sure that the family had a good supply of food. The families depended on wives and mothers and grandmothers to make moccasins, jackets, and mitts out of hides. To make these things, Native women had to know how to take the skins of moose and deer and scrape them and wash them and oil them. Not only did that skill mean that

the family would be clothed, but also the moccasins, mitts, and jackets could be traded for clothing from white people, or sold for money.

45   How well a family survived often depended on the ability of the wife to do the things that my mother and Bella, and Mrs. John herself, did so easily. I had none of the skills that a good Native wife should have had. . . .

46   How often my mother-in-law was mad at me in the months after the wedding! "Don't you know how to do anything?" she would ask me.

47   I wanted to say to her, "I wasn't trained to do these things! It was my stepsister Bella who went out with my parents, who trapped and scraped hides and dried fish. I always stayed home and looked after the kids. That was the work I learned. I was more of a baby-sitter than anything else. Please, please don't blame me!"

48   Of course I didn't answer back. I didn't say one word! A young bride did not talk back to her mother-in-law. I kept silent, but there was no happiness in my silence. Deep down, I felt that her impatience was unfair.

49   When we are young and unhappy, we cannot imagine that people will change, that the person who despises us today will come to love us tomorrow. And yet that is what happened in my relationship with my mother-in-law. Before she died in the 1950s, we had grown very close to each other. When she was old and needed care, I was the one who looked after her. Every day I would go to her, make up her fire in the morning, take her a cup of tea. She was thankful to have me around.

50   But that was many years later—in 1929 and for some years after that, neither one of us could have believed that one day she would say to me, "Lazare got himself a good wife!"

51   Poor Lazare! In the first few months I was submissive, but as I came to know him better, I began to demand, quietly at first, but with increasing push as the years passed, that we live in a place of our own. I was not much of a fighter, but as year followed year, I became more and more determined that we must leave our corner of the downstairs room in the John home.

52   It wasn't a very even struggle, which is why it lasted so long. On the one side was a possessive mother and a son who would do anything to avoid making his mother sad. On the other side was a young girl who had never before stood up for herself, who had been trained to respect her husband and her elders and who had always done as she was told.

53   "When can we get our own cabin?" I would ask.

54   "Pretty soon," he would say.

55   Then I began to have babies. Winnie in 1930 when I was seventeen, Helen in 1932. And still we lived in that one room.

56   "Lazare," I would say, "you have to find us a place."

57   "Pretty soon," he would say.

58   I think that what finally forced him to break the ties with his mother was the fighting. In the end, when there wasn't an argument going on between his mother and me—with his mother doing most of the talking—there was an argument between me and Lazare. I was determined to get a home of my own.

59   The struggle to get my own place, the need for some privacy, for freedom from criticism and rejection, made me lose some of my shyness. In that struggle with Lazare and his mother, I was finally able to stand up for myself. I never became much of a fighter, but I did learn in the first four years of my marriage to wear away at my husband, like water flowing in a gentle but never-ending stream over a rock.

60   Finally, in 1933, Lazare could stand the bickering no longer. "Lazare," I said, "Your aunt will let us have her dead husband's shack. It is only one room, it is very small, but it will be big enough for us for the time being."

61   I waited for him to say "Pretty soon." He didn't. He said, "All right."

62   And so, after nearly five years of marriage spent in the home of my inlaws, Lazare and I and our two little girls finally had our own home.

63   It was so small, I was expecting again and I could see that with another baby in the shack, we would hardly be able to move in that tiny room. After a few months, I said to Lazare, "Let's start building."

64   I expected him to say "Pretty soon." He surprised me again. He said, "All right."

65   In those days, there was no help of any kind from the Department of Indian Affairs. We knew that if we wanted new housing, we were on our own. We saved a little bit of money to buy nails and other necessities, Lazare worked for some white people to get rough lumber for the floors and walls and ceiling, and we made the shakes for the roof ourselves. Within one year after we left the John home, we moved into our own two room cabin, one room downstairs, one room upstairs, furnished with a table and benches and beds that Lazare had made.

66   We moved in before the building was finished, but to me, finished or not, that cabin was heaven. There was room in it to move around, a place for the children to sleep upstairs, and above all, we were alone as a family. For ten years, that cabin was our home.

DISCUSSION QUESTIONS

1. Mary John writes that "the village of Stoney Creek was my world and I loved it." What was it about her life there that appealed to her?
2. Mary John says that not being allowed to enter any cafes in Vanderhoof didn't bother her as a little girl. Why do you think it didn't?
3. Were Mary John's first reactions to being married normal in your opinion?
4. In general, what is the mood of this autobiographical excerpt?

WRITING TOPICS

1. List the advantages and disadvantages of an arranged marriage and then incorporate these two lists into a paper in which you discuss the pros and cons of such an arrangement.
2. Assume you are Lazare John, and write a paragraph or two telling of your feelings upon being told you are to wed Mary.
3. Write an short essay contrasting Carrier seasonal food catching and processing with the steady supply of food purchased for cash in a supermarket.

THE MARRIAGE OF RED PAINT AND WHITE MAN'S DOG

James Welch

James Welch's *Fools Crow* is a richly textured novel filled with fascinating characters. The book opens a window on a world secure in traditional customs, language, and religion. The year is 1870 and the place is northwestern Montana where the Lone Eaters, a small band of Blackfeet, or Pikunis, are camped in the Two Medicine Territory near the Rocky Mountains, the "Backbone" of their universe. Encroaching Napikwans are a fearful threat, but these Americans have yet to destroy the Blackfeet world. (The terms *Blackfoot* and *Blackfeet* are used interchangeably.)

Welch focuses on three families to carry his story. The families of White Man's Dog and Red Paint are central to their community. White Man's Dog, the young protagonist, is learning from his father Rides-at-the-Door to become a Pikuni leader. In this family lodge, Rides-at-the-Door lives with three wives, Double Strike Woman, her sister Striped Face, and the young Kills-close-to-the-lake. Double Strike Woman is the mother of White Man's Dog and Running Fisher.

In a nearby lodge, Red Paint lives with her father Yellow Kidney, her mother Heavy Shield Woman, and her two young brothers. Not far away stands the lodge of Boss Ribs and his rebel son, Fast Horse. The Medicine Man Mik-api is another important member of the community. He teaches White Man's Dog about healing and spiritual power. The renegade Owl Child and his followers pursue a precarious path of attacking Napikwan settlements, thereby endangering Pikuni lives.

Welch reveals Pikuni values and beliefs through the maturation of the novel's major character, White Man's Dog. As a young boy, he received his name from following Victory Robe White Man, an old storyteller, about camp. At eighteen, the youth begins to earn a new name, Fools Crow, which will identify him as a mature husband, healer, and hero.

Prior to the excerpt from the novel reprinted here, one of the trials White Man's Dog must complete is a successful horse raid. Yellow Kidney, a great warrior and scout, leads the raid against the enemy Crows. Fast Horse and other young men accompany Yellow Kidney on this dangerous and exciting strike. During the raid, White Man's Dog distinguishes himself, but his friend Fast Horse commits a foolish act leading to Yellow Kidney's capture. In a dream, "Cold Maker" has told Fast Horse to move a big rock blocking an ice spring, and to provide warm hides and coals for his daughters. Having failed to locate the spring, Fast Horse should have turned back from the raid because his failure can endanger the expedition. Moreover, he recklessly runs into the Crow camp taunting the Crow warriors. He shouts a boast that endangers the success of the raid and the lives of his companions. Consequently, the Crows capture Yellow Kidney, cut off his fingers, and hold him awhile, before sending him home as an example. His mutilation mars the rest of his life. When the others return home without Yellow Kidney, his absence is a mystery that only Fast Horse understands. He alone knows his guilty secret.

Spirituality guides all aspects of Pikuni life. Hoping that Yellow Kidney still lives, his wife Heavy Shield Woman vows to lead the sacred Sun Dance, seeking spiritual help to bring her husband home. Yellow Kidney returns, and White Man's Dog rides to tell the other bands to gather for the Sun Dance. The excerpt continues with White Man's Dog return from visiting the other bands. The ceremony involves telling the myth of Feather Woman, herself a wife and mother. Her son Poia (Scar Face) is the hero who instructed the Blackfeet about the purpose of the Sun Dance and how to conduct the ceremony.

1　　White Man's Dog had settled down into the routine of the winter camp but there were days when he longed to travel, to experience the excitement of entering enemy country. Sometimes he even thought of looking for Yellow Kidney. In some ways he felt responsible, at least partially so, for the horse-taker's disappearance. When he slept he tried to will himself to dream about Yellow Kidney. Once he dreamed about Red Old Man's Butte and the war lodge there, but Yellow Kidney was not in it. The country between the Two Medicine River and the Crow camp on the Bighorn was as vast as the sky, and to try to find one man, without a sign, would be impossible. And so he waited for a sign.

2　　In the meantime, he hunted. Most of the blackhorn herds had gone south, but enough remained to keep the hunters busy. It was during this season that the hides were prime, and the big cows brought particularly high prices. Very few of the men possessed the many-shots gun, so they hunted with bows and arrows. Their muskets were unwieldy, sometimes they misfired, and always they had to stop the chase to reload. Every man was determined to pile up as many robes as he could in order to buy a many-shots gun the following spring. It was rumored that the traders were bringing wagonloads of the new guns.

3   Most of the time White Man's Dog hunted with Rides-at-the-door and Running Fisher and a couple of his father's friends. Because the many-shots gun was so scarce, not even Rides-at-the-door possessed one, but the hunting group had grown adept at surprising the blackhorns, riding down on them and among them and getting off their killing shots. They kept Double Strike Woman, Striped Face and Kills-close-to-the-lake busy tanning the hides. Once in a while, White Man's Dog would go off by himself to hunt nearer the Backbone. On those occasions he spent much of his time staring off at the mountains. He longed to cross over them to see what he might encounter, but the high jagged peaks and deep snow frightened him. There were no blackhorns in that country, but there were many bighorns and long-legs. Once he came upon two long-legs who had locked antlers during a fight and were starving to death. Both animals were on their knees, their tongues hanging out of their mouths. Although they were large animals, their haunches had grown bony and their ribs stuck out. White Man's Dog felt great pity for the once-proud bulls. He got down from his horse and walked up to them. They were too weak to lift their heads. He drove an arrow into each bull's heart and soon their heads dropped and their eyes lost depth. He did not even think to dig out their canine teeth, which were much valued as decorations for dresses. As he climbed on his gray horse, he thought of next summer when these bulls would be just bones, their antlers still locked together. He went home without killing anything more that day.

4   But he killed many animals on his solitary hunts and he left many of them outside the lodge of Heavy Shield Woman. Sometimes he left a whole blackhorn there, for only the blackhorn could provide for all the needs of a family. Although the women possessed kettles and steel knives, they still preferred to make spoons and dippers out of the horns of the blackhorn. They used the hair of the head and beard to make braided halters and bridles and soft-padded saddles. They used the hoofs to make rattles or glue, and the tails to swat flies. And they dressed the dehaired skins to make lodge covers and linings and clothes and winding cloths. Without the blackhorn, the Pikunis would be as sad as the little bigmouths who howled all night.

5   Because there were always dogs lurking about, White Man's Dog would halloo the lodge and then turn and ride off. Once, Red Paint emerged before he could get away, and he stammered something about meat and galloped his horse clear out of camp. But he had looked on her, and afterward her vision came frequently. Sometimes when he imagined himself in his own lodge, her face would float across the fire from him. She was almost a

woman and he didn't know when this had happened. It seemed less than a moon ago she had been a skinny child helping her mother gather firewood or dig turnips; now, her eyes and mouth had begun to soften into those of a young woman and her dress seemed to ride more comfortably on her shoulders and hips. Except for that one time she had surprised him, White Man's Dog observed her only from a distance. He had acted foolish and he knew she would scorn him.

6   One day while he stood on the edge of camp watching the children slide down a long hill on their blackhorn-rib sleds, he had the uncomfortable feeling that he too was being watched. For an instant he thought it might be Red Paint, but when he looked up the hill behind him he saw Fast Horse, arms folded, near the brow. They had not talked much since returning from the raid, had rarely sought each other out. On the few occasions they did get together, Fast Horse seemed sullen. He no longer made jokes at White Man's Dog's expense; he no longer joked with anybody. He didn't brag about his buffalo-runner or flirt with the girls. He didn't hunt with the others and he tended his horses poorly, allowing them to wander a good distance from camp. Most of the time the day-riders would bring them back, but once seven of them disappeared and Fast Horse accepted the loss with a shrug. If the weather was good, he would go off to hunt by himself, seldom returning with meat. When the storms came down from the north, from Cold Maker's house, he would go inside his father's lodge and sulk. His father, Boss Ribs, keeper of the Beaver Medicine, often asked White Man's Dog to talk to Fast Horse, to try to learn the nature of this mysterious illness. Boss Ribs was sure that a bad spirit had entered his son's body. But Fast Horse would have little to do with his friend. Once White Man's Dog almost told Boss Ribs of his son's dream of Cold Maker, but to tell another's dream could make one's own medicine go bad, so he held his tongue. But it troubled him that Fast Horse had not made good on his vow to Cold Maker. The helping-to-eat moon was nearly over and Fast Horse had not yet acquired the prime blackhorn hides for Cold Maker's daughters. To break this vow was unthinkable; it could make things hard for all the Pikunis. But White Man's Dog had another reason for wanting the vow honored. It had come to him one night while lying in bed listening to the wind blow snow against the lodge. Perhaps Cold Maker, not the Crows, held Yellow Kidney prisoner. Perhaps he was waiting for the vow to be fulfilled before he would set the warrior free.

7   The next day White Man's Dog caught up with Fast Horse just as the young man was starting out on a hunt.

8   "Fast Horse, I would like to talk."

9   Fast Horse glanced at him. A fog had come down during the night and the air was gray between them. "Hurry, then. You see I am off to hunt."

10   "That night you caught up with us at Woman Don't Walk—you told us about a vow you made to Cold Maker."

11   Fast Horse looked away toward the Backbone.

12 "You vowed two hides. And you vowed the red coals for the eyes of his daughters. Because of these vows you said he spared your life."

13 "You stop me to tell me what I already know?"

14 "I have come to tell you to fulfill your vows. The helping-to-eat moon is passing and soon it will be too late. If a vow—"

15 Fast Horse laughed. "So you think I am incapable of keeping my word. You think Fast Horse has become a weakling, without honor."

16 "No, no! But I wish to hunt with you. I would like to help you acquire the hides." White Man's Dog hesitated, but he knew he would have to go on. "You see, I have it in my mind that Cold Maker holds Yellow Kidney prisoner and will not let him go until this vow is fulfilled. It is your failure that keeps Yellow Kidney from his people."

17 The look on Fast Horse's face almost frightened White Man's Dog. It was a look of hatred, cold and complete. For an instant White Man's Dog thought of taking back his words. But then he saw another look come into the eyes, a combination of fear and hopelessness, and he knew he had been right to confront his friend.

18 "I will get the blackhorns. I do not need you—or anybody. I am a man and have done no wrong." Fast Horse kicked the buffalo-runner he had acquired from the Crows in the ribs and led the two packhorses away from camp.

19 As White Man's Dog watched him ride away, he knew there was something going on inside of Fast Horse that he didn't understand. But it had to do with something other than his vow to Cold Maker. It had to do with Yellow Kidney.

20 White Man's Dog had given five of his best horses to Mik-api upon returning from the Crow raid. They had sweated together and prayed together, thanking the Above Ones for the young man's return. White Man's Dog thanked Mik-api and gave him a horsehair bridle he had made the previous winter. He left the old man's lodge feeling pure and strong.

21 But he was back the next day, this time with some real-meat that his mother had given him. The two men ate and talked, and then White Man's Dog left. But he came back often, always with food, for he had never seen any provisions in the old many-faces man's lodge. Mik-api lived alone on the edge of camp and received few visitors. He performed healing ceremonies to drive out the bad spirits, and White Man's Dog grew fascinated with his powers. He had never paid much attention to heavy-singers-for-the-sick. Their way seemed like magic to him, and he was fearful to learn too much. But sometimes as he and Mik-api talked, the old man would mix up his medicines or sort through his powerful objects and White Man's Dog did not see much to be afraid of.

22 One day Mik-api asked White Man's Dog to prepare the sweat lodge, and that was the beginning of the young man's apprenticeship. As he repaired the willow frame and pulled the blackened hides in place, he

thought of his actions as a favor to Mik-api. He built up a great fire and rolled the stones into the hot coals. He carried a kettle of water into the sweat lodge. He added more wood to the fire. He felt strong and important, and he was glad to help the old man.

23   When Mik-api and his patient, a large middle-age man with yellow skin, were settled in the sweat lodge, White Man's Dog carried the large stones with a forked stick into the lodge. He set them, one by one, into a rock-lined depression in the center. Then he stood outside and listened to the water explode with a hiss as the many-faces man flicked it on the stones with his blackhorn-tail swab.

24   Sometimes Mik-api would go into the sweat lodge alone to purify himself when he had to go to a person who was gravely ill. White Man's Dog would hold Mik-api's robe while listening to the old man sing and pray. He was always surprised at how thin and pale Mik-api was. He always reminded himself that he would have to bring even more meat next time. He had taken to accompanying Mik-api to the sick person's lodge, carrying the healing paraphernalia. Mik-api would clear the lodge and step inside. White Man's Dog would wait outside for as long as he could, listening to the singing, the prayers, the rattles and the eagle-bone whistle. Often these healings took all day, sometimes more. Eventually, White Man's Dog would go to his father's lodge to eat or nap, but he would come back to see if Mik-api needed anything.

25   Later, in Mik-api's lodge, as he tended the fire, White Man's Dog would watch the frail old man sleep his fitful sleep and wonder at his power. But the young man had not thought to possess such power. He was just happy to help.

26   One day while Mik-api was sorting through various pigments he said, "Now that we have changed your luck and you have proven yourself a great thief of Crow horses, you must begin to think of other things." Often Mik-api teased him, so White Man's Dog waited for the joke. And it occurred to him that the others had quit teasing him so unmercifully. He was no longer the victim of jokes, at least not more so than any of the others. No one had called him dog-lover since the raid on the Crows. He hadn't really noticed it until now, but the people seemed to respect him. He felt almost foolish with this knowledge, as though he had grown up and hadn't noticed that his clothes no longer fit him.

27   And now Mik-api was telling him about a dream he had the night before. "As I slept, Raven came down to me from someplace high in the Backbone of the World. He said it was behind Chief Mountain and there he dwelt with several of his wives and children. One night as they were bedding down he heard a great commotion in the snow beneath their tree, and then he heard a cry that would tear the heart out of the cruelest of the two-leggeds. When Raven looked down in the almost-night, he could see that it was a four-legged, smaller than a sticky-mouth but with longer claws and hair thicker than the oldest wood-biter. The creature looked up at Raven and said, 'Help

me, help me, for I have stumbled into one of the Napikwans' traps and now the steel threatens to bite my leg off.' Well, Raven jumped down there and tried to pull the jaws apart, but they wouldn't budge. Then he summoned his wives and children to help, but nothing would make those jaws give." Mik-api stopped and lit his pipe with a fire stick. He leaned back against his backrest and smoked for a while. "Then Raven remembered his old friend Mik-api, and so he came last night and told me of his sorrow. We smoked several pipefuls and finally Raven said, 'I understand you now have a helper who is both strong and true of heart. It will take such a man to release our four-legged brother. My hearts breaks to see him so, and his pitiful cries keep my wives awake. If you will send this young man, I will teach him how to use this creature's power, for in truth only the real-bear is a stronger power animal.' Then my brother left, and when I awoke I found this dancing above the fire." Mik-api handed White Man's Dog a pine cone. It was long and oval-shaped and came to a point at one end. "I believe this came from Raven's house up in the Backbone."

28   White Man's Dog felt the pine cone. It had hairs coming out from under its scales. He had never seen such a pine cone. "How will I find this place?" he said.

29   Mik-api broke into a smile. "I will tell you," he said.

30   Red Paint sat outside her mother's lodge in the warm sunshine of mid-morning. Her robe, gathered around her legs. was almost too warm. Her shiny hair was loose around her neck, framing a bird-bone and blue-bead choker. Her light, almost yellow eyes were intent on the work before her. She had passed, over the winter, from child to woman with hardly a thought of men, although judging by the frequency with which they rode by her mother's lodge, the young men had thought plenty about her. It was clear that when or if Yellow Kidney returned, he would be besieged with requests to court his daughter. But for now, as she bent over her beadwork, she was concerned with other things. Her mother, Heavy Shield Woman, had become so preoccupied with her role as Medicine Woman at the Sun Dance that she hadn't noticed her two sons were becoming boastful and bullying to their playmates. One Spot had even tried to kill a dog with his bow and arrow. And, too, Red Paint was worried about a provider. Although White Man's Dog still kept them in meat, she felt that one day he would grow weary of this task. Without a hunter, they might have to move on to another band, to the Many Chiefs, to live with her uncle, who had offered to take them in.

31   She held up the pair of moccasins she had been beading. She had taken up beadwork for other people, particularly young men who had no one to do it for them. She was good and her elaborate patterns were becoming the talk of the camp. In exchange, the young men gave her skins and meat, cloth, and the Napikwans' cooking powder. They brought her many things for her work, they tried to outgive each other, but she paid attention only to their goods. Now she looked for flaws in the pattern on the moccasins.

She wanted them to be perfect. They were for her mother to wear at the Sun Dance ceremony. She stretched her neck and allowed her eyes to rest on the figure astride the gray horse moving away from camp in the direction of the Backbone. The white capote[1] that the rider wore blended in with the patches of snow and tan grass. Beyond, the mountains looked like blue metal in the bright light. Red Paint bent once again to her work, sewing the small blue beads with an intensity that made her eyes ache.

32   In a draw just below the south slope of Chief Mountain, White Man's Dog made his camp. He built a shallow lean-to of sticks and pine boughs and covered the floor with branches of fir. He had enough branches left over to cover the entrance. Then, in the dying light, as the sun turned Heart Butte to the south red, he gathered the wispy black moss from the surrounding trees and balled it up. He struck his fire steel into this ball until he coaxed a yellow flame. He piled on pieces of rough bark stripped from the lower dead twigs of the trees and soon had a fire. He put several twigs on the fire and sat back. Even three moons ago he would have been afraid to be alone in the mountains of the Backbone. As he watched the chunk of meat on a tripod before him sizzle and splatter the fire, he felt comfortable and strong. The fat real-bears would still be sleeping in their dens and the bigmouths would be hunting in packs on the plains.

33   The young man thought about the following day, for it would be the most important in his life. He knew where to find the four-legged trapped in the steel jaws. Mik-api had given him good directions, and the spot was less than half a day distant. He put the hood of his capote over his head and felt the hunger gnawing at his belly. If his luck stood up, he would find the spot behind Chief Mountain, release the four-legged and be back to this site by nightfall. He was certain that the animal was a wolverine. Mik-api would not call it by name, for to name another man's power animal would rob that man of its medicine. So Mik-api had pretended dumb. But White Man's Dog knew that the skunk-bear was the only animal as fierce as the real-bear, although smaller. He took the roasted meat off the fire, and when it cooled he cut off a small piece and placed it carefully in the fork of a tree a short distance away. Then he ate greedily, for it was his first food since morning. The yellow fire reflected off the silvery needles of the firs around him.

34   The croak was so deep and close, he thought he had been awakened by his gut rumbling. It took a moment to realize he was not in his father's warm lodge. He pushed aside the boughs covering the entrance and looked out into the gray light. He had slept well in his small shelter, but now his breath told him that it was very cold—and still. He heard the croak again and looked up into the trees. The sky was lighter above them. The granite face of the great mountain loomed through the trees, and the yellow light

---

[1] *capote:* a long cloak with a hood.

of Sun Chief struck the very top. He rolled out and stood up, and there in the pine where he had placed the meat sat a fat raven.

35   White Man's Dog ate a piece of cold meat and the patient raven watched him. When he had finished and gathered up his gear, the raven flew away through the trees, away to the west into the mountains. White Man's Dog looked down into the clearing where his hobbled horse grazed. There was enough grass showing thorough the snow and a stream nearby. He turned and followed the raven.

36   The shiny black bird led him up into the mountains, following a game trail on the side of a deep ravine. The winds had scoured the side, leaving only an occasional drift of snow behind rocks and downed timber. Then the bird flew up and across a massive slide of scree, dipping and bobbing its effortless way through the late morning sun. It disappeared over the top of a ridge. The way was harder for White Man's Dog, for although the scree was mostly frozen and offered firm footing, sometimes it gave way and he slid some way down the slope. Four times he slid off the hardly-there trail; each time took a little more effort to climb back up.

37   Finally he stood at the top of the ridge, sweating and panting, and looked around. To the south and west he could see Heavy Shield Mountain and, at the base, Jealous Woman Lake. Beyond, he could make out Old Man Dog Mountain; then, south again, Rising Wolf and Feather Woman—all mountains of the Backbone—and he prayed to Old Man, Napi, who had created them, to guide him and allow him to return to his people. He looked down the other side of the ridge and saw the raven, sitting in a snag beside a pothole lake that was covered with snow. Below the lake, in a grove of quaking-leaf trees, he made out the shiny ice and open water of a spring that led away to the north. "Oh, Raven," he cried, "do not lead me too far from my people, for the day approaches its midpoint." At that, the raven glided down to the shiny ice and lit on a rock beside the bubbling dark hole of water.

38   The footing was good on this side of the ridge, and White Man's Dog trotted down on a slant, now one way, now the other, until he was circling the lake, his heavy fur moccasins leaving a soft flat imprint in the wet snow. He slid down the steep incline on the far side of the lake. The snow was firm, but going back would not be easy. Once down, he pulled his musket from its tanned hide covering and tapped some powder in the barrel from his blackhorn flask. Then he heard the raven call to him. He was sitting on a branch of one of the delicate quaking-leaf trees not fifty paces ahead. "You do not need your weapon, young man. There is nothing here to harm you."

39   White Man's Dog felt his eyes widen, and his heart began to beat like a drum in his throat. Raven laughed the throaty laugh of an old man. "It surprises you that I speak the language of the two-leggeds. It's easy, for I have lived among you many times in my travels. I speak many languages. I converse with the blackhorns and the real-bears and the wood-biters. Bigmouth and I discuss many things." Raven made a face. "I even deign to speak once in a while with the swift silver people who live in the water—but they are

dumb and lead lives without interest. I myself am very wise. That is why Mik-api treats me to a smoke now and then."

40 White Man's Dog dropped his weapon and fell to his knees. "Oh, pity me, Raven! I am a nothing-man who trembles before your power. I do not wish to harm my brothers. I was afraid of this place and what I might find."

41 "It is proper that you humble yourself before me, White Man's Dog, for in truth I am one of great power." Raven allowed himself a wistful smile. "But my power is not that of strength. Here you see your brother, Skunk Bear, is caught in the white man's trap and I have not the strength to open it. In all of us there is a weakness." Raven dropped down out of the tree behind a patch of silvery willows. "Here," he croaked.

42 White Man's Dog crept around the willows and saw a large dark shape in the white snow. Behind it the spring gurgled out of the earth's breast. The wolverine lifted his head, and his eyes looked darkly at the young man.

43 "So you see how it is," said Raven. "He has been trapped for four days, and now he is too weak to cry out. You may release him."

44 "He will not bite me?"

45 Raven laughed, the harsh *caw! caw!* echoing around the white field. "You are his enemy for sure, but even Skunk Bear has a little common sense."

46 White Man's Dog approached the animal from the rear. The big spring trap had bitten the left hind leg. The reddish-brown hair was caked with blood, and White Man's Dog could see gnawed bone where the wolverine had tried to chew his leg off. He must have been too weak, for the bone was still in one piece. White Man's Dog placed the trap on the tops of his thighs and pushed down with all his strength on the springy steel on either side of the jaws. The jaws gaped open and the leg came free. With a hiss the animal tried to scramble away but he only dug into the snow. He showed his teeth but the head drooped and finally rested on his forelegs.

47 "Throw him some of your real-meat, for it has strength in it to fix up this beast. I brought him some pine cones but he is not equipped to dig out the seeds. In four days he has eaten only one mouse who got too curious." Raven hopped over to the trap and looked at it. "You see, this animal has a weakness too—he is a glutton and cannot live long without food."

48 White Man's Dog watched the wolverine chew off bits of the meat and swallow them. He marveled at the animals' long thick fur with the dirty yellow stripes along the flanks. The claws that held the meat were as long as his own fingers.

49 "And now you must get down the mountain. I have medicine that will fix up this glutton's leg. I would guide you down but my wives are irritable with lack of sleep. If they had their way they would pluck out this creature's eyeballs at the first opportunity. You may leave a little of that meat for them. This time of year the pickings are lean."

50 White Man's Dog thanked Raven and as he turned to leave, he glanced at the wolverine. The animal was watching him with a weak ferocity.

51   "By the way," called Raven, "when you enter your close-to-the-ground house tonight, lie on your left side, away from the entrance. Dream of all that has happened here today. Of all the two-leggeds, you alone will possess the magic of Skunk Bear. You will fear nothing, and you will have many horses and wives. But you must not abuse this power, and you must listen to Mik-api, for I speak through him, that good many-faces man who shares his smoke."

*   *   *   *

52   White Man's Dog came that evening just as Sun Chief ended his journey. Families were getting together to feast and sing and to compare their new possessions. In the middle of camp, young men sat around a large fire, weapons across their laps, and sang wolf songs. Young women strolled arm in arm around the perimeter, sometimes doing a dance step, other times trailing a robe over the head of a young man. Running Fisher was part of a drum group, and he sang and watched the girls.

53   White Man's Dog led the gray horse into camp, watching the various activities. From time to time, he heard the *pop* of a rifle or the taunting yodel of a young brave, meant to frighten an imaginary enemy.

54   A small boy fell in step with White Man's Dog. "What happened to your horse?"

55   "He stepped on a sharp rock." White Man's Dog recognized the boy as One Spot, Red Paint's younger brother. He wore only a breechcloth and moccasins. His cheeks were painted a bright yellow.

56   "Couldn't you ride him?"

57   "Not since morning. He's been lame all day."

58   They walked in silence for a way. Then the boy said, "I have a faster horse," and darted between two lodges to join some children who were playing with a gopher.

59   Rides-at-the-door greeted his son outside the lodge. He had been standing there, smoking, watching the drum group. "My son! It is good to see you."

60   The two men embraced and White Man's Dog knew his father had been worried. "I would have come sooner but I stayed a night with the Black Patched Moccasins. Then this horse came up lame. Mad Plume sends you his greetings."

61   "Ah, a good man, Mad Plume. Come inside and eat, my son. Your mother has been worried about you."

62   Later that night the two men walked over to the lodge of Three Bears. White Man's Dog followed his father in and when he straightened up he was surprised to see so many people present. Three Bears sat at the head of the fire, away from the entrance.

63   "Welcome, my son. Come here and sit beside me. You have been gone too long."

64   White Man's Dog looked at his father. Rides-at-the-door smiled. And so the young man sat in the place of honor and told of all the greetings that had been sent to Three Bears and the Lone Eaters. He told them of Mountain Chief's flight to Canada.

65   "Was Owl Child with them?"

66   "No one knew. But most felt he was, that the seizers had chased Owl Child and his gang to the camp of the Many Chiefs. That's why they all had to run."

67   Three Bears muttered his disgust. All the people fell silent. And that's when White Man's Dog noticed Red Paint. She was sitting beside her mother, a black cloth shawl over her head. He glanced at Heavy Shield Woman; then he looked around the group. Yellow Kidney was not among them. Although Red Paint was several paces away, this was the closest White Man's Dog had been to her She was watching him.

68   "And what about the purpose of your travels?"

69   White Man's Dog looked at Three Bears as if he hadn't understood. But he recovered his wits. "I went from band to band—the only people I didn't see were the Many Chiefs—and they all expressed their approval. They were happy to learn of Heavy Shield Woman's vow and of her good fortune in having Yellow Kidney return to her. They said they knew she was a virtuous woman and would help to make the Sun Dance ceremony a success. They also said they would do anything she required of them. Many prayers were said, and many of the women said they would assist Heavy Shield Woman."

70   Three Bears picked up his medicine pipe. He looked at Heavy Shield Woman. "It would seem that all of our people are in agreement with your desire, sister. The way is clear for you to begin your preparations. You have witnessed the Sun Dance many times and you have seen the role of the Sacred Vow Woman. Many women would not accept such a role because the way is arduous. Only the strongest of our women have made such a vow, because one needs great strength to prepare for and carry out her duties. If you are successful, the Pikunis will prosper and enjoy favor with the spirit world. If you fail, if you are not strong or virtuous enough, great harm will come to us." Three Bears looked slowly from face to face within the circle. "We are one, sister, in our approval. Do you accept the role of the Sacred Vow Woman?"

71   Heavy Shield Woman did not hesitate. "I made this vow in a time of great distress. My heart had fallen down, but I told my children that their father would return to them. I don't know now if I believed it then. But I prayed to the Above Ones, to Sun Chief, to our Mother Earth, to allow my man to come home to me. My heart lightened somewhat because I knew the spirits had listened to me and took pity. They would not desert me and my children in our time of sadness. That's when I came to you, Three Bears. I knew when I talked with you that Yellow Kidney would be returned." Here, Heavy Shield Woman's voice almost faltered as she thought of her pitiful husband. "That has happened, and so I say to you,

and to the others present, I am strong and glad in my heart to be the Sacred Vow Woman."

72 "We will smoke this pipe," said Three Bears. "We will pray for our sister's success."

73 Outside the lodge, White Man's Dog breathed in the fresh air and looked up at the stars. His father had stayed to talk with Three Bears. He looked at the stars and listened to the drumming and singing and he was happy. He would sleep well.

74 "I wish to thank you, White Man's Dog."

75 He turned his head to the voice and saw Heavy Shield Woman and Red Paint. He was too tired to be startled.

76 "I know your journey was long and you missed out on the trading. Your mother told me."

77 "No, I—I wanted to make the journey. It was good."

78 "Your words tonight set my heart at ease." Heavy Shield Woman smiled, and White Man's Dog felt the warmth of it. "There have been times when I wished another had made a similar vow. I would have gladly relinquished mine. But when I saw your face I knew there were no others and it made me happy."

79 "The other women, they were happy too. They said Heavy Shield Woman is one of great resolve, of great virtue, of great, great . . ."

80 The woman laughed at White Man's Dog's struggle for fine words. Red Paint laughed, and then he laughed. He laughed long and loud. He had never been this happy—or exhausted. His feet ached, he was weary in his bones, but being near Red Paint made even his weariness seem a thing of joy.

81 He wiped away the tears and Heavy Shield Woman said, "And thank you—for hunting for us. You can't know—" She turned and walked away quickly.

82 Red Paint had not spoken and she didn't speak now. She stepped forward and touched his arm. She smiled but there were tears in her eyes. Then she turned and followed her mother.

83 "And what about you, young man? Now that you are rich and powerful, it is time for you to take a wife." Mik-api lay just inside the entrance to his lodge. The Lone Eaters had returned the day before to the Two Medicine River from the trading house, and the trip had tired him. The lodge skins were raised and he could see White Man's Dog from where he lay.

84 White Man's Dog sat just outside in the warm sun, rubbing an oily cloth over his new single-shot. He had been firing it earlier that morning, and he was still in awe of its power and accuracy. On his third shot, he had killed a prairie hen at a hundred paces. When he retrieved it, he found only a tangle of feathers and bone.

85 "As a heavy-singer-for-the-sick I encounter many people. Sometimes they want my healing, other times just to talk. They think they want me to tell them important things, but most often it's the other way around. Just the

other day I was invited into the lodge of my friend Yellow Kidney. In passing he mentioned that he would be forever grateful to you for sharing your kills with his family. I told him that you were now a man and becoming adept in the ways of medicine. I told him you had acquired power much stronger than that of the other young ones, that you would one day distinguish yourself among our people. Of course, I was joking to cheer the poor man up."

86   White Man's Dog smiled.

87   "Then I happened to notice Red Paint, who sat across the lodge engaged in her beadwork, and I mentioned that it was too bad our young women seem to favor these beads over quillwork. Yellow Kidney agreed with me but said Red Paint did it for others in exchange for goods. Then he became very sad and held up his fingerless hands and said that he was worse than useless to his family, that Red Paint would grow up poor and no man would have her."

88   White Man's Dog turned around to face the old man. Mik-api sucked on his pipe and looked out the entrance at nothing in particular. His eyes crinkled as though he were straining to see something.

89   "I felt sorry for the poor man and, like a fool, said that I might know somebody who would keep her well. Of course, that person would have to hunt for the whole family now. But now that I think on it, perhaps there is nobody that rich and powerful among the Lone Eaters. Perhaps Yellow Kidney will have to seek out such a person among the Small Brittle Fats or the Hard Topknots. I understand there are among them a few young men rich and powerful enough."

90   "Would you speak for me, Mik-api?" White Man's Dog heard the voice far away. His heart was too far in his throat for the words to come from him.

91   "Slow down, you foolish young one. You're getting as bad as me. First, you must go to your father and mother and tell them of your intentions. If they agree, I will talk to Yellow Kidney. But what makes you think Red Paint would want such a fool?"

92   White Man's Dog suddenly slumped back. He remembered Little Bird Woman, Crow Foot's daughter. But only Double Strike Woman had mentioned her as a possible wife. Perhaps Rides-at-the-door and Crow Foot were not aware of such an arrangement. Nothing had happened. He had not even spoken to Little Bird Woman. White Man's Dog jumped up. "I will speak with them now, Mik-api. I'll be back."

93   Double Strike Woman argued that it would be advantageous for the two families to be united; that Little Bird Woman was sought after by many men, young and old; that she was built to bear many children.

94   "Just think of Crow Foot. Many say he will be the next head chief of the Pikunis. They say he is already more important than Mountain Chief, because Mountain Chief is always on the run."

95   "I don't mind you wanting to marry off this young man, but next time you will consult with me before you do such a thing." Rides-at-the-door was angry. Most of the time, he left things in the lodge up to his sits-beside-him

wife, but he too had been thinking of his son's future. In truth, he had been just as surprised, shocked even, as Double Strike Woman at White Man's Dog's request. He hadn't known of his son's interest in Red Paint. And if he were to be honest with himself, he would have admitted that the idea was not appealing to him, not because of Red Paint but because White Man's Dog would have to provide for the entire family.

96 "I only want what is best for my son," said Double Strike Woman. "If he were to marry into Crow Foot's family, he would have more opportunities."

97 "You can see he doesn't want Little Bird Woman. He wants to marry Red Paint. He is a man now."

98 "And what about Yellow Kidney? He will have to marry Yellow Kidney, too, and support him and that whole family! People will make jokes. People will say, There goes Rides-at-the-door's son, he marries whole families."

99 And what about you, my son? Do you think you can take such jokes?"

100 "They will not joke for long," said White Man's Dog.

101 Rides-at-the-door studied his son.

102 Kills-close-to-the-lake looked up from her quillwork. She had been following the conversation intently. In the brief silence, she too studied White Man's Dog. Without thinking about it, she had been anticipating this time when White Man's Dog would leave the lodge. But she couldn't believe it was actually happening. With him gone, there would be nothing left for her. But there had been nothing anyway—only his presence and some vague hope. Now it was all gone."

103 "Your mother and I give you our permission, son. You may propose a marriage to Red Paint and her family. She is a good young woman and will make you happy."

104 White Man's Dog sneaked a look at his mother, but she was busy cutting meat. He stood and walked to the entrance. "Thank you," he said. He looked down at Kills-close-to-the-lake, but she was bent over her quillwork. "Thank you," he said again. He ducked out of the lodge and ran all the way to Mik-api's.

105 Four sleeps later the families got together and exchanged gifts. White Man's Dog gave Yellow Kidney three of his best horses. His father gave Yellow Kidney four horses, three ropes of tobacco and a full headdress he had taken from a Parted Hair. Yellow Kidney gave White Man's Dog four horses and a beaded shirt. He gave Rides-at-the-door five horses and a Napikwan saddle. Double Strike Woman gave Red Paint a pair of white beaded medallions for her hair. She hugged the girl briefly.

106 Earlier, Rides-at-the-door had presented his new many-shots gun to White Man's Dog. "You're going to have to do a lot of hunting now." White Man's Dog then gave his single-shot to his father. "Between you and Running Fisher, you now have two shots."

107 White Man's Dog had left nothing to chance. The day before, he had gone to the camp of the Grease Melters to look up a man who specialized

in Liars' Medicine. The man constructed two bark figures—a man and a woman—and poured the magic liquid between them. That would ensure good loving. He charged his client a large packhorse he had noticed during the trade.

108   Now, on the twenty-third day of the new-grass moon, Red Paint moved her things into the small tipi beside the big lodge of Rides-at-the-door. That night the families and friends feasted on boss ribs and tongues and buffalo hump. One of the men had brought a tin of the white man's water, and the feast soon turned loud and boisterous. White Man's Dog drank the liquor and talked and laughed, but he was a little disappointed that Kills-close-to-the-lake and Mik-api were not there. Mik-api had said, "I am an old man. Celebrations are for the young." White Man's Dog drank some more and laughed louder. Red Paint sat beside him, twirling her feather fan. All the noise had made her shy—but more than that, she couldn't believe she was a married woman. Less than seven sleeps ago, marriage had been the furthest thing from her thoughts. She had sought only to help her mother prepare for the Sun dance. Could it have been only seven sleeps ago that she had touched White Man's Dog's arm and smiled at him? Even then she had no thought that this might happen. And tonight—tonight they would go to their own lodge. She had thought occasionally of what it would be like to lie with a man, but there had been no reality to it. Her mother had said it would happen naturally and it would be good with the right man. Would White Man's Dog be the right man? She glanced at him and his face was shiny with sweat and oil. He sensed her eyes on him and turned. For a moment they looked upon each other; for the first time they looked into each other's eyes. Then Red Paint lowered her eyes to the twirling fan.

109   White Man's Dog stood and walked outside. He walked away from the lodge and stood in a small field. He smelled the fresh bite of sage grass and looked up at the stars, trying to locate the Seven Persons. His head was fuzzy with the liquor, but he became aware of a small hand on his. "The Seven Persons do not look upon us tonight," he said softly.

110   "They ride to the west, over there," said a voice that did not sound right to his ears. He turned and looked into the face of Kills-close-to-the-lake. Although she had not been at the feast, she was wearing her elkskin dress and rose medallions in her hair. The sharp sage grass gave way to the scent that made him lightheaded. She said, "I am very happy for you, White Man's Dog. I wish you to have this." And she turned and hurried off into the dark.

111   He watched her until he couldn't see her anymore. Then he unfurled the object. It was a soft-tanned scabbard for his new rifle. In the faint light of the fire-lit lodges, he could just make out the quillwork thunderbird design. Then the design blurred and he wiped his eyes.

112   Some time between the moon of flowers and Home Days, with the high hot sun turning the grass from green to pale straw, the Pikuni people began

to pack up their camps to begin the four-day journey to Four Persons Butte near the Milk River. Here, the Sacred Vow Woman and her helpers had determined to build a lodge for the Sun Chief, and here they meant to honor him with sacred ceremonies, songs and dances.

113   Heavy Shield Woman had purchased the Medicine Woman bundle from her predecessor, and her relatives in the camps had procured the sacred bull blackhorn tongues.

114   On the first day the people assembled near the confluence of the Two Medicine River and Birch Creek. Most of the bands arrived within the compass of the midmorning and midafternoon sun. As each band arrived, members of the All Crazy Dogs, the police society, showed them where to set up. Soon a great circle was formed, as the last of the bands, the Never Laughs, filled the perimeter. The Sacred Vow Woman's lodge was erected in the center and Heavy Shield Woman entered. Then the camp crier rode among the lodges, calling forth all the women who had vowed to come forward to the tongues. He beat his small drum and called for their husbands to accompany them. He stopped before the lodge of Heard-by-both-sides Woman, who had been a Sacred Vow Woman two years earlier, and called her to instruct Heavy Shield Woman in her duties.

115   When the chosen had been assembled in the lodge, Heard-by-both-sides Woman lifted one of the tongues above her head and asked Sun Chief to affirm that she had been virtuous in all things. All of the women did this. Then the dried tongues were boiled and cut up and placed in parfleches. Heavy Shield Woman began her fast.

116   The next day she led the procession to the second camp. On her travois she carried the Medicine Woman bundle and the sacred tongues. Four days they camped in four different locations, arriving at last on a flat plain beneath Four Persons Butte. Each day Yellow Kidney and the many-faces man, wise in the ritual of the Sun Dance, purified themselves in the sweat lodge.

117   The dawn of the fifth day, Low Horn, a celebrated warrior and scout, left his lodge, saddled his buffalo-runner and galloped down off the plain to the valley of the Milk River. As he rode, he examined the big-leaf trees around him. Across the river he spotted one that interested him. It was stout but not too thick. It was true and forked at just the right height. He looked at the tree, the way the sun struck it, and decided it was the chosen one.

118   When he reached camp—by now everyone was up and the breakfast fires were lit—he rode among the lodges, calling to the men of the Braves society. He ate a chunk of meat while the others saddled their horses. Then he led them back to the spot. Everybody-talks-about-him had been selected to chop it down, and he set upon it with his ax. He had killed many enemies. At midmorning, his bar back shiny with sweat, he gave a final blow and the tree groaned and swayed and toppled into a stand of willows. The men who had been waiting jumped upon the tree and began

to slash and hack, cutting off the limbs as though they were the arms and
legs of their enemies. Not too long ago, these would have been traditional
enemies; now, more than one of the Braves was killing the encroaching
Napikwans.

119   Heavy Shield Woman sat in the Sacred Vow lodge, her face drawn and
gray with her fast. Soon it would be over, but the thought of food had
become distant and distasteful. She listened to her helpers talk quietly
among themselves, but the words were not clear to her ears. She prayed to
the Above Ones, to the Below Ones and to the four directions for strength
and courage, but each time she began her prayers, her mind drifted and
she saw her husband as he had appeared at her lodge door after his long
absence. She had greeted him with high feelings, with much crying, hugging and wailing. She was overjoyed to have her man return. But later, as
they sat quietly, she had been surprised to feel only pity for him. He was
not the strong warrior who had left camp in that moon of the falling
leaves. This man was a shadow who looked at her with stone eyes, who no
longer showed feelings of love or hate or even warmth. And he had not
changed in the ensuing moons. He was no longer a lover, hardly even a
father to his children. Was he still a man? Had a bad spirit taken him over?
But she, Heavy Shield Woman, had changed too.

120   Her thoughts were interrupted by the entrance of Heard-by-both-sides
Woman and her husband, Ambush Chief. He carried the Medicine Woman
bundle and would serve as ceremonial master during the transfer. When all
the helpers, clad in gray blankets with red painted stripes, had seated
themselves, Ambush Chief began to open the bundle, praying and singing
as he did so. The first object he held up was the sacred elkskin dress. He
sang of the origin of the garment while the women put the dress on Heavy
Shield Woman. Then they draped an elkskin robe over her shoulders. One
by one, he removed the sacred objects: the medicine bonnet of weasel
skins, feather plumes and a small skin doll stuffed with tobacco seeds and
human hair; the sacred digging stick that So-at-sa-ki, Feather Woman, had
used to dig turnips when she was married to Morning Star and lived in the
sky with him and his parents, Sun Chief and Night Red Light. She and
Morning Star had an infant son named Star Boy.

121   Ambush Chief told of the time So-at-sa-ki, while digging turnips, had
dug up the sacred turnip, creating a hole in the sky. She looked down and
saw her people, her mother and father, her sister, on the plains and she
grew homesick. Night Red Light, upon hearing of her daughter-in-law's
act, became angry, for she had warned Feather Woman not to dig up the
sacred turnip. Sun Chief, when he returned from his journey, became
angry with Morning Star, for he had not kept his wife from doing this, and
so he sent Feather Woman back to earth to live with her people. She took
Star Boy with her because Sun did not want him in his house. She also
took the elkskin dress, the bonnet, the digging stick. She and her son rode

down the wolf trail back to her people, and she was happy to be with them. She hugged them and rejoiced, for she was truly glad to be home. But as the sleeps, the moons, went by, she began to miss her husband. Each morning she would watch him rise up. She shunned the company of her mother and father, her sister, even her son, Star Boy. She became obsessed with Morning Star, and soon she began to weep and beg him to take her back. But each morning he would go his own way, and it was not long before Feather Woman died of a broken heart.

122   As Star Boy began to grow up, a scar appeared on his face. The older he grew, the larger and deeper the scar grew. Soon his friends taunted him and called him Poia, Scar Face, and the girls shunned him. In desperation he went to a many-faces man who gave him directions to Sun Chief's home and whose wife made Scar Face moccasins for his journey. After much traveling, he reached the home of Sun Chief far to the west. Sun had just returned from his long trip across the sky and he was angry with Scar Face for entering his home. Sun Chief decided to kill him, but Night Red Light interceded on behalf of the unlucky young man. Morning Star, not knowing the youth was his son, taught him many things about Sun and Moon, about the many groups of Star People. Once, while on a hunt, seven large birds attacked Morning Star, intending to kill him, but Scar Face got to them first, killing them. When Morning Star told his father of this brave deed, Sun Chief removed the scar and told the youth to return to his people and instruct them to honor him every summer and he would restore their sick to health and cause the growing things and those that fed upon them to grow abundantly. He then gave Poia two raven feathers to wear so that the people would know he came from the Sun. He also gave him the elkskin robe to be worn by a virtuous medicine woman at the time of the ceremony. Star Boy then rode down the wolf trail to earth and instructed the Pikunis in the correct way, and then he returned to Sun's home with a bride. Sun made him a star in the sky. He now rides near to Morning Star and many people mistake him for his father. That is why he is called Mistake Morning Star. And that is how the Sun ceremony came to be.

123   While Ambush Chief related this story of Scar Face, three helpers were building an altar near the lodge door. They stripped off the sod and dry-painted Sun, Moon and Morning Star. They painted sun dogs on either side of Sun's face to represent his war paint. Then the helpers chanted and shook their rattles to pay homage to Sun and his family. When they finished, Ambush Chief stood and lifted his face.

124   "Great Sun! We are your people and we live among all your people of the earth. I now pray to you to grant us abundance in summer and health in winter. Many of our people are sick and many are poor. Pity them that they may live long and have enough to eat. We now honor you as Poia taught our long-ago people. Grant that we may perform our ceremony in the right way. Mother Earth, we pray to you to water the plains so that the

grass, the berries, the roots may grow. We pray that you will make the four-leggeds abundant on your breast. Morning Star, be merciful to your people as you wee to the one called Scar Face. Give us peace and allow us to live in peace. Sun Chief, bless our children and allow them long lives. May we walk straight and treat our fellow creatures in a merciful way. We ask these things with good hearts."

125   Before they left the lodge, the helpers with brushes obliterated their dry paintings, just as Sun had removed the scar from Poia.

126   Red Paint stood next to her husband and watched the procession. The ground was already becoming dusty from the people and horses. Earlier the people had been busy setting up their lodges, getting water from the clear, deep creek that came out of Four Persons Butte, gathering firewood. But now they were all here, watching the procession, moving to the beat of a single small drum. Red Paint was shocked at how old and bent her mother looked. She wasn't even certain that the woman was her mother. Her face was hidden by hanging the weasel skins. Two helpers held her up.

127   The procession circled halfway around the unfinished Medicine Lodge. Then they entered a sun shelter to the west of it. Here, the tongues were distributed to the sick, the poor, the children, to all who desired such communion. The women who had vowed to come forward to the tongues opened the parfleches and distributed pieces to the faithful. Heavy Shield Woman, weak from her lack of food, watched the people chew the tongues and she prayed, moving her lips, without words.

128   It was nearly dark by the time the men of the warrior societies began the task of erecting the center pole of the Medicine Lodge. With long poles they advanced from the four directions, singing to the steady drumbeat. With rawhide lines attached to their poles, they raised the cottonwood log until it stood in the hole dug to receive it. Heavy Shield Woman watched the proceedings with prayers and apprehension, for if it failed to stand straight, she would be accused of not being a virtuous woman. But it did stand, and the men began hurriedly to attach to it posts and poles around the perimeter of the lodge. Younger men began to pile brush and limbs over the structure. Now Heavy Shield Woman sighed and slumped into the arms of two of her assistants. They carried her back to her lodge, where the hot berry soup awaited her. She could break her fast.

129   For the next four days the weather dancers danced to the beat of rattles against drum. Warriors enacted their most courageous exploits and hung offerings on the center pole. For each deed they placed a stick on the fire until it blazed high night and day. In other lodges Sacred Pipe men and Beaver Medicine men performed their ceremonies for those who sought their help.

DISCUSSION QUESTIONS

1. Welch uses Raven as a character who helps White Man's Dog gain wolverine's power. Do you think Raven's role and actions are an effective device? Explain your answer with evidence from the text.
2. Does Welch have White Man's Dog perform for his prospective in-laws what Dorris called "groom service?" Justify your answer.
3. The author invents names that reflect a Pikuni point of view such as "many-shots" guns. Find other examples of this technique, and tell what they mean.
4. What is the function of the Feather Woman-Poia myth in relation to the Sun Dance ritual?
5. Find four examples of Pikuni religious or spiritual behavior and explain their significance.

WRITING TOPICS

1. Review the Lakota Sun Dance described by Luther Standing Bear in Chapter 3. Write an essay that contrasts and compares this Sun Dance with the Blackfeet Sun Dance Welch describes.
2. Select one of the following characters, and explain his or her role in the context of Pikuni life. Mik-api, Fast Horse, White Man's Dog, Red Paint, Heavy Shield Woman, Raven, Yellow Kidney.
3. Write two or three paragraphs on "The Spiritual Life of the Pikunis."

EARTH AND I GAVE YOU TURQUOISE

N. Scott Momaday

N. Scott Momaday, one of the premier poets of American literature, began writing poetry as a student at the University of New
Mexico and published his first poem "Earth and I Gave you
Turquoise," in the *New Mexico Quarterly* in 1959. This was probably
one of the poems in the collection that Momaday submitted to a creative writing contest sponsored by Stanford University. The distinguished poet Yvor Winters, who judged the poetry entries, awarded
Momaday a Wallace Stegner Creative Writing Fellowship to Stanford.
Winters admired Momaday's immense talent and became his mentor,
his friend, and a major influence on his early career. He convinced
the young student to pursue doctoral studies in American literature.
Momaday earned his Ph.D. in 1963 and later taught English and comparative literature in the University of California (both Santa Barbara
and Berkeley) and at Stanford. Since 1981, he has been Regents professor of English at the University of Arizona.

In 1974 Momaday taught for a year at the University of Moscow.
That year his first book of poems *Angle of Geese and Other Poems*
was published as a handsome chapbook followed by *The Gourd
Dancer* in 1976. These small volumes represent approximately
twenty years of poetic effort, suggesting that Momaday followed
Winter's advice: "any poet with a critical conscience will publish a
small body of work." *In the Presence of the Sun, Stories and Poems
1961–1991* contains some new poems.

"Earth and I Gave You Turquoise" reflects the Southwestern landscape, spiritually and physically. This stately poem seems to pause
between life and death as the lover slowly moves to join his beloved.
Momaday, who grew up among the Navajo, mentions place names
that locate his poem clearly within Navajo landscape and culture.
Chinle is a small town near the dramatic Canyon de Chelly area on
the Navajo Reservation in Arizona. This cultural context clarifies
many images.

Turquoise is cherished by Navajos as a bringer of good fortune
and well-being. Many Native Americans, including Navajos, believe

the owl signifies death. The final line of the first stanza expresses the hope for a reunion of the two lovers on Black Mountain, west of Chinle. The dancers who eat mutton and drink coffee follow typical Navajo patterns. Horses having a primary position in Navajo society, the narrator jubilantly tells his beloved that she will hear him racing toward her. Surrounded by real and perceived dangers, Navajos do not risk uttering the name of a deceased person for fear that his or her spirit will hear and think that it is being summoned. So the poem's narrator and his younger brother "have not spoken of you" although they sang sad songs. The same taboo makes "I will speak your name many times" an extremely poignant signal that the narrator anticipates being reunited in death with "you." Left bereft by her death, the poetic persona dreams of a full life blessed with abundant crops and children.

Earth and I gave you turquoise
    when you walked singing
We lived laughing in my house
    and told old stories
5 You grew ill when the owl cried
We will meet on Black Mountain

I will bring corn for planting
    and we will make fire
Children will come to your breast
10   You will heal my heart
I speak your name many times
The wild cane remembers you

My young brother's house is filled
    I go there to sing
15 We have not spoken of you
    but our songs are sad
When Moon Woman goes to you
I will follow her white way

Tonight they dance near Chinle
20   by the seven elms
There your loom whispered beauty
    They will eat mutton
and drink coffee till morning
You and I will not be there

25   I saw a crow by Red Rock
       standing on one leg
       It was the black of your hair
       The years are heavy
       I will ride the swiftest horse
30   You will hear the drumming hooves

Discussion Questions

1. Identify at least two clues that "you" and the narrator lived happily together.
2. What happened to the "you" in the poem, and how do you know?
3. In what sense do you think the speaker hopes to be reunited with the one who will heal his heart?
4. Why do you think the speaker includes "earth" in the title?

Writing Topics

1. There are numerous allusions to nature in this poem. In a short paper, discuss the effect of these allusions on the theme of the poem.
2. Read the poem aloud, emphasizing the rhythm. In a paragraph, discuss the metrical form (syllabics) of the poem, and explain the impact of this technique on the reader.

LOVE POEM

Leslie Silko

Leslie Silko weaves cosmological characters and symbols from Pueblo myth into her stories and poems. If you listen closely, you can hear old singers and old songs "spilling out into the world" through her images. Ancestral Pueblo stories tell that the Mother Creator is female, and Silko shapes fertility images of the Earth as Woman. Yellow Woman, who represents all women for Silko, is one of many aspects of this feminine principle. She is associated with yellow butterflies and yellow flowers. The mythic masculine principle may appear as Buffalo Man, Whirlwind Man, Mountain Lion Man, Sun Man, and others. In "When Sun Came to Riverwoman," a companion poem to "Love Song," Sun loves Riverwoman and leaves her to sing "for rainclouds swelling in the northwest sky/ for rainsmell on pale blue winds."

For the Laguna Pueblo people, water in any form means fertility and life. In a letter to poet James Wright, Silko wrote, "If you have not waded in the San Jose River below the village, if you have not hidden in the river willows and sand with your lover, then even as the teller relates a story, you will miss something which people from the Laguna community would not have missed."

Given the place of water in Laguna mythology and in real life, it is not surprising that water metaphors and images abound in Silko's poems. Rain brings summer green and new life. Images of rain and wind, green grass and blue sky, sand dunes and cottonwood leaves illuminate the story of Earth Woman and her lover.

(late spring Navajo Nation, 1972)

Rain smell comes with the wind
                    out of the southwest.
Smell of sand dunes
                    tall grass glistening
5   in the rain.
Warm raindrops that fall easy
                    (this woman)
The summer is born.
Smell of her breathing new life
10   small gray toads on damp sand.
(this woman)
            whispering to dark wide leaves
            white moon blossoms dripping
                                tracks in the sand.
15 Rain smell
            I am full of hunger
            deep and longing to touch
wet tall grass, green and strong beneath.

This woman loved a man
20 and she breathed to him
                    her damp earth song.
I am haunted by this story
I remember it in cottonwood leaves
                                their fragrance in the shade.
25 I remember it in the wide blue sky
when the rain smell comes with the wind.

Discussion Questions

1. "I" appears in lines 16–18 and 22–25. What observations can you make about this persona?
2. List images evoked by the smell of rain for the narrator.
3. What is the story that "I" remembers?

Writing Topics

1. Write a paragraph about what this poem says to you.
2. In your literary journal, write some related images that remind you of love, a certain season, and a particular place or landscape.
3. Write a letter to Leslie Silko telling her what you think of her poem. Give reasons for your opinions.

SUMMARY WRITING TOPICS

1. How effective is this chapter in presenting aspects of love and friendship in Native American societies? Are these aspects universal in human societies or not?
2. Prepare a reader's theatre dramatization of one of the prose selections in this chapter and, with other students, present it before the class.
3. Prepare and present an oral interpretation of "Raisin Eyes" and "Earth and I Gave you Turquoise."
4. Find at least one other poem by N. Scott Momaday, Luci Tapahonso, or Leslie Marmon Silko, reread it several times, and prepare and give an oral interpretation of it for the class.
5. Research courtship and marriage customs in one of the Native American societies represented in this chapter and report to the class. A subtopic might be "kinship" or "kin groups" in one or more of these tribes: Navajo; Spokane; Coeur d'Alene; Chippewa; Winnebago; Lakota, Cheyenne, Flathead; Modoc; Carrier; Blackfeet; Kiowa; and Laguna Pueblo.
6. Write an essay comparing Lipsha in "Bingo Van" and High Horse in "High Horse's Courting." These are some possible topics for comparison and contrast: the roles of men and women in the society; housing; transportation; values; aspects of everyday life.
7. Which character or real person in this chapter would you like to have for a friend? What are some similarities and differences between your life and the life of this imaginary friend? Explain the reason for your choice.
8. Consider your opinions, experiences, and values about love and friendship. Which selection is closest to your views and experiences? Which selection is the most unlike your views and experiences?
9. Reread the mother-daughter characterizations of Red Paint-Heavy Shield woman in "The Marriage of Red Paint and White Man's Dog," and Marie-Blanche in "Groom Service." Identify three differences in the characters and their settings. Write an essay on your conclusions, citing examples from the text.

CHAPTER EIGHT

LANGUAGE AND LEARNING IN TWO WORLDS

> About 16th of March (1621) a certain Indian came boldly
> among them and spoke to them in broken English, which they
> could well understand but marvelled at. . . . At length they under-
> stood by discourse with him, that he was not of these parts, but
> belonged to the eastern parts where some English ships had come
> to fish, with whom he was acquainted and . . . amongst whom he
> had got his language.
>
> William Bradford, *History of Plimouth Plantation*

The Pilgrims "marvelled" at Samoset's speaking English because they landed
on the New England coast full of inaccurate conceptions of native peoples.
While in Holland, the Puritans considered migrating to "those vast and
unpeopled countries of America, which are fruitful and fit for habitation,
being devoid of all civil inhabitants, where there are only savage and brutish
men which range up and down, little otherwise than the wild beasts . . ."
(*History of Plimouth Plantation*). The Pilgrims "marvelled" even more after
Samoset introduced them to Squanto, who had been in England and could
speak better English than Samoset. Squanto became the Pilgrims' indispensable interpreter, inasmuch as the newcomers did not learn Algonquian. The
bilingual Squanto taught them how to survive by growing native crops,
exploiting the rich fishery, and profiting from trade with natives beyond the
colony.

During early contacts between Native Americans and Europeans, the
two peoples learned about, and sometimes from, each other. Explorers, fish-
ermen, trappers, traders, missionaries, and early settlers acquired knowledge
from Native Americans about routes and distances and about the waterways

and natural features of the land. They learned of Indian healing methods and gardening practices. They learned Indian words for places and for animals and plants that did not exist in Europe. Thousands of Indian words name places across North America today, including Massachusetts, Oklahoma, and Arizona. Other words such as *squash, moccasin, hickory, hominy,* and *succotash* were adopted into English. As Euro-Americans expanded westward, they continued the process. *Toboggan, potlatch, kiva,* and *Appaloosa* are all later borrowings from Indian languages. In all, some one thousand Indian words, most from the Algonquian languages, entered the English language.

Borrowing worked both ways. Roger Williams, founder of Rhode Island, wrote that the Narragansetts borrowed English words for objects new to them, and Western and Southwestern Indians often borrowed words from Spanish. Except for some artists, travelers, and writers, fewer and fewer Euro-Americans were interested in learning from or about Indians, however. For a variety of motives, they endeavored instead to impose their own culture, religion, and language on native peoples.

Native American literature presents an immediately apparent paradox. It is usually written and published in the English language, regardless of the author's native language. Very few Native American authors have published in Native American languages, most of which are still oral. Some Native Americans have resisted learning English. Understandably, therefore, Native Americans write a good deal about the linguistic and cultural learning process. A few thoroughly bilingual Native Americans have written in English about their "maternal" language. Albert White Hat, Sr.'s discussion of his Lakota language, which begins this chapter, exemplifies this kind of language-conscious literature. His essay clarifies why some Native American nations make speaking the ancestral language a requirement for membership: "It is our bloodline."

Linguists estimate that there were at least three hundred languages in North America in 1492. Many of them have disappeared entirely, along with the people who spoke them. For example, the Timucuan language of Florida, now extinct, was spoken by as many as 722,000 people in the sixteenth century. By the early seventeenth century, disease had reduced the number to less than 37,000. Today the people are gone and the language is no longer spoken. This was the fate of many languages following the European invasion of the Western Hemisphere. It is a sad fact that Native American languages surviving today continue to be endangered. Some, like the Tlingit language of Nora Dauenhauer and other Indians of Alaska, are near extinction. When children no longer speak the language of their parents or grandparents, that language disappears. Nonetheless Nora Dauenhauer published serious scholarship and playful poetry in Tlingit and in English. Note her "Tlingit Concrete Poem."

The Census Bureau in 1990 recognized one hundred and seventy different Native American languages. Of the more than three hundred thousand Native Americans who speak a native language at home, more than one hundred thousand are Navajos, who occupy a large reservation in the Southwest. In contrast, seventy-four different native languages are spoken within California. The 1990 Census records show that at least one Native American language is still spoken in every state.

What is the future of Native American languages? Some languages, such as Navajo, spoken by large populations will thrive. More Indians, including Luci Tapahonso and Shonto Begay, speak Navajo than any other Indian language. Most native languages, however, face an uncertain future. Reportedly, one hundred and thirty-six languages had less than two thousand speakers in 1960. There were only ten people speaking each of thirty-four dwindling languages. It is unlikely that these languages will survive to the twenty-first century.

In 1990, Congress passed the Native American Languages Act, which declares that it is federal policy to "preserve, protect, and promote the rights and freedom of natives to use, practice, and develop Native American languages." The act further states that Native Americans may use their languages in "publicly supported education programs." This act is in stark contrast to the policies enforced in Bureau of Indian Affairs (BIA) boarding schools described in this volume by Luther Standing Bear, Zitkala-Ša, Shonto Begay, and others.

Authors in this chapter reflect facets of Indian education from traditional times to the present. Luther Standing Bear's "At Last I Kill a Buffalo" is the best description of how native education worked. Native Americans have always educated their children. Children learned the language of their people in an environment where everyone spoke the same language. Young people were taught skills for practical survival and producing artistic work, proper behavior for rituals and ceremonies, family and tribal histories, and ways to respond to family and tribal members. Teaching methods included telling stories and setting examples.

Formal English-language teaching to Indians in North America began early, particularly in missionary schools. Since Colonial settlers in New England were committed to teaching literacy so that everyone could read the Bible, Protestant missionaries quickly started classes in the English language for Indians. William Apess and Elias Boudinot, both represented in this anthology, were two eastern Indians who became fluent in spoken and written English. Zitkala-Ša studied at a missionary school in the 1870s, and Albert White Hat, Sr. attended a mission school in the 1950s. As a result of early missionary activity, the so-called Five Civilized Tribes established tribally financed and controlled academies and seminaries after their removal. This was the earliest Native American attempt to control curriculum taught to their children in the English language. By 1851, the Cherokees in Oklahoma had opened male and female seminaries to educate young Cherokees.

In the 1870s, policymakers in Washington decided that the best way to "civilize" Indians was through removing children from their homes and placing them in faraway boarding schools. Boarding schools became the bedrock of the government's ambitious, but flawed, program, and learning English was required. Established in 1879, Carlisle Indian School in Pennsylvania became the model institution for authoritarian discipline. Boarding schools closely supervised students for an average of ten months a year and often placed them with non-Indian families and businesses during the summer. Some Indian children benefited from boarding schools. They established friendships with members of other tribes, learned English, and found a way to make a living. Luther Standing Bear took pride in becoming fluent in English and writing it well. His "First Days at Carlisle" stands out as eyewitness history of the first class at Carlisle Indian School.

Many students suffered in this atmosphere, however. Being separated from friends and family traumatized them, and they experienced homesickness and difficult periods of adjustment to a foreign environment. In addition, many died of disease. Hundreds died of tuberculosis and other contagious diseases because of poor diet, inadequate medical care, and unhealthful surroundings. Many contracted trachoma, a serious inflammation of the eyes, which is also contagious. Small wonder that many Indian pupils fled, as Louise Erdrich dramatizes in "Indian Boarding School: The Runaways." Once students returned home, many had difficulty adjusting to reservation life and to living with their elders who could not speak or write English. Zitkala-Ša, known as Gertrude Bonnin in English, provides a Sioux teacher's perspective on the early Indian boarding school system. Like Standing Bear, she took pride in her accomplishments, but she remained quite ambivalent about the process and policy. By 1899, twenty-five residential schools had been established in fifteen states. Total enrollment reached twenty thousand students.

As part of Franklin D. Roosevelt's New Deal of the 1930s, the Indian New Deal began to transform these boarding schools into day schools. Even after the Bureau of Indian Affairs shifted its educational emphasis, native students did not universally adjust well to day schools, as Sherman Alexie makes clear in "Indian Education." In contrast, N. Scott Momaday holds fond memories of his days at Jemez Pueblo Day School where his parents were teachers.

As a pivotal decade, the 1960s witnessed the beginning of self-determination in Indian education. Navajo Community College, the first Indian-controlled and Indian-directed college in the country was founded in 1968. As of 1998, there were some thirty community colleges, most of them on reservations, making an impact on Indian education. Located in Indian communities, the colleges provide tribal language and cultural instruction, publish classroom materials, and employ fluent bilingual teachers. Anna Lee Walters and Albert White Hat, Sr. both teach in such institutions.

Speakers of languages that are not threatened may wonder why the loss of or changes in a language are lamented. Albert White Hat, Sr. and N. Scott Momaday in "The Man Made of Words" make clear the connections among language, learning, and identity. One's sense of self is derived in part from family stories. These stories become part of one's cultural heritage—a heritage that can be transmitted only through language. Many native peoples are now able to study their heritage in Native American courses in colleges and universities. "Enchanted Enchanted Rattlesnake" illustrates one collaboration between a university professor committed to preservation of oral literature and one Indian community ceremonialist. Such collaborations and courses are open to non-Indians as well, for as Momaday writes, "in a certain sense we are all made of words."

LAKOTA LANGUAGE

Albert White Hat, Sr.

For more than twenty-five years, Albert White Hat, Sr. has been a remarkable scholar and teacher of the Lakota language. An instructor at Sinte Gleska University since 1982, White Hat has lived at St. Francis, South Dakota, on the Rosebud Reservation. This enrolled member of the Rosebud Sioux Tribe has served in political, religious, and educational arenas. He was elected to two terms on the Tribal Council from 1978 to 1982. Committed to traditional Lakota ceremonies, he assisted with the Sun Dance and studied with a medicine man for ten years before leading the Sun Dance. White Hat has fulfilled his Sun Dance vows as a dancer.

Born in 1938 to Joseph D. White Hat and Emily Hollow Horn Bear, young Albert spoke only Lakota until he entered Spring Creek Day School. He graduated from St. Francis Mission School and returned to teach there in 1971 after attending Sinte Gleska University. He published *Lakota Ceremonial Songs* in 1983.

In "Lakota Language," White Hat explains the history of a Lakota-developed orthography, which is used in his textbook, *Writing and Reading the Lakota Language* (1999). Most of White Hat's language education comes from speaking Lakota and from listening to the words of elders and medicine men. With the establishment of Oglala Lakota College in 1970 and Sinte Gleska College in 1971, Lakota people became more involved with developing a standardized Lakota alphabet. In 1973, White Hat was teaching at St. Francis Indian School and experimenting with an alphabet. He recalls, "At that time, I had no teaching experience—all that I had was a twelfth-grade diploma and I was bilingual." He struggled to formulate a successful teaching approach. "However, I wasn't comfortable with our results because the sentence structure didn't sound right. . . . I was afraid to question the linguist because, to me, she was the expert. I was afraid to say, 'No, this is the way we say it in Lakota.'" Nevertheless, the instructor continued to learn from his students and older Lakota speakers. In 1982, he chaired the Committee for the Preservation of the Lakota Language. The association voted in 1995 to create a Lakota dictionary utilizing an alphabet system of eighteen letters representing English sounds and twenty-two letters representing sounds unique to the Lakota language.

White Hat prefers the translations that reflect oral history and contributions of Lakota elders even when their words and explanations contradict earlier writings. "I am aware of such contradictions. Despite what has been written, I was taught to value their words. Grammar without philosophy is teaching a dead language. My language is alive. It invokes feelings and it embodies a history. These stories must be told."

1   Language is vital to Lakota culture. It is our bloodline. History has demonstrated that how we handle our language, how we develop it, can cause the Lakota people to grow or can destroy us. Two hundred years ago the language built us up to a point where we were a progressive and strong people. Within two hundred years, misuse of the language almost destroyed us.

2   *Očeti Šakowiŋ* (The Seven Council Fires), most commonly referred to as the Sioux Nation, comprises seven tribes that fall into three distinct dialect groups. Four tribes speak Dakota (Mdewa-kaŋtuŋ, Wahpetuŋ, Wahpekute, Sisituŋ), two tribes speak Nakota (Ihaŋktunwaŋ, Ihaŋktunwaŋi), and one tribe, the Titunwaŋ (People of the Prairie), the most populous of the three divisions, speaks Lakota. Today, most Lakota speakers live west of the Missouri River on various reservations within South Dakota. (The Lakota orthographic system[1] used here was developed in 1982 by the Committee for the Preservation of the Lakota Language.)

3   The Lakota language, like most Native American languages, was not originally a written language. The first people to transcribe Lakota into a written alphabet were early missionaries and anthropologists. In 1834, the Episcopal missionaries Samuel W. Pond, Gideon H. Pond, Stephen R. Riggs, and Dr. Thomas S. Williamson created a Dakota alphabet. This alphabet system was adapted and extended to the "L" dialect by Ella Deloria and Franz Boas during the 1930s. Since then, three other spelling systems have been created. In 1939, the Reverend Eugene Buechel published a Lakota grammar book that contains his spelling system. In 1976 another alphabet system for the Lakota language was introduced by Allen Taylor and David Rood of the University of Colorado at Boulder.

4   The most recent Lakota alphabet was created in 1982 by Lakota language instructors from the South Dakota area who were frustrated by the wide variety of written forms of our language. The group of instructors—

---

[1] *orthographic system:* System of spelling, either by an alphabet or by other symbols.

from the Rosebud Reservation, the Pine Ridge Reservation, the Cheyenne River Reservation, and Rapid City—organized the Committee for the Preservation of the Lakota Language. This committee wanted to standardize the alphabet and to learn more about the philosophy of the language from tribal elders.

5   In the spring of 1982, the committee members created a "recommended alphabet system" that we believe combined the best elements of the existing systems. The forty letters in our system function as a pronunciation guide for the Lakota language. Though this system is not the official alphabet system for the Sioux Nation, it does address all forty Lakota sounds and is simple enough for children to use.

6   After listening to tribal elders from the various reservations, the committee identified two central ideas to be emphasized in teaching the language. First, the language is *wakaŋ*, "very powerful." We use it to communicate with the other nations: the Deer Nation, the Eagle Nation, the Buffalo Nation, and so forth. We talk to the *wamakakaŋ*, living beings of the earth, through spiritual communications. Language must be taught with this in mind. Second, when teaching the language to younger people, its good and evil powers must also be taught. Children need to understand that language contains great power, that it can be used to injure peoples' feelings or to compliment the achievements of another human being, that it can be used to harm or to honor and bless. Young people need to understand that language contains the power to give life or to take it away and that it therefore must be used with respect.

7   The committee's ideas challenged Western language teaching by emphasizing the importance of philosophy in the Lakota language. This can be seen in the Lakota use of gender endings—words at the end of the sentence that indicate whether the speaker is a woman or a man. For example, to ask if something is good, a woman says, *"Waśte he?"* while a man says, *"Waśte huwho?"* To answer, "Yes, it is good," a woman responds by saying, *"Haŋ waśte ksto,"* and a man responds by saying, *"To waśte yelo."*

8   These differences in male and female speech patterns reflect Lakota philosophy. Men and women have distinct roles in our society. Women represent beauty, softness, and the goodness of birth, of giving life. Though all these qualities are more gentle than those of a man, they imply just as much strength and determination. A woman's softer approach is evident by both her behavior and her speech. Traditionally, a woman lets the man address her first, out of respect for him and for his role. In addition, female expressions sound more gentle because they often contain nasal vowels.

9   Men, on the other hand, are the protectors of the circle and as a result, in the Lakota view they are more aggressive and rough. Their behavior and speech reflect their role in Lakota society. Men's speech tends to be loud and rugged, filled with many guttural sounds. Also, their behavior is more aggressive, especially if they are called to protect the values of the circle. Thus gender endings reinforce Lakota philosophy.

10   The Lakota language also reflects the Lakota environment. It affirms spirituality. It supports music, dance, good times, sad times. All those feelings are in it. Lakota teachers need to steep themselves in their language. A Lakota speaker needs to feel and understand every word in order to express true emotions.

11   Before World War II our people were conditioned to read and to write the Lakota language. Through this process, the language changed to reflect the Christian perspective of early missionaries. Words began to have as many as four different interpretations. For example, *wakaŋ,* used as a noun, means "energy." It teaches that all creation has the power to give life or to take it away. Christians understood this word to mean "something sacred." Anthropologists translated *wakaŋ* as "mystery." In such ways traditional Lakota meanings get corrupted and, eventually, lost. Lakota speakers in the classroom become fearful and uneasy when they hear a traditional translation. Their fear reminds me of my own struggles when I first started teaching the language. The language I spoke, although it was Lakota, reflected a Catholic philosophy. At that time I, too, was afraid of the traditional interpretation of the language. At Catholic boarding schools, I was taught that the traditional language represented evil. Once I had identified that old belief in myself, I could apply my own experience to the classroom. I could see whether a student was Catholic or Episcopalian, and then I could understand his or her perspective. Each would have a different interpretation of the language, and both would fear the traditional translation.

12   During the 1940s and 1950s, communities began to deteriorate as Lakota speakers became increasingly dependent on authority figures from churches, the Bureau of Indian Affairs, or tribal programs. These circumstances created an ideal setting for alcoholism. When you drank, you could temporarily escape authority and practice a type of independence. Independence is a feature of Lakota tradition, but such alcohol-supported behavior was artificial.

13   By the 1960s a new culture with its own language had developed—what I call the reservation subculture and the reservation language. Young people thought that this was normal Lakota speech. When I asked students what *makuje* (I am sick) meant, they responded, "Hangover." When I asked what *oteh'i* (difficult to endure) meant, they responded, "You have one hell of a hangover. You are flat broke with absolutely no resources for another drink." This particular culture, which was aggressive and was practiced daily, challenged the other three (Catholic, Episcopalian, Lakota). Today, in an attempt to reverse this change in language, we deliberately use words in their traditional form. Today, we have more powwows, more Sun Dances, more giveaways, more naming ceremonies, more honoring ceremonies. We use our words in settings and situations where they truly belong. It is our hope that, through these community activities, people will feel able to adjust their lifestyles to reflect the true meaning of their language.

14   In class, I explain the different cultures. My intention is to clarify our current situation. We are all Lakota. In the classroom, I try to explain how the different influences have conditioned students' lives and how that affects them today. I try to make students conscious of what each culture represents. You have a traditional Lakota spirituality. You have a Catholic spirituality. You have an Episcopalian spirituality. You should respect each other and honor each other's choices. I honor my people and respect them. Whatever decisions they have made I will honor.

15   This new approach has forced me to redefine my role as a language instructor. As an instructor, I realize that I have to demonstrate Lakota values and morals in my own daily life so that students not only learn the Lakota words but also see examples of what I am teaching. I find that this work, though challenging, frees me from concepts and uses of my language that I never chose. It is a process of deconditioning and liberation. Our language was invaded, just as our lands were. We need to bring back our language with all its spiritual values and its moral force, just as we fight to reclaim the Black Hills and the other sacred sites within our domain.

DISCUSSION QUESTIONS

1. The author says that language has great power—both good and evil, and he mentions spiritual communication and the power of language to harm or to bless. In a small group, discuss and give some examples of what he means with reference to your own language.
2. How do differences in male and female speech patterns reflect Lakota philosophy, according to the author?
3. Explain the process by which traditional Lakota meanings for words are corrupted and lost.
4. Why would Lakota speakers become fearful and uneasy at traditional translations?
5. The author says that he tries to explain to students how "different influences have conditioned students' lives" and that the Lakota language "was invaded." Explain what he means.
6. Can a language have "moral force," as the author maintains? Explain.

Writing Topics

1. All languages change, but at the same time, in order for communication to take place, speakers must agree on the meanings of words. Would Albert White Hat, Sr., agree or disagree with this statement? Explain in a short paper.

2. Suppose that your native language was "invaded" and that meanings of words in your language took on meanings from a culture or belief system different from yours. What would be your reaction? Discuss this question in an essay, giving hypothetical examples of words like *courage, home, father,* or *prayer,* or similar-meaning words in your own language.

FIRST DAYS AT CARLISLE

Luther Standing Bear

Luther Standing Bear, a Teton Sioux, was enrolled by his father in the Carlisle Indian Industrial School in Pennsylvania in 1879. This boarding school, founded that same year, was strictly for native children. Its first director was an army officer, Richard Henry Pratt, who had previously headed an Indian prisoner-of-war camp in Florida. In keeping with Pratt's stated purpose to "kill the Indian and save the man," the use of native languages was forbidden. Upon his arrival at Carlisle, Standing Bear was assigned the name "Luther," although he had been enrolled as Ota K´te (Plenty Kills), son of Standing Bear. His hair was cut, and he began vocational training.

The tinsmithing skill he had learned proved useless when he returned to the Rosebud Reservation, and he subsequently was in charge of a school on the Pine Ridge Reservation and later worked as a clerk, an assistant in a post office, and a minister's aide.

He auditioned for a part in Buffalo Bill's Wild West Show in 1902, got the role, and traveled with the show for eleven months in England. He was then chosen to replace his deceased father as chief of his extended family group in 1903 but, finding it impossible to improve the lives of his people on the reservation, he soon left. After he gained citizenship, which meant that he could move off and on the reservation without permission from the U.S. agent, he went to California in 1912 and found work as a movie actor. He acted in silent films and in "talkies," all of them Westerns. Among his films are *The Santa Fe Trail* (1930) and *Fighting Pioneer* (1935). He died in 1939 in California during filming of *Union Pacific*.

In this excerpt from his autobiography *My People, the Sioux*, Standing Bear writes of his first days at the Indian school. Although the date of his birth is not certain, Luther states that he was twelve years old when he arrived at the school.

1   At last the train arrived at a junction where we were told we were at the end of our journey. Here we left the train and walked about two miles to the Carlisle Barracks. Soon we came to a big gate in a great high wall. The gate was locked, but after quite a long wait, it was unlocked and we marched in through it. I was the first boy inside. At that time I thought nothing of it, but now I realize that I was the first Indian boy to step inside the Carlisle Indian School Grounds.

2   Here the girls were all called to one side by Louise McCoz, the girls' interpreter. She took them into one of the big buildings, which was very brilliantly lighted, and it looked good to us from the outside.

3   When our interpreter told us to go to a certain building which he pointed out to us, we ran very fast, expecting to find nice little beds like those the white people had. We were so tired and worn out from the long trip that we wanted a good long sleep. From Springfield, Dakota, to Carlisle, Pennsylvania, riding in day coaches all the way, with no chance to sleep, is an exhausting journey for a bunch of little Indians.

4   But the first room we entered was empty. A cast-iron stove stood in the middle of the room, on which was placed a coal-oil lamp. There was no fire in the stove. We ran through all the rooms, but they were all the same—no fire, no beds. This was a two-story building, but we were all herded into two rooms on the upper floor.

5   Well, we had to make the best of the situation, so we took off our leggins and rolled them up for a pillow. All the covering we had was the blanket which each had brought. We went to sleep on the hard floor, and it was so cold! We had been used to sleeping on the ground, but the floor was so much colder.

6   Next morning we were called downstairs for breakfast. All we were given was bread and water. How disappointed we were! At noon we had some meat, bread, and coffee, so we felt a little better. But how lonesome the big boys and girls were for their far-away Dakota homes where there was plenty to eat! The big boys seemed to take it worse than we smaller chaps did. I guess we little fellows did not know any better. The big boys would sing brave songs, and that would start the girls to crying. They did this for several nights. The girls' quarters were about a hundred and fifty yards from ours, so we could hear them crying. After some time the food began to get better; but it was far from being what we had been used to receiving back home.

7   At this point I must tell you how the Carlisle Indian School was started. A few years previously, four or five tribes in Oklahoma had some trouble. They were Cheyennes, Arapahoes, Comanches, and Wichitas. There was another tribe with them, but I have forgotten the name. The Government arrested some braves from these various tribes and took them to Virginia as prisoners. Captain Pratt was in charge of them. He conceived the idea of placing these Indians in a school to see if they could learn anything in that manner. So they were put into the Hampton School, where Negroes were

sent. They were good-sized young men, having been on the war-path already, but old as they were, they were getting on splendidly with their studies.

8   That gave Captain Pratt another idea. He thought if he could get some young Indian children and educate them, it would help their people. He went to the Government officials and put the proposition up to them, and asked permission to try the experiment. They told him to go ahead and see what he could do, providing he could get any Indians to educate. Captain Pratt was not at all sure he could do this.

9   He had nothing prepared to start such a school, but the Government gave him the use of some empty buildings at Carlisle, Pennsylvania. He brought some of the Indian prisoners from Virginia with him, and they remained in the Carlisle Barracks until Captain Pratt could go to Dakota and return with his first consignment of "scholars." Carlisle School had been a soldiers' home at one time so at the start it was not built for the education of the Indian people.

10   I had come to this school merely to show my people that I was brave enough to leave the reservation and go East, not knowing what it meant and not caring.

11   When we first arrived at Carlisle, we had nothing to do. There were no school regulations, no rules of order or anything of that sort. We just ran all over the school grounds and did about as we pleased. . . .

12   For some time we continued sleeping on the hard floor, and it was far from being as comfortable as the nice, soft beds in our tipis back home. One evening the interpreter called us all together, and gave each a big bag. He said these were to be our mattresses, but that we would have to fill them ourselves with straw. He said, "Out behind the stable is a large haystack. Go there and fill these bags all full."

13   So we all ran as fast as we could to the haystack and filled our sacks as quickly as possible, pushing and scuffling to see who would get finished first. When the bags were all full, we carried them to one of the big rooms on the second floor. Here the bags were all laid out in a row. We little fellows certainly did look funny, lugging those great bags across the yard and upstairs.

14   That night we had the first good sleep in a long time. These bags were sewed all around, and in the center there was a slit through which they were filled with the straw; but there was nobody to sew the slit up after the bag was filled. We had no sheets and no extra blankets thus far—nothing but the blankets we had brought from the reservation.

15   The next day we played back and forth over these bags of straw, and soon it began to filter out through the slits. Presently it was scattered all over the floor, and as we had no brooms with which to sweep it up, you can imagine the looks of the room at the starting of our school!

16   Although we were yet wearing our Indian clothes, the interpreter came to us and told us we must go to school. We were marched into a schoolroom, where we were each given a pencil and slate. We were seated at sin-

gle desks. We soon discovered that the pencils made marks on the slates. So we covered our heads with our blankets, holding the slate inside so the other fellow would not know what we were doing. Here we would draw a man on a pony chasing buffalo, or a boy shooting birds in a tree, or it might be one of our Indian games, or anything that suited our fancy to try and portray.

17   When we had all finished, we dropped our blankets down on the seat and marched up to the teacher with our slates to show what we had drawn. Our teacher was a woman. She bowed her head as she examined the slates and smiled, indicating that we were doing pretty well—at least we interpreted it that way.

18   One day when we came to school there was a lot of writing on one of the blackboards. We did not know what it meant, but our interpreter came into the room and said, "Do you see all these marks on the blackboard? Well, each word is a white man's name. They are going to give each one of you one of these names by which you will hereafter be known." None of the names were read or explained to us, so of course we did not know the sound or meaning of any of them.

19   The teacher had a long pointed stick in her hand, and the interpreter told the boy in the front seat to come up. The teacher handed the stick to him, and the interpreter then told him to pick out any name he wanted. The boy had gone up with his blanket on. When the long stick was handed to him, he turned to us as much as to say, "Shall I—or will you help me—to take one of these names? Is it right for me to take a white man's name?" He did not know what to do for a time, not uttering a single word—but he acted a lot and was doing a lot of thinking.

20   Finally he pointed out one of the names written on the blackboard. Then the teacher took a piece of white tape and wrote the name on it. Then she cut off a length of the tape and sewed it on the back of the boy's shirt. Then that name was erased from the board. There was no duplication of names in the first class at Carlisle School!

21   Then the next boy took the pointer and selected a name. He was also labeled in the same manner as Number One. When my turn came, I took the pointer and acted as if I were about to touch an enemy. Soon we all had the names of white men sewed on our backs. When we went to school, we knew enough to take our proper places in the class, but that was all. When the teacher called the roll, no one answered his name. Then she would walk around and look at the back of the boys' shirts. When she had the right name located, she made the boy stand up and say "Present." She kept this up for about a week before we knew what the sound of our new names was.

22   I was one of the "bright fellows" to learn my name quickly. How proud I was to answer when the teacher called the roll! I would put my blanket down and half raise myself in my seat, all ready to answer to my new name. I had selected the name "Luther"—not "Lutheran" as many people call me. "Lutheran" is the name of a church denomination, not a person.

23   Next we had to learn to write our names. Our good teacher had a lot of patience with us. She is now living in Los Angeles, California, and I still like to go and ask her any question which may come up in my mind. She first wrote my name on the slate for me, and then, by motions, indicated that I was to write it just like that. She held the pencil in her hand just so, then made first one stroke, then another, and by signs I was given to understand that I was to follow in exactly the same way.

24   The first few times I wrote my new name, it was scratched so deeply into the slate that I was never able to erase it. But I copied my name all over both sides of the slate until there was no more room to write. Then I took my slate up to show it to the teacher, and she indicated, by the expression of her face, that it was very good. I soon learn to write it very well; then took a piece of chalk downstairs and wrote "Luther" all over everything I could copy it on.

25   Next the teacher wrote out the alphabet on my slate and indicated to me that I was to take the slate to my room and study. I was pleased to do this, as I expected to have a lot of fun. I went up on the second floor, to the end of the building, where I thought nobody would bother me. There I sat down and looked at those queer letters, trying hard to figure out what they meant. No one was there to tell me that the first letter was "A" the next "B" and so on. This was the first time in my life that I was really disgusted. It was something I could not decipher, and all this study business was not what I had come East for anyhow—so I thought.

26   How lonesome I felt for my father and mother! I stayed upstairs all by myself, thinking of the good times I might be having if I were only back home, where I could ride my ponies, go wherever I wanted to and do as I pleased, and, when it came night, could lie down and sleep well. Right then and there I learned that no matter how humble your home is, it is yet home.

27   So it did me no good to take my slate with me that day. It only made me lonesome. The next time the teacher told me by signs to take my slate to my room, I shook my head, meaning "no." She came and talked to me in English, but of course I did not know what she was saying.

28   A few days later, she wrote the alphabet on the blackboard, then brought the interpreter into the room. Through him she told us to repeat each letter after her, calling out "A," and we all said "A"; then "B," and so on. This was our real beginning. The first day we learned the first three letters of the alphabet, both the pronunciation and the reading of them.

29   I had not determined to learn anything yet. All I could think of was my free life at home. How long would these people keep us here? When were we going home? At home we could eat anytime we wished, but here we had to watch the sun all the time. On cloudy days the waits between meals seemed terribly long.

30   There soon came a time when the school people fixed up an old building which was to be used as our dining-room. In it they placed some long tables, but with no cover on. Our meals were dished up and brought to each

plate before we entered. I very quickly learned to be right there when the bell rang, and get in first. Then I would run along down the table until I came to a plate which I thought contained the most meat, when I would sit down and begin eating without waiting for any one.

31 We soon "got wise" when it came to looking out for the biggest portion of meat. When we knew by the sun that it was near dinner time, we would play close to the dining-room, until the woman in charge came out with a big bell in her hand to announce that the meal was ready. We never had to be called twice! We were right there when it came meal-time!

32 After a while they hung a big bell on a walnut tree near the office. This was to be rung for school hours and meals. One of the Indian boys named Edgar Fire Thunder used to sneak around the building and ring the bell before it was time to eat. Of course we would all rush for the dining-room, only to find the doors locked. Nobody seemed to object to this boy playing such pranks, but we did not like it.

33 We were still wearing our Indian clothes. One of the Indian prisoners was delegated to teach us to march in to the dining-room and to school. Some of the boys had bells on their leggins, which helped us to keep time as we stepped off.

34 One day we had a strange experience. We were all called together by the interpreter and told that we were to have our hair cut off. We listened to what he had to say, but we did not reply. This was something that would require some thought, so that evening the big boys held a council, and I recall very distinctly that Nakpa Kesela, or Robert American Horse, made a serious speech. Said he, "If I am to learn the ways of the white people, I can do it just as well with my hair on." To this we all exclaimed "Hau!"–meaning that we agreed with him.

35 In spite of this meeting, a few days later we saw some white men come inside the school grounds carrying big chairs. The interpreter told us these were the men who had come to cut our hair. We did not watch to see where the chairs were carried, as it was school time, and we went to our classroom. One of the big boys named Ya Slo, or Whistler, was missing. In a short time he came in with his hair cut off. Then they called another boy out, and when he returned, he also wore short hair. In this way we were called out one by one.

36 When I saw most of them with short hair, I began to feel anxious to be "in style" and wanted mine cut, too. Finally I was called out of the school-room, and when I went into the next room, the barber was waiting for me. He motioned for me to sit down, and then he commenced work. But when my hair was cut short, it hurt my feelings to such an extent that the tears came into my eyes. I do not recall whether the barber noticed my agitation or not, nor did I care. All I was thinking about was that hair he had taken away from me.

37 Right here I must state how this hair-cutting affected me in various ways. I have recounted that I always wanted to please my father in every way pos-

sible. All his instructions to me had been along this line: "Son, be brave and get killed." This expression had been moulded into my brain to such an extent that I knew nothing else.

38　But my father had made a mistake. He should have told me, upon leaving home, to go and learn all I could of the white man's ways, and be like them. That would have given a new idea from a different slant; but Father did not advise me along that line. I had come away from home with the intention of never returning alive unless I had done something very brave.

39　Now, after having had my hair cut, a new thought came into my head. I felt that I was no more Indian, but would be an imitation of a white man. And we are still imitations of white men, and the white men are imitations of the Americans.

40　We all looked so funny with short hair. It had been cut with a machine and was cropped very close. We still had our Indian clothes, but were all "bald-headed." None of us slept well that night; we felt so queer. I wanted to feel of my head all the time. But in a short time I became anxious to learn all I could.

41　Next, we heard that we were soon to have white men's clothes. We were all very excited and anxious when this was announced to us. One day some wagons came in, loaded with big boxes, which were unloaded in front of the office. Of course we were all very curious, and gathered around to watch the proceedings and see all we could.

42　Here, one at a time, we were "sized up" and a whole suit handed to each of us. The clothes were some sort of dark heavy gray goods, consisting of coat, pants, and vest. We were also given a dark woolen shirt, a cap, a pair of suspenders, socks, and heavy farmer's boots.

43　Up to this time we had all been wearing our thin shirts, leggins, and a blanket. Now we had received new outfits of white men's clothes, and to us it seemed a whole lot of clothing to wear at once, but even at that, we had not yet received any underwear.

44　As soon as we had received our outfits, we ran to our rooms to dress up. The Indian prisoners were kept busy helping us put the clothes on. Although the suits were too big for many of us, we did not know the difference. I remember that my boots were far too large, but as long as they were "screechy" or squeaky, I didn't worry about the size! I liked the noise they made when I walked, and the other boys were likewise pleased.

45　How proud we were with clothes that had pockets and with boots that squeaked! We walked the floor nearly all that night. Many of the boys even went to bed with their clothes all on. But in the morning, the boys who had taken off their pants had a most terrible time. They did not know whether they were to button up in front or behind. Some of the boys said the open part went in front; others said, "No, it goes at the back." There is where the boys who had kept all their clothes on came in handy to look at. They showed the others that the pants buttoned up in front and not at the back. So here we learned something again.

46   Another boy and I received some money from home. His name was Waniyetula, or Winter, and he was my cousin. We concluded we might as well dress up like white men; so we took all our money to the interpreter and asked him if he would buy us some nice clothes. He promised he would.

47   We did not know the amount of money which we handed over to him, but we gave him all we had received, as we did not know values then. He took the money and went to town. When he returned he brought us each a big bundle. We took them and went into an empty room to dress up, as we did not want the other boys to see us until we had the clothes on. When we opened the bundles, we were surprised to see how many things we had received for our money. Each bundle contained a black suit of clothes, a pair of shoes and socks, stiff bosom shirt, two paper collars, a necktie, a pair of cuffs, derby hat, cuff buttons, and some colored glass studs for our stiff shirt fronts.

48   We were greatly pleased with our purchases, which we examined with great curiosity and eagerness. As it was nearly time for supper, we tied the bundles together again and took them into one of the rooms where an Indian prisoner was staying, asking him to keep the bundles for us until the next day. We had to talk to him in the sign language, as he was from a different tribe. The sign language, by the way, was invented by the Indian. White men never use it correctly.

49   We felt very proud of our new purchases and spent most of that evening getting off by ourselves and discussing them. We found out later that our wonderful clothes cost all together about eleven dollars. The interpreter had bought the cheapest things he could get in the town of Carlisle.

50   All the next day we were together. We kept our eyes on our disciplinarian, Mr. Campbell, because we wanted to see how he put on his collar. We were studying not very far away from him and we watched him constantly, trying to figure out how he had put that collar on his shirt.

51   When evening came at last, we carried our bundles up to the second floor where we could be alone. Here we opened the things up and started to dress up. While we were thus engaged, in came the prisoner with whom we had left the bundles the night before. We were glad, in a way, that he had come in, because he knew more about how the clothes ought to be worn than we did, and he helped us dress.

52   Just as we were through, the bell rang for supper. The other boys were already in line. We came down the outside stairway, and when they observed us, what a war-whoop went up! The boys made all kinds of remarks about our outfits, and called us "white men." But our teachers and the other white people were greatly pleased at our new appearance.

53   We had only two paper collars apiece, and when they became soiled we had to go without collars. We tried our best to wear the ties without the collars, but guess we must have looked funny.

54   It was now winter and very cold, so we were supplied with red flannel underwear. These looked pretty to us, but we did not like the warmth and

the "itching" they produced. I soon received some more money from my father, and another boy named Knaska, or Frog, and I bought us some white underwear. This was all right, but we did not dare let any one else know it, as the rules were that we had to wear the red flannels. So every Sunday morning we would put the red ones on, because they held inspection on Sunday morning. Captain Pratt and others always looked us over that day very carefully; but as soon as the inspection was through, we would slip into our white underclothes and get ready to attend Sunday School in town.

55   All the boys and girls were given permission to choose the religious denomination which appealed to them best, so they were at liberty to go where they pleased to Sunday School. Most of us selected the Episcopal Church. I was baptized in that church under the name of Luther.

56   In our room lived a boy named Kaici Inyanke, or Running Against. While not exactly bad, he was always up to some mischief. His father's name was Black Bear, so when the boy was baptized he took his father's name, while his Christian name was Paul. He is yet living at Pine Ridge Agency, South Dakota. More than once Captain Pratt had to hold Paul up. He would play until the very last minute and then try to clean his shoes and comb his hair, all at once seemingly. On this particular Sunday Paul rushed in and was so busy that he did not get half finished. He had combed his hair, but had applied too much water, which was running down his face, while one of his shoes was cleaned and the other was dirty.

57   We had been taught to stand erect like soldiers when Captain Pratt, Dr. Givens, and others entered the room for inspection. First, Captain Pratt would "size us up" from head to foot, notice if we had our hair combed nicely, if our clothes were neatly brushed, and if we had cleaned our shoes. Then he would look the room over to see if our beds were made up right, often lifting the mattresses to see that everything was clean underneath. Often they would look into our wooden boxes where we kept our clothes, to see that everything was spick and span.

58   Paul Black Bear had not been able—as usual—to finish getting ready for inspection, and when Captain Pratt looked at his feet, Paul tried to hide the shoe that was not polished, by putting it behind the other one. Captain Pratt also noticed the water running down his face. We all expected to see Paul get a "calling down" but Captain Pratt only laughed and told Paul to do better next time.

59   At Carlisle it was the rule that we were not to be permitted to smoke, but Paul smoked every time he had a chance. One day he made a "long smoke" and stood by one of the big fireplaces, puffing away very fast. All at once he got sick at the stomach and fainted. We had to drag him out of the fireplace and pour water on him.

60   One day our teacher brought some wooden plates into the schoolroom. She told us they were to paint on. She gave me about half a dozen of them.

We each received a small box of water-colors. I painted Indian designs on all my plates. On some of them I had a man chasing buffalo, shooting them with the bow and arrow. Others represented a small boy shooting at birds in the trees. When I had them all painted, I gave them back to the teacher. She seemed to be well pleased with my work, and sent them all away somewhere. Possibly some persons yet have those wooden plates which were painted by the first class of Indian boys and girls at Carlisle.

61   About this time there were many additions to the school from various tribes in other States and from other reservations. We were not allowed to converse in the Indian tongue, and we knew so little English that we had a hard time to get along. With these other tribes coming in, we were doing our best to talk as much English as we could.

62   One night in December we were all marched down to the chapel. When the doors were opened, how surprised we were! Everything was decorated with green. We all took seats, but we could not keep still. There was a big tree in the room, all trimmed and decorated. We stretched our necks to see everything. Then a minister stood up in front and talked to us, but I did not mind a thing he said—in fact, I could not understand him anyway.

63   This was our first Christmas celebration, and we were all so happy. I saw the others were getting gifts from off that tree, and I was anxious to get something myself. Finally my name was called, and I received several presents, which had been put on the tree for me by the people for whom I had painted the plates. Others were from my teacher, Miss M. Burgess, and some from my Sunday-School teacher, Miss Eggee. I was very happy for all the things I had received.

64   I now began to realize that I would have to learn the ways of the white man. With that idea in mind, the thought also came to me that I must please my father as well. So my little brain began to work hard. I thought that some day I might be able to become an interpreter for my father, as he could not speak English. Or I thought I might be able to keep books for him if he again started a store. So I worked very hard.

65   One day they selected a few boys and told us we were to learn trades. I was to be a tinsmith. I did not care for this, but I tried my best to learn this trade. Mr. Walker was our instructor. I was getting along very well. I made hundreds of tin cups, coffee pots, and buckets. These were sent away and issued to the Indians on various reservations.

66   After I had left the school and returned home, this trade did not benefit me any, as the Indians had plenty of tinware that I had made at school.

67   Mornings I went to the tin shop, and in the afternoon attended school. I tried several times to drop this trade and go to school the entire day, but Captain Pratt said, "No, you must go to the tin shop—that is all there is to it," so I had to go. Half school and half work took away a great deal of study time. I figure that I spent only about a year and a half in school, while the rest of the time was wasted, as the school was not started properly to begin

with. Possibly you wonder why I did not remain longer, but the Government had made an agreement with our parents as to the length of time we were to be away.

68 A short time later, some boys, myself among the number, were called into one of the schoolrooms. There we found a little white woman. There was a long table in front of her, on which were many packages tied in paper. She opened up one package and it contained a bright, shining horn. Other packages disclosed more horns, but they seem to be different sizes.

69 The little white woman picked up a horn and then looked the boys over. Finally she handed it to a boy who she thought might be able to use it. Then she picked out a shorter horn and gave it to me. I learned afterward that it was a B-flat cornet. When she had finished, all the boys had horns in their hands. We were to be taught how to play on them and form a band.

70 The little woman had a black case with her, which she opened. It held a beautiful horn, and when she blew on it it sounded beautiful. Then she motioned to us that we were to blow our horns. Some of the boys tried to blow from the large end. Although we tried our best, we could not produce a sound from them. She then tried to talk to us, but we did not understand her. Then she showed us how to wet the end of the mouthpiece. We thought she wanted us to spit into the horns, so we did. She finally got so discouraged with us that she started crying.

71 We just stood there and waited for her to get through, then we all tried again. Finally, some of the boys managed to make a noise through their horns. But if you could have heard it! It was terrible! But we thought we were doing fine.

72 So now I had more to occupy my attention. In the morning I had one hour to practice for the band. Then I must run to my room and change my clothes and go to work in the tin shop. From there I had to run again to my room and change my clothes and get ready for dinner. After that, I had a little time to study my lessons.

73 Then the school bell would ring and it was time for school. After that, we played or studied our music. Then we went to bed. All lights had to be out at nine o'clock. The first piece of music our band was able to play was the alphabet, from "a" to "z." It was a great day for us when we were able to play this simple little thing in public. But it was a good thing we were not asked to give an encore, for that was all we knew!

74 After I had learned to play a little, I was chosen to give all the bugle calls. I had to get up in the morning before the others and arouse everybody by blowing the morning call. Evenings at ten minutes before nine o'clock I blew again. Then all the boys would run for their rooms. At nine o'clock the second call was given, when all lights were turned out and we were supposed to be in bed. Later on I learned the mess call, and eventually I could blow all the calls of the regular army.

75   I did these duties all the time I was at Carlisle School, so in the early part of 1880, although I was a young boy of but twelve, I was busy learning everything my instructors handed me.

76   One Sunday morning we were all busy getting ready to go to Sunday School in town. Suddenly there was great excitement among some of the boys on the floor below. One of the boys came running upstairs shouting, "Luther Standing Bear's father is here!" Everybody ran downstairs to see my father. We had several tribes at the school now, many of whom had heard of my father, and they were anxious to see him.

77   When I got downstairs, my father was in the center of a large crowd of the boys, who were all shaking hands with him. I had to fight my way through to reach him. He was so glad to see me, and I was so delighted to see him. But our rules were that we were not to speak the Indian language under any consideration. And here was my father, and he could not talk English!

78   My first act was to write a note to Captain Pratt, asking if he would permit me to speak to my father in the Sioux tongue. I said, "My father is here. Please allow me to speak to him in Indian." Captain Pratt answered, "Yes, my boy; bring your father over to my house."

79   This was another happy day for me. I took my father over to meet Captain Pratt, who was so glad to see him, and was very respectful to him. Father was so well dressed. He wore a gray suit, nice shoes, and a derby hat. But he wore his hair long. He looked very nice in white men's clothes. He even sported a gold watch and chain. Captain Pratt gave father a room with Robert American Horse, in the boys' quarters. He allowed the boys to talk to him in the Indian tongue, and that pleased the boys very much. Here Father remained for a time with us.

DISCUSSION QUESTIONS

1. What did Luther Standing Bear learn about the difference between Indian and Euro-American ideas about time?
2. Judging by Luther Standing Bear's various experiences at Carlisle, how was "civilization" defined?
3. The teachers Luther had at Carlisle do not seem to have been very skilled at teaching non-English speakers. How might they have improved their methods?
4. Luther seems to have accepted most of his experience at Carlisle with cheerfulness, although he was often bewildered. How can you account for his generally good humor?

WRITING TOPICS

1. In an essay, tell what you would have done differently if you had been hired to oversee Carlisle Indian School in 1879. Would you have followed any of the same procedures that were followed when Luther was there?

2. In an essay, recall your first days in school as a first-grader or your first days in a new school. Were any of your feelings the same as Luther Standing Bear's feelings?

THE SCHOOL DAYS OF AN INDIAN GIRL

Zitkala-Ša (Gertrude Bonnin)

Born in 1876 in South Dakota, Zitkala-Ša (Gertrude Simmons Bonnin), a Yankton Sioux, left home at the age of eight to attend White's Indian Manual Labor Institute in Wabash, Indiana, a Quaker-sponsored school. After three years, she returned home, but she was unable to adjust to reservation life with her mother. After three more years of missionary schooling, she continued her education at Earlham College against her mother's wishes. She then went to Pennsylvania in 1898 to teach at the Carlisle Indian Industrial School. Zitkala-Ša criticized the "anti-Indian educational principles" and assimilation policy promoted at Carlisle, and her strong disagreements with Captain Pratt led to the end of her service there. She bitterly reflected on the aim of Indian education and her role as a teacher in her essay "An Indian Teacher Among Indians."

After leaving Carlisle, Zitkala-Ša studied briefly at the New England Conservatory of Music. Later, she returned to the reservation to collect stories for her first book, *Old Indian Legends* (1901). During that period, Zitkala-Ša began writing articles and short stories, publishing three autobiographical pieces in the *Atlantic Monthly* (1900), which were later reprinted along with short stories and essays in her book *American Indian Stories* (1921). The following text is an abridgement of the *Atlantic Monthly* essay series. It recounts episodes in the author's life from age eight to about twenty-four.

In 1902 Zitkala-Ša married Raymond T. Bonnin, a Yankton Sioux, who worked for the Indian Service. They lived at the Uintah Ouray Ute Agency in Utah from 1902 to 1916, where their only child was born. While there, she became associated with the Society of American Indians (SAI) and when she was elected secretary in 1916, the Bonnins moved to Washington, D.C. to enable her to serve in that position. She edited the *American Indian Magazine* (1918–1919), which provided a forum for her writing. After the disintegration of SAI, Bonnin founded the National Council of American Indians in 1926 and served as its president until her death in 1938. She is buried in Arlington National Cemetery.

Like Sarah Winnemucca, Bonnin was a pioneer among Native American writers. Claiming her heritage in print as an American Indian woman at a time when few Indian women were published, she never moderated her critical tone. In spite of her criticism of boarding school education, Bonnin effectively wielded the written word to support her fight for just treatment of Native Americans. Her skills in the English language began when the small eight-year-old first went to boarding school. She polished her command of English as a tireless and eloquent public speaker, campaigning for Indian rights and lobbying Congress for Indian citizenship. In this selection, she begins by telling of her desire to go to school in a "Wonderland" where she could pick red apples.

THE BIG RED APPLES

1   The first turning away from the easy, natural flow of my life occurred in an early spring. It was in my eighth year; in the month of March, I afterward learned. At this age I knew but one language, and that was my mother's native tongue.

2   From some of my playmates I heard that two paleface missionaries were in our village. They were from that class of white men who wore big hats and carried large hearts, they said. Running direct to my mother, I began to question her why these two strangers were among us. She told me, after I had teased much, that they had come to take away Indian boys and girls to the East. My mother did not seem to want me to talk about them. But in a day or two, I gleaned many wonderful stories from my playfellows concerning the strangers.

3   "Mother, my friend Judéwin is going home with the missionaries. She is going to a more beautiful country than ours; the palefaces told her so!" I said wistfully, wishing in my heart that I too might go.

4   Mother sat in a chair, and I was hanging on her knee. Within the last two seasons my big brother Dawée had returned from a three years' education in the East, and his coming back influenced my mother to take a farther step from her native way of living. First it was a change from the buffalo skin to the white man's canvas that covered our wigwam. Now she had given up her wigwam of slender poles, to live, a foreigner, in a home of clumsy logs.

5   "Yes, my child, several others besides Judéwin are going away with the palefaces. Your brother said the missionaries had inquired about his little sister," she said, watching my face very closely.

6   My heart thumped so hard against my breast, I wondered if she could hear it.

7   "Did he tell them to take me, mother?" I asked, fearing lest Dawée had forbidden the palefaces to see me, and that my hope of going to the Wonderland would be entirely blighted.

8   With a sad, slow smile, she answered: "There! I knew you were wishing to go, because Judéwin has filled your ears with the white men's lies. Don't believe a word they say! Their words are sweet, but, my child, their deeds are bitter. You will cry for me, but they will not even soothe you. Stay with me, my little one! Your brother Dawée says that going East, away from your mother, is too hard an experience for his baby sister."

9   Thus my mother discouraged my curiosity about the lands beyond our eastern horizon; for it was not yet an ambition for Letters[1] that was stirring me. But on the following day the missionaries did come to our very house. I spied them coming up the footpath leading to our cottage. A third man was with them, but he was not my brother Dawée. It was another, a young interpreter, a paleface who had a smattering of the Indian language. I was ready to run out to meet them, but I did not dare to displease my mother. With great glee, I jumped up and down on our ground floor. I begged my mother to open the door, that they would be sure to come to us. Alas! They came, they saw, and they conquered!

10   Judéwin had told me of the great tree where grew red, red apples; and how we could reach out our hands and pick all the red apples we could eat. I had never seen apple trees. I had never tasted more than a dozen red apples in my life; and when I heard of the orchards of the East, I was eager to roam among them. The missionaries smiled into my eyes, and patted my head. I wondered how mother could say such hard words against them.

11   "Mother, ask them if little girls may have all the red apples they want, when they go East," I whispered aloud, in my excitement.

12   The interpreter heard me, and answered: "Yes, little girl, the nice red apples are for those who picked them; and you will have a ride on the iron horse if you go with these good people."

13   I had never seen a train, and he knew it.

14   "Mother, I am going East! I like big red apples, and I want to ride on the iron horse! Mother, say yes!" I pleaded. My mother said nothing. . . .

15   The next morning came, and my mother called me to her side. "My daughter, do you still persist in wishing to leave your mother?" she asked.

16   "Oh, mother, it is not that I wish to leave you, but I want to see the wonderful Eastern land," I answered.

17   My dear old aunt came to our house that morning, and I heard her say, "Let her try it."

18   I hoped that, as usual, my aunt was pleading on my side. My brother Dawée came for mother's decision. I dropped my play, and crept close to my aunt.

---

[1] *letters:* learning or knowledge, especially of literature.

19 "Yes, Dawée, my daughter, though she does not understand what it all means, is anxious to go. She will need an education when she is grown, for then there will be fewer real Dakotas, and many more palefaces. This tearing her away, so young, from her mother is necessary, if I would have her an educated woman. The palefaces, who owe us a large debt for stolen lands, have begun to pay a tardy justice in offering some education to our children. But I know my daughter must suffer keenly in this experiment. For her sake, I dread to tell you my reply to the missionaries. Go, tell them that they may take my little daughter, and that the Great Spirit shall not fail to reward them according to their hearts."

20 Wrapped in my heavy blanket, I walked with my mother to the carriage that was soon to take us to the iron horse. I was happy. I met my playmates, who were also wearing their best thick blankets. We showed one another our new beaded moccasins, and the width of the belts that girdled our new dresses. Soon we were being drawn rapidly away by the white man's horses. When I saw the lonely figure of my mother vanish in the distance, a sense of regret settled heavily upon me. I felt suddenly weak, as if I might fall limp to the ground. I was in the hands of strangers whom my mother did not fully trust. I no longer felt free to be myself, or to voice my own feelings. The tears trickled down my cheeks, and I buried my face in the folds of my blanket. Now the first step, parting me from my mother, was taken, and all my belated tears availed nothing. . . .

The Land of Red Apples

21 . . . It was night when we reached the school grounds. The lights from the windows of the large buildings fell upon some of the icicled trees that stood beneath them. We were led toward an open door, where the brightness of the lights within flooded out over the heads of the excited palefaces who blocked the way. My body trembled more from fear than from the snow I trod upon.

22 Entering the house, I stood close against the wall. The strong glaring light in the large whitewashed room dazzled my eyes. The noisy hurrying of hard shoes upon a bare wooden floor increased the whirring in my ears. My only safety seemed to be in keeping next to the wall. As I was wondering in which direction to escape from all this confusion, two warm hands grasped me firmly, and in the same moment I was tossed high in midair. A rosy-cheeked paleface woman caught me in her arms. I was both frightened and insulted by such trifling. I stared into her eyes, wishing her to let me stand on my own feet, but she jumped me up and down with increasing enthusiasm. My mother had never made a plaything of her wee daughter. Remembering this I began to cry aloud.

23 They misunderstood the cause of my tears, and placed me at a white table loaded with food. There our party were united again. As I did not hush my crying, one of the older ones whispered to me, "Wait until you are alone in the night."

24 It was very little I could swallow besides my sobs, that evening.

25 "Oh, I want my mother and my brother Dawée! I want to go to my aunt!" I pleaded; but the ears of the palefaces could not hear me.

26 From the table we were taken along an upward incline of wooden boxes, which I learned afterward to call a stairway. At the top was a quiet hall, dimly lighted. Many narrow beds were in one straight line down the entire length of the wall. In them lay sleeping brown faces, which peeped just out of the coverings. I was tucked into bed with one of the tall girls, because she talked to me in my mother tongue and seemed to soothe me.

27 I had arrived in the wonderful land of rosy skies, but I was not happy, as I had thought I should be. My long travel and the bewildering sights had exhausted me. I fell asleep, heaving deep, tired sobs. My tears were left to dry themselves in streaks, because neither my aunt nor my mother was near to wipe them away.

THE SNOW EPISODE

28 A short time after our arrival we three Dakotas were playing in the snow-drifts. We were all still deaf to the English language, excepting Judéwin, who always heard such puzzling things. One morning we learned through her ears that we were forbidden to fall lengthwise in the snow, as we had been doing, to see our own impressions. However, before many hours we had forgotten the order, and we were having great sport in the snow, when a shrill voice called us. Looking up, we saw an imperative hand beckoning us into the house. We shook the snow off ourselves, and started toward the woman as slowly as we dared.

29 Judéwin said: "Now the paleface is angry with us. She is going to punish us for falling into the snow. If she looks straight into your eyes and talks loudly, you must wait until she stops. Then, after a tiny pause, say, 'No.'" The rest of the way we practiced upon the little word "no."

30 As it happened, Thowin was summoned to judgment first. The door shut behind her with a click.

31 Judéwin and I stood silently listening at the keyhole. The paleface woman talked in very severe tones. Her words fell from her lips like crackling embers, and her inflection ran up like the small end of a switch. I understood her voice better than the things she was saying. I was certain we had made her very impatient with us. Judéwin heard enough of the words to realize all too late that she had taught us the wrong reply.

32 "Oh, poor Thowin!" she gasped, as she put both hands over her ears.

33 Just then I heard Thowin's tremulous answer, "No."

34 With an angry exclamation, the woman gave her a hard spanking. Then she stopped to say something. Judéwin said it was this: "Are you going to obey my word the next time?"

35 Thowin answered again with the only word at her command, "No."

36   This time the woman meant her blows to smart, for the poor frightened girl shrieked at the top of her voice. In the midst of the whipping the blows ceased abruptly, and the woman asked another question: "Are you going to fall in the snow again?"

37   Thowin gave her bad password another trial. We heard her say feebly, "No! No!"

38   With this the woman hid away her half-worn slipper, and led the child out, stroking her black shorn head. Perhaps it occurred to her that brute force is not the solution for such a problem. She did nothing to Judéwin nor to me. She only returned to us our unhappy comrade, and left us alone in the room.

39   During the first two or three seasons misunderstandings as ridiculous as this one of the snow episode frequently took place, bringing unjustifiable frights and punishments into our lives.

40   Within a year I was able to express myself somewhat in broken English. As soon as I comprehended a part of what was said and done, a mischievous spirit of revenge possessed me. One day I was called in from my play for some misconduct. I had disregarded a rule which seemed to me very needlessly binding. I was sent into the kitchen to mash the turnips for dinner. It was noon, and steaming dishes were hastily carried into the dining room. I hated turnips, and their odor which came from the brown jar was offensive to me. With fire in my heart, I took the wooden tool that the paleface woman held out to me. I stood upon a step, and, grasping the handle with both hands, I bent in hot rage over the turnips. I worked my vengeance upon them. All were so busily occupied that no one noticed me. I saw that the turnips were in a pulp, and that further beating could not improve the, but the order was, "Mash these turnips," and mash them I would! I renewed my energy; and as I sent the masher into the bottom of the jar, I felt a satisfying sensation that the weight of my body had gone into it.

41   Just here a paleface woman came up to my table. As she looked into the jar, she shoved my hands roughly aside. I stood fearless and angry. She placed her red hands upon the rim of the jar. Then she gave one lift and a stride away from the table. But lo! the pulpy contents fell through the crumbled bottom to the floor! She spared me no scolding phrases that I had earned. I did not heed them. I felt triumphant in my revenge, though deep within me I was a wee bit sorry to have broken the jar.

42   As I sat eating my dinner, and saw that no turnips were served, I whooped in my heart for having once asserted the rebellion within me.

FOUR STRANGE SUMMERS

43   After my first three years of school, I roamed again in the Western country through four strange summers.

44   During this time I seemed to hang in the heart of chaos, beyond the touch or voice of human aid. My brother, being almost ten years my senior,

did not quite understand my feelings. My mother had never gone inside of a schoolhouse, and so she was not capable of comforting her daughter who could read and write. Even nature seemed to have no place for me. I was neither a wee girl nor a tall one; neither a wild Indian nor a tame one. This deplorable situation was the effect of my brief course in the East, and the unsatisfactory "teenth" in a girl's years.

45 It was under these trying conditions that, one bright afternoon, as I sat restless and unhappy in my mother's cabin, I caught the sound of the spirited step of my brother's pony on the road which passed by our dwelling. Soon I heard the wheels of a light buckboard, and Dawée's familiar "Ho!" to his pony. He alighted upon the bare ground in front of our house. Tying his pony to one of the projecting corner logs of the low-roofed cottage, he stepped upon the wooden doorstep.

46 I met him there with a hurried greeting, and, as I passed by, he looked a quiet "What?" into my eyes.

47 When he began talking with my mother, I slipped the rope from the pony's bridle. Seizing the reins and bracing my feet against the dashboard, I wheeled around in an instant. The pony was ever ready to try his speed. Looking backward, I saw Dawée waving his hand to me. I turned with the curve in the road and disappeared. I followed the winding road which crawled upward between the bases of little hillocks. Deep water-worn ditches ran parallel on either side. A strong wind blew against my cheeks and fluttered my sleeves. The pony reached the top of the highest hill, and began an even race on the level lands. There was nothing moving within that great circular horizon of the Dakota prairies save the tall grasses, over which the wind blew and rolled off in long, shadowy waves.

48 In a little while I came in sight of my mother's house. Dawée stood in the yard. I asked Dawée about something.

49 "No, my baby sister, I cannot take you with me to the party to-night," he replied. Though I was not far from fifteen, and I felt that before long I should enjoy all the privileges of my tall cousin, Dawée persisted in calling me his baby sister.

50 That moonlight night, I cried in my mother's presence when I heard the jolly young people pass by our cottage. They were no more young braves in blankets and eagle plumes, nor Indian maids with prettily painted cheeks. They had gone three years to school in the East, and had become civilized. The young men wore the white man's coat and trousers, with bright neckties. The girls wore tight muslin dresses, with ribbons at neck and waist. At these gatherings they talked English. I could speak English almost as well as my brother, but I was not properly dressed to be taken along. I had no hat, no ribbons, and no close-fitting gown. Since my return from school I had thrown away my shoes, and wore again the soft moccasins.

51 While Dawée was busily preparing to go I controlled my tears. But when I heard him bounding away on his pony, I buried my face in my arms and cried hot tears.

INCURRING MY MOTHER'S DISPLEASURE

52   In the second journey to the East I had not come without some precautions. I had a secret interview with one of our best medicine men, and when I left his wigwam I carried securely in my sleeve a tiny bunch of magic roots. This possession assured me of friends wherever I should go. So absolutely did I believe in its charms that I wore it through all the school routine for more than a year. Then, before I lost my faith in the dead roots, I lost the little buckskin bag containing all my good luck.

53   At the close of this second term of three years I was the proud owner of my first diploma. The following autumn I ventured upon a college career against my mother's will.

54   I had written for her approval, but in her reply I found no encouragement. She called my notice to her neighbors' children, who had completed their education in three years. They had returned to their homes, and were then talking English with the frontier settlers. Her few words hinted that I had better give up my slow attempt to learn the white man's ways, and be content to roam over the prairies and find my living upon wild roots. I silenced her by deliberate disobedience.

55   Thus, homeless and heavy-hearted, I began anew my life among strangers.

56   As I hid myself in my little room in the college dormitory, away from the scornful and yet curious eyes of the students, I pined for sympathy. Often I wept in secret, wishing I had gone West, to be nourished by my mother's love, instead of remaining among a cold race whose hearts were frozen hard with prejudice.

57   During the fall and winter seasons I scarcely had a real friend, though by that time several of my classmates were courteous to me at a safe distance.

58   My mother had not yet forgiven my rudeness to her, and I had no moment for letter-writing. By daylight and lamplight, I spun with reeds and thistles, until my hands were tired from their weaving, the magic design which promised me the white man's respect.

59   At length, in the spring term, I entered an oratorical contest among the various classes. As the day of competition approached, it did not seem possible that the event was so near at hand, but it came. In the chapel the classes assembled together, with their invited guests. The high platform was carpeted, and gayly festooned with college colors. A bright white light illuminated the room, and outlined clearly the great polished beams that arched the domed ceiling. The assembled crowds filled the air with pulsating murmurs. When the hour for speaking arrived all were hushed. But on the wall the old clock which pointed out the trying moment ticked calmly on.

60   One after another I saw and heard the orators. Still, I could not realize that they longed for the favorable decision of the judges as much as I did.

Each contestant received a loud burst of applause, and some were cheered heartily. Too soon my turn came, and I paused a moment behind the curtains for a deep breath. After my concluding words, I heard the same applause that the others had called out.

61 Upon my retreating steps, I was astounded to receive from my fellow students a large bouquet of roses tied with flowing ribbons. With the lovely flowers I fled from the stage. This friendly token was a rebuke to me for the hard feelings I had borne them.

62 Later, the decision of the judges awarded me the first place. Then there was a mad uproar in the hall, where my classmates sang and shouted my name at the top of their lungs; and the disappointed students howled and brayed in fearfully dissonant tin trumpets. In this excitement, happy students rushed forward to offer their congratulations. And I could not conceal a smile when they wished to escort me in a procession to the students' parlor, where all were going to calm themselves. Thanking them for the kind spirit which prompted them to make such a proposition, I walked alone with the night to my own little room.

63 A few weeks afterward, I appeared as the college representative in another contest. This time the competition was among orators from different colleges in our state. It was held at the state capital, in one of the largest opera houses.

64 Here again was a strong prejudice against my people. In the evening, as the great audience filled the house, the student bodies began warring among themselves. Fortunately, I was spared witnessing any of the noisy wrangling before the contest began. The slurs against the Indian that stained the lips of our opponents were already burning like a dry fever within my breast.

65 But after the orations were delivered a deeper burn awaited me. There, before that vast ocean of eyes, some college rowdies threw out a large white flag, with a drawing of a most forlorn Indian girl on it. Under this they had printed in bold black letters words that ridiculed the college which was represented by a "squaw." Such worse than barbarian rudeness embittered me. While we waited for the verdict of the judges, I gleamed fiercely upon the throngs of palefaces. My teeth were hard set, as I saw the white flag still floating insolently in the air.

66 Then anxiously we watched the man carry toward the stage the envelope containing the final decision.

67 There were two prizes given, that night, and one of them was mine!

68 The evil spirit laughed within me when the white flag dropped out of sight, and the hands which furled it hung limp in defeat.

69 Leaving the crowd as quickly as possible, I was soon in my room. The rest of the night I sat in an armchair and gazed into the crackling fire. I laughed no more in triumph when thus alone. The little taste of victory did not satisfy a hunger in my heart. In my mind I saw my mother far away on the Western plains, and she was holding a charge against me.

A TRIP WESTWARD

70   One sultry month I sat at a desk heaped up with work. Now, as I recall it, I wonder how I could have dared to disregard nature's warning with such recklessness. Fortunately, my inheritance of a marvelous endurance enabled me to bend without breaking.

71   Though I had gone to and fro, from my room to the office, in an unhappy silence, I was watched by those around me. On an early morning I was summoned to the superintendent's office. For a half hour I listened to his words, and when I returned to my room I remembered one sentence above the rest. It was this; "I am going to turn you loose to pasture!" He was sending me West to gather Indian pupils for the school, and this was his way of expressing it.

72   I needed nourishment, but the midsummer's travel across the continent to search the hot prairies for overconfident parents who would intrust their children to strangers was a lean pasturage. However, I dwelt on the hope of seeing my mother. I tried to reason that a change was a rest. Within a couple of days I started toward my mother's home.

73   The intense heat and the sticky car smoke that followed my homeward trail did not noticeably restore my vitality. Hour after hour I gazed upon the country which was receding rapidly from me. I noticed the gradual expansion of the horizon as we emerged out of the forests into the plains. The great high buildings, whose towers overlooked the dense woodlands, and whose gigantic clusters formed large cities, diminished, together with the groves, until only little log cabins lay snugly in the bosom of the vast prairie. The cloud shadows which drifted about on the waving yellow of long-dried grasses thrilled me like the meeting of old friends.

74   At a small station, consisting of a single frame house with a rickety board walk around it, I alighted from the iron horse, just thirty miles from my mother and my brother Dawée. A strong hot wind seemed determined to blow my hat off, and return me to olden days when I roamed bareheaded over the hills. After the puffing engine of my train was gone, I stood on the platform in deep solitude. In the distance I saw the gently rolling land leap up into bare hills. At their bases a broad gray road was winding itself round about them until it came by the station. Among these hills I rode in a light conveyance, with a trusty driver, whose unkempt flaxen hair hung shaggy about his ears and his leather neck of reddish tan. From accident or decay he had lost one of his long front teeth.

75   Though I call him a paleface, his cheeks were of a brick red. His moist blue eyes, blurred and bloodshot, twitched involuntarily. For a long time he had driven through grass and snow from this solitary station to the Indian village. His weather-stained clothes fitted badly his warped shoulders. He was stooped, and his protruding chin, with its tuft of dry flax, nodded as monotonously as did the head of his faithful beast.

76   All the morning I looked about me, recognizing old familiar sky lines of

rugged bluffs and round-topped hills. By the roadside I caught glimpses of various plants whose sweet roots were delicacies among my people. When I saw the first cone-shaped wigwam, I could not help uttering an exclamation which caused my driver a sudden jump out of his drowsy nodding.

77　　At noon, as we drove through the eastern edge of the reservation, I grew very impatient and restless. Constantly I wondered what my mother would say upon seeing her little daughter grown tall. I had not written her the day of my arrival, thinking I would surprise her. Crossing a ravine thicketed with low shrubs and plum bushes, we approached a large yellow acre of wild sunflowers. Just beyond this nature's garden we drew near to my mother's cottage. Close by the log cabin stood a little canvas-covered wigwam. The driver stopped in front of the open door, and in a long moment my mother appeared at the threshold.

78　　I had expected her to run out to greet me, but she stood still, all the while staring at the weather-beaten man at my side. At length, when her loftiness became unbearable, I called to her, "Mother, why do you stop?"

79　　This seemed to break the evil moment, and she hastened out to hold my head against her cheek.

80　　"My daughter, what madness possessed you to bring home such a fellow?" she asked, pointing at the driver, who was fumbling in his pockets for change while he held the bill I gave him between his jagged teeth.

81　　"Bring him! Why, no, mother, he has brought me! He is a driver!" I exclaimed.

82　　Upon this revelation, my mother threw her arms about me and apologized for her mistaken inference. We laughed away the momentary hurt. Then she built a brisk fire on the ground in the tepee, and hung a blackened coffeepot on one of the prongs of a forked pole which leaned over the flames. Placing a pan on a heap of red embers, she baked some unleavened bread. This light luncheon she brought into the cabin, and arranged on a table covered with a checkered oilcloth.

83　　My mother had never gone to school, and though she meant always to give up her own customs for such of the white man's ways as pleased her, she made only compromises. Her two windows, directly opposite each other, she curtained with a pink-flowered print. The naked logs were unstained, and rudely carved with the axe so as to fit into one another. The sod roof was trying to boast of tiny sunflowers, the seeds of which had probably been planted by the constant wind. As I leaned my head against the logs, I discovered the peculiar odor that I could not forget. The rains had soaked the earth and roof so that the smell of damp clay was but the natural breath of such a dwelling.

RETROSPECTION

84　　Leaving my mother, I returned to the school in the East. As months passed over me, I slowly comprehended that the large army of white teachers in Indian schools had a larger missionary creed than I had suspected.

85   It was one which included self-preservation quite as much as Indian education. When I saw an opium-eater holding a position as teacher of Indians, I did not understand what good was expected, until a Christian in power replied that this pumpkin-colored creature had a feeble mother to support. An inebriate paleface sat stupid in a doctor's chair, while Indian parents carried their ailments to untimely graves, because his fair wife was dependent upon him for her daily food.

86   I find it hard to count that white man a teacher who tortured an ambitious Indian youth by frequently reminding the brave changeling that he was nothing but a "government pauper."

87   Though I burned with indignation upon discovering on every side instances no less shameful than those I have mentioned, there was no present help. Even the few rare ones who have worked nobly for my race were powerless to choose workmen like themselves. To be sure, a man was sent from the Great Father to inspect Indian schools, but what he saw was usually the students' sample work *made* for exhibition. I was nettled by this sly cunning of the workmen who hoodwinked the Indian's pale Father at Washington.

88   My illness, which prevented the conclusion of my college course, together with my mother's stories of the encroaching frontier settlers, left me in no mood to strain my eyes in searching for latent good in my white co-workers.

89   At this stage of my own evolution, I was ready to curse men of small capacity for being the dwarfs their God had made them. In the process of my education I had lost all consciousness of the nature world about me. Thus, when a hidden rage took me to the small white-walled prison which I then called my room, I unknowingly turned away from my one salvation.

90   Alone in my room, I sat like the petrified Indian woman of whom my mother used to tell me. I wished my heart's burdens would turn me to unfeeling stone. But alive, in my tomb, I was destitute!

91   For the white man's papers I had given up my faith in the Great Spirit. For these same papers I had forgotten the healing in trees and brooks. On account of my mother's simple view of life, and my lack of any, I gave her up, also. I made no friends among the race of people I loathed. Like a slender tree, I had been uprooted from my mother, nature, and God. I was shorn of my branches, which had waved in sympathy and love for home and friends. The natural coat of bark which had protected my oversensitive nature was scraped off to the very quick.

92   Now a cold bare pole I seemed to be, planted in a strange earth. Still, I seemed to hope a day would come when my mute aching head, reared upward to the sky, would flash a zigzag lightning across the heavens. With this dream of vent for a long-pent consciousness, I walked again amid the crowds.

93   At last, one weary day in the schoolroom, a new idea presented itself to me. It was a new way of solving the problem of my inner self. I liked it. Thus I resigned my position as teacher; and now I am in an Eastern city, following the long course of study I have set for myself.

DISCUSSION QUESTIONS

1. Why did the author's mother allow her to go away with the missionaries?
2. What caused "fright and punishments" during the first few seasons at the school?
3. What were the causes of the author's unhappiness during her summers at home?
4. What caused the author's mother's displeasure?
5. What was the reason for the author's unhappiness in college despite her triumphs?
6. Why was Bonnin unhappy teaching at Carlisle?

WRITING TOPICS

1. Analyze the imagery in paragraphs 73–83, noting the senses to which it appeals and telling how Bonnin conveys a sense of movement from the time she gets on the train until she leans her head against the logs in her mother's house.
2. Using Bonnin's descriptions in paragraphs 73–83 as a model, write of a journey, long or short, you have made.
3. Characterize Bonnin in a short essay, supporting your observations with remarks and events from these excerpts from her autobiography.

INDIAN BOARDING SCHOOL: THE RUNAWAYS

Louise Erdrich

Louise Erdrich, whose work appears in earlier chapters, said in an interview with Joseph Bruchac that she liked the rhythm of her poem, "Indian Boarding School: The Runaways." Although she never ran away from school, Erdrich poignantly depicts the plight of students who tried to escape from school only to be returned by the authorities. She commented to Bruchac that these students were running to home, not away: "The kids who are talking in this poem are children who've been removed from their homes, their cultures, by the Bureau of Indian Affairs. . . . So, it is about the hopelessness of a child in that kind of situation. There is no escape." Fortunately, today's boarding school students have choices about being in such schools.

Erdrich, who grew up near the Turtle Mountain Chippewa Reservation in North Dakota, in a sense also returns "home" in her writing. Many of her novels and poems are drawn from the Chippewa part of her heritage. For Native American writers like Erdrich, going home through their writing is a way to recover and restore parts of their Indian heritage. Magical beadwork forms the central metaphor of her sixth novel, *The Antelope Wife* (1998). Mythic twins bead and thread lives in a multiple strand of destinies and a balanced world. Mortal Chippewa twins sew intricate designs of their lives into their beautiful beadwork.

Erdrich worked at a variety of jobs—waitress, lifeguard, psychiatric aide, and poetry teacher—before she achieved success as a writer. A turning point in her writing career was her 1981 marriage to Michael Dorris after graduating from Johns Hopkins in 1979. Dorris encouraged Erdrich to write and helped her break into print. They collaborated on the novel *The Crown of Columbus* (1991). Indeed, Erdrich and Dorris have stated that they consulted on everything either of them wrote.

Home's the place we head for in our sleep.
Boxcars stumbling north in dreams
don't wait for us. We catch them on the run.
The rails, old lacerations that we love,
5 shoot parallel across the face and break
just under Turtle Mountains. Riding scars
you can't get lost. Home is the place they cross.

The lame guard strikes a match and makes the dark
less tolerant. We watch through cracks in boards
10 as the land starts rolling, rolling till it hurts
to be here, cold in regulation clothes.
We know the sheriff's waiting at midrun
to take us back. His car is dumb and warm.
The highway doesn't rock, it only hums
15 like the wing of long insults. The worn-down welts
of ancient punishments lead back and forth.

All runaways wear dresses, long green ones,
the color you would think shame was. We scrub
the sidewalks down because it's shameful work.
20 Our brushes cut the stone in watered arcs
and in the soak frail outlines shiver clear
a moment, things us kids pressed on the dark
face before it hardened, pale, remembering
delicate old injuries, the spines of names and leaves.

DISCUSSION QUESTIONS

1. A motif of disfigurement and hurt runs through this poem. Find the words that suggest this motif, and in a small group discuss what this motif tells you about the experience of the runaways.
2. Why are the rails referred to as lacerations in line 4, and why would they be loved?
3. In the last stanza, the runaways who scrub the sidewalks seem to see pictures in the "watered areas," including "the spines of names and leaves." What kind of names might they envision?

WRITING TOPICS

1. Write a brief essay in which you analyze how Erdrich achieves the tone of her poem. (Tone is the author's attitude toward her subject.)
2. Think of a time when you wanted to run away—either away from home or toward home—and write a poem about this time.

INDIAN EDUCATION

Sherman Alexie

Sherman Alexie, an energetic young poet, short-story writer, and novelist often performs his works for live audiences. Aware that poetry must be heard to be fully appreciated, Alexie commented at the 1998 Taos Poetry Circus, "Poetry is a bardic tradition. . . . They were doing this a thousand years ago." Alexie estimated that he gave 290 readings throughout the United States in 1992 and 1993, performing to audiences ranging in size from six to one thousand. A popular performer among young people, he takes his works on the road to many high schools, on and off reservations.

Alexie attended school on the Spokane Reservation in Wellpinit, Washington. He later studied at Gonzaga University and at Washington State University.

Alexie says his grandmother was his strongest link to tradition, telling him funny tribal stories. In an interview in the Spring 1998 issue of *Indian Artist,* Alexie says, "She knew I was weird. . . . She was really supportive of who I was. Big Mom would go to Goodwill shopping or garage-sale shopping, and she would always bring back books for 'Junior.' She wouldn't even look at what kind of books they were; she would just see a book and bring it home. So I'd end up with these Harlequin romances, or auto-repair manuals—it didn't matter."

Alexie describes himself as "kind of mixed up, kind of odd, not traditional. I'm a rez kid who's gone urban, and that's what I write about." In fact, he had ten books published by age thirty. The following excerpt from "Indian Education" appears in *The Lone Ranger and Tonto Fistfight in Heaven* (1993), a collection of stories which was made into a movie. The film, *Smoke Signals,* was co-produced by Alexie and premiered at the Sundance Film Festival. He is also working on another book of poetry and the screenplay based on his book *Indian Killer* (1996).

"Indian Education" is a recital of the trials of various school years for an Indian boy.

First Grade

1   My hair was too short and my U.S. Government glasses were horn-rimmed, ugly, and all that first winter in school, the other Indian boys chased me from one corner of the playground to the other. They pushed me down, buried me in the snow until I couldn't breathe, thought I'd never breathe again.

2   They stole my glasses and threw them over my head, around my out-stretched hands, just beyond my reach, until someone tripped me and sent me falling again, facedown in the snow.

3   I was always falling down; my Indian name was Junior Falls Down. Sometimes it was Bloody Nose or Steal-His-Lunch. Once, it was Cries-Like-a-White-Boy, even though none of us had seen a white boy cry.

4   Then it was a Friday morning recess and Frenchy SiJohn threw snowballs at me while the rest of the Indian boys tortured some other *top-yogh-yaught* kid, another weakling. But Frenchy was confident enough to torment me all by himself, and most days I would have let him.

5   But the little warrior in me roared to life that day and knocked Frenchy to the ground, held his head against the snow, and punched him so hard that my knuckles and the snow made symmetrical bruises on his face. He almost looked like he was wearing war paint.

6   But he wasn't the warrior. I was. And I chanted *It's a good day to die, it's a good day to die,* all the way down to the principal's office.

Second Grade

7   Betty Towle, missionary teacher, redheaded and so ugly that no one ever had a puppy crush on her, made me stay in for recess fourteen days straight.

8   "Tell me you're sorry," she said.

9   "Sorry for what?" I asked.

10   "Everything," she said and made me stand straight for fifteen minutes, eagle-armed with books in each hand. One was a math book; the other was English. But all I learned was that gravity can be painful.

11   For Halloween I drew a picture of her riding a broom with a scrawny cat on the back. She said that her God would never forgive me for that.

12   Once, she gave the class a spelling test but set me aside and gave me a test designed for junior high students. When I spelled all the words right, she crumpled up the paper and made me eat it.

13   "You'll learn respect," she said.

14   She sent a letter home with me that told my parents to either cut my braids or keep me home from class. My parents came in the next day and dragged their braids across Betty Towle's desk.

15   "Indians, indians, indians." She said it without capitalization. She called me "indian, indian, indian."

16   And I said, *Yes, I am. I am Indian. Indian, I am. . . .*

Fourth Grade

17 "You should be a doctor when you grow up," Mr. Schluter told me, even though his wife, the third grade teacher, thought I was crazy beyond my years. My eyes always looked like I had just hit-and-run someone.

18 "Guilty," she said. "You always look guilty."

19 "Why should I be a doctor?" I asked Mr. Schluter.

20 "So you can come back and help the tribe. So you can heal people."

21 That was the year my father drank a gallon of vodka a day and the same year that my mother started two hundred different quilts but never finished any. They sat in separate, dark places in our HUD house and wept savagely.

22 I ran home after school, heard their Indian tears, and looked in the mirror. *Doctor Victor,* I called myself, invented an education, talked to my reflection. *Doctor Victor to the emergency room. . . .*

Sixth Grade

23 Randy, the new Indian kid from the white town of Springdale, got into a fight an hour after he first walked into the reservation school.

24 Stevie Flett called him out, called him a squawman, . . . and called him a punk.

25 Randy and Stevie, and the rest of the Indian boys, walked out into the playground.

26 "Throw the first punch," Stevie said as they squared off.

27 "No," Randy said.

28 "Throw the first punch," Stevie said again.

29 "No," Randy said again.

30 "Throw the first punch!" Stevie said for the third time, and Randy reared back and pitched a knuckle fastball that broke Stevie's nose.

31 We all stood there in silence, in awe.

32 That was Randy, my soon-to-be first and best friend, who taught me the most valuable lesson about living in the white world: *Always throw the first punch. . . .*

Ninth Grade

33 At the farm town high school dance, after a basketball game in an overheated gym where I had scored twenty-seven points and pulled down thirteen rebounds, I passed out during a slow song.

34 As my white friends revived me and prepared to take me to the emergency room where doctors would later diagnose my diabetes, the Chicano teacher ran up to us.

35 "Hey," he said. "What's that boy been drinking? I know all about these Indian kids. They start drinking real young."

36 Sharing dark skin doesn't necessarily make two men brothers. . . .

ELEVENTH GRADE

37   Last night I missed two free throws which would have won the game against the best team in the state. The farm town high school I play for is nicknamed the "Indians," and I'm probably the only actual Indian ever to play for a team with such a mascot.

38   This morning I pick up the sports page and read the headline: INDIANS LOSE AGAIN.

39   Go ahead and tell me none of this is supposed to hurt me very much.

TWELFTH GRADE

40   I walk down the aisle, valedictorian of this farm town high school, and my cap doesn't fit because I've grown my hair longer than it's ever been. Later, I stand as the school board chairman recites my awards, accomplishments, and scholarships.

41   I try to remain stoic for the photographers as I look toward the future.

42   Back home on the reservation, my former classmates graduate: a few can't read, one or two are just given attendance diplomas, most look forward to the parties. The bright students are shaken, frightened, because they don't know what comes next.

43   They smile for the photographer as they look back toward tradition.

DISCUSSION QUESTIONS

1. What kinds of stereotypical thinking does the narrator encounter? How does he react to this thinking?
2. What lessons does the narrator learn throughout his school career?
3. How does the reader know that the narrator learns some academic things as well?
4. Would you classify this selection as satire? Explain.

WRITING TOPICS

1. Analyze the tone of "Indian Education," and in a brief essay tell how it is achieved.
2. Write about some of the trials in your various years in school.
3. Alexie's sense of humor qualifies him to be a class comic. Select a friend or classmate who has a great sense of humor and the wit to express it. Write a profile of this person and include some of his or her funny stories and comments.

TLINGIT CONCRETE POEM

Nora Dauenhauer

Born and reared in Juneau, Alaska, Nora Marks Dauenhauer comes from a family of noted carvers and beadwork artists. She has a degree in anthropology and is one of Alaska's best-known native linguists. Respected for her translations of traditional texts and performances by Tlingit elders, she is a committed teacher, scholar, and traditional dancer.

This Tlingit woman has collected numerous traditional texts in the Tlingit language and translated them into English. Her poems have been published in the *Greenfield Review, Northward Journal, Raven's Bones Newsletter,* and other publications. She and her husband, Richard Dauenhauer, a translator of European poetry with a doctoral degree in comparative literature, have been a collaborative writing team for over twenty years. They are the authors of *Beginning Tlingit* (1976). They have edited three massive volumes of Tlingit texts. *Haa Shuká, Our Ancestors: Tlingit Oral Narratives* appeared in 1987. *Haa Tuwunáagu Yis, for Healing Our Spirit* (1990) is a book of Tlingit oratory recorded in performance. *Haa Kutseeyí, Our Culture: Tlingit Life Stories* (1994) presents life histories of more than fifty men and women.

```
                          t'a    n
                       a               i
                     a   k
         x'aax'x'aax'x'aax'x'aax'x'aax
        aax'x'aax'x'aax'x'aax'x'aax'x'aax'x
       'x'aax'x'aax'x'aax'x'aax'x'aax'x'aax'x'a
      x'x'aax'x'aax'x'aax'x'aax'x'aax'x'aax'x'aax
     aax'x'aax'x'aax'x'aax'x'aax'x'aax'x'aax'x'aax'
    'aax'x'aax'x'aax'x'aax'x'aax'x'aax'x'aax'x'aax'x
   x'aax'x'aax'x'aax'x'aax'x'aax'x'aax'x'aax'x'aax'x'
  'x'aax'x'aax'x'aax'x'aax'x'aax'x'aax'x'aax'x'aax'x'
  'x'aax'x'aax'x'aax'x'aax'x'aax'x'aax'x'aax'x'aax'x'a
  'x'aax'x'aax'x'aax'x'aax'x'aax'x'aax'x'aax'x'aax'x'a
 x'x'aax'x'aax'x'aax'x'aax'x'aax'x'aax'x'aax'x'aax'x'a
 x'x'aax'x'aax'x'aax'x'aax'x'aax'x'aax'x'aax'x'aax'x'a
 x'x'aax'x'aax'x'aax'x'aax'x'aax'x'aax'x'aax'x'aax'x'a
 x'x'aax'x'aax'x'aax'x'aax'x'aax'x'aax'x'aax'x'aax'x'a
  'x'aax'x'aax'x'aax'x'aax'x'aax'x'aax'x'aax'x'aax'x'a
  'x'aax'x'aax'x'aax'x'aax'x'aax'x'aax'x'aax'x'aax'x'
  'x'aax'x'aax'x'aax'x'aax'x'aax'x'aax'x'aax'x'aax'x'
   x'aax'x'aax'x'aax'x'aax'x'aax'x'aax'x'aax'x'aax'x'
    'aax'x'aax'x'aax'x'aax'x'aax'x'aax'x'aax'x'aax'x
    'aax'x'aax'x'aax'x'aax'x'aax'x'aax'x'aax'x'aax'
     aax'x'aax'x'aax'x'aax'x'aax'tl'ukwx'aax'x'aax'
      ax'x'aax'x'aax'x'aax'x'aax'x'aax'x'aax'x'aax
       x'x'aax'x'aax'x'aax'x'aax'x'aax'x'aax'x'aa
        'x'aax'x'aax'x'aax'x'aax'x'aax'x'aax'x'a
         'aax'x'aax'x'aax'x'aax'x'aax'x'aax'x
          ax'x'aax'x'aax'x'aax'x'aax'x'aax
           'x'aax'x'aax'x'aax'x'aax'x'a
            'aax'x'aax'x'aax'x'aax'x'
             x'aax'x'aax'x'aa
              'x'aa
```

Akat'ani = stem
x'aax' = apple
tl'ukwx = worm

⊡

DISCUSSION QUESTIONS

1. What do you think was the author's purpose in writing a visual poem such as this? Do you think she achieved her purpose?

2. In small groups, discuss whether a visual poem has a different impact on the reader than a conventional poem and why.

WRITING TOPICS

1. A concrete poem is both graphic and literary art that uses the shapes of letters and sentences to express meaning, as in Dauenhauer's poem and the examples below. Write your own concrete poem.

   a. ZZZZ
      (.) (.)
         ..
         ~

   b.   hopper   hopper
      grass grass   grass grass grass

2. Research and write an essay about the culture, language, and history of the Tlingits.

ENCHANTED ENCHANTED RATTLESNAKE

Yaqui Song
Translated by Larry Evers and Felipe Molina

Late in the nineteenth century, Mexico's national government conducted military operations aimed at exterminating the Yaqui tribe living along the Yaqui River. It sought rich lands for its non-Indians. The Yaqui towns in northwestern Mexico resisted conquest and land loss until 1927. Many individuals fled, however, to the United States. There the refugees earned a living mainly as agricultural workers.

These Yaqui refugees who congregated at Pascua (Easter) Village on the outskirts of Tucson, Arizona, tried to carry out ethnic calendrical rituals as though Pascua were a Yaqui River town. In 1987, some Pascua men and youths formed what they called a Bow Leaders dance group to perform the Coyote Dance that had lapsed there in 1941. Name and dance recalled Yaqui bow companies organized during Spanish colonial times. Yaqui soldiers became members of a sacred military society called the Coyotes during Mexican times, if not before.

After helping to organize the 1987 revival, Felipe Molina sang the Coyote songs to which the new Coyotes danced. He had learned them from transcriptions furnished by Larry Evers and made by Amos Taub in the 1950s from Yaqui elders, including Ignacio Alvarez and Refugio Savala. Molina sang "Enchanted Enchanted Rattlesnake," among other Coyote songs.

ENCHANTED ENCHANTED RATTLESNAKE

Enchanted enchanted rattlesnake
in the cactus is lying

Siirisiiri sounding
siirisiiri sounding
5   siirisiiri sounding

Sounding
sounding
sounding
sounding

10 Remember
he is frightened of the day
already in the cactus lying

Siirisiiri sounding
siirisiiri sounding
15 siirisiiri sounding

Sounding
sounding
sounding
sounding[1]

YOYO A'AKAME

yoyo a´akame
sevipo vo´oka

siirisiiriti hia
siirisiiriti hia
5   siirisiiriti hia

hia
hia
hia
hia

10 katikun
taewalita sumeiyaka
haivusu sevipo vo´oka

siirisiiriti hia
siirisiiriti hia
15 siirisiiriti hia

hia
hia
hia
hia

DISCUSSION QUESTIONS

1. Does the onomatapoetic *siirisiiri* evoke in your mind the sound of a rattlesnake's agitated rattles?
2. The note states that dancers enact the song. Would you think the music and drums would be soft or loud?

WRITING TOPICS

1. Write a poem that includes the sounds that an animal or bird makes.
2. In a brief essay, comment on the effectiveness the use of onomatopoeia in "Enchanted Enchanted Rattlesnake."

---

[1] This is a play song. When Felipe sings it, the dancers dance all the way out during the repetitions of the first stanza as usual but when the concluding stanza begins, "when the drum calls them back" they get down on the ground and slither like snakes.

THE MAN MADE OF WORDS

N. Scott Momaday

The man made of words motif moves throughout the writing of N. Scott Momaday. For three decades, he has explored this unique concept of language. "The Man Made of Words" was originally published in 1971. Indeed, we are all made of words, according to Momaday. Language is a miracle of symbols and sounds that enables us to define ourselves. Applying imagination to language, we may create ourselves in stories and literature.

Momaday grew up in the midst of two languages, Kiowa and English. His father told him stories from the Kiowa oral tradition even before his son could talk. Those stories lived within the sensitive child and nourished his imagination ever after. "They are among the most valuable gifts that I have ever been given."

Momaday says that his father loved to tell him the story of the arrowmaker and the youngster loved hearing it. He thinks, perhaps, this metaphorical "man made of words" was the first story his father told him. "One does not come to the end of such a story. I have lived with the story of the arrowmaker for many years, and I am sure that I do not yet understand it in all of its consequent meanings." Momaday continues, "Nor do I expect to understand it so. The stories I keep close to me, day by day, are those that yield more and more of their spirit in time." Internalizing such ancient oral literature, Momaday has mastered the art of writing versions that retain the emotional and intellectual impact of the oral originals.

A section from *The Way to Rainy Mountain* (1969), which Momaday refers to in "The Man Made of Words," appears in Chapter Five. The following selection is the text of a talk Momaday made in 1970. In his talk, Momaday skillfully ties many ideas together—ideas about history, imagination, ecology, storytelling, and the power of words.

1   I want to try to put several different ideas together this morning. And in the process, I hope to indicate something about the nature of the relationship between language and experience. It seems to me that in a certain sense we are all made of words; that our most essential being consists in language. It is the element in which we think and dream and act, in which we live our daily lives. There is no way in which we can exist apart from the morality of a verbal dimension.

2   In one of the discussions yesterday the question "What is an American Indian?" was raised.

3   The answer of course is that an Indian is an idea which a given man has of himself. And it is a moral idea, for it accounts for the way in which he reacts to other men and to the world in general. And that idea, in order to be realized completely, has to be expressed.

4   I want to say some things then about this moral and verbal dimension in which we live. I want to say something about such things as ecology and storytelling and the imagination. Let me tell you a story.

5   One night a strange thing happened. I had written the greater part of *The Way to Rainy Mountain*—all of it, in fact, except the epilogue. I had set down the last of the old Kiowa tales, and I had composed both the historical and the autobiographical commentaries for it. I had the sense of being out of breath, of having said what it was in me to say on that subject. The manuscript lay before me in the bright light. Small, to be sure, but complete, or nearly so. I had written the second of the two poems in which that book is framed. I had uttered the last word, as it were. And yet a whole, penultimate piece was missing. I began once again to write.

6   During the first hours after midnight on the morning of November 13, 1833, it seemed that the world was coming to an end. Suddenly the stillness of the night was broken; there were brilliant flashes of light in the sky, light of such intensity that people were awakened by it. With the speed and density of a driving rain, stars were falling in the universe. Some were brighter than Venus; one was said to be as large as the moon. I went on to say that the event, the falling of the stars on North America, that explosion of meteors which occurred 137 years ago, is among the earliest entries in the Kiowa calendars. So deeply impressed upon the imagination of the Kiowas is that old phenomenon that it is remembered still; it has become a part of the racial memory.

7   "The living memory," I wrote, "and the verbal tradition which transcends it, were brought together for me once and for all in the person of Ko-sahn." It seemed eminently right for me to deal, after all, with that old woman. Ko-Sahn is among the most venerable people I have ever known. She spoke and sang to me one summer afternoon in Oklahoma. It was like a dream. When I was born she was already old; she was a grown woman when my grandparents came into the world. She sat perfectly still, folded over on herself. It did not seem possible that so many years—a century of years—could be so compacted and distilled. Her voice shuddered, but it did

not fail. Her songs were sad. An old whimsy, a delight in language and in remembrance, shone in her one good eye. She conjured up the past, imagining perfectly the long continuity of her being. She imagined the lovely young girl, wild and vital, she had been. She imagined the Sun Dance:

8   There was an old, old woman. She had something on her back. The boys went out to see. The old woman had a bag full of earth on her back. It was a certain kind of sandy earth. That is what they must have in the lodge. The dancers must dance upon the sandy earth. The old woman held a digging tool in her hand. She turned towards the south and pointed with her lips. It was like a kiss, and she began to sing:

> We have brought the earth.
> Now it is time to play.

9   As old as I am, I still have the feeling of play. That was the beginning of the Sun Dance.

10   By this time I was back into the book, caught up completely in the act of writing. I had projected myself—imagined myself—out of the room and out of time. I was there with Ko-sahn in the Oklahoma July. We laughed easily together; I felt that I had known her all of my life—all of hers. I did not want to let her go. But I had come to the end. I set down, almost grudgingly, the last sentences:

11   It was—all of this and more—a quest, a going forth upon the way of Rainy Mountain. Probably Ko-sahn too is dead now. At times, in the quiet of evening, I think she must have wondered, dreaming, who she was. Was she become in her sleep that old purveyor of the sacred earth, perhaps, that ancient one who, old as she was, still had the feeling of play? And in her mind, at times, did she see the falling stars?

12   For some time I sat looking down at these words on the page, trying to deal with the emptiness that had come about inside of me. The words did not seem real. I could scarcely believe that they made sense, that they had anything whatsoever to do with meaning. In desperation almost, I went back over the final paragraphs, backwards and forwards, hurriedly. My eyes fell upon the name Ko-Sahn. And all at once everything seemed suddenly to refer to that name. The name seemed to humanize the whole complexity of language. All at once, absolutely, I had the sense of the magic of words and of names. Ko-sahn, I said, and I said again KO-SAHN.

13   Then it was that the ancient, one-eyed woman Ko-sahn stepped out of the language and stood before me on the page. I was amazed. Yet it seemed entirely appropriate that this should happen.

14   "I was just now writing about you," I replied, stammering. "I thought— forgive me—I thought that perhaps you were . . . that you had . . ."

15   "No," she said. And she cackled, I thought. And she went on. "You have imagined me well, and so I am. You have imagined that I dream, and so I do. I have seen the falling stars."

16 "But all of this, this imagining," I protested, "this has taken place—is taking place in my mind. You are not actually here, not here in this room." It occurred to me that I was being extremely rude, but I could not help myself. She seemed to understand.

17 "Be careful of your pronouncements, grandson," she answered. "You imagine that I am here in this room, do you not? That is worth something. You see, I have existence, whole being, in your imagination. It is but one kind of being, to be sure, but it is perhaps the best of all kinds. If I am not here in this room, grandson, then surely neither are you."

18 "I think I see what you mean," I said meekly. I felt justly rebuked. "Tell me, grandmother, how old are you?"

19 "I do not know," she replied. "There are times when I think that I am the oldest woman on earth. You know, the Kiowas came into the world through a hollow log. In my mind's eye I have seen them emerge, one by one, from the mouth of the log. I have seen them so clearly, how they were dressed, how delighted they were to see the world around them. I must have been there. And I must have taken part in that old migration of the Kiowas from the Yellowstone to the Southern Plains, near the Big Horn River, and I have seen the red cliffs of Palo Duro Canyon. I was with those who were camped in the Wichita Mountains when the stars fell."

20 "You are indeed very old," I said, "and you have seen many things."

21 "Yes. I imagine that I have," she replied. Then she turned slowly around, nodding once, and receded into the language I had made. And then I imagined I was alone in the room.

22 Once in his life a man ought to concentrate his mind upon the remembered earth, I believe. He ought to give himself up to a particular landscape in his experience, to look at it from as many angles as he can, to wonder about it, to dwell upon it. He ought to imagine that he touches it with his hands at every season and listens to the sounds that are made upon it. He ought to imagine the creatures that are there and all the faintest motions in the wind. He ought to recollect the glare of noon and all the colors of the dawn and dusk.

23 The Wichita Mountains rise out of the Southern Plains in a long crooked line that runs from east to west. The mountains are made of red earth, and of rock that is neither red nor blue but some very rare admixture of the two like the feathers of certain birds. They are not so high and mighty as the mountains of the Far West, and they bear a different relationship to the land around them. One does not imagine that they are distinctive in themselves, or indeed that they exist apart from the plain in any sense. If you try to think of them in the abstract they lose the look of mountains. They are preeminently in an expression of the larger landscape, more perfectly organic than one can easily imagine. To behold these mountains from the plain is one thing; to see the plain from the mountains is something else. I have stood on the top of Mt. Scott and seen the earth below, bending out into the whole circle of the sky. The wind runs always close upon the slopes, and

there are times when you can hear the rush of it like water in the ravines.

24   Here is the hub of an old commerce. A hundred years ago the Kiowas and Comanches journeyed outward from the Wichitas in every direction, seeking after mischief and medicine, horses and hostages. Sometimes they went away for years, but they always returned, for the land had got hold of them. It is a consecrated place, and even now there is something of the wilderness about it. There is a game preserve in the hills. Animals graze away in the open meadows or, closer by, keep to the shadows of the groves: antelope and deer, longhorn and buffalo. It was here, the Kiowas say, that the first buffalo came into the world.

25   The yellow grassy knoll that is called Rainy Mountain lies a short distance to the north and west. There, on the west side, is the ruin of an old school where my grandmother went as a wild young girl in blanket and braids to learn of numbers and of names in English. And there she is buried.

> Most is your name the name of
> this dark stone.
> Deranged in death, the mind to
> be inheres
> 5   Forever in the nominal unknown,
> Who listens here and now to
> hear your name.
> The early sun, red as a hunter's
> moon,
> 10   Runs in the plain. The mountain
> burns and shines;
> And silence is the long approach
> of noon
> Upon the shadow that your name
> 15 defines—
> And death this cold, black
> density of stone.

26   I am interested in the way that a man looks at a given landscape and takes possession of it in his blood and brain. For this happens, I am certain, in the ordinary motion of life. None of us lives apart from the land entirely, such an isolation is unimaginable. We have sooner or later to come to terms with the world around us—and I mean especially the physical world, not only as it is revealed to us immediately through our senses, but also as it is perceived more truly in the long turn of seasons and of years. And we must come to moral terms. There is no alternative, I believe, if we are to realize and maintain our humanity; for our humanity must consist in part in the ethical as well as the practical ideal of preservation. And particularly here and now is that true. We Americans need now more than ever before—and indeed more than we know—to imagine who and what we are with respect to the earth

and sky. I am talking about an act of the imagination essentially, and the concept of an American land ethic.

27   It is no doubt more difficult to imagine in 1970 the landscape of America as it was in, say, 1900. Our whole experience as a nation in this century has been a repudiation of the pastoral ideal which informs so much of the art and literature of the nineteenth century. One effect of the Technological Revolution has been to uproot us from the soil. We have become disoriented, I believe; we have suffered a kind of psychic dislocation of ourselves in time and space. We may be perfectly sure of where we are in relation to the supermarket and the next coffee break, but I doubt that any of us knows where he is in relation to the stars and to the solstices. Our sense of the natural order has become dull and unreliable. Like the wilderness itself, our sphere of instinct has diminished in proportion as we have failed to imagine truly what it is. And yet I believe that it is possible to formulate an ethical idea of the land—a notion of what it is and must be in our daily lives—and I believe moreover that it is absolutely necessary to do so.

28   It would seem on the surface of things that a land ethic is something that is alien to, or at least dormant in most Americans. Most of us in general have developed an attitude of indifference toward the land. In terms of my own experience, it is difficult to see how such an attitude could ever have come about.

29   Ko-sahn could remember where my grandmother was born. "It was just there," she said, pointing to a tree, and the tree was like a hundred others that grew up in the broad depression of the Washita River. I could see nothing to indicate that anyone had ever been there, spoken so much as a word, or touched the tips of his fingers to the tree. But in her memory Ko-sahn could see the child. I think she must have remembered my grandmother's voice, for she seemed for a long moment to listen and to hear. There was a still, heavy heat upon that place; I had the sense that ghosts were gathering there.

30   And in the racial memory, Ko-sahn had seen the falling stars. For her there was no distinction between the individual and the racial experience, even as there was none between the mythical and the historical. Both were realized for her in the one memory, and that was of the land. This landscape, in which she had lived for a hundred years, was the common denominator of everything that she knew and would ever know—and her knowledge was profound. Her roots ran deep into the earth, and from those depths she drew strength enough to hold still against all the forces of chance and disorder. And she drew strength enough to hold still against all the forces of change and disorder. And she drew therefrom the sustenance of meaning and of mystery as well. The falling stars were not for Ko-sahn an isolated or accidental phenomenon. She had a great personal investment in that awful commotion of light in the night sky. For it remained to be imagined. She must at last deal with it in words; she must appropriate it to her understanding of the whole universe. And, again, when she spoke of the Sun Dance, it was an essential expression of her relationship to the life of the earth and to the sun and moon.

31   In Ko-sahn and in her people we have always had the example of a deep, ethical regard for the land. We had better learn from it. Surely that ethic is merely latent in ourselves. It must now be activated, I believe. We Americans must come again to a moral comprehension of the earth and air. We must live according to the principle of a land ethic. The alternative is that we shall not live at all.

32   Ecology is perhaps the most important subject of our time. I can't think of an issue in which the Indian has more authority or a greater stake. If there is one thing which truly distinguishes him, it is surely his regard of and for the natural world.

33   But let me get back to the matter of storytelling.

34   I must have taken part in that old migration of the Kiowas from the Yellowstone to the Southern Plains, for I have seen antelope bounding in the tall grass near the Big Horn River, and I have seen the ghost forests in the Black Hills. Once I saw the red cliffs of Palo Duro Canyon. I was with those who were camped in the Wichita Mountains when the stars fell. "You are very old," I said, "and you have seen many things." "Yes, I imagine that I have," she replied. Then she turned slowly around, nodding once, and receded into the language I had made. And then I imagined that I was alone in the room.

35   Who is the storyteller? Of whom is the story told? What is there in the darkness to imagine into being? What is there to dream and to relate? What happens when I or anyone exerts the force of language upon the unknown?

36   These are the questions which interest me most.

37   If there is any absolute assumption in back of my thoughts tonight, it is this: We are what we imagine. Our very existence consists in our imagination of ourselves. Our best destiny is to imagine, at least, completely, who and what, and *that* we are. The greatest tragedy that can befall us is to go unimagined.

38   Writing is recorded speech. In order to consider seriously the meaning of language and of literature, we must consider first the meaning of the oral tradition.

39   By way of suggesting one or two definitions which may be useful to us, let me pose a few basic questions and tentative answers:

40   (1) What is the oral tradition?

41   The oral tradition is that process by which the myths, legends, tales, and lore of a people are formulated, communicated, and preserved in language by word of mouth, as opposed to writing. Or it is a *collection* of such things.

42   (2) With reference to the matter of oral tradition, what is the relationship between art and reality?

43   In the context of these remarks, the matter of oral tradition suggests certain particularities of art and reality. Art, for example . . . involves an oral dimension which is based markedly upon such considerations as memorization, intonation, inflection, precision of statement, brevity, rhythm, pace, and dramatic effect. Moreover, myth, legend, and lore, according to our

definitions of these terms, imply a separate and distinct order of reality. We are concerned here not so much with an accurate representation of actuality, but with the realization of the imaginative experience.

44   (3) How are we to conceive of language? What are words?

45   For our purposes, words are audible sounds, invented by man to communicate his thoughts and feelings. Each word has a conceptual content, however slight, and each word communicates associations of feeling. Language is the means by which words proceed to the formulation of meaning and emotional effect.

46   (4) What is the nature of storytelling? What are the purposes and possibilities of that act?

47   Storytelling is imaginative and creative in nature. It is an act by which man strives to realize his capacity for wonder, meaning and delight. It is also a process in which man invests and preserves himself in the context of ideas. Man tells stories in order to understand his experience, whatever it may be. The possibilities of storytelling are precisely those of understanding the human experience.

48   (5) What is the relationship between what a man is and what he says—or between what he is, and what he thinks he is?

49   This relationship is both tenuous and complicated. Generally speaking, man has consummate being in language, and there only. The state of human *being* is an idea, an idea which man has of himself. Only when he is embodied in an idea, and the idea is realized in language, can man take possession of himself. In our particular frame of reference, this is to say that man achieves the fullest realization of his humanity in such an art and product of the imagination as literature—and here I use the term "literature" in its broadest sense. This is admittedly a moral view of the question, but literature is itself a moral view, and it is a view of morality.

50   Now let us return to the falling stars. And let me apply a new angle of vision to that event—let me proceed this time from a slightly different point of view.

51   In this winter of 1833 the Kiowas were camped on Elm Fork, a branch of the Red River west of the Wichita Mountains. In the preceding summer they had suffered a massacre at the hands of the Osages, and Tai-me, the sacred Sun Dance Doll and most powerful medicine of the tribe, had been stolen. At no time in the history of their migration from the north, and in the evolution of their plains culture, had the Kiowas been more vulnerable to despair. The loss of Tai-me was a deep psychological wound. In the early cold of November 13 there occurred over North America an explosion of meteors. The Kiowas were awakened by the sterile light of falling stars, and they ran out into the false day and were terrified.

52   The year the stars fell is, as I have said, among the earliest entries in the Kiowa calendars, and it is permanent in the Kiowa mind. There was symbolic meaning in that November sky. With the coming of natural dawn there began a new and darker age for the Kiowa people; the last culture to evolve

on this continent began to decline. Within four years of the falling stars the Kiowas signed their first treaty with the government; within twenty, four major epidemics of smallpox and Asiatic cholera destroyed more than half their number; and within scarcely more than a generation their horses were taken from them and the herds of buffalo were slaughtered and left to waste upon the plains.

53   Do you see what happens when the imagination is superimposed upon the historical event? It becomes a story. The whole piece becomes more deeply invested with meaning. The terrified Kiowas, when they had regained possession of themselves, did indeed imagine that the falling stars were symbolic of their being and their destiny. They accounted for themselves with reference to that awful memory. They appropriated it, recreated it, fashioned it into an image of themselves—imagined it.

54   Only by means of that act could they bear what happened to them thereafter. No defeat, no humiliation, no suffering was beyond their power to endure, for none of it was meaningless. They could say to themselves, "Yes, it was all meant to be in its turn. The order of the world was broken, it was clear. Even the stars were shaken loose in the night sky." The imagination of meaning was not much, perhaps, but it was all they had, and it was enough to sustain them.

55   One of my very favorite writers, Isak Dinesen, said this: "All sorrows can be borne if you put them into a story or tell a story about them."

56   Some three or four years ago, I became interested in the matter of "oral tradition" as that term is used to designate a rich body of preliterate storytelling in and among the indigenous cultures of North America. Specifically, I began to wonder about the way in which myths, legends, and lore evolve into that mature condition of expression which we call "literature." For indeed literature is, I believe, the end-product of an evolutionary process, a stage that is indispensable and perhaps original as well.

57   I set out to find a traditional material that should be at once oral only, unified and broadly representative of cultural values. And in this undertaking, I had a certain advantage, because I am myself an American Indian, and I have lived many years of my life on the Indian reservations of the southwest. From the time I was first able to comprehend and express myself in language, I heard the stories of the Kiowas, those "coming out" people of the Southern plains from whom I am descended.

58   Three hundred years ago the Kiowa lived in the mountains of what is now western Montana, near the headwaters of the Yellowstone River. Near the end of the seventeenth century they began a long migration to the south and east. They passed along the present border between Montana and Wyoming to the Black Hills and proceeded southward along the eastern slopes of the Rockies to the Wichita Mountains in the Southern Plains (Southwestern Oklahoma).

59   I mention this old journey of the Kiowas because it is in a sense definitive of the tribal mind; it is essential to the way in which the Kiowas think

of themselves as a people. The migration was carried on over a course of many generations and many hundreds of miles. When it began, the Kiowas were a desperate and divided people, given up wholly to a day-by-day struggle for survival. When it ended, they were a race of centaurs, a lordly society of warriors and buffalo hunters. Along the way they had acquired horses, a knowledge and possession of the open land, and a sense of destiny. In alliance with the Comanches, they ruled the southern plains for a hundred years.

60   That migration—and the new golden age to which it led—is closely reflected in Kiowa legend and lore. Several years ago I retraced the route of that migration, and when I came to the end, I interviewed a number of Kiowa elders and obtained from them a remarkable body of history and learning, fact and fiction—all of it in the oral tradition and all of it valuable in its own right and for its own sake.

61   I compiled a small number of translations from the Kiowa, arranged insofar as it was possible to indicate the chronological and geographic progression of the migration itself. This collection (and it was nothing more than a collection at first) was published under the title *The Journey of Tai-me* in a fine edition limited to 100 hand printed copies.

62   This original collection has just been re-issued, together with illustrations and a commentary, in a trade edition entitled *The Way to Rainy Mountain*. The principle of narration which informs this latter work is in a sense elaborate and experimental, and I should like to say one or two things about it. Then, if I may, I should like to illustrate the way in which the principle works, by reading briefly from the text. And finally, I should like to comment in some detail upon one of the tales in particular.

63   There are three distinct narrative voices in *The Way to Rainy Mountain*— the mythical, the historical, and the immediate. Each of the translations is followed by two kinds of commentary; the first is documentary and the second is privately reminiscent. Together, they serve, hopefully, to validate the oral tradition to an extent that might not otherwise be possible. The commentaries are meant to provide a context in which the elements of oral tradition might transcend the categorical limits of prehistory, anonymity, and archaeology in the narrow sense.

64   All of this is to say that I believe there is a way (first) in which the elements of oral tradition can be shown, dramatically, to exist within the framework of a literary continuance, a deeper and more vital context of language and meaning than that which is generally taken into account; and (secondly) in which those elements can be located, with some precision on an evolutionary scale.

65   The device of the journey is peculiarly appropriate to such a principle of narration as this. And *The Way to Rainy Mountain* is a whole journey, intricate with notion and meaning; and it is made with the whole memory, that experience of the mind which is legendary as well as historical, personal as well as cultural.

66   Without further qualification, let me turn to the text itself.

67   The Kiowa tales which are contained in *The Way to Rainy Mountain* constitute a kind of literary chronicle. In a sense they are the milestones of that old migration in which the Kiowas journeyed from the Yellowstone to the Washita. They recorded a transformation of the tribal mind, as it encounters for the first time the landscape of the Great Plains; they evoke the sense of search and discovery. Many of the tales are very old, and they have not until now been set down in writing. Among them there is one that stands out in my mind. When I was a child, my father told me the story of the arrowmaker, and he told it to me many times, for I fell in love with it. I have no memory that is older than that of hearing it. This is the way it goes:

68   If an arrow is well made, it will have tooth marks upon it. That is how you know. The Kiowas made fine arrows and straightened them in their teeth. Then they drew them to the bow to see that they were straight. Once there was a man and his wife. They were alone at night in their tipi. By the light of a fire the man was making arrows. After a while he caught sight of something. There was a small opening in the tipi where two hides had been sewn together. Someone was there on the outside, looking in. The man went on with his work, but he said to his wife, "Someone is standing outside. Do not be afraid. Let us talk easily, as of ordinary things." He took up an arrow and straightened it with his teeth; then, as it was right for him to do, he drew it to the bow and took aim, first in this direction and then in that. And all the while he was talking, as if to his wife. But this is how he spoke: "I know that you are there on the outside, for I can feel your eyes upon me. If you are a Kiowa, you will understand what I am saying, and you will speak your name." But there was no answer, and the man went on in the same way, pointing the arrow all around. At last his aim fell upon the place where his enemy stood, and he let go of the string. The arrow went straight to the enemy's heart.

69   Heretofore the story of the arrowmaker has been the private possession of a very few, a tenuous link in that most ancient chain of language which we call the oral tradition; tenuous because the tradition itself is so; for as many times as the story has been told, it was always but one generation removed from extinction. But it was held dear, too, on that same account. That is to say, it has been neither more nor less durable than the human voice, and neither more nor less concerned to express the meaning of the human condition. And this brings us to the heart of the matter at hand: The story of the arrowmaker is also a link between language and literature. It is a remarkable act of the mind, a realization of words and the world that is altogether simple and direct, yet nonetheless rare and profound, and it illustrates more clearly than anything else in my own experience, at least, something of the essential character of the imagination—and in particular of that personification which in this instance emerges from it: the man made of words.

70   It is a fine story, whole, intricately beautiful, precisely realized. It is worth thinking about, for it yields something of value; indeed, it is full of provocation, rich with suggestion and consequent meaning. There is often an inherent danger that we might impose too much of ourselves upon it. It is informed by an integrity that bears examination easily and well, and in the process it seems to appropriate our own reality and experience.

71   It is significant that the story of the arrowmaker returns in a special way upon itself. It is about language, after all, and it is therefore part and parcel of its own subject; virtually, there is no difference between the telling and that which is told. The point of the story lies, not so much in what the arrowmaker does, but in what he says—and indeed that he says it. The principal fact is that he speaks, and in so doing he places his very life in the balance. It is this aspect of the story which interests me most, for it is here that the language becomes most conscious of itself; we are close to the origin and object of literature, I believe; our sense of the verbal dimension is very keen, and we are aware of something in the nature of language that is at once perilous and compelling. "If you are a Kiowa, you will understand what I am saying, and you will speak your name." Everything is ventured in this simple declaration, which is also a question and a plea. The conditional element with which it begins is remarkably tentative and pathetic; precisely at this moment is the arrowmaker realized completely, and his reality consists in language, and it is poor and precarious. And all of this occurs to him as surely as it does to us. Implicit in that simple occurrence is all of his definition and his destiny, and all of ours. He ventures to speak because he must; language is the repository of his whole knowledge and experience, and it represents the only chance he has for survival. Instinctively, and with great care, he deals in the most honest and basic way with words. "Let us talk easily, as of ordinary things," he says. And of the ominous unknown he asks only the utterance of a name, only the most nominal sign that he is understood, that his words are returned to him on the sheer edge of meaning. But there is no answer, and the arrowmaker knows at once what he has not known before; that his enemy is, and that he has gained an advantage over him. This he knows certainly, and the certainty itself is his advantage, and it is crucial; he makes the most of it. The venture is complete and irrevocable, and it ends in success. The story is meaningful. It is so primarily because it is composed of language, and it is in the nature of language in turn that it proceeds to the formulation of meaning. Moreover, the story of the arrowmaker, as opposed to other stories in general, centers upon this procession of words toward meaning. It seems in fact to turn upon the very idea that language involves the elements of risk and responsibility; and in this it seeks to confirm itself. In a word, it seems to say, everything is a risk. That may be true, and it may also be that the whole of literature rests upon that truth.

72   The arrowmaker is preeminently the man made of words. He has consummate being in language; it is the world of his origin and of his poster-

ity, and there is no other. But it is a world of definite reality and of infinite possibility. I have come to believe that there is a sense in which the arrow-maker has more nearly perfect being than have other men, by and large, as he imagines himself, whole and vital, going on into the unknown darkness and beyond. And this last aspect of his being is primordial and profound.

73   And yet the story has it that he is cautious and alone, and we are given to understand that his peril is great and immediate, and that he confronts it in the only way he can. I have no doubt that this is true, and I believe that there are implications which point directly to the determination of our literary experience and which must not be lost upon us. A final word, then, on an essential irony which marks this story and gives peculiar substance to the man made of words. The storyteller is nameless and unlettered. From one point of view we know very little about him, except that he is some-how translated for us in the person of an arrowmaker. But, from another, that is all we need to know. He tells us of his life in language, and of the awful risk involved. It must occur to us that he is one with the arrowmaker and that he has survived, by word of mouth, beyond other men. We said a moment ago that, for the arrowmaker, language represented the only chance of survival. It is worth considering that he survives in our own time, and that he has survived over a period of untold generations.

DISCUSSION QUESTIONS

1. When Momaday speaks the name Ko-sahn, "she stepped out of the language and stood before me on the page." Can you think of a time when a story made someone "come alive"? If so, tell about that time.
2. Comment on Momaday's statement that most people "have developed an attitude of indifference toward the land." Why does this disturb him? How does he tie this idea to the story about Ko-sahn and the Kiowas?
3. Ko-sahn could not have seen the falling stars in 1833, but Momaday says that she had seen them "in the racial memory." Explain how this could be so.
4. Reread paragraph 37, and discuss in a small group what this paragraph might mean for each member of the group.
5. Momaday says that "when the imagination is superimposed upon the historical event [the event] becomes a story." How did this process work after the event of the falling stars?
6. Momaday says that the story of the arrowmaker turns "upon the very idea that language involves the elements of risk and responsibility." Explain how the story of the arrowmaker illustrates this.

WRITING TOPICS

1. Retell in writing a family story that you have heard. Include whether you would want to tell this story to your children.

2. In an essay discuss the relationship between myth and history, perhaps using examples from your own culture. Is one more important than the other?

3. In today's media-saturated world, it is possible to see, hear, and read hundreds of stories every year. How would you distinguish between the kind of stories presented every evening on television and the kinds of stories Momaday writes about in this selection? Write an essay giving your views.

SUMMARY WRITING TOPICS

1. Assume that you have just encountered someone on your street from another planet. You can't speak this person's language. How will you indicate who you are, how will you welcome (or not) your visitor, and how will you convey what you want to know about that person?
2. Suppose that this being from another planet wants to teach you his or her language. How will you respond?
3. Assume that more people from a distant planet arrive and tell you that while they are with you, you are forbidden to speak your own language. What is your first thought?
4. Does the Native American experience with European strangers predict extraterrestrial beings' interaction with earthlings? How were language experiences between Indians and Europeans similar to and different from your imagined experiences with the aliens?
5. If possible, learn about an ancestor you have never known. Sit for a few minutes, and think about what you have learned about that person. Then write what you think this person might tell you.
6. As you review "The Way to Rainy Mountain" (Chapter Five) and "The Man Made of Words," jot down responses about Momaday's ideas on the role of language in our lives. Organize your first impressions into an essay on Momaday and language.
7. Research one Indian language that is spoken today. You may select one spoken in your state. In your report, these are some questions to consider. Who speaks the language? How many people speak it? Does it have an orthography? Can you find examples of it in written texts? What are some points that relate the language to culture and history of those who speak it? What is its future? You may begin by browsing the Internet. Check web sites for Indian community colleges.
8. Many voters are lobbying Congress and state legislators to establish English as the official language for school instruction. Others wish to eliminate or severely limit bilingual education. What is your response to these proposals?
9. If you speak a language other than English as your first language, write about some of your experiences with both languages.
10. Everyone in the United States and Canada except American Indians is an immigrant or has immigrant ancestors. (And many Native Americans have immigrant ancestors as well.) How, then, does this fact affect your ideas about language, storytelling, and mythmaking, if it does? Explore your thoughts in a personal essay.

CHAPTER NINE

WE SURVIVE

A cry arises across Indian country, "We are alive!" N. Scott Momaday, Joy Harjo, and other writers celebrate this survival in their prose and poetry. In "The Story of Our Survival," Joy Harjo is awed that any Indians are here: "Who would believe the fantastic and terrible story of all of our survival, those who were never meant to survive?" Approximately ten million people lived in North America in 1490. Four hundred years of wars of conquest, famine, and disease decimated that dense population. Smallpox, measles, malaria, yellow fever, plague, typhus, and influenza killed Indians susceptible to Old World pathogens. In 1890, the U.S. Census Bureau counted only about two hundred and fifty thousand Indians in the United States, only 2.5 percent of the original number.

According to Henry Dobyns in *Native American Historical Demography*, "Smallpox became the single most lethal disease Europeans carried to the New World." Smallpox swept through the Pueblos in 1800, 1815, 1836 (worsened by typhoid fever or typhus), 1853, 1862, and 1896. Kiowa traders contracted the disease from the Pueblos in 1816 and 1861, carrying the virus home to decimate their own tribe; Osage visitors carried smallpox south to Kiowas in 1839. Forty-niners transmitted cholera to Kiowas; hundreds died. Measles killed many Kiowa children in 1877, 1882 (combined with whooping cough), and 1892.

Scholars calculate that only about 13,000 Cherokees survived the Trail of Tears. Concentrating the small, scattered Cherokee populations created ideal conditions for smallpox. The highly infectious disease killed most of the more than four thousand Cherokee casualties.

When smallpox spread from Pueblos to Bosque Redondo, where thirteen thousand Navajos had been forcibly detained in 1863, thousands of

Navajos perished. Nonetheless, U.S. censuses toward the end of the twenti-eth century show Navajos and Cherokees as the two largest contemporary Native American peoples.

The near annihilation of American Indians affected the historical and cultural contexts of native literature. According to Francis Paul Prucha in *The Indians in American Society,* the epidemics "weakened the Indian eco-nomic systems and dispirited the people, whose world order seemed to have collapsed in the face of unknown forces." This collapse opened up lands for European colonization. The North American continent was not the virgin land many have called it. Native depopulation widowed the land, leaving it strewn with abandoned towns and ruined fields. Finally, an unknown amount of Native American oral literature was forever lost, along with the millions of composers, performers, and storytellers who perished. N. Scott Momaday based his admonition that oral tradition is always only a genera-tion from disappearance on historic reality.

Native North American population fell to its lowest numbers between 1890 and 1920. The long decline fostered and reinforced the stereotype of the "vanishing Indian." Since 1920, Native American numbers have increased at a rapid rate, however, although the stereotype still lingers. Native American authors find considerable satisfaction, therefore, in pub-lishing works that celebrate and emphasize Native American persistence.

One Native American trait that has helped tribal peoples to survive is a strong sense of humor. Making fun of impossible situations is one means of coping with them. Pointing out the irony of others' actions and attitudes is another such means. Native American ironic writing has a long history. Early Indian author William Apess pinpointed the discrepancy between Protestant preaching and behavior in "An Indian's Looking-Glass for the White Man," appealing ironically to "respectable gentlemen and ladies."

Resilient family networks and humor have been the two most important factors in maintaining and restoring Native American morale. As Vine Deloria, Jr., points out, newcomers got their stereotype of the "granite-faced grunting redskin" all wrong. Surviving Indian peoples "are exactly opposite of the popular stereotype."

Much as humor helped Native Americans to cope with and survive demoralizing circumstances, frequent biological threats and colonial domi-nation have exacted a heavy psychological toll. Most of the selections in this chapter reflect that reality. Sherman Alexie makes quite explicit in a few poetic lines his view that the holocaust label applies to post-Columbian native North American depopulation as well as to German World War II genocide against Jews. Alexie labels both Jews and Native Americans as sur-vivors in the strictest sense of that word.

In her poem "I Give You Back," Joy Harjo touches on a "generation of warfare, slaughter, and massacre in this country." Harjo writes of her per-sonal transformation, which occurred at the Institute of American Indian Arts, in the essay "Metamorphosis." As a mature poet, she created a metaphor for all women fighting for survival in "The Woman Hanging from the Thirteenth Floor Window." Hope undergirds Harjo's message: "I want us all to know as women, as Indian people, as human beings that there is always hope, that we are whole, alive, and precious."

Like members of other minority groups in the United States, Native Americans in disproportionate numbers fought for this nation in Vietnam. As Colville poet Ted Palmanteer put it in the vocabulary of the men who served the United States during that war, "We Saw Days." Nez Perce poet Phil George also served in Vietnam. In "Battle Won Is Lost," the elders state their pious platitudes and are countered by a young warrior's terse two-syllable responses. Some Native American men went not to Vietnam but to prison. In Duane Niatum's "Street Kid," the speaker differentiates himself from fellow juvenile offenders behind bars by turning his vision outward.

Native Americans have had to cope not only with high mortality but, like many Americans, with tornadoes, blizzards, and floods. Christine Quintasket, under her more romantic pen-name "Mourning Dove," poignantly tells how her family survived the deep snow of the winter of 1892–1893 and a devastating Columbia River flood the next spring. Her mother's food-gathering skills in the wild plus native community cooperation and the kindness of one white woman saw them through, hungry but alive.

In "The Man to Send Rainclouds," Leslie Marmon Silko illustrates how Pueblo peoples have retained traditional religious beliefs and rituals and, since Spanish colonial times, have made a fine art of keeping their customs hidden.

The Navajos are the largest tribe in North America today. Geographic dispersion protected families from some diseases, and animal protein in their diet augmented resistance to disease. In Chahadineli Benally's family story, "Captured by the Enemy," Benally portrays another fundamental survival factor—the indomitable will of Navajo women.

INDIAN HUMOR

Vine Deloria, Jr.

Vine Deloria, Jr., frequently analyzes Native American issues from legal and religious viewpoints. If he seems sometimes to preach, his forebears furnished him with ministerial role models. His great-grandfather was a Yankton native curer. His grandfather, a Yankton chief, converted to Christianity in the 1870s and spent the rest of his life as a missionary to the Standing Rock Sioux Reservation population. Deloria's father, Vine Deloria, Sr., served for thirty-seven years as an Episcopal missionary.

Perhaps Deloria's career betrays a small element of youthful rebellion against family tradition. He enlisted in the United States Marine Corps before attending Iowa State University. With a B.A. in hand, he worked as a welder for four years. Then family heritage seems to have won; Deloria enrolled in Augustana Lutheran Seminary, graduating with a B.D. in 1963. Rather than preach to a congregation, however, he sought pulpits that enabled him to reach much larger audiences.

In 1964, Deloria became Executive Director of the National Congress of American Indians (NCAI), the pioneer and premier national organization of reservation executive officers and other influential Native Americans. From 1967 to 1970, he earned his law degree at the University of Colorado. He then founded the Institute for the Development of Indian Law in Washington, D.C. From 1978 to 1990, he taught law and political science at the University of Arizona, where he helped to found an Indian Studies Program. Since 1990, he has been professor of law at the University of Colorado in Boulder.

"Indian Humor" originally appeared in Deloria's first and best known book, *Custer Died for Your Sins* (1969). That title illustrates Deloria's delight in turning Euro-American icons on themselves. Custer, for example, symbolizes greed, arrogance, and aggression. This book won the 1970 Anisfield Wolf award for writing on race relations. Deloria's writing, teaching, and political activism have been crucial to Indians and others. He has informed the American public of the long history and the present state of Indian affairs, correcting misconceptions, exposing stereotypes, and explaining historical issues.

◉

1   One of the best ways to understand a people is to know what makes them laugh. Laughter encompasses the limits of the soul. In humor life is redefined and accepted. Irony and satire provide much keener insights into a group's collective psyche and values than do years of research.

2   It has always been a great disappointment to Indian people that the humorous side of Indian life has not been mentioned by professed experts on Indian Affairs. Rather the image of the granite-faced grunting redskin has been perpetuated by American mythology.

3   People have little sympathy with stolid groups. Dick Gregory did much more than is believed when he introduced humor into the Civil Rights struggle. He enabled non-blacks to enter into the thought world of the black community and experience the hurt it suffered. When all people shared the humorous but ironic situation of the black, the urgency and morality of Civil Rights was communicated.

4   The Indian people are exactly opposite of the popular stereotype. I sometimes wonder how anything is accomplished by Indians because of the apparent overemphasis on humor within the Indian world. Indians have found a humorous side of nearly every problem and the experiences of life have generally been so well defined through jokes and stories that they have become a thing in themselves.

5   For centuries before the white invasion, teasing was a method of control of social situations by Indian people. Rather than embarrass members of the tribe publicly, people used to tease individuals they considered out of step with the consensus of tribal opinion. In this way egos were preserved and disputes within the tribe of a personal nature were held to a minimum.

6   Gradually people learned to anticipate teasing and began to tease themselves as a means of showing humility and at the same time advocating a course of action they deeply believed in. Men would depreciate their feats to show they were not trying to run roughshod over tribal desires. This method of behavior served to highlight their true virtues and gain them a place of influence in tribal policy-making circles.

7   Humor has come to occupy such a prominent place in national Indian affairs that any kind of movement is impossible without it. Tribes are being brought together by sharing humor of the past. Columbus jokes gain great sympathy among all tribes, yet there are no tribes extant who had anything to do with Columbus. But the fact of white invasion from which all tribes

have suffered has created a common bond in relation to Columbus jokes that gives a solid feeling of unity and purpose to the tribes.

8   The more desperate the problem, the more humor is directed to describe it. Satirical remarks often circumscribe problems so that possible solutions are drawn from the circumstances that would not make sense if presented in other than a humorous form.

9   Often people are awakened and brought to a militant edge through funny remarks. I often counseled people to run for the Bureau of Indian Affairs in case of an earthquake because nothing could shake the BIA. And I would watch as younger Indians set their jaws, determined that they, if nobody else, would shake it. We also had a saying that in case of fire call the BIA and they would handle it because they put a wet blanket on everything. This also got a warm reception from people.

10   Columbus and Custer jokes are the best for penetration into the heart of the matter, however. Rumor has it that Columbus began his journey with four ships. But one went over the edge so he arrived in the new world with only three. Another version states that Columbus didn't know where he was going, didn't know where he had been, and did it all on someone else's money. And the white man has been following Columbus ever since.

11   It is said that when Columbus landed, one Indian turned to another and said, "Well, there goes the neighborhood!" Another version has two Indians watching Columbus land and one saying to the other, "Maybe if we leave them alone they will go away." A favorite cartoon in Indian country a few years back showed a flying saucer landing while an Indian watched. The caption was, "Oh, no, not again."

12   The most popular and enduring subject of Indian humor is, of course, General Custer. There are probably more jokes about Custer and the Indians than there were participants in the battle. All tribes, even those thousands of miles from Montana, feel a sense of accomplishment when thinking of Custer. Custer binds together implacable foes because he represented the Ugly American of the last century and he got what was coming to him.

13   Some years ago we put out a bumper sticker which read "Custer Died for Your Sins." It was originally meant as a dig at the National Council of Churches. But as it spread around the nation it took on additional meaning until everyone claimed to understand it and each interpretation was different.

14   Originally, the Custer bumper sticker referred to the Sioux Treaty of 1868 signed at Fort Laramie in which the United States pledged to give free and undisturbed use of the lands claimed by Red Cloud in return for peace. Under the covenants of the Old Testament, breaking a covenant called for a blood sacrifice for atonement. Custer was the blood sacrifice for the United States breaking the Sioux treaty. That, at least originally, was the meaning of the slogan.

15   Custer jokes, however, can barely be categorized, let alone sloganized. Indians say that Custer was well-dressed for the occasion. When the Sioux found his body after the battle, he had on an Arrow shirt.

16   Many stories are derived from the details of the battle itself. Custer is said to have boasted that he could ride through the entire Sioux nation with his Seventh Cavalry and he was half right. He got half-way through.

17   One story concerns the period immediately after Custer's contingent had been wiped out and the Sioux and Cheyennes were zeroing in on Major Reno and his troops several miles to the south of the Custer battlefield.

18   The Indians had Reno's troopers surrounded on a bluff. Water was scarce, ammunition was nearly exhausted, and it looked like the next attack would mean certain extinction.

19   One of the white soldiers quickly analyzed the situation and shed his clothes. He covered himself with mud, painted his face like an Indian, and began to creep toward the Indian lines.

20   A Cheyenne heard some rustling in the grass and was just about to shoot.

21   "Hey, chief," the soldier whispered, "don't shoot, I'm coming over to join you. I'm going to be on your side."

22   The warrior looked puzzled and asked the soldier why he wanted to change sides.

23   "Well," he replied, "better red than dead."

24   Custer's Last Words occupy a revered place in Indian humor. One source states that as he was falling mortally wounded he cried, "Take no prisoners!" Other versions, most of them off color, concentrate on where those **** Indians are coming from. My favorite last saying pictures Custer on top of the hill looking at a multitude of warriors charging up the slope at him. He turns resignedly to his aide and says, "Well, it's better than going back to North Dakota."

25   Since the battle it has been a favorite technique to boost the numbers on the Indian side and reduce the numbers on the white side so that Custer stands out as a man fighting against insurmountable odds. One question no pseudo-historian has attempted to answer, when changing the odds to make the little boy in blue more heroic, is how what they say were twenty thousand Indians could be fed when gathered into one camp. What a tremendous pony herd must have been gathered there, what a fantastic herd of buffalo must have been nearby to feed that amount of Indians, what an incredible source of drinking water must have been available for fifty thousand animals and some twenty thousand Indians!

26   Just figuring water-needs to keep that many people and animals alive for a number of days must have been incredible. If you have estimated correctly, you will see that the Little Big Horn was the last great *naval* engagement of the Indian wars.

27   The Sioux tease other tribes a great deal for not having been at the Little Big Horn. The Crows, traditional enemies of the Sioux, explain their role as Custer's scouts as one of bringing Custer where the Sioux could get at him! Arapahos and Cheyennes, allies of the Sioux in that battle, refer to the time they "bailed the Sioux out" when they got in trouble with the cavalry.

28   Even today variations of the Custer legend are bywords in Indian country. When an Indian gets too old and becomes inactive, people say he is "too old to muss the Custer anymore."

29   The early reservation days were times when humorous incidents abounded as Indians tried to adapt to the strange new white ways and occasionally found themselves in great dilemmas.

30   At Fort Sisseton in Dakota territory, Indians were encouraged to enlist as scouts for the Army after the Minnesota Wars. Among the requirements for enlistment were a working knowledge of English and having attained twenty-one years of age. But these requirements were rarely met. Scouts were scarce and the goal was to keep a company of scouts at full strength, not to follow regulations from Washington to the letter.

31   In a short time the Army had a company of scouts who were very efficient but didn't know enough English to understand a complete sentence. Washington, finding out about the situation, as bureaucracies occasionally do, sent an inspector to check on the situation. While he was en route, orders to disband the scouts arrived, and so his task became one of closing the unit and making the mustering-out payments.

32   The scouts had lined up outside the command officer's quarters and were interviewed one by one. They were given their choice of taking money, horses, or a combination of the two as their final severance pay from the Army. Those who could not speak English were severely reprimanded and tended to get poorer horses in payment because of their obvious disregard of the regulations.

33   One young scout, who was obviously in violation of both requirements, was very worried about his interview. He quizzed the scouts who came from the room about the interview. To a man they repeated the same story: "You will be asked three questions, how old you are, how long you have been with the scouts, and whether you want money or horses for your mustering-out pay."

34   The young scout memorized the appropriate answers and prepared himself for his turn with the inspector. When his turn came he entered the room, scared to death but determined to do his best. He stood at attention before the man from Washington, eager to give his answers and get out of there.

35   The inspector, tired after a number of interviews, wearily looked up and inquired:

36   "How long have you been in the scouts?"

37   "Twenty years," the Indian replied with a grin.

38   The inspector stopped short and looked at the young man. Here was a man who looked only eighteen or twenty, yet he had served some twenty years in the scouts. He must have been one of the earliest recruits. It just didn't seem possible. Yet, the inspector thought, you can't tell an Indian's age from the way he looks, they sure can fool you sometimes. Or was he losing his mind after interviewing so many people in so short a time? Perhaps it was the Dakota heat. At any rate, he continued the interview.

39   "How old are you?" he continued.

40   "Three years."

41   A look of shock rippled across the inspector's face. Could this be some mysterious Indian way of keeping time? Or was he now delirious?

42   "Am I crazy or are you?" he angrily asked the scout.

43   "Both" was the reply and the scout relaxed, smiled, and leaned over the desk, reaching out to receive his money.

44   The horrified inspector cleared the window in one leap. He was seen in Washington, D.C., the following morning, having run full speed during the night. It was the last time Indian scouts were required to know English and applications for interpreter were being taken the following morning.

45   The problems of the missionaries in the early days provided stories which have become classics in Indian country. They are retold over and over again wherever Indians gather.

46   One story concerns a very obnoxious missionary who delighted in scaring the people with tales of hell, eternal fires, and everlasting damnation. This man was very unpopular and people went out of their way to avoid him. But he persisted to contrast heaven and hell as a carrot-and-stick technique of conversion.

47   One Sunday after a particularly fearful description of hell he asked an old chief, the main holdout of the tribe against Christianity, where he wanted to go. The old chief asked the missionary where *he* was going. And the missionary replied that, of course, he as a missionary of the gospel was going to heaven.

48   "Then I'll go to hell," the old chief said, intent on having peace in the world to come if not in this world.

49   On the Standing Rock reservation in South Dakota my grandfather served as the Episcopal missionary for years after his conversion to Christianity. He spent a great deal of his time trying to convert old Chief Gall, one of the strategists of Custer's demise, and a very famous and influential member of the tribe.

50   My grandfather gave Gall every argument in the book and some outside the book but the old man was adamant in keeping his old Indian ways. Neither the joys of heaven nor the perils of hell would sway the old man. But finally, because he was fond of my grandfather, he decided to become an Episcopalian.

51   He was baptized and by Christmas of that year was ready to take his first communion. He fasted all day and attended the Christmas Eve services that evening.

52   The weather was bitterly cold and the little church was heated by an old wood stove placed in the center of the church. Gall, as the most respected member of the community, was given the seat of honor next to the stove where he could keep warm.

53   In deference to the old man, my grandfather offered him communion first. Gall took the chalice and drained the entire supply of wine before

returning to his seat. The wine had been intended for the entire congregation and so the old man had a substantial amount of spiritual refreshment.

54 Upon returning to his warm seat by the stove, it was not long before the wine took its toll on the old man who by now had had nothing to eat for nearly a day.

55 "Grandson," he called to my grandfather, "now I see why you wanted me to become a Christian. I feel fine, so nice and warm and happy. Why didn't you tell me that Christians did this every Sunday. If you had told me about this, I would have joined your church years ago."

56 Needless to say, the service was concluded as rapidly as possible and attendance skyrocketed the following Sunday.

57 Another missionary was traveling from Gallup to Albuquerque in the early days. Along the way he offered a ride to an Indian who was walking to town. Feeling he had a captive audience, he began cautiously to promote his message, using a soft-sell approach.

58 "Do you realize," he said, "that you are going to a place where sinners abound?"

59 The Indian nodded his head in assent.

60 "And the wicked dwell in the depths of their iniquities?"

61 Again a nod.

62 "And sinful women who have lived a bad life go?"

63 A smile and then another nod.

64 "And no one who lives a good life goes there?"

65 A possible conversion, thought the missionary, and so he pulled out his punch line: "And do you know what we call that place?"

66 The Indian turned, looked the missionary in the eye, and said, "Albuquerque. . . ."

67 The years have not changed the basic conviction of the Indian people that they are still dealing with the United States as equals. At a hearing on Civil Rights in South Dakota a few years ago a white man asked a Sioux if they still considered themselves an independent nation. "Oh, yes," was the reply, "we could still declare war on you. We might lose but you'd know you'd been in a terrible fight. Remember the last time in Montana?"

68 During the 1964 elections Indians were talking in Arizona about the relative positions of the two candidates, Johnson and Goldwater. A white man told them to forget about domestic policies and concentrate on the foreign policies of the two men. One Indian looked at him coldly and said that from the Indian point of view it was all foreign policy.

69 The year 1964 also saw the emergence of the Indian vote on a national scale. Rumors reached us that on the Navajo reservation there was more enthusiasm than understanding of the political processes. Large signs announced, "All the Way with LJB."

70 The current joke is that a survey was taken and only 15 percent of the Indians thought that the United States should get out of Vietnam. Eighty-five percent thought they should get out of America. . . .

71   . . . When the War on Poverty was announced, Indians were justly skeptical about the extravagant promises of the bureaucrats. The private organizations in the Indian field, organized as the Council on Indian Affairs, sponsored a Capital Conference on Poverty in Washington in May of 1966 to ensure that Indian poverty would be highlighted just prior to the passage of the poverty program in Congress.

72   Tribes from all over the nation attended the conference to present papers on the poverty existing on their reservations. Two Indians from the plains area were asked about their feelings on the proposed program.

73   "Well," one said, "if they bring that War on Poverty to our reservation, they'll know they've been in a fight."

74   At the same conference, Alex Chasing Hawk, a nationally famous Indian leader from Cheyenne River and a classic storyteller, related the following tale about poverty.

75   It seemed that a white man was introduced to an old chief in New York City. Taking a liking to the old man, the white man invited him to dinner. The old chief hadn't eaten a good steak in a long time and eagerly accepted. He finished one steak in no time and still looked hungry. So the white man offered to buy him another steak.

76   As they were waiting for the steak, the white man said, "Chief, I sure wish I had your appetite."

77   I don't doubt it, white man," the chief said. "You took my land, you took my mountains and streams, you took my salmon and my buffalo. You took everything I had except my appetite and now you want that. Aren't you ever going to be satisfied? . . ."

78   One-line retorts are common in Indian country. Popovi Da, the great Pueblo artist, was quizzed one day on why the Indians were the first ones on this continent. "We had reservations," was his reply. Another time, when questioned by an anthropologist on what the Indians called America before the white man came, an Indian said simply, *"Ours."* A young Indian was asked one day at a conference what a peace treaty was. He replied, "That's when the white man wants a piece of your land."

79   The best example of Indian humor and militancy I have ever heard was given by Clyde Warrior one day. He was talking with a group of people about the National Indian Youth Council, of which he was then president, and its program for a revitalization of Indian life. Several in the crowd were skeptical about the idea of rebuilding Indian communities along traditional Indian lines.

80   "Do you realize," he said, "that when the United States was founded, it was only 5 percent urban and 95 percent rural and now it is 70 percent urban and 30 percent rural?"

81   His listeners nodded solemnly but didn't seem to understand what he was driving at.

82   "Don't you realize what this means?" he rapidly continued. "It means we are pushing them into the cities. Soon we will have the country back again."

83 Whether Indian jokes will eventually come to have more significance than that, I cannot speculate. Humor, all Indians will agree, is the cement by which the coming Indian movement is held together. When a people can laugh at themselves and laugh at others and hold all aspects of life together without letting anybody drive them to extremes, then it seems to me that that people can survive.

DISCUSSION QUESTIONS

1. What reason does Deloria give for Indians having developed their extensive repertoire of humor?
2. Why is George Armstrong Custer such an "enduring subject of Indian humor"?
3. Select one satiric statement by Deloria which you think effectively supports his purpose in the essay. Read it aloud to your classmates and discuss why you chose it.

WRITING TOPICS

1. Many of Deloria's humorous statements may stimulate cartoon captions. With a group of your classmates, use one of his ideas or sentences as a springboard for creating a cartoon or a humorous collage.
2. According to Deloria, "One of the best ways to understand a people is to know what makes them laugh." Collect jokes from students in your school and write an essay combining their jokes with your comments about what the examples reveal about the group you surveyed. For example, do the jokes fall into particular topics or themes?
3. Research the humor of a particular ethnic group, and write conclusions about what you found.
4. Beginning with paragraph 1, outline the major points in this essay. Consult your outline and write an essay in which you discuss Deloria's structure (organization).

I GIVE YOU BACK

Joy Harjo

"I Give You Back" is one of the poems highlighted in Joy Harjo's interview with journalist Bill Moyers. Harjo revealed that by repeating "my heart" four times, she mimicked the rhythm of the human heart beat. She also employed repetition to give a ceremonial sound to her poetic sermon. Her paternal grandfather was a Creek Baptist minister, and Harjo once said, "I always recognize something of his life in what I am doing." Harjo has also said that when she writes, she has often felt the presence of Creek ancestors. While "I Give You Back" is intensely personal, it is simultaneously Pan-Indian. As a member of a recent generation, Harjo turns fear into an ally instead of an enemy. "It's a poem that I wrote specifically to get rid of fear. . . . I'm trying to understand this destructive force and, in some way, to take it into myself. Otherwise, it's always going to be the enemy."

This poem discloses probably as clearly as any of Harjo's writing that she has lived with demons and cast them out. "We each have our own particular gifts, but I've had to take what has been, to me, a symbol of destruction and turn it into creative stuff." When Moyers commented that many of Harjo's poems begin with fear and end with love, she explained that writing itself is a process of transformation and reconciliation. "Poetry has given me a voice, a way to speak, and it has certainly enriched my vision so that I can see more clearly." Poetry carries her message to all Americans. "I know that language is alive and living, so I hope that in some small way my poems can transform hatred into love." Horrible events have caused bitter experiences for American Indians, but Harjo hopes that people throughout the world can learn lessons from these experiences and seek healing, forgiveness, and renewal, "instead of killing each other and hurting each other through all the ways that we have done it. . . . We're not separate. We're all in this together."

I release you, my beautiful and terrible
fear. I release you. You were my beloved
and hated twin, but now, I don't know you
as myself. I release you with all the
5   pain I would know at the death of
my daughters.

You are not my blood anymore.

I give you back to the white soldiers
who burned down my home, beheaded my children.
10 I give you back to those who stole the
food from our plates when we were starving.

I release you, fear, because you hold
these scenes in front of me and I was born
with eyes that can never close.

15 I release you, fear, so you can no longer
keep me naked and frozen in the winter,
or smothered under blankets in the summer.

I release you
I release you
20 I release you
I release you

I am not afraid to be angry.
I am not afraid to rejoice.
I am not afraid to be black.
25 I am not afraid to be white.
I am not afraid to be hungry.
I am not afraid to be full.
I am not afraid to be hated.
I am not afraid to be loved.

30 to be loved, to be loved, fear.

Oh, you have choked me, but I gave you the leash.
You have gutted me but I gave you the knife.
You have devoured me, but I laid myself across the fire.

I take myself back, fear.
35 You are not my shadow any longer.
I won't hold you in my hands.

You can't live in my eyes, my ears, my voice
my belly, or in my heart my heart
my heart my heart

40 But come here, fear
I am alive and you are so afraid
of dying.

Discussion Questions

1. Harjo expels or releases fear from all parts of her body. Locate examples of this approach and read them aloud to your classmates.
2. The poet often uses opposites or polarities to accentuate her images. Find three examples of this technique in the poem.
3. Personification of fear lends a personal quality to this poem. What examples do you think are effective?
4. Explain the meaning of lines 31 through 33.

Writing Topics

1. Completing the line, "I am not afraid to be (your words)," write a short poem or paragraph that expresses your feelings.
2. Harjo explains that she has learned to make fear an ally instead of an enemy. Write an essay about a time when you overcame fear, dispelled it, or made it an ally.
3. Read the poem aloud and listen for the repetition. Write your observations about Harjo's use of repetition to create a ritual chantlike effect. Support your ideas with specific references from the poem.
4. Prepare a choral reading script for this poem, and, with other classmates, perform the poem for the rest of the class.

AN INDIAN'S LOOKING-GLASS
FOR THE WHITE MAN

William Apess

William Apess's early years are recounted in the excerpt from his autobiography, *Son of the Forest,* in Chapter 6. Apess, who was still an indentured servant in 1813, ran away, enlisted, and served in the War of 1812. After living in Canada at the end of the war, he returned to Connecticut in 1818 and was ordained as a minister by the Protestant Methodist Church in 1829–1830. He and Mary Wood, who had also been an indentured servant, were married in 1821 and had three children.

In 1831, the New York Annual Conference of Protestant Methodists sent Apess to preach to the Pequots. Little is known concerning his 1831–1833 activities, but during those years he wrote *The Experiences of Five Christian Indians of the Pequod Tribe, or, An Indian's Looking-Glass for the White Man.* This work was, in effect, a printed sermon in which Apess addressed Euro-Americans who ignored his oral preaching, much as they deluded themselves that no Native Americans survived in New England. Apess's text provided the looking-glass for those who professed to believe the Christian Bible and to behave as it commanded. An eloquent orator, Apess also wrote in an oratorical style, quoting from the Bible and appealing to the emotions of his audience. At that time slavery was only beginning to become a major political issue among Euro-Americans, and Apess clearly discerned that Native Americans and African Americans both suffered discrimination based on racism.

Becoming an evangelical Christian enabled Apess to affirm his worth as a human being and his identity as an Indian while he championed tribal causes. Many leaders of both church and state opposed an Indian's preaching Christianity, but Apess "felt convinced that Christ died for all mankind—that age, sect, colour, country, or situation made no difference. I felt an assurance that I was included in the plan of redemption with all my brethren."

Critic Barry O'Connell emphasized the impact of Apess's writing and his place in our literature: "He was an inventive survivor, a man who refused to be extinguished and who understood that he could not live on unless his people also did. So they have. The Pequots are still with us . . . not as a saving remnant, not noble or bloody savages, but Americans of a mixed heritage and proud history."

1   Having a desire to place a few things before my fellow creatures who are traveling with me to the grave, and to that God who is the maker and preserver both of the white man and the Indian, whose abilities are the same and who are to be judged by one God, who will show no favor to outward appearances but will judge righteousness. Now I ask if degradation has not been heaped long enough upon the Indian? And if so, can there not be a compromise? Is it right to hold and promote prejudices? If not, why not put them all away? I mean here, among those who are civilized. It may be that many are ignorant of the situation of many of my brethren within the limits of New England. Let me for a few moments turn your attention to the reservations in the different states of New England, and, with but few exceptions, we shall find them as follows: the most mean, abject, miserable race of beings in the world. . . .

2   Let a gentleman and lady of integrity and respectability visit these places, and they would be surprised; as they wandered from one hut to the other they would view, with the females who are left alone, children half-starved and some almost as naked as they came into the world. . . . One reason why they are left so is because their most sensible and active men are absent at sea. Another reason is because they are made to believe they are minors and have not the abilities given them from God to take care of themselves, without it is to see a few little articles, such as baskets and brooms. Their land is in common stock, and they have nothing to make them enterprising.

3   Another reason is because those men who are Agents, many of them are unfaithful and care not whether the Indians live or die; they are much imposed upon by their neighbors, who have no principle. They would think it no crime to go upon Indian lands and cut and carry off their most valuable timber, or anything else they chose; and I doubt not but they think it clear gain. Another reason is because they have no education to take care of themselves; if they had, I would risk them to take care of their own property.

4   Now I will ask if the Indians are not called the most ingenious people among us. And are they not said to be men of talents? And I would ask: Could there be a more efficient way to distress and murder them by inches than the way they have taken? And there is no people in the world but who may be destroyed in the same way. Now, if these people are what they are

held up in our view to be, I would take the liberty to ask why they are not brought forward and pains taken to educate them, to give them all a common education, and those of the brightest and first-rate talents put forward and held up to office. Perhaps some unholy, unprincipled men would cry out, "The skin was not good enough"; but stop, friends—I am not talking about the skin but about principles. I would ask if there cannot be as good feelings and principles under a red skin as there can be under a white. And let me ask: Is it not on the account of a bad principle that we who are red children have had to suffer so much as we have? And let me ask: Did not this bad principle proceed from the whites or their forefathers? And I would ask: Is it worthwhile to nourish it any longer? If not, then let us have a change, although some men no doubt will spout their corrupt principles against it, that are in the halls of legislation and elsewhere. But I presume this kind of talk will seem surprising and horrible. I do not see why it should so long as they (the whites) say that they think as much of us as they do of themselves.

5   This I have heard repeatedly, from the most respectable gentlemen and ladies—and having heard so much precept, I should now wish to see the example. And I would ask who has a better right to look for these things than the naturalist himself—the candid man would say none.

6   I know that many say that they are willing, perhaps the majority of the people, that we should enjoy our rights and privileges as they do. If so, I would ask, Why are not we protected in our persons and property throughout the Union? Is it not because there reigns in the breast of many who are leaders a most unrighteous, unbecoming, and impure black principle, and as corrupt and unholy as it can be—while these very same unfeeling, self-esteemed characters pretend to take the skin as a pretext to keep us from our unalienable and lawful rights? I would ask you if you would like to be disenfranchised from all your rights, merely because your skin is white, and for no other crime. I'll venture to say, these very characters who hold the skin to be such a barrier in the way would be the first to cry out, "Injustice! awful injustice!"

7   But, reader, I acknowledge that this is a confused world, and I am not seeking for office, but merely placing before you the black inconsistency that you place before me—which is ten times blacker than any skin that you will find in the universe. And now let me exhort you to do away that principle, as it appears ten times worse in the sight of God and candid men than skins of color—more disgraceful than all the skins that Jehovah ever made. If black or red skins or any other skin of color is disgraceful to God, it appears that he has disgraced himself a great deal—for he has made fifteen colored people to one white and placed them here upon this earth.

8   Now let me ask you, white man, if it is a disgrace for to eat, drink, and sleep with the image of God, or sit, or walk and talk with them. Or have you the folly to think that the white man, being one in fifteen or sixteen, are the only beloved images of God? Assemble all nations together in your

imagination, and then let the whites be seated among them, and then let us look for the whites, and I doubt not it would be hard finding them; for to the rest of the nations, they are still but a handful. Now suppose these skins were put together, and each skin had its national crimes written upon it—which skin do you think would have the greatest? I will ask one question more. Can you charge the Indians with robbing a nation almost of their whole continent, and murdering their women and children, and then depriving the remainder of their lawful rights, that nature and God require them to have? And to cap the climax, rob another nation to till their grounds and welter out their days under the lash with hunger and fatigue under the scorching rays of a burning sun? I should look at all the skins, and I know that when I cast my eye upon that white skin, and if I saw those crimes written upon it, I should enter my protest against it immediately and cleave to that which is more honorable. And I can tell you that I am satisfied with the manner of my creation, fully—whether others are or not. . . .

9   What then is the matter now? Is not religion the same now under a colored skin as it ever was? If so, I would ask, why is not a man of color respected? You may say, as many say, we have white men enough. But was this the spirit of Christ and his Apostles? If it had been, there would not have been one white preacher in the world—for Jesus Christ never would have imparted his grace or word to them, for he could forever have withheld it from them. But we find that Jesus Christ and his Apostles never looked at the outward appearances. Jesus in particular looked at the hearts, and his Apostles through him, being discerners of the spirit, looked at their fruit without any regard to the skin, color, or nation; as St. Paul himself speaks, "Where there is neither Greek nor Jew, circumcision nor uncircumcision, Barbarian nor Scythian, bond nor free—but Christ is all, and in all" [Col. 3:11]. If you can find a spirit like Jesus Christ and his Apostles prevailing now in any white congregations, I should like to know it. I ask: Is it not the case that everybody that is not white is treated with contempt and counted as barbarians? And I ask if the word of God justifies the white man in so doing. When the prophets prophesied, of whom did they speak? When they spoke of heathens, was it not the whites and others who were counted Gentiles? And I ask if all nations with the exception of the Jews were not counted heathens. And according to the writings of some, it could not mean the Indians, for they are counted Jews. And now I would ask: Why is all this distinction made among these Christian societies? I would ask: What is all this ado about missionary societies, if it be not to Christianize those who are not Christians? And what is it for? To degrade them worse, to bring them into society where they must welter out their days in disgrace merely because their skin is of a different complexion. What folly it is to try to make the state of human society worse than it is. How astonished some may be at this—but let me ask: Is it not so? Let me refer you to the churches only. And, my brethren, is there any agreement?

Do brethren and sisters love one another? Do they not rather hate one another? Outward forms and ceremonies, the lusts of the flesh, the lusts of the eye, and pride of life is of more value to many professors than the love of God shed abroad in their hearts, or an attachment to his altar, to his ordinances, or to his children. But you may ask: Who are the children of God? Perhaps you may say, none but white. If so, the word of the Lord is not true. . . .

10   By what you read, you may learn how deep your principles are. I should say they were skin-deep. I should not wonder if some of the most selfish and ignorant would spout a charge of their principles now and then at me. But I would ask: How are you to love your neighbors as yourself? Is it to cheat them? Is it to wrong them in anything? Now, to cheat them out of any of their rights is robbery. And I ask: Can you deny that you are not robbing the Indians daily, and many others? But at last you may think I am what is called a hard and uncharitable man. But not so. I believe there are many who would not hesitate to advocate our cause; and those too who are men of fame and respectability—as well as ladies of honor and virtue. There is a Webster, an Everett, and a Wirt, and many others who are distinguished characters—besides a host of my fellow citizens, who advocate our cause daily. And how I congratulate such noble spirits—how they are to be prized and valued; for they are well calculated to promote the happiness of mankind. They well know that man was made for society, and not for hissing-stocks and outcasts. And when such a principle as this lies within the hearts of men, how much it is like its God—and how it honors its Maker— and how it imitates the feelings of the Good Samaritan, that had his wounds bound up, who had been among thieves and robbers.

11   Do not get tired, ye noble-hearted—only think how many poor Indians want their wounds done up daily; the Lord will reward you, and pray you stop not till this tree of distinction shall be leveled to the earth, and the mantle of prejudice torn from every American heart—then shall peace pervade the Union.

DISCUSSION QUESTIONS

1. Reread paragraphs 4, 6, 8, and 9. Select one paragraph and discuss the rhetorical questions Apess uses to persuade his audience.
2. What are four reasons Apess lists for the poor conditions of his fellow Indians?
3. What does Apess recommend to correct these problems?
4. Why do you think Apess and other Indians used Christianity to bolster their appeal to Euro-American audiences?

WRITING TOPICS

1. Apess repeats rhetorical questions, usually in a series, to advance his arguments. For example in the first paragraph, he introduces his thesis for the sermon with questions. "Now I ask if degradation has not been heaped long enough upon the Indians? And if so, can there not be a compromise? Is it right to hold and promote prejudice? If not, why not put them all away?" Find four other examples of rhetorical questions you think are effective and explain in a paragraph how they relate to Apess's argument.

2. Assume you are a reader of Apess's sermon in 1833. First, describe your background, religious views, and other information that defines your identity. Next, write a column for a Massachusetts newspaper in which you defend or attack three points in Apess's argument.

3. Apess's persuasive techniques include rhetorical questions and telling personal anecdotes. Write a persuasive essay about some modern-day injustice in which you attempt to convince an audience who disagrees with you.

THE GAME BETWEEN THE JEWS AND THE INDIANS IS TIED GOING INTO THE BOTTOM OF THE NINTH INNING

Sherman Alexie

Survival is an omnipresent theme in all of Sherman Alexie's books. A recent book of poems, *The Summer of Black Widows,* addresses prejudice, genocide, and tolerance. "Inside Dachau," links American Indian experiences with those of Jewish people. Prior to his visit to Dachau, he imagines he will write poetry about the cold death camp. After seeing brutal images of Jewish suffering, he knows his earlier plan was selfish, "What could I say about Dachau when I had never suffered through any season inside its walls?" Reflecting on the image of an "american indian holocaust museum," the poet wants to weep for victims of both holocausts. At the end of the poem, he concludes, "I have nothing new to say about death." The lines of a different poem "The Museum of Tolerance" beat with war, war, war as he regretfully remembers the twentieth century. Forgiveness is possible, and the Museum of Tolerance remains open all night, but "nobody can agree on the price of admission."

So, now, when you touch me
my skin, will you think
of Sand Creek, Wounded Knee?
And what will I remember

5   when your skin is next to mine
Auschwitz, Buchenwald?
No, we will only think of the past
as one second before

where we are now, the future
10　just one second ahead
but every once in a while
we can remind each other

that we are both survivors and children
and grandchildren of survivors.

DISCUSSION QUESTIONS

1. What did you expect this poem to be about when you first read the title?
2. What is the most important characteristic of "we"?
3. If Alexie had titled the poem "The Survivors," do you think it would have been more effective? Why or why not?
4. What images are brought to mind by the mention of Sand Creek, Wounded Knee, Auschwitz, and Buchenwald? What is the effect?

WRITING TOPICS

1. Research the story of one Nazi death camp, and write a report, poem, or other response to your information.
2. Locate other Alexie poems in a library and write an essay analyzing his theme of survival and survivors. Consider using a comparison/contrast organization.
3. Find a recent newspaper or magazine photograph of victims of violence, resulting from racial or religious conflicts. In a descriptive paragraph or a poem, write your feelings about what you see and what caused the violence.

THE MAN TO SEND RAINCLOUDS

Leslie Silko

Leslie Silko was still a University of New Mexico student when she wrote "The Man to Send Rainclouds," which was published in the *New Mexico Quarterly*. As her first important publication, it established her literary reputation almost overnight.

Editor Kenneth Rosen republished it promptly in an anthology that he named for it, *The Man to Send Rainclouds: Contemporary Stories by American Indians* (1974). This Rosen anthology itself was the first collection of stories by Native American authors to emerge from the Native American literary renaissance. Rosen included in the anthology three additional stories by Silko, thus emphatically recognizing her fine short fiction.

In her story, Silko shows that Pueblo people have not abandoned their traditions, which have been under attack for more than two hundred and fifty years. The title alludes to the Pueblo belief that the dead are associated with cloud beings who bring rain.

1   They found him under a big cottonwood tree. His Levi jacket and pants were faded light blue so that he had been easy to find. The big cottonwood tree stood apart from a small grove of winterbare cottonwoods which grew in the wide, sandy arroyo. He had been dead for a day or more, and the sheep had wandered and scattered up and down the arroyo. Leon and his brother-in-law, Ken, gathered the sheep and left them in the pen at the sheep camp before they returned to the cottonwood tree. Leon waited under the tree while Ken drove the truck through the deep sand to the edge of the arroyo. He squinted up at the sun and unzipped his jacket—it sure was hot for this time of year. But high and northwest the blue mountains were still in snow. Ken came sliding down the low, crumbling bank about fifty yards down, and he was bringing the red blanket.

2   Before they wrapped the old man, Leon took a piece of string out of his pocket and tied a small gray feather in the old man's long white hair. Ken

gave him the paint. Across the brown wrinkled forehead he drew a streak of white and along the high cheekbones he drew a strip of blue paint. He paused and watched Ken throw pinches of corn meal and pollen into the wind that fluttered the small gray feather. Then Leon painted with yellow under the old man's broad nose, and finally, when he had painted green across the chin, he smiled.

3   "Send us rain clouds, Grandfather." They laid the bundle in the back of the pickup and covered it with a heavy tarp before they started back to the pueblo.

4   They turned off the highway onto the sandy pueblo road. Not long after they passed the store and post office they saw Father Paul's car coming toward them. When he recognized their faces he slowed his car and waved for them to stop. The young priest rolled down the car window.

5   "Did you find old Teofilo?" he asked loudly.

6   Leon stopped the truck. "Good morning, Father. We were just out to the sheep camp. Everything is O.K. now."

7   "Thank God for that. Teofilo is a very old man. You really shouldn't allow him to stay at the sheep camp alone."

8   "No, he won't do that any more now."

9   "Well, I'm glad you understand. I hope I'll be seeing you at Mass this week—we missed you last Sunday. See if you can get old Teofilo to come with you." The priest smiled and waved at them as they drove away.

10   Louise and Teresa were waiting. The table was set for lunch, and the coffee was boiling on the black iron stove. Leon looked at Louise and then at Teresa.

11   "We found him under a cottonwood tree in the big arroyo near sheep camp. I guess he sat down to rest in the shade and never got up again." Leon walked toward the old man's bed. The red plaid shawl had been shaken and spread carefully over the bed, and a new brown flannel shirt and pair of stiff new Levi's were arranged neatly beside the pillow. Louise held the screen door open while Leon and Ken carried in the red blanket. He looked small and shriveled, and after they dressed him in the new shirt and pants he seemed more shrunken.

12   It was noontime now because the church bells rang the Angelus. They ate the beans with hot bread, and nobody said anything until after Teresa poured the coffee.

13   Ken stood up and put on his jacket. "I'll see about the gravediggers. Only the top layer of soil is frozen. I think it can be ready before dark."

14   Leon nodded his head and finished his coffee. After Ken had been gone for a while, the neighbors and clanspeople came quietly to embrace Teofilo's family and to leave food on the table because the gravediggers would come to eat when they were finished.

15   The sky in the west was full of pale yellow light. Louise stood outside with her hands in the pockets of Leon's green army jacket that was too big

for her. The funeral was over, and the old men had taken their candles and medicine bags and were gone. She waited until the body was laid into the pickup before she said anything to Leon. She touched his arm, and he noticed that her hands were still dusty from the corn meal that she had sprinkled around the old man. When she spoke, Leon could not hear her.

16 "What did you say? I didn't hear you."

17 "I said that I had been thinking about something."

18 "About what?"

19 "About the priest sprinkling holy water for Grandpa. So he won't be thirsty."

20 Leon stared at the new moccasins that Teofilo had made for the ceremonial dances in the summer. They were nearly hidden by the red blanket. It was getting colder, and the wind pushed gray dust down the narrow pueblo road. The sun was approaching the long mesa where it disappeared during the winter. Louise stood there shivering and watching his face. Then he zipped up his jacket and opened the truck door. "I'll see if he's there."

21 Ken stopped the pickup at the church, and Leon got out; and then Ken drove down the hill to the graveyard where people were waiting. Leon knocked at the old carved door with its symbols of the Lamb. While he waited he looked up at the twin bells from the king of Spain with the last sunlight pouring around them in their tower.

22 The priest opened the door and smiled when he saw who it was. "Come in! What brings you here this evening?"

23 The priest walked toward the kitchen, and Leon stood with his cap in his hand, playing with the earflaps and examining the living room—the brown sofa, the green armchair, and the brass lamp that hung down from the ceiling by links of chain. The priest dragged a chair out of the kitchen and offered it to Leon.

24 "No thank you, Father. I only came to ask you if you would bring your holy water to the graveyard."

25 The priest turned away from Leon and looked out the window at the patio full of shadows and the dining-room windows of the nuns' cloister across the patio. The curtains were heavy, and the light from within faintly penetrated; it was impossible to see the nuns inside eating supper. "Why didn't you tell me he was dead? I could have brought the Last Rites anyway."

26 Leon smiled. "It wasn't necessary, Father."

27 The priest stared down at his scuffed brown loafers and the worn hem of his cassock. "For a Christian burial it was necessary."

28 His voice was distant, and Leon thought that his blue eyes looked tired.

29 "It's O.K., Father, we just want him to have plenty of water."

30 The priest sank down into the green chair and picked up a glossy missionary magazine. He turned the colored pages full of lepers and pagans without looking at them.

31 "You know I can't do that, Leon. There should have been the Last Rites and a funeral Mass at the very least."

32 Leon put on his green cap and pulled the flaps down over his ears. "It's getting late, Father. I've got to go."

33 When Leon opened the door Father Paul stood up and said, "Wait." He left the room and came back wearing a long brown overcoat. He followed Leon out the door and across the dim churchyard to the adobe steps in front of the church. They both stooped to fit through the low adobe entrance. And when they started down the hill to the graveyard only half of the sun was visible above the mesa.

34 The priest approached the grave slowly, wondering how they had managed to dig into the frozen ground; and then he remembered that this was New Mexico, and saw the pile of cold loose sand beside the hole. The people stood close to each other with little clouds of steam puffing from their faces. The priest looked at them and saw a pile of jackets, gloves, and scarves in the yellow, dry tumbleweeds that grew in the graveyard. He looked at the red blanket, not sure that Teofilo was so small, wondering if it wasn't some perverse Indian trick—something they did in March to ensure a good harvest—wondering if maybe old Teofilo was actually at sheep camp corraling the sheep for the night. But there he was, facing into a cold dry wind and squinting at the last sunlight, ready to bury a red wool blanket while the faces of his parishioners were in shadow with the last warmth of the sun on their backs.

35 His fingers were stiff, and it took him a long time to twist the lid off the holy water. Drops of water fell on the red blanket and soaked into dark icy spots. He sprinkled the grave and the water disappeared almost before it touched the dim, cold sand; it reminded him of something—he tried to remember what it was, because he thought if he could remember he might understand this. He sprinkled more water; he shook the container until it was empty, and the water fell through the light from sundown like August rain that fell while the sun was still shining, almost evaporating before it touched the wilted squash flowers.

36 The wind pulled at the priest's brown Franciscan robe and swirled away the corn meal and pollen that had been sprinkled on the blanket. They lowered the bundle into the ground, and they didn't bother to untie the stiff pieces of new rope that were tied around the ends of the blanket. The sun was gone, and over on the highway the eastbound lane was full of headlights. The priest walked away slowly. Leon watched him climb the hill, and when he had disappeared within the tall, thick walls, Leon turned to look up at the high blue mountains in the deep snow that reflected a faint red light from the west. He felt good because it was finished, and he was happy about the sprinkling of the holy water; now the old man could send them big thunderclouds for sure.

DISCUSSION QUESTIONS

1. What did the short story title mean to you before you read the story? Did your interpretation change after you read the story? Explain.
2. What does the reader learn about the priest from details in the story?
3. What is the relationship between the priest and his parishioners? Cite specific examples.
4. Find two examples of irony during the interaction between Leon and Father Paul.

WRITING TOPICS

1. Research symbols and funerary practices of a non-Pueblo society and write an essay comparing and contrasting your information with the ceremony for old Teofilo.
2. Write a short essay on the role of the setting in this story.
3. In a brief essay, describe the conflict in this story that moves the plot forward.

METAMORPHOSIS

Joy Harjo

Like the legendary Phoenix, Joy Harjo has risen brilliantly from the ashes of history and her troubled youth. This personal transformation began when she entered the Institute of American Indian Arts (IAIA). In 1969, IAIA was an exciting place to interact with other students. Some of the faculty stimulated students selected for their high potential to create works of art in whatever medium they preferred.

Like many young people from a mixed heritage, Joy Harjo struggled to come to terms with her identity. Her acceptance of both parts of herself came in stages. "There were times when I went through a period of really hating myself for being a mixture of both races." Harjo wanted to be either all of one or all of the other, "but at the same time part of my lesson in this life is to recognize myself as a whole person." Accepting her unique heritage taught Harjo that she had a gift too precious to squander. "I learned a long time ago, after much difficulty and near suicide, that I would not allow the duality of blood and cultures to destroy me." In a way, her association with other Indians and her development of her artistic talents at IAIA saved her life, once she had reconciled her polarities. "The paradox was in my own blood, in my own body. It was difficult to decide for one or the other because I loved and hated both parts of myself. As a poet, I learned to bring all this despairing history together."

For this talented young woman, writing became a means of survival: "I don't believe I would be alive today if it hadn't been for writing. There were times when I was conscious of holding onto a pen and letting words flow painful and from the gut, to keep from letting go of it all." This poet-musician-singer credits writing with her metamorphosis: "Writing helped me give voice to turn around a terrible silence that was killing me."

1   When I started Indian School in Santa Fe in 1967, I knew I had escaped
the emotional winter of my alcoholic childhood home. There was no one to
talk to except the invisible world, nothing to move me but the music I heard
on the radio—the shout and flame of James Brown, the crooning of the
Four Tops, and the brash bands of the English Invasion. There were family
stories about Monahwee, my great-great-grandfather, who led the Red Stick
War[1] in the early 1800s, one of the largest Indian wars in this country, but
as a teenager I had difficulty placing that history on the template of my
childhood. And yet those stories of resistance kept my heart beating toward
an unknown possibility, a promise of creative change.

2   It was in the fire and creativity of Indian school, newly renamed the
Institute of American Indian Arts, that my spirit made steps back from the
assaults of childhood, of culture. It was not a solitary journey. Rather, it was
made with a collective of students that included Inuit from Alaska,
Miccosukee from Florida, and many tribes in-between. Yet we made
alliances, or rather they were often made for us according to tribal history.

3   The Siouxs hung together; the Pawnees avoided them. The Pueblos
clung together, as did the Navajos. And then there were the Washington
State Indians who were an active political force. I belonged to the "Civilized
Tribes," which included the Creeks, Choctaws, Cherokees, Chickasaws, and
Seminoles. And there were divisions within the divisions. You were either a
cowboy or a hippie, a freak or a straight. Yet we were all "skins" traveling
together in an age of metamorphosis, many of us facing the same tests of
rage, locked grief, alienation. History still talked to us, still lived, and we
were direct evidence of the struggles of our great-grandparents, though
many of us wore bell-bottoms and Lennon glasses and listened to the psy-
chedelic music of the exploding times. We felt united.

4   In the Civilized Tribes, some of us were considered black because of
intermarriages and alliances with African-Americans. A Choctaw student
who was a fine piano player and a sweet gentleman was obviously part black
and sometimes excluded for that reason. I, too, despite my light skin, was
teased because of my family's black history.

5   To be Indian was difficult because of the demands of culture, of color,
but to be of African blood was to carry a load that was nearly impossible. Yet
my light skin invoked privilege—not among my peers but with some of the
teachers who'd been in the Bureau of Indian Affairs for years and who were
hired when the teaching philosophy had been to rehabilitate Indian students
to become urban citizens. Light skin was evidence of the civilizing process.

6   One of our school buildings was originally constructed to teach apartment living. The previous generation of students had been taught house-
keeping, milking, janitorial tasks, and other vocational skills. Only a few
years before, the fine-arts program that we were being taught—someone

---

[1] *Red Stick War:* The Red Stick faction of the Creek Confederacy fought the Tennessee militia. General
Andrew Jackson defeated the Red Sticks in 1814 at the battle of Horseshoe Bend.

had "discovered" that we were gifted in the arts—would have been considered beyond the minds and talents of Indians.

7   We embodied this cultural racism just as our parents had, and yet we were the headwaters of the tribal cultural renaissance, poised at the edge of an explosion of images and ideas that would shape contemporary Indian art. The energy crackled, the same kind of energy needed to shift continental plates, to propel a child into the world to start all over again. We honed ourselves on that energy, were tested by it, destroyed by it, re-created. We all changed and will never forget.

8   This Indian-school world was rife with paradox. Formerly run like a military camp by the Bureau of Indian Affairs, the school had been hastily transformed into a school for Native arts. Almost overnight, the staff, mostly old BIA employees, were asked to accommodate a fine-arts curriculum and faculty—an assortment of idealistic and dedicated artists, both Indian and non-Indian. This was a messy war.

9   We were given materials and encouraged to create, and we often did until three or four in the morning. Then we were awakened at exactly 5:30 A.M. to report to details—jobs that included working in the kitchen or cleaning studios and offices. We slept in academics, but not purely out of exhaustion. The classes were poorly taught. In my junior English class we were forced to read aloud from fourth-grade readers. I especially remember a story about a white banker who swept his sidewalk every morning before opening his bank. I looked around at our class, made up of students who were gifted storytellers, speakers, and artists, many fluent in two or more languages. We sometimes felt ashamed at this lack of respect. We were insulted and bored. While the story droned on, we wrote poems to each other, read Thomas Hardy novels, and then discussed them after class.

10   We struggled with this clash of systems just as we battled the whirlwinds of troubled families and history we could never leave behind. These tensions often erupted in violence with the urging of alcohol, drugs, and pure frustration.

11   One of the students, Danny, of classic Sioux looks and quick humor, was the same age as I. We were to have graduated together. One afternoon, our drawing class had an assignment to draw from nature. We scattered across the campus to luxuriate in one of the first warm days of spring. We were intoxicated by the smell of the Earth as she throws off heat. I sat on the steps of the theater building with a few other students. We smoked and contemplated the afternoon. Our past, present, and future drifted by us. We were momentarily content. Then Danny sprang by, lit up with a fierce anger. We were all surprised as he leapt brutally onto the hoods of every car in the administration parking lot, crushing them one by one. There was no mercy. But this didn't satisfy his anger, an anger larger than the tall cottonwoods watching our intense human drama. He grew with the anger and kicked in each set of windows lining the academic building. Around him a whirling halo glowed a brownish red. Within the whirl were racial epithets, his baby-self abandoned by his mother for a drink, the running-away ghost of his

father. Two teachers grabbed him and threw him to the ground. Tears ran from me, tears made of the same anger.

12 Years later, as I drove up on his reservation in South Dakota, I was nearly knocked down by the force of events called power that encircled a land so beautiful you wept. I understood the boy who kicked through a little tear in the fabric so many years ago. The discrepancy between his world of loss and images of horses on the plains could only be met first with anger.

13 Women often turn their anger inward, and at Indian school it was no different. We manifested it by mutilating ourselves or less often by attacking others. Yet each scar was evidence that we wished to live. We had to keep knives away from one Pueblo student, one of the best painters. We often carried another student to the Indian hospital to have her stomach pumped. She was a stunningly beautiful dancer. We had to hunt down another friend before she froze to death in the snow. She was trying to go home—to a home that was not there. We never really talked about any of this. We did what we could to save each other in the moment.

14 Just as our bodies were impressed with our anger, they also provided the canvas of our most intimate art. Once some of my roommates decided to tattoo themselves with needles and black ink. I contemplated what I would tattoo on my hands, but I was not in love enough with anyone to tattoo their initials and L-O-V-E on my knuckles as another girl was doing. Besides, it looked like it hurt. It was an initiation of sorts. There was no ice-numbing here. Only a few girls endured it, either for love or as a mark of blood to show their bravery or to note a particular event, a breakup, an accomplishment.

15 Twenty-five years later when I picked my daughter up from Rehoboth Indian School near Gallup and met the boyfriend who had made her soggy with grief for summer vacation, his hand blazed with her initials. They were still seeping blood. I knew I had trouble.

16 I marked myself once with a knife. I was disappearing into the adolescent sea of rage and destruction, but the mark of pain assured me of my own reality. The cut could speak. It had a voice that cried out when I could not make a sound in my defense. I knew that blood could talk. It was full of the stories that call us human, that link us with stars as well as the Earth. I thought I did not want to live, yet a shining sound burned at the center of my heart, urging me to stand like a tall cedar pole pointed toward the apex of the starry sky. It rescued me from the oblivion of unknown terrors of memory.

17 It was the stuff of my generation, we who came of age in that best and worst of times. We broke the surface of memory with stories of our anger and great love. We were mixed rage and beauty. And we moved from that place to remake the world in our image.

DISCUSSION QUESTIONS

1. Harjo uses specific details about music, dress, emotions, and language to define her generation. What are ten important details that define your generation? Include historical as well as personal details.
2. How do you explain Danny's anger? Do you think violent acts are often an expression of anger? Why did Harjo cry when the teachers grabbed him and threw him to the ground?
3. Select four sentences that you think are important in conveying Harjo's message about education, about her personal life, or about her classmates.

WRITING TOPICS

1. Write about a time in your life that could be described as a metamorphosis, a time of significant change. You may wish to use some of the images of dress, music, and other details you have discussed with your friends to define your generation.
2. Harjo writes, "And we moved from that place to remake the world in our image." If your generation could change three things in the contemporary world, what would you choose to alter? Explain your choices in your literary journal.
3. Harjo names "divisions within the divisions" in the student group. Write an article for your school newspaper in which you name and describe the divisions among students in your school. Then examine the possibility that the divisions also unite as well as separate students.
4. Write your immediate thoughts in response to these quotes from the essay.

"We were mixed rage and beauty."
"History still talked to us, still lived."
"We sometimes felt ashamed at this lack of respect."
"We all changed and will never forget."

THE WOMAN HANGING FROM THE THIRTEENTH FLOOR WINDOW

Joy Harjo

Harjo explained to interviewer Bill Moyers that the impetus for this poem came from her first visit to Chicago. In the angular, hard Chicago Indian Center, Harjo noticed a rocking chair "which actually shocked me in its roundness." That chair appeared at the edge of her vision for a couple of years. "Finally, this woman came and sat—she had probably gone to Chicago on one of the relocation programs, or maybe her parents had—but she appeared in the rocking chair and she would not let me get up from my typewriter until I wrote the poem." Harjo considered the woman a muse whose spirit followed her from Chicago. Despite poverty and incredible odds, the woman had sometimes found beauty and survived.

Harjo believes that the poem grew from the seed of "a woman's need to speak, to be seen in a cityscape that deemed her invisible." The woman made her presence known, "so I could not deny her or escape her, for to do so was to deny or escape myself." Sitting at the edge of the poet's memory, the woman refused to move, and Harjo wrote the poem in recognition of all women. The poet embraced her responsibility because, "I wanted recognition for all of us past the shame, the destruction, the lies. Women must have courage and must find a voice."

More than eighty writers representing nearly fifty nations find their voices in Harjo's landmark anthology *Reinventing the Enemy's Language* (1997). This collection of Native American women authors ranging from Wilma Mankiller, Cherokee Chief, to Rigoberta Menchu, Mayan winner of the Nobel Peace Prize, has garnered high praise. Alice Walker welcomed the anthology as "a book I have been yearning for all my life." Walker celebrated the fact that "native ancestral grandmothers who are the reason so much of Native American life and spirit still exists, have been honored by their granddaughters," telling their grandmother's stories and their own.

The anthology evoked a dramatic response from Walker. "I sat before a blazing fire, reading this gift: enthralled, enchanted, in tears, in happiness and hope."

She is the woman hanging from the 13th floor
window. Her hands are pressed white against the
concrete moulding of the tenement building. She
hangs from the 13th floor window in east Chicago,
5 with a swirl of birds over her head. They could
be a halo, or a storm of glass waiting to crush her.

She thinks she will be set free.

The woman hanging from the 13th floor window
on the east side of Chicago is not alone.
10 She is a women of children, of the baby, Carlos,
and of Margaret, and of Jimmy who is the oldest.
She is her mother's daughter and her father's son.
She is several pieces between the two husbands
she has had. She is all the women of the apartment
15 building who stand watching her, watching themselves.

When she was young she ate wild rice on scraped down
plates in warm wood rooms. It was in the farther
north and she was the baby then. They rocked her.

She sees Lake Michigan lapping at the shores of
20 herself. It is a dizzy hole of water and the rich
live in tall glass houses at the edge of it. In some
places Lake Michigan speaks softly, here, it just sputters
and butts itself against the asphalt. She sees
other buildings just like hers. She sees other
25 women hanging from many-floored windows
counting their lives in the palms of their hands
and in the palms of their children's hands.

She is the woman hanging from the 13th floor window
on the Indian side of town. Her belly is soft from
30 her children's births, her worn levis swing down below
her waist, and then her feet, and her heart.
She is dangling.

The woman hanging from the 13th floor hears voices.
They come to her in the night when the lights have gone
35 dim. Sometimes they are little cats mewing and scratching
at the door, sometimes they are her grandmother's voice,
and sometimes they are gigantic men of light whispering
to her to get up, to get up, to get up. That's when she wants
to have another child to hold onto in the night, to be able
40 to fall back into dreams.
And the woman hanging from the 13th floor window
hears other voices. Some of them scream out from below
for her to jump, they would push her over. Others cry softly
from the sidewalks, pull their children up like flowers and gather
45 them into their arms. They would help her, like themselves.

But she is the woman hanging from the 13th floor window,
and she knows she is hanging by her own fingers, her
own skin, her own thread of indecision.

She thinks of Carlos, of Margaret, of Jimmy.
50 She thinks of her father, and of her mother.
She thinks of all the women she has been, of all
the men. She thinks of the color of her skin, and
of Chicago streets, and of waterfalls and pines.
She thinks of moonlight nights, and of cool spring storms.
55 Her mind chatters like neon and northside bars.
She thinks of the 4 a.m. lonelinesses that have folded
her up like death, discordant, without logical and
beautiful conclusion. Her teeth break off at the edges.
She would speak.

The woman hangs from the 13th floor window crying for
the lost beauty of her own life. She sees the
sun falling west over the grey plane of Chicago.
She thinks she remembers listening to her own life
break loose, as she falls from the 13th floor
window on the east side of Chicago, or as she
climbs back up to claim herself again.

DISCUSSION QUESTIONS

1. Why do you think Harjo located the woman on the thirteenth floor?
2. Harjo anchors her poem on "the woman hanging from the 13th floor window." Locate the places this line occurs and discuss the context of each line in that stanza.
3. Explain lines 16–18.
4. Find the references to children. Why do you think Harjo included them?

WRITING TOPICS

1. Write one additional stanza in which you tell what happened to the woman.
2. Select five images that contribute to the impact of the poem. In a brief essay, explain why each is important.
3. In a short essay, tell whether you think the woman is literally hanging from the window or whether this image is a figurative symbol. Support your conclusion with evidence from the poem.

THE BIG SNOW AND FLOOD RAMPAGE OF 1892–1893

Mourning Dove [Christine Quintasket]

In 1888, Christine Quintasket, by her own account, was born in a canoe while her mother was crossing the Kootenay River, near Bonner's Ferry, Idaho. Besides her English name, she was given the name Humishuma, or Mourning Dove, which she later used as her pen name. Her mother's family were Colville tribal leaders and her father was from the Okanagans. The Lucy and Joseph Quintasket family lived on the Colville Reservation in eastern Washington. Mourning Dove first attended the Goodwin Mission School of the Sacred Heart Convent in Ward, Washington, where she acquired a few years of formal schooling. Punished for speaking Salish, she was lonely and traumatized by school experiences, but determined to learn. When her mother died in 1902, Mourning Dove left a Colville public school to help care for four younger sisters and brothers.

Despite scant schooling, poverty, and multiple hardships, Mourning Dove was absolutely determined to write. Being virtually uneducated and laboring hard as a housekeeper, migrant worker, and at other jobs did not diminish her ambition to write in order to challenge stereotypes about Indians and to promote social justice for her people. In 1912 at age twenty-four, she enrolled in a Calgary, Alberta, business school to learn to type and to improve her English.

By 1914, she had written the first draft of her novel *Cogewea, the Half-Blood: A Depiction of the Great Montana Cattle Range.* Mourning Dove drew on her own life as a person of mixed genetic heritage in writing this novel, published as a Western genre romance. In 1915 at the Walla Walla Frontier Days celebration, she met Lucullus McWhorter, who became her mentor and editor for twenty years. McWhorter collaborated with Mourning Dove on *Cogewea* and managed to get it published in 1927. This was only the second novel by an Indian woman depicting the complex dilemma of the mixed bloods: "Regarded with suspicion by the Indian; shunned by the Caucasian; where was there any place for the despised breed!" It appeared to Mourning Dove there was no place for the Métis among either race. "Yes, we are between two fires, the Red and the White. Our Caucasian brothers criticize us as a shiftless class, while the Indians disown us as abandoning our own race."

In 1919 Mourning Dove and her husband Fred Galler, a Wenatchee, became migrant workers, moving from crop to crop, picking hops and thinning apples. They pitched tents and camped in all kinds of conditions. Everywhere they traveled, Mourning Dove lugged her battered typewriter and wrote after long hours of back-breaking labor in the fields or orchards. It is remarkable that Mourning Dove wrote at all since she had to write for most of the night in a tent or cabin.

Mourning Dove: A Salishan Autobiography appeared in 1990. Mourning Dove, who died in 1936, left voluminous pages recounting her life in the context of historical and ethnographic information. Editor Jay Miller rewrote her unfinished drafts and published the text a century after Mourning Dove and her family had survived the tremendous snowstorm and terrible flood of 1892–93. Miller explained, "In rewriting I attempted to apply standard English conventions of syntax, spelling, and grammar while retaining Mourning Dove's words."

1   We were settling in our winter home when the men decided to take the ponies far into the heart of the reservation so they could graze on the lush grass there and get fat before the snow came. Most of Father's horses were of the cayuse type, much smaller than regular horses but with greater endurance, able to work long and hard on meager food. They were almost as vigorous as the deer of the forest and could live on the same foods.

2   In previous years, Father took his ponies thirty-five miles up the Kettle River in Canada. The Canadians did not think it was worth the effort to set up a customs office along the Indian trail, though there had been one at Lake Osoyoos since 1860. Hence we could come and go as we pleased. The pasture was located at the first big bend of the river in an open valley with rocky cliffs and small boulders. It got less snow than the other areas, or perhaps the numerous rocks helped to melt the snow faster and keep the bunchgrass clear for feeding animals.

3   The men gathered their fat, sleek horses into a log corral. The ponies snorted and frisked, with quivering nostrils and wild eyes. Father smiled with satisfaction when his herd left the corral, kicking and playing. The hair of my pinto shone in the late fall sunshine glistening off the crusted snow. On the day set, the men moved the horses to the winter pasture and returned on

foot three days later, resigned to stay around camp for the long days of winter. Cooking utensils and saddles were cached at the pasture in preparation for spring roundup. After their return, the men had a holiday, their hard work done for the year. Some of the old men made holes in the ice at the edge of the river and fished, while others helped the women gather firewood. The men seldom carried water, as that was considered a chore for women and children.

4   Before the snow, Sulee and I played with the other children, making tipis out of the thick green moss that carpeted rocks beside the creek. When the snow deepened, we amused ourselves by climbing young saplings and swinging back and forth. We used to see who could climb highest and spy the fishery that most of us called home.

5   The long and tedious winter evenings were devoted to visiting and feasting, and it was the proper time to tell stories, legends, and sagas. The old people told their families about past tribal customs, laws, habits, and wars. In the quiet of winter, much of our important traditional knowledge was passed on to a willing audience. Our tipi was a favorite gathering place because my parents were generous hosts. As a child I found the stories monotonous, but I always stayed awake beside my father.

6   We children played in our section of the tipi until visitors came; then we were hushed and told to sit quietly and listen while our elders conversed. We were not allowed to ask questions or interrupt the conversation.

7   The snow came down slowly at first, but by midwinter it filled the sky and ground with a vengeance. It was as high as my father's knees. Blinding white sheets came down faster every day until it was waist deep by the time of the church holidays at St. Regis Mission. We were anxious to celebrate Christmas (First Shoot) Day. The day before, some Indians crossed the river in canoes and walked on foot with backpacks of blankets and food to spend the night at the mission. My mother went with them, but Sulee and I stayed home with Father. The holiday continued until Last Shoot Day or New Year, when guns were also fired at midnight.

8   A few days after, Father grew worried about his horses, laced on snowshoes early one morning, and put on his pack to trek to the pasture. He was gone for more than a week, returning sad and disheartened. After walking for two days, he had made a desperate attempt to save the ponies in the deep snow, but to no avail. The horses were pawing up the snow, but it was too deep and crusted for them to reach the grass. They were starving when he reached them. For a week he used a slab of wood to try to expose enough feed for all of them, but he could not. He was especially concerned about my pinto, but by then my pony was too thin to save. Father lost his fine herd of horses.

9   We were not the only ones hard hit that winter. Everyone lost their herds, whites and Indians alike. The deer came down low and tried desperately to survive the long, cold winter. Many of them starved beside the Columbia. They were at the mercy of Indians on snowshoes. The small

hoofs of the deer sank into the crusted snow, burying them to the belly, where they were easily taken by hunters. From this and other small favors, Indians were able to keep somewhat happy and indifferent to fate for the rest of the winter. People became restless only at the first signs of spring when the snow began to thaw.

10   Just before spring, hundreds of deer died, unable to exist on tree moss, pine needles, or bush tops. Game was very scarce for the next several years. In the Buttercup Moon (March), Father dressed me warmly and sent me outdoors to play until he said I could come home. He said my mother was ill. It was a very windy day that shook the tipis in the slushy snow, but the sun was shining. I went out and joined a group of children riding down a nearby hillside using mats with bark runners as sleds. We had great fun, but our moccasins got wet. While some used the sleds, the rest of us scrambled over the ice sheet to bare patches to pick the buttercups just coming into bloom. Spring was in the air, and we were happy.

11   Some of the children wandered farther into the deep ravines to jump into the snowdrifts there. They worked hard to extract themselves until they reached safety at the edges, laughing the whole time. Our parents seemed indifferent to our health, since they let us stay in our wet moccasins. Every spring was the same as we came home soaking wet, covered with snow and mud, and gathered around the central fire to get dry. Yet their indifference seemed justified, because we never caught cold. We were very happy and free. We did not go to school and set our own schedules, playing and eating when we wanted. We had pure, clean air both outside and inside the tipi. We lived among friends and relations, free to enter every home and eat there.

12   Late that evening, Father called me from one of these homes. As we entered the doorway of the tipi, I heard a funny noise that sounded like a baby crying. Then I saw a wee babe in my mother's arms and appreciated that we had a new member of the family and I had another sister. She was tiny, with a wrinkled face that I liked to watch as her mouth opened in search of food. It reminded me of the little birds my friends had found the summer before. Sulee cried from the grief she suffered at the tragedy of being replaced as the youngest in the family.

13   Father always wanted a son, so his disappointment was great when this third daughter arrived. She was given Keleta as a pet name. This was the last in a series of disappointments Father had that spring. He had lost his horses, his food rack was disappearing, and his family increased. He lost his jovial spirit and looked sad [brooding around the tipi]. He did not laugh or talk as much as before.

14   The snow slowly melted away, but the nights would freeze the water into ice to thaw in the sun of the next day. The ground was bare in spots.

15   Early one morning I overheard my parents talking. They decided the family should stay in the winter camp while Father went across the river to the white towns to seek work. This was necessary because we had no horses or ponies to carry all of us to another place. The rest of the day, he prepared

for his departure. The next morning he put on clean clothing and gave what few coins he had to Mother. He had no blankets or food, nor did he have a destination. He was desperate and in need of food for his family.

16   After he left, Mother held Keleta to her breast and cried in silence. Sulee and I did not understand any of this and so played around the dying embers of our fire. She had always been generous to the poor and needy with our food. All winter long she had given away some of the food Father had saved the previous summer. Father said nothing because he also believed in helping the needy. That was the reason we were short of food before the spring plants were ready.

17   It was only when I was much older that I realized the sacrifices made by my gentle mother. She would cook a very small piece of venison and divide it equally into three pieces. Sulee and I would swallow ours almost whole. Mother would then divide the third piece again and go without any food for herself. I did not stop to wonder why she fed the baby after each meal with tears in her eyes. It was because she was hungry. Our childish selfishness did not understand that our mother was going without to keep us alive while she yet had to nurse a third. My heart aches with remorse as I write this. She died long before I realized any of this, and now I cannot ask her to forgive me for being so selfish. When we cried for food, she could only turn her back to the fire, away from us, and weep quietly. While neighbor women were complaining and [broadcasting their troubles], Mother remained silent. She never complained of her ailments or misfortunes and never aired her troubles in public.

18   Mother was a reserved woman, almost to the point of coldness, and many people misunderstood her aloofness and the hidden warmth of her character. She had a heart of gold that showed only to the poor and unfortunate. I knew her to give away our own food to the needy so that we went without for a time. It was the way she and Father were raised, and they had watched their own parents do the same.

19   When all our food was gone, Mother did the next best thing. She dressed us each morning and bathed the baby before lacing her into the cradleboard. She took her digging stick and led us to the hillsides to dig up the tender shoots of the balsam sunflower and feed them to us. We did this for two weeks until the shoots were high enough to develop a thin skin that had to be peeled off. These shoots were called "famine food" because they were the first fresh food available each spring. It tasted like celery and was considered an aid to digestion. It was best mixed with other food and meat because a steady diet of it was not healthy.

20   One day Mother led us up the Kettle River to gather mussels from the shoals to eat with the shoots. Back home she buried the shells under the fire to bake in the sandy loam. Even so, they were tough and we had to work very hard to chew them. Still, we enjoyed this change of food.

21   Mother trapped ground squirrels when they first emerged from their burrows after winter hibernation. Groundhogs were fatter but had a

stronger scent than the squirrels. They were a luxury we all enjoyed. As always, Mother divided our catch with the old people in camp. We also ate tree squirrels and all kinds of birds Mother snared with a hemp string.

22   That spring of 1893 everyone was starving. Those who were able-bodied had moved on in search of food, work, or money. We were stranded in camp with the old and feeble because of our lack of horses.

23   Early one morning I awakened to hear the singing of meadowlarks. I had had no supper, and my stomach ached for food. I could not abide the happy sound of the "tattler" of legend and began to cry quietly to myself. By now I had learned to be patient and not complain, for it was useless to share my grief with Mother. She remained true to her education and was stoic with everyone. Mother did this even with her own children, never cuddling us or saying soft words. I was [a bit] afraid of her and in consequence held her words in great respect.

24   Yet that day my mother was very kind and understanding. She interrupted my tears by saying, "What is the matter Kee-ten?" using my pet name. It was too much to bear, and I told her I was hungry and lonesome for Father. I heard her sigh as she got up to start the fire. I got up quickly, dried my eyes, and warmed myself at the fire. We said nothing else, but we had shared our sorrow.

25   Mother dressed Sulee and the baby in clean but worn clothes, better than we wore for every day. I wondered why we were wearing them but was afraid to ask. My questions or inquisitiveness were always rebuked because it was not the Indian way to learn anything.

26   Instead, I waited to see what would happen. When we were dressed and ready, Mother placed the cradleboard with Keleta on her back, and we went directly across the river in a fragile canoe lent to us for the trip to Marcus. Mother placed her daughters on the bottom and paddled from the stern. With each dip of the oar, the boat leaped forward. Mother was expert with a canoe, and we went in speedy safety.

27   At the little city of Marcus, we followed Mother from one house to another as she knocked on the back door to ask for food for her family. At each door she was refused admittance and would silently leave while Sulee begged and cried for food in our language. Perhaps this prevented whites from learning the true nature of our distress. By afternoon the sun beat on my bare head and I felt weak [from hunger]. Mother stopped in the shade of some jack pines near three lone houses set in this shade. She rested there for some time before she determined to go to the door of a house where we could hear men and women laughing hilariously.

28   A woman came to the door wearing a long dress with many ruffles along the bottom and her hair curled and piled high in a roll behind her head. Her smile was sweet and dimpled. She was beautiful, with pink skin, red lips, eyes as blue as the sky. Mother talked to her and she nodded. She came outside and shut the door, giving each of us children a pat on the head. Then she went back inside and returned with some fluffy, lacy clothing for my mother

to wash and mend. She also brought out some bread and food that Sulee and I ate in haste under the jack pines.

29   Out of respect for the dead and their kind deeds, I will not use the real name of this woman but will supply a substitute. The city of Marcus was filled with nice churchgoers who did not believe in associating with a prostitute like Nellie. She made her money from providing the nightlife in the sleepy little burg of Marcus, a character of the Gay Nineties with a kind heart who was shunned by the decent society of this pioneer town. Yet she alone was willing to help and provide our salvation until Father returned. Every week Mother went to get washing and mending from Nellie and returned with food and spare clothing. Mother had no idea where or how Father was. She could only wait for him patiently and continue to support the family by digging roots, trapping animals, and doing laundry. She never stopped dividing our food with those less fortunate, even though the worst was yet to come.

30   As the days passed and the spring sun melted the snow, the Columbia rose with increasing speed until it became a roaring and ferocious monster. One morning Mother shook me awake because the water was at our doorway. I helped her gather up our most necessary possessions, and we escaped to higher ground. Mother went back and forth all day to move everything to safety. She also helped the old people move away from the flood. She did not rest until everyone was safe on higher benchland.

31   Within a few days the river rose to threaten us again, and we had to move up farther to be safe. It was a sight I will never forget. We children stood in a group while driftwood and other debris passed by our tipi. It was so dense that nothing could get across. It included whole trees, houses, barns, chicken coops, fence rails, intact haystacks, and ferryboats. Some of the homes were complete even to the floors. Once a chicken coop went by with a rooster and some hens sitting on the roof. As it passed close to the bank, the rooster crowed. All these things were destined to be smashed to splinters at the falls just below.

32   The flood went on for some time before the water receded. The high water left grayish rings around the pine trees as high as fifteen feet above the ground. These marks were evident for years, bearing witness to the force of the destruction.

33   The Creator had been kind to provide the famine food that got us through the early spring as it had our ancestors for eons before. But nature had whims of its own, playing havoc with the property of Indians and whites who lived along the Columbia. The big snow destroyed all the ponies, preventing us from searching for food, and the melting snow caused the rampage that wiped out everything else. We had to start over and became stronger than before as a result. Anyone who had food or a warm place shared it with others so that all might survive.

34   Father returned to plant a garden, but when harvest time came he had to borrow tools to bring it in. When he began to build up his herds again,

he needed hay and had to borrow a scythe and wooden rake to collect bunchgrass. He could not find a wagon to borrow to haul it, so he devised a pole sled to haul it to storage. His only remaining personal tool was an ax, and he used it to start a new log cabin. This was too slow, and my parents decided that my father would go back to working at Fort Steele in British Columbia until he could save enough money to start over.

35   All of this was hard work, but the important lesson for us all during that time of hardship was that we could best survive by working together. We learned the important thing about being Indians was the willingness to share whatever we had and the determination to survive with renewed intent and wisdom after any calamity.

DISCUSSION QUESTIONS

1. List five adjectives you would use to describe Mourning Dove's mother.
2. What are three things you learn about life on the Colville Reservation during this time?
3. Find two examples in the selection that illustrate "the important thing about being Indians was the willingness to share whatever we had and the determination to survive. . . ."

WRITING TOPICS

1. Write about the time a relative or some other person sacrificed for your benefit. Give details about that person's character and the act of sacrifice.
2. Write a paragraph on the importance of horses for the Colville people at this time.
3. In a brief essay, discuss the values important to Mourning Dove which she reveals in this chapter from her life.
4. In a personal essay, recall a time when your family or someone you know survived a disaster. Give details about life before and after the disaster and the changes it caused.

Street Kid

Duane Niatum

Duane Niatum, skillful poet and influential editor, was born in Seattle in 1938, of Klallam, French, and Irish ancestry. During his childhood, he learned Klallam traditions from his grandfather, who taught him to hunt, fish, and survive in the countryside. "I was the black sheep of my family, and he took my side, always, and gave me support all through my life until he died." His grandfather died when Niatum was seventeen, but "he had laid the groundwork for my art without my knowing it." Niatum recalls his growing up as troubled and confused. After three stints in reform schools, he enlisted in the United States Navy at seventeen.

The young prisoner in "Street Kid" echoes the author's experiences. Niatum explains that the poem's setting is Martinez, a reform school in California where he spent two months. Speaking of his adjustment to the horrors of being incarcerated, Niatum observed, "What I've grown to admire about humanity is its incredible ability to survive." In the poem, the locked-up thirteen-year-old seeks survival in solitude, building a nest of self like the meadowlark he watched through the barred window.

The maturing Niatum learned how to transform his youthful struggles into art. At the University of Washington, he became caught up by the excitement and camaraderies of the creative writing program. He honed his own poetic skills studying under such prominent poets as Theodore Roethke and Elizabeth Bishop. Niatum graduated with a B.A. in English in 1970. By the time he had received an M.S. in creative writing from Johns Hopkins University in 1972, he had published his first poetry collection, *After the Death of an Elder Klallam* (1970). This first book, like his subsequent ones, paid tribute to his Native American heritage.

I stand before the window that opens
to a field of sagebrush——
California country northeast of San Francisco.
Holding to the earth and its shield of silence,
5   The sun burns my thirteen years into the hill.
The white breath of twilight
Whirrs with insects crawling down the glass
Between the bars. But is the meadowlark
Warbling at the end of the fence
10 That sets me apart from the rest of the boys,
The cool toughs playing ping pong
And cards before lock-up.
When this new home stops calling on memory,
As well as my nickname, Injun Joe,
15 Given to me by the brothers,
The Blacks, the Chicanos, the others growing
Lean as this solitude, I step
From the window into the darkness
Reach my soul building a nest against the wall.

DISCUSSION QUESTIONS

1. What does the meadowlark symbolize?
2. Is "Injun Joe" a positive or negative nickname? Explain.
3. How is the title related to the poem?

WRITING TOPICS

1. Contrast the "cool toughs" and the speaker in a paragraph.
2. Niatum contrasts imagery of freedom and beauty of the natural world
   with imagery of confinement. Find at least five images for each category
   and write an essay contrasting the imagery in "Street Kid."
3. Describe the tone of this poem in a few sentences, using examples from
   the text.

BATTLE WON IS LOST

Phil George

Phil George, who calls the Puget Sound area home, wrote "Battle Won Is Lost" while a student at the Institute of American Indian Arts in Santa Fe. His work has appeared in several anthologies including *Voices of the Rainbow, Contemporary Poetry by American Indians* edited by Kenneth Rosen. George has read his poetry for Radio Free Europe, and it has been translated into several languages. His first chapbook *Kautsas* (Grandmothers) is distributed by the Nez Perce National Historical Park in Spaulding, Idaho. There his poetry enhances museum cases and walls. He wrote, produced, and narrated "A Season of Grandmothers" for PBS (1977).

In much of his prose and poetry, George honors his Nez Perce heritage. He dedicated his poem "Prelude to Memorial Song" to the "Descendants of the War of 1877, Chief Joseph Band of Nez Perce." The poem's speaker celebrates, "I am alive. Nemipu are breathing humans: We Are Alive." In "Battle Won Is Lost," the young poet questions a traditional rationale for warfare. The poem may be read as specifically tribal or as a universal protest poem.

They said, "You are no longer a lad."
    I nodded.
They said, "Enter the council lodge."
    I sat.
5 They said, "Our lands are at stake."
    I scowled.
They said, "We are at war."
    I hated.
They said, "Prepare red war symbols."
10   I painted.
They said, "Count coups."
    I scalped.

They said, "You'll see friends die."
      I cringed.
15 They said, "Desperate warriors fight best."
      I charged.
They said, "Some will be wounded."
      I bled.
They said, "To die is glorious."
20   They lied.

DISCUSSION QUESTIONS

1. Do you think the poem's title is ironic? Explain, using evidence from the poem.
2. The poet achieves rhythm through repetition and parallelism. Discuss four examples.
3. Were you surprised by the last line? Explain why or why not.
4. Select three strong images in the poem and explain their relationship to the rest of the poem.

WRITING TOPICS

1. Summarize the relationship between the young warrior, or soldier, and the leaders, beginning with the first line and proceeding to the end of the poem.
2. Recall an experience you have had with an older person who gave you advice that you rejected. In an essay, describe the person, the advice, and your response. Include how you feel about your decision today.
3. Write a brief essay on the following topic. In "The Battle Won Is Lost," Phil George uses repetition and parallelism to achieve rhythm and structure.

WE SAW DAYS

Ted Palmanteer

Ted Palmanteer was born June 28, 1943. Late June is apple-thin-ning season in Washington, and Palmanteer's mother kept working in the orchards until she did not have time to reach the hospital. Consequently, Palmanteer was born in a laborer's cabin.

Palmanteer attended Coulee Dam High School until he trans-ferred to the Institute of American Indian Arts in Santa Fe. He stayed there for two post-graduate years studying writing, sculpture, and painting. He then enrolled at Hartnell College in Salinas, California, to study sociology, but his draft board called him up at the end of his first year.

Sent to Vietnam after his basic training, Palmanteer was wounded during the 1968 Tet Offensive. Evacuated to Japan on a stretcher, he later spent nearly a year recovering at Madigan General Hospital near Fort Lewis, Washington. His autobiographical poem "We Saw Days" illustrates that the U.S. armed forces integrated young men from diverse ethnic backgrounds into a single fighting organization.

Once discharged from the hospital, Palmanteer spent three months on a lookout tower regaining his civilian perspective on life. He then enrolled at Yakima Valley College. Later he continued his painting and writing as a teacher of fine arts.

I sometimes think of 'Nam and the boys.
We used to say,
"If you goin' to be one,
be a Big Red One.
5   That's us, baby,
Delta Duds,
Third Herd, man."

We saw death's face
Smelled life's blood as it left,
10 and death's face.
We knew fear,
Boredom.
We saw days.

The sun pulsated like a huge blood clot
15 in the artery of the sky.
Concertina wire cut stitches in the clot's face.
Night reached out to ensure the vision of another day.

We hoped with hidden desperation
to live another night,
20 another day.
We talked,
Passive talk.

Someone told me,
"Don't let anyone push you without pushing back, Chief."
25 I said, "The hell you say."
He said, "We care."
We laughed.
Another night;
Another day.

DISCUSSION QUESTIONS

1. Why do you think the poet repeats "day/days" four times including the title?
2. What does the conversational tone add to the poem?
3. Do you think free verse form is effective in this poem? If so, why?

WRITING TOPICS

1. Both Phil George and Ted Palmanteer spent time in Vietnam. Write an essay comparing the tone, images, rhythm, and structure of their poems.
2. Research United States military involvement in Vietnam in the library or on the Internet. Write a report on the information you find.
3. Interview someone who served in Vietnam. Turn your interview information into a poem, paragraph, or report to share with your classmates.

CAPTURED BY THE ENEMY

Chahadineli Benally

When Chahadineli Benally related this story, he was approximately eighty-five years old, and he lived between Many Farms and Chinle at the mouth of Canyon de Chelly, Arizona. That is more or less the center of the Navajo Indian Reservation. A well-known medicine man, he had a wide reputation as a storyteller and Navajo historian. One of his grandmothers told him this account, which had been in the oral tradition of his family for three generations.

A century before his birth, Navajos and New Mexicans (Hispanics) raided each other for sheep, horses, and people. Sometimes outlaws from both groups joined together to prey on both peoples. Navajos captured and kept many Hispanic women, so this matrilineal tribe includes a Mexican Clan consisting of descendants of those captive women. Benally's story was published in *Navajo Stories of the Long Walk Period.* The selection presents in translation his family's oral history of New Mexicans capturing a young woman and little boy. With the aid of a Mexican woman, the young Navajo woman escaped and made her perilous journey home to her loved ones. His great-grandmother told Benally that she never went to Fort Sumner on the forced Long Walk. She spent that terrible four years hiding on top of a mountain along with other relatives, surviving mostly on goat and horse milk and wild animals.

———

1   My great-grandmother's sister had four daughters and one boy. The youngest of the four daughters was taken captive by the enemies. The story was related to me by her (my late grandmother), and I will tell you as much as I can remember. After all, it did not happen yesterday nor a year ago.

2   The family was living close to Black Mesa, west of the mesa where *Hastliin* (Mister) *Tsébicha'í* (Rock It Has a Hat) lives now. The enemies, the Mexicans, must have camped overnight in a nearby valley because it was

early in the morning when they came to attack. They were out killing and capturing our people at the time.

3   One of the girls said her sister left the family camp early that morning without looking for enemies who might be close by or approaching from any direction. She took a five-year-old boy, a close kin, with her. They walked quite a distance from the camp to the cornfields, where there also was a small patch of potatoes which were ripe and ready for gathering. While the little boy played nearby, she dug potatoes. Suddenly she saw a group of Mexicans riding out from behind a large rock about half a mile away. They must have spotted the little boy for they headed in his direction, and there was nothing to do but to try and hide. The girl guessed that they had been spotted, but, if by any chance they had not been seen, which was possible, she crawled underneath a large bush of greasewood, pulling the boy with her.

4   The riders stayed on the main horse trail, but, just as they were passing, four of them turned their horses and headed toward the potato patch, searching for the two Navajos. They pulled their horses right up to the bush, and they all dismounted. They had long rifles in scabbards tied to their saddles. One of them stepped forward, held out his hand for the little boy and pulled him forward. A second man did the same to the girl who was to become my grandmother. One of the men opened a bag of potatoes that my grandmother had picked, glanced in it and threw it away. He put the boy behind him on his horse, and the girl was helped upon a horse behind another man with whom she rode all through the journey.

5   This is how they were captured, and the journey started through *Tsé'abe'i* (Breast Rock). Along about noon they stopped near *Tsélichíí Dah Azkání* (Red Rock) where they unsaddled the horses and prepared to eat lunch. The little boy came running to my grandmother, crying. They were given a little food, and, together, they ate. The Mexicans threw an armful of long-ear corn to the horses, and this looked very tempting. The girl, who still was hungry, wished she could get hold of some.

6   After lunch, the journey continued toward *Lók'aahnteel* (Ganado). Once in a while one of the men would pull something from his pocket, glance at it and put it back. (Later the girl came to know that it was called a watch. At that time it was kept in a pocket instead of on the wrist.) The journey slowly advanced toward *Tsé Bínii Dziní* (Rock Standing Against the Wall), and some of the riders were sleeping in the saddle as they rode along. Had there been an ambush, they would not have had a chance. They all would have been killed. Right above *Be'ek'idhatsoh* (Big Lake), where there was plenty of grass, they unsaddled their horses at sunset and prepared to camp for the night. One of the men tried to get the little boy to sleep with him, but the boy kept crying and wouldn't settle down; so the man brought him over, and the girl tucked him beside her and they went to sleep. The men were up at daylight and prepared breakfast. The captives were fed, as they were for the rest of the journey.

7   Preparations for the day's ride—packing several mules with blankets, food, etc.—took time. At last the men covered the fire with sand, being cautious not to start a fire in the tall grass that grew all around. At noon they stopped for lunch at *Na'ásho'iító'i* (Snake Water). After lunch they went on below *Lók'aahnteel* (Ganado), and from there to *Lééyí'tó* (Klagetoh). Overnight camp was made not far from there. The next day, they stopped for lunch in the region of *Ch'ilzhóó'* (Chambers). That was as far as she knew the places, the areas and the names of them. From there everything was unfamiliar and strange. They traveled across deserts, plains, mountains and rivers, traveling toward some large mountains, very dimly seen in the distance; and the journey continued toward those mountains heading straight south. She thought that she knew *Tsoodzil* (Mount Taylor) near which they spent the night.

8   Then, another day, they camped across *Tooh* (Rio Grande River). Then there were more mountains which they traveled through, getting nearer to their destination which was in the territory of New Mexico. It had been very far, and it seemed to the girl like traveling would never end, when they finally came to a wide river. After crossing it the party separated; some of the men rode on, taking the little boy with them. The others lived near the river, and an older Mexican in the party took her to his house where she met his wife.

9   As they came into the room, his wife rushed to him, crying. They embraced and hugged each other for a while. The wife was an elderly woman with hair almost all white. The Navajo girl shook hands with her, and the woman said something, but all the girl understood was "my friend."

10   By that time she knew that she was pregnant with a baby for her husband whom she had left behind along with the rest of the family. Back home, they had been missed by the family that same day, and, from the tracks and evidence left behind, they knew what had happened. Some relatives went looking for them and saw the riders from a distance, with the woman and the boy, but they had no hope of saving them.

11   That evening, in the Mexican home, she was given two blankets and a sleeping pad, also space inside the same house that the couple lived in. From that time on she got acquainted with the Mexican woman, and she helped with the cooking, house work and whatever chores that needed to be done. Soon, the two women got so used to each other that they were almost inseparable. The Mexican man didn't bother her; he went about attending to his daily chores.

12   It was in the fall. Winter was just around the corner, and she was growing bigger with the baby inside her.

13   She caught on to the language fast, and soon the two women were communicating fluently in the Mexican language. The Mexican woman didn't like the idea of the girl being captured and held captive in her pregnant condition, and she expressed her opinion by saying, "This will not be permitted. No! We won't permit anything bad to happen, no matter what he says

(referring to her husband). I don't like it! There is no sense in your captivity! There is no use in having you suffer. You will go home!"

14 My grandmother liked the idea.

15 After being there five months, a caravan of Mexican men approached, riding side by side in twos. The woman told her the purpose of the visit was to buy her. Then she added, "But I won't let them have you; my answer will be 'no'! You are already given to me; so you belong to me. I shall never agree to let them take you."

16 The couple had no children of their own—just the two of them living there. And now the Navajo captive. There were other neighbors, friends who lived close by who would come for visits. Sometimes they would get into conversation about the Navajos, and one elderly woman said, "The people named *Diné* are very brave; no other tribe can match their braveness. If the Navajo people as a whole would fight against a single tribe, the other tribe would not have a chance. They all would be killed. As it is now, almost all other tribes have become allies to fight against the Navajo people. They have no friends among the other tribes here. Their only friends are *Beehai* (Jicarilla Apaches), but they live far off up north; and one other tribe in the east." Then she added, to the girl, "But I am your friend and I am on your side. Should a time ever come that I would get captured by your people, I'm willing to live among them."

17 At the time the Mexican men came, slave trading went on not too far from the house. There was a special meeting house for the purpose. The caravan that arrived had camped there, and the old Mexican man was over there talking with the people. In the meantime, the two ladies were busy, preparing meals for the visitors, setting out food on the long table. When this was ready the men were called to come in to eat. As they went into the room, they gave the girl hard looks.

18 The next day, just as the morning star appeared, the two women started cooking again, and, at sunrise, the visitors had their breakfast. The trading was postponed to another date. The visitors brought their horses and prepared to leave. In the slave trading, the girl was one who was to be sold, but the Mexican woman kept her word. She had a hot discussion with her husband. The husband wanted to sell the Navajo, but her Mexican friend flatly refused. Later, the woman found out that there was some correspondence going on between her husband and another man who was interested in buying the woman, but he had kept the letters hidden from his wife. Somehow, she got hold of them. In one letter it was written that the man was willing to pay a high price for her and that he would come any day now. His wife was furious, tore up the letter and threw it in the fire, saying to her husband, "I will never permit you to do this." They had a fight over this, and some friends had to break it up. The man was pretty angry.

19 On the day of the appointment, toward sunset, the same caravan of Mexicans returned. After their arrival at the meeting place, the discussion of slave trading got started. Some time toward dawn, the girl's Mexican friend

came back from the meeting and she told her what had taken place and how she absolutely refused to let her be sold, regardless of the cost. She had told the men that she wanted to have the Navajo lady keep her company now that she was in her old age. She had said, "Let her stay with me; I can't let you take her." With that she had left the room.

20 Afterward there was a long discussion, for the old man kept hoping his wife would give in. But, the next day, they left again after they ate breakfast.

21 Seven months had passed, and my grandmother's baby was growing bigger. The old Mexican man was still angry and pouting. He had left home for several weeks.

22 During that time, the Mexican woman made a plan for her. She said, " I don't want my husband to sell you. He'll never guess or find out how I'm to let you go. I want to release you to go home."

23 My grandmother hugged the woman to her, calling her sister in the Mexican language which she could understand and speak very well. The elderly woman said, "I know the journey will be very hard and fearful, but you'll make it back all right. The faith and belief within you will guide you home safe. I will let you take one of these long swords; there are a lot of them in there. It will come in handy in case you are attacked, perhaps by vicious animals. I will hide a sword along with a knife for you near the river." Then she added, after thinking a while, "A month from now they will return, and by then there will be a definite decision. I'm sure they'll take you then, if you are still here."

24 From that time she made plans and preparations for my grandmother's escape. She thought that, after the men returned, and while they were deeply involved with the meeting, would be a good time for her to take off; she started to get ready the things that the young woman would need to take on her journey. All these were to be fixed ahead of time so that there wouldn't be any delay when the day came for her to leave. The Mexican woman and her husband were in a happy mood, talking about the butchering of a steer for their visitors. Four days before their arrival a big animal was butchered, and the meat prepared for a feast. At the same time, the woman prepared some meat into jerky for her friend.

25 In the meantime, my grandmother was busy, too. Among other things, she cooked some blue corn and made it into heavy mush. Her food was packed into a container, along with a jug of water. The old woman also gave my grandmother two blankets, one black, and one red, which were brand new. All the things were fixed into a bundle, tied with a rope on each end and arranged so that it could be carried over the back.

26 Toward evening on a certain day, the visitors arrived, tables were set with food and they all came in to eat.

27 The Mexican woman had given my grandmother instructions, telling her how to get across the river and how she should go toward a certain mountain and hide there until the men gave up looking for her. It was the opposite direction from where she had been brought. So, she slipped away late

that evening, after the Mexican woman returned from the meeting house and said that it was safe for her to leave. She arranged the pack on her back and started for the river, following her friend's instructions. By that time she was about eight months pregnant. After crossing the river without any difficulty, she came upon some horses that were grazing. Had she got hold of one of them, no doubt she could have traveled a great distance in a single night. However, she climbed the mountain, just as the woman had told her; and, almost at the top, she found a good hiding place where she settled down. From that point, she barely could see the lights where the houses were. She kept looking, trying to see what was happening. Later, she knew that the search was on. She could see torches carried around by searchers, looking for her tracks. They finally gave up toward dawn.

28   However, early the next morning, just before sunup, they started gathering their horses, and, soon, a group of riders really were searching, riding around appearing to look for her tracks. The search mostly went on in the direction opposite to where she was hiding. The riders split into several groups as they searched. And they all did their searching in the other direction. Soon one group went over the hill toward another mountain, while the rest stayed behind, still looking for her tracks. This went on all day, and, finally, at sundown, they all came riding in to the houses.

29   In the meantime, my grandmother stayed hidden. Now and then she would look out and watch the activities in the distance below. She took a nap, and it was late in the afternoon when she awoke. Late in the evening she was ready to leave. She started walking carefully down the slope of the mountain. After reaching the bottom, she kept close to the slope, taking care not to make her tracks obvious, walking mostly on rocks and grass. She would take only a mouthful of water now and then because she wanted to make it last for as long as possible. By daybreak she had reached another mountain in the opposite direction from the house from where she had been. She found a cave where she hid because she didn't want to take a chance on being seen. She slept in the cave all day; then, as it was getting dark, she climbed out and started walking again. After she was sure she was going in the right direction, she walked all night. At dawn she crawled under a large cedar tree whose branches hung thickly to the ground, and she went to sleep. She still didn't want to take a chance on traveling in the daytime; so she slept during daylight and traveled at night.

30   Again, she started out when darkness came, and she traveled all night. By that time she knew she had put a great distance behind her and that there would be little danger of being seen, even if she traveled during the day; so she traveled day and night. She would stop just long enough to rest a while and eat a little of the food, saving it as long as possible. After traveling without sleep for almost two days, she was exhausted; and she found a place to spend the night.

31   Next morning, she came to the edge of a mountain from where she could see miles and miles in every direction. In one direction, she could see

a white tent several miles away. "Probably a sheepherder's camp," she thought, and she avoided it. After traveling several more days and nights, toward evening, as she was still walking, she thought of continuing all night, but she heard the howl of a wolf, and she knew danger was approaching. Nearby were some large trees, thin of foliage at the bottom and thick with branches and leaves at the top. She climbed one of the trees and settled near the top, making herself as comfortable as possible—not knowing how long she'd be up there.

32   Soon the wolf came running, growling and showing his long white teeth. It kept charging up the tree, but fell each time. Then the woman heard another sound, and two more wolves appeared. They all would run and try to climb the tree. They were there all night. Finally, my grandmother got impatient. "This has gone on long enough," she thought; so she climbed down to near the bottom of the tree, the sword ready in one hand, prepared to attack the animals. She placed her legs wide apart and planted one foot against a big branch, while she held onto another branch tightly with one hand. In the other she held the long weapon. One animal was very vicious, clawing the tree and growling. When it tried to climb the tree again she thrust the long sword into its throat. The wolf made a strangling noise, fell backward and died almost instantly. The other two wolves went over, sniffed the blood that was flowing from the mouth of the dead wolf and left, running fast over the hill and howling after they had gone quite a distance. Much later, they howled far off in the mountains.

33   After the danger had passed, my grandmother climbed down (it was daylight by that time), and she walked all day. There were few signs of life anywhere, not even many tracks. Once in a while she would come upon coyote tracks as she walked across the valleys, mountains, plains and desert lands. Before she reached another mountain, the sun disappeared, and it began to get dark fast. She was exhausted, and she started looking for a place to rest for the night. She came upon a small stream where she decided to stay. She took out her holy corn pollen and prayed to Mother Earth, saying, "Hear me! Let no one see me or find me throughout my journey as I go in the unknown direction. Let someone direct and guide me. Mr. Owl, I know you live above in the high cliffs. In time of trouble, I am in need of your guidance. I trust you will guide me."

34   After her prayers, she sat down and took out some cornmeal, which she ate with water. Before long, an owl hooted a short distance away. Soon it came to rest on top of a nearby rock. Once more, she pleaded with the owl, saying, "I will follow you. Hoot at intervals so that I will know which way I'm going as you guide me toward my homeland."

35   It was very dark as she started walking, following the owl. After a short distance the owl hooted again, and she walked in the direction from which the sound came. This continued all night—the owl hooting at intervals, and the woman following at a distance—until early dawn. At that time the owl left her. She had reached another mountain; and, after climbing to the top,

she stopped to rest and to eat more blue cornmeal. From there she could see for miles around in all directions. In the far-off distance she could see a large herd of sheep grazing in a valley. Nearby was a tent, and she figured it was another sheepherder's camp.

36   After resting for several hours, she continued her journey through a wide section of mountain forest. Just as she reached the ridge of the mountain, she heard the barking of a dog behind her. It sounded quite close, and, with a frightened feeling, she looked around. She thought that search dogs might be coming after her, and she looked for a place to hide. Directly ahead she saw the shell of an old tree stump, with the insides rotted out. It would be a safe place, she thought, as she climbed inside the stump and stood there. At this moment, a big yellow dog ran up, with another (white with black spots) following right behind. Both dogs barked and ran back and forth. Then one charged up, ready to attack. The moment it came near my grandmother stuck the sword into its heart, and the dog fell dead. As the second one attacked, she did the same thing. She left both dogs lying there and walked away quickly, for she feared there might be riders behind them. She hastily went over the ridge and almost ran down to the level ground below. From there she could see a region thick with trees, and she aimed for them. The sun had gone down again.

37   She did not know how many days and nights she had traveled. She had come from the east, from somewhere beyond and below *Tóta'* (Farmington). That she later figured out, but, at the time, she didn't know. Upon her capture she had been taken toward the southeast. She thought that, somewhere, coming back, she had lost her way after she had made her escape from the Mexicans.

38   Anyway, she walked all night, until, at dawn, when she was almost exhausted, she came to an area where there was a lot of green grass; and she decided to rest. She unpacked her blankets and some food and prepared a bed on the ground. After eating and drinking a little water, she went to sleep. Just before sundown, a coyote howled back where she had come from; and, looking carefully, she saw the coyote tracking her. The animal saw her, too. It stood looking at her for a while, and then slowly advanced. It seemed to be uncertain of itself, hesitating a moment before each step. When it had come quite near, she said, "What is it?" The coyote slunk along the ground. She had frightened it. She tried to decide what she should do to it—perhaps kill it with the sword. Then, on second thought, she decided against this and decided to just plead with it to help her find her way home. "Mr. Coyote, that howls with the early dawn of the mornings, great things have been said about you. Turquoise you carried. I want to get home. I'm in very poor condition and barely making it on my journey."

39   As she talked, she noticed that the coyote was watching her. It tried to stand up, but it didn't seem able to raise its back end; so it dragged itself to within a short distance of her with its two front arms until, suddenly, it got up and ran over the hill without looking back.

40   She then fixed her pack and left. She started through *Tsénaajin* (Black Rock Cliff) and finally came to *Tooh* (San Juan River). She noticed that the river was running low. At the shore, she took all her clothes off, put them into a bundle, along with the rest of her pack, and prepared to cross the river. With both hands holding the bundle above her head, she got into the water and started to cross. Before long, the water was above her knees. About halfway across, it came up to her chest and soon was to her chin. However, she got across and sat down to get dry before putting her clothes on.

41   A familiar mountain was in view in the distance, and from there she recognized the different directions. From one of the Navajo late leaders she remembered hearing of an old horse trail that led from about where she was toward the mountain, and suddenly she knew exactly where she was. She realized that somewhere along the way she had lost the direction toward her homeland, but now she knew it. She began to walk again.

42   Her baby was about due. She stopped to rest, ate some blue cornmeal, which was about gone. She had filled the small jug with water at the river. Feeling very tired, she took a short nap before continuing her journey on through *Tsénaajin*. She finally found the horse trail that she had heard about. It was in the afternoon by the time she reached the other side of *Lók'ai'jígai* (Lukachukai) at a place called *Há'jishzhíis* (Where He Came Out Dancing). After walking through there, she came upon the ridge overlooking *Tó Diłhił* (Whiskey Creek). There she stopped to rest when she felt some sharp pains and knew her time was drawing near. She knew, too, that she would have to get prepared before the sun went down. But, first, she had to find a good place.

43   Her pains began to come at closer intervals as she worked. She cleared a hollow in the sand under a thick cedar tree, gathered some firewood and built a fire. Then she gathered a supply of wood. She also brought some big flat rocks and put them into hot ashes. Then she lay down, waiting for the rocks to get hot. After they were hot, she placed the rocks and ashes under her, right against her lower back. She was glad that she knew what to do in a case like this. She had observed, and helped with, some babies being delivered at home. Once in a while, she gave a good massaging to her abdomen. While she massaged she sang the sacred song for the safe arrival of the baby.

44   When the morning star rose over the horizon, the baby came. . . .

45   At sunup she was ready to leave. She ate the last of the blue cornmeal, with water, and then she walked away. . . .

46   She became very exhausted as she walked on and on. In the region of *Díwózhiibii'tó* (Upper Greasewood, Arizona) she couldn't go any farther; so she set fire to an old stump and spent the night by the fire. In another day and a half she crossed the valley between *Tséhílí* (Tsaile) and *Baanijighάz* (Slip Off Mesa). By noon of that last day, she came back to the place where she and the boy had been captured. It had been almost nine months from the time they had been captured to when she returned.

47   Having the baby had made her very weak, and she got exhausted easily. So, once more, she stopped to rest under some thick greasewood. She had been seen by her relatives from a good distance, where the families were living. The people were curious, asking one another who it could be. A man (it happened to be her husband) went out to see. He kept out of sight as he walked toward the person, keeping his bow and arrows ready. By that time it was in the afternoon, and she felt rested and ready to continue her journey. The man was quite near, and he could see that it was a woman dressed in Mexican style. He stayed hidden as he watched her, and, when she started walking again, he recognized her. He was about to catch up with her when she saw him, carrying his bow and arrows. Suddenly, she recognized him, and she stood there, startled. He came and embraced her, with tears in his eyes.

48   It was the custom that when a person had been captured and held in captivity a certain length of time, upon his or her return, a certain ceremonial had to be performed over the person before he or she could begin to associate again with family and relatives. The husband took her pack and ran home ahead of her, bearing the news. The family was living right below *Tsénineezí* (Tall Rock), where there are some authentic old hogans today. While she was walking in, the family started preparations for the ceremonial. Upon her arrival she undressed some distance from the hogan where the ceremonial was to take place. The medicine man came out of the hogan, singing and carrying a prayer stick in one hand. He extended one end of the prayer stick to her, and together they walked into the hogan where yucca soap was ready. She was bathed and then dried with white cornmeal. The medicine man started his prayers, which continued until evening. When they were over, she was greeted by each member of the family. Tears of joy were shed, and they were happy. Together they shared the blessing of yellow corn pollen.

49   This is the story of how my grandmother came home from captivity. She was of the *Kinyaa'áanii* (Tall House) clan. She died of old age. Also, my grandfather died of old age. Both were buried with white corn, which is the custom when a person dies of old age.

50   The boy who was captured with her never was found.

DISCUSSION QUESTIONS

1. Give five adjectives you would use to describe the young Navajo captive.
2. How was she able to escape?
3. What do you think was the most difficult part of her perilous journey? Explain.

WRITING TOPICS

1. Choose one of the other grandmothers portrayed in this anthology to compare, in a brief essay, to Benally's grandmother for strength of character, contribution to family, and relationship to future generations.
2. Select one intense episode in this story, and write it as if the young Navajo woman is the narrator.
3. With a group of your classmates, select a part of this story to turn into a play. Create dialogue, and if necessary, soliloquies, plus stage directions for the actors. Read or perform your script for the class.

Summary Writing Topics

1. Assume that a classmate remarks to you that Vine Deloria is too critical of non-Indian attitudes and actions in "Indians Today, The Real and Unreal" (Chapter 1) and "Indian Humor." Respond to this criticism in an essay that defends Deloria's arguments. Using evidence from the selections, point out to your classmate reasons for at least four of Deloria's statements.

2. Imagine you are a freelance reporter writing an article on discrimination. Reread Sherman Alexie's "Tiny Treaties" (Chapter 7) and "The Game Between the Jews and the Indians Is Tied Going into the Bottom of the Ninth Inning." Using Alexie's ideas plus your own views, write an article in which you review the status of discrimination in your surroundings and offer three proposals for improving it.

3. In "The Man to Send Rainclouds" and "Lullaby" (Chapter 5) Silko explores the theme of two cultures in conflict. Write an essay on this theme in which you cite examples from both stories.

4. Strong women appear in several selections in this chapter. Select one from the following list that you would like to meet. Give at least three questions you would ask her. Explain your choice: Mourning Dove's mother; the woman hanging from the thirteenth floor window; or Benally's grandmother.

5. Phil George and Ted Palmanteer write about war experiences. After rereading their poems, make a list of questions and interview someone who has served in the military. From the information you gather, write an essay, lyric poem, or record of the interview to share with your classmates.

6. In "Captured by the Enemy," Benally tells vivid details of a story that has been passed down through generations. In "Metamorphosis," Joy Harjo writes of her own experiences. Which story seems the most believable to you and why?

7. Contrast the purpose and style of Apess' "Son of the Forest" and "An Indian's Looking-Glass for the White Man."

8. This chapter focuses on the theme of survival, which is articulated by Joy Harjo in her three selections. Identify and discuss at least two passages in each of her selections that speak to this theme.

CHAPTER TEN

MEMORY ALIVE

This chapter takes its title from Joy Harjo's lyrical line "I am memory alive," in her poem "Skeleton of Winter." In one way or another, the theme of memory permeates the following selections. It's no accident that James Welch begins his intimate reminiscence with "I remember" and that Linda Hogan honors the memory of her forebears, "From them I still remember to honor life, mystery, and this incomparable ongoing creation." These and other authors illustrate, indeed celebrate, the fundamental fact that memory and oral tradition are two cornerstones on which contemporary Native American writers build their works. Living without written words, early Native Americans preserved literature, history, and culture in their memories.

In "The Warriors," Pawnee-Otoe Anna Lee Walters embeds in her short story a fictional biography of the narrator's Pawnee uncle. Walters gently sketches how traditional tribal and contemporary society's values can conflict in a person until the conflict consumes him or her. Still, the positive message resonates: "Our battle is for beauty."

Choctaw-Cherokee Louis Owens' "Water Witch" is his father, who periodically took his family from California back to Mississippi Choctaw country on the Yazoo River. In his autobiographical essay about growing up in the Salinas River Valley, Owens discloses that the dominant society also has its psychopaths.

Shonto Begay creates beauty. This Navajo artist is one of the best children's book illustrators in the country. He has the twin advantages of living in a beautiful mesa-and-canyon landscape and having been reared by artistic parents. His mother wove woolen textiles using traditional designs; his medicine man father created sacred curing pictures with colored grains of sand and minerals.

In her essay "Seeing, Knowing, Remembering," Linda Hogan dramatically focuses on female transmission of native biological and cultural heritages: "The line where my grandmother ends and I begin is no line at all."

Alonzo Lopez packs his people's dancing, feasting, and games into his concise poem "Celebration." The narrator of Phil George's somber "Proviso" prescribes his funeral rites. Nonetheless, the poet states a counterpoint to death: "I'll drum. I'll sing." In Peter Blue Cloud's poetic creation story, the sun "found a nation of golden children playing flutes which were Creation songs." Blackfeet-Gros Ventre James Welch remembers the hot summer day a voice singing to the sun entered his nine-year old bones "and I was Blackfeet and changed forever."

The Native American past these authors present from different perspectives is prelude to the present space age. Color photographs of Earth taken from space vehicles emphasize to Linda Hogan how isolated this world really is. In "The Voyagers," she calls Earth "a world whose intricately linked together ecosystem could not survive the continuing blows of exploitation." Hogan emphasizes, "We are delicate and our world is fragile." In this essay, she analyzes the spacecraft the United States launched in 1977 and describes the hope in the varied images and sounds the spacecraft carries into deep space for the year 8,000,000.

SKELETON OF WINTER

Joy Harjo

In "Ancestral Voices," an interview with Bill Moyers, Joy Harjo tells about writing her first poem: "One day in the 8th grade the teacher came in and said, 'All right, everyone's got to write a poem.' We were dumb-founded—a poem?" So all the students wrote poems. Harjo lamented, "Mine was terrible." She then wrote rock songs for an all-Indian rock band. "I hope none of those survive." Years later, this author has come full circle as a major poet. She arranges poems as lyrics for her all-Indian band, Poetic Justice, which plays tribal rhythms with jazz and reggae. In 1998 Harjo received a Wallace Reader's Digest Writers' Award. She plans to use the $105,000 award to celebrate the Native American literary tradition by honoring native writers in their home cities through writing workshops and public readings.

Harjo's poems and songs rise out of her Creek heritage. Describing her tribal memories as powerful and deep, she notes, "I carry my tribal past with me, the same as this body carries the heart as a drum." In her writing, Harjo makes connections between her inner tribal memories and the outer world. Memory, "the other-sight," gives the speaker vision to see her heart beating within the cosmic web of sun and stars. For her, memory is not only associated with past events but with ongoing stories and events moving into the future. She merges symbols of ancient Indian life with symbols of a restless cosmos in a single spectrum.

These winter days
I've remained silent
as a whiteman's watch
keeping time
5   an old bone
empty as a fish skeleton

at low tide.
It is almost too dark
         for vision
10 these ebony mornings
but there is still memory,
the other-sight
and still I see.

Rabbits get torn under
15 cars that travel at night
but come out the other
side, not bruised
breathing soft
like no fear.

20 And sound is light, is
movement. The sun revolves
and sings.

There are still ancient
symbols
25   alive
I did dance with the prehistoric horse
years and births later
near a cave wall
late winter.

30 A tooth-hard rocking
in my belly comes back,
something echoes
all forgotten dreams
            in winter.

35 I am memory alive
         not just a name
but an intricate part
of this web of motion,
meaning: earth, sky, stars circling
40 my heart

        centrifugal.

DISCUSSION QUESTIONS

1. Harjo chooses each word carefully. Explain the difference in her choice of "skeleton" and "winter" for the title instead of "Skeleton of Summer" or "Skeleton of Spring." What connotations does the word "skeleton" have for you? Write down as many as you can think of.
2. According to the first ten lines, what effect has winter had on the speaker?
3. The speaker seems to feel that memory is stored in her body as well as in her mind. What lines in the poem support this idea?

WRITING TOPICS

1. The speaker begins with "I" and progresses through the poem to the cosmos and back to her heart. Describe this journey through time and space in a lyrical paragraph.
2. Taking Harjo's idea "I am memory alive" create a poem, personal story, or collage that expresses memories important to you.
3. Write a short essay on the specific images Harjo uses to convey movement through time and space in "Skeleton of Winter."
4. In lines 11 and 12, the speaker refers to memory as the "other-sight." In a brief essay, explain what you think the speaker means.
5. In a paragraph, tell what you think is the theme of this poem. First jot down some of the topics mentioned in the poem; then state the theme in two or more sentences.

THE WARRIORS

Anna Lee Walters

"The Warriors" appeared in *The Sun Is Not Merciful* (1985), a volume of eight short stories. Story themes include cultural and self-identity and Indian survival. Reviewing this collection, Jo Whitehorse Cochran wrote that Walters "comes around sideways through her characters' experiences and words to tell about the spiritual aspects and connections of being, of the people."

In 1992 Walters published *Talking Indian: Reflections on Survival and Writing,* in which she combined essays, stories, poems and photographs. Reviewing that volume, Joseph Bruchac noted that "The enduring presence of the sacred in American Indian life has always been the underlying message in the writing of Anna Lee Walters." In this vein, Walters also co-edited with Peggy V. Beck a valuable textbook, *The Sacred: Ways of Knowledge, Sources of Life* (1977).

Born on 9 September 1946, in Pawnee, Oklahoma, Walters is Pawnee-Otoe. She attended the Institute of American Indian Arts in Santa Fe, New Mexico. She married Harry Walters, a Navajo, and moved to his reservation. There she joined him on the staff of Navajo Community College at Tsaile where he is curator of the Navajo Museum. After directing the college press, Walters became a full-time professor of humanities.

1   In our youth, we saw hobos come and go, sliding by our faded white house like wary cats who did not want us too close. Sister and I waved at the strange procession of passing men and women hobos. Just between ourselves, Sister and I talked of that hobo parade. We guessed at and imagined the places and towns we thought the hobos might have come from or had been. Mostly they were white or black people. But there were Indian hobos, too. It never occurred to Sister and me that this would be Uncle Ralph's end.

2   Sister and I were little, and Uncle Ralph came to visit us. He lifted us over his head and shook us around him like gourd rattles. He was Momma's

younger brother, and he could have disciplined us if he so desired. That was part of our custom. But he never did. Instead, he taught us Pawnee words. "*Pari* is Pawnee and *pita* is man," he said. Between the words, he tapped out drumbeats with his fingers on the table top, ghost dance and round dance songs that he suddenly remembered and sang. His melodic voice lilted over us and hung around the corners of the house for days. His stories of life and death were fierce and gentle. Warriors dangled in delicate balance.

3   He told us his version of the story of *Pahukatawa*, a Skidi Pawnee warrior. He was killed by the Sioux, but the animals, feeling compassion for him, brought *Pahukatawa* to life again. "The Evening Star and the Morning Star bore children and some people say that these offspring are who we are," he often said. At times he pointed to those stars and greeted them by their Pawnee names. He liked to pray for Sister and me, for everyone and every tiny thing in the world, but we never heard him ask for anything for himself from *Atius,* the Father.

4   "For beauty is why we live," Uncle Ralph said when he talked of precious things only the Pawnees know. "We die for it, too." He called himself an ancient Pawnee warrior when he was quite young. He told us that warriors must brave all storms and odds and stand their ground. He knew intimate details of every battle the Pawnees ever fought since Pawnee time began, and Sister and I knew even then that Uncle Ralph had a great battlefield of his own.

5   As a child I thought that Uncle Ralph had been born into the wrong time. The Pawnees had been ravaged so often by then. The tribe of several thousand when it was at its peak over a century before were then a few hundred people who had been closely confined for more than a hundred years. The warrior life was gone. Uncle Ralph was trapped in a transparent bubble of a new time. The bubble bound him tight as it blew around us.

6   Uncle Ralph talked obsessively of warriors, painted proud warriors who shrieked poignant battle cries at the top of their lungs and died with honor. Sister and I were little then, lost from him in the world of children who saw everything with children's eyes. And though we saw with wide eyes the painted warriors that he fantasized and heard their fierce and haunting battle cries, we did not hear his. Now that we are old and Uncle Ralph has been gone for a long time, Sister and I know that when he died, he was tired and alone. But he was a warrior.

7   The hobos were always around in our youth. Sister and I were curious about them, and this curiosity claimed much of our time. They crept by the house at all hours of the day and night, dressed in rags and odd clothing. They wandered to us from the railroad tracks where they had leaped from slow-moving boxcars onto the flatland. They hid in high clumps of weeds and brush that ran along the fence near the tracks. The hobos usually traveled alone, but Sister and I saw them come together, like poor families, to share a can of beans or a tin of sardines that they ate with sticks or twigs. Uncle Ralph also watched them from a distance.

8   One early morning, Sister and I crossed the tracks on our way to school and collided with a tall, haggard white man. He wore a very old-fashioned pin-striped black jacket covered with lint and soot. There was fright in his eyes when they met ours. He scurried around us, quickening his pace. The pole over his shoulder where his possessions hung in a bundle at the end bounced as he nearly ran from us.

9   "Looks just like a scared jackrabbit," Sister said, watching him dart away.

10   That evening we told Momma about the scared man. She warned us about the dangers of hobos as our father threw us a stern look. Uncle Ralph was visiting but he didn't say anything. He stayed the night and Sister asked him, "Hey, Uncle Ralph, why do you suppose they's hobos?"

11   Uncle Ralph was a large man. He took Sister and put her on one knee. "You see, Sister," he said, "hobos are a different kind. They see things in a different way. Them hobos are kind of like us. We're not like other people in some ways and yet we are. It has to do with what you see and feel and when you look at this old world."

12   His answer satisfied Sister for a while. He taught us some more Pawnee words that night.

13   Not long after Uncle Ralph's explanation, Sister and I surprised a black man with white whiskers and fuzzy hair. He was climbing through the barbed-wire fence that marked our property line. He wore faded blue overalls with pockets stuffed full of handkerchiefs. He wiped sweat from his face. When it dried, he looked up and saw us. I remembered what Uncle Ralph had said and wondered what the black man saw when he looked at us standing there.

14   "We might scare him," Sister said softly to me, remembering the white man who had scampered away.

15   Sister whispered, "Hi," to the black man. Her voice was barely audible.

16   "Boy, it's sure hot," he said. His voice was big and he smiled.

17   "Where are you going?" Sister asked.

18   "Me? Nowheres, I guess," he muttered.

19   "Then what you doing here?" Sister went on. She was bold for a seven-year-old kid. I was older but I was also quieter. "This here place is ours," she said.

20   He looked around and saw our house with its flowering mimosa trees and rich green mowed lawn stretching out before him. Other houses sat around ours.

21   "I reckon I'm lost," he said.

22   Sister pointed to the weeds and brush further up the road. "That's where you want to go. That's where they all go, the hobos."

23   I tried to quiet Sister but she didn't hush. "The hobos stay up there," she said. "You a hobo?"

24   He ignored her question and asked his own. "Say, what is you all? You not black, you not white. What is you all?"

25   Sister looked at me. She put one hand on her chest and the other hand on me. "We Indians!" Sister said.

26   He stared at us and smiled again. "Is that a fact?" he said.

27   "Know what kind of Indians we are?" Sister asked him.

28   He shook his fuzzy head. "Indians is Indians, I guess," he said.

29   Sister wrinkled her forehead and retorted, "Not us! We not like others. We see things different. We're Pawnees. We're warriors!"

30   I pushed my elbow into Sister's side. She quieted.

31   The man was looking down the road and he shuffled his feet. "I'd best go," he said.

32   Sister pointed to the brush and weeds one more time. "That way," she said.

33   He climbed back through the fence and brush as Sister yelled, "Bye now!" He waved a damp handkerchief.

34   Sister and I didn't tell Momma and Dad about the black man. But much later Sister told Uncle Ralph every word that had been exchanged with the black man. Uncle Ralph listened and smiled.

35   Months later when the warm weather had cooled and Uncle Ralph came to stay with us for a couple of weeks, Sister and I went to the hobo place. We had planned it for a long time. That afternoon when we pushed away the weeds, not a hobo was in sight.

36   The ground was packed down tight in the clearing among the high weeds. We walked around the encircling brush and found folded cardboards stacked together. Burned cans in assorted sizes were stashed under the cardboards, and there were remains of old fires. Rags were tied to the brush, snapping in the hard wind.

37   Sister said, "Maybe they're all in the boxcars now. It's starting to get cold."

38   She was right. The November wind had a bite to it and the cold stung our hands and froze our breaths as we spoke.

39   "You want to go over to them boxcars?" she asked. We looked at the Railroad Crossing sign where the boxcars stood.

40   I was prepared to answer when a voice roared from somewhere behind us.

41   "Now, you young ones, you git on home! Go on! git!"

42   A man crawled out of the weeds and looked angrily at us. His eyes were red and his face was unshaven. He wore a red plaid shirt with striped gray and black pants too large for him. His face was swollen and bruised. An old woolen pink scarf hid some of the bruise marks around his neck, and his topcoat was splattered with mud.

43   Sister looked at him. She stood close to me and told him defiantly, "You can't tell us what to do! You don't know us!"

44   He didn't answer Sister but tried to stand. He couldn't. Sister ran to him and took his arm and pulled on it. "You need help?" she questioned.

45   He frowned at her but let us help him. He was tall. He seemed to be embarrassed by our help.

46   "You Indian, ain't you?" I dared to ask him.

47   He didn't answer me but looked at his feet as if they could talk so he wouldn't have to. His feet were in big brown overshoes.

48   "Who's your people?" Sister asked. He looked to be about Uncle Ralph's age when he finally lifted his face and met mine. He didn't respond for a minute. Then he sighed. "I ain't got no people," he told us as he tenderly stroked his swollen jaw.

49   "Sure you got people. Our folks says a man's always got people," I said softly. The wind blew our clothes and covered the words.

50   But he heard. He exploded like a firecracker. "Well, I don't! I ain't got no people! I ain't got nobody!"

51   "What you doing out here anyway?" Sister asked. "You hurt? You want to come over to our house?"

52   "Naw," he said. "Now you little ones, go on home. Don't be walking round out here. Didn't nobody tell you little girls ain't supposed to be going round by themselves? You might git hurt."

53   "We just wanted to talk to hobos," Sister said.

54   "Now, you don't. Just go on home. Your folks is probably looking for you and worrying 'bout you."

55   I took Sister's arm and told her we were going home. Then we said "Bye" to the man. But Sister couldn't resist a few last words, "You Indian, ain't you?"

56   He nodded his head like it was a painful thing to do. "Yeah, I'm Indian."

57   "You ought to go on home yourself," Sister said. "Your folks probably looking for you and worrying 'bout you."

58   His voice rose again as Sister and I walked away from him. "I told you kids, I don't have no people!" There was exasperation in his voice.

59   Sister would not be outdone. She turned and yelled, "Oh yeah? You Indian ain't you? Ain't you?" she screamed. "We your people!"

60   His topcoat and pink scarf flapped in the wind as we turned away from him.

61   We went home to Momma and Dad and Uncle Ralph then. Uncle Ralph met us at the front door. "Where you all been?" he asked looking toward the railroad tracks. Momma and Dad were talking in the kitchen.

62   "Just playing, Uncle," Sister and I said simultaneously.

63   Uncle Ralph grabbed both Sister and I by our hands and yanked us out the door. "*Awkuh!*" he said, using the Pawnee expression to show his dissatisfaction.

64   Outside, we sat on the cement porch. Uncle Ralph was quiet for a long time, and neither Sister nor I knew what to expect.

65   "I want to tell you all a story," he finally said. "Once, there were these two rats who ran around everywhere and got into everything all the time. Everything they were told not to do, well they went right out and did. They'd get into one mess and then another. It seems that they never could learn."

66   At that point Uncle Ralph cleared his throat. He looked at me and said, "Sister, do you understand this story? Is it too hard for you? You're older."

67   I nodded my head up and down and said, "I understand."

68   Then Uncle Ralph looked at Sister. He said to her, "Sister, do I need to go on with this story?"

69   Sister shook her head from side to side. "Naw, Uncle Ralph," she said.

70   "So you both know how this story ends?" he said gruffly. Sister and I bobbed our heads up and down again.

71   We followed at his heels the rest of the day. When he tightened the loose hide on top of his drum, we watched him and held it in place as he laced the wet hide down. He got his drumsticks down from the top shelf of the closet and began to pound the drum slowly.

72   "Where you going, Uncle Ralph?" I asked. Sister and I knew that when he took his drum out, he was always gone shortly after.

73   "I have to be a drummer at some doings tomorrow," he said.

74   "You a good singer, Uncle Ralph," Sister said. "You know all them old songs."

75   "The young people nowadays, it seems they don't care 'bout nothing that's old. They just want to go to the Moon." He was drumming low as he spoke.

76   "We care, Uncle Ralph," Sister said.

77   "Why?" Uncle Ralph asked in a hard, challenging tone that he seldom used on us.

78   Sister thought for a moment and then said, "I guess because you care so much, Uncle Ralph."

79   His eyes softened as he said, "I'll sing you an *Eruska* song, a song for the warriors."

80   The song he sang was a war dance song. At first Sister and I listened attentively, but then Sister began to dance the man's dance. She had never danced before and tried to imitate what she had seen. Her chubby body whirled and jumped the way she'd seen the men dance. Her head tilted from side to side the way the men moved theirs. I laughed aloud at her clumsy effort, and Uncle Ralph laughed heartily, too.

81   Uncle Ralph went in and out of our lives after that. We heard that he sang at one place and then another, and people came to Momma to find him. They said that he was only one of a few who knew the old ways and the songs.

82   When he came to visit us, he always brought something to eat. The Pawnee custom was that the man, the warrior, should bring food, preferably meat. Then, whatever food was brought to the host was prepared and served to the man, the warrior, along with the host's family. Many times Momma and I, or Sister and I, came home to an empty house to find a sack of food on the table. Momma or I cooked it for the next meal, and Uncle Ralph showed up to eat.

83   As Sister and I grew older, our fascination with the hobos decreased. Other things took our time, and Uncle Ralph did not appear as frequently as he did before.

84   Once while I was home alone, I picked up Momma's old photo album. Inside was a gray photo of Uncle Ralph in an army uniform. Behind him were tents on a flat terrain. Other photos showed other poses but only in one picture did he smile. All the photos were written over in black ink in Momma's handwriting, *Ralphie in Korea,* the writing said.

85   Other photos in the album showed our Pawnee relatives. Dad was from another tribe. Momma's momma was in the album, a tiny-gray-haired woman who no longer lived. And Momma's momma's dad was in the album; he wore old Pawnee leggings and the long feathers of a dark bird sat upon his head. I closed the album when Momma, Dad, and Sister came home.

86   Momma went into the kitchen to cook. She called me and Sister to help. As she put on a bibbed apron, she said, "We just came from town, and we saw someone from home there." She meant someone from her tribal community.

87   "This man told me that Ralphie's been drinking hard," she said sadly. "He used to do that quite a bit a long time ago, but we thought it had stopped. He seemed to be all right for a few years." We cooked and then ate in silence.

88   Washing the dishes, I asked Momma, "How come Uncle Ralph never did marry?"

89   Momma looked up at me but was not surprised by my question. She answered, "I don't know, Sister. It would have been better if he had. There was one woman who I thought he really loved. I think he still does. I think it had something to do with Mom. She wanted him to wait."

90   "Wait for what?" I asked.

91   "I don't know," Momma said, and sank into a chair.

92   After that we heard unsettling rumors of Uncle Ralph drinking here and there.

93   He finally came to the house once when only I happened to be home. He was haggard and tired. His appearance was much like that of the white man that Sister and I met on the railroad tracks years before.

94   I opened the door when he tapped on it. Uncle Ralph looked years older than his age. He brought food in his arms. "*Nowa,* Sister," he said in greeting. "Where's the other one?" He meant my sister.

95   "She's gone now, Uncle Ralph. School in Kansas," I answered. "Where you been, Uncle Ralph? We been worrying about you."

96   He ignored my question and said, "I bring food. The warrior brings home food. To his family, to his people." His face was lined and had not been cleaned for days. He smelled of cheap wine.

97   I asked again, "Where you been, Uncle Ralph?"

98   He forced himself to smile. "Pumpkin Flower," he said, using the Pawnee name, "I've been out with my warriors all this time."

99   He put one arm around me as we went to the kitchen table with the food. "That's what your Pawnee name is. Now don't forget it."

100   "Did somebody bring you here, Uncle Ralph, or are you on foot?" I asked him.

101   "I'm on foot," he answered. "Where's your Momma?"

102   I told him that she and Dad would be back soon. I started to prepare the food he brought.

103   Then I heard Uncle Ralph say, "Life is sure hard sometimes. Sometimes it seems I just can't go on."

104   "What's wrong, Uncle Ralph?" I asked.

105   Uncle Ralph let out a bitter little laugh. "What's wrong?" he repeated. "What's wrong? All my life, I've tried to live what I've been taught, but Pumpkin Flower, some things are all wrong!"

106   He took a folded pack of Camel cigarettes from his coat pocket. His hand shook as he pulled one from the pack and lit the end. "Too much drink," he said sadly. "That stuff is bad for us."

107   "What are you trying to do, Uncle Ralph?" I asked him.

108   "Live," he said.

109   He puffed on the shaking cigarette a while and said, "The old people said to live beautifully with prayers and song. Some died for beauty, too."

110   "How do we do that, Uncle Ralph, live for beauty?" I asked.

111   "It's simple, Pumpkin Flower," he said. "Believe!"

112   "Believe what?" I asked.

113   He looked at me hard. "*Awkuh!*" he said. "That's one of the things that is wrong. Everyone questions. Everyone doubts. No one believes in the old ways anymore. They want to believe when it's convenient, when it doesn't cost them anything and they get something in return. There are no more believers. There are no more warriors. They are all gone. Those who are left only want to go to the Moon."

114   A car drove up outside. It was Momma and Dad. Uncle Ralph heard it too. He slumped in the chair, resigned to whatever Momma would say to him.

115   Momma came in first. Dad then greeted Uncle Ralph and disappeared into the back of the house. Custom and etiquette required that Dad, who was not a member of Momma's tribe, allow Momma to handle her brother's problems.

116   She hugged Uncle Ralph. Her eyes filled with tears when she saw how thin he was and how his hands shook.

117   "Ralphie," she said, "you look awful, but I am glad to see you."

118   She then spoke to him of everyday things, how the car failed to start and the latest gossip. He was silent, tolerant of the passing of time in this way. His eyes sent me a pleading look while his hands shook and he tried to hold them still.

119   When supper was ready, Uncle Ralph went to wash himself for the meal. When he returned to the table, he was calm. His hands didn't shake so much.

120   At first he ate without many words, but in the course of the meal he left

the table twice. Each time he came back, he was more talkative than before, answering Momma's questions in Pawnee. He left the table a third time and Dad rose.

121   Dad said to Momma, "He's drinking again. Can't you tell?" Dad left the table and went outside.

122   Momma frowned. A determined look grew on her face.

123   When Uncle Ralph sat down to the table once more, Momma told him, "Ralphie, you're my brother but I want you to leave now. Come back when you're sober."

124   He held a tarnished spoon in midair and put it down slowly. He hadn't finished eating, but he didn't seem to mind leaving. He stood, looked at me with his red eyes, and went to the door. Momma followed him. In a low voice she said, "Ralphie, you've got to stop drinking and wandering—or don't come to see us again."

125   He pulled himself to his full height then. His frame filled the doorway. He leaned over Momma and yelled, "Who are you? Are you God that you will say what will be or will not be?"

126   Momma met his angry eyes. She stood firm and did not back down.

127   His eyes finally dropped from her face to the linoleum floor. A cough came from deep in his throat.

128   "I'll leave here," he said. "But I'll get all my warriors and come back! I have thousands of warriors and they'll ride with me. We'll get our bows and arrows. Then we'll come back!" He staggered out the door.

129   In the years that followed, Uncle Ralph saw us only when he was sober. He visited less and less. When he did show up, he did a tapping ritual on our front door. We welcomed the rare visits. Occasionally he stayed at our house for a few days at a time when he was not drinking. He slept on the floor.

130   He did odd jobs for minimum pay but never complained about the work or money. He'd acquired a vacant look in his eyes. It was the same look that Sister and I had seen in the hobos when we were children. He wore a similar careless array of clothing and carried no property with him at all.

131   The last time he came to the house, he called me by my English name and asked if I remembered anything of all that he'd taught me. His hair had turned pure white. He looked older than anyone I knew. I marvelled at his appearance and said, "I remember everything." That night I pointed out his stars for him and told him how *Pahukatawa* lived and died and lived again through another's dreams. I'd grown, and Uncle Ralph could not hold me on his knee anymore. His arm circled my waist while we sat on the grass.

132   He was moved by my recitation and clutched my hand tightly. He said, "It's more than this. It's more than just repeating words. You know that, don't you?"

133   I nodded my head. "Yes, I know. The recitation is the easiest part but it's more than this, Uncle Ralph."

134   He was quiet, but after a few minutes his hand touched my shoulder. He said, "I couldn't make it work. I tried to fit the pieces."

135 "I know," I said.

136 "Now before I go," he said, "do you know who you are?"

137 The question took me by surprise. I thought very hard. I cleared my throat and told him, "I know that I am fourteen. I know that it's too young."

138 "Do you know that you are a Pawnee?" he asked in a choked whisper.

139 "Yes Uncle," I said.

140 "Good," he said with a long sigh that was swallowed by the night.

141 Then he stood and said, "Well, Sister, I have to go. Have to move on."

142 "Where are you going?" I asked. "Where all the warriors go?" I teased.

143 He managed a smile and a soft laugh. "Yeah, wherever the warriors are, I'll find them."

144 I said to him, "Before you go, I want to ask you . . . Uncle Ralph, can women be warriors too?"

145 He laughed again and hugged me merrily. "Don't tell me you want to be one of the warriors too?"

146 "No, Uncle," I said, "Just one of yours." I hated to let him go because I knew I would not see him again.

147 He pulled away. His last words were, "Don't forget what I've told you all these years. It's the only chance not to become what everyone else is. Do you understand?"

148 I nodded and he left.

149 I never saw him again.

150 The years passed quickly. I moved away from Momma and Dad and married. Sister left before I did.

151 Years later in another town, hundreds of miles away, I awoke in a terrible gloom, a sense that something was gone from the world the Pawnees knew. The despair filled days, though the reason for the sense of loss went unexplained. Finally, the telephone rang. Momma was on the line. She said, "Sister came home a few days not too long ago. While she was here and alone, someone tapped on the door, like Ralphie always does. Sister yelled, 'Is that you, Uncle Ralphie? Come on in.' But no one entered."

152 Then I understood that Uncle Ralph was dead. Momma probably knew too. She wept softly into the phone.

153 Later Momma received an official call confirming Uncle Ralph's death. He had died from exposure in a hobo shanty, near the railroad tracks outside a tiny Oklahoma town. He'd been dead for several days and nobody knew but Momma, Sister, and me.

154 Momma reported to me that the funeral was well attended by the Pawnee people. Uncle Ralph and I had said our farewells years earlier. Momma told me that someone there had spoken well of Uncle Ralph before they put him in the ground. It was said that "Ralphie came from a fine family, an old line of warriors."

155 Then years later, Sister and I visited briefly at Momma's and Dad's home. We had been separated by hundreds of miles for all that time. As we sat

under Momma's flowering mimosa trees, I made a confession to Sister. I said, "Sometimes I wish that Uncle Ralph were here. I'm a grown woman but I still miss him after all these years."

156 Sister nodded her head in agreement. I continued. "He knew so many things. He knew why the sun pours its liquid all over us and why it must do just that. He knew why babes and insects crawl. He knew that we must live beautifully or not live at all."

157 Sister's eyes were thoughtful, but she waited to speak while I went on. "To live beautifully from day to day is a battle all the way. The things that he knew are so beautiful. And to feel and know that kind of beauty is the reason that we should live at all. Uncle Ralph said so. But now, there is no one who knows what that beauty is or any of the other thinks that he knew."

158 Sister pushed back smoky gray wisps of her dark hair. "You do," she pronounced. "And I do, too."

159 "Why do you suppose he left us like that?" I asked.

160 "It couldn't be helped," Sister said. "There was a battle on."

161 "I wanted to be one of his warriors," I said with an embarrassed half-smile.

162 She leaned over and patted my hand. "You are," she said. Then she stood and placed one hand on her bosom and one hand on my arm. "We'll carry on," she said.

163 I touched her hand resting on my arm. I said, "Sister, tell me again. What is the battle for?"

164 She looked down toward the fence where a hobo was coming through. We waved at him.

165 "Beauty," she said to me. "Our battle is for beauty. It's what Uncle Ralph fought for, too. He often said that everyone else just wanted to go to the Moon. But remember, Sister, you and I done been there. Don't forget, after all, we're children of the stars."

DISCUSSION QUESTIONS

1. In this story there are various "warriors." Cite specific references that explain each.
2. The narrator writes of men—the hobos—who lived apart from mainstream society in a culture that her Uncle Ralph eventually belonged to. What seem to have been the reasons for Ralph's wandering?
3. Uncle Ralph teaches the narrator and her sister Pawnee words, tells them Pawnee stories, and sings a war dance song. Why do you think he persisted in trying to keep the old ways alive?
4. How were Uncle Ralph's efforts to preserve his culture eventually realized?

WRITING TOPICS

1. Write an essay in which you analyze why Walters devotes so much description to the hobos and what these descriptions add to her account.

2. The last time the narrator sees her uncle, he says, "I couldn't make it work. I tried to fit the pieces." In a paragraph, explain what you think he meant.

3. Write three paragraphs in which you explore three important points about your cultural roots. What images best express your feelings about your heritage?

4. Write about the role of the older sister as the narrator of the story. In your analysis, consider possible differences in the story if the author had chosen the younger sister or Uncle Ralph as the narrator.

WATER WITCH

Louis Owens

"My formative years were spent in a two-room cabin a stone's throw from the Yazoo River in Mississippi," Louis Owens says. After his Mississippi years, Owens grew up in rural parts of California, "where my eight brothers and sisters and I could invariably pick up a gun and start hunting rabbits, quail, or deer a few steps out the back door." These youthful experiences gave the author a spatial axis between Mississippi and California. So each of his stories "arises out of a place I know, out of the feelings and smells and sounds and tastes of specific landscapes: the rotting mud of my childhood along the Yazoo River and the rich odor that hung in the viney forest between our cabin and that river; the warm oat hills and oak canopies of the California coast range."

"Water Witch" features Owens's father, who worked from time to time as a "water witch" for California ranchers desperate for well water. Winter rains clothe the rolling hills of the central coast with rich grasses, especially wild oats. Livestock flourish on this feed but must drink daily. A cow can travel at most about five miles between pasture and water, but the grass-covered hills lack surface water. Owens' father was able to guide a well-driller to spots above the invisible underground water fed by the Salinas River.

Most of this condensed autobiography celebrates growing up in the California coast range. Owens remembers when he could still catch trout in the local creek, even if they were tainted by chicken-plant waste, before it was mechanically "cleared." He remembers hunting deer before big city hunters crowded the hills to shoot anything that moves or makes a noise. Owens evokes, in other words, a coastal California that exists no more.

Owens attended California universities, earning a B.A. in 1971 and an M.A. in 1974 from the University of California-Santa Barbara and a Ph.D. from the University of California-Davis in 1981. The National Endowment for the Humanities in 1987 awarded Owens a fellowship; the National Endowment for the Arts awarded him a grant in 1989. A charismatic teacher, Owens writes novels, criticism,

and essays for both academic and general readers. He has contributed more than one hundred articles and reviews to a wide variety of periodicals.

Owens has identified several basic motivations in his writing.
First, he writes "to explore my own identify as a mixed-blood
American of Choctaw, Cherokee, and Irish-American heritage." With
wider vision, he writes "to explore the dilemmas of all mixed-bloods
in America." Beyond human relationships Owens writes "to illuminate our relationships with the natural world." Finally, he writes
"because it is the greatest pleasure."

1   For a while, when I was very young my father was a water witch. He took
us with him sometimes, my older brother and me, and we walked those
burned-up central California ranches, wherever there was a low spot that a
crop-and-cattle desperate rancher could associate with a dream of wetness. The
dusty windmills with their tin blades like pale flowers would be turning tiredly
or just creaking windward now and then, and the ranch dogs—always long-
haired, brown and black with friendly eyes—would sweep their tails around
from a respectful distance. The ranches, scattered near places like Creston,
Pozo, San Miguel, and San Ardo, stretched across burnt gold hills, the little
ranch houses bent into themselves beneath a few dried up cottonwoods or
sycamores, some white oaks if the rancher's grandfather had settled early
enough to choose his spot. Usually there would be kids, three or four ranging
from diapers to hotrod pickups, and like the friendly ranch dogs they'd keep
their distance. The cattle would hang close to the fences, eyeing the house and
gray barn. In the sky, red-tailed hawks wheeled against a washed-out sun while
ground squirrels whistled warnings from the grain stubble.

2   He'd walk, steps measured as if the earth demanded measure, the willow
fork held in both hands before him pointed at the ground like some kind of
offering. We'd follow a few yards behind with measured paces. And nearly
always the wand would finally tremble, dip and dance toward the dead wild
oats, and he would stop to drive a stick into the ground or pile a few rock-dry
clods in a cairn.

3   A displaced Mississippi Choctaw, half-breed, squat and reddish, blind in
one eye, he'd spit tobacco juice at the stick or cairn and turn back toward the
house, feeling maybe the stirring of Yazoo mud from the river of his birth as
if the water he never merely discovered, but drew all that way from a darker,
damper world. Within a few days he'd be back with his boss and they'd drill a
well at the spot he'd marked. Not once did the water fail, but always it was
hidden and secret, for that was the way of water in our part of California.

4   When I think now of growing up in that country, the southern end of
the Salinas Valley, a single mountain range from the ocean, I remember first

the great hidden water, the Salinas River which ran out of the Santa Lucias and disappeared where the coastal mountains bent inland near San Luis Obispo. Dammed at its headwaters into a large reservoir where we caught bluegill and catfish, the river never had a chance. Past the spillway gorge, it sank into itself and became the largest subterranean river on the continent, a half-mile-wide swath of brush and sand and cottonwoods with a current you could feel down there beneath your feet when you hunted the river bottom, as if a water witch yourself, you swayed at every step toward the stream below.

5   We lived first in withdrawn canyons in the Santa Lucias, miles up dirt roads into the creases of the Coast Range where we kids squirmed through buck brush and plotted long hunts to the ocean. But there were no trails and the manzanita would turn us back with what we thought must be the scent of the sea in our nostrils. Rattlesnakes, bears, and mountain lions lived back there. And stories of mythic wild boars drifted down from ranches to the north. In the spring the hills would shine with new grass and the dry creeks would run for a few brief weeks. We'd hike across a ridge to ride wild horses belonging to a man who never knew that the kids rode them. In summer the grasses burned brown and the clumps of live oaks on the hillsides formed dark places in the distance.

6   Later we lived down in the valley on the caving banks of the river. At six and eight years we had hunted with slingshots in the mountains, but at ten and twelve we owned rifles, .22s, and we stalked the dry river brush for quail and cottontails and the little brush rabbits that, like the pack rats, were everywhere. Now and then a deer would break ahead of us, crashing thickets like the bear himself. Great horned owls lived there and called in drumming voices, vague warnings of death somewhere. From the river bottom we pinged .22 slugs off new farm equipment gliding past on the flatcars of the Southern Pacific.

7   Once in a while, we'd return to Mississippi, as if my father's mixed blood sought a balance never found. Seven kids, a dog or two, canvas water bags swaying from fender and radiator, we drove into what I remember as the darkness of the Natchez Trace. In our two-room Mississippi cabin, daddy longlegs crawled across the tar papered walls, and cotton fields surged close on three sides. Across the rutted road through a tangle of tree, brush, and vine, fragrant of rot and death, was the Yazoo River, a thick current cutting us off from the swamps that boomed and cracked all night from the other shore.

8   From the Yazoo we must have learned to feel water as a presence, a constant, a secret source of both dream and nightmare, perhaps as my father's Choctaw ancestors had. I remember it as I remember night. Always we'd return to California after a few months, as much as a year. And it would be an emergence, for the Salinas was a daylight world of hot, white sand and bone-dry brush, where in the fall, red and gold leaves covered the sand, and frost made silver lines from earth to sky. Here, death and decay seemed unrelated things. And here, I imagined the water as a clear, cold stream through white sand beneath my feet.

9   Only in the winter did the Salinas change. When the rains came pounding down out of the Coast Range, the river would rise from its bed to become a half-mile-wide terror, sweeping away chicken coops and misplaced barns; whatever had crept too near. Tricked each year into death, steelhead trout would dash upstream from the ocean, and almost immediately the flooding river would recede to a thin stream at the heart of the dry bed, then a few pools marked by the tracks of coons, then only sand again and the tails and bones of big fish.

10   When I think of growing up in California, I think always of the river. It seemed then that all life referred to the one hundred and twenty miles of sand and brush that twisted its way northward, an upside-down, backwards river that emptied into the Pacific near Monterey, a place I didn't see till I was grown. As teenagers, my brother and I bought our own rifles, a .30-.30 and an ought-six, and we followed our father into the Coast Range after deer and wild boar. We acquired shotguns and walked the high coastal ridges for band-tail pigeon. We drove to fish the headwaters of the Nacimiento and San Antonio rivers. And from every ridge top we saw, if not the river itself, then the long, slow course of the valley it had carved, the Salinas. Far across were the rolling Gabilan Mountains, more hawk hills than mountains, and on the valley bottom, ranches made squares of green and gold with flashing windmills and tin roofs.

11   After school and during summers we worked on the ranches, hoeing sugar beets, building fences, bucking hay, working cattle (dehorning, castrating, branding, ear-clipping, inoculating, all in what must have seemed a single horrific moment for the bawling calf). We'd cross the river to drive at dawn through the dry country watching the clumps of live oak separate from the graying hillsides. Moving shadows would become deer that drifted from dark to dark. Years later, coming home from another state, I would time my drive so that I reached that country at daybreak to watch the oaks rise out of night and to smell the damp dead grasses.

12   Snaking its way down through our little town was a creek. Dipping out of the Coast Range, sliding past chicken farms and country stores, it pooled in long, shadowed clefts beneath the shoulders of hills and dug its own miniature canyon as it passed by the high school, beneath U.S. 101, around the flanks of the county hospital and on to the river where it gathered in a final welling before sinking into the sand. Enroute it picked up the sweat and stink of a small town, the flotsam and jetsam of stunted aspirations, and along its course in tree shadow and root tangle, under cutbank and log, it hid small, dark trout we caught with hook and handline. From the creek came also steelhead trapped by a vanished river, and great blimp-bellied suckers which hunkered closed to the bottom, even a single outraged bull-head which I returned to its solitary pool. At the place where the chicken-processing plant disgorged a yellow stream into the creek, the trout grew fat and sluggish, easily caught. We learned every shading and wrinkle of the creek, not knowing then that it was on the edge already, its years numbered. I more than anyone, fisher of tainted

trout, kept what I thought of as a pact with the dying creek: as long as the water flows and the grass grows.

13   Up on Pine Mountain, not so much looming as leaning over the town of my younger years, a well-kept cemetery casts a wide shadow. From this cemetery, one fine summer evening, a local youth exhumed his grandmother to drive about town with her draped across the hood of his car, an act so shocking no punishment could be brought to bear. Later, when I asked him why, he looked at me in wonder. "Didn't you ever want to do that?" he asked. That fall, after a bitter football loss, members of the high-school letterman's club kidnapped a bus full of rooters from a rival school, holding them briefly at gunpoint with threats of execution. The summer before, an acquaintance of mine had stolen a small plane and dive-bombed the town's hamburger stand with empty beer bottles. The town laughed. Later, he caught a Greyhound bus to Oregon, bought a shotgun in a small town, and killed himself. It was that kind of place also. Stagnant between Coast Range and river, the town, too, had subterranean currents, a hot-in-summer, cold-in-winter kind of submerged violence that rippled the surface again and again. Desires to exhume and punish grew strong. Escape was just around a corner.

14   Behind the cemetery, deep in a wrinkle of the mountain, was an older burial ground, the town's original graveyard, tumbled and hidden in long grasses and falling oaks. Parting the gray oat stalks to read the ancient stone, I felt back then as astonished as a Japanese soldier must have when he first heard the words of a Navajo code talker. Here was a language that pricked through time, millennia perhaps, with painful familiarity but one that remained inexorably remote.

15   A year ago, I drove back to the house nine of us had lived in on the banks of the river. The house was gone, and behind the empty lot the river had changed. Where there had been a wilderness of brush and cottonwoods was now only a wide, empty channel gleaming like bone. Alfalfa fields swept coolly up from the opposite bank toward a modern ranch house. "Flood control" someone in the new Denny's restaurant told me later that afternoon. "Cleaned her out clear to San Miguel," he said.

Discussion Questions

1. How would you describe the organization of this essay?
2. Owens writes as much of dry landscape as he does water. What is the effect of this contrast?
3. What is the contrast between the Yazoo River and its surroundings and the Salinas River and its surroundings?
4. How does Owens connect the characterization of the town he lived in with the river?

WRITING TOPICS

1. In an essay, analyze Owens's use of sensory imagery in this essay, and tell what the cumulative effect is.
2. An important element of Owens's style is the use of strong verbs. Make a list of the strong verbs in paragraphs 1, 2, and 12.
3. Write a description of a body of water near you or one that you have visited. Describe some aspect of life that exists in or near the water. Try to be as specific in your descriptions as Owens is in his and use strong verbs.
4. Think of a place that has made an important impact on your life. Using Owens' sense of place and vivid description as a model, write about your place, including the people and the environment.

THE VIEW FROM THE MESA

Shonto Begay

Shonto Begay, maker of images in paint and in words, was born in 1954 at Shonto, Arizona, on the vast Navajo Reservation. This talented author and artist was the fifth child in a family of sixteen children. His mother, like most Navajo women of her day, wove rugs from the wool of their sheep to earn income for the family. His father, a traditional healer, performed ceremonies and taught his children lessons through stories.

Federal officials started Begay in a boarding school at age five. He could see his parents only during a two-week Christmas break and the summers until he was in the eighth grade. During his early school years, teachers forbade him and other students to speak their Navajo language. Young Shonto learned to speak, read, and write English, but boarding school left him determined to preserve his Navajo heritage.

After high school, Begay attended the Institute of American Indian Arts in Santa Fe, earning an Associate of Fine Arts Degree in 1976. He received a Bachelor of Fine Arts degree from the California College of Arts and Crafts in Oakland, California, in 1980. Since 1981 the artist has been a ranger at Navajo National Monument. He has designed museum exhibits, taught fine arts for Northern Pioneer College, and lectured on Navajo traditions and art. Begay's paintings have appeared in over thirty exhibitions, and his art can be found in collections throughout the world.

Begay expanded his artistic range by illustrating trade and textbooks. He has also published children's books, including *The Mud Pony* (1988) and *Mai'ii and Cousin Horned Toad* (1992), which have been highly praised. Illustrating led Begay to begin writing. His *Navajo: Visions and Voices Across the Mesa* (1995) presents color paintings, poems, and stories for a mature audience.

One painting with special meaning to Shonto hangs in the Phoenix Public Library. It illustrates the intimate relationship between his writing and painting. Entitled "Story Rock," it shows a young Navajo boy reading atop a special rock. Begay says he rested there while herding sheep, imagining he was transcending time and space. "This is my spot. My childhood time machine, my dream machine," Shonto wrote of that lichen-covered boulder, an enchanted feature of the Shonto Plateau. "There were no Nintendo games then, so I sat there and day-dreamed and read Mark Twain, James Fenimore Cooper, Jules Verne, Louis L'Amour, even Hitchcock collections. I saw patterns and figures in the lichens that cover the rock. It was my flying carpet, my personal Mecca, my Sistine Chapel," Arizona's prize-winning artist recalls. In "The View from the Mesa," Begay writes lyrically about it. That rock "exists today for future generations. Everyone has such a space somewhere, if not within."

1   Sitting here, atop this mesa, I survey all that is home to me. The wide valley of Kethla yawns before me. In the distance, to the east, Black Mesa lies heavy, its northernmost tip rising above the town of Kayenta to the northeast. Far to the South, its body merges with the dusty earth of Tonalea. To the South, Wildcat Peak sits on the horizon. To the West, White Mesa, home of the Lightening Beings, lies bright against the distant violet of vermillion cliffs. It awakens summer thunder, bringing life to our thirsty land. To the Northwest, Navajo Mountain, dark blue against the milky turquoise sky. The head of the Mother. The birthplace of my grandfather. To the North, the massive uplift of the Shonto Plateau humbles the vision, yet lifts the spirit. On a clear day, when the Navajo Generating Station in Page, Arizona is not spewing out too much filth, I can even see the Sacred Mountain of the West. San Francisco Peaks shimmer like a mirage far to the Southwest. (As a child, when a cloud appeared in a peaked formation over the west, I thought it to be this mountain. I watched in awe.) Below me, patterns of gray-green hues of the upper Sonoran desert plant life wash the valley. Streaks of flesh-colored sand dunes ripple up the valley. Dark greens of the piñon and juniper trees spill off this mesa. Halfway across the valley, it gets sparse until it runs into an invisible barrier beyond which no tree grows. Patchworks of slick rocks hug the land, breaking up the sagebrush plains and rolling hills. From where I sit, I look into the sanctuary of my childhood.

2   In my earliest recollections, my environment was just as far as my eyes could see. My world was the circular line of the horizon. This was the place that harbored the ancient gods and animal beings that are so alive in our legends. The Hero-Twins once again ride upon the rainbow in their battle against the *Yé'iitsoh* (Monster Gods), on thundering male rain summer days, during the battles in the war to reclaim the Fourth World. The beautiful White Shell Woman, once again, spreads her blanket of mist on days of gen-

tle female-rain. The chorus of happy frogs sounds the white shells of her blanket. The land is scarred with erosions of rain, yet the corn stands tall, offering yellow pollen for another year. The wet clay binds the tires of trucks, immobile machines roaring in frustration. Yet, the watering holes for livestock are overflowing. Such are the contradictions of nature, such is the contradiction of creation.

3   As a child, I slept on my sheepskin in the southern cycle of the *hooghan* among my brothers and sisters. I slept next to an old trunk containing the wealth of the family. Medicine bundles and turquoise jewelries of my father, velveteen and weaving tools of my mother. Upon this old trunk, I saw patterns night after night where the white paint was chipping off. By the light of the kerosene lamp, to the rhythm of the cracking fire in an old oil drum stove, the nightly ritual of my imagination began. Contorted beings, heroic figures, *Yé'iitsoh* and familiar faces marched across the trunk as I created epic after epic until my mother gently blew out the lamp. In the dark, colors licked my eyelids. Sounds from about the *hooghan* evoked imagination. In this manner, I entertained myself to sleep. Until I saw my first black and white television at my uncle's trailer in Flagstaff, I had never experienced a readily available source of movements on blank spaces. The old trunk in the corner never had commercial breaks.

4   Like many young Navajos my age, the Bureau of Indian Affairs boarding school left an impression upon my early life. It was a very strict and controlling surrogate parent to us for ten years. I recall these impressions as either very bad or almost pleasant, going from the hearth of our *hooghan* into the cold metal framed desk that was my introduction into the outside world. Years of campaigns to assimilate and acculturate us only made my resistance to these attempts stronger. Missionaries tried to place teachings upon us to renounce our "heathen" ways, but the inspiration and values of our grandparents never budged. Little did they know, it seemed, that these values and humanity, shared in the name of love and mercy, were universal. In this family of man, despite our ritual differences, we offered to the same deity. On the positive side, these years with other young people shaped views of the encroaching outside world, our reactions to intrusions into our traditions and those compromises we deemed necessary. For the first time outside of the immediate related family, friends were made and kept, friends whose views complimented or contrasted with our own like sand dunes amidst a fertile valley. We realized each other's values and needs. We understood that we were not alone in our journeys to meet the outside world. But, creative young minds were not nurtured nor encouraged by the schools.

5   At home, I watched my mother weave rugs. To my innocent eyes, I just saw colors and patterns composed on a loom. I did not see the significance of the designs. The passions of the native dyes, the recreation of the Spider Women stories in my mother's eyes as strands of wool flowed out of her hand. The spiritual connection she pushed down with every row wove her

deeper into the heart of the pattern. My eyes were too "dazzled" to see a minute line she allowed from the center to the edge of the rug. Upon this line, she will travel back out of the pattern so she can continue to create other fine rugs. I remember sitting on a sheepskin next to her with a magazine, showing her images she should try. She never got interested in product logos and other "alien" patterns that so intrigued me. Many years later, in 1969, my aunt wove her first pictoral rug depicting the first moon landing. A human visitation to a celestial body, a recurring theme in our legend, certainly was worth recording. That hot June night, my brothers and I lay on our backs in the cornfield looking up at the full moon past the young stalks and felt a oneness with the night sky. Even the coyote up the canyon felt the need to cry out. In my soul, I felt a strange wind of discontent, knowing that another pattern of conquest was left behind . . . up there.

6   Some of my mother's rugs became saddle blankets we and the horses sorely needed. Most went to the local trader down at Shonto. Our needs were few. Thus we were raised comfortably on what little subsistence she got in return.

7   From my perch upon this mesa, I see far below my mother's *hooghan* a cluster of other buildings and shacks. A sheep pen and horse and cow corral. Odd specks of colors where old junked car bodies lie here and there. The cows are just specks resting on slick rock next to the homesite. A pond remains most of the year there. The area around there looks windswept and barren. Years of our impact. Closer to me, at the foot of the mesa, are two earthen *hooghans* blending so well into the earth. My father's ceremonial *hooghan* and retreat. The other is where I was raised. Farther to the north, through the juniper and piñon forest is an old homesite, now a bare patch of ground choked with sagebrush. This is the site where I was born. That is the place my wife Rita and I are building our *hooghan*. I can barely see the top of the *hooghan* from here. Way off in the distance, towards Black Mesa, out on the edge of the sand dunes, my grandmother's house sits alone. If you look hard, you can see a thread of dirt road connecting these homes. In a flurry of activity, piñon jays burst from a juniper tree below me. A lone raven streaking just above the tree line must have scared it. A tinkling of sheep bells to the north gives away the sparse herd of my aunt just over the mesa. She often walks these mesas after her sheep, guarding the place that holds my umbilical cord.

8   Giant shadows move across the landscape like returning *Yé'iis* of old. Shadows darken juniper and piñon flats, giving them an instant burst of motion. As the sun regains control of the land at the heel of these shadows, slickrock outcroppings radiate with new light. The land undulates in color and energy in this manner. An opera of the land, a symphony of the sky. I believe I have the best seat on the Shonto plateau at the moment. Silence roars in my ears like waves of ocean.

9   The wind picks up from the southwest. The mesa top is suddenly alive with the whispering forest passing secrets: creaking branches and rustling

boughs. Far below me, a dust devil forms out of nowhere. Twisting and swaying, it ominously travels the dirt road down the mesa. It circles our winter *hooghan* and passes through the brush arbor where it re-emerges as two, as if one was waiting there all along. Dust devils were always an object of mystery and fear for us growing up. We were told to avoid being contaminated by one. They were a visible form of *Ch'iidii* (ghosts). My mother told me long ago if you hit one with a stick, you can hear a sound like hitting a dry, stiff sheepskin. I have thrown sticks towards them, yet never stuck around to listen. Recently I was told that only the ones spinning in a counter-clockwise fashion are to be avoided. If one runs over your *hooghan*, you scream words of prayers after it to avoid its "disease." Sometimes just obscenities seem to work for me. Far above me, beyond passing clouds in the deep blue sky, a jet stream slowly reaches out, beading the high wispy clouds. Another mystery.

10   There were other mysteries I grew up with which affect my art life to this day. Mysteries of powerful beings, elements and animals I was told never to reproduce on paper. Images never to be placed upon rocks. I was told that this is the way the Anasazi (ancient ones) disappeared. It is said that these people fell victims to their own creations. These people, whose villages are so intact in canyon walls today, were blessed in every way and manner. Their fertile valley knew no boundaries; their architectural skills, their trade systems and artistic outpourings were all guided by this mystery. They were to stay within certain boundaries in their rituals of healings, their creative expressions and views of themselves. As years went by, the population grew and pride evolved. Sickness became common. Ceremonies of the Windway were practiced to curtail these sicknesses. This particular ceremony became so overdone and trivialized that even newborns were given this ritual. The people contaminated themselves and angered the spirit of the wind. (Sort of like an overdose of vitamins.) The art upon the face of the cliff *no longer* was done exclusively as a recording and offering, a sacred undertaking. As a result, altars were desecrated. Designs on potteries became bold and colorful. Swirling patterns of the wind were used. It is said that the pottery designs broke the final barrier that held back the wrath of the wind. Within days, the wind purged the canyon of its inhabitants but left the structures standing. The people were either buried by blowing sand or completely removed from the canyons. With this lesson in a story, I was always told that there is a limit to what I have the freedom of drawing. I must be careful not to draw lightning, snakes and sandpaintings, to name some of them. Today, I see copies of sandpaintings sold along roadsides, at flea markets and at every outlet catering to tourist trade. I see this marketing of sacred symbols—very disturbing. It is done, I know, under the guise that certain elements are removed from the symbol, thus making it powerless. I have seen more than one young sandpainter quit the business because of the ill effects it had on them. Economic conditions are such that our young

people are compromising more than they should today. My father is a medicine man of some renown. We grew up assisting him on occasions in making these mandalas. We sat in ceremonies where healing took place and reverence emanated out of every face. The sand absorbs the illness upon which the patient sits. The painting is disposed of before darkness. It is not taboo, it is respect above all that has prevented me from copying this thus far. Besides, it's too detailed and disciplined for me.

11   It is hard to be an art critic in this time and place. The reservation artist of today is just responding to the conditions around him the best way he can. Unemployment is high, technical skills are low. These talents that seem so natural to so many are used to survive these times. I'm even surprised to find some young artists and craftspeople do not consider themselves "artists"; they feel their skills are marketable just as would a mechanic or a gardener. Survival takes precedent over any serious applications of aesthetics. This is why, on some evenings, I drive out towards the edge of Monument Valley and see the colors and shades a little duller, muted and hazier. So much life has been taken from it in order to "capture" its "essence," it came to a point where we see the same expression of the beauty of this place over and over again until it gets laborious to view. Talents and achievement of these artists attest to the fact that this needn't be.

12   In the air now, I feel a new excitement, a slight surge of energy, a new light of a new dawn. This anticipation is like grass in the path of a distant approaching thunderstorm. I feel that the "spirit line" out of our complacencies in art has been drawn. A fresh expression of our passions, our joys and pains is in the making. A new generation of interpretations of our legends and stories, strengths and weaknesses as Navajo people are replacing the images of stoic tribalisms that so pervaded our recent art history. To paraphrase another artist, "realness instead of redness." I feel as do other young fine artists of the northern reservation, that there is much potential for individual expression of beauty, of power, of mysteries to be created within the perimeter of our culture in this time. But what inspires us young Navajo artists to create these interpretations of our culture? What force drives us to seek fresher means of expression? We all have our reasons and means to do this. It may be money, it may be recognition or self-satisfaction. For me, it is a means of confronting myself, my fears and mysteries. A means of coming to terms with childhood phobias and a recognition of my strength and weaknesses in this day. In Navajo society, it is necessary to journey that road to self-discovery. To attain a spiritual growth, we will have to go beyond the world we retreat into. We must recognize and acknowledge this new high tech world, yet still maintain an identity. We must draw a line beyond which we don't venture. Be able to compromise wisely and know how much to expose of ourselves. Know ourselves and our past, yet still have faith in the future. We are a segment of a society that has been thrust into the twentieth century all within thirty years. We will not

allow ourselves to become casualties in this collision of cultures. The art that we represent must be flexible and adaptable, like the nature of our grandfather, if it is to survive, lest we become brittle and blow away like shells of dry piñon nuts. The art that we represent, like the role of the medicine man of today, must help in creating a positive evolution into this new era for our people and those coming after us. It will scream of tomorrow, yet be dressed in the truth of our past. I believe this to be a collective therapy for us, for our culture and our art.

13   I am back atop this mesa. From the base of this gnarly old juniper tree I'm sitting under, as if sharing the same umbilical cord to the mother, round leaf buffalo berry bush cascades over the edge of the mesa. A blanket of greenish-silver plant. Sweet aroma of the cliffrose catches my senses every so often. What a beautiful plant. I am sitting among food and medicine of all sorts. Truly the Mother provides. Where I am sitting, the ground no longer feels hard: I just feel a fusion with her, a clear sensation like billions of molecules flowing up from the center through my body and gently rising into the sky. The teachings that we are all one in the universe, an integral part of the great cycle stands true. Everything is inter-related and inter-dependent. I am no more or no less important to this mystery than a blade of grass, a late afternoon rainbow or a grain of sand. These, I am taught, are all a part of us and we are a part of it. From our Mother—the earth—all creation springs. We are responsible for maintaining and respecting this relationship for all time. From the foot of the Four Sacred Mountains, our contentment flows; from their bodies, our strength, and from their peaks, our prayers. In this journey of life, we experience many emotions, some good, some bad. Pain and illness occur when we choose to detach ourselves from this connection. We choose to embrace "alien" conveniences too soon, too much, too long. We choose to be strangers to our family and travel against the cycle of all that is holy to us.

14   When I was around four years old, I traveled with my grandmother to the foot of the Sacred Mountain of the West. During this time, she told me many things. She told me that we are responsible in maintaining and nurturing a good identity with our grandparents every single day. Each day before the sun rises, we should greet the new coming day with pollen and re-affirm our relationship with it. To a young piñon tree, we greet "*Yá'áhtééh shima'sání*" (Hello, my grandmother); to a young juniper tree; "*Yá'áhtééh shí'cheii*" (hello, my grandfather). In this manner, we bring new light and life to our world. At this age I learned to feel, see and smell my world. I still associate lots of pieces of past experiences, painful and pleasant, to these subtleties. There are few things more pleasant than waking up in the morning to see dew on blades of grass, or to hear rolling of the thunder as dark clouds gather on spring days. To smell wet sand and hear the raindrops dancing on parched ground. The cornstalks weeping for joy. Forming figures from clay and feeling like a god. The soft crunching sound in the snow as I make my way home with a rabbit or two on moonlit winters night, or

even being momentarily lost in a blizzard. To feel as a tumbleweed rolling across rough landscape, to see the last ray of sunlight hitting the mesa after an autumn day, light reflecting off a distant passing car makes me feel vulnerable and sad at times. These past feelings and experiences, associated with time and places, I regard as a reservoir of my inspiration.

15   Like most young Navajos my age, we spent many winter nights gathered around our father, listening to stories passed down through generations. We sat in expectation as we journeyed up from the womb of the Mother in creation stories. We sat mezmerized by coyote stories. Laughing at his antics and frightened by his cruelties. We sat in awe as First Man and First Woman brought forth life upon the Fourth World. We journey back from the west, the home of Changing Woman, into the midst of the Four Sacred Mountains after the creation of our clans. "Slayer of Enemies" and "Born for Water," the hero and savior of the fourth world, came alive for us these nights. I felt the pain of their fathers' testing in the roaring fire of the hearth. Their war with the Monster Gods raged as the snow storm dusted outside our door, snow sifting through the cracks of the door. Shadows leaping on cribbed wall of the *hooghan* brought to life the animal beings as the shoe game was created. As the nights wore on, the youngest ones of us fell asleep where we sat. My mother's spindle scratching the floor set the tempo of these late night journeys . . . back.

16   From these sources I draw my inspirations. I am humbled by its beauty and strengthened by its power. With great respect, I relive this in every creation, every all-night Blessingway chant and every vision of glory upon this land. With good intentions, I recreate this in every piece of art: intentions of preserving and passing on, intentions of sharing and inviting all good-willed people for the sake of us as American Indians in general, as Navajos in particular and the beauty of our culture. This culture through art, in whatever form, however expressed, will endure.

17   The sun is low now. The clouds awashed in gold. The shadows move across the valley ever so slowly. Smoke of the evening fire drifts from my mother's *hooghan* below. Far off, on the edge of the shadow, a few cows make their way slowly towards the windmill, to wash another day of dust from their throats. A trail of dust out on the clay flat where someone is driving out towards our home. A patient my father was expecting all day is finally coming. Tuba City, was it? Down below, at the base of the mesa, the sheep start back towards the pen. A tinkling bell or bleating of the lambs breaks the silence every once in a while. The sheep dogs, alert and busy, have spotted me. A bittersweet feeling washes over me. Thoughts of lost friends and relatives cross my mind. "Pah pah" I whisper as I pick my way back of the mesa. The full moon will rise tonight.

DISCUSSION QUESTIONS

1. What aspects of Shonto Begay's descriptions tend to confirm that he is a visual artist?
2. At the end of the first paragraph, Begay refers to the "sanctuary" of his childhood. What does the word connote?
3. Begay expresses two views of the Bureau of Indian Affairs boarding school. What are they?
4. In referring to reservation artists, Begay says that "a fresh expression of our passions, our joys and pains is in the making." Why does he say this is necessary, and how did his aunt recognize this necessity?
5. Begay combines his recollections of earlier experiences with descriptions of what he sees from atop a mesa. How do these two strands help to express what seems to be his main idea—that "this culture through art . . . will endure"?

WRITING TOPICS

1. Begay says that "these past feelings and experiences associated with time and places, I regard as reservoir of my inspiration." Think of a time when you created something. What was the source of your inspiration? Write about your creation and the source of inspiration.
2. Begay has written, "We all experience beauty of our cultures in our own way. This is my way of expressing my culture." Reread paragraphs 1, 2, 3, 10, and 15. Write a paper on important elements in Navajo culture that the author expresses in these paragraphs.
3. Sit in one place like Shonto Begay did. Describe the landscape or cityscape around you with strong images. First jot down immediate impressions, and then organize your images into a poem or a piece of prose.

SEEING, KNOWING, REMEMBERING

Linda Hogan

Linda Hogan opens a door to her Oklahoma past through her Chickasaw grandmother. While growing up, the author's family moved from post to post as her father was transferred by the army. She also spent time in Oklahoma with her father's relatives. In a 1990 interview with Patricia Clark Smith, Hogan remembers, "I think Oklahoma was where magic lived for me, and still does, in the fire-flies, and in the breezy motion of trees, and the stillness. . . . I know, in my mind, that the air and earth and my body are all really home, but my heart home is there, in Chickasaw country."

Hogan's ancestors had been removed to Oklahoma (Indian Territory) in the 1830s along with other southeastern tribes including the Cherokees and Choctaws. For centuries the Chickasaws had farmed and hunted in their vast, fertile land located in present-day Mississippi, Alabama, and Tennessee. After forced removal, they slowly rebuilt their lives in the West. But in the early 1900s, the United States government again disrupted Chickasaws' lives when it dissolved the Chickasaw Nation and divided the tribal territory into individually owned tracts, many of which were soon illegally acquired by non-Indians. In the allotment scandals, Indian women were particularly at risk because a non-Indian man who married a Chickasaw woman could claim her land under Oklahoma state law.

In this essay Hogan aligns herself with uncounted generations of Native American women who have borne new natives, even when they were forced to marry newcomers. She labels her grandmother's Euro-American father "a thief of Indian lands, a killer" and a source of family terror instead of love. Expressing her grief and admiration for her grandmother, Hogan turns her vision toward the future by recognizing, "I am the grandmother now."

1   On the day my grandmother died, the black and shining wet frog with golden eyes leapt against the wall, hitting it with a force that broke its spine. The grief for my grandmother was still too large for weeping, so I held the frog in my palm and cried for it. With fascination, I had watched the amphibious development of the frog, rescued from science-worshipping people. It seemed to reflect my own human growing, the way an egg divides, the pushing out of legs, how my own gill slit in the womb before birth vanished back into my still-wet skin. Like the frog, my grandmother and I lived between the elements, born to two worlds, Indian and white. And that white world was one that had come down, for Indian people, like a wall we were thrown against, a wall that turned our lives inside out, a wall that broke the spine of our societies.

2   Recently, Suzan Shown Harjo, director of the Morning Star Foundation, said, "When white people came here they threw a blanket over our heads. We are just now beginning to lift the corner of that blanket and see ourselves again." We are rising from the murky waters of history, surfacing like the crawfish of our tradition who brought clay up from unformed waters and fashioned the Earth. And it is true, we are just beginning to see and know each other, our pasts, our people. Only now is it safe. And we find ourselves still on the interrupted journey that our ancestors began. And coming into the light of this vision, I am beginning to see my grandmother.

3   Come from the Mound Builders,[1] the brilliant calculators of time who stretched their hands in reverence toward the new moon, granddaughter of tribal leader Winchester Colbert, she was born in 1883. My grandmother lived through times that were astonishing in their horror: the Wounded Knee Massacre, deliberate policies of starvation and wars of extermination, the banning of Indian religions. The continent-wide stories of the suffering that befell other tribes traveled into Oklahoma, where the unbelievable tragedies were whispered in the night, and everyone knew it was a danger-ous thing to be Indian. She witnessed what some would call the end, sur-viving through treaty-breaking times, gunpowder times, and later, the whirling sands of the Depression in a deforested Oklahoma. It was a time when belief and hope were assassinated, when it was understood that the white people feared and hated what was Indian, what was, to them, any form of wilderness or darkness or ancient ways.

4   There was a hole in the world through which life itself was escaping. It was dangerous at home; my grandfather's sisters were forced to marry white men who wanted their land. There was no safety within the family; my grandmother's own father was an ambitious and dangerous man, a thief of Indian lands, a killer. Terror lived inside the familiar, inside what should have been love.

5   Like all other Chickasaw girls, my grandmother, Lucy, was a student at Bloomfield Academy, an Indian girls' school started by missionaries in Indian

---

[1] *Mound Builders:* Ancient Native Americans who built large earthworks believed to be used for mortuary and ritual use. The earliest mounds, in Louisiana, date from about 4000 B.C. Two well-known mounds, in Cahokia, Illinois, and in Adams County, Ohio, were probably constructed about 2,000 years ago.

Territory with the purpose of Americanizing the girls. I found her graduation exercises in the *Chronicles of Oklahoma*. She played a piano solo at commencement. Her sister recited "The Lotus Eaters" by Tennyson. Rev. Burris, an Indian orator, delivered the invocation in Chickasaw. The girls were educated as if they were white, but leaving there, they returned to the Indian world.

6   Living in rural poverty, without water, my grandmother became a quiet, tender woman. The double knot of America was tied about her and inescapable. Like most of the Chickasaw women, she became an active churchgoer, practicing the outward shape of Christianity while retaining the depth of Indian traditional religion, a reverence for all life. She lived outside the confines of the white world within an older order, holding the fragments of an Indian way closed within her hands. She was the face of survival, the face of history and spirit in a place where even women were forced to take up arms to protect themselves. At death, she made a statement of resistance; her gravestone disavowed Oklahoma statehood, the white world. It reads: Born and died in Berwyn Indian Territory.

7   I remember her as the old Indian woman of the turtles, who spoke to them and they listened, who wore aprons and cleaned fish, who cooked platters of eggs to feed her many grandchildren. She was the woman with never-cut hair. She was the blue-eyed Indian who used lye and ash to turn corn into white, tender hominy, cooking *pashofa* in a black kettle. There is even a recipe for "Lucy's Lye Soap." She was the woman, forced into English, who used snuff and healed her children with herbs, home remedies, and the occasional help of a black Chickasaw freedwoman named Aunt Rachel, a root worker. My grandmother was the beautiful lover of land, people, and quiet Oklahoma nights full of remembered fear, wet heavy air, fireflies, and the smell of pecan trees, the land with tarantulas and rattlesnakes, the numerous and silencing sounds of gunshots in the night.

8   Like the old redwood forests, when a mother tree falls, a young one springs from its death. I am one of the trees grown out of my grandmother's falling at a time when Indian dances were still outlawed, gatherings suspect. One of the bare survivors of this history, lighter-skinned, broken, I rose out of the forbidden ways, a frog waking beneath the mud, feeling the vibration of rain, smelling water, digging out.

9   The line where my grandmother ends and I begin is no line at all. I am a child that once lived inside her, that was carried inside the builders of the mounds, the cells of mourners along the Trail of Tears. From them I still remember to honor life, mystery, and this incomparable ongoing creation.

10   And living at the secret heart of this creation, I am the grandmother now, traveling among those who cannot see or know me, learning the healing of plants, caring for children, struggling against the madness called progress, and believing the sun's old ways. I know this land is charged with life. I know what has happened to it, and to us. And I know our survival.

DISCUSSION QUESTIONS

1. What is the mood of this essay?
2. How effective is Hogan's frog-wall metaphor for you? Discuss an experience that left you feeling like you had run into a wall.
3. In paragraph two, Hogan speaks of "the interrupted journey that our ancestors began." Assuming that a journey has a destination, what is a destination for a people or family? How in Hogan's family's case was the journey interrupted?

WRITING TOPICS

1. In a paragraph, respond to one of the following sentences from the essay.

"There was a hole in the world through which life itself was escaping." (paragraph 4)

"She was the face of survival, the face of history and spirit in a place where even women were forced to take up arms to protect themselves." (paragraph 6)

"The line where my grandmother ends and I begin is no line at all." (paragraph 9)

2. Write a comparison of three differences or similarities between the life of one of your grandmothers, or an older person you know, and Hogan's grandmother.
3. Write a character sketch of an older relative, perhaps interviewing that person before you begin.
4. This is the fourth selection in this chapter on the theme of memory. Choose two of the selections and, in an essay, compare and contrast them. Consider the subject matter, purposes, writing style, and mood.

OF ALL TOMORROWS

Peter Blue Cloud

Peter Blue Cloud lives at Kahnawake, Quebec, where he was born and attended school. Concerning his name, he wrote "My Indian name is Aroniawenrate. 'Blue Cloud' is a present give me by some Paiutes."

Blue Cloud experiments with form in many of his poems, including this one. He says, "I like to think I'm writing songs and chants rather than poems." "Of All Tomorrows" picks up the beat of the dance or the chant, repeating sounds and rhythms. Here the poet swirls metaphors in dizzying succession through the orderly lines and stanzas.

The poet crowds at least one major cosmological metaphor into each compact three-line stanza on the left. Although the title speaks of the future, the verse plays upon the traditional past—apparently a pan-tribal mythology. The action takes place in mythic time. "As a poet," wrote critic James Ruppert, Blue Cloud "is a seeker, a crier of visions, a meditator on the world spirit. His poems are songs of vision and illumination."

Time flies away on the wings
of yesterday, he said,
spreading out a night blanket.

He emptied his sack of bones
5 at the feet of bent saplings
white-haired with snow.

The brittle music of cracked
bones splintered the night
with puffs of frost.

And
they
played

a
lonely
farewell

as
we
departed.

10 He reached further into his sack pulling out an obsidian ball which was the sleeping moon.	And they forgot
Look, he said, this globe is the owl's own dreaming 15 etched in forgotten charcoal.	and forgot again
He reached again into his sack and drew forth a necklace of star fingers;	all the pain
When dawn washes all this away, 20 he said, we will have long since departed this desolate place.	of their birth.
Then from his sack he took a flute of newly polished bone fashioned from my thigh.	And he smiled
25 He played a shower of seeds which fell upon the snow as tiny, blue children.	and told me
He folded the blanket of night about their naked bodies 30 and continued to play.	that a promise
And now the flute was crying of dreams the raven's wings enfold thru all eternities.	had been given
He smiled a breath of stars 35 which fell around us softly, giving substance to the night.	us this night.
Then he played dawn's own song, and maybe had changed his mind, for we had not departed.	And the promise
40 He smiled again, and said okay, let us together call the sun to witness our first meeting.	is that life

And the sun found a nation of
golden children playing flutes
45 which were Creation songs.

And each and every note was
a plant, or insect, or bird
spreading out from their circle.

Now, he said, let us leave
50 and let night be a part
of all their dreaming:

we, after all, are but myths
etched on old bones and boulders
like memories of all tomorrows.

born
of
youth

thru
old
teachings

is
the
fabric

of
all
tomorrows.

DISCUSSION QUESTIONS

1. The speaker in this poem seems to be a spirit or supernatural, since in lines 23–24 a flute is fashioned from his thigh bone. How does knowing this affect your understanding of the poem?
2. How would you describe the role of "he" in the poem?
3. What references to time do you notice in the poem? How would you describe this time element?
4. The poem has a unique structure. Explain the tone and action in stanzas 1–7. Beginning with stanza 8, the tone and actions change and continue until the end of stanza 18. The actions change again in the brief stanzas on the right. Describe these changes.

WRITING TOPICS

1. In a paragraph entitled "Creation Song," discuss the theme of creation. You may wish to begin with the first stanza and progress through the poem.
2. Prepare this poem as a script for readers' theater and perform it with your classmates.

3. In your response journal, give some ideas about the meaning of the title "Of All Tomorrows" and how it relates to "the promise."
4. In the last stanza, the speaker says that we "are but myths etched on old bones and boulders." In an essay, explain what you think this means. Does the "we" refer to spirits of those long gone or to living people today?
5. In a short paper, analyze the figurative language in this poem. Include specific examples of imagery, personification, and metaphor.

PROVISO

Phil George

Like Peter Blue Cloud, Phil George writes poetry that connects to his people's traditional values and sacred places. "Proviso" focuses on the sacred geography in and around Wallowa Valley in Oregon. As a Nez Perce, George often writes lyrically about Appaloosas, the horse breed the Nez Perce developed. George's great-grandfather, for whom he is named, owned hundreds of Appaloosa horses.

The author wrote this piece when he was a young man. Yet, the persona's voice speaks with maturity in addressing those transporting his body to burial. In counterpoint, the voice drums and sings. The poet fills these ostensible funeral directions with metaphors of traditional Nez Perce ways of life and territory. George composed this poem almost a century after Yellow Wolf refused to surrender his rifle after the Nez Perce defeat at Bear Paw. The contemporary poet demonstrates that Nez Perce pride lives on in a new generation.

After my wake, oh people of my lodge,
Place a drum upon my chest
And lay me on a travois—
An ancient, gentle travois.
5 In the dawn, not eventide, I beg,
Take me far away.
        I'll drum.
        I'll sing.

Carry me in regalia of bygone days
10 Plumed by the morning breath of Appaloosas,
Across the meadow of the camas,[1]
Through satin dew upon Wallowa's shadow,
There leave me far away.

---

[1] *camas:* A plant producing an edible root that constituted a staple food for Nez Perce.

I'll drum.
15   I'll sing.

Hold me without bruising, as in embrace,
Carpeted on palms of loving hands.
Move through the camps from west to east,
For my sun rises, does not set,
20 And lifts me far away.
    I'll drum.
    I'll sing.

DISCUSSION QUESTIONS

1. How do you explain the title in relation to the rest of the poem?
2. Images of Nez Perce life abound in this poem. What examples do you notice?
3. What is the tone of the poem? Cite evidence from the text to support your answer.
4. What lines reveal the speaker's feeling for the past?

WRITING TOPICS

1. Imagine that Yellow Wolf and Phil George meet in the year 2025. Write a conversation that they may have about Nez Perce past and future.
2. In a short essay, examine how the poet achieves a sense of movement in the poem. How does this sense contribute to the meaning?
3. In a critical essay, compare "Proviso" and "Old Man, the Sweat Lodge" (Chapter 2). Use examples of imagery and symbolism. Also discuss form (structure) and tribal perspective.

CELEBRATION

Alonzo Lopez

Alonzo Lopez's "Celebration" appeared in *The Whispering Wind* in 1972. Lopez attended Sells Consolidated School on the Tohono O'odham (Papago) Reservation until he transferred to the Institute of American Indian Arts in Santa Fe. He went from IAIA to Yale University for a year's study and then transferred to Wesleyan University. There Lopez recorded his native language for anthropology department faculty members. In other words, Lopez wrote "Celebration" in his second language; no interpreter filtered his Piman into English.

I shall dance tonight.
When the dusk comes crawling,
There will be dancing
    and feasting.
5   I shall dance with the others
    in circles
        in leaps,
            in stomps.
Laughter and talk
10   will weave into the night,
Among the fires
    of my people
Games will be played
And I shall be
15   a part of it.

Discussion Questions

1. What does this poem reveal about the speaker?
2. How does the speaker know what will happen at dusk?

Writing Topics

1. Write a poem or a paragraph about a celebration in your life.

I REMEMBER

James Welch

James Welch writes from inside Indian country in Montana. In "I Remember," he brings to life a moving montage from his childhood as he evokes his nine-year-old perception of a tribal Sun Dance. Images of the sacred vow woman and the Blackfeet camp resemble images in his novel *Fools Crow*. In this short, simple reminiscence, the sometimes surrealistic poet and complex novelist, uses simple, lyrical language. "Thirty four years later the image of that Sun Dance procession is still with me, and in my novels and poems I have tried to maintain the spirit of that moment."

1   I remember standing beside my father on a hot summer day on a plain southwest of Browning, near the Two Medicine River. I was standing beside my father and we were standing in the middle of an encampment of traditional painted tepees. There were many straight-sided canvas tents around the perimeter of the camp. Pickups and beaten cars glinted harshly beneath a roaring sun. Dogs barked and horses grunted and whickered and somewhere not far off a child cried. Perhaps the child was my young brother, held high in my mother's arms, squirming to see over the headdresses and roaches[1] of the people in front of us. The air smelled of smoky buckskin and sagebrush and the burning sweetgrass. The people grew silent and attentive. We were watching a tepee not far to the west of the big half-finished medicine lodge. Behind me I heard the whirr of a home movie camera. I was a little frightened, I remember.

2   Then the lodge flap was lifted away and the first head appeared. My father nudged me. One by one they emerged, these holy Blackfeet. The master of ceremonies, large and far-seeing, led the procession. Behind him slowly strode the medicine woman's husband, his body blackened by charcoal, symbols of moon and sun on chest and back, his face lined with sun

---

[1] *roach:* A Plains Indian dancer's headpiece fashioned from hair from a horse's mane.

dogs. Next came the previous year's sacred vow woman, who had transferred the paraphernalia in an elaborate ceremony within the lodge. Then came the medicine woman with her helpers behind her. She wore an elkskin dress, an elkskin cape, and a headdress made of buffalo hide, weasel skins, and feathers. Attached to the front was a doll stuffed with tobacco seeds and human hair. It was a sacred headdress. In her arms she held a sacred digging stick. Two of her assistants walked close beside her, holding those arms, for she was weak and frail from her fast. In my youthful distortion (I was nine at the time), I imagined her to be ninety years old, but now I suspect she was closer to fifty. Her helpers carried in their parfleches the sacred tongues, once buffalo, now beef or elk—I don't remember—to be distributed to the people. As they made their way to the medicine lodge, a voice, high and distant, sang to the sun and it entered my bones and I was Blackfeet and changed forever. I remember.

3 Thirty-four years later the image of that Sun Dance procession is still with me, and in my novels and poems I have tried to maintain the spirit of that moment.

DISCUSSION QUESTIONS

1. How would you describe the tone or "the spirit of the moment" for the author?
2. What can you infer about why the Sun Dance procession made such an impression on the author as a boy?
3. The author employs imagery that appeals to several senses. In four columns, jot down the images that appeal to hearing, sight, smell, and touch.

WRITING TOPICS

1. "I Remember" inspires and organizes Welch's imagination. Taking a cue from him, write your initial impressions from a scene in your childhood that greatly impressed you. You may begin "I remember. . . ."
2. Ceremonies are common in all societies and are known as far back as recorded history. Why do you think humans feel a need for various types

of ceremonies? Think of some ceremonies of which you have been a part and then examine this question in a paper.
3. Recall a ceremony, parade, or procession that you have witnessed or been a part of and describe it, appealing to as many of the five senses as you can.

THE VOYAGERS

Linda Hogan

Linda Hogan typically turns a sensitive lens on earthly things—a golden-eyed frog, a steaming sweat lodge, her grandmother's aging face. She skillfully transforms these ordinary images into strong metaphors. In "The Voyagers," the essayist leaves earth's limits and follows a probe into the cosmos. In 1977, NASA launched Voyagers 1 and 2. They carried a special kind of videodisk upon which was encoded scientific information as well as a medley of earthly sights and sounds, sort of an interstellar version of "The Earth's Greatest Hits." Photographs show the Red Sea, a snowflake, an X-ray of a hand, dolphins, a supermarket, and children. Greetings in many languages range from Arabic to English. On the disk are sounds of earth, including surf, a whale, a hyena, rain, laughter, a baby, and a kiss. A passage from Mozart's "The Magic Flute," Peruvian pan pipes, Louis Armstrong's "Melancholy Blues," and Beethoven's "Symphony #5" exemplify earth's musical repertoire. NASA designed the complex collection of the Interstellar Record for a curious and friendly alien, an intelligent being interested in us. Hogan examines the contents of this time capsule speeding through space. For her, the video memories encode "the sacred language of life that we ourselves have only just begun to remember."

1   I remember one night, lying on the moist spring earth beside my mother. The fire of stars stretched away from us, and the mysterious darkness traveled without limit beyond where we lay on the turning earth. I could smell the damp new grass that night, but I could not touch or hold such black immensity that lived above our world, could not contain within myself even a small corner of the universe.

2   There seemed to be two kinds of people; earth people and those others, the sky people, who stumbled over pebbles while they walked around with their heads in the clouds. Sky people loved different worlds than I loved;

they looked at nests in treetops and followed the long white snake of vapor trails. But I was an earth person, and while I loved to gaze up at night and stars, I investigated the treasures at my feet, the veined wing of a dragonfly opening a delicate blue window to secrets of earth, a lusterless beetle that drank water thirstily from the tip of my finger and was transformed into sudden green and metallic brilliance. It was enough mystery for me to ponder the bones inside our human flesh, bones that through some incredible blueprint of life grow from a moment's sexual passion between a woman and a man, walk upright a short while, then walk themselves back to dust.

3   Years later, lost in the woods one New Year's eve, a friend found the way home by following the north star, and I began to think that learning the sky might be a practical thing. But it was the image of earth from out in space that gave me upward-gazing eyes. It was that same image that gave the sky people an anchor in the world, for it returned us to our planet in a new and loving way.

4   To dream of the universe is to know that we are small and brief as insects, born in a flash of rain and gone a moment later. We are delicate and our world is fragile. It was the transgression of Galileo to tell us that we were not the center of the universe, and now, even in our own time, the news of our small being here is treacherous enough that early in the space program, the photographs of Earth were classified as secret documents by the government. It was thought, and rightfully so, that the image of our small blue Earth would forever change how we see ourselves in context with the world we inhabit.

5   When we saw the deep blue and swirling white turbulence of our Earth reflected back to us, says photographer Steven Meyers, we also saw "the visual evidence of creative and destructive forces moving around its surface, we saw for the first time the deep blackness of that which surrounds it, we sensed directly, and probably for the first time, our incredibly profound isolation, and the special fact of our being here." It was a world whose intricately linked-together ecosystem could not survive the continuing blows of exploitation.

6   In 1977, when the Voyagers were launched, one of these spacecraft carried the Interstellar Record, a hoped-for link between earth and space that is filled with the sounds and images of the world around us. It carries parts of our lives all the way out to the great Forever. It is destined to travel out of our vast solar system, out to the far, unexplored regions of space in hopes that somewhere, millions of years from now, someone will find it like a note sealed in a bottle carrying our history across the black ocean of space. This message is intended for the year 8,000,000.

7   One greeting onboard from Western India says: "Greetings from a human being of the Earth. Please contact." Another, from Eastern China, but resembling one that could have been sent by my own Chickasaw people, says: "Friends of space, how are you all? Have you eaten yet? Come visit us if you have time."

8   There is so much hope in those greetings, such sweetness. If found, these messages will play our world to a world that's far away. They will sing out the strangely beautiful sounds of Earth, sounds that in all likelihood exist on no other planet in the universe. By the time the record is found, if ever, it is probable that the trumpeting bellows of elephants, the peaceful chirping of frogs and crickets, the wild dogs baying out from the golden needle and record, will be nothing more than a gone history of what once lived on this tiny planet in the curving tail of a spiral galaxy. The undeciphered language of whales will speak to a world not our own, to people who are not us. They will speak of what we value the most on our planet, things that in reality we are almost missing.

9   A small and perfect world is traveling there, with psalms journeying past Saturn's icy rings, all our treasured life flying through darkness, going its way alone back through the universe. There is the recorded snapping of fire, the song of a river traveling the continent, the living wind passing through dry grasses, all the world that burns and pulses around us, even the comforting sound of a heartbeat taking us back to the first red house of our mothers' bodies, all that, floating through the universe.

10   The Voyager carries music. A Peruvian wedding song is waiting to be heard in the far, distant regions of space. The Navajo Night Chant travels through darkness like medicine for healing another broken world. Blind Willie Johnson's slide guitar and deep down blues are on that record, in night's long territory.

11   The visual records aboard the Voyager depict a nearly perfect world, showing us our place within the whole; in the image of a snow-covered forest, trees are so large that human figures standing at their base are almost invisible. In the corner of this image is a close-up of a snow crystal's elegant architecture of ice and air. Long-necked geese fly across another picture, a soaring eagle. Three dolphins, sun bright on their silver sides, leap from a great ocean wave. Beneath them are underwater blue reefs with a shimmering school of fish. It is an abundant, peaceful world, one where a man eats from a vine heavy with grapes, an old man walks through a field of white daisies, and children lovingly touch a globe in a classroom. To think that the precious images of what lives on earth beside us, the lives we share with earth, some endangered, are now tumbling through time and space, more permanent than we are, and speaking the sacred language of life that we ourselves have only just begun to remember.

12   We have sent a message that states what we most value here on earth; respect for all life and ways. It is a sealed world, a seed of what we may become. What an amazing document is flying above the clouds, holding Utopia. It is more magical and heavy with meaning than the cave paintings of Lascaux, more wise than the language of any holy book. These are images that could sustain us through any cold season of ice or hatred or pain.

13   In *Murmurs of Earth,* written by members of the committee who selected the images and recordings, the records themselves are described in

a way that attests to their luminous quality of being: "They glisten, golden, in the sunlight, . . . encased in aluminum cocoons." It sounds as though, through some magical metamorphosis, this chrysalis of life will emerge in another part of infinity, will grow to a wholeness of its own, and return to us alive, full-winged, red, and brilliant.

14   There is so much hope there that it takes us away from the dark times of horror we live in, a time when the most cruel aspects of our natures have been revealed to us in regions of earth named Auschwitz, Hiroshima, My Lai, and Rwanda, a time when televised death is the primary amusement of our children, when our children are killing one another on the streets.

15   At second glance, this vision for a new civilization, by its very presence, shows us what is wrong with our world. Defining Utopia, we see what we could be now, on earth, at this time, and next to the images of a better world, that which is absent begins to cry out. The underside of our lives grows in proportion to what is denied. The darkness is made darker by the record of light. A screaming silence falls between the stars of space. Held inside that silence are the sounds of gunfire, the wailings of grief and hunger, the last, extinct song of a bird. The dammed river goes dry, along with its valleys. Illnesses that plague our bodies live in this crack of absence. The broken link between us and the rest of our world grows too large, and the material of nightmares grows deeper while the promises for peace and equality are empty, are merely dreams without reality.

16   But how we want it, how we want that half-faced, one-sided God.

17   In earlier American days, when Catholic missions were being erected in Indian country, a European woman, who was one of the first white contacts for a northern tribe of people, showed sacred paintings to an Indian woman. The darker woman smiled when she saw a picture of Jesus and Mary encircled in their haloes of light. A picture of the three kings with their crowns and gifts held her interest. But when she saw a picture of the crucifixion, the Indian woman hurried away to warn others that these were dangerous people, people to fear, who did horrible things to one another. This picture is not carried by the Voyager, for fear we earth people would "look" cruel. There is no image of this man nailed to a cross, no saving violence. There are no political messages, no photographs of Hiroshima. This is to say that we know our own wrongdoings.

18   Nor is there a true biology of our species onboard because NASA officials vetoed the picture of a naked man and pregnant woman standing side by side, calling it "smut." They allowed only silhouettes to be sent, as if our own origins, the divine flux of creation that passes between a man and a woman, are unacceptable, something to hide. Even picture diagrams of the human organs, musculature, and skeletal systems depict no sexual organs, and a photograph showing the birth of an infant portrays only the masked, gloved physician lifting the new life from a mass of sheets, the mother's body hidden. While we might ask if they could not have sent the carved stone gods and goddesses in acts of beautiful sexual intimacy on temple walls in

India, this embarrassment about our own carriage of life and act of creative generation nevertheless reveals our feelings of physical vulnerability and discomfort with our own life force.

19　　From an American Indian perspective, there are other problems here. Even the language used in the selection process bespeaks many of the failings of an entire system of thought and education. From this record, we learn about our relationships, not only with people, but with everything on earth. For example, a small gold-eyed frog seen in a human hand might have been a photograph that bridges species, a statement of our kinship with other lives on earth, but the hand is described, almost apologetically, as having "a dirty fingernail." Even the clay of creation has ceased to be the rich element from which life grows. I recall that the Chilean poet Pablo Neruda wrote "What can I say without touching the earth with my hands?" We must wonder what of value can ever be spoken from lives that are lived outside of life, without a love or respect for the land and other lives.

20　　In *Murmurs of Earth,* one of the coauthors writes about hearing dolphins from his room, "breathing, playing with one another. Somehow," he says, "one had the feeling that they weren't just some sea creatures but some very witty and intelligent beings living in the next room." This revealing choice of words places us above and beyond the rest of the world, as though we have stepped out of our natural cycles in our very existence here on earth. And isn't our world full of those rooms? We inhabit only a small space in the house of life. In another is a field of corn. In one more is the jungle world of the macaw. Down the hall, a zebra is moving. Beneath the foundation is the world of snakes and the five beating hearts of the earthworm.

21　　In so many ways, the underside of our lives is here. Even the metals used in the record tell a story about the spoils of inner earth, the laborers in the hot mines. Their sweat is in that record, hurtling away from our own galaxy.

22　　What are the possibilities, we wonder, that our time capsule will be found? What is the possibility that there are lives other than our own in the universe? Our small galaxy, the way of the milk, the way of sustenance, is only one of billions of galaxies, but there is also the possibility that we are the only planet where life opens, blooms, is gone, and then turns over again. We hope this is not the case. We are so young we hardly know what it means to be a human being, to have natures that allow for war. We barely even know our human histories, so much having unraveled before our time, and while we know that our history creates us, we hope there is another place, another world we can fly to when ours is running out. We have come so far away from wisdom, a wisdom that is the heritage of all people, an old kind of knowing that respects a community of land, animals, plants, and other people as equal to ourselves. Where we know the meaning of relationship.

23　　As individuals, we are not faring much better. We are young. We hardly know who we are. We face the search for ourselves alone. In spite of our search through the universe, we do not know our own personal journeys.

We still wonder if the soul weighs half an ounce, if it goes into the sky at the time of our death, if it also reaches out, turning, through the universe.

24   But still, this innocent reaching out is a form of ceremony, as if the Voyager were a sacred space, a ritual enclosure that contains our dreaming the way a cathedral holds the bones of saints.

25   The people of earth are reaching out. We are having a collective vision. Like young women and men on a vision quest, we seek a way to live out the peace of the vision we have sent to the world of stars. We want to live as if there is no other place, as if we will always be here. We want to live with devotion to the world of waters and the universe of life that dwells above our thin roofs.

26   I remember that night with my mother, looking up at the black sky with its turning stars. It was a mystery, beautiful and distant. Her body I came from, but our common ancestor is the earth, and the ancestor of earth is space. That night we were small, my mother and I, and we were innocent. We were children of the universe. In the gas and dust of life, we are voyagers. Wait. Stop here a moment. Have you eaten? Come in. Eat.

DISCUSSION QUESTIONS

1. What does Hogan say gave her "upward gazing eyes"?
2. How does Hogan use contrast to structure her essay?
3. What does she say is revealed by our failure to include "a true biology of our species"?
4. In paragraph 20, Hogan says that "we have stepped out of our natural cycles in our very existence here on earth." Reread this paragraph and discuss whether this is a justifiable conclusion based on her examples.
5. Explain what you think Hogan means by saying "we are all voyagers." How can this be true?

WRITING TOPICS

1. In a brief essay, explain how the ideas in this essay are related to the title of this chapter, "Memory Alive."
2. In a journal entry, imagine that you could send a message to distant, possibly inhabited planets. What would you say?

SUMMARY WRITING TOPICS

1. Reread lines 35–41 of the first poem in this chapter, "Skeleton of Winter," and in an essay compare Harjo's statement with statements made in Linda Hogan's essay "The Voyagers."
2. Write impressions in your literary journal about the part memory—even painful memory—plays in the life of Native Americans.
3. Prepare a multimedia program based on this chapter. You may mark scripts for oral interpretation and choral reading, research and show images of Native American art, and play recordings of Native American music.
4. Imagine that NASA deploys Voyager 3 in the year 2000. Your class has been asked to be one of several to represent American students' views of the twentieth century on a videodisk. Prepare a class exhibit that includes the following items from each student: a message of less than one hundred words; one photograph; and one musical selection. Your goal is to exhibit a composite view of twentieth-century America from young people to a being who has never been to earth.
5. In an essay, relate Harjo's line "I am memory alive" to her poems "Remember" (Chapter Five) and "I Give You Back" (Chapter Nine). Compare and contrast the three poems on these points: imagery, meaning, and form.
6. There are four Navajo writers anthologized in this text: Shonto Begay, Luci Tapahonso, Howard Gorman, and Chahadineli Benally. After reading the Navajo cosmology selections in Chapter Two, review the works by these four authors. Jot down points you consider important. Using your notes, write a report on what you have learned about Navajo life and literature in your study of the selections in this anthology.
7. Review Linda Hogan's essays in this anthology: "The Two Lives" (Chapter One), "All My Relations" (Chapter Two), and "Seeing, Knowing, Remembering" and "The Voyagers" (Chapter Ten). Write down important points as you review. Then organize your notes and write an essay on Hogan's writing and life as revealed in the four essays.
8. Organize a class exhibit on the theme "I Am Memory Alive." You may include individual paintings, group murals, drawings, personal stories, imaginary narratives, and poems. Add sound effects and music. Consider designing a computer component as part of your exhibit for other students and faculty to visit.

ACKNOWLEDGMENTS

Alexie, Sherman. "13/16" by Sherman Alexie. Reprinted from *The Business of Fancydancing* copyright © 1992 by Sherman Alexie, with permission of Hanging Loose Press. "The Game Between the Jews and the Indians Is Tied Going Into the Bottom of the Ninth Inning" and "Tiny Treaties" by Sherman Alexie. Reprinted from *First Indian on the Moon* copyright © 1993 by Sherman Alexie, with permission of Hanging Loose Press. "The Lone Ranger and Tonto Fistfight in Heaven" and "Indian Education" from *The Lone Ranger and Tonto Fistfight in Heaven* by Sherman Alexie. Copyright © 1993 by Sherman Alexie. Used by permission of Grove/Atlantic, Inc.

Apess, William. Reprinted by permission from *On Our Own Ground: The Complete Writings of William Apess, A Pequot*, ed. Barry O'Connell (Amherst: The University of Massachusetts Press, 1992), copyright © 1992 by The University of Massachusetts Press.

Baca, Lorenzo. From "Ten Rounds" by Lorenzo Baca. Copyright © 1993 by Lorenzo Baca. Reprinted by permission of the author.

Bass, Althea. From *The Arapaho Way* by Althea Bass. Copyright © 1966 by Mrs. John Harvey Bass. Reprinted by permission of Crown Publishers, Inc.

Bates, Russell. "Rite of Encounter" by Russell Bates. First appeared in *The Magazine of Fantasy and Science Fiction*, May 1973. © 1973 by the Mercury Press, Inc. Reprinted by permission of the author.

Begay, Shonto. Courtesy of the Wheelwright Museum of the American Indian.

Bell, Betty Louise. From *Faces in the Moon* by Betty Louise Bell. Copyright © 1994 by Betty Louise Bell. Reprinted by permission of the University of Oklahoma Press as publisher.

Benally, Chahadineli. From "Chahadineli Benally" from *Navajo Stories of the Long Walk Period* published by Navaho Community College Press, 1973. Reprinted by permission of the publisher.

Blue Cloud, Peter. "Hawk Nailed to a Barn Door" and "Of All Tomorrows" by Peter Blue Cloud. Reprinted by permission of Aroniawenrate/Peter Blue Cloud, Turtle Clan, Mohawk Nation, Kahnawake, Quebec, Canada.

Bruchac, Joseph. "Time" from *Translator's Son* by Joseph Bruchac, Cross Cultural Communications, Merrick, NY 1980. Reprinted by permission of Barbara S. Kouts, Literary Agent. "Ellis Island" from *The Remembered Earth*, Red Earth Press, Albuquerque, 1979 edited by Geary Hobson. Reprinted by permission of Barbara S. Kouts, Literary Agent. From "Notes of a Translator's Son" by Joseph Bruchac. Reprinted from *I Tell You Now: Autobiographical Essays by Native American Writers*, edited by Brain Swann and Arnold Krupat, by permission of the University of Nebraska Press. Copyright © 1987 by the University of Nebraska Press.

Burns, Diane. "Sure You Can Ask Me a Personal Question" by Diane Burns. Reprinted by permission of the author.

CallingThunder, Debra. From "Voices of the Invisible" by Debra Calling Thunder from *A Circle of Nations: Voices and Visions of American Indians.* © 1993 Beyond Words Publishing, Inc., 1-800-284-9673.

Campbell, Maria. Reprinted from *Halfbreed* by Maria Campbell by permission of the University of Nebraska Press. Copyright © 1973 by Maria Campbell. Also, used by permission McClelland & Stewart, Inc., The Canadian Publishers.

Dauenhauer, Nora Marks. "Tlingit Concrete Poem" by Nora Dauenhauer. Copyright © by Nora Marks Dauenhauer; used with permission of the author.

Deloria, Vine, Jr. Excerpted with the permission of Simon & Schuster from *Custer Died for Your Sins: An Indian Manifesto* by Vine Deloria, Jr. Copyright © 1969 by Vine Deloria, Jr.

Deloria, Philip J. Abridged from "Mascots" by Philip J. Deloria from *Encyclopedia of North American Indians* edited by Frederick E. Hoxie. Copyright © 1996 by Houghton Mifflin Company. Reprinted by permission of Houghton Mifflin Company. All rights reserved.

Dorris, Michael. "Groom Service" by Michael Dorris. Copyright © 1989 by Michael Dorris. Reprinted by permission of the Author's Estate. This story first appeared in *Louder Than Words,* 1989, republished by Henry Holt & Company in *Working Men.* Excerpts from *Paper Trail* by Michael Dorris. Copyright © 1994 by Michael Dorris. "Rayona's Ride," reprinted by permission of HarperCollins Publishers, Inc. From *A Yellow Raft in Blue Water* by Michael Dorris. © 1987 by Michael Dorris. Reprinted by permission of Henry Holt & Co., Inc.

Erdrich, Louise. From "Skunk Dreams" from *The Blue Jay's Dance* by Louise Erdrich. Copyright © 1993 by Louise Erdrich. Reprinted by permission of HarperCollins Publishers, Inc. From "Morning Glories and Eastern Phoebes" from *The Blue Jay's Dance* by Louise Erdrich. Copyright © 1995 by Louise Erdrich. Reprinted by permission of HarperCollins Publishers, Inc. Chapter 7 "The Bingo Van" from *The Bingo Palace* by Louise Erdrich. Copyright © 1994 by Louise Erdrich. Reprinted by permission of HarperCollins Publishers, Inc. "Dear John Wayne," "Indian Board School: The Runaways" and "The Strange People" from *Jacklight Poems* by Louise Erdrich. Copyright © 1984 by Louise Erdrich. Reprinted by permission of Henry Holt & Co., Inc.

Evers, Larry and Felipe S. Molina. "Enchanted Enchanted Rattlesnake" and "Yoyo A'akame" are included with the permission of Chax Press, publisher of *Wo'i Bwikam Coyote Songs* by Larry Evers and Felipe S. Molina.

George, Phil. "Battle Won is Lost," "Old Man, the Sweat Lodge" and "Proviso" by Phil George from *The Whispering Wind* by Terry Allen. Copyright © 1972 by the Institute of American Indian Arts. Used by permission of Doubleday, a division of Bantam Doubleday Dell Publishing Group, Inc. "My Indian Name" and " Name Giveaway" by Phil George. Reprinted by permission of Phil George, Nez Perce.

Glancy, Diane. "Black Kettle National Grasslands, Western Oklahoma" by Diane Glancy from *Offering: Poetry & Prose* (Holy Cow! Press, 1988). Reprinted by permission of the publisher. Excerpt from *Pushing the Bear* by Diane Glancy, copyright © 1996 by Diane Glancy, reprinted by permission of Harcourt Brace & Company.

Gorman, Howard W. From "Howard W. Gorman" from *Navajo Stories of the Long Walk Period* published by Navaho Community College Press, 1973. Reprinted by permission of the publisher.

Gunn Allen, Paula. Excerpt from "Iyani: It Goes This Way" by Paula Gunn Allen from *The Remembered Earth* edited by Geary Hobson, retitled "We Are the Land." Reprinted by permission of Paula Gunn Allen.

Hale, Janet Campbell. From *Bloodlines: Odyssey of a Native Daughter* by Janet Campbell Hale. Copyright © 1993 by Janet Campbell Hale. Reprinted by permission of Random House, Inc.

Harjo, Joy. "I Give You Back," "Remember," "Skeleton Of Winter," and "The Woman Hanging From The Thirteenth Floor Window" from the book *She Had Some Horses* by Joy Harjo. Copyright © 1983 by Thunder's Mouth Press. Used by permission of the publisher, Thunder's Mouth Press. "Metamorphosis" by Joy Harjo from *A Circle of Nations: Voices and Visions of American Indians.* © 1993 Beyond Words Publishing, Inc., 1-800-284-9673.

Hobson, Geary. "Buffalo Poem #1" from *The Remembered Earth* edited by Geary Hobson. © Geary Hobson. Reprinted by permission of the author.

Hogan, Linda. "All My Relations" and "The Voyagers" from *Dwellings: A Spiritual History of the Living World* by Linda Hogan. Copyright © 1995 by Linda Hogan. Reprinted by permission of W.W. Norton & Company, Inc. "The Truth Is," reprinted by permission from *Seeing Through the Sun* by Linda Hogan (Amherst: University of Massachusetts Press, 1985), Copyright © 1985 by Linda Hogan. Reprinted by permission of University of Massachusetts Press. Excerpt from *Solar Storms,* reprinted with the permission of Scribner, a division of Simon & Schuster from *Solar Storms* by Linda Hogan. Copyright © 1995 by Linda Hogan. "Seeing, Knowing, Remembering" by Linda Hogan from *A Circle of Nations: Voices and Visions of American Indians.* © 1993 Beyond Words Publishing, Inc., 1-800-284-9673. "The Two Lives" by Linda Hogan. Reprinted from *I Tell You Now: Autobiographical Essays by Native American Writers* edited by Brian Swann and Arnold Krupat, by permission of the University of Nebraska Press. Copyright © 1987 by the University of Nebraska Press.

Hopkins, Sarah Winnemucca. From *Life Among the Piutes* by Sarah Winnemucca Hopkins, reprinted 1994 by University of Nevada Press.

Kenny, Maurice. From *On Second Thought* by Maurice Kenny. Copyright © 1995 by Maurice Kenny. Reprinted by permission of the University of Oklahoma Press as publisher. "Waiting at the Edge" by Maurice Kenny. Reprinted from *I Tell You Now: Autobiographical Essays By Native American Writers* edited by Brian Swann and Arnold Krupat by permission of the University of Nebraska Press. Copyright © 1987 by the University of Nebraska Press.

Kroeber, Karl. Reprinted from *Traditional Literatures of the American Indian: Texts and Interpretatations* compiled and edited by Karl Kroeber by permission of the University of Nebraska Press. Copyright © 1981 by the University of Nebraska Press.

Lame Deer, John Fire and Richard Erdoes. Reprinted with the permission of Simon & Schuster from *Lame Deer Seeker of Visions* by John Fire Lame Deer and Richard Erdoes. Copyright © 1972 by John Fire/Lame Deer and Richard Erdoes.

Lopez, Alonzo. "Celebration" by Alonzo Lopez from *The Whispering Wind* by Terry Allen. Copyright © 1972 by the Institute of American Indian Arts. Used by permission of Doubleday, a division of Bantam Doubleday Dell Publishing Group, Inc.

McNickle, D'Arcy. "Going to School" from *The Hawk Is Hungry & Other Stories* by D'Arcy McNickle. Reprinted by permission of The Newberry Library.

McWhorter, Lucullus Virgil. From *Yellow Wolf* by Lucullus Virgil McWhorter. Copyright © The Caxton Printers, Ltd. Caldwell, Idaho.

Midge, Tiffany. From "Beets" by Tiffany Midge. Reprinted by permission of the author, a member of The Standing Rock Sioux Reservation.

Miller, Jay. Reprinted from *Mourning Dove: A Salishan Autobiography* edited by Jay Miller by permission of the University of Nebraska Press. Copyright © 1990 by the University of Nebraska Press.

Momaday, N. Scott. "Carriers of the Dream Wheel," "Earth and I Gave You Turquoise," and "The Delight Son of Tsoai-talee" from *The Gourd Dancer* by N. Scott Momaday. © N. Scott Momaday. Reprinted by permission. From *The Names* by N. Scott Momaday. © N. Scott Momaday. Reprinted by permission. "Introduction" from *The Way to Rainy Mountain* by N. Scott Momaday, University of New Mexico Press, 1969. Reprinted by permission of the publisher. "The War God's Horse Song" from *House Made of Dawn* by N. Scott Momaday. © N. Scott Momaday. Reprinted by permission. "The Man Made of Words" by N. Scott Momaday. © N. Scott Momaday. Reprinted by permission. "December 29, 1890." Copyright © 1992 by N. Scott Momaday. From *In the Presence of the Sun* by N. Scott Momaday. Reprinted by permission of St. Martin's Press, Incorporated.

Moran, Bridget. Reprinted with permission from *Stoney Creek Woman* by Bridget Moran (Arsenal Pulp, 1988).

Neihardt, John G. Reprinted from *Black Elk Speaks* by John G. Neihardt by permission of the University of Nebraska Press. Copyright 1932, 1959, 1972 by John G. Neihardt. Copyright © 1961 by the John G. Neihardt Trust.

Niatum, Duane. "Street Kid" from *Digging Out the Roots* by Duane Niatum. Copyright © 1978 by Duane Naitum. Reprinted by permission of HarperCollins Publishers, Inc.

Ortiz, Simon J. "My Father's Song" from *Going for the Rain* by Simon Ortiz. Permission to reprint granted by the author, Simon J. Ortiz.

Owens, Louis. "Soul-Catcher" and "Water Witch" by Louis Owens. Reprinted by permission of the author.

Palmanteer, Ted. "We Saw Days" by Ted Palmanteer from *The Whispering Wind* by Terry Allen. Copyright © 1972 by the Institute of American Indian Arts. Used by permission of Doubleday, a division of Bantam Doubleday Dell Publishing Group, Inc.

Ramsey, Jarold. From "The Origin of Eternal Death" by Jarold Ramsey from *The North American Indian*, Vol. 8 by Edward Curtis (Norwood, MA: Plimpton Press, 1911) pp. 127–129. Included in Jarold Ramsey, ed. *Coyote Was Going There* (Seattle: University of Washington Press, 1977) pp. 81-84. Reprinted by permission of Professor Jarold Ramsey.

Reid, Bill and Robert Bringhurst. From *The Raven Steals the Light* by Bill Reid and Robert Bringhurst, copyright © 1984, 1996, published by Douglas & McIntyre. Reprinted with permission of the Douglas & McIntyre and the University of Washington Press.

Riley, Patricia. "Adventures of an Indian Princess" by Patricia Riley. Reprinted by permission of the author. Copyright © 1993.

Rose, Wendy. From "Neon Scars" by Wendy Rose. Reprinted from *I Tell You Now: Autobiographical Essays By Native American Writers* edited by Brian Swann and Arnold Krupat by permission of the University of Nebraska Press. Copyright © 1987 by the University of Nebraska Press. "Three Thousand Dollar Death Song" by Wendy Rose. © 1994 Wendy Rose. From *Bone Dance*, University of Arizona Press. Reprinted by permission of the author.

Silko, Leslie Marmon. Excerpt from *Storyteller* entitled "Giant Bear" by Leslie Marmon Silko. © 1981 by Leslie Marmon Silko, reprinted with the permission of The Wylie Agency, Inc. "Indian Song: Survival" by Leslie Marmon Silko. © 1981 by Leslie Marmon Silko, reprinted with the permission of The Wylie Agency, Inc. "Love Poem" by Leslie Marmon Silko. © 1974 by Leslie Marmon Silko, reprinted with the permission of The Wylie Agency, Inc. "Lullaby" by Leslie Marmon Silko. © 1981 by Leslie Marmon Silko, reprinted with the permission of The Wylie Agency, Inc. "I Still Trust the Land," reprinted with the permission of Simon & Schuster from *Yellow Woman and a Beauty of the Spirit: Essays on Native American Life Today* by Leslie Marmon Silko. Copyright © 1996 by Leslie Marmon Silko. "Slim Man Canyon" by Leslie Marmon Silko. © 1974 by Leslie Marmon Silko, reprinted with the permission of The Wylie Agency, Inc. "The Man to Send Rain Clouds" by Leslie Marmon Silko. © 1981 by Leslie Marmon Silko, reprinted with the permission of The Wylie Agency, Inc. "The Time We Climbed Snake Mountain" by Leslie Marmon Silko. © 1981 by Leslie Marmon Silko, reprinted with the permission of The Wylie Agency, Inc.

Standing Bear, Luther. "At Last I Kill a Buffalo" reprinted from *My Indian Boyhood* by Luther Standing Bear by permission of the University of Nebraska Press. Copyright 1931 by Luther Standing Bear. Copyright © renewed 1959 by May M. Jones.

Swann, Brian. "Song of the Sky Loom" from *Wearing The Morning Star* by Brian Swann. Copyright © 1996 by Brian Swann. Reprinted by permission of Random House, Inc.

Tapahonso, Luci. "In 1864," "Raisin Eyes," "It Was a Special Treat," and "They Were Alone in Winter" from *Saanii Dahataal: The Women Are Singing* by Luci Tapahonso. Copyright © 1993 Luci Tapahonso. Reprinted by permission of The University of Arizona Press as publisher. "What I Am" from *Anii Anaadaalyaa'lgii: Recent ones that are made.* Courtesy of the Wheelwright Museum of the American Indian.

Underhill, Ruth M. Excerpt from *Papago Women* by Ruth M. Underhill, copyright © 1979 by Holt, Rinehart and Winston, reprinted by permission of the publisher.

Vizenor, Gerald. From *Interior Landscapes* by Gerald Vizenor. Reprinted by permission of University of Minnesota Press. "Prologue" from *The People Named the Chippewa* by Gerald Vizenor. Reprinted by permission of University of Minnesota Press.

Walters, Anna Lee. "The Warriors" from *The Sun Is Not Merciful* by Anna Lee Walters. Reprinted by permission of Firebrand Books, Ithaca, New York. Copyright © 1995 by Anna Lee Walters.

Welch, James. Excerpt from *Fool's Crow* by James Welch. Copyright © 1986 by James Welch. Used by permission of Viking Penguin, a division of Penguin Books USA Inc. "Forward" by James Welch from *The Reservation Blackfeet, 1882–1945* by James Welch. Reprinted by permission of the University of Washington Press. "Plea To Those Who Matter," "The Man From Washington," and "Snow Country Weavers" by James Welch. Reprinted by permission of James Welch. From *Riding the Earthboy, 40*, Harper & Row, 1976. Copyright © 1976 by James Welch. All rights reserved.

AUTHOR-TITLE INDEX